THE PAGEANT OF
YEARS

SIR PHILIP GIBBS, K.B.E.

THE PAGEANT OF
THE YEARS

AN AUTOBIOGRAPHY

BY

PHILIP GIBBS

WILLIAM HEINEMANN LTD
LONDON   ::   TORONTO

Dedicated
with the author's love
to
PHILIP MARTIN GIBBS
and
FRANCES GIBBS
of the younger generation
and to a very small boy named
RICHARD ROWLAND
who looks out on life with laughing eyes,
and to many small people
who are the author's friends

FIRST PUBLISHED 1946

————

THIS BOOK IS PRODUCED IN COMPLETE
CONFORMITY WITH THE AUTHORISED
ECONOMY STANDARDS

————

PRINTED IN GREAT BRITAIN AT THE WINDMILL PRESS
KINGSWOOD, SURREY

CONTENTS

PART I

A World That Has Passed 1

The Old Rhythm, 1. Family Life, 3. Home Influence, 6. Friends of Boyhood, 9. Adolescence, 12. Victorian Flirtation, 15. Young Ecstasy, 16. Marriage of Babes, 17. Frock-coated Youth, 22. Ancient Burial, 23. Italy in London, 24. The Boer War, 26. Babes in the Wood, 27. Young Birds, 28.

PART II

The Street of Adventure 31

Literary Syndicate, 31. Back from the North, 34. A Changing World, 37. The New Journalism, 39. Sacked, 43. Intellectual Mansions, S.W., 46. Reporter of Life, 47. Shakespeare and Others, 50. Grub Street and Alsatia, 54. Holland Street, Kensington, 56. The Tribune Tragedy, 59. Men of Letters, 62. The Old Prison, 65. Death in Bouverie Street, 66. Free Lance Again, 68. The Royal Poet, 70. The Battle of Sidney Street, 71. The Birth of a Princess, 75. The Lure of Paris, 77. The Strange Affair of Dr. Cook, 82.

PART III

War in the Balkans 91

Servia Stands to Arms, 91. Scenes in Sofia, 94. Te Deum, 97. Peasants and Prisoners, 99. The Cross and the Crescent, 102. Fox Ferdinand, 103. Pushed Out, 107.

PART IV

Before the Storm 109

Adventure in Lisbon, 109. The Lady with a Big Appetite, 115. Death of a King, 116. Coronation, 119. The Last of the Bourbons, 121. The Golden Years, 123. The Butterfly Ball, 124. Labour Trouble, 125. The Suffragettes, 127. Trouble in Ireland, 129. The Menace of Germany, 131.

PART V

The First World War 135

Across the Channel, 135. The Call to Arms, 136, Mobilised, 138. Tout Va Bien!, 141. Behind the Veil, 143. Retreat from Mons, 144. The German Tide, 147. Paris in Danger, 148. Stragglers, 149. A Silent City, 152. Dead and Wounded, 153. The Flames of Dixmude, 156. Nuns and Nurses, 158. Under Arrest, 160. Comrades All, 162. No Health Resorts, 169. Loos, 172. Lloyd George in France, 174. Strange Encounters, 177. Near to Enemy, 179. On the Somme, 181. Fear and Courage, 185. Some of Our Generals, 188. The Coming of the Tanks, 192. Bernard Shaw Looks at War, 195. German Retreat, 197. Vimy and Arras, 198. Gordon Highlanders, 201. The Mines Go Up, 202.

PART V (*Continued*)

The King at the Front, 203. The Hell of Flanders, 205. Forgotten Heroes, 207. Private Conversation, 210. Military Hospital, 212. Grim Foreboding, 214. The Great Attack, 215. Rescue of Amiens, 220. The Northern Attack, 221. Backs to the Wall, 222. The Last Reserves, 224. England in Wartime, 225. The Way to Victory, 228. Liberation, 231. Armistice, 232. Dancing Mania, 234. Into Germany, 235.

PART VI

IN QUEST OF PEACE 242

The Future Hope, 242. Man of Peace, 243. The Accolade, 244. Berlin After the War, 245. Spartacists, 247. Viennese Tragedy, 248. The Spirit of Hungary, 250. The Peace-Makers, 253. Danse Macabre, 255. The Little Gentleman in Rome, 256. Victory March, 261. Country Life, 263.

PART VII

AMERICAN JOURNEYS 267

Stage Fright, 267. Odd Happenings, 271. Lecture Tours, 272. President Harding, 274. Irish Americans, 276. Important People, 281. People of Destiny, 282. Crossing the Atlantic, 284.

PART VIII

THE NEAR EAST 287

The Sea of Enchantment, 287. Constantinople, 290. The Enchanted Garden, 293. Russian Refugees, 294. A Ship Goes to Smyrna, 298. The Doomed City, 300. Greek Faith, 302. English Residents, 304. Beauty of Athens, 305. The Coming of Kemal, 306.

PART IX

SOVIET RUSSIA 311

Journey to Moscow, 311. Forgotten Tragedy, 314. Behind the Scenes, 316. Glimpses of Life, 318. In the Kremlin, 320. Petrograd, 324. The Road to Famine, 326. Down the Volga, 328.

PART X

THE POST-WAR YEARS 333

The Defeated, 333. Conference in Cannes, 335. Occupation of the Ruhr, 338. German Episodes, 341. Surrey Gardens, 343. The Great Actor, 346. Glorious Editor, 347. Egypt, 349. The Pleasure Hunters, 351. General Strike, 354. The Dream of Geneva, 358. Briand and Stresemann, 361.

PART XI

EUROPEAN JOURNEY   365

Paris in Ferment, 365. Fear in France, 367. The Building of a Palace, 369. Fascist Italy, 373. The Wisdom of the Old, 376. Powder Magazine, 378. Marching Youth, 379. An Ambassador Talks, 382. Those Who Were Bored, 385. The Evil Spell, 386. What For?, 388. Invasion of Austria, 391.

PART XII

THE FOUR HORSEMEN PREPARE TO RIDE .   .   399

My Scientist, 399. Merrie England, 400. Low and High, 403. The Stricken North, 407. Farming Folk, 409. Prime Minister, 410. Bildens, 412. Madam, Will You Walk?, 413. Gallant Brother, 416. English Anxieties, 418. Abyssinia, 421. Winston, 422. Traffic in Arms, 425. The King's Camp, 430.

PART XIII

THE DARKENING SHADOW   434

The Mood of England, 434. The Last Hope, 436. The Last Attempt for Peace, 439. Satan's Right Hand, 441. Last Contacts, 443. Descendants of Kings, 444. Gürtelrosen, 446. Laughing Italian, 448. Leopold of the Belgians, 449. The Man of Munich, 451. A Forecast, 454. So It Came, 456.

PART XIV

SECOND WORLD WAR   457

Ghosts, 457. The New Crowds, 459. Censorship, 460. All the World's a Stage, 462. Maginot Line, 465. Our Weak Defences, 466. Encounters in France, 469. Those in Command, 471. The King Receives Us, 472. The Grim Winter, 473. Gracie Fields, 474. Christmas Party, 475. Private Report, 476. A Family in France, 479. French Defeat, 480.

PART XV

THE WAR AT HOME   485

The Deadly Menace, 485. Air Armadas, 487. Blitz, 488. Refugees, 488. The Amazing Summer, 489. Night Shelters, 492. Down the Tubes, 494. War in the Air, 495. Across the Atlantic, 497. The American Idea, 499. A Rare Bird, 501. I Didn't Die in Omaha, 503. Pearl Harbour, 504. The Great Man, 505. Henry Wallace, 507. The Old Cottage, 508. Dim Light, 510. The Miracles, 513. The "Things" Arrive, 514. Deliverances, 516. Labour Wins, 518. What Hope?, 523.

LIST OF ILLUSTRATIONS

SIR PHILIP GIBBS, K.B.E.   *Frontispiece*

A LITERARY FAMILY   *facing page* 8

ANTHONY GIBBS—SIR PHILIP'S NOVELIST SON   9

LADY GIBBS AND HER SON ANTHONY   16

PHILIP GIBBS   17

THE BATTLE OF SIDNEY STREET

THE AFFAIR OF DR. COOK   *Between*

BOARDING DR. COOK'S SHIP   72–73

BEERBOHM TREE AS "CALIBAN"

"A LONG, LONG WAY TO TIPPERARY"   168

PHILIP GIBBS WRITING HIS DESPATCHES   169

THE FIRST JOURNALIST TO INTERVIEW THE POPE   256

BERLIN CATHEDRAL   257

LYON

BOLZANO   *Between*

GREEK REFUGEES FROM ASIA MINOR   392–393

INNSBRUCK

HIGH STREET, GUILDFORD   416

BILDENS, EWHURST   417

PART I

A WORLD THAT HAS PASSED

1

THE OLD RHYTHM

WE were close to the England of Dickens when I was a boy, though the change in social life during the last quarter of Queen Victoria's golden days (for those who had the gold) was hurrying on apace. Since then almost everything has changed and we live in a different kind of world, which would have been unbelievable to the minds of the eighties and nineties if suddenly they had seen a vision of what is now familiar to us.

They would not have believed that one day, if they lived so long, they would be walking through the ruins of London, just noticing in a casual way, because of familiarity, some new heap of rubble and brick and twisted iron, caused by the latest arrival of a V-2. They would have refused to believe a nightmare dream that great numbers of their fellow citizens in London and other cities would sleep for months, and even years, in tube stations and other underground shelters, while above them flying demons dropped tons of high explosives, and the night sky throbbed with scarlet flames from fires raging in the streets below.

The minds of my contemporaries in childhood could not have imagined even the tube stations, or the roar of motor traffic in the streets, or the drone of aeroplanes overhead. We came into a world before the invention of the internal combustion engine which speeded up the *tempo* of life—and death. In many parts of the country away from the railway lines, the pace of a horse was our quickest speed, as it had been since the beginning of man's adventure. Down in Somerset, where I went a-courting as a young man, it was a whole day's expedition to drive from Stoke-under-Ham to Yeovil—a matter of ten miles or so—walking up hill to ease the horse. Now one can get there and back in twenty minutes by motor car, and not have such a good time with a pretty girl and lots of laughter on the way. There seemed more time to do things then, though speed is supposed to save time. Our minds moved to a different rhythm, more leisurely, with more time for reading, and more time for thought—if we thought. We had the blessing of peace, though unconscious of it, and we were without any dark forebodings of two world wars which some of us might have to endure.

In Kensington where I was born one May day in 1877—though I

1

can't believe it—and afterwards in Clapham Park, to which my impecunious family migrated, the klip-klop of horses' hoofs, so romantic now when they are reproduced by the B.B.C., were familiar to our young ears drowsing off to sleep, with the sudden slither of poor beasts on wet roads and the lash of the whip on their thin ribs. More than once, when later I rode in hansoms on journalistic adventures, the driver's lash stung across my face, or the horse came down with a scatter of sparks from hoofs, and staggered up with bleeding knees. I do not sentimentalise over the passing of the old cab-horse and those 'gondolas' of London as they were called, though I drove in them now and then with beauty by my side.

Out of the nursery windows we children of the eighties looked into the glamorous dusk of London streets, and watched the lamplighter making his magic at the end of a long pole, until all the lamp-posts in the street were shining on wet pavements or made a golden haze through a night of fog. The muffin man still went his rounds, ringing his bell, and muffins and crumpets seemed to taste better in those days when we had to make a rush for that passer-by before he vanished with his tray on his head.

There were still horse-busses after the first tramcars went clanging down the Clapham road. They put straw inside on wet days to keep one's feet warm. Many times I sat beside the driver who raised his whip to other Jehus, talked genially to City gentlemen who were regular customers, and swore most dreadful oaths to enemies on the road. One of them tied a noose in his whip and held it up as a fellow bus-driver passed, raising a clenched fist.

"What's the meaning of that?" asked one of the City gentlemen.

" 'Is brother was 'anged yesterday," answered the driver, with a laugh below the scarf tied round his neck and mouth. "One must 'ave one's little bit of 'umour."

In those boyhood days of mine Sam Weller and Tony Weller had not disappeared from our human types. On Derby Day they all came out in gigs, and pony carts, and char-a-bancs, and donkey carts, and coaches, roaring down the road to Epsom with a blare of tin trumpets and concertinas. The coster girls wore big hats with long feathers. The sporting gentlemen wore loud check suits with horseshoe pins. It was a noisy good-humoured pageant of English life belonging to the pages of Dickens, and the songs of Albert Chevalier, and the caricatures of 'Ally Sloper'. In the East End old Fagin still had his school for thieves, and there were thousands of Bill Sikes and Artful Dodgers.

Round the gin palaces there were always fights and screams on Saturday nights, when drunken women were carried off on stretchers after fighting and scratching half a dozen Bobbies. I saw scenes like that as a boy exploring life in London. It has all passed now. They were the last scenes in a squalid old drama—an old melodrama—which is no longer on the stage. Into the gin palaces went the Salvation Army lassies with their tinkling tambourines and their call to Jesus. The frightful, grinding, soul-destroying poverty of the eighties and nineties has mostly passed. There have been good wages in munition factories of war time. That drunken world, caused by poverty and foul social conditions, has passed. Other things have passed since I was a boy—the quietude of family life in the prosperous middle class, some elegance and some charm among those who were called the gentlefolk, stately homes and lovely parks, a lot of character, and an age of genius which flowered into great literature and art.

2

FAMILY LIFE

My father was a civil servant in the Education Department, Whitehall, and in the course of time had a family of seven—five boys and two girls, of whom I came fifth. We were, as I can say now without vanity, being past all that, a handsome crowd of youngsters and, in spite of poverty, or, at least, lack of luxury, we had a romantic idea that by blood and family tradition we belonged to the old aristocracy. It was, I think, due to the fact that my father was born in Windsor Castle, that my grandfather was a Queen's Messenger, and that my Aunt Kate had nursed most of the Royal babies, and after her retirement received visits from two or three of these princesses, who drove up in a carriage-and-pair with red on the collars of the coachman and the Royal Crown on the panels. Besides, did not my father write 'O.H.M.S.' even on his private letters, thereby saving the cost of postage stamps? Then there was a family secret whispered by elder brothers to younger brothers which added to our sense of family romance. An aunt of ours who lived in Royal Avenue, Chelsea—the house still stands in spite of many bombs in its neighbourhood—had been the mistress of a Duke's son, who had in his veins the blood of Charles II by a very naughty lady. After the birth of a daughter this young gentleman settled a fair sum upon our Aunt—a pretty woman as I remember her—and she lived comfortably, but not happily, I fear, with her little daughter, who grew up to be a handsome, high-spirited young woman.

Always now when I pass St. James's Palace, on the way to my club in Pall Mall, I look up at two small windows facing the courtyard where the Changing of the Guard takes place. Those were the windows of my grandfather's rooms, and to this day I remember going there as a very small boy when the Prince of Wales was holding a levée. My grandfather was in uniform, which I seem to remember was chocolate brown with a broad red stripe down the trousers. He carried an imposing sword and was, to my young eyes, a fine figure with side whiskers in the Victorian style. As a Queen's Messenger he travelled over Europe, and from Balmoral to Windsor or Whitehall, with those long letters which Queen Victoria wrote with desperate industry to her Ministers and to her family. He travelled in post chaises and coaches as did young Charles Dickens, though farther afield than Dickens. Stirring adventures he had, according to family legend, with spies who tried to steal his despatch case and romantic adventures on the way to the Court of Napoleon III and the Empress Eugénie.

The Queen was kind to him, as she was to all who served her. To this day I have a beautiful little portrait, like a large-sized miniature of the little Queen in girlhood, which she gave to him. I have two cut-glass decanters—one without a stopper now—which was another gift from her, and after my grandfather died the walls of my dining-room were hung with large Winterhalter prints of the Queen, and the Prince Consort (with luxuriant whiskers) and several of the Princesses in billowing frocks. They were steel engravings, and signed in Queen Victoria's beautiful handwriting with the long 'V'. My wife could not bear to live with them and one day, after some years, packed the whole lot off to a secondhand furniture dealer who bought them for a few shillings apiece. I was annoyed, but understood her point of view. They were rather oppressive on our walls.

My grandmother must have been a beauty as a young woman, but I remember her only as an old lady with a pippin-like face and very blue eyes behind a pair of spectacles which she was always losing, as now I lose mine. My brothers teased her unmercifully but I was more tender-hearted and spent hours with her on many days of my boyhood playing cribbage, which now I have forgotten except for a claim to 'one for his nob' and putting little pegs into a small board of inlaid wood.

My grandmother was a great reader, but in her old age she read only one book. It was *Evelina*, by Fanny Burney, that dear young lady who was so much admired by Dr. Johnson and his friends. As soon as the last page of this novel was finished my little old grandmother would sigh happily and begin again at the first page.

This family history is unimportant except as a calling back of ghosts and the time in which they lived before two world wars. I had, for instance, an Uncle Bill who was a hell of a fellow and helped to make history. I remember him as a tall man, with a heavy and long moustache, who used to curdle my young blood by turning up a trouser leg and exhibiting a deep hole plugged by a bullet. He had fought in the American Civil War on the Northern side—though for some romantic reason we youngsters always preferred to believe that he had fought for the Southerners. When I went out to the United States, for the first time after the last war, and visited the marvellous State Library in Washington, one of the librarians asked me whether I would like to turn up anything as a test of efficiency.

"Yes," I said. "Will you turn up my Uncle Bill? His name was Colonel William Gibbs."

In less than two minutes I had the military history of Uncle Bill. There was quite a bit about him. He had fought in many battles of the Civil War. As the librarian remarked with enthusiasm "he was certainly the hell of a fellow and a very gallant gentleman."

He married a bad-tempered lady who must have tormented his later life. She was a German, and we knew her as Aunt Sophie and detested her, especially as one day she called at our house when my father was out and, after making a great scene—I still remember her guttural fury—walked off with the clock on the drawing-room mantelpiece which she said, most untruthfully I believe, was the rightful property of Uncle Bill.

Aunt Kate and I had a charming friendship which was never broken until her death. She had a tragic life after leaving the Queen's service, for both her husband and her grown-up daughter died and she was left alone and miserable. For a time she took to drink, poor dear, and drank madly. At those times the younger members of the family were told that 'Aunt Kate was unwell', but somehow we all found out and whispered it to each other as a dead secret. As a young woman she was, as my father told me, a pretty thing, known to many a young gallant as "the Rose of Windsor", which I can well believe, for even in her time of white hair she was handsome and vivacious. She told me many stories of her life in the Royal Household of which I remember a few. One was about a young maid-of-honour who was so tired of standing for a long time among a bevy of other ladies in the presence of the Widow of Windsor that she supported herself for a moment by half sitting against the window sill. But the Queen had the sharpest eyes, and in a voice of icy rebuke cried out: "How dare you sit in the presence of your Queen?" The maid-of-honour stood up trembling, turned deathly pale and nearly swooned. There was also a terrible incident when a little white button from the underclothing of one of the maids-of-honour fell into the very centre of the polished floor and caused a lady-in-waiting to giggle. She was sent out of the room for most improper behaviour.

Aunt Kate's only claim to fame as an historical character put her

very high indeed in the estimation of her young nephews and nieces.
She once spanked the Kaiser. That was when he was a very naughty
little boy on a visit to Windsor.

As a young journalist I used to be sent to describe the arrival of the
German Emperor on his visits to England, and I had the honour of
lunching with him—from afar—under the old roof of the Guidhall,
destroyed by German high explosives later in history. On his arrival at
the railway station on State visits he bore himself proudly, and was
certainly a most impressive figure in full dress uniform, in spite of his
withered arm. He dramatised himself and was theatrical in his manner.
But there was a smile inside my mind when I was an onlooker of such a
scene. I thought "an aunt of mine gave you a spanking once, my fine
and mighty fellow!" Not that I had any grudge against him at that time.

3

HOME INFLUENCE

I hope I have not given the impression that my family basked in the
presence of royalty. As boys and girls we lived in a shabby old house on
the edge of Clapham Park (then an old-fashioned suburb), and had very
little pocket money for our hobbies. We belonged definitely to that
shabby genteel middle class which, however, produced in the Victorian
era so much quality and character.

Looking back on that time I am still staggered by the way in which
my father and mother brought up a big family on the most meagre
remuneration paid to civil servants. I doubt whether my father ever
earned more than £800 a year and that only towards the end of his
service. I should think that in our early days it was only £400 or £500.
Yet somehow or other he and my mother fed us, clothed us—seven of
us—and provided, by some miracle, a well furnished home, in the
comfortable mid-Victorian style. I can remember still the drawing-
room with its cabinets and what-nots, and a series of water-colours by a
well-known artist of that time, and my mother's most priceless possession—the grand piano—upon which she played adorably. How did
our fathers—your grandfathers or great grandfathers, my little ones
—perform such miracles of economy on such miserable salaries? One
answer, of course, is that money was worth more in those days when
income tax was 4d. in the pound, and when the English sovereign was of
real gold, carried about in little silver purses just large enough to hold
the coins which flicked open at a touch, as well I know, because until the
beginning of the first World War I had one in my waistcoat pocket.

But what courage our parents must have had, what anxieties, what sleepless nights, must have come to them often when things were not going well in family life, or the burden was becoming too heavy. How were they going to pay the school bills, the doctor's bills, the tailors' bills, for a growing family of boys and girls with big appetites and lengthening limbs? My mother was always sewing and mending. The whirr of the sewing machine was a constant rhythm in the ears of a small boy with his head over a book.

My father cut out the expense of school fees by educating us himself, or rather encouraging us to educate ourselves after our early years of boyhood. Public schools, he said, were sinks of iniquity, and most horrible dens of bullying and brutality. I am inclined to believe he was right, judging from the stories I have heard about the school-days of my contemporaries who were unmercifully flogged for trivial offences by sadistic pedagogues, and who, in this brutalising system, took it out of new boys and juniors by ingenious and imaginative tortures. That is not an exaggeration, I am told, of what happened at Marlborough, Rugby, Winchester and other schools in the eighties and nineties, and even later than that. But in any case my father could not afford to send his sons to those institutions, and he acted before and after office hours as our philosopher and friend.

We had no formal lessons, but he fired us with his own enthusiasm for all good books and for the study of foreign languages. He was equally enthusiastic for a game of cricket any morning when we felt more like play than work, and on Saturdays and Sundays we would take the train to some rural station and set off on a long walk through Surrey lanes and woods, stopping for lunch of bread and cheese and shandy-gaff in some old inn, like the White Horse at Leatherhead or the Bear at Esher.

We played cricket now and then with our Hamilton cousins who in those days had a house on the edge of Epping Forest with its old wild beauty. I was a small and delicate boy, and I still remember my ordeal of courage in standing up to the ferocious bowling of my cousins Charles and Geoff who were strong, sturdy, and terrifying fellows on a cricket pitch. Charles afterwards became the husband—for a time—of a lady now famous as Mary Agnes Hamilton, for whom I have a high regard. But in a book of hers called *Remembering My Friends*, her contempt for me is blighting. I wish she had not remembered me with such affection!

My father, before ill health broke him down at last, was an enchanting companion, gay, overflowing with "wise saws and modern instances", interested in all aspects of life and character, with a fine memory for poetry which he would recite down country roads, and a merry eye for a pretty wench, as frequently, with a wink to each other, we observed. He loved, and really knew, his Shakespeare, Scott, Dickens, Thackeray, George Eliot, Anthony Trollope, Charles Reade (now neglected), and the older masters of the novel—Fielding and Smollett. He was a devoted Johnsonian and quoted the old doctor on all occasions. He knew his Pepys. He loved Montaigne. He had read most essays from Bacon to Emerson. He had what most of us now would consider a misguided reverence for Thomas Carlyle, to whom he doffed his hat when they passed each other in Chelsea. He was enslaved by the drudgery of a desk in Whitehall. He would have made a good actor, for he always dramatised his stories and himself, causing us self-conscious boys considerable embarrassment at times because of his exuberant personality. He would stand drinks to a bunch of yokels in a country pub and play the part of the Colonel or the Squire.

People told him their most intimate life-stories on the top of a bus, or across the table of a tea shop. His sense of humour carried him to strange adventures, as when in Normandy he travelled in a hearse because no other transport was available, and jumped on the back of a French peasant, who tried to throw him off, when he wanted a pick-a-back to the local inn, because the road was ankle-deep in mud and he had only one pair of boots.

My mother was a saint and a martyr, like so many other Victorian wives, poor ladies. She was always sewing and mending and darning to keep the boys' clothes decent and to make frocks for the two girls. Yet we had a succession of maids—two at a time—who all seemed to come from Newbury in Oxfordshire, and sometimes were pretty enough to attract the adolescent attentions of my elder brothers.

Once we had a mother's help—a bonny girl—and many years later when I was in America I had a little note from her inviting me to go and see her. She had married an American and was one of the great ladies of California. She gave me a gold nugget for a tie pin—which I lost within a few weeks.

Now our home life may be interesting to readers of to-day, I think, not because it belonged to me—that only matters to myself—but because it was fairly typical of thousands of other English homes in that far off period, and especially homes in which there was a great deal of interest in books and pictures and music. We made our own entertainment and our own music, without turning a knob to switch it on, as now is done. My brothers played the violin, to my mother's accompaniment on the piano. My brother Cos had a fair tenor and sang "On the Road to Mandalay", "My Old Dutch", and other ballads. Perhaps my best memories of boyhood are those when I lay on a sofa, by a flickering fire and an oil lamp, listening to my mother playing Handel and Beethoven

HENRY GIBBS : FATHER

COSMO HAMILTON

FRANK HAMILTON GIBBS

ARTHUR HAMILTON GIBBS

A LITERARY FAMILY

ANTHONY GIBBS—SIR PHILIP'S NOVELIST SON

and Schubert and Chopin and Mendelssohn and many other masters, with an exquisite touch.

She loved reading also, and read out to us some of the books which she liked best. I remember laughing so much over her reading of Martin Chuzzlewit that I had to implore her to stop lest I should die a-laughing. One of her great favourites was *The Cloister and the Hearth*, by Charles Reade, and I remember reading it in a cottage at Leatherhead which we took one year.

And that reminds me of a very odd incident which happened forty years afterwards when I went into a little old bookshop in the old part of Leatherhead and was browsing about when I saw a French book beautifully illustrated. It was *L'Histoire d'un Paysan*, that great story of the French Revolution by Erckmann-Chatrian. I remembered with a sense of ghostliness that my father had been reading this when I was absorbed in *The Three Musketeers* and *Twenty Years After*, by Alexandre Dumas, as a young boy of fourteen or fifteen. This was the very same book. There on the margins were my father's notes in his fine hand-writing. I bought it for a few shillings and have it now.

A trivial memory of young boyhood comes back to me with that mention of old Leatherhead. It is hardly worth telling except for my own pleasure. I walked one day to an avenue of ancient yew trees—two thousand years old said the nature lovers—called the Druid's Grove, near Mickelham. I walked with awe between the old trees, and then lay down among them and fell asleep on that summer day. When I awoke and opened my eyes there was a circle of bunnies sitting up and watching that young human who was me. At my first movement they bolted away to their warren in the sandy bank, but for some reason I had a moment of pure delight which I have never forgotten, because it seemed to me that I had entered the fairy world in that moment of awakening.

4

FRIENDS OF BOYHOOD

In those days we, like many Victorian families, had an "At Home" one evening a week. For refreshment there were sandwiches, buns and coffee. Entertainment was provided by the family and guests, after the usual etiquette of diffidence and reluctance broken down by polite pleadings, and the discovery that a musical friend had left a few pieces in the hall. There were also recitations, and as boys we delighted in one called "The Bahgpeeps" delivered in the broadest Scotch by an honoured friend of ours, named Hope Moncrieff. He was the first

editor of *The Boy's Own Paper* which we devoured for serial stories by
Talbot Baines Reid, and by Hope Moncrieff himself, who wrote grand
stories for boys under the name of Ascot R. Hope. My father, under
pressure, which he really did not need, recited "Bouillabaisse" by
Thackeray—"Quel vin M'sieu désire-t-il?"—or some other ballad from
his rich store of memory. Henry Lawrence, the painter, played the
piano on these evenings at home, but he knew only three pieces by
heart and we used to hide our smiles when he would preface his performance by saying: "I think you must have heard this before."
Now on the wireless when I hear one of those pieces—"The Har-
monious Blacksmith"—I am carried straight back to those evenings at
home when I was a boy in an Eton collar. Henry Lawrence was a man
of private means in those days, and we regarded him as being rich. He
had a studio in Elm Park Gardens, and with his silver hair and beard,
and clothes designed by a Savile Row tailor was a man of elegance,
unlike his contemporary artists of Chelsea. He was a shy man of charm
and kindness, devoted to my mother and to all us youngsters. In his old
age he fell into poverty through some fraudulent stockbroker, and I was
shocked when he asked my help to obtain for him an old-age pension
and was kept from utter penury by this small help and a little allowance
made to him by my wife and myself.

Many of our friends were literary and artistic, and my father gave me
a glimpse now and then of some of the lions of that time when he took
me to the Whitefriars Club, of which he was a member. It was, and still
is, a literary club and I was proud to see my father's portrait hanging up
in their picture gallery. Around him at table sat G. A. Henty, the
famous author of historical novels for boys, with his big flowing beard,
and George Manville Fenn, and, on Guest nights, famous men like
Henry Irving and Johnston Forbes-Robertson, afterwards, in his old
age, a dear friend of mine.

My father, though a civil servant, had qualified for membership of a
literary club as the author of two or three novels—one enormously long
novel of French life called *A Long Probation*—which his friends
thought better than anything produced by his sons. He was also a
frequent contributor of essays to the old *Globe* "turnover" written by
many brilliant pens. It was one of his articles which led to the purchase
of Carlyle's house in Cheyne Row as a memorial for the nation. A
committee was formed, and his name is there in the book, still, as one
of the Founders of the Trust. I went with him when I was a boy, and
at least thirty years later I went again. An old lady opened the door to
me, and when I told her that I was the son of Henry Gibbs she said:
"I well remember you coming with your father when you were a small
boy. I have been caretaker here ever since, and we have had thousands

of visitors, but I still remember your father because he was so kind to me when I was a young girl."

Some years ago my friend Filson Young gave a broadcast from Carlyle's house, and one heard the jangle of the little bell which poor dear Jane heard so often when the errand boys, or Mr. Tennyson, or Mr. John Stuart Mill, came to pay a call. Filson Young brought back to life the painful scene when Mill came to tell Carlyle that his manuscript of the French Revolution had been burnt by a servant maid. It was wonderfully done and brought tears to many eyes and mine. The frightful tragedy, the splendid courage of old Carlyle, the fine steel of Mrs. Carlyle's spirit! I am glad that my father had something to do with the public possession of the little house where those ghosts walk, and he would have been glad that I was one of those who, shortly before this war, handed it over to the National Trust for long-term preservation.

At the meeting when this was done in Cheyne Row a tall old man, with side whiskers of the variety once called "weepers", arrived rather late and took a seat. He rose to make a speech in a trumpet voice and told many stories of calling upon the Carlyles and being given a basket of fruit by Mrs. Carlyle, and hearing the old man growling upstairs. Thomas Carlyle has been dead for nearly sixty years. There are ghosts about, I thought. It would not surprise me at all if the old man himself were to make an appearance among us. The old gentleman was Sir James Crichton-Browne, family physician, then aged something over ninety.

Once a week, at least, my father lunched with a group of friends at Gatti's in the Strand. Always among them was his lifelong and most intimate friend, Tom Thorpe, who was known as Uncle Tom by us children. He was a round little man with the face of a middle-aged cherub—if a cherub ever reaches middle age. The soul of good nature, and a born merry-maker in any nursery full of children, with a passion for poetry, and endless notebooks stored with the wit and wisdom of the ages, he was the simplest and most modest of men, and we youngsters tended to regard him as the Sancho Panza to my father as Don Quixote. In fact I think he would have put himself in the same subordinate and humble place in his relationship with my father, to whom he was devoted and for whom he had a profound and touching admiration. One day at this table at Gatti's the company of friends were making up epitaphs for famous men. "Write one for me," said Uncle Tom.

"Certainly," said my father.

Thorpe's
Corpse.

I suppose it was in the Whitefriars Club that my father became very friendly with G. D. Williams who for a long span of years was head of

Reuters' with its great and splendid tradition. Our two families visited each other from time to time and we came to know a bevy, or bouquet, of dark-haired, dark-eyed, Gypsy-looking Williams girls, each one named after a flower, and two boys, Valentine and Douglas. It never entered my imagination then that, one day later in life, I should walk into a hell on earth called Souchez with young Valentine, when the Germans were on the Vimy ridge above and when the French soldiers of "Le Feu" were holding that heap of ruins under enemy observation. I never dreamed that with Douglas, his brother, I should be billeted in the old Hôtel de l'Univers in Arras in a second World War after going through the first. Both of them have had brilliant careers as special correspondents. Valentine was Berlin correspondent for Reuters' and did fine work before becoming the author of *Clubfoot* and other detective novels. In the first World War he began as a war correspondent and ended as a captain of the Irish Guards. His autobiography is most interesting and modest and deserves its great success.

5

ADOLESCENCE

Remembering back again to those evening at home at the old house in Clapham Park it is astonishing to think now that our drawing-room was illumined by candlelight with one or two oil lamps.

At eleven o'clock my father, with a pretence of absent-mindedness, which did not deceive his family who knew this trick, would put out one of the candles. Five minutes later he would put out another. It was a signal for his guests to go. If they did not take the hint almost total darkness would creep upon them.

Among our friends at that time was an old man—we youngsters thought him almost as old as death, though he had a young family who were our own contemporaries—named James Weale. He walked about Clapham and South Kensington in a black skull cap which he wore indoors and out, and a long black coat over a dark suit green with age. He was the greatest authority on Flemish art, and as librarian and custodian of South Kensington Museum was a connoisseur of early printed books, tapestries, crystals and medieval carvings. It was he who found the famous Judith crystal, now in the British Museum, after it had been missing for hundreds of years. A battle for its possession had been fought by two bodies of monks before it disappeared from history. One day one of old Weale's assistants reported to him that a tray of crystals had been offered to the Museum.

"Not worth anything I should say. But there's one old crystal which is rather interesting. It's carved with the story of Judith and Holofernes."

Mr. Weale turned pale. Could it possibly be the Judith crystal? It was, and he bought it for a small price with an odd-job lot.

Once an old lady sent in a box of old books and asked £7 10. 0 for them. Among them was an original folio edition of Shakespeare's works.

James Weale's household was very austere. We used to pity his family who all looked undernourished, thinly clad, and harshly treated by the old man, who lived only for scholarship and religion, and frowned upon all the pleasures and frivolities of life.

Of quite a different character was another man to whom the rare name of genius can justly be given. He had a young family with whom we boys played and flirted. This was Bentley, the architect of Westminster Cathedral. He was a burly, sulky-looking man, very silent among his chattering family, but with now and again a humorous gleam in his eyes and kindly words to a young visitor like myself. He had a passion for Byzantine art and was a master builder in line with those who raised our great cathedrals in the past.

Apart from my father, I had my first encouragement as a writer from him when as a boy of fifteen I went to Bruges and Brussels and wrote letters to the Bentley family describing what I had seen—the old canals in Bruges, the great belfry, the Beguinage, the lace makers, the picture galleries, and the people.

"That boy can write," he told one of his daughters.

We were devotees of the stage, seen by us mostly from the gallery, but sometimes, by some miracle, from a stage box. Like G. K. Chesterton and other small boys of the Victorian era I had begun this passion for the theatre by having one of my own—that is to say a wooden stage, three feet by one, with cardboard characters, penny plain and twopence coloured, which were drawn off and on by fixing them into metal slides. It had romantic back scenes and wings which gave the illusion—to me— of real trees. With my brothers and sisters, who read out different parts while concealed behind curtains, we gave a dramatic performance of the famous *Miller and His Men* to a large audience of friends. It was unfortunate, but inevitable, that in the middle of the last act, the toy theatre caught fire because its scenery was touched by a candle flame in the light of which we had been reading our parts. There was a panic in the audience, or part of it, when the curtains caught fire, and one of my aunts—the lady who had been the mistress of a Duke's son—clasped her daughter to her breast and cried out: "Let us die together!" Needless to say the daughter did not want to die at all, nor did she, for my father's prompt action extinguished the flames.

Later in family history our theatrical enterprises became more ambitious and we gave a notable performance in the flesh—no cardboard characters this time—of *Pygmalion and Galatea*. My father was a born actor, so that mostly he took the chief parts, but on this occasion the honours were carried off by my brother Cos who brought the house down—the house being the big playroom downstairs—by his interpretation of the comic part. For the role of Galatea we had a beautiful and talented girl by name of May Jobling, afterwards a professional actress of distinction. Her mother had played the original part of Galatea in Gilbert's famous play and she came to see her daughter carry on the family tradition.

It was a stupendous success among our circle of friends, many of whom said (sincerely but mistakenly) that it could not have been done better by professionals. My own part was the humble one of a young slave who has a fight in his master's studio with another slave—played by cousin Geoff Hamilton, who afterwards fought more seriously against the Boers.

The D'Oyley Carte Company gave us, and millions like us, a great gift of joy by their performances of the Gilbert and Sullivan operas. It was from a stage box at the Savoy that we saw and heard them all with rapture. They were not the original performances—those took place even before my time—but they were still played by the great company which included Grossmith and Rosina Brandon, and Rutland Barrington, and the whole delightful cast. The players were always interested and amused by the big family in the stage box and sometimes smiled at us and even whispered a word or two. Afterwards my mother would play the music of *The Yeomen of the Guard*, *Patience*, and all the others, and we would sing them and finger them out for ourselves on one finger or ten.

It would be hard to exaggerate the amount of pure pleasure given to the nation by Gilbert and Sullivan—those two sensitive and quick-tempered men who quarrelled, and wrangled, and tormented each other over trivial details, while producing their delightful work, as described by my brother Cos in a book called *Discord and Harmony*.

I paid only twopence to see and hear another famous opera, *Les Cloches de Corneville*. It was in a theatre on the Surrey side, and a full company gave a most excellent performance which held us spellbound as we sat aloft among coster girls who were sucking oranges and spitting the pips at the people in the pit below. Heaven knows the hardships, the semi-starvation, the frightful lodgings, the squalor, which had to be endured by a company of players like that, touring the country in one-night stands. Dickens knew as well as Heaven. So did the father of an actress still living, who was once so hungry that he grabbed the first twopence, put down for a gallery seat, and bought himself a bun to ease the aching void. So for a time did my brother Cos though he was never quite so hard pressed as that, but experienced for a year or two the life of a small-part actor in touring companies, before he became a playwright and made easy money and a lot of it.

6

VICTORIAN FLIRTATION

My elder brothers had their little love affairs and two of them—Cos and Frank—were great flirts in a boyish way. To the end of his life Cos could never resist the attraction of a pretty woman, as far as an amusing flirtation might lead him, and in adolescence when he, like Frank, was remarkably handsome, and a most humorous lad, there were plenty of pretty girls in the neighbourhood whose hearts beat a little faster when he appeared.

There was a family of McGuinness girls who were great friends of ours. Needless to say they were Irish. Their father—Major McGuinness—was a regular soldier of the old school, simple, gallant and debonair. They were all, of course, staunch Catholics, and the Major was so sure of his faith that like the Jongleur of Notre Dame he could be a little merry even before the altar. One morning at early Mass with his family he put a gong under his waistcoat and at the moment when the priest says the words "mea culpa", and the faithful are supposed to tap their breasts as a sign of contrition, he struck his waistcoat and the gong below it, to the horror of his lady wife and the delight of his girls.

There were four McGuinness girls, and Frank fell in love with all of them, as he confided to me. This caused him much heart-searching and perplexity, because he liked them all so much he could not choose one. When Maude, the youngest, arrived from a convent school we were all startled by her beauty with big dark eyes and long dark lashes in a little delicate Madonna-like face—poor darling. She made an unhappy marriage and died young. The other McGuinness girls never married. Ethel types my books and is still very kind to me.

It was because of my friendship with this family that I went for a time to the Irish Literary Society when I was still a boy, and on grand nights met W. B. Yeats and Algernon Percival Graves, the author of *Father O'Flynn*, and the father of Robert Graves and Charles Graves.

Yeats was a young man then, and looked more like a poet than any poet ought to look. A long lock of brown hair fell over his forehead and over his eyes, like the fringe of a Yorkshire terrier, so that he had to keep on brushing it back with a long, thin, delicate hand, showing a length of bare wrist because the sleeves of a shabby jacket had become too short for him. I suspect he was as poor as a church mouse. But when he spoke his personality was glorified, for he had a golden voice and a great gift of oratory, and words of magic and loveliness poured from his lips.

There was another family of girls who kept open house whenever we liked to call, even at breakfast time. I was too young for amorous adventures with them but my brothers liked them a good deal, and Frank especially paid his attentions to them. They were the Follett family whose father—a most kindly man—had one of those big old mansions in Clapham Park, surrounded by lawns and full-grown trees, which were built for rich city merchants in the early Victorian era, when they drove to their offices in comfortable broughams. Now it happened that my father liked to have a little flirtation now and then with the Follett girls whom he found remarkably intelligent, and, as one of them told me, he was disconcerted and annoyed when young Frank, alluring in his youth and Byronic beauty, turned up and put him in his place.

7

YOUNG ECSTASY

Before I reached the age of seventeen I knew what my ambition was in the adventure of life. I wanted to write and started writing. God help me, I have never left off!

I was sixteen when I had my first article accepted and printed. Curiously enough it was in the old *Daily Chronicle*, then the most literary newspaper in London, which afterwards I served for years as special correspondent at home and abroad. I received 7s. 6d. for a vignette describing the sea gulls screaming over London Bridge on a winter afternoon. Then I started writing fairy tales which were published now and then in *Little Folks*.

I remember turning to my father one day when I had no less than two cheques for small amounts at the breakfast table and saying :

"I think I may really call myself a literary gent."

He looked into my shining eyes and smiled.

"You're making a good start," he said; "but there's a long road ahead old boy, and it's a perilous adventure."

At that age of adolescence I had moments of ecstasy or—shall I say—of being carried outside myself, which I have not known since, at least so intensely and poignantly. The first may blossom, lying like snow on

LADY GIBBS AND HER SON ANTHONY

PHILIP GIBBS
War correspondent on the Western Front, 1914-1918

the branches of the trees on Surrey commons, stirred me with a sense of earth's beauty and loveliness. It was perhaps a kind of pantheism when I felt myself to be a part of this universe and of all life. I remember leaning out of my bedroom window on a summer night and seeing the glow of London—no air raid then!—above the chimney pots, and hearing the murmur of its traffic. The human drama of London seemed to enter into me, and take possession of me, so that I was aware, as it seemed, of all the suffering, the agony, the heartbreak, and the hopes, of all those millions in this half-sleeping city. It was an intense awareness of life and of the beating pulse of humanity of which I was one insignificant boy.

I was at that time a shy, sensitive, lad, without any armour to protect myself against the brutalities, or even the unkindnesses, of the rough world about me. I blushed at any coarseness of speech. I had no toughness of fibre, none of the ease and assurance which are acquired by a public school education. I was deplorably self-conscious and diffident in company. Worse than that for myself, I was far too sensitive to the tragedy of life and to other people's pain and suffering, so that I agonised over the martyrdom of man, and even over the imaginary tortures of fictitious characters in novels and plays. It took a long time to harden me in the Street of Adventure where most men get hardboiled. I am not quite hardened yet.

8

MARRIAGE OF BABES

I fell in love and three years later, at the age of twenty-one, married my love. Her name was Agnes. She was the daughter of a country parson, the Revd. W. J. Rowland, who had the living of Stoke-under-Ham, and afterwards of Crewkerne and Middle Chinnock, down in Somerset, where as I said in the old phrase I went a-courting.

Agnes had been brought to our house in Clapham by my sister Helen, with whom she had been to a convent school in Belgium, near to the Ardennes at Paliseul where in the second World War the Americans fought some of their stiffest battles. When I saw her first I knew that all my happiness lay with her, though I hardly dared hope that she would care for me, because my brothers, Cos and Frank, were so much more amusing and made her laugh far more than I could ever do. She had the gift of laughter all her life, having a merry wit and a sense of humour never killed by desperate illnesses and much spiritual unhappiness in later years.

As a young girl she had a rose-like beauty, and it is among roses that I like to remember her for she tended them in many gardens. I saw her first among roses in the garden of her aunt's house at Elstree, where, in a white frock which would look very oldfashioned now, and a big straw hat, she stood with a pair of scissors snipping off the dead blossom from a marvellous show of summer glory. Shyly I went towards her, and saw her laughing eyes, and heard her cry of "Hullo, Pip!"

Her aunt was her father's sister Alice who had married a distinguished and sinister man named Dr. Ernest Hart. He was for many years Editor of *The British Medical Journal*, and stood high in his profession. He was a rich man with a house in Wimpole Street, filled with a priceless collection of Japanese bronzes and porcelain.

For a time he gave house-room to Agnes in return for secretarial service and enslavement, and to Wimpole Street went I in a top hat, tail coat, and striped trousers, when old Hart was well off the premises, and when the footman—he was I thought an insolent fellow—gave me a wink as much as to say "the old man's out".

My future father-in-law had another sister who married a remarkable man, more benevolent—though grotesquely ugly—than Dr. Ernest Hart. This was Canon Barnett who, with his wife Henrietta, founded Toynbee Hall in Whitechapel as a centre of life and learning and social welfare in the East End. Afterwards Mrs. Barnett became Dame Henrietta and helped to found Hampstead Garden Suburb in which once I gave a lecture, pleasing the old lady, who was a combination of Queen Victoria and Mrs. Jellyby, with a touch of Becky Sharp, by referring to her as "my amazing aunt".

My future wife's relations took me into unknown ways in those years before our marriage. I came to know the life of a country rectory and of many parsonages in its neighbourhood, and of country squires and local characters including some who made a stir in the world of letters, like the three Powys brothers. I came to know intimately and with some affection the greatest character of all—my future father-in-law.

The Revd. W. J. Rowland had been a military chaplain in India. That was why my wife's first language was Hindustani, and her first memory of life a vision of Cashmere. Being a man of private means he and his first wife had lived in some style out there with carriages and native servants. It had been a gay life, especially for my wife's mother who was a Domville of Devonshire and a beautiful lady of the old quality, elegant, a little masterful, but easy in her ways with gardeners and grooms and gamekeepers and sextons. A little too gay perhaps, that life in India. When I knew her afterwards—long afterwards—I understood that as a clergyman's wife she was out of place. She had no reverence in her laughing heart. She was an incurable flirt. She was witty and, poor dear, a little wicked. One night in England when they had left India for a spell she said good-night to each of her sleeping children, of whom there were four. One of them grew up to be Sydney Rowland, a brilliant bacteriologist and an expert on spinal meningitis, of which he died as a martyr to science, in World War I. Another was my wife, then a little girl of seven or so. She remembered a strange glitter in the eyes of her mother who bent over her and gave her a string of beads and then slipped away. She slipped away with an officer in the Indian Army.

I do not know whether my future father-in-law was more stricken by the loss of a beautiful lady or by the expense of the divorce she cost him, but I think the latter. He was embittered also by the impossibility of getting promotion in the Church, which at that time regarded a clergyman who had divorced his wife and then married again—he married again—as ineligible for ecclesiastical preferment. He was given poor parishes in the depths of Somerset, instead of being made a Canon or a Bishop according to his intellectual ability and ambition.

He was a great scholar in the full sense of the word. I have never met a more learned man, or a man more passionately devoted to study. All his life he rose, winter and summer, at 5.30, washed his face in cold water, and sat down for a couple of hours reading before breakfast. He was always reading, except when "parish poking" as he called it, when he visited the old and sick and fulfilled his duties as a country clergyman, which he did conscientiously but without enthusiasm. He was a fine classical scholar but vastly interested in almost every branch of knowledge, except science. He studied architecture, and could tell the date of any part of a church or any bit of decoration within twenty-five years. He read history deeply.

He was a profound student of art and of all its masters. He studied old furniture, porcelain, sculpture, medieval craftsmanship. He read vast tomes on the history of Rome and every volume of Frazer's *Golden Bough*, and every authority on early civilisations.

But in spite of this scholarship he had a rich sense of humour—very Elizabethan at times—and was fond of a flirtation with any pretty woman, if she had intelligence as well as good looks. He found much food for his humour among the neighbouring clergy, to all of whom he gave nicknames kept dark as a family secret. I remember "Dirty Shirt", who had a vicarage not far away. His wife was placed in the portrait gallery as "The Light of the Harem". In a carefully locked drawer of the Vicar's desk was a manuscript book bound in red leather and filled with most dangerous stuff, but very mirth provoking when occasionally he let me have a glimpse of it. Into this book he wrote squibs, satires, and ironical verse about his relations and neighbours, with occasional sallies into the political field. His sister Henrietta Barnett, and her husband the Canon, were among his most bitter satires.

"Have nothing to do with your relations," was his constant advice to his family, uttered as an almost daily slogan.

Certainly his brothers and sisters, and nephews and nieces, were a very queer crowd, rather feckless and disorderly. They had all inherited small fortunes from a very rich father who was one of the most celebrated men in England, being none other than the proprietor of Rowland's Macassar Oil which originated the Victorian antimacassars, on every horsehair-stuffed chair, in every Victorian household. Byron wrote about him in *Childe Harold*. His name was as familiar as a household word, and his oil was as precious balm to the luxuriant whiskers of Victorian dandies. As a young man he went to Germany and brought back a little German wife whose portrait hangs in my drawing-room now, a pretty and pathetic little lady, childlike and delicate, but the mother of a big family before she died, poor dear. She was, of course, my wife's grandmother, and once Agnes and I, being in the Rhineland, went to find her family "Schloss" at Honef-am-Rhein of which we had a drawing. The driver of the car to whom we confided our quest became quite excited and sentimental. He stopped several citizens of Honef and informed them of the object of our journey.

"The *Herrschaften* seek the Schloss of their German grandmother."

"Ach! That is very romantic. Surely it is the Schloss now inhabited by Herr von Diercksen," or whatever the name might be.

We were taken to several Schlosses. The driver would stop below a flight of steps and say: "This is the Schloss of your grandmother."

But it was not the Schloss of my wife's grandmother, according to the drawing we had. At the fourth time we yielded, and pretended that certainly it was the Schloss and gazed at it with sham sentimentality which satisfied the romantic soul of our German driver.

My father-in-law-to-be inherited a somewhat Germanic character from his little German mother and her ancestry. That may have accounted for the severity with which he brought up his family. His three sons hated him because of his bullying, though he sent them to public schools and spent a lot of money on their education, which greatly reduced his inheritance.

He sent Agnes to a convent school in Belgium, as I have said, for the sake of economy, and then was violently angry when she told him one day that she had become a Catholic. He treated her in a medieval way, shutting her up in her room, after denouncing the Catholic Church and all its works. He even wrote a letter to the Pope, but His Holiness ignored it. It was a long time before he became reconciled to this change of faith, but he had mellowed when I went down to Somerset with Agnes before our marriage.

Every morning before breakfast we joined in family prayers in his study. I can remember the smell of his room—old leather, old books, and the tobacco of many pipes. This combination of scents was heavily stored up in that big study because its owner did not believe in what he called "foul fresh air". Another saying of his was that he "never drank what he washed in". He was a great beer-drinker like his mother's ancestors, and was a big, burly man with a brown moustache and beard and plump fair-complexioned cheeks. I came to like him a great deal and we were always friends, though at first sight of me he told Agnes that I was no match for her, which indeed was true.

He had a passion for foreign travel and after my marriage I went abroad with him several times, mostly to France, staying in Paris and going to the Louvre every day for a couple of hours at least. Once we went as far as the Pyrenees where to my astonishment I saw a real live bear on a snow-topped peak. On these journeys he was a good companion, and when we visited cathedrals, and churches, and galleries, and castles his immense knowledge was an education to me.

His second wife was a tiny little lady, very prim and old-fashioned, like a character in a Jane Austen novel. She had been to school in Belsize Park with the Caltrops and the Novellos and the Boucicaults. There she learnt the "use of the globes", read the letters of Madame de Sévigné and received the "ladylike" education of that time. She also went to all the operas, and when she became an old lady and came to stay with me her greatest pleasure was to remember the enchantment of Verdi, and Offenbach, and Mozart, and Bizet. She loved music, and played very charmingly even when her little hands were knotted with rheumatism, and when she had to peer through spectacles to see the notes. I made a pencil sketch of her at the piano and it is very like her. She became the mother of two girls, one of whom is now a Reverend Mother, always gay and quick to laugh. I shall have to tell a story about her when I come to the first World War. The other daughter is now the mother of a tall Saxon-looking young gunner—Adrian Harbottle Reed—who has the scholarly nature of his grandfather and something of his look.

9

FROCK-COATED YOUTH

My first job as a boy of eighteen was in the publishing house of Cassell and Company, whose premises were in La Belle Sauvage Yard, at the foot of Ludgate Hill. It was on the site of an old inn of that name, called after little Pocahontas who was brought over from Virginia by Captain Smith in the reign of James I.

Although I started low down on the ladder I advanced to my work every morning in a top hat and frock coat, impressing as a "young toff" rough fellows hauling enormous rolls of paper in the courtyard to feed the printing machines and winking at each other as I passed.

I was in the illustration department to start with, under the direction of a youngish man named Smith, who was very kind to his new junior. My colleagues were all middle-aged men on small salaries, which were just sufficient to maintain their wives and families above the starvation line. My own salary was not enormous but I paid over part of it to my father with whom I still lived. One day I was robbed of a golden sovereign or two, and not caring to confess to this loss made my lunch for a month on two pennyworth of dried figs, bought in a paper bag from a fruiterer's shop in old Holywell Street where, during lunch time, I used to browse among the secondhand book shops. For years afterwards I dared not look a fig in the face.

One could pick up treasures in Holywell Street which, with its neighbour, Wych Street (do you remember Stacy Aumonier's story *Which is Wych Street?*) was swept away for the making of Aldwych.

My friend of Cassell's bought an old book for a shilling which he discovered to be highly valuable. It was a copy of Hudibras with the first-known illustrations of Hogarth when he was a goldsmith's apprentice. Not even the British Museum had a copy and Smith sold it for a large sum of money. It created a sensation among the connoisseurs in literary journals.

My first step up on the ladder of success was due to my effort to learn German. I was puzzling out a novel in that language one day, while there was nothing much to do at my desk, when I heard a pleasant voice behind me.

"Do you read German?"

"I'm trying to," I answered.

I turned round and saw a tall curly-haired man with the bluest eyes I have ever seen in a human face. They were a deep china blue. He asked me a few questions about my work and then said: "Come and see me upstairs one day. I am often there between twelve and one."

"Thanks," I answered.

When he had gone I spoke to Smith.

"Who is that?"

Smith smiled.

"Our great chief. The Managing Director of this house, and Minister for War. H. O. Arnold-Forster. Grandson of Dr. Arnold."

Within a few weeks I was sitting at a desk in the same room as this blue-eyed gentleman, and some time later I was put in charge of his department which had to do with educational books and the sales thereof. My main job was to bring them to the notice of elementary and other schools.

Arnold-Forster was an astonishing man, the soul of courtesy to his subordinates, and so punctilious that I once saw him take a grubby printer's devil down a passage to show him his way. To his equals in social rank he was sometimes the rudest man imaginable, and I saw him treat distinguished visitors like dirt. He had an immense amount of knowledge in his head, and in that room where I worked with him he dictated a whole History of England—the best that has ever been written for young people. He dictated this to an unfortunate secretary named Tasker whose job it was to fill in dates and names of places when required.

To me he was always kind and I think my youth and shyness appealed to him. It was due to a word from him that I was commissioned by Cassell and Company to write my first book *Founders of the Empire*, for which he wrote a preface as a very particular favour. That little book, beautifully illustrated, had a great success, and went on selling for years.

10

ANCIENT BURIAL

While I was at Cassell's I attended the funeral of an old gentleman named Baskerville, who had been a traveller in school books produced by my department. He had been charming to me, and was a very cultured old man, who had been a schoolmaster. One evening a sharp wind cut him like a knife at the end of his street—a street of mean little houses—and he dropped down dead.

"It's nice of you to come, dearie," said Mrs. Baskerville when I went to her house for the funeral. "William was always very fond of you."

Mr. and Mrs. Baskerville's relatives and friends had rallied for the sad occasion. The blinds were drawn and by gas-light we partook of sherry and biscuits before the arrival of the undertakers who came in strength. Their chief—a most lugubrious gentleman in black from head to foot with a black scarf round his top hat—presented each member of the funeral party with a pair of black gloves. The neighbours all had their blinds down, but many of them stood in the street to watch the pageant of death. It was an oldfashioned funeral in the best style. That is to say the hearse was drawn by four black steeds with long tails which almost swept the ground. They had big black plumes on their heads, and the coachmen of the carriages which conveyed us to the cemetery wore long trailing scarves round their top hats like the gentleman with the gloves.

"It's just as he would have liked it, poor dear!" said Mrs. Baskerville peeping through the window curtain before we started.

It must have been very expensive and I fancy that the pomp and circumstance of burial has departed with its black plumes from the mean streets of London.

11

ITALY IN LONDON

During the luncheon hour at Cassell's I used to explore as much of London as lay within reach of my legs, after a hurried meal of which my limit in cost was 1s. 2d. with 1d. for the waiter.

One district beyond Holborn always fascinated me. It was the Italian quarter, approached by way of Leather Lane, where at lunch time there were many cheap Jacks extolling the all-healing qualities of sarsaparilla, and selling trash by whirlwind oratory and all the guile of Autolycus. The Italian quarter in the neighbourhood of Hatton Garden was completely foreign, with narrow courtyards crowded with dark-eyed children, and young Italian women at the washtubs. At the corner of one alley I often heard growling and the rattle of chains. It was where two fellows in blue bérets kept a dancing bear. In the cellars slept the young Italian boys who went round with hurdy-gurdies, and little monkeys in red caps and jackets. The boys were as much enslaved as the monkeys, being farmed out to a *padrone*, who beat them if they did not bring back good earnings after their day's wandering through the residential streets of London, where coppers were thrown to them from nursery windows. I went into a factory where Italian craftsmen, powdered white from head to foot, made plaster casts of Greek gods and goddesses, and busts of Napoleon, Nelson, Wellington, and Queen Victoria.

I also went into the workshop of an old Italian, whose hair was curled and crinkled as though the music in his soul—for he was a *maestro*—was bursting out of his head in quavers and semiquavers. He sat at a piano organ, with its front taken off, exposing a big roll of cartridge paper upon which he stabbed innumerable little holes with a bodkin. The little holes ran up and down the roll of cartridge paper which turned on a handle, and afterwards, wherever there had been a hole there was a steel spike in a cylinder, after being cast in metal. These spikes struck the notes of the piano organ and reproduced all the trills and flourishes with which this old Italian with his plump fingers had filled out an ancient ballad or a new tune. Now and then a young musician starving in a garret awoke to find that one of his melodies was being played through the streets of London, whistled by butcher boys, and trilled by kitchen maids down in the basements. It was the way to fame and fortune, and my little old man in his workshop had this destiny in his hands, at the point of his bare bodkin, though unknown in his lair at the end of Leather Lane.

One day I wrote an article about all this and it was illustrated with photographs by a young friend of mine in Cassell's—his name was Powell—and accepted by a London magazine. Shortly afterwards we strolled into the Italian quarter to show our friends there the illustrated article about themselves, thinking it would please them mightily. But something had gone wrong. The young women at the washtubs looked at us angrily and spoke excited Italian which we failed to understand. Somebody gave a shrill whistle. The courtyard in which we stood was suddenly crowded with men and boys all jabbering Italian, all looking very fierce. A number of them drew their knives—long murderous-looking knives—and flashed them too near to our noses to be pleasant.

"What on earth is the matter?" asked my friend Powell.

"It doesn't look too good," I answered.

Greatly to our relief a London Bobby, hearing the uproar, strolled into the courtyard.

"Now, what's all this abaht?" he asked in the usual formula.

His presence had a chastening effect. Many of the men slipped away. We discovered from one of them who spoke English that the Italian community had greatly disliked my description of their way of life, because it suggested that they were a dirty lot, living in foul conditions from which came the twopenny licks of ice cream eaten by their English customers.

I had not intended to convey that impression. I was sorry about it because I liked these people, and it was the first lesson I had that writing is apt to lead one into trouble of the gravest kind, including libel

B

and other terrors. Since then I know it to be one of the dangerous trades and costly in its penalties.

The Italian quarter disappeared at the beginning of the first World War.

The men with the bears, the monkey boys, the trays of plaster casts, the Italian ice-cream merchants, the young women with bare arms at their washtubs, have now passed into the dream world of memory, with much else that was picturesque.

12

THE BOER WAR

One morning during those early days at Cassell's I stood outside the Guildhall during lunch time. I was not alone. A dense crowd stood packed in the old courtyard, excited, noisy, cheering. The Lord Mayor of London appeared in his robes and made a speech to the crowd. I cannot remember his exact words, but they announced that after intolerable insults from an old man named Kruger, Her Majesty's government had declared war upon the South African Boers. There was terrific and tumultuous cheering. Top hats were flung up after the crowd had sung "God Save the Queen". I don't believe I joined in the cheering. Certainly I did not fling up my top hat. Brought up in the Gladstonian tradition of the Liberals, and being, anyhow, a liberal-minded youth hostile to the loud-mouthed jingoism of the time, I was not swept by enthusiasm for a war which seemed to me, as it did to others, a bit of bullying by the big old British Empire— was it not invincible and invulnerable?—against a poor little pastoral people. The Jameson raid which preceded it had seemed to me a dirty business. It was only when that poor little pastoral people, as I had thought of them, put up a stiff fight, outmanœuvred our generals, ambushed our infantry, and caused dreadful casualties among our officers and men that I realised that we were not going to have a walk-over. There was a dreadful Black Sunday when the news came of a disaster at Magersfontein and when the casualty lists looked long and horrible—a frightful blow to British morale before a World War had accustomed us to bigger massacres of youth.

I saw the C.I.V. ride through London and heard the cheering crowds.

I heard Kipling's ballad of "Pay, Pay, Pay!" I saw the rush to the recruiting booths. I was one of those who clutched at the evening papers for the news of war. In my lifetime there has been too much war—for all of us who have lived so long. Little did I guess that day when I stood outside the Guildhall that I should become a war correspondent and should walk for years across battlefields and trenches strewn with the bodies of dead youth, with the stench of death in my nostrils and with a horror of war in my mind.

13

BABES IN THE WOOD

My chief—Arnold-Forster—became Secretary of the Navy, and was destined for a high political career, but his health broke down and he died comparatively young, leaving behind two young sons.

One day when I was in his room the door opened and a girl popped her head in, said: "Hullo!" and then retreated hurriedly when she saw that I was not alone.

"Who's that pretty girl?" asked Arnold-Forster.

"A friend of mine," I told him.

I hadn't the courage to tell him it was my wife. We both looked so young. People laughed when they heard we were husband and wife. I was married when I was twenty-one. I was much younger in mind, and character, and lack of sophistication, than a boy of twenty-one to-day, who perhaps is a veteran of war. I married on £120 a year.

What a perilous adventure! What high audacity of youth! What a fairy tale of two Babes in the Wood, who went hand in hand through the enchantment of life with a hungry wolf round the corner, with many man-traps hidden in the undergrowth, with many devils and goblins waiting to trip us up, but kept at bay by our innocence and courage! It was Agnes who had most of the courage and who led the way.

I am astonished to remember, when I look back upon my early married life, that Agnes and I were able to afford a holiday in Paris during our first year of marriage. Out of that £120 a year, with perhaps a few extra guineas earned by a fairy tale or an article, we spent a fortnight abroad, and were so rich at the end of it that we bought presents for our family. We stayed at a tiny hotel called the Dauphin, in the rue St. Roch, out of the rue St. Honoré, within a few yards of that church where the young Napoleon placed a battery of guns and seized power by "a whiff of grapeshot". The *patron* and his wife—a young couple then—were amused and touched by our youth and innocence. They had only one bedroom available, and that was very small and barely furnished on the top floor, but they let us have it for a few francs a night with coffee and rolls for breakfast. They fell in love with us, that couple, and we kept friendly with them for years after they had become fat and middle-aged. But they were the only people friendly to us in Paris at that time, for our visit coincided with an incident in history which made the English very much disliked. It was the time of Fashoda, when a French general named Marchand raised the tricolor over a bit of desert in Africa, which Kitchener considered to be within the British sphere of influence. Kitchener's right-hand man at that time was a little fellow named Reginald Wingate, afterwards Sirdar of Egypt. Nearly thirty years afterwards I sat next to him at a London dinner table and he described that affair of Fashoda, when Kitchener and he informed General Marchand, very politely, that he would have to haul down his flag and fade out of the picture. Marchand stormed and wept, while in Paris our ambassador was having a painful time with the French government. We were close to war, and so excited was French public opinion that when two harmless young people, who were Agnes and myself, walked along the Grands Boulevards, French workmen spat as we passed, and French students and midinettes jeered at us and cried out *"Conspuez les Anglais!"* Still we enjoyed ourselves vastly, exploring old Paris and wandering through the Louvre, walking hand in hand through the Bois de Boulogne, and looking at the little shops in the Palais Royal where one day Camille Desmoulins had called the people to attack the Bastille in the name of Liberty.

14

YOUNG BIRDS

My marriage—an anxious affair for my father and mother—was another break in the old family life. The birds were leaving the parent nest. My eldest brother, Henry, was the first to go. He went as far as South America to a bank in Buenos Aires where his gift for languages— French, German, Italian, and Spanish—was useful to him. He married a beautiful Argentine, and in due course had several Spanish-speaking children, and came to look like a Spanish hidalgo, being dark with a long thin face.

My brother Frank also went far afield, landing in a surf-boat on the coast of West Africa where he became a "palm oil ruffian", though he had a Byronic look and never became really "tough".

He went into the jungle and was in charge—the only white man—of a rubber plantation with two thousand black people working for him. Often his life hung only on white man's prestige and the look in his eyes, and the strength of his wrist when he had to flog a man who defied him and tried to raise rebellion. He was only about twenty-three, and must have had astonishing moral courage to endure the fevers and all the terrors of jungle life. He took his violin with him, and used to play to himself in his thatched hut. One night while he played he heard a curious sound outside. It was like the deep rhythmic breathing of some prehistoric monster. It was the breathing of his black labourers who had crept up to hear the white man's music. Music ceased for him one day, for an army of white ants marched through his hut and ate his violin, so that only a little powder was left on the floor. During those years in West Africa he wrote three novels on life out there, and years afterwards Edgar Wallace told me that they were the best books he had ever read on West Africa, and had been very useful to him as atmosphere for his own stories. They had plenty of atmosphere. Reading them one could smell the jungle, and hear the little noises of creeping things, or the enormous silence. One sweated with blackwater fever. One could, if one liked, learn pidgin English. Some years later I had a telegram asking me to meet him at Victoria station. He had been put so nearly dead into a boat that the skipper said: "We don't take corpses in this ship." I met a living skeleton at Victoria station. There was only brown skin on its bones. It wore a sun-helmet and a loose overcoat over white ducks which clung about him. In one hand the skeleton carried a gun, and in the other a canary in a golden cage. It was my brother Frank.

I have said that Cos became an actor, but that was not for long. He wrote a little novel called *Which is Absurd*, which was published in the Pseudonym Library by Fisher Unwin. It had a considerable success and he followed it by other novels under the pen name of Cosmo Hamilton—taking our mother's surname—by which finally he became so well known that, mistakenly I think, he adopted it as his own. But it was first as a playwright that he made quite a little fortune at a very early age. He collaborated with Seymour Hicks. Together they produced the *Catch of the Season* which had a stunning success, followed by *The Beauty of Bath* and *The Belle of Mayfair*.

I saw very little of him in those golden days of his. He took a fine old house at West Drayton, was part owner of a race-horse—Sal Gal—and consorted with very smart people, including the theatrical world who were outside my "beat". He was a terrific worker, and besides writing plays and novels was editor of *The World*, for which he wrote innumerable articles, stories, and reviews. How he escaped the law on libel I do not understand to this day, for he was a biting critic and satirist, careless of the staid old tradition of the Yates family who had founded that weekly journal of social life.

He married Beryl Faber, still remembered by old playgoers at the St. James's Theatre under George Alexander. She was a beautiful woman —the sister of that fine actor Aubrey Smith—and exquisite on the stage.

She was ambitious for my brother, and he lost all the money he had made, and something more, by running a theatre of his own. Perhaps this worried her. One evening she arrived from the theatre and said: "I feel very tired." She was so tired that she fell asleep that night for ever.

Cosmo Hamilton had for his secretary my youngest brother Arthur, whom he had sent to St. John's College, Oxford, where he did well and produced a handsome book called *Rowlandson's Oxford*. He won several cups for Archery, was a good rowing man, and was a light-weight boxer. Now and then young Arthur wrote my brother's articles for *The World* and other papers when Cos was hard pressed. It was a good apprenticeship, and later, after serving as a gunner in the first World War and reaching the rank of major, this "kid-brother" of mine, as I always thought of him, wrote a novel called *Soundings*, which had one of those typhoon successes in the United States, establishing him as a novelist in that country where now he lives.

One of my sisters named Helen also produced fiction for a time, so that out of that disorderly home-made education in the old house at Clapham came a group of writers not without success, and anyhow remarkable for their literary output.

For my parents, left very lonely after the old rowdiness and activity of family life—especially as my father's health broke down—this breaking away was sad. It is the eternal tragedy of parenthood. I was sorry for them. I owed so much to them, and years after they had died, even until recently, I had a recurrent dream. It was always that I had not gone to see them for a very long time, and that I had been neglectful. I went to see them in my dream and woke up with a pain in my heart. That old home life had been the most abiding influence in my mind and sub-consciousness. Not even my wife would believe that I was home-sick after my marriage. But I was.

PART II

THE STREET OF ADVENTURE

1

LITERARY SYNDICATE

MY way to Fleet Street, which my ghost will haunt, was by a roundabout route which took me to the North of England.

I heard one day that there was a good job going as editor of the biggest literary syndicate in England, situated, strangely, in a Lancashire town called Bolton, and owned by some people called Tillotson.

What they did as a literary syndicate was a mystery to me, but I understood, rightly, that they bought stories and articles from well-known writers and syndicated them in provincial newspapers with a profit on the deal.

I applied for this post by letter, and, as I was told afterwards, I was selected among many candidates because of one sentence I wrote therein: "Like the younger Pitt," I wrote, "I am guilty of the damnable crime of being a young man."

Now this quotation made an instant appeal to the Tillotsons because their syndicate was run by three young brothers. One of them, Fred Tillotson, a very charming fellow as I found, had just come down from Oxford, and this reference to Pitt tickled him a good deal. Their father had founded the business after making a fortune by having the monopoly of printing pawn tickets. He then started the *Bolton Evening News*, and it occurred to him one day that it would be a good idea to run a serial story. Somewhat ambitiously he bought one by Miss Braddon, then one of the most popular novelists, and as it cost a considerable sum of money the thought came to him that he might share this expense with other provincial newspapers, not conflicting with his own area of circulation. Not only did he cover his outlay but he made a profit, and this suggested the idea of syndication on a big scale, covering the whole provincial press, as well as the Colonial Press, who thereby would be able to publish famous authors and smaller fry at a moderate cost. It succeeded admirably.

My wife and I plunged into the unknown when we travelled north with few impedimenta, having few. To this day I remember waking for the first time in the capital city of Cotton, and hearing the clatter of the clogs, as thousands of factory girls, with shawls over their heads and wooden shoon, were going to the mills in a bleak dawn. The trams went clanging down Bradshawgate. Darkness and a damp fog enveloped this unbeautiful city with its tall factory chimneys and blackened buildings of most hideous architecture, with streets of small brick houses, all alike in ugliness for that big population of mill hands.

My first impression of Bolton was very unfavourable and I felt darkly depressed at having come to such a place, but I learnt before long that one can make one's own little paradise in the blackest environment, that kind people matter more than the houses in which they live, and that there were pleasant quarters and good country beyond the mean streets and the tall chimneys.

We took a house in the Westwood Road, much to the astonishment of Lever Tillotson, my immediate chief, who knew the slender packet which came to me each week. For it appeared that the "best people" lived in the Westwood Road, which turned out of the Chorley New Road, inhabited by the cotton kings and the rich industrialists of Bolton.

My wife knew what she was about, and we cut our coats according to our cloth by rigid economy. Our furniture was procured on the hire-purchase system. Somehow or other we made a pleasant-looking home, where presently we received many visitors attracted, perhaps, by our youth, and careless of our poverty. We made good friends among them and the cotton kings, like the Haslams and Lomaxes, invited us to their dinner tables.

Culture had reached out to Bolton here and there. There were witty and widely read women who gave us their friendship. One was our next door neighbour by name of Mrs. Nash. The other was a bird-like little woman with a mind as sharp as a needle and a most whimsical sense of humour, who was Mrs. Hall, the wife of the Public Prosecutor, with two adorable children whom we fed with immoderate quantities of buns when they came to tea.

In Bolton I widened my knowledge and kept my pen busy, reading and writing after a full day's work. This was the reading and the marketing of novels and stories by writers like Conan Doyle, Hornung, Katherine Tynan, "Rita" and most of the well-known writers of the day. Once we bought a story by Kipling—one of his best—and the Tillotsons made quite a bit of money by spotting a new literary lion— Arnold Bennett—before he knew his own value. We syndicated his amusing novel *The Grand Babylon Hotel*.

But in order to pay the butcher's bill, and the doctor's bill, and other expenses hardly covered by my salary, I started a series of articles which were syndicated in *The Weekly Scotsman*, and many other papers. It was called "Knowledge is Power", and like Sir Francis Bacon I took all knowledge for my province, undertaking to answer any question which might be addressed to me. I confess that my knowledge was not always more than a week old, being based on books which I had devoured the week before, as a pupil-teacher keeps in advance of his class. But all the reading I had done as a boy, all my youthful enthusiasm for Shakespeare, Milton, Scott, Thackeray, Dickens, George Eliot, and Hardy, and the great masters, all my study of history—not very deep but fairly wide— was a great source of supply now when I sat down to write about great books, and the wisdom of the ages, and the love of poetry and art and drama and all beauty. These articles of mine had a surprising success, far beyond the British Isles, for *The Weekly Scotsman* in which they appeared among other papers, as I have said, went to far outposts wherever a Scot had established himself, and I had letters from all parts of the world discussing the subjects with which I had dealt, and finding pleasure in my essays on books and writers.

One day a very tall broad-shouldered man whose visiting card announced that he was Cutcliffe Hyne, the author of *Captain Kettle*, and many adventure books, came into my room at the Tillotson's and after a glance at me began to laugh heartily.

"What's the matter?" I asked.

"Good heavens!" he exclaimed. "I've been reading your articles called 'Knowledge is Power'. I thought you were an old baldheaded man with a long white beard, and I find you a fair-faced youth!"

Years afterwards I came to know the famous preacher, R. J. Campbell, with his snow-white hair and big, dark, romantic eyes. He told me that he always kept a copy of *Knowledge is Power* by his bedside—it had been published in book form—and found it helpful to him. I was abashed, remembering my youth and innocence at the time of writing those essays. But they are still selling in book form and perhaps that young idealism accounts for it.

I started another series of articles written by a small group of contributors and myself. Payment was on the lowest scale—half a guinea an article—and the writers were mostly amateur who wrote for the fun of the thing, and a little pocket money. Among them was a friend of mine named R. P. Croom-Johnson with whom I played in amateur theatricals when we were very young. He is now Sir Reginald Croom-Johnson, one of His Majesty's Judges of the High Court. Not long ago I had lunch with him when he was on circuit. The Judge's lodgings as he called them, were in a fine old mansion surrounded by a park. Not knowing its whereabouts I lost my way down a long country road and seeing a police inspector asked if he could direct me.

"What do you want to go there for?" he asked suspiciously.

"I am taking lunch with Mr. Justice Croom-Johnson."

"How am I to know that?" he asked. "How can you prove it?"

I couldn't prove it, but I showed him my identity card and he seemed satisfied, and told me he was standing at the very gate.

Presently a car arrived, as I stood in an immense room with a big fire on the hearth, the door opened and in came Croom-Johnson in his Judge's robes and wig, followed by a chaplain ready to put on the black cap in case of need. He reminded me of those good old days when he had written innumerable articles for the Tillotsons at half a guinea apiece.

2

BACK FROM THE NORTH

During this time at Bolton our son Anthony was born, and Agnes thought it would be pleasant to take a country cottage beyond the pall of smoke. We could not afford much, but we could go as far as 9d. a week which was the rent charged us for a tumbledown labourer's cottage on the slope of Rivington Pike. Our landlord was the Soap King who became Lord Leverhulme. He had a very fine bungalow furnished with great luxury on the top of the hill, with a far view of the Black Country round about, with its innumerable chimneys faintly pencilled in the blue distance.

To Agnes and myself the cottage was a paradise and our life in it a fairy tale, but it was not the lap of luxury. When there was heavy rain, as often there was, with a howling gale, we had to sleep under umbrellas because of a leaky roof. It was also rat infested, at least in its bit of ground with a coal shed and outhouse. We became familiar with three large rats, one of which had lost its tail. Alarmed lest they should bite her baby, Agnes paid them Danegeld, and put out bread for them against the garden wall.

To this cottage one day came a carriage and pair with a coachman and footman. Inside the carriage was a handsome gentleman in a grey top hat and a fawn coloured coat and trousers. By his side, as presently I saw when she stepped out of the carriage, was a most beautiful lady in a Watteau gown of painted silk.

I was digging in a potato patch. I was alarmed when the footman descended and enquired across the wall whether I could tell him the whereabouts of Mr. Philip Gibbs's country house.

"Well, as a matter of fact," I stammered, "I am Philip Gibbs."

I don't know whether the footman said "Good God!" but he looked it.

Our visitors, as afterwards we learned, were Mr. and Mrs. Horace Bleackley. I had been in correspondence with Bleackley over some excellent cricket stories he had written, which we had bought for a good price, though being very rich the price did not matter to him. He had assumed that the editor of Tillotson's Syndicate was a man of some standing, with a country mansion for his week-ends. Not by the flicker of an eyelid did either of them show the least surprise at finding us in a labourer's hovel. Agnes accepted the situation with her usual gaiety, and we gave them some kind of a meal at the end of which Mrs. Bleackley, that most lovely lady, tucked up her gown of painted silk and helped to wash up. Bleackley abandoned writing cricket stories and wrote books on the Eighteenth Century, of which he was a great student. His life of Wilkes was a brilliant and scholarly work.

Mr. Lever in his fine bungalow at the top of Rivington Pike was equally indifferent to the poverty of his two young tenants who paid him ninepence a week. He invited us to dine up there and used to pace up and down his verandah, talking very often about Napoleon for whom, as a self-made man with great ambitions, he had a hero worship. At his works in Port Sunlight he had a fine collection of Napoleonic relics, which I suppose are still there.

Here then is a glimpse of our life in Bolton which lasted for two and a half years. It was, as I have said, my way to Fleet Street, for one day I had a letter from Alfred Harmsworth of the *Daily Mail* suggesting that I should go and see him.

I went, and that handsome, fascinating, man was very civil to me in his big room in Carmelite House, and, after a little conversation about syndicating and other subjects, offered me the editorship of Page Four, which was the literary page of the *Daily Mail*, and a very exalted position, I thought, for a young man like myself. I was to be paid £6 a week, which seemed to me beyond the dreams of avarice, with an extra £3 for any article I might write. I was then twenty-three years old.

When I presented myself at the *Daily Mail* office some six weeks later I was kept waiting a longish time before being admitted to the presence of the Chief, as he was always called. At last I was summoned to his room. He held out his hand but seemed doubtful of my identity.

"Let me see," he said. "Oh yes, I remember. Didn't I ask you to join us?"

"Yes," I answered. "You offered me the editorship of Page Four."

He looked surprised.

"Did I? Well, that's a little awkward. I've given it to a brilliant young fellow named Filson Young."

My spirits sank to zero. Agnes and I had burned our boats. We had brought our furniture to London. We had taken a flat in Prince of Wales Road, Battersea Park. We only had a few poor pounds in the bank.

"Perhaps I had better get Young to come down," said Harmsworth.

He rang the bell, and told the boy who answered it to ask Mr. Filson Young to come down.

A tall, good-looking, pale-faced young man gave me a flabby hand when I was introduced to him.

"This is Philip Gibbs," said Harmsworth. "He tells me I offered him the editorship of Page Four."

Filson Young looked surprised, and gave a little uneasy laugh.

"I'm afraid he's going to be disappointed."

"Well, he can work under you for a time," said Harmsworth. "He can write plenty of articles for you. Later on perhaps—one never knows—he may take over the editorship of Page Four."

It was a suggestion to Filson Young that he might be ousted from his chair unless he took care. It was an awkward situation, but I must say that Filson Young behaved very well to me and seemed to like the stuff I wrote for him. I managed to get in about two articles a week, and some time afterwards I took the editorial chair when Young was sent off to Ireland to write a series of articles, which he did brilliantly, and then was given other work during my time on the *Mail*.

That was shortly after the death of Queen Victoria, which ended an era in the history of England and began another with the old world passing, and great changes just behind the curtain on the world's stage. The Boer War was still dragging on. There had been the night of Mafeking which put a new word into the English language. On that night when London went mad top hats skimmed over the heads of the crowds, young men and women danced on the dinner tables of public restaurants, and there was a din of tin trumpets and whistles, and the shrieks of coster girls, and the yells of excited mobs.

When at last peace came—the Peace of Vereenigen, wasn't it?—there was no public excitement or jubilation. A friend of mine named Smith of the Press Association—he was always known as "Smith of the P.A." went down to Windsor with the idea that King Edward would take note of the event by a Royal Message of thanksgiving. Smith specialised in Royal affairs, and was well known to the King's household, including Lord Knollys for whom he asked.

Lord Knollys informed Smith that the King had no idea of issuing a message, and hinted that Smith was an impertinent fellow to suggest it.

"I think His Majesty may care to do so," answered Smith. "Perhaps it hasn't occurred to him. I shall be glad if you will mention it."

Lord Knollys said the King was out and not likely to return for some hours.

"I'll wait," said Smith.

He waited a long time. Hour after hour passed and then Lord Knollys came into the room and said that it was quite useless for Smith to wait any longer. The King would only be back in time to change for dinner. There would be no time for him to write a message, even if he wanted to do so.

"Well," said Smith, "while I've been waiting I've drafted out something which the King might care to glance at."

Smith was familiar with Royal proclamations. He knew their style and phraseology. He could write them with his eyes shut.

Lord Knollys did not disguise his conviction that Smith was a damned nuisance and a most obstinate cuss. But he took the bit of paper.

Presently there were "noises off" as they say on the stage. The King had returned to the Castle for a rapid change before dinner. Three quarters of an hour passed. Then Lord Knollys reappeared with the sheet out of Smith's notebook. It was signed *Edward R.I.*

So it went out to the world.

3

A CHANGING WORLD

It was a world changing in social life, manners, and morals. In this country it was a change over from the Victorian era to the Edwardian, with an improvement in the conditions of the working classes, with a better standard of education among the masses, and with less hypocrisy and smugness in the upper classes who did not know that their power, and wealth, and old tradition of elegance, splendour, and privilege, were in their last phase.

King Edward was a devotee of horse racing, and I saw him at many races in England and Ireland. The Irish races were the liveliest and gayest, and a bevy of beauty—English and Irish—assembled at Punchestown and Leopardstown in the elaborate frocks and hats of the Edwardian era. I had a great time one day at Punchestown where I met Sir Reginald Pole Carew whom I happened to know a little.

"Hullo!" he said. "Anything I can do for you, young fellow?"

"I want to meet the prettiest girls in Ireland," I told him as a jest.

He took it seriously.

"By jingo! I can help you over that. They're all here and bewitching beyond words. Come along."

He introduced me to a number of lovely girls who were much amused when he told them of my quest and there was laughter, and a little shyness, in their Irish eyes.

At one of these meetings I was with a friend of mine from Fleet Street who was always called Skipper Williams because once he had been master of a merchant ship. He looked like that, wearing a bowler hat and a blue reefer jacket. One morning before the arrival of the King he had an idea that the Royal stand would be the best place for him, and interested to see what would happen I followed him there. We stood on the top row of seats and presently the King arrived. A number of Irish and English peers stood on either side of the gangway and the King shook hands with each as he came up the stairs. At the top he encountered Skipper Williams who grasped his hand warmly —so warmly that King Edward was startled. A few moments later one of the officials approached Williams and after enquiries about his identity asked him politely to depart. I was left unchallenged. The King was in very good humour and slapped a young man on the back.

"It's time you were married, young fellow," he said.

"Think so, sir?" answered the young man with a laugh.

It was Prince Arthur of Connaught, who married a beautiful lady soon afterwards.

King Edward's visit at this time was a great success, though three jockeys died to make a Royal holiday. He went down to Waterford first and stayed at the Duke of Devonshire's house where there was salmon to be had in the Blackwater river at Lismore. On the way he was to receive a royal address at some station whose name I have forgotten. The Mayor had roped off a place on the platform for himself and his officials, and had given orders that no journalists were to be allowed on the platform at all. This seemed to be annoying and just before the arrival of the Royal train I spoke about it to General Pole Carew who was in command of all arrangements.

"Ridiculous!" he exclaimed. "I'll put that Mayor in his right place."

He gave him a dressing down, made him remove himself and his officials from the roped-in stand and put us in that position.

I was at Epsom when King Edward's horse Minoru won the Derby. Vast crowds were massed on the heath and around the rails. It was Merrie England in its most rowdy and hilarious mood, of the old tradition. There were jolly luncheon parties on the lines of coaches. Away back were the Gypsy camps. The bookies shouted themselves hoarse. The costers who had driven to Epsom in donkey carts and pony carts were playing concertinas to their Dinahs in their big feathered hats. The Grand Stands were crowded with all the fashion and the quality. In the Royal Box were the Prince and Princess of Wales and many of their friends. No one heard the Four Horsemen of the Apocalypse getting ready to ride forth over the fields of Europe.

Minoru! . . . Minoru! . . . Minoru!

A tidal wave of cheers swept along the course, rising to a storm round Tattenham Corner to the winning post.

The King's horse won.

The crowd went absolutely mad with enthusiasm and to show their loyalty and delight nearly killed the King. According to custom as owner of the winner he left the Royal Stand and went out beyond its rails to lead in his horse and jockey. The Prince of Wales stood by his side. The pressure of the crowd became dangerous. Thousands of cheering men surged forward to get near to the King. They got too near and were unable to keep at any distance because of this vast moving mass of excited humanity behind them. For a few minutes the King was in great danger. Some of us standing near him linked arms and tried to form a barrier. The King's detective, Spencer, a tall powerful man, struck out with his fists. King Edward stood there quietly but his heart was beating heavily and he seemed to be panting, with quick short breaths. The Prince of Wales, afterwards George V, looked deeply alarmed. A few moments later the King regained the safety of the Royal Stand.

4

THE NEW JOURNALISM

Fleet Street revealed and interpreted these changes. The New Journalism had arrived, and the *Daily Mail* under Alfred Harmsworth for whom I worked was its founder and pioneer.

There were violent critics of this new type of journalism. They thought it vulgar, trashy, and lacking altogether in the dignity of the old-time Press. "The *Daily Mail*" said one of them "is a paper written by office boys for officer boys". But Alfred Harmsworth knew what he was doing, and did it with genius. He knew that a public had grown up which took an intelligent interest in things not previously considered part of newspaper chronicles. Food; fashions; the drama of life in low places as well as high; sport of all kinds; the human story wherever it might be found; the adventure of science as it affected everyday life. Harmsworth knew that women's interests had been left out mainly from the oldfashioned newspapers, and he knew that here was an enormous field for increasing circulation. He scorned the deadly dullness of the newspaper Press which had preceded him, with its long and dreary reports of political speeches, its portentous leaders, its blindness towards the little things of everyday life and their infinite variety.

Harmsworth's success was due not a little to the closeness of his own mind to the mood and *tempo* of his time. He was interested in all these things. He looked out upon life with a boyish zest for new discoveries, new fields of interest, new fashions, new ideas. And he refused to be bored by pomposity or portentousness, or the dullness of leaden-minded writers. Everything in his paper had to be bright, sparkling, and pointed. He wanted his young writers to dramatise their news stories. In fact everything had to be a "story" rather than a report. He sent them out to search for oddities of character, strange ways of life, out-of-the-way adventure. In the description of an historic scene, or an affair of public ceremony, he gave his praise to the descriptive writer who had observed some little touch of oddity behind the scenes, or who had avoided the obvious by seeing the human stuff on the side walk while some pompous pageant passed.

That was the spirit of the new journalism into which I came, and Alfred Harmsworth soon had many imitators and rivals, though none with his own quality and genius.

Every day at three o'clock in the afternoon Harmsworth held a conference of editors and reporters. It was open to anyone on the editorial staff. Harmsworth presided in an easy informal way. A handsome man with a square clean-cut face and brown, vivid, eyes he was always well dressed and insisted that even the most junior reporter should be smart in his clothes. In summer he used to turn up in very light suits and looked well in them. Sitting at his desk, upon which there was a bronze of the young Napoleon, whom he certainly resembled a little, or making himself easy in a deep armchair, he would go through the scheme for the next day's paper and ask for any ideas which might be put into the pool to make it more attractive. If some cub reporter put up an idea which pleased him he would turn to that young man with a warm word of encouragement.

Edgar Wallace was there, always smoking cigarettes through a long holder. Charlie Hands turned up at times from some foreign country, or from some provincial city where he had been discovering the oddest things which only Charlie Hands would find and notice.

One of Harmsworth's bright young men during my time was Holt White, reporter and descriptive writer. He was very bright indeed, tall, gay, and debonair, in clothes almost too elegant and exquisite. Hamilton Fyfe, as good-looking as George Alexander, scholarly and critical, was one of Harmsworth's editors and writers. Hannen Swaffer, straight out of the pages of Dickens, was making his *début* as a reporter.

Tom Marlowe was the editor of the *Daily Mail* then and for many years afterwards. He was always at these conferences, which he regarded I am sure as a waste of time, except that they pleased the Chief who had to be humoured. Tom Marlowe knew that the King's favourite of to-day would have his head chopped off to-morrow. He knew that other men were intriguing to take his job from him if he left the editorial chair for half an hour. He knew that lots of these ideas put forward at the Conference would have to be ironed out when next day's paper went to press. Heavy-jowled with a grumpy, deep-throated voice which was belied by the humour of his eyes he survived many palace revolutions, and remained loyal to his chief as Harmsworth always kept loyal to him. They had arrived together from poverty to power.

With them was another man who helped to build up the fortune of the Harmsworth Press, being strong on the financial side. This was Kennedy Jones who rose to great wealth, but once knew the direst poverty. One day, as he told in his recollections, he went into the Press restaurant in Fleet Street and ordered a meal, knowing that he had no money to pay for it. He had a good meal and then spoke to the waiter who was reading an evening newspaper behind the counter.

"Waiter," said Kennedy Jones, "I haven't any money to pay for this dinner."

He expected that he would be given in charge to the nearest Bobby.

"That's all right," said the waiter. "Pay next time."

Charlie Hands, whom I mentioned just now, is one of the famous ghosts of Fleet Street, among whom my own ghost walks. He was a little man, with a bowler hat jammed tightly on his head and the look of a jockey or a music hall comedian. He had done good work as a correspondent in the Boer War, and afterwards wandered about the world finding good stories behind the scenes of history—many of which he never wrote. There was something in him, his dead honesty of mind, his whimsical humour, his gift of comradeship with all manner of men, which made friends for him in many ports and cities. I remember once going to a banquet with him in the Guildhall when the Kaiser was lunching there. Many Princes and great Lords, Generals and Admirals and Ambassadors arrived in their carriages. But it was Charlie Hands, and not the Kaiser, who stole the play, as they say in the theatrical world. He was clapped on the shoulder by Admirals in much gold braid.

"Hullo, Charlie! . . . Haven't seen you for an age. Do you remember . . . ?"

His arm was grabbed by a General whose breast glittered with decorations.

"Hullo, Charlie! . . . Well, I'm damned! If it isn't Charlie Hands. The last time we met . . ."

They roared with laughter at secret and joyous reminiscences. Everyone loved Charlie Hands.

Harmsworth had an affection for him and gave him more rope than he would have allowed any other man. The story is well known of his disappearance for quite a time. At the Conference Harmsworth would remark: "Has anybody seen Charlie Hands? He seems to have disappeared."

He was discovered in a hotel up North.

"Good God!" exclaimed one of his colleagues. "The Chief is searching for you everywhere. Where have you been all this time?"

"Hush!" said Charlie who was in his shirt sleeves chalking a billiard cue. "I was sent up here to await instructions. I'm still waiting for them and improving my game."

During my time on the *Mail* he lingered behind at the Conference and asked Harmsworth to lend him £100.

"Certainly not," said Harmsworth. "You know I never lend money, Charlie."

But he wrote out a cheque for £100 and gave it to him.

Hands knew the side streets of life in many cities and countries. He made friends with the *patrons* of French restaurants and the waiters in Italian hotels, and the cooks and chambermaids. He could find a good dinner in the midst of ruin, or in a war-beleaguered city. I was hungry and undernourished in Sofia when the Balkan wars began.

He whispered to me one evening.

"Come with me, my boy. Don't say a word."

He took me down narrow alleys in a city eaten out by the mobilisation of a army.

"There's a friend of mine who will give us a good meal," he told me. "It's not much of a place to look at, but he cooks like an angel."

We had a good dinner washed down by excellent wine.

Edgar Wallace became a friend of mine in those early Fleet Street days, and we met from time to time on journalistic adventures, on race courses, and, when the miracle of flight happened, on aerodromes. It was before he became famous as a writer of thrillers, and as a playwright. I knew nothing of his private life which was unhappy, but as a friend in Fleet Street he was always kindly, and generous, and good humoured, though very quiet and unboisterous. He was a born gambler at the card table or on the turf. Once we were together in an old inn at Doncaster, and I joined him, rashly, in a game of poker. He had a Royal Flush—the rarest thing—and scooped the pool. Our landlord who had been watching the game thought it looked good and offered to take a hand. Wallace bid him up for high stakes. The landlord thought he was bluffing. But, incredible as it seems, Wallace put down his cards and revealed another Royal Flush! The landlord departed, a sadder and a wiser man, and we laughed with sham incredulity at this run of luck. But nobody would ever have accused Wallace of manipulating his cards. He was as straight as a yardstick.

5

SACKED

After I had been at the *Daily Mail* for some time Harmsworth invited me down for a week-end to Sutton Place, near Guildford, which he had rented from the Duke of Sutherland. It is a lovely old Tudor mansion, and was the home of young Weston, the lover of Anne Boleyn, who lost his head for his love, as she did, poor lady. It is astonishing that Henry, after his fury and anguish, quartered himself here on the boy's father.

When I went down there Harmsworth had a house party of journalists, among whom I remember Andrew Caird, a dour Scot, who was a convinced Free Trader until one day, after I had left the *Mail*, he was told by Harmsworth to change his tune and support Joseph Chamberlain in his campaign for Tariff reform. We were down at Newport for one of Chamberlain's speeches and Caird, suffering moral torture because of this violation of his inmost convictions, ordered a bottle of red wine and tried to drown his sorrow. But he had a harder head than mine, and when I listened to the great man's speech the hall swung around me, and I had to struggle against the fumes of that filthy wine while writing my report.

At Sutton Place I failed to see the ghosts of Tudor England, but was aware of the incongruity of the company in this stately old house. The talk was all about Fleet Street "shop". In the Minstrels' gallery a group of journalists smoked Harmsworth's cigars and drank his port. Harmsworth himself was a charming host, and was the only one whose personality and dignity—for he had that—was not out of tune with the vibrations of this old mansion.

After lunch on Sunday he took me apart for private conversation.

"You know all about syndicating," he said, referring to my experience with the Tillotsons. "Tell me about it."

He listened to my statement of the case and put a dramatic proposal to me.

"How would you like to start a syndicate in London? The British Empire Syndicate Ltd. We should have to smash the Tillotsons. My name wouldn't appear. It would be your show and I would come in now and then and see how things were getting on."

I hesitated, not liking that idea of smashing the Tillotsons who had been very kind to me.

"Now, I tell you what," said Harmsworth. "You can go back to the office this afternoon and say you've got the sack. Then you will go to the Riviera with your wife for a few months. It will do you good. When you come back you will find a nice little office waiting for you in Fleet Street—The British Empire Syndicate Ltd. You'll have a lot of fun with it and might make a lot of money."

Again I hesitated, and he who hesitated with Harmsworth was lost. He wanted instant enthusiasm and the optimism of youth. I asked for a couple of days to think it over.

"That's all right," he said. "But you're a cautious young man."

I saw that he was disappointed with me, but he told me that he was going to Germany for a few weeks and that I could draw up a report on the syndicate idea during his absence. He would read it when he came back.

I was excited by this proposal but decided to seek advice from a man who knew Harmsworth well.

"My dear lad," he told me, "I know exactly what will happen. You will tell the *Daily Mail*—Tom Marlowe—that you have got the sack. That, to Carmelite House, means your job has gone. You will go to the South of France with your wife and spend a lot of money—far more than you can afford. When you return to Fleet Street there will be no little office waiting for you. Harmsworth will have forgotten all about the idea. So there you will be—in the cart."

Now I believe that he was wrong. If I had jumped at the offer Harmsworth would have been as good as his word, and I should have become a rich unhappy man, missing all the fun of life as a writer. It was my lack of quick enthusiasm which damped down Harmsworth's interest. He was away I think a couple of months. When he returned I presented my report and I never heard a word about it.

Perhaps that was one little nail in my coffin as a *Daily Mail* editor. Later Harmsworth became critical of the articles on Page 4. He thought they were getting dull and condemned about a dozen which I showed him in galley proof.

"Send them back," he said. "They're no good."

"I can't send them back," I told him, "I've commissioned them."

"I've asked you to send them back," he answered sternly.

A week later he asked to see some more of these articles and was in a better humour, smoking a cigar and reading with one leg over the arm of a deep leather chair. I had mixed up the articles previously shown to him with a number of others.

He glanced through them all.

"Now, these are good," he exclaimed, mentioning a few titles. "Why didn't you show me these before?"

I didn't tell him that they were the same articles that he had condemned as devilish dull. I had a reprieve.

One day he asked me to go to see old General Booth of the Salvation Army, who was very fierce about something which had annoyed him in the *Daily Mail*.

"Put it all right with the old man," said Harmsworth. "We don't want to quarrel with him."

I went on this diplomatic mission, and for the first time came in touch with that remarkable old gentleman whom afterwards I met many times. His spirit was like a white flame. He had a burning fire within him. There was nothing of the gentle saint about him, and sometimes he had a terrifying anger, as once I saw, which scorched and blasted those who had betrayed him or had done some dirty work. He was a militant soldier of the Lord, like one of the Old Testament prophets, but with one strange difference. He had a sense of humour, and for the sake of "saving souls" would make himself a buffoon—dancing on a public stage with old grannies or leading one of the Salvation Army songs with a clapping of hands and loud cries like a negro revivalist. On that day I went to see him, on behalf of the *Daily Mail*, he started by being angry, and then softened. Presently he seized me by the wrist and dragged me down to my knees beside him.

"Let us pray for Alfred Harmsworth," he said.

He prayed long and earnestly for Harmsworth, and Fleet Street, and the newspaper Press that it might be inspired by the love of truth and charity and the Spirit of the Lord.

Now I don't know whether that prayer did a bit of good to Alfred Harmsworth, afterwards Lord Northcliffe, but some little time later I got the sack.

As a matter of fact I anticipated the Order of the Sack by handing in my resignation first. I had overheard some ominous words by Kennedy Jones to the Chief who gave a nod. My time is up, I thought, and going upstairs wrote my resignation and sent it down by a messenger boy. Half an hour later there was a tap at my door and I called "Come in."

A very little man appeared and said: "Good evening."

"Who is it?" I asked.

"Mee," he answered.

"Sorry," I told him, "I'm afraid I don't know you. What name?"

"Mee," he answered.

"Yes," I said, "but I would like to know your name."

It was Arthur Mee who informed me in a kindly way that he had come to succeed me as editor of Page 4.

Later he became editor of the Children's Encyclopædia, thereby giving great delight and much knowledge to millions of children from one generation to another. He also made a lot of money.

I walked out into the street. I was without a job and I had a wife and child. I told Agnes, and she took the news cheerfully, having no fear of poverty and some faith in my pen.

Now it's strange but true that, as far as I know, no one felt a grudge against Harmsworth for having been given the sack, and I parted from him with no ill feeling. He had no ill feeling against me and was always kind. Some years later I came face to face with him in the Temple Gardens and he stopped.

"You're not looking well," he said. "What are you doing?"

"Looking for a job," I answered, not very seriously. It was one of my times when I had turned my back on Fleet Street to write books, and short stories, and free lance articles, with enough success to keep the wolf from the door. A day later I had a letter from him and it was very kind. He was not quite sure, he wrote, whether I really wanted a new post. If so he would be glad to give me anything that was going in Carmelite House. I did not take advantage of his offer. And some years later again I had a message from him delivered to me by Beach Thomas. It was in the middle of a world war. Would I care to become War Correspondent of *The Times* (of which he was now proprietor) on the Western Front?

It was an offer of some honour, but I was War Correspondent of the *Daily Chronicle*, the *Daily Telegraph*, and about forty other papers and I hated the idea of swapping horses when crossing the stream.

"Care to give me your answer to-morrow?" asked Beach Thomas.

"I'll give it you now," I told him. "No—thanks very much."

"A quick decision, old man," said Beach Thomas.

6

INTELLECTUAL MANSIONS, S.W.

During my first years as a journalist I lived in the Prince of Wales Road facing Battersea Park. Almost all the poor intellectuals lived there at one time.

I had a ground floor flat in Overstrand Mansions, with a little garden where my baby boy, Tony, could dig in a sand pit and watch life passing through the railings. There was quite a lot of life, including squadrons of bicycles ridden by ladies in bloomers, and lovely specimens of the male and female Smart Set, who had a sudden passion for cycling and made Battersea Park a rendezvous of fashion for a season or two.

Above us lived a very big man. He was so big that I sometimes feared he might come through the ceiling and squash us all. He was G. K. Chesterton, then in the full glory of his great girth, and in the springtime of his genius. He observed a morning ritual which became familiar to us. Some time in the middle of the morning a hansom cab would draw up. It had a very old driver and a very old horse. Chesterton kept it waiting quite a time. Then he would emerge in a big black cloak and a floppy black hat, looking like a portrait of a Dutch *Burgermeister* by Franz Hals. With him sometimes came Mrs. Chesterton, a fragile little lady. Chesterton would get into the cab first, and the old horse would stagger in its shafts, giving a see-saw to the old driver on his high perch. Mrs. Chesterton would follow, and I had the conviction that if ever she climbed in first she would never come out alive, because of her massive husband and his heavy weight.

Chesterton would drive to the *Daily News* office, which published his wit and wisdom for many years, and often he would finish an article in the Press Café where journalists nudged each other as he chuckled over his own epigrams. I came to know him fairly well, as I shall tell, and read every word he wrote with admiration and joy.

He was a man who had a high regard for local patriotism, and for a time this was centred in the Prince of Wales Road, Battersea Park. He always had the desire to be wrecked on a desert island, as once he wrote, but only on condition that the inhabitants of the Prince of Wales Road —the poor artists, the poor musicians, the poor intellectuals, should be wrecked with him. Conversation with such a crowd would never flag. I wrote a novel about the Prince of Wales Road called *Intellectual Mansions, S.W.* It had for its theme the Suffragette struggle, and the pioneers of Votes for Women bought up an edition, bound it in Suffragette colours and killed it stone dead because of their unpopularity.

7

REPORTER OF LIFE

There was a beaten track between the *Daily Mail* office and the office of the *Daily Express*. Every young reporter sacked from the *Mail* followed this track unerringly, and joined the staff of the rival paper, owned by Arthur Pearson, and edited by R. D. Blumenfeld.

I followed this tradition and was appointed special correspondent of the *Daily Express*.

I came to know all the folly and amusement of stunt journalism, not as an editor this time but as a reporter of contemporary events.

I went down to Windsor when the Kaiser was there, and followed the routine of a royal visit which included a State banquet and a *battue* of birds, and drives in Windsor forest.

We reporters put up at the Castle Hotel, having viewed the day's proceedings at a respectful distance, or found out something about them from officers of the Household. It was before the the days of press photography, and artists of the *Daily Graphic*, and the *Illustrated London News*, came down to do black-and-white drawings. One of them was named Macpherson. He was a brilliant black-and-white man and he had one special gift which greatly entertained us. With a table napkin skilfully folded and placed on his head, and with puffed cheeks and careful arrangement of his facial expression, he could make himself astoundingly like Queen Victoria.

I remember those old days at the Castle for their ribald stories and their gusts of laughter. I was the youngest of the crowd and this kind of thing was new to me though it had, I thought, the true Shakespearean touch. We had a Falstaff among us—the correspondent of the *Morning Post* who spoke in Falstaffian style, quaffed wine immoderately, accosted the chambermaids as though they were the Merry Wives of Windsor, and broke into snatches of song in a deep dramatic voice. He was a great comedian and a good companion.

None of us imagined that the guest of honour in Windsor Castle would be the Supreme War Lord of great armies entrenched against us in France and Flanders.

I have forgotten many of the "stories", the pageants, the interviews with the great, and the adventures upon which I was sent by the *Daily Express*. My time with them was not long—perhaps the inside of a year. But one day I was sent for by Arthur Pearson. He stood on his hearth-rug and held out his hand to me.

"I want you to write a special series of articles," he said. "I'm sure you'll do them well."

"Many thanks," I answered.

"I want you to write a set of articles proving that Bacon was the author of the so-called Shakespeare Plays. There's a lot of evidence. You will have to dig it out and make it interesting and convincing."

"I'm afraid I can't write those articles," I told him. "I don't believe in the Baconian theory. It's all nonsense."

"I'm telling you to write them," said Pearson, rather harshly. "A journalist writes from a brief."

Now that raised a point of principle which faces every journalist in his career. Is he willing to write against his own convictions, as a barrister pleads for one side or the other according to his brief? I have always held myself that it is bad morality and bad policy for a journalist to do this, though many newspaper men do not take this view. I do not see how one can write against one's inmost convictions without pro-stituting one's pen and betraying truth itself. I have always refused to do so, and I refused Arthur Pearson then. I walked out of his office and risked penury again, with nothing between my little home and the sharp-jawed wolf but some sheets of blank paper and a penny bottle of ink.

Years afterwards I met Sir Arthur Pearson again many times. He had gone blind, and by that blindness acquired a nobility of courage and service of the highest quality. During the first World War he came out to France, and I went with him into Peronne which we had just captured. The ruined streets were still on fire. In the Grand' Place the Germans had made an effigy of a French soldier hanging by his neck, and there was a big placard on the pedestal of a statue on which were the words "*Nicht aergern nur wundern*" ("Don't be angry—only astonished"), the significance of which I have never understood. That evening Pearson and I dined in an officers' mess, and he made a speech, telling the company what he had "seen" in Peronne. He had touched things, smelt things, listened and absorbed the atmosphere of the scene in which he had stood utterly blind. But his description of Peronne was like that of a sighted man. I noticed also at table how never once did he fumble or look clumsy. On sitting down he had felt for his wine glass, his knife and fork, and other things about him. After that he was perfectly at ease. "It is a question of memory," he told me. "One has to train one's memory for every detail. I hate knocking things over."

At St. Dunstan's in Regent's Park, where I went to see him several times, he was an inspiration to all the blinded soldiers, and his courage and cheerfulness, and refusal to indulge in self-pity, taught them to make the best of blindness and carry on. He had mellowed since those days at the *Daily Express*. All that was best in him came through, and he found light in his darkness.

During my time in "Intellectual Mansions" I did a job for a little Jew who was a great scholar with a heart of gold. This was Israel Gollancz, professor of Anglo-Saxon and Early English at Oxford. He was inspired with the idea of founding a Shakespeare Memorial Theatre, and enlisted my aid in forming the first Committee to support this scheme and raise funds. Bernard Shaw was enthusiastic for the idea, and I succeeded in getting some great names on the list. In some cases it needed personal visits, and there was one which led me into trouble. I took a hansom cab—it was still in that period—to the house of the Lord Chief Justice Alverstone, in Kensington. I wore a top hat and tail coat and with a clatter of hoofs arrived in style at the door of that red brick mansion. The footman who opened the door informed me that his Lordship had been on circuit but would be back in half an hour. Deceived by my appearance into the belief that I was a young gentleman of rank, personally known to his master, he invited me to wait and showed me into the study of the Lord Chief. After waiting half an hour I became uneasy. It occurred to me that I ought not to be sitting in this room. The desk was open, and was strewn with legal-looking papers. Bundles of documents lay on the chairs. A criminal might have had a fine time in this room. I was not a criminal, but I felt uncomfortable. The Lord Chief Justice might not like a stranger in his holy of holies. The Lord Chief Justice did not like it. Presently I heard the arrival of a carriage and heavy footsteps in the hall and an angry voice speaking loudly.

"In my study? Who the devil is it?"

The door opened violently. The Lord Chief glared at me.

"Who are you?" he asked. "What do you want?"

I mentioned the name of William Shakespeare and the purpose of my visit. It had a mollifying effect.

"Good God!" he exclaimed, "I thought you might be a crook among my private papers. A Shakespeare memorial?"

He joined the Committee.

I called at another door on this mission. It was in Portland Place. Another footman asked my business.

"May I see Lord Roberts for a few minutes?"

"Come in," said a pleasant voice.

In the hall stood a little man in the uniform of a Field Marshal, with rows of stars and medals on his breast, not brighter than his eyes which twinkled at me.

I used the name of Shakespeare as my introduction.

"Will Shakespeare!" he exclaimed. "I would do anything for that fellow. I owe him a very great debt."

He joined the Committee and put his name down for a bit of money.

I sent out the invitations for the first general meeting at the Mansion House. Agnes and I addressed innumerable letters. Tony, aged four, had great fun in trundling them in a wheelbarrow to the nearest pillar box, which we filled up to the brim. It was a marvellous meeting. Bernard Shaw made a brilliant speech. Beerbohm Tree made another. All the literary and theatrical world came to the Mansion House. Enough money was subscribed to buy a site for the Memorial Theatre. That site still stands, but as yet no brick has been laid upon it. Will Shakespeare still awaits his Memorial in London. Two wars have delayed it.

8

SHAKESPEARE AND OTHERS

I became friendly with Beerbohm Tree, and Shakespeare again was the introduction to his dressing room at His Majesty's Theatre.

He was playing Caliban, and looked most hideous when I was shown in between the acts. I desired to interview him for the provincial Press on the subject of Shakespeare.

"Shakespeare? . . . Shakespeare? . . ." he said in a dreamy voice. "Do I know that name?"

In answer to various questions from me he professed complete ignorance about Shakespeare and all his works.

"My dear lad," he said, "what can I say in five minutes between the acts? In five minutes I have to go on and play my part. I daresay you know quite a lot about Bill Shakespeare. Go away and write it. Put my name to it. Write what you like."

I went away and wrote quite a lot about Shakespeare in two long articles signed Beerbohm Tree. They did not appear for nearly a year. I took for granted the proofs had been sent to him.

Then one day out of the blue I had a telegram from Tree.

"My dear Philip Gibbs. I am greatly indebted to you. Will you favour me by accepting two stalls at His Majesty's and come to see me between the acts?"

Agnes and I sat in the stalls. Between the acts I went to Tree's dressing room. When my name was announced he embraced me.

"It was a miracle!" he exclaimed. "The other night my man reminded me that I had promised to give a lecture on Shakespeare at the London Polytechnic. 'Impossible!' I told him. 'Shakespeare? What can I say about Shakespeare on the spur of the moment? Don't you know that I am in the midst of a new production?'

" 'You'll have to do it,' said my man.

" 'Go away!' I told him.

"On my dressing table among other letters was a packet with a green wrapper. Press cuttings. I opened them and found two long articles interviewing me on the subject of Shakespeare.

"I read them with amazement. Had I said all that? Had a young man named Philip Gibbs dragged all that out of me? I went to the London Polytechnic and delivered my lecture by reading out your articles. My dear lad, I am very much in your debt and I shall never forget it."

He never forgot it, and I lunched with him many times in the dome above His Majesty's, and at the Garrick Club, listening to his carefully prepared epigrams and his completely untruthful stories, and his overdramatised views on life and the stage. He was immensely entertaining, witty, and emotional. Once when I came to see him at the theatre in the middle of the first World War he listened to things I told him about the fighting and then flung himself with both hands raised against the wall of his dressing room and groaned in anguish of spirit.

"O God! O God!" he cried. "The martyrdom of man! Will it never cease?"

I remember one of his stories. He was taking his company to New

York and opening in that city with *Hamlet*. On the way across the Atlantic Lionel Brough, who was playing the grave-digger, lost his false teeth overboard. The loss dejected him, but he cheered up towards the end of the voyage after reading an advertisement in the *Saturday Evening Post*. It was an advertisement for a set of self-masticating teeth. Upon arrival Lionel Brough took a cab and bought the teeth. That night the curtain was raised on the scene at the grave of Yorick. Brough's head appeared above the grave. But no sooner had he uttered his first words than the false teeth sprang out of his mouth, and went yapping about the stage until they fastened on to the calf of Beerbohm Tree as Hamlet. The curtain had to be lowered hurriedly. . . . Believe it or not.

During times of my exile from Fleet Street I wrote a novel or two, and one or two historical books—*Men and Women of the French Revolution. George Villiers, First Duke of Buckingham. King's Favourite.* I put a lot of work into *George Villiers* and obtained much material, never before published, about that romantic man "Dogge Steenie" who was the favourite of James I, the friend of Charles, and the lover of the French Queen. Dumas had written about him in *Twenty Years After*, and the plot centres round some diamond studs given by the King of France to his Queen, and by her to Buckingham. Suspicious of her the King demanded that she should wear them at a State Ball and the three musketeers came to England to get them back in time. Now I found out something that Dumas would have liked to know. The Queen gave Buckingham not some diamond studs but a jewelled garter which the King had given her. More incriminating!

Through this book I came to know Lord Denbigh and his family of sons and daughters in the old house of Newnham Paddox. Descended from the sister of George Villiers who had married the first Earl of Denbigh, the Lord Denbigh whom I came to know had some fine portraits of George and his wife and family by Vandyke. He also had a chest full of letters, which he allowed me to use, from Lady Buckingham to her husband—some of the most beautiful letters in the English language.

Agnes and I stayed at Newnham Paddox and had a charming time there with a rowdy and attractive family. But I had one *mauvais quart d'heure*. It was when I took my turn for the bathroom among the young people, of whom the eldest was the pretty dark-eyed girl, Lady Dorothy Feilding. There was a kind of anteroom to the bathroom and when my turn came I dropped my pyjamas and dressing gown on the floor of this little outer room before taking my bath. When I emerged there were no pyjamas and no dressing gown.

I could hear squeals of laughter outside, and scuttling of feet, and then silence. The family had gone down to breakfast. What was I going to do about it? I had no courage to walk down a long corridor stark naked. Outside the door a maid was sweeping. I mounted a chair and spoke through the fanlight, and explained the situation to this girl outside. She gave a hearty laugh with a cry of: "Those young varmints!" She went away and after what seemed to me a long time returned and pushed my pyjamas through the fanlight at the end of her broom.

At breakfast I was greeted with cheerful "Good mornings". "Had a nice bath?" asked one of the Feilding boys who was a midshipman. "Fine!" I told him. No more was said.

Afterwards, some years later, I met Lady Dorothy Feilding on the field of battle in Belgium, and had strange adventures with her, and was covered with blood in her service as I shall tell later.

The first World War, and the ferocious taxation which followed it, impoverished the old landed gentry of England and caused a social revolution. Ancestral mansions had to be abandoned, and lovely parks sold for building estates. Lord Denbigh had to sell his Vandyke portraits and could not keep up Newnham Paddox.

My book *Men and Women of the French Revolution* was a fine-looking volume and handsomely illustrated by French prints and mezzotint portraits of the 18th century. I obtained these from a little old man somewhere in the neighbourhood of Stoke Newington. I was introduced to him by a romantic and adventurous friend of mine, named J. H. Bailey, who was the editor and part proprietor of the *Connoisseur*. The little man was a passionate collector of prints—mostly French—upon which he spent all his money. He lived in squalor, and when I went to see him there was hardly room to sit down, because of the packing cases stored with his collections which filled up his floor space. Mice infested the room and he threw crumbs to them from his breakfast table. When he was in need of money to pay the baker's bill or the rent he would take a print to one of the dealers and cash it as though it were a cheque. But he had no regard for money and gave his unique collection of Marie Antoinette prints to Queen Alexandra. Nor did he charge anything to me for permission to reproduce those I wanted for my own book. It gave me a thrill one day to see *Men and Women of the French Revolution* in Galignani's book shop in Paris, but if there was credit in it there was little cash. I think I made about £100 out of *George Villiers, Duke of Buckingham*, and perhaps less for other historical books upon which I had done a lot of original research. I knew that if I relied upon history for a living my wife and child would go hungry. I went back to Fleet Street, this time as a literary editor, in charge of the magazine page of the *Daily Chronicle*.

9

GRUB STREET AND ALSATIA

I remember the old *Daily Chronicle* office when it was ramshackle and rat infested. In those days the editor worked in his shirt sleeves and sent out for his supper from the Red Lion round the corner. Editors in those days stood aloof, mostly, from the social round and the tables of the great. They were autocrats in their own world, and both critics and judges of social and political life, not aspiring to public honours or exalted titles. The lower class of journalist was a disreputable fellow, badly dressed, and a hard drinker, though once he might have been a scholar and a gentleman. The penny-a-liner was often no more than a tout for news, haunting the police courts and greedy for murder, fires, and horrible accidents. To obtain news about society he went round to the servants' entrance and bribed the butlers and the ladies' maids. In the higher ranks were men of learning and strong political convictions which they would not barter for gold, and writers of ponderous prose sprinkled with Greek and Latin tags.

A few of these types of the old style hung on when I entered Fleet Street but were fast disappearing under the influence of Harmsworth and the new school of journalism. The old buildings were pulled down or reconstructed, the rats were smoked out. The newspaper men were a better dressed crowd, though not exactly Beau Brummels. Anyhow, Grub Street was not quite so squalid, and Alsatia was not so crowded with Pyms and Bardolphs.

One of the last of the Alsatians was an old fellow named O'Dell. I had met him at Whitefriars Club and afterwards saw him about Fleet Street. He had been a Shakespearean actor and still dressed the part in a big black hat, and a long black cloak now green with age. Nobody knew where he lived or how he lived. He kept his dwelling place a dark secret—probably he went from one dosshouse to another—and one night he led some newspaper men a dance when they tried to follow him home. On the heights of Hampstead he turned upon them and said: "Gentlemen, this is not where I live. I hope you have enjoyed your walk."

He had a tongue touched with vitriol. Once he told my father that he had had a slight quarrel with a well-known publisher.

"I told him that he stank in my nostrils and—strange fellow!—he took umbrage."

Travelling one day in an omnibus late at night the conductor looked at his cadaverous face under the black broad-brimmed hat and called up to the driver:

"Say Bill, we've got Cardinal Manning aboard."

"Bet you a bob it ain't," answered the driver who had seen O'Dell come to his bus.

"Right!" said the conductor.

He addresses O'Dell.

"Beg your pardon, sir, but are you Cardinal Manning?"

"Go to hell!" said O'Dell in his sepulchral voice.

"I've won, Bill. It is 'is 'Oliness!"

Not long before the second World War Agnes and I went to a big banquet at the Mansion House—one of those formal affairs of infinite boredom, unless one sits next to interesting people. Afterwards there was an assembly under the awning outside, when duchesses and dames and other guests waited for their cars while rain streamed down and beat upon the pavement. A very tall man, then one of His Majesty's Judges of the High Court, grabbed my arm and spoke to me.

"Seeing you here, Gibbs, reminds me of my early days in Fleet Street when Perris threw my first week's earnings wrapped up in a bit of paper out of the window of the London Press Agency. It amounted to 7s. 6d."

As editor of the magazine page of the *Daily Chronicle* I had a little office of my own in Fleet Street, round the corner from Whitefriars Street, where the main office stood. It was an independent kingdom, though subject to the approval of the Editor-in-Chief, Robert Donald, and the criticism of the news editor, Perris.

I had three black-and-white artists working with me. One was Alfred Priest, who betrayed his conscience later as a painter of melo-dramatic pictures for the Royal Academy such as "The Dope Fiend" and "Mother! Mother!"

Another was Stephen Reid, a nephew of Robert Donald. He was a fine black-and-white artist—he did all decorative and tail pieces for the *Connoisseur*—and gained a well-deserved reputation for his historical paintings and landscapes. The third was Edgar Lander known as "Pingers" in the Press Club and the Three Arts, but afterwards more widely known as "Uncle" by a great number of adopted nephews and nieces who sketched with him, worked in his studio, and painted Chelsea red with him.

He was the husband of Hilda Cowham, whose long-legged children are still remembered, and who is still an exquisite artist of little hill-top towns in Italy and France. Many an adventure I have had with Edgar Lander in enchanting places of Europe—Avignon, Arles, Nimes, La Rochelle, and old cathedral cities in France, where I went sketching with him and staying in cheap hotels and old inns. He and his wife are still my friends, though Lander's views on life are often opposed to mine, at least in argument and verbal violence.

In those old days in Fleet Street where first I met him—a dark-haired fellow, with merry eyes, and a scathing tongue, devoted to Kipling, Meredith and the "Yellow Book"—we four made a friendly and industrious team in that high room above the roar of Fleet Street. We were keen on our jobs. I wrote innumerable articles descriptive of contemporary scenes—a Royal levée, floods in England, London life in many aspects—and they were illustrated by these artists, who talked incessantly as they did their work, arguing about everything, quoting the poets, criticising contemporary artists, dragging down the charlatans and getting hot in disagreement. But we turned out a first-class page day by day, with untiring toil and a touch of pride.

Then one day it all came to an end. A new era had begun. Some ingenious fellow discovered a way of reproducing photographs on a rotary press. Photography killed black-and-white drawings. Ernest Perris conveyed the news to me and I broke it to the three artists. They were no longer wanted for the magazine page.

10

HOLLAND STREET, KENSINGTON

Agnes and I shifted from the Prince of Wales Road and took a little house in Holland Street, Kensington. It is still there, having survived the blitz which created ruin all around it, and especially in Church Street into which it goes.

Holland Street was charmingly oldfashioned. There was, and is, a row of Queen Anne houses at the Church Street end, and, on the opposite side, an old mansion inhabited at that time by a famous and now forgotten artist—Walter Crane—who belonged to the William Morris school in revolt against the hideous taste of the early Victorian era. He designed wall papers and stained glass windows and illustrated books with sylvan scenes and long-legged young women and did cartoons of winged angels and classical ladies. I took tea with him now and then, and found him a melancholy man, strangely sad with a dead spirit, because somehow he had failed.

Opposite our small house was Mr. Cotton, the tailor, whose shop and dwelling place caught fire one night and created a pandemonium in the street when the fire-engines arrived with clanging bells. Once a week a German band played pom-pom and toot-toot under our windows. On another day, as regularly as the calendar went round, there was the squawk of Punch, and the oldest drama in the world collected small boys and babes and nursemaids. The muffin man came ringing his bell.

The chimes of St. Mary Abbots, now a ruin, were pleasant in the night. Round the corner was the Carmelite Church, which is now a wreck of rubble. A little alley up from Kensington High Street still leads into Holland Street, and then as now it had a cobbler's shop and a toy shop, against whose window panes my son Tony pressed his nose, and a little bun shop. In Hornton Street lived very grandly, I thought, my friend E. W. Hornung, whose wife was the sister of Conan Doyle. In little Holland House, where once Watts lived with his child wife, Ellen Terry, who ran away from him to liberty and fame and romantic love, I had another friend who invited me to see how a rich literary man might live, surrounded by works of art and many treasures. This was Lewis Hind a literary critic of some eminence, and the editor for a time of the *Academy*. He was a rich literary man, not because of wealth obtained from criticism, but from an American wife who had many dollars. One day he was sentenced to death by his doctors who diagnosed cancer. They gave him only a week or so to live. But a week or so later I saw him crossing Holland Street in a very sprightly way. "Good God!" I cried, "I thought you were in a desperate state."

He looked at me with a smile and gave a queer laugh.

"I have been cured of cancer," he said, "by Christian Science, in which I didn't believe. It was my wife who was the Christian Scientist. Very odd, isn't it?"

Next door to our little house in Holland Street was a gentleman of strange habits. He never went through the front door, but after looking up and down the street in a furtive way climbed through the drawing-room window. Sometimes we observed grim-looking men watching the house for quite a time. It seemed that the gentleman was very much in debt, owing to an unnatural thirst, and that he avoided being served with a writ, or allowing the bailiffs to enter to seize his goods, by using the window instead of the door, thereby taking advantage of some ancient law. At last he flitted in the night with his sticks of furniture in a hired van. Apart from that episode it was a very respectable little street with nice people in its old houses.

There were frequent rat-tat-tats at our door knocker and on Saturday and Sunday afternoons our small drawing-room, running the length of the house, was apt to be overcrowded. Those friends of ours are mostly gone or scattered. Now and then when I go down Holland Street and stand for a moment opposite our former dwelling place I feel that they are ghosts and that I am ghostly.

Some of them were young then. There was a talkative young fellow called Arthur Ransom, who went to Russia afterwards and had strange adventures before writing children's books which have given delight to millions of young people. Other young literary men appeared and disappeared. Now and again a very odd little man, who spoke ex-

c

plosively with a stutter, came to stay the week-end as a hideaway from old ladies and worshipful women. It was Father Hugh Benson, one of the three famous brothers. We put him into a tiny bedroom upstairs and there he used to write one of his novels, or innumerable postcards which he filled with a close script.

"What is your idea of Heaven?" I asked him once.

He answered without hesitation.

"My idea of Heaven is to be writing a novel which is going well and never finishes."

He was a famous preacher, and wherever he preached the church was crowded. But I found him distressing as a preacher because I was always afraid that he would hurl himself out of the pulpit. He literally used to fling himself over its edge with an intensity of eloquence by which he lost his stutter.

A few poets passed our way and remained for a cup of tea. One of them will always have a place in English anthology. It was Katharine Tynan who has some of her poems, lovely in their simplicity and touch of magic, in the Oxford Book of English Verse. She looked not at all like a poet. She looked like the wife of an Irish farmer. She spoke with a strong brogue and was as Irish as the peat of Connemara.

Byam Shaw, admirable artist and big, good-natured fellow, was one of those who came in to see us now and then, though I cannot remember how I came to know him. One day he called about Christmas time and my wife said: "Draw me a Christmas card."

He drew instantly a caricature of himself with a dog, and I have it still in a little frame.

My wife took Italian lessons from an old lady who spoke abominable English with great vivacity. My small boy listened in and when the postman came down the street announced the fact by a shout of "Ecco il postino!"

So at times our little house was crowded with pleasant and amusing people who did not mind our poverty and fell in love with Agnes, because of her loveliness and her merry wit and her spiritual beauty.

Always we had with us a little maid named Amy who stood by us in good times and bad, in ill health and sadness. She was with us when my son was born. She was with me when my wife died. I owe a great debt to little old Amy who is now pensioned off but comes to see me from time to time.

But we reinforced her services, and I remember we had one mother's help who turned out to be the daughter of the Chief Justice of the Transvaal. She was of course a lady in the oldfashioned sense of the word, and I found myself carrying in scuttles of coal for her, or doing household jobs which really belonged to her part of the contract.

Agnes and I also found that being a vivacious girl she was pleased to entertain our guests while we handed round the cake and bread and butter. After she left us she became a lady in waiting to the Queen of Spain—a great rise from a little house in Holland Street—and came back from Madrid from time to time, looking very elegant, and bringing gifts. She brought me a Spanish walking stick with a leather handle and thong which one wore round one's wrist.

We were happy, on the whole, in Holland Street, but my life as a journalist was full of vexations, insecurity of tenure, and desperate interferences with home life. The hours were long and utterly uncertain. A little dinner party was more than likely to be without its host because he had been sent off somewhere at a moment's notice, or was rushing an article through the last edition some time about midnight. There was no mercy in Fleet Street for a home-loving man or a waiting wife. Agnes was always waiting, waiting, waiting. Nine o'clock? Not home yet. Ten o'clock—No. Those were not his footsteps down the street. Eleven o'clock, and a wife still sitting by a dwindling fire. Midnight. Two in the morning, perhaps, when a tired wife had gone to sleep. So often it was like that and very wearing to the nerves, and spoiling to all domestic and social plans.

In those days Fleet Street was a hellish place in which to have a husband or a lover.

11

THE TRIBUNE TRAGEDY

A sensation came to Fleet Street with the news that a big new daily Liberal paper was to be published under the title of the *Tribune*. Being out of a job and extremely hard up I applied for the position of literary editor, and was accepted as such by a little old gentleman named William Hill, who was to be Editor-in-Chief. He was a North countryman, and had been news editor under Massingham, of that very fine paper, the *Westminster Gazette*, sometimes called "The Sea-green Incorruptible".

Now I think I owed my acceptance to Hill's private secretary who was a poet named John Irving Taylor. He had read *Knowledge is Power*, and thought a lot of it. William Hill thought a lot of him.

The proprietor of the new paper was a romantic-looking young man, extraordinarily handsome in a Spanish way, named Franklin Thomasson. He was the son of a very rich old cotton spinner up in Bolton who would quarrel over a farthing change though he left something like a million of money to young Franklin. In his will he put a clause, more or less obliging his son to found a Liberal newspaper.

Franklin Thomasson, whom I had met in Bolton, knew nothing whatever about Fleet Street or newspapers, but relied upon the advice of William Hill, that little old man with a game leg which went dot-and-carry-one down the passages of the *Tribune* office, newly built in the grand style in Bouverie Street. He was advised that it would be a good thing to get Augustine Birrell—that charming and scholarly essayist and critic—to act nominally as literary editor and chief literary adviser while I and others would do the daily drudgery. I went with Thomasson and Hill to put this proposition before Augustine Birrell. He received us "most politely", according to the famous song by Harry Fragson, and was very genial, with twinkling eyes behind his spectacles, in a study walled in by books. He declined the offer, and at the end of the conversation put his hand on Franklin Thomasson's shoulder.

"My dear fellow," he said, "I knew your father and had a great respect for him. If you take my advice you will write me a cheque for £300,000 and *not* start the *Tribune*. It will save you a lot of money."

It is queer that he should have mentioned £300,000, for that is just about the amount which Thomasson lost over this adventure, which proved disastrous.

I was in at the beginning, but had a shock when I met a friend of mine down one of the passages a few days before the paper first appeared. His name was Edward Hawke, formerly of "Intellectual Mansions, S.W.".

"Hullo, Hawke!" I exclaimed. "What are you doing here?"

"I'm the new literary editor," he told me.

"That's very odd," I answered. "I also am the new literary editor."

It was an awkward situation. We found that old Hill had also engaged two news editors in a spirit of megalomania or absent-mindedness. Hawke and I had been equally hard up and in need of a regular salary. We decided that we would share up the literary side of the paper, he taking over the book reviews and I looking after the special articles and other literary items. Hill accepted this arrangement.

Certainly he had engaged a brilliant staff. No newspaper in London, not even *The Times*, to which afterwards several of them drifted, had such distinguished men on the editorial and reporting side. L. T. Hobhouse, J. L. Hammond, H. Brailsford, highly distinguished as political writers on the *Manchester Guardian* and as men of letters, were our chief leader writers. A first class journalist named Drysdale was our parliamentary reporter. Our regular contributors, gathered by myself for special articles, combined all the talents of the time. Among them was G. K. Chesterton whom I had persuaded, rather reluctantly, because of his loyalty to the *Daily News*, to write for us frequently, provided he did not abandon his old paper. He agreed partly, I am sure, as a personal favour to me.

Franklin Thomasson had the idea, or had it suggested to him, that for publicity reasons and prestige it would be good to have a reception in the *Tribune* office a night or two before the first issue.

I was put in charge of a dummy paper which would be printed while the guests were present and handed to each one during the evening with full reports of that day's news. This reception was organised regardless of cost. The hall and stairways of the *Tribune* office were hung with baskets of orchids and trailing creepers. The Carlton restaurant provided the refreshments, including champagne *ad libitum*.

Now that kind of thing was unusual in Fleet Street, and overexcited some of the members of the new staff on the business and reporting side. Anxious lest the flow of champagne should dry up rapidly when the guests arrived they had the forethought to come early and drink the health of the new paper before the crush. One of them was an extremely tall young man, with pale blue eyes in a clean-shaven face, with just a suspicion of side whiskers in the style of the Early Victorians. He dressed in that style, I fear at the expense of his tailor, in fawn coloured frock coats, tight waisted and wide skirted, with peg top trousers. His tall hats were masterpieces, probably from Lock in St. James's Street—still there with its old hats in the window despite the fury of the German blitz in its close neighbourhood. His name was Randal Charlton, and he became a friend of mine and the hero of my novel *The Street of Adventure*, though he was not pleased with my portrait as I shall have to tell.

The guests arrived, a very distinguished crowd of literary and social personalities. Mr. and Mrs. Thomasson received them. Among them was the noble figure of my friend G. K. Chesterton with a thousand little curls on his head, as though his whimsical thoughts were bursting out of his brain, as indeed they always were, and with a benevolent smile for me whom he pretended to regard as one of his patrons.

Among them also was Augustine Birrell, bland and bespectacled. In spite of his warning and half-serious advice the paper was going to be started. Randal Charlton had been appointed as a reporter on the *Tribune* by the influence of Mr. Birrell, and it was unfortunate that before the evening had gone by Charlton, pale as death because of a careless repetition of precious liquids provided free, fell like a lily at the feet of his patron.

Other regrettable incidents were happening behind the scenes. One of the office boys, who, somehow, had had access to the champagne, started fighting one of the business staff, and after being knocked down was put on a lift for printing paper and sent aloft.

The guests were mostly unaware of any unseemly happenings. There were speeches proposing the success of the *Tribune*. G. K. Chesterton out of the kindness of his heart made generous references to me, somewhat to the annoyance of Franklin Thomasson who had the cotton spinner's point of view of one of his "hands" or subordinate employees. A good time was had by all, as the provincial reporter used to say. The guests drifted away. Some of the staff remained. It was a pity not to do justice to the efforts of the Carlton restaurant. Now the long green neon lights outside the offices in Bouverie Street had attracted a crowd of night birds, the down-and-outs of the Embankment, who were drawn like moths to this scene of splendour with many richly dressed people and a concourse of carriages. (It was still before the time of motor cars except for a few pioneers.) One of the staff, who shall be nameless even at this distant date (the law of libel is very terrible) was touched by the contrast between these human derelicts and the rich scene within. He too had released his inhibitions and had been moved to tearful emotion by the magic of a sparkling wine. He invited the down-and-outs to carry off the baskets of orchids.

"Help yourselves, my poor fellows," he said.

His generosity increased as the minutes fled.

He invited those tramps to carry off from the hall a grandfather's clock which had deep and lovely chimes. Astonished and gratified by this invitation they took the gentleman at his word, and Franklin Thomasson returned unexpectedly—I think he was one of those who drove up in a car—anxious as to what was happening, after a telephone message, and saw to his consternation the removal of that piece of furniture which he was only just in time to save.

12

MEN OF LETTERS

On the first day of publication the bus horses of London were caparisoned in white sheets bearing the name of the *Tribune*, and announcing the advent of this great Liberal daily. By bad luck it was one of London's foul days, with a gusty wind, and rain beating down on the roads and pavements. Very soon the white sheets were splashed with gobs of mud and soaked with rain until they became dirty, wind-blown rags, with their words indecipherable to the passers-by.

The first number had not been produced without a struggle. The very night before there had been an editorial revolt in which I took part. Poor little William Hill had a passion for snippets, and he had assigned no less than five daily columns to this kind of pot-pourri, one of them being called, I remember, the "Tribune Jorum". The editorial staff, including the leader writers, begged the old gentleman to abandon at least four of these columns, which we thought would make us all ridiculous. Hill refused. He was very obstinate about it. So were we. He became white with anger. Thomasson, loyal to his Editor-in-Chief, backed him up, but finally there was a compromise and three of the snippety features were wiped out. The truth is that William Hill, shrewd and experienced as a news gatherer, was unequal to the editorship of a paper like this, and his intelligence and education were lower than the level of his staff. Also he had no order or method in his mind. His desk became a horror of unanswered and higgledy-piggledy letters and manuscripts. His secretary, the poet, John Irving Taylor, was not himself a master of tidiness, his thoughts being with the gods and goddesses of ancient Greece, with Milton, Shelley, Keats and Byron. Franklin Thomasson, a business man, though not a newspaper man, blenched at the sight of so much disorder.

Nevertheless the paper appeared in due time every day, though the chief printer nearly went mad because of alterations in red ink scribbled on every column at the eleventh hour by William Hill. Because of its distinguished staff and contributors it was filled with articles of high quality. Hobhouse and Brailsford and J. L. Hammond preached the pure gospel of Liberalism—too pure, I fear, and too highbrow for the little man in the corner of the railway carriage, and too exalted for the typist girls, the shop girls, and suburban women in the horse-drawn busses and tramcars. They preferred the *Daily Mail* or the *Daily Express*. The *Tribune* was too good, and there was too much of its goodness. This was due partly to the scarcity of advertisements. We were not backed by the big advertisers because they said, very truly no doubt, that our readers were not their customers. Smart millinery, corsets, furs, and hats, would not find a great market with the *Tribune* public, they said. That left us with many columns to fill, and the general effect was a paper with too many articles for the average man or woman to absorb in the course of a busy day.

I kept filling up those pages day by day with articles by distinguished contributors and by some of my own. I tried to brighten those pages now and then by concessions to popular taste, a few grades lower than our intellectual standards, and in a misguided moment wrote to Marie Corelli asking her to write something for us. She answered that she would be willing to do so if I assured her that it would not be cut or edited in any way. In another misguided moment I agreed, and I received from her a very gratifying postcard on which was written: *"You are the only gentleman in Fleet Street."*

Cheered by this unsolicited testimonial I pinned it over my desk for my friends and colleagues to see when they came into my room.

But when the article arrived I read it with consternation. It was a violent and libellous attack upon almost every other newspaper. It was an impossible thing to publish and I sent it back with an expression of great regret.

I received another postcard. On it was written in Marie Corelli's bold script:

"*You are an unspeakable cad.*"

I pinned it above my desk side by side with the other.

William Hill was conscious that our paper was over serious and without a sufficient attention to Women's Interest. With this idea he engaged a man of wit and social standing to deal each day with London society and social gossip. This member of our staff was Captain Harry Graham, who was well known for his satirical verse and amusing plays. He moved in fashionable circles, or at least was supposed to do so by William Hill who regarded the "West End" as a romantic and not too virtuous realm to which he had no entry. Now I noticed that Harry Graham seemed very loth to get going on the social column. He drew quite a good salary for any work he might do but he did not work very hard.

"I find it all very difficult," he told me.

But one day he did produce a column of social chit-chat, and the chief item, which seemed to me unexciting, was that Mr. Balfour had attended a dance the night before and chosen as his partner a little girl of tender age. But this item was Graham's downfall. It transpired that Mr. Balfour had refused an important engagement under the plea that he was confined to his bed. He wrote a furious letter to Harry Graham who had been present at the dance, and Graham resigned his position on the *Tribune* to make fame and fortune elsewhere.

One figure of picturesque appearance comes to my mind when I think back to those days of the *Tribune*.

This was J. L. Hammond, distinguished sociologist and author of many good books on the industrial era. He had a touch of lung trouble and was told by his doctor to keep in the open air as much as possible. To fulfil this advice he selected a spot in the *Tribune* office at the end of a corridor down which the wind howled as it entered from a wide window. Hammond at that time was a bearded man, and his beard waved in the wind. To keep his feet warm he laid down straw which blew about him as he wrote. He was like a wild man of the woods.

More picturesque still was G. K. Chesterton, who used to come to my room from time to time to deliver his script and have a chat. But I lived high up above many stone steps, and Chesterton's progress to my

room was by degrees. At the top of one flight he would pause for five or
ten minutes not only to take breath but to correct or amplify his latest
screed, pointing a witty aphorism and shaking with mirth at some jest
which had surprised himself. So, many times, I saw him on my way
downstairs.

One afternoon I had invited him to take tea with me at Anderton's
Hotel in Fleet Street, a rat-infested place in those days.

Tea was brought, but Chesterton looked wistful.

"Do you think I might have some port instead of tea?" he asked.

I ordered a bottle of port, and during two hours of brilliant conversation he drank it to the dregs. It was a hot August afternoon.

13

THE OLD PRISON

For the *Tribune* I wrote a series of articles called "London Pictures"
—about fifty or sixty of them. They were descriptions of London life,
high and low, from the London Docks and the Jewish quarter to a
garden party at Buckingham Palace, or to the studio of Vandyke, the
photographer, when the *débutantes* came to have their portraits taken
after presentation at Court.

I found material for one article unexpectedly. I was passing the Old
Bailey when I remembered that this ancient court and prison was about
to be pulled down for a new building on its site. I went inside and found
extraordinary scenes going on. The police had cleared out, and the
criminal population of London had come to see the last of the old place
where many of them had been sentenced for thefts and drunkenness and
other offences against the law. It was a queer riff-raff. Old drunks and
pickpockets and prostitutes had taken possession of the court room
and were exploring the cells below. Among them were Dickens
characters who I thought had disappeared for ever from London life.
Old Fagin and the Artful Dodger were there with Bill Sykes and Nancy
and the convict in *Great Expectations*. Some of them had swarmed into
the Judge's chair, and were sentencing each other to death with sham
solemnity ending in shrieks of laughter. Others were addressing the
Court.

"M'lud. May it please your ludship——"

I went among them down to the cells which were very grim. They
remembered having spent nights there. They were my guides to the
very cell from which Jack Sheppard had made his escape.

Wandering around I saw piles of papers strewn on the floors. They
were encrusted in black soot but I picked up some of them and shoved

them in my pocket. On one of the tables was lying a big book. It was the charge sheet of the Old Bailey going back a century. I was tempted to carry it off, and regret not having done so, but I was afraid of being pinched for a theft under the very roof of the Old Bailey, not being quite sure that the police were well out of the way.

When I went back to the office I examined the papers I had brought away. They were full of tragic interest. One of them was a list of a hundred and twenty convicts, mostly condemned to death but "graciously reprieved" by His Majesty William IV and sentenced to be transported for life to Botany Bay.

Among them were a girl sentenced for stealing an apron, and boys for stealing potatoes, and men for breaking threshing machines which they thought would take away their work. I sent this to John Burns, who had shown me his wonderful collection of books on London. I am sorry now that I did because he neglected to thank me for the gift. He lived on the North Side of Clapham Common, and once had taken me about London, showing me among other things the iron rings and shiny parapets on the Thames Embankments where the convicts had sat before being put on the hulks.

14

DEATH IN BOUVERIE STREET

Poor old William Hill received the sack from Franklin Thomasson when the paper was losing a lot of money and showing no sign of success. He was followed by a little reddish-haired man named S. J. Pryor who had been with the Harmsworth Press for many years. He was a charming and humorous little man whom I liked enormously, but he was the wrong man to choose for the *Tribune*, not being a convinced Liberal and the Harmsworth style of journalism not being really in tune with our public, such as it was. He brightened the paper, but we fell between two stools, not attracting the popular crowd and offending serious Liberals by a note of flippancy and the new appeal to the lighter side of life. Gradually Thomasson began to realise that he was pouring his money into a deep well of failure, and he didn't like it. Perhaps if he had held on we might have turned the corner. Advertising was improving just when he decided that he would bring this costly adventure to an end. Those of us who heard that the paper was doomed were deeply distressed, not only because we should lose our jobs, but because, in spite of ill success, we had made a living thing of this *Tribune* and had put our best work into it, and after two years had the feeling towards it which naval men have for a ship in which they have served. We hated the idea that it should go down with all hands.

Some of us decided to save it if we could by raising new money, and we obtained a respite of two weeks from Franklin Thomasson. Randal Charlton, that tall romantic fellow who dressed in the Early Victorian style, was one of those who set forth in search of fairy gold. He had been one of my assistants on the literary side, and I had pardoned many transgressions due to his mode of life which took him into the sporting world of pugilists and bookies and touts, and into taverns of Alsatia where there was great talk and much wine. During his time on the *Tribune* he had produced two remarkable novels in the Eighteenth Century style: *The Virgin Widow* and *The Bottomless Bed*. They had a touch of genius, a kind of Elizabethan quality not apparent in his conversation or self-revelation. Anyhow, the idea occurred to him that his patron Augustine Birrell, now Irish Secretary in Dublin, might and should save the paper for the sake of the Liberal Party. Taking with him the sporting editor, a tiny little man named Benison with a bowler hat jammed on his brow, Charlton donned his best silk hat and this remarkable couple, so tall and so short, crossed the Irish Sea together one night and advanced upon Mr. Birrell in Dublin Castle. When they were shown in Randal Charlton put his silk hat on Mr. Birrell's desk and addressed him in dramatic and sepulchral words.

"Mr. Birrell, is the *Tribune* going to die?"

Augustine Birrell blinked through his spectacles and made answer.

"May the *Tribune* die that death it so richly deserves."

There was no rescue from Mr. Birrell or the Liberal Government.

I set out on the same quest but in a different direction. I had come in touch somehow or other with one of the grand old dames of England. She was the Countess of Carlisle, a sturdy Liberal and a great Temperance advocate. I went down to her country house and found a family party assembled at the dinner table. Among them was her son, Geoffrey Howard, a brilliant gay-hearted fellow and a Liberal Member of Parliament. No serious conversation was possible during the meal which was rowdy. Geoffrey Howard threw bread at his relatives who retaliated with great spirit. Afterwards I had a talk with the old lady who was genuinely distressed at the plight of a paper for which she had a high respect. She agreed to meet its editor S. J. Pryor and discuss the possibility of rescue. Pryor was slightly alarmed at the prospect of meeting this formidable old dame, who was a fanatic on temperance, and whom he was to take out to lunch. It was his habit to have a glass of whisky with his meal, but he staggered the waiter by ordering a glass of milk.

The Countess of Carlisle listened to the facts about the financial condition of the *Tribune*. She was blunt and businesslike when she made a very generous offer. She was willing to guarantee the expenses of the paper, paying all salaries and wages for two weeks, during which time we might get some syndicate to buy the paper and carry it on.

We had two more weeks of life, but failed to go beyond that. There were distressing scenes when the last night came. The printers and compositors assembled to hear the sentence of death. Their little ones were in jeopardy. They might have to walk the streets. The editorial staff were equally distressed and one man wept. Some of us might find it hard to get new places and looked forward to lean days. One man, who was our naval expert, shot himself.

That night Randal Charlton and I stood outside the office in Bouverie Street. We had been talking for hours. Suddenly the long green lights went out. Our ship had gone down with all hands.

Charlton gave a kind of sob.

"Dead ! . . . Dead!" he cried with deep emotion, taking off his hat.

It was the end of the *Tribune*, and the end of a great adventure in which we had been very keen, putting in our best work, neglecting our home life, sacrificing our leisure, for the sake of "the rag", with a sense of loyalty and team work and comradeship. All that had gone for nothing. Ahead of us there was a bleak outlook.

15

Free Lance Again

My wife did not flinch when she heard of the death of the *Tribune*. She was used to these ups and downs of fortune, and these periods of free-lancing when there was nothing between us and the direst poverty but a wad of blank paper and a bottle of ink.

"Better write a novel about it!" she suggested. "Let's have a holiday at the seaside. Then you can do some writing. It will do Tony good."

We took a tiny coast-guard's cottage at Littlehampton and there, to the noise of a merry-go-round on the green, and the squawk of a Punch and Judy, and the shouts of the children, I wrote *The Street of Adventure*. It was the first novel about Fleet Street behind the scenes, and I made the *Tribune* the centre of it. Almost every character in the book, apart from two young women, much romanticised, was a portrait. My editor in the novel was S. J. Pryor. My hero was Randal Charlton, whom I called Christopher Codrington. I wrote it all at a great pace, working for bread and butter, against time and the hungry wolf. It seemed to go well and I was pleased with it. I thought all the characters in the book would be equally pleased when they recognised my portraits, slightly caricatured now and then, in the friendliest way. Alas, they were not pleased!

Having completed the novel I returned to town where we still lived in Holland Street. On the way up I left the manuscript on the mantelshelf of a railway waiting room, and had been in London two hours before I became aware of its loss. In frantic anxiety I wired to the station-master, and in due course received an answer that the manuscript had been found. Afterwards I was sorry that it had been found, because immediately upon its publication by William Heinemann, who thought well of it, I received several letters threatening me with libel actions. I was greatly astonished. Had I not been very kind? Had I not described Fleet Street and its denizens in a friendly and favourable light, though I had not concealed its slavery and hardships?

Only one of the threatened libel actions was carried through, and this was done by the man who had been, I thought, my hero of the novel, my friend Randal Charlton.

He was annoyed, it seemed, by my slight touches of caricature. Through his lawyer he accused me of depicting him as a disreputable and worthless character, holding him up to ridicule and contempt, and jeopardising his journalistic career. This was very annoying of him because I had sent him proofs in advance, offering to alter anything to which he might object.

Heinemann was alarmed and sent me to his lawyers, Lewis and Lewis. They took a serious view of the case. They briefed Counsel. They employed detectives to keep an eye on the private life of Randal Charlton. It was all going to be very costly and I should have to bear the cost with blue ruin staring me in the face.

On the day before it was coming into Court I met Charlton in Fleet Street and we shook hands, I laughed at him and told him that he was going to make a fool of himself in Court. "My Counsel will tear you to bits," I told him. "He will just make a laughingstock of you."

Charlton looked uneasy, and I thought he looked hungry.

"Come and have a bite of lunch," I suggested.

He hesitated only a second, and then accepted. We had a meal in a Fleet Street restaurant and talked in a friendly way.

"Why don't you withdraw?" I suggested. "There's still time. It will save us both a lot of money."

"No," he said, "it's gone too far. I can't withdraw now. Besides, I have a very good case."

We talked about other things. He let me pay his bill.

I had an appointment that afternoon with Lewis and Lewis. When I told them that Charlton and I had had lunch together, and that I had paid his bill, they were dumbfounded and horrified. "It makes the whole case ridiculous," they said. "For the two principals to get together like this is outrageous."

Upon their advice I sought out Charlton that evening and said: "We had better come to an agreement. You shouldn't have let me pay for your lunch. It seems to have knocked things edgewise."

He saw the point. I don't think he was anxious to appear in court. He withdrew his action in writing. But for years afterwards I was paying off the bill run up by Lewis and Lewis out of my royalties.

The Street of Adventure went on selling year after year, decade after decade. It is still selling, although it must seem archaic to the younger generation when they read of my characters going about in hansom cabs. But somehow it appeals because of a youthful spirit in it, and its story of newspaper life behind the scenes. It was meant as a dread warning to journalistic aspirants, but I am told that it has lured great numbers of young men to Fleet Street where afterwards, no doubt, they have cursed my name.

16

THE ROYAL POET

During one of my free lance periods I earned some easy money with the *Daily Graphic*, then quietly approaching its end. The editor asked me to suggest a good subject for letters from readers. Their contributions would cost nothing, and if the series were successful I should be paid at the rate of two guineas a column. I suggested "Curiosities of Coincidence", and sat down to write to many famous people in *Who's Who* asking if they had had any interesting and unusual coincidences in life. I enclosed a penny stamp for reply. Now it was astonishing that most of them had had the most astounding coincidences and were pleased to narrate them at some length. To this day I find it hard to believe some of them, which were fantastic. The long arm of coincidence seems to stretch very far. But it provided most entertaining reading, afterwards put into a book, and I drew two guineas a column to the great satisfaction of the butcher, the baker, the tailor, and the grocer, whose bills were promptly paid. Miraculous as it may seem, never once did we get into debt, owing to the household economy of Agnes who had a horror of unpaid bills.

About this time, when our little house in Holland Street was still a rendezvous of pleasant people, I made friends with a very high old bird, and it used to amuse me to take tea from my poverty round the corner with the Duke of Argyll in Kensington Palace. He was the husband of Princess Louise, daughter of Queen Victoria, and he liked a good talk about books and authors, being of a literary turn of mind and in his youth, as Marquis of Lorne, a poet. Often we talked until dusk crept into the room through the long windows of the old palace where Dutch William had lived, and though he must have noticed my rather thread-bare clothes, baggy at the knees, he was always very affable and chatty, and seemed to regard it as a favour that I should sit with him.

Sometimes at the approaching end of our talk the door would open and a lady would appear and address us in a clear and pleasant voice. It was Princess Louise.

"You two gentlemen have talked enough! It's time to change for dinner."

"Oh, Lord! So it is, my dear," said the Duke, rising from his big armchair.

At Windsor after the funeral of King Edward, when many princes and exalted people came out of St. George's Chapel, my newspaper colleagues were astounded to see me walking arm in arm with a noble Duke, magnificent in full uniform. It was my old friend of Kensington Palace.

A great number of years later—almost a lifetime later—I met Princess Louise again. She was over ninety and came to Charing Cross Hospital, of which I am Vice Chairman, and of which she was President. It was not long before the second World War. It was during the Civil War in Spain when Franco was fighting the Reds and when our Leftists were clamouring for intervention.

I escorted the old lady to the door, after she had presided at our meeting and made a nice little speech. She leaned heavily on her stick and as though addressing a public meeting said in very clear tones:

"We should do well as a nation if we refrained from putting our fingers into other people's pies."

It seemed to me a very sound piece of advice. Not very long after-wards we were up to our neck in "other people's pies", which I suppose was inevitable as our own pie was so close to the red-hot oven of our neighbours.

17

THE BATTLE OF SIDNEY STREET

I was driven back to Fleet Street again by the spur of poverty, and by that bug which, if it bites one, is almost incurable—the bacillus of journalism. Fleet Street puts a spell upon a man. Away from it he feels exiled, and outside the arena of life. As a journalist, and especially as a special correspondent, he sees behind the scenes of the whirligig, and is one of its recorders. He hears the news before it is published to the world. He is present at the pageants of the historic scene, and is sometimes very close to its exalted actors. He talks with them sometimes—the men and women who are making history. He is to some extent their judge. He observes their vanities or their pomposities. It is he who brings them alive to the public and takes down the words they speak on great occasions—words of wisdom maybe, or words of folly, or words of doom which pronounce sentence of death on masses of youth who go willingly to sacrifice because of their leadership or their lies.

The reporter, as Edgar Wallace liked to call himself—he chose that word to describe his life upon his memorial tablet—gets the thrill of being an eye-witness of passing events. The word "Press" opens many barriers which the mob cannot pass. It takes him to the front seats of the peep-show. It is an 'Open Sesame' to hidden chambers, or the stage door of life's melodrama—a murder trial, a Coronation, the funeral of a hero, the wedding of a great lady, the death-bed of a King-Emperor where once I stood. It is the Spell of the Street which has bewitched many men, though now and then they cursed themselves for fools, because of its enslavement and utter indifference to those who get tired, and to those who get old in the service of this monster, with its insatiable appetite for news which is dead before to-day becomes tomorrow.

So back I went to Fleet Street as special correspondent of the *Daily Chronicle* at home and abroad.

Robert Donald was still Editor-in-Chief and Ernest Perris news editor, and the best in London, being a tiger for work, inspiring his staff with his own enthusiasms for new "scoops" and the excitement of the chase. Contemporary events assumed an exaggerated importance. We were mostly chroniclers of small beer before that beverage turned into blood and tears for the greater part of humanity.

One of the most sensational incidents of London life was the so-called "Battle of Sidney Street". I turned up at the office rather early and the news editor said: "You had better get along to Whitechapel. There's something exciting going on there. A bunch of anarchists have barricaded themselves in a house in Sidney Street and are defying the police with automatic pistols."

I took a cab as near as possible and found some of my Fleet Street friends already on the scene, standing at the end of the street.* One of them was leaning on his walking stick but suddenly gave a lurch and nearly fell over. A bullet had cut his stick in two.

"That's very odd!" he exclaimed.

* One of them was my friend I. P. Eddy who later became a Judge in India and is now back in chambers as a K.C. Later he has written this story of the Battle of Sidney Street for the Crimes Club.

THE BATTLE OF SIDNEY STREET
(By F. Matania)

BEERBOHM TREE AS " CALIBAN "
(By F. Matania)

It was certainly very odd. A moment later a bullet took a bite out of a policeman's helmet. Bullets were chipping bits out of a wall on the opposite side of the road and ricochetting down the street.

"Now, gentlemen," said the policeman, "it's quite silly standing here. Don't want to get killed, do you?"

We were careless of being killed because, at the time of history, we were not familiar with death by Tommy-guns or other weapons, especially in a London street. An old woman went across the road with some washing under her arm. Anarchists or no anarchists she was going to do her job.

I heard the story as far as it was known. There had been the murder of a young Russian in a house in a neighbouring street. His body, dripping blood, had been carried there by two or three men. One of the men had been identified as Peter the Painter, another Russian. The police had got on his trail. They located him with two other men in the Sidney Street house. When they went to arrest him the men inside the house had opened fire and three policemen were killed and three severely wounded. Now they were preventing the police from getting near by constant fire, and they were good shots, who could make a pattern no bigger than a playing card on any spot they used for their target. It was certain death for any Bobby who exposed himself for a second. There were masses of Bobbies, but they crouched under the wall running at right angles from the house, and were under orders not to get killed needlessly.

"Now, you can't stand here!" shouted the policeman nearest to us. "You gentlemen of the Press must take cover. We don't want this street littered with corpses."

We decided to get a good observation post on the Rising Sun which was almost immediately opposite the anarchists' house, a three-storey building of red brick. The man who kept the pub decided to make hay while the sun shone. He demanded a "quid" from anyone who wished to go on his roof. We all wished to go there, but I had no golden sovereign in my purse and only 1s. 6d. in my pocket. A friend came to my rescue. It was Macer Wright of the *Westminster Gazette* who offered generously to lend me the "quid". So on to the roof we went, and looked at a slight angle into the windows of the red brick villa. All view inside was concealed by dirty curtains. Presently a body of Scots Guards came up and deployed at the end of the street and then lay down on their stomachs on newspaper placards, sniping at the windows from which the bullets were issuing in spasms of fire. They seemed to have no lack of ammunition, those anarchists.

"Good Lord!" said a voice at my side presently, "there's Winston. Just like him to come here and watch the fun."

There he was standing by a bunch of Bobbies, smoking a cigar and peering round the corner towards the anarchists' lair. He wore a kind of square bowler like a farmer. He was then Home Secretary in a Liberal Government.

We watched for a couple of hours, I should say. The Guardsmen were plugging through the windows. Some of them had occupied the opposite houses and had stuffed their own windows with mattresses leaving chinks through which they could fire.

Suddenly some of us on the Rising Sun were aware of smoke and bits of charred paper floating above one of the chimney pots.

"They're burning their papers," said someone.

"They're burning the blooming house," said someone else.

Little flames began to lick out of the windows opposite. They charred the curtains. Out of one curtain leapt a tongue of fire. Very soon the whole house was a furnace. No human being was visible inside. But, as the last act in this drama, a hand and an arm were stretched out from one of the windows and took a final shot. Not long afterwards the whole house collapsed and the police rushed it. Two dead bodies were found inside. Peter the Painter, it was said, had escaped and was heard of later in the Russian Revolution.

My friend and colleague J. P. Eddy, came with me to explore the East End and to dive down to its underworld and the haunts of its "anarchists".

For some reason we were anxious to put up in the house where the young murdered man had been found, but the door was slammed in our face. They took us to be police "narks". The problem that night was to get a lodging somewhere and we knocked at door after door. Nobody spoke English in that quarter. Everybody spoke Yiddish, but could understand a bit of German in which I addressed them. Not for love or money could we get a lodging until late at night we found one room fairly clean in Sidney Street itself. For a week or two we haunted the East End. One of our guides was a young thief who had done time and had had "the cat". To this day I remember the shudder of horror which passed through him when he told us of that torture inflicted upon his body. He took us into strange places—the rendezvous of pickpockets and flash burglars.

One evening we managed to get into a meeting of so-called "anarchists". There was a big gathering of these "Reds", as we should now call them, English and foreign. They were crowded up the stairs, listening to oratory from an upper room too packed to enter. We had made our identity known. They were not hostile to representatives of the *Daily Chronicle*, the London Oracle of Liberalism. Some of them were well educated, though mostly they belonged to the shop assistant and sempstress class, the Russian women with flat Slav faces and hair looped over their ears. I remember having a long and academic argument on the philosophy of Communism with a glib-tongued fellow, and a woman of some intellectual brilliance in the small bathroom adjoining the room where the meeting was in progress. It was the only space available for private conversation. I wonder now as I write whether any of the leaders of the future Revolution in Russia were present that night—Lenin or Trotsky or their fellow conspirators.

One place I visited, in order to get better acquainted with Russian exiles in London, was a cigarette factory which employed a considerable number of them. It was run by an old man—a very old man—who, strange as it may seem, was the first manufacturer of cigarettes in London. Previously to the Crimean War smoking in England was restricted to pipes and cigars. Cigarettes were regarded as effeminate, and were only known by the select few. But British officers in the Crimea learnt to smoke the cigarette and this Russian came to England to take advantage of the new fashion.

When I saw him his factory was turning out hand-made cigarettes, and his "hands" were political exiles from Russia with many Jews among them. Some of them were handsome and intelligent-looking men, wearing Russian blouses and smoking as they worked. Some of them were University men who had been in trouble with the Czar's secret police because of their revolutionary ideas. One of their leaders in London was Prince Kuropatkin whom I met once or twice. He was a scholar and a noble-minded man, living poorly in a mean street. He believed in Liberty but his soul would have been shocked had he foreseen the blood and cruelty of revolution as it happened in Russia.

18

THE BIRTH OF A PRINCESS

I was sent on an amusing and somewhat ludicrous mission to Holland which gave me an opportunity, unduly prolonged, to see the lovely old towns and fine galleries of art in that enchanting country.

Now it happened that Queen Wilhelmina expected to have a child, and for some absurd reason, apart from the natural jubilation of the Dutch people, there was much excitement about it in England and other countries. If anything happened to the Queen the next heir to the throne was a German Prince—Henry the 33rd of Reuss. International troubles might arise. Anyhow, to the Hague I went and found myself in the company of various international journalists, including Hamilton

Fyfe of the *Daily Mail*, and a young *Times* correspondent whose name I have forgotten.

We were received most hospitably by the officials of the Court in the old palace of the Hague. Every night a banquet was prepared for us and we were led thereto by powdered and knee-breeched flunkeys holding lighted candles. Every night the Jonkheer van Geen, the Court Chamberlain, made a little speech in five languages.

"Gentlemen, the happy event for which we all wait cannot be far ahead. Her Majesty's health is excellent. It is with patience and joy that we restrain our emotions."

Something of the sort.

But the astonishing thing was that day after day passed without the joyful news being brought to us. When we arrived an old plane tree outside the palace was bare of buds or leaves, but gradually we saw it break out into spring foliage.

For a time we remained close to the palace lest anything should happen in our absence. Hamilton Fyfe read Nietzsche and other philosophers. *The Times* correspondent, a young man anxious to fulfil his duty, sat up most of the night every night. After several days of this we—Hamilton Fyfe and I—decided that we would risk day excursions provided we returned early enough to send off the news, if the news arrived, in time for the morning papers in England. The news did not arrive. We studied the art gallery in the Hague, and its priceless treasures of Flemish art. We went to Amsterdam, and stood entranced by the old tall houses along the canals, and by Rembrandt's "Night Watch" in the art gallery.

We went to Delft and found it charming. We saw the tulip fields stretching as far as the eye could see with lovely colours like a patchwork quilt woven by fairy fingers. We even learnt Dutch well enough to read the morning papers.

"This is absurd!" said Hamilton Fyfe.

"It's all very amusing," I answered.

Then one night, or, rather, early one morning, at about seven o'clock, I think, the unexpected happened, for we had given up expecting it. The Jonkheer van Geen with tears in his eyes came to announce that Her Majesty had been delivered of a daughter, and that both were doing well. Now the young *Times* correspondent had taken a night off, sceptical of any baby being born during his absence. But it appeared, as we knew, that King Edward was greatly interested in this event and that *The Times* correspondent had undertaken to inform him directly it occurred. Not wanting to let him down I undertook this duty for him.

Fyfe and I made a dash for the Post Office. Our running feet seemed to arouse the people of the Hague, and women in dressing gowns came out on to the balconies, and I shouted out the word "Princess": By the time we had sent off our messages the Hague was alive and riotous with joy. It went on being riotous with joy for three days and nights. The Dutch army had already celebrated the event one night previously on a false rumour, but they celebrated it again in the good old Dutch way, with lots of *schnapps* and lots of marching and cheering, and dancing with Dutch girls in their flowered petticoats. Heralds and trumpeters made formal proclamations. The Dutch government—its "grave and reverend signors"—came out into the street and did a kind of dance with linked hands. It was as though Mr. Lloyd George and Mr. Winston Churchill and their colleagues had done a barn dance down Whitehall. Hamilton Fyfe and I hired an old four-wheeled cab and drove about seeing the sights of this national jubilation. For the first and last time in my life I had a fight.

It was with a Dutch photographer of great bulk who climbed up on our cab which lurched to and fro under his weight. I asked him to get down and when he refused pulled him down. He came at me like a bull and I hit out at him. Hamilton Fyfe said I hit him below the belt. Certainly he collapsed like a pricked balloon. It was all very laughable. Hamilton Fyfe laughed delightedly at what he described as a battle between a white rabbit and a Dutch boar.

So I became the literary accoucheur of Princess Juliana.

19

THE LURE OF PARIS

I went to Paris now and then on special missions, and learnt to know that city by day and night from Montparnasse to the hill of Montmartre. For me Paris has always been the city of enchantment, and intellectual liberty, and, at its best, of beauty touched by the ghost world of its history. I have seen it between two wars and during two wars, when each time it was drenched in sunlight under cloudless blue, and when, at night, the gardens of the Tuileries had some magical beauty beyond the ordinary senses, under a sky of stars, when the grass between the paths and flower beds was of emerald green, and the statues of nymphs and graces were of unspotted white in the whiteness of the moonlight. I came to know the people of Paris in the *bistros* and the markets, in the student quarter, and in the apartments of the intellectuals. I have seen them in their most tragic days of history and have heard the sound of guns very close to their city. To me all foreign journeys should start in Paris. I have to get back to its atmosphere, to smoke a cigarette at one of its café tables, to watch its citizens hurrying past the Dôme, some of them hand in hand as lovers, not ashamed of love, or sitting even on chilly autumn nights round the café tables, sheltered by a screen of glass and warmed a little, but not much, by charcoal stoves.

I like the common people of Paris—the woman behind the *zinc*, the garage hand in a cheap eating house, an old fellow selling books at a stall on the Seine—better than the smart set into which now and then I have been received. But the hours I have loved best in Paris were those when I walked with Agnes through the Bois, or rowed to the Chalet des Iles for a rose-tinted ice under the shelter of a sunshade.

The *Daily Chronicle* had an office in Paris, not far from the Madeleine. A young Frenchman—young then—held the fort, and sent off the news of the day when his chief was away on some adventure, and it was then that I used to take over. Bourdin and I became close comrades, and from him I learnt all that I knew about French politics and personalities. He had a passion for the drama, and after our work, late at night, when we were waiting for further news, he would tell me the stories of the plays he had seen or read, acting every part and dramatising his narrative in a vivid way.

As an assistant he had a little old man who looked like a gnome, though much to his amusement I called him Abdul Hamid, the terrible Turk. His clothes were shabby and threadbare, but he kept himself spotlessly clean, and was always washing his hands. He spoke the *argot* of Paris with great fluency. He had lived there for years as assistant on many English and American papers, always losing his job because of one fatal weakness—absinthe. He would work diligently and well, and then on a day of crisis when his assistance was most needed, he would fail to turn up and remain away for several weeks. Everybody knew the cause of absence. Everybody who had employed him laughed with a shake of the head at the mention of his name. "Hopeless!" they would say, and yet they had a soft spot in their heart for him and would pass him a bit of work because underneath it all— his frightful language learnt in low haunts of Paris, and his gradual descent into the abyss of squalor—there was the gentleman still, and a man of wit and intelligence who knew more about Paris and its political history than any other Englishman.

Often he did little acts of kindness and courtesy which disarmed his judges.

Not very long before the second World War I had a visit from a venerable man with a straggling beard and moustache. His hair and beard were almost white. His clothes were in the last stage of disintegration, but his hands were very clean.

"Do you remember," he asked, "Abdul Hamid?"

I remembered him, though he was greatly changed. The sinner had turned into a saint. He looked like one of the apostles in old age. He was utterly destitute, living in a dosshouse, but my wife and I helped him a bit until he died. So ended an old journalist who had been his own worst enemy, but is still remembered by his friends.

Those were my two office companions in Paris, and I knew them over a long term of years when terror and despair took the place of light-heartedness and humour. Bourdin loathed the first war and was dragged from journalism to be a French *poilu* in filthy barracks and dirty places. In the second World War he escaped with his wife to England where I met them both. But they were agonising over a young son who had been an interpreter with the B.E.F. but failed to get away at Dunkirk. Months went by and they heard no word of him and Madame Bourdin died of heartbreak in this English exile.

One time when I went to Paris, before all that, there was a general strike during the premiership of Aristide Briand. It was a dangerous affair and reminiscent, I thought, of the French Revolution.

Street battles were taking place between the police and the strikers. The *terrassiers*, or labourers, of Paris came out in strength, and barricaded themselves in blocks of half built tenements where I saw them charged by the *Garde Républicaine*. Students of the Latin Quarter came from the Left Bank carrying lanterns, because the street lights had gone out when the electricians ceased work. The students seemed all in favour of the strikers and kept up a lugubrious chant of "*A bas la Police! A bas la Police!*" until here and there the police, exasperated, charged them with their batons and put them to flight. I got mixed up in these crowds and had narrow escapes from baton charges and horses' hoofs.

One night when Jaurès, the Socialist, addressed the *cheminots*, or railwaymen, in a big riding school in the slum quarter, I decided to hear his speech if I could get in. Dense crowds surged round the building, and I had difficulty in forcing my way through. The door leading in to the meeting place was heavily guarded by strikers and the crowd around me told me that there was no room inside for a mouse. A young man at the door asked what I wanted and who I was. When I mentioned the *Daily Chronicle*, he shook my hand warmly and said that he had always read that paper when he was in a barber's shop in Soho.

"I will get you in somehow," he said, and somehow I squeezed into a big barn-like hall where, I should say, about two thousand *cheminots* were packed. They were all sweating in a damp heat which came up from the tan. The stench of human bodies was strong. The smell of the tan mingled with it. On the platform stood Jaurès, a big powerful man with a far-carrying voice and a clenched fist which he struck against the palm of his other hand with sledgehammer blows. I have forgotten the gist of his oration but remember only that he was very eloquent and aroused the cheers of the *cheminots*. Presently I sickened and nearly swooned. "If I don't get out of this," I thought, "I shall faint." I got out and saw that the crowds were being pressed back by a squadron of *Gardes Républicaines*.

I had an idea that it would be good to get a view from the top window, or roof, of one of the tall tenement buildings round an open square in which the crowds were surging. I banged at a door and pulled the chain of an old bell which clanged.

A surly-looking man answered.

"What do you want?"

"I want to see what happens down below from one of your windows."

He refused sullenly, but his sullenness was mollified when I offered him twenty francs for the favour.

"That makes a difference," he admitted.

He led me into a squalid house which I soon saw was a low-class lodging house. On the way upstairs we passed through several big rooms with rows of beds. Men and women lay on them, or sat on them, half dressed. Some of the women were combing their hair. Some of the men were playing cards. Others were sleeping with snuffling snores. No one paid the least attention to a riot outside. From the roof of the tenement house I looked down upon it. Jaurès had just left the hall with his army of *cheminots*. The mounted police, with their red plumes caught by the light of street lamps, were trying to block certain ways from the surge of the vast mob. Several of the mounted men were unseated and crashed heavily from their horses. The others had drawn their sabres and were beating the foremost ranks with the flat sides.

It was all reminiscent of the French Revolution. There were the types who shouted "*à la lanterne!*" to hunted aristocrats. There on the beds of the cheap lodging house were women like the *tricoteuses* who gossiped below the guillotine while waiting for more heads to roll into the basket.

The strike was ended abruptly by a dramatic act of Aristide Briand, head of the French Government. He had been one of the leaders of the Left. He had in his time drawn up plans for a general strike. But now he saw that it would lead to chaos and anarchy, and that it was an attack not only on the French Government but on the people of France, deprived of light, fuel, and railway transport. It was, he thought as Prime Minister of France, an attack against democracy. Something of the sort he told me when I was presented to him by his *Chef du Cabinet*. He came into the room and held out his hand, and for the first time I saw a man who, later in history, was the greatest orator in France with a passionate endeavour—which failed—to establish peace in Europe, even with Germany, through the League of Nations. At that time he was well dressed, and his black hair and moustache were neatly brushed and oiled. His dark liquid eyes looked into mine and he spoke gravely about the political state of France. Years later I used to see him at Geneva—a shabby old man hunched up in his seat, smoking innumerable cigarettes, with scurf on his shoulders, until he was called upon to speak, when he would draw himself up and pace up and down like an old caged lion, and pour forth words which stirred the emotion even of cynical men. "An old play actor," they called him, but they could not resist the spell of his oratory.

He ended the general strike by calling the strikers to the colours and putting them under martial law. Tradition and discipline were too strong to be resisted by the railway men. They obeyed the summons. The machinery of life worked again. The strike was over.

One day at the end of July 1914, the name of Jaurès, the man whom I had heard speaking to the crowd of *cheminots*, was shouted out in the streets by newsvendors rushing down the boulevards with their bundles of papers.

"*Jaurès, Assassiné! . . . Jaurès . . . Jaurès.*"

That evening I had dined with my friend Bourdin in a little restaurant called Le Croissant in the rue Montmartre. It was open all night for journalists and other night workers. I had often been there for meals at two in the morning, which might have been supper or might have been breakfast. That evening at the end of July of 1914, when the world held its breath because of a fearful menace to all living men, Bourdin and I sat on a plush-covered seat with our backs to the window, and ate whatever food there was on our plates as men do, even if civilization is crumbling beneath their feet. An hour or so later, when we had left, our places were taken by Jaurès and a friend. They too sat on the plush-covered seat with their backs to the window. A young man stopped outside the window. He fired a pistol at Jaurès, who fell dead over the table with its check-covered cloth.

Jaurès had worked for peace even with Germany. That was why they killed him, though he loved France and was one of its most stalwart patriots. The French Government and public men, knowing that France was on the edge of war, were scared by his assassination. It might break the unity of France in this mortal crisis. They followed his coffin to the grave. His political enemies were there with his friends in the Socialist ranks. I saw many Ministers and Ambassadors and famous men marching slowly beneath the blood-red banners carried by the leaders of the Left. It was a demonstration of unity which abolished all political and party feuds when France was in danger.

20

THE STRANGE AFFAIR OF DR. COOK

One afternoon after a sea voyage I sat in a café in Copenhagen and began a strange adventure.

The café did not look much of a place, though it had excellent coffee, but I learnt afterwards that it was the rendezvous of Danish poets, explorers, and intellectuals.

I had a talk with a waiter who spoke good English.

"Have you ever heard of Dr. Cook, an American explorer?"

He laughed.

"All Denmark is talking about Dr. Cook! They talk of nothing else. He has discovered the North Pole."

I confided to this friendly waiter that I had been sent out by an English newspaper to get an interview with this Dr. Cook. Did the waiter happen to know whether he had arrived?

"Not yet. According to the evening papers—the *Politiken*, the earliest he can arrive is to-morrow. His ship, the *Hans Egede*, is somewhere beyond the Kattegat."

That was a bit of luck for me. I had not arrived too late.

"There are many journalists here," said the waiter, "from all countries. They are all anxious to interview the man who has been first to reach the North Pole. They are waiting in Copenhagen to meet him when he arrives."

That was not good news. I wondered if by some desperate enterprise I could go out to meet Dr. Cook before he reached Copenhagen and get ahead of my newspaper rivals. That idea seemed hopeless when I came to think of it. I turned to the *Politiken* and glanced at its pages. The name of Cook was printed many times in large letters. Obviously the Danes were excited by the news of his coming arrival.

Presently, after I had smoked several cigarettes over my coffee, I saw a lady in white furs with a white fur cap enter the café with a young man. She was rather beautiful I thought. The others stared at her and one or two nudged each other.

The friendly waiter whispered to me.

"Did you see that lady in white furs? It is Mrs. Rasmussen. Her husband is a very famous explorer. He was the last to see Dr. Cook before he set out for the North Pole and helped him with his dogs and sledges."

That information interested me. It seemed to me important to any story I might have to tell. I was a shy man, but no journalist if I failed to talk to that lady. After some hesitation I approached her table and ventured to introduce myself as an English journalist sent out to meet Dr. Cook. Might I have the honour of a few words with her?

She answered in perfect English.

"I don't know much about Dr. Cook. It is my husband who knows him."

The young man at her side invited me to sit at their table and introduced himself as Peter Freuken, whom afterwards I came to know as an Arctic explorer and one of the greatest authorities on the Eskimos. His books are well known to English readers.

I sat at their table and had another coffee and several more cigarettes. These two Danes were very charming. Mrs. Rasmussen—half an Eskimo—had a very nice smile and big dark eyes in a sun-tanned face. Her black hair was looped over her ears in the Russian style. She told me something about her husband. She had not heard from him for a long time, but in his last letter he had mentioned Dr. Cook whose ambition was to reach the North Pole. Rasmussen had provided him with some of his dogs.

"Is there any chance of meeting Cook out at sea?" I asked.

Mrs. Rasmussen glanced at Peter Freuken. They spoke in Danish to each other in low voices. Presently Freuken spoke to me in English again.

"We must ask you to keep a secret. Do you mind?"

I promised to be as secret as the grave.

"We know somebody," he said, "a gentleman of importance, who has a small steamship at Elsinore. He is putting out to sea to meet Dr. Cook's ship, the *Hans Egede*, in the Kattegat. Possibly he will start at dawn to-morrow. Mrs. Rasmussen and I have a hope of making that little trip. Many other people would like to go, but Mrs. Rasmussen may have first claim as it was her husband who was the last man to see Dr. Cook before he went to the North Pole. If you would care to come with us we might get permission for you also. But that is the merest chance and I'm afraid most unlikely. We are motoring to-night to Elsinore. We should be happy to take you with us."

Now, that was a noble offer. My heart gave a lurch. It would be an extraordinary bit of luck if I should be the only English journalist to get aboard the *Hans Egede* and meet Dr. Cook on his way back to Copenhagen. It was asking too much of luck, but I was keen to take the chance.

In slight return for their kindness I invited these two new-found friends to dinner and had a pleasant time with them over good food and good wine. It must have been, I suppose, about ten o'clock when we set out in a car for Elsinore. We went at a great speed through the darkness, and there were moments when I thought that we should all have our necks broken before reaching that haven. It was before dawn when we arrived.

Mrs. Rasmussen was nervous.

"I'm afraid we have brought you on a wild goose chase," she told me. "I'm afraid our friend will not take us in his boat. So many people have asked him for this favour."

Her friend was a pompous little man of high authority in the Danish navigation service. He had a long and earnest conversation with Mrs. Rasmussen and Freuken. It did not seem to be going too well, judging from their looks of disappointment and the little man's gesture of regret.

"Nothing doing!" I thought. "Still it has been amusing."

To my amazement Freuken told me that he and Mrs. Rasmussen had been turned down. There would be great trouble if they were given this special favour, refused to many other people of importance—but I should be allowed to go. As a journalist all the way from England I should be given this privilege.

I felt embarrassed. My new friends had been so generous. It seemed a dirty thing to leave them in the lurch. But I had to think of my paper, and they urged me to go. That night I found myself steaming out to sea. It was all fantastic, like a dream story.

Early next morning we saw, far ahead and very small in one's vision, a ship which we knew to be the *Hans Egede* bringing Dr. Cook to Copenhagen. Slowly the ship seemed to grow bigger. At last we were within hail of her. We could see men in furs leaning over the rail. They waved to us. A rope ladder was lowered and while our boat slowed down several men sprang on to the ladder and climbed aboard the ship. My turn came. I didn't like the look of it. "If I miss that rope ladder that's the end of this adventure," I thought. In an overcoat and felt hat, looking very unseamanlike, I grabbed the rope, got a foothold, and clambered aboard. There on the top deck stood a tall, fair-skinned, blue-eyed man of powerful build and heavy jaw, in furs and snow boots, surrounded by Eskimo dogs. I shook hands with Dr. Cook who had announced his discovery of the North Pole. Next to him was a Danish giant, whom I came to know as Norman Hansen, poet and explorer.

Now, I knew nothing about Polar exploration in any technical way, but somehow on that voyage down the Kattegat I came to doubt the integrity of this man Cook. He allowed myself, and one or two foreign journalists, and one Press agency man, who had also come aboard to question him for a long time in his cabin. He was out for publicity, but did not like some of the questions I put to him in all innocence. I was anxious to get some written narrative from him which I could put over the wires, thus safeguarding myself from scientific errors, and telling the story in his own words.

He said he had nothing in writing.

"But surely," I said, "you have kept a diary?"

He said that all the notes he had made were in the hands of a man named Whitney, who would arrive back from the Arctic some months later.

That seemed to me strange. Having claimed the discovery of the North Pole it seemed to me that this man must have some documents to back up his claim.

"Won't people want to read your diary?" I asked. "Haven't you anything at all in writing?"

He said he had nothing in writing.

I pressed him again for his astronomical observations. Suddenly he became very angry and said: "Don't you believe me? Do you doubt my story? Haven't other explorers come back and given their word which has been believed? Why do you disbelieve me?"

Those may not have been his exact words but that was the gist of his defence, shouted out with violence.

I had not disbelieved him. I was prepared to accept anything he told me, and had made copious notes in all good faith of what he told us all. But this man protests too much, I thought. Why this anger with an innocent? A doubt crept into my mind. "I believe this fellow is lying," I thought. "I believe he's a charlatan."

This scepticism about Cook's integrity deepened in my mind when we were nearing Copenhagen. All Denmark seemed to be coming to meet our ship, in steamboats and launches and skiffs and rowing boats.

The Crown Prince of Denmark was coming to greet the man who said he had reached the North Pole. Pennants fluttered, sirens shrieked, whistles shrilled over the dancing waters. It was a welcome for a hero by a nation of seamen. But here was no hero. Cook cowered in his cabin.

He was brought out almost forcibly by that Danish giant, Norman Hansen. Cook was green. He looked like a criminal who has lost his nerve and knows that discovery is inevitable.

The little devil doubt was growing big in my brain.

When I got ashore in Copenhagen I saw a battalion of journalists from all parts of Europe awaiting Dr. Cook. Among them was W. T. Stead, veteran editor and journalist. There also was my young friend

Alphonse Courlander of the *Daily Express*. He was astounded to see me come off the *Hans Egede*.

"Hullo Gibbs!" he shouted. "Got a good story?"

I had a very good story and I was not willing to share it.

To his chagrin I dodged him and took to my heels, determined to avoid all contact with newspaper men until my narrative was on the wire. I wrote it in an obscure hotel. I wrote several columns, describing my meeting with Dr. Cook and narrating his own story. All through my account there was the strong suggestion of doubt as to the truth of his claim. I did not call him a liar and a charlatan, but every reader would know that I disbelieved him. I took a big chance, and looking back on it one which was too dangerous and not quite justified. I had no proof whatever that he was a fraud.

But later I obtained that proof. My news editor in London, Ernest Perris, printed every line of what I had written and kept me in touch with his own work of investigation with the aid of scientific men who did not believe Cook's claim to the North Pole. One of them was Commander Bernacchi, who was with the Scott and Shackleton expeditions. In Copenhagen I had the help and advice of Danish explorers and students of Arctic life, who came to me and suggested certain questions which Cook ought to answer regarding the number of his dogs, the weight they pulled, the journeys they made, and the detail of his time-table. One of them was Peter Freuken. Another was Sverdrup.

The Crown Prince gave a banquet in honour of Dr. Cook in the palace of the Tivoli Gardens. Many distinguished people of Denmark were invited, and the Press representatives of that country were given seats. I was among them but was in a difficulty regarding evening clothes which were essential for an affair of this kind. I had come in a blue serge suit, having been sent off hurriedly one evening without time to pack. How could I get hold of an evening suit? I thought of my friendly waiter in the café, and willingly he lent me his second best suit. It was not a good fit. The sleeves were too long. The trousers were like concertinas however much I braced them up. There was grease on the waistcoat. Thus clad, and feeling self-conscious, I took a cab to the Tivoli Gardens and arrived rather late. There was a flight of marble steps going up to the great restaurant where the banquet was in progress. Feeling like Leslie Henson in a musical comedy I climbed the marble steps. Then I was startled by a fantastic happening. I was being saluted by a Guard of Honour of the English Life Guards, who drew their sabres at my miserable approach. Afterwards I discovered that they were ladies of the ballet dressed in these uniforms. It was unbelievable.

At the banquet, where the long tables were strewn with flowers, Dr. Cook sat on the right hand of the Crown Prince, who at the right time proposed his health and acclaimed his achievement as the first man to reach the North Pole.

"Now Cook will tell us his story," said a man sitting near me. "We have been waiting for it. He will give us all the details."

But Cook did not tell his story. He said he was keeping it for the book he was writing. He spoke evasively and said nothing which illuminated the darkness of his claim. The company was deeply disappointed. Some of them thought it very extraordinary behaviour. Alphonse Courlander, sitting near me, made funny faces like a codfish.

Owing to the kindness of the American Ambassador in Denmark, who was extremely friendly to me, I was able to meet Dr. Cook several times in the American Embassy at tea time. He knew that I was the English journalist who disbelieved him and that my paper was denying his claim. He looked at me sullenly but, strangely enough, answered various questions I had put to him as suggested by my Danish friends, and his answers, in their opinion, proved conclusively that he had not reached the North Pole. Day by day I went on with the campaign of "debunking" him and Ernest Perris in London carried on the attack.

My fellow journalists in Copenhagen warned me that I was endangering my career. Alphonse Courlander gazed at me with amusement and alarm. He admired my courage, he said, but was aghast at the risks I was taking with the law of libel. Anyhow he believed that Cook was an honest man.

Old W. T. Stead was an enthusiastic believer in Dr. Cook and deplored my scepticism. He put his hands firmly on my shoulders and spoke gravely.

"Young man, you are not only ruining yourself but you are ruining the *Daily Chronicle* for which I have a great respect."

I was the most unpopular man in Copenhagen. The Danish people had hailed Dr. Cook as a hero. The Danish Crown Prince had given him high honours. They bitterly resented the despatches in the *Daily Chronicle*, quoted every day in their own Press, making him out to be a fraud. When I went into a restaurant to get some food I was booed by the people at the little tables. The *Politiken* published a frightful portrait of me, and underneath it put the caption: "The Murderer Gibbs".

There were moments when I had frightful doubts about the line I was taking. Supposing after all Cook had been to the North Pole? Supposing I was maligning an honest and heroic man?

One such moment came to me when an honorary degree was conferred on Cook by the University of Copenhagen and when Cook, expressing his thanks from a kind of pulpit, said in a dramatic way: "I hold out my hands. They are clean!"

Another of these moments was when the *Politiken* published a statement that the Rector of the University had examined Dr. Cook's scientific notes and observations, and had found in them complete proof that he had reached the North Pole. If that were true I was undone. But how could it be true? Cook himself had told me that he had not brought back any notes or scientific data. Either he had lied to me or this was a false report.

I went to Stead and asked him a favour. "Will you come with me to the University and be my witness when I question the Rector about this report?"

Stead agreed, and suggested that I should also take as witness a French journalist who was a man of reputation and honour.

My interview with the Rector of the University was extraordinary and painful. For a long time he would not answer my questions. He argued that he had no authority to give an interview which would be published in the Press.

"I only want to ask one question and to have one answer," I told him. "Did you or did you not examine any notes and scientific observations by Dr. Cook?"

For a long time he remained silent, shifting in his chair uneasily. He was a big heavy man with a handsome florid face and blue eyes which looked to me honest and honourable. He was a man of dignity and courtesy, but desperately uneasy.

"I do not want to get involved in this controversy," he said. "The reputation of my University . . ."

Stead, very generously, pressed my case. "This young man's reputation is also at stake," he said. "In any case the report in the Press that you have examined Dr. Cook's documents should be confirmed or denied."

Finally the Rector of the University answered. It was the answer I had wanted.

"I have seen no papers from Dr. Cook which confirm his claim to the discovery of the North Pole."

W. T. Stead gripped my arm when we went out.

"That was important," he said. "You are lucky. I'm glad to have been of service to you."

Crossing the square in Copenhagen one afternoon a young Danish journalist pulled a copy of the *Politiken* out of his pocket and said: "Have you seen this?"

Not knowing Danish I could not read something on the front page to which he pointed except my own name and that of Norman Hansen, the giant Dane, who was a poet and explorer.

"What's it all about?" I asked.

"Norman Hansen challenges you to a duel. He has constituted himself the champion of Dr. Cook."

I may have blenched. I knew that if I fought a duel with Norman Hansen I should die. He was a very tall man.

"He will send you his seconds," said the young Dane.

The seconds did not arrive that day, or the next, or the one after, and I was much relieved by this respite from death. But I was too busy to worry about it much.

A frightful thing happened to me. Mrs. Rasmussen, that lovely lady, had been very friendly. We had taken tea together several times and then dinner, mostly with Peter Freuken. Over one of the dinner tables she had produced a letter just received from her husband who had helped Cook on his journey.

"I will translate a bit of it," she told me. "It's about Dr. Cook."

It was a bit in which Rasmussen, this famous Arctic explorer denounced Cook as a charlatan and a rogue who certainly had never been anywhere near the North Pole.

"May I publish that?" I asked. "It's vastly important to me."

She hesitated but agreed. Freuken wrote down the English translation of that passage in the letter. When published in the *Daily Chronicle* and wired back to Denmark it created a sensation. If Rasmussen said that Cook was a liar . . .

But a few days later a letter was published in the Danish papers from Mrs. Rasmussen. She denied that she had shown me one of her husband's letters, or that any such words appeared in one. It was to me a a knock-down blow.

I tried to find her but she had disappeared from Copenhagen. What was I going to do about it? My own truthfulness and honour were utterly at stake. I published a letter in the Danish Press asking for a committee to be appointed with Mrs. Rasmussen's consent to read the last letter received from her husband. If no such words were found in the letter, I would give a certain sum of money to any Danish charity agreed upon by the Committee.

Mrs. Rasmussen never answered that letter. I never saw her again. I learned afterwards that she had weakened under great political and social pressure from high quarters. I have long forgiven her.

Dr. Cook departed in due course from Cophengen with a wreath of flowers round his bowler hat. Great crowds had assembled to see his going. I was on the quayside and after the ship had warped away the

D

crowd split and made way for a very tall man. It was Norman Hansen who had challenged me to a duel.

"Very unpleasant," I thought, with an uneasy feeling at the pit of the stomach.

But the Danish giant held out a big hand and laughed.

"We will fight with the pen and not with the sword," he told me.

It was good news for me.

Not long afterwards he wrote to me saying that he had lost all faith in Cook, and afterwards I had friendly little letters from him. W. T. Stead was another man who wrote to me when Cook was finally disbelieved and disproved by the University of Copenhagen which had honoured him, and by our own Royal Society.

"You were right and I was wrong," wrote Stead, and he was generous in his praise of a young journalist to whom afterwards he was always very kind. Always he insisted on kissing my wife—he kissed every pretty woman—and he went down on his knees to her and called her 'Mother Hubbard', which was the nickname of my heroine in *The Street of Adventure*.

PART III

WAR IN THE BALKANS

1

SERVIA STANDS TO ARMS

IN 1912 I had my first glimpse of war and the first stench of it. Early in September of that year Europe became alarmed by events in the Balkans. There were reports of general mobilisation in Bulgaria, Servia, Montenegro, and Greece, for a combined challenge against the Turks. The liberation of Macedonia from Turkish rule was the watchword for this alliance, but the Balkan States had other interests. Servia had long set her heart upon "an open window" on the shores of the Adriatic. Montenegro coveted the Sanjak of Novi Bazar, Bulgaria was anxious to bring within her frontiers the rich country of Thrace and to thrust the Turk back into Asia Minor. Greece was out for Crete. All these allies in the Balkan federation had old scores which they were eager to wipe out in Turkish blood.

The Great Powers became active, and were intriguing against each other behind the scenes. Russian sympathy was with Servia. Germany had her agents in Bulgaria. As we know now, this Balkan war was a dress rehearsal for the World War of 1914.

I went out to Servia for the *Daily Graphic* as a war artist, as well as special correspondent. My art was elementary, but I provided rough sketches from which Frank Dadd and other black-and-white men worked up elaborate pictures. Before I started on this adventure the editor of the *Graphic*—my very good friend John Bulloch, Scot of the Scots, with a grim humour with which he tried to shock my sensitive soul (as he was pleased to call it) said: "Laddie, this may be useful to you." He opened a drawer in his desk and pulled out a heavy Browning. I declined the offer, having an idea that I might be the first victim of that weapon, and the conviction, which I still hold, that an unarmed man is least likely to get into trouble.

I crossed Europe to Belgrade and my first view of that city was from the broad waters of the Danube in a ferry boat from the Hungarian bank. Its white walls and red roofs were bathed in sunshine. At the sight of it three young men on the ferry boat raised their hats and cheered. They were Servians who had come from Austria as volunteers. One of them looked like a young actor, with a pale face and long black hair. He pointed to a soldier pacing the fortifications with the sun glinting on his bayonet.

"In a little while," he said, "we shall all be chasing the Turks. We'll show them how the Servians can shoot!"

A girl by his side put her hand on his shoulder with a caressing touch and laughed gaily, as though he had spoken a good jest. A man in a bowler hat and black overcoat, like a city clerk, spoke to me in German.

"I am an agent for aeroplanes," he told me. "I am bringing over three biplanes. It's a wonder the Austrians let them through."

It was the first war in which man's victory of the air was used for the destruction of his fellow men, but not on the scale of fury by aerial armadas which afterwards flung death from the skies upon great cities and their civilian populations.

On the quayside when I landed my passports were scrupulously examined by a very fat officer in a gorgeous uniform, and then my luggage was pounced on by a band of hairy brigands who, without paying the slightest attention to me, proceeded to fight amongst themselves for my bags. They shouted and cursed each other and exchanged lusty blows, and it was full twenty minutes before the victors piled my luggage on to a miserable-looking cab drawn by two lean horses and allowed me to depart after heavy payment. I now found that I was in extreme peril, for my coachman whipped up his steeds and started off on a wild career over the roads of Belgrade—that is to say over rock-strewn quagmires, gaping pits, and ruts like deep ditches. The carriage lurched from one side to the other with its wheels deep in the ruts or perched high upon piles of loose stones, and at times it seemed as though only a miracle could save me from instant death. Never had I seen anything like the streets of Belgrade before the war, when an elaborate plan for repairing them had been checked in the midst of chaos by the calling up of all able-bodied workmen to the colours.

I found the city still waiting for the declaration of war, which seemed so long delayed after the preliminary challenge that people were becoming sceptical of its beginning. There were crowds of men in the streets who slouched about in an aimless way with bundles on their backs. They belonged to the last reserves and were waiting for the word to join their battalions. Many of them had come from remote Servian villages, and their costumes were of startling variety and colour. Some wore sheepskin coats with the shaggy wool inside, and the skin decorated with crude paintings or garish embroidery. Nearly all of them wore loose gaiters worked with red stitches, or woollen buskins of elaborate patterns.

Through the streets of Belgrade came a clattering cavalcade. They were mounted peasants from the country districts, and as wild a set of men as one might find in Europe. Their horses were lean and shaggy, with wooden saddles made of sticks tied together, and with reins and stirrups of a coarse rope. The men had long black hair beneath sheep-skin caps, and short brown jackets with loose shirts tied about with coloured sashes.

Women were doing men's work in the fields and market places. Immense crowds of them came from the churches where they had been praying for their sons and husbands. They seemed to carry their household goods about with them, having come into Belgrade from the country. They were laden with great bundles which were hung on to heavy notched sticks, from which also were suspended earthenware bottles and boots, and domestic utensils. These women were ablaze with gaudy colour. They wore heavy woollen kirtles, generally of red and blue stripes, and woollen or leather aprons embroidered with floral patterns.

I had not been in Belgrade long before I was arrested as a spy. In my innocence of war I did not realise that a man who makes sketches is under instant suspicion. I was scribbling a sketch of reservists round the railway station when a heavy hand was put on my shoulder and I was swung round by a Servian soldier. He seized my sketch book, examined my bit of drawing upside down, and marched me off with two English companions through the town, attracting the hostile attentions of the crowd who booed and scowled. After a long walk over the abominable roads we were taken to police headquarters and locked up in a room. We were hungry and a trifle anxious. This was a bad beginning. Presently we were taken before a young officer with a solemn face and suspicious eyes. He examined my sketch and seemed to take a grave view of it, as well he might if judged as a work of art.

He could not speak one word of English, French or German, but, undaunted by this, interrogated me at length in his own tongue and seemed to think that my silence was due to guilt.

My friends and I pulled out our passports and other documents and exhausted ourselves in the endeavour to prove our identity as English correspondents. The officer examined the passports, but it was obvious that they only served to increase his horrible suspicion. He motioned us to our seats, spoke some rapid sentences to the guard, and then, ignoring us completely, smoked a cigarette and stared up at the window. My friends and I shifted in our seats, exchanged uneasy glances, whispered, coughed, smiled while the young officer smoked on with sublime impassivity. I began to be seriously alarmed, not for my safety, but for my dinner. I was getting very hungry.

Finally our suspense was ended by the appearance of a dirty, blear-eyed old man who announced himself as police interpreter. Through him we were interrogated by the officer. The first question was: "Are you Austrian?" which we answered with a chorus of "No!" The second question was: "Are you Italian?" Again we protested our entire innocence of any blood but pure English. After a great deal of questioning as to our business in Belgrade, and especially as to the meaning and purpose of my unfortunate sketch, the officer had a long and whispered conversation with the blear-eyed old man and finally told us that we were free to leave Belgrade at the earliest possible moment. It was a doubtful kind of compliment, but we accepted it gladly and after shaking hands with the young officer breathed again the air of liberty.

It was characteristic of the tension in Belgrade, when every foreigner was suspected of being an Austrian until the contrary was proved.

I sat with Servian officers in their cafés and found them gay fellows, but it seemed to me that when they laughed and raised their glasses and said: "To our first dinner in Constantinople!" their gaiety was a little forced and covered a secret anxiety. They were not quite sure then of the weakness or strength of the Turk. They were wondering what Austria would do in the event of Servian victories or defeats. They were uneasy also with a tense expectancy, and the delay in declaring war was setting their nerves on edge.

When darkness fell Belgrade was very quiet. Only solitary figures hurried through the ill-lighted streets, and after ten o'clock no one seemed alive except a few soldiers. Outside the King's palace—a new building which had taken the place of an old one where Alexander and his Queen Draga had been murdered—sentries paced up and down with fixed bayonets, and their footsteps echoed in the solitude. Away on the hill, above the Danube, the great building of the Headquarters staff had lighted windows across which shadows passed. From the ramparts came now and then the shrill note of a bugle.

A Servian friend pacing by my side listened to the bugle note, and grasping my arm said: "To-morrow I think the war will begin."

"Are you anxious?" I asked.

"War is a dangerous game," he answered. "Who can tell which way it will go?"

At that moment there was no man in Europe who could tell. But in a few weeks the revelation came, for the Turks were already in retreat before the Greeks and Bulgarians.

2

SCENES IN SOFIA

A crowd of correspondents had come to Belgrade from different countries—far too many of them. Among the British contingent was

H. W. Nevinson, even then a veteran war correspondent. He was a hater of war, though a lover of liberty, passionate in his championship of the little nations and the underdogs everywhere. A handsome man with a little beard and moustache streaked with silver, and a ruddy complexion and blue eyes, he was the most distinguished of them all. Charlie Hands of the *Daily Mail* had come, and McHugh of the *Telegraph*, and little reddish-haired S. J. Pryor formerly editor of the *Tribune*, whom I had portrayed in my novel *The Street of Adventure*. Another man of the old brigade of war correspondents, who had been through the South African war and other campaigns, was Bennett Burleigh—a bluff, boisterous man, who greeted Nevinson with a heartiness received rather coldly. The fact was that the old time war correspondents had conducted their campaigns with ruthless rivalry to get a "beat" on the news at all costs. Burleigh had once thrown Nevinson's baggage out of a train to prevent his getting ahead. Nevinson had not forgotten that episode.

There were younger men who came out to the Balkan war in a new profession, the first of their kind. They were not war correspondents but war photographers. I linked up with two of them. One was Horace Grant, whom I came to know as a good comrade on whose loyalty and courage one could count always. The other was a young Italian named Console, working for English newspapers. He was excitable and amusing, and he had a habit of pouring olive oil—of which he seemed to have an inexhaustible reserve—on any food which came his way.

I found myself accredited to the Bulgarian Second Army, and said farewell to some of my friends in Belgrade when I set forth for Sofia. They wished me good luck, and envied me, for stories had reached them of the generous things in store for war correspondents in Bulgaria. It seemed that we were to be provided with horses and servants, that we were to be fed by the army, and that we were to have full facilities to get to the front. Little did they know the painful truth awaiting me!

The journey to Sofia was abominable. Before the train started there was a wild stampede on the platform by a battalion of peasant reservists, and all sorts and conditions of people who had been waiting for the last chance of getting through to Nish and on to Bulgaria. I narrowly escaped death from naked bayonets which jabbed about in the midst of a maelstrom of surging humanity storming the doorways and clambering upon the roof of the train. When at last I got on board I found myself wedged in the corridor between piles of baggage, soldiers, and peasants. I had only a piece of cheese and a little drop of brandy, and fellow passengers prophesied that it would be two days before we reached Sofia, with luck. The prophecy was fulfilled. We stopped at every wayside station and at night we were turned out on to the platform of

Sarabrot, hungry, chilled to the bone by a biting wind and a hard frost.
There was no shelter and I lay down amidst a mass of Servian soldiers
whose peaked caps jabbed me as they turned their heads restlessly in
their sleep. But amidst all the soldiers and peasants one man excited
my admiration as he stood immaculate in a tall hat and frock coat, as
though he had just stepped out of the rue de Rivoli. He was a French
journalist on his way to the front.

Outside the station of Sarabrot there was, all night long, the tramp of
soldiers as battalion after battalion of Servian troops marched up to
entrain for the front.

Before dawn a troop train came in to Sarabrot and the soldiers were
packed into open trucks so tightly that they could not move. Their
bayonets made a quickset hedge above each truck. They were very
silent. There was no laughing or singing. I realised the grim reality of
all this business in the darkness. There was something rather horrible
in the sight of all those peasants being carried away like cattle to the
fighting lines. They were like dumb beasts going to the slaughter house.

It was a night of queer conversation. One man sloped up to me in
the dim light and said: "I guess you're an Englishman." I returned the
compliment and said: "You're an American." But I was wrong. He
was a Bulgarian born and bred, but had been in the United States, and
now had come back, in a thin flannel suit and a straw hat, from a main
street in the Middle West.

"I heard the call," he said, "and was ready to take my place in the
firing line. I shall be glad to give hell to the Turks."

The war spirit reigned in Sofia, the capital of Bulgaria, which since the
eighties had grown from a Turkish village into a great city with many
good buildings. Outside the old white Mosque with its tall and slender
minaret, the one thing of beauty inherited from the Turks, there passed
all day small companies of soldiers heavily laden in their field kit, and
bands of Macedonian exiles who had volunteered for the war. Through
the street was the rumble of bullock wagons and forage carts, dragged
by buffaloes who stared at this activity with sullen eyes.

As in Belgrade there were more women than men in the town, and
they stood in the market place with children clinging to their skirts,
watching the guns go by. These brown-skinned, black-haired, liquid-
eyed women in their embroidered skirts, striped kirtles, white petticoats,
and red stockings, were amazingly picturesque.

With grave dignity priests of the Orthodox Church, wearing high
black caps and long black gowns, passed among the crowd of soldiers
and peasants, and now and then a young man ran across the street to
kiss the hand of one of these bearded priests and bend a knee before his
blessing.

I watched the army of Macedonian recruits pass through Sofia, and followed them on to the Plain of Slivnica, the old battleground between the Servians and Bulgarians. They marched with a long and swinging stride—elderly men who remembered many a massacre of their brethren by the Turks and many orgies of wild and terrible revenge, and young lads who had inherited the tradition of hatred against the Moslems, who had made Macedonia a place of terror. Among them were young girls from eighteen to twenty, dressed in the rough sheepskin jackets and white woollen trousers worn by the men, and taking their places in the ranks. The drummers beat their pigskins with wild passion which stirred the Macedonian blood and there was the squeak of primitive bagpipes.

3

Te Deum

War was not yet declared. As it grew inevitably nearer all able-bodied men of Bulgarian nationality were called to the colours and passed away to the wild country on the Turkish frontier. It was the first time that I saw the meaning and the drama of general mobilisation—the calling up of civilians for military service. Little then did I think that it would happen in England, twice in my own lifetime. I sat with men in the cafés who a few weeks before had been teaching art, history, or economics to University students, and with men who had been busy in all the enterprises of a modern city. They found their uniforms strange and uncomfortable. They seemed to be living in a fantastic dream in which all that matters in daily life became shadowy and insignificant. They were going to fight, to lie out on wild hills, to suffer hunger and frost under the great sky in the darkness of mountain passes, to kill or be killed.

In a little while all these educated men, most of them spoke several languages, left Sofia with the battalions of armed peasants and the Macedorians in their sheepskins. I saw the last troops of mounted infantry ride past my windows. They had twined scarlet flowers about their caps and upon their rifles and in the bridles of their horses.

One evening in Sofia I saw the Turkish ambassador drive to the station where a train was waiting for him. He had handed in his papers. King Ferdinand had signed the declaration of war. I was one of the few who knew this but it was held back from the Bulgarian people for twenty-four hours. Then in the early morning of October 18th I heard the sound of shouts in the streets. The people knew at last. Cheer after cheer rose from them with the wild exaltation of war fever, and this noise mingled with the screaming of the jackdaws which seldom ceased in the gardens of the Royal Palace.

At ten o'clock the bells of Sofia began to ring. They were the big deep bells of the old Cathedral in which a Te Deum was to be sung, and the silvery chimes of many churches rang together. They all blended into a vague and beautiful harmony of clashing notes like Debussy's *"Cloches à travers les feuilles"*.

It was market day, and thousands of peasant women had come in from the country districts. Their white headdresses, and short embroidered kirtles, and lace petticoats made a good picture as they all went their way to the Cathedral. The Cathedral square itself was filled with Macedonian peasants still awaiting their rifles before going to the front, and in their sheepskins and white woollen breeches they stood in long ranks, bareheaded and reverent. Among them were remarkable faces of young men with flaxen hair parted in the middle and waving out each side like pictures of John the Baptist by the primitives.

In the Cathedral the scene was solemn and beautiful. Queen Eleanor came—the King had left for his headquarters in Stara Zagora—which my friend Ludovic Nodeau insisted on calling Cascara Sagrada—and knelt down before the sanctuary steps. The music of the choir throbbed under the roof. A young priest preached from the pulpit outside the sanctuary and his words were translated to me.

"We have done all that we could to obtain justice for our Christian brothers and yet to obtain peace. Peaceful methods have failed and now we must obtain justice and peace by the sword. God calls us to help our brethren and He will aid us now that we answer the call. It is the Cross against the Crescent."

Once again the Christian Church blessed her soldiers and inflamed the ardour of men who needed no spur when the smell of blood was in their nostrils. It was proclaimed a just war. But in that Cathedral of Sofia two years later the same prayers were said to the same God invoking his aid, when King Ferdinand—old Fox Ferdinand as he was called—flung his nation into another war by the side of Germany with Turkey as his ally. It is rash to call upon God to smite the enemy of to-day who is the friend of to-morrow.

In Sofia I read the regulations for war correspondents and their severity was appalling. We were forbidden to describe the disposition of troops, to give the names of generals, the names and numbers of the wounded, the success or failure of Bulgarian forces, the state of the soldiers' health, the conditions of the climate.

I put a polite question to the chief censor.

"Will you tell me sir if there is anything about which we shall be allowed to write?"

He thought deeply for a moment and then answered with great gravity: "There is much interest in Bulgarian literature."

"Perhaps I may also be permitted to describe the song of the birds?" I enquired.

"By all means!" said the censor very cordially.

It was fantastic. In the Hotel Bulgarie would-be war correspondents were playing billiards and telling stories of ancient things. At last however the call came. Most of us were given permits to join the Second Army. Each of us donned a brassard bearing the letter B.K. which being interpreted meant war correspondent, and a train was ready to take us to the army headquarters at Stara Zagora. We looked forward to those adventures with the troops which now seemed assured to us, even if we could not write about them. I did not know then that intensive shell fire takes all the romance out of such adventures.

4

PEASANTS AND PRISONERS

The journey to Stara Zagora lay along the chain of the Rhodope mountains and the distant range of the Balkan mountains. On the slopes the leaves of stunted oak trees glistened with the gold of autumn tints, and here and there on the high peaks was the pure beauty of new-fallen snow. At night a crescent moon rose and a bright star hung beyond it—the symbol of the Turkish flag. In an article I wrote describing this I said the star was between the horns of the crescent moon, and for years afterwards I had postcards protesting that this phenomenon was contrary to nature. I had indulged in a little poetic licence.

Stara Zagora, for a time the general headquarters of the Bulgarian army, was of a typical Turkish character. Tall and slender minarets rose, as white as columns of snow, above the little old houses of a town, where the memory of a massacre in the Russo-Turkish war still haunted the imagination of its inhabitants. In the wild retreat from the Russian guns the Turks swept the town of human life leaving the corpses of women and children lying in the snow and choking the wells with dead bodies.

Now many Turks in Stara Zagora were living on friendly terms with their Bulgarian neighbours. Indeed, apart from the soldiers, most of the people here were Moslems, and it is to the credit of the Bulgars in this time of war that these Turks were not molested. I watched them curiously, for it seemed a strange thing to see these men in the red fez of the Mohammedan enemy sitting cross-legged in the streets, cooking hot cakes over open ovens, and chaffering their wares as though there were no conflict between the Cross and the Crescent.

Through the market place moved silent figures, in the white yashmak with which the Turkish women veiled their heads, and long robes draped about their bodies, revealing, as they walked, baggy trousers tight at the ankles. It was as picturesque as old Baghdad in the time of Haroun al Raschid, and I found it difficult to believe that I was still in Europe.

Here in Stara Zagora I saw the business of war behind the lines. Battalion after battalion of peasant soldiers tramped over the uneven roads on their way to the trenches and the fighting line. As I watched the army of reservists in a never ending tide the faces of thousands of men seemed to blend into one face, the typical face of the Bulgarian soldier, square cut, with a short beard, sullen eyed and the look of one of his own oxen, beastlike and menacing.

With them went great guns drawn by long teams of buffaloes, and flocks of sheep to feed the army, the tremendous convoys of supplies.

Other processions passed through the town day by day and told the other side of the story. They were the first prisoners captured by the Bulgarians. These Turkish soldiers came in with a hang-dog look, spent with fatigue, their faces drawn and pinched by hunger and despair. One of the officers told me stories of the sheer starvation of the Turkish army—a pound and a half of bread between ten men each day, and afterwards no bread at all but only uncooked maize and roots in the fields.

The first batch of prisoners who were brought in had been taken in a skirmish in which most of their comrades were slain.

"The Bulgarians cut us up into small pieces," said the officer, as he calmly lighted a cigarette.

Now and again a crowd gathered to see the King. He came driving down in his automobile with his two sons, Prince Boris and Prince Cyril, from a brewery on the hillside where he had taken up his residence. I saw him several times, and once had a talk with him, a tall handsome man with a soft grey beard and a long hooked nose, and eyes that smiled with a strange inscrutable smile. The people did not cheer him. They stood very quiet, as though overawed by the sovereign presence. It was the oriental attitude in the presence of kingship, and Ferdinand treated them as an oriental Monarch would, ignoring them utterly after the first grave salute. He passed amongst them as a Sultan.

The military attachés of many nations were with us in general head-quarters, in a strange variety of uniforms, and holding converse with each other in a strange variety of tongues. They dined in a villainous little shanty called the *Zlaten Lev* or Golden Lion, where I had a small cell called a bedroom, infested with mice which ran along the bedrail and played merry games with me at night as I lay in a coffin-like box called a bed. The catering in the *Zlaten Lev* was supplied by a German Jew, who charged enormous sums for the vilest food. The attachés had the first call, and correspondents like myself had to be content with licking our lips, and scenting the meats from afar, until the attachés had satisfied their appetites, when we partook of the crumbs that fell from the rich men's table.

While we were waiting to go further forward I wandered one day outside the town and went into a Gypsy encampment which was one of the most extraordinary places I have ever seen. I was glad to escape with my money and my life. There were streets of mud huts, not bigger than pigsties, and so low that to get inside the Romany tribe had to crawl through the doorways like beasts. The place was filthy beyond description, and it was pervaded by pestilential smells. Hundreds of children, many of them stark naked, played about the open patches, fighting and screaming like a forest full of monkeys. Squatting in the shadows of the wall, or drawing water from the wells, or pacing slowly through the Lilliputian streets, was the adult population of this Romany camp. There were many beautiful women and girls among them, dressed in loose trousers tight at the ankle, and in cotton jackets tied with gaudy sashes. One of them came running up to me, showing her white teeth and flashing her black eyes, and then seizing me by the wrist made signs that she wanted to tell my fortune. In less than a minute I was surrounded by half the population all clamouring for *baksheesh*, all plucking at my clothes, while among them stood tall Gypsy fellows armed with long sticks. I had anxious thoughts about a belt full of gold pieces round my waist. An old man, who seemed to be chief of the tribe, brought up a young girl completely naked and as beautiful as a Greek bronze, and I understood that he was willing to sell her to me for a few coins. I wondered what would have happened if I took this wild little animal back to Holland Street, Kensington, but I resisted the temptation. By good luck a police officer came riding through the village, and suddenly at the sight of him there was a shrill whistle and a general scamper like rabbits frightened to their holes. I followed the mounted policeman until I was clear of the village, and though he could speak nothing but Bulgarian I understood his words to mean that the Gypsy camp was not a nice place for a Christian gentleman.

When I went back to Stara Zagora I received the welcome news that we were to move on, and that this time we should see something of the fighting in Turkish territory and the siege of Adrianople.

5

THE CROSS AND THE CRESCENT

Europe was sceptical of the first victories against the Turk. Military writers at home described them as frontier skirmishes and believed that the Turks would rout the allied armies. But very quickly in the first weeks of war the Turkish armies on all fronts were in retreat, demoralised, ill equipped, badly fed, and outgeneralled. The Montenegrins had made the first dash and captured great numbers of prisoners. They were helped by the Christian mountaineers of Albania, who for years had been carrying on a sporadic warfare with Moslem tribes, with intermittent success, so that Moslem and Christian villages were delivered to the flames as each side gained the upper hand.

The Greeks were attacking Turkish ports, occupying Turkish islands in the Aegean Sea and advancing northwards to join hands with the Servians at Monastir and Salonica.

But it was upon the Servians and Bulgarians that the fate of the Balkan confederation depended, and the Servians showed that they were carrying out their part of the contract with almost incredible success. The first great battle was at a place called Kumanovo. Here the Turks had twenty-five thousand men, a large number of guns of the most modern type, enormous stores, and a most formidable defensive position. But under General Patnik the Servian army flung themselves against the enemy's lines with reckless courage for two days and nights. They charged with the bayonet to the very muzzle of the Turkish guns. Then the Turks broke and ran. In a little while the remnants of their army became a frightful rout. They flung away their rifles and ammunition, the guns were abandoned, there was no attempt to save the stores and, utterly demoralised, they stampeded along the road to Uskub. Here a new panic seized upon them, Uskub was abandoned, and the Servians entered it in triumph upon a road strewn with dead bodies and all the litter of a great rout. The city was deserted by its garrison who had left behind them a mass of artillery, ammunition, and weapons.

It was from the time of that defeat that the Turks became paralysed by the fear of Servian and Bulgarian bayonets. The very name of "*la nosche*" or the knife, as they called that weapon, was like a dreadful spell, which scattered a Turkish force even before a man had died. In Uskub the cry of "The Servians are coming with the knife!" made it impossible for the officers to rally their troops or check the retreat, and later in the war I heard a hundred times from Bulgarian officers, that when a bayonet charge was ordered the Turkish lines would begin to waver and break.

So it happened in the Bulgarian victory of Kirk Kilissa after the storming of the Turkish outposts along a chain of hills stretching northwards of the city. The Bulgarian regiments advanced singing the Slivnica March, while the heavy guns behind bombarded the Turkish batteries and silenced them.

"We came up in waves," I was told by a Bulgarian officer, "and my own men were like tigers. They were utterly indifferent to the storm of bullets, and advanced over hundreds of their dead comrades as though their corpses were but paving stones to victory. I was struck down on the last rush and knew no more until the business was over and the Bulgarian flag flew over Kirk Kilissa."

The next great victory of the Bulgarians was at Lüle Burgas where there was ferocious fighting on both sides and enormous casualties. The Turkish retreat from Lüle Burgas was an accumulation of horror. It began in something like order. It degenerated into a fierce wild and chaotic flight. Its way was strewn with dead bodies. The Turks escaped from one foe but found another and even more terrible one in ambush. Not even the shells of the Bulgarians were so deadly as the cholera which attacked the retreating Turks.

The Bulgarian Second Army were now investing the great city of Adrianople after an advance towards Mustafa Pasha on the Maritza river from which the Turkish outposts fell back. The town was deserted by most of its inhabitants, all but the Christian population fleeing in terror to the shelter of Adrianople. Before retiring the Turks made an ineffectual attempt to blow up the great bridge over the Maritza which leads into the town, but did their work so badly that very little damage was done. It was one of their fatal acts of incompetency. The one bridge was worth a victory to the Bulgarians, for it became the passage way of thousands of troops, of vast convoys of bullock wagons, and of all their great siege guns, as I saw day after day. The Bulgarian flag was hoisted over the headquarters of General Ivanoff commanding the Bulgarian Second Army in Mustafa Pasha, and the Crescent was hauled down and torn in half. By a curious trick of fate the remnant of it is in my study now as I write these words.

6

FOX FERDINAND

Horace Grant, Console, and I, were billeted in a Turkish farmhouse, outside the town of Mustafa Pasha. It was kept by a peasant and his family who regarded us as strange beings with inexplicable habits. While I was writing or drawing my sketches for the *Graphic* the man would stand before me with grave puzzled eyes. The whole family would assemble to see us washing in the morning, stripped to the waist. At night we slept on divans with caps pulled down about our ears and rugs heaped upon us to keep out the cutting draughts and the intense coldness of the nights. The farmhouse shook to the noise of gunfire, the great Bulgarian siege guns, and the thunder of Turkish batteries on the outer lines defending Adrianople. The Maritza river overflowed its banks, and the roads and fields round Mustafa Pasha were quagmires through which we trudged along piles of stones above deep mud.

Turkish villages were burning and smouldering along the roads to Adrianople. We went into them, and I saw for the first time, but not for the last, the devastation and filth of war and smelt the stench of death. As the days and nights passed I seemed to be living in a nightmare full of black and white beasts—buffaloes and oxen—with long horns prodding at me and armed men surging like a living tide, and gun-carriages, and bullock wagons, and bayonets glistening like silver, and bearded faces, and black eyes staring at me, as a great army passed and passed. There were shouts and curses and slashing of whips, as heavy carts lurched over boulders and into deep ruts.

The noise of all this struggling mass of men and beasts made me dazed, almost drunk. On the way back to my farmhouse there were bullocks in all the lanes, up to their bellies in mud and water, and in the darkness, illumined only by the flash of gunfire. Threading my way through a tangle of traffic I felt warm breath upon my face from the nostrils of the oxen, whose fat curly horns I clutched to prevent myself being trampled to death.

The wounded were already coming back. Day after day they came back in a long crawling tide of Red Cross wagons and ox-carts, lying on straw, groaning pitifully as the wheels lurched into the ruts, many of them dying before journey's end.

At one place whose name I have forgotten, I saw the King decorating a number of wounded officers. Some of them seemed on the point of death. Others were horribly crippled. Their bandages were soaked in blood. One man had lost both his legs. Others were blinded. The King pinned medals on their breasts. He did not speak a word to them. They stared at him with grave eyes, if they had eyes, and no light came into them. It was a *macabre* scene.

One day King Ferdinand stopped to talk to me on the bridge over the Maritza. I was dressed in Bulgarian clothes, because of the climate, with a sheepskin jacket and high fur cap, but I had no Bulgarian look. The King spoke perfect English and was very civil. I felt at ease with him, though a German correspondent was almost prostrating himself. I have forgotten what he talked about except that he said the war was going well, and that the Turk was up to his old game of murder and massacre in towns from which he retreated.

An English photographer appeared on the scene and held up his camera.

The King started back and raised his stick.

"Tell that fellow to go away!" he said angrily. "If he doesn't, I'll strike him down!"

"He's quite harmless," I said. "It's his profession."

"Photography is not a profession," said King Ferdinand. "It's a disease."

I heard afterwards that Fox Ferdinand was afraid of assassination under the pretence of snap-shooting him.

I seemed to get on very well with this long-nosed Bourbon. He made a few jokes at which I laughed politely. He hoped we were getting on well, and I told him we were anxious to see more of the war. I had an idea that I had done a good turn to all of us, but a few days later I happened to be in a place where the King appeared again. It was a place where, for some reason unknown to me, he did not wish a foreign correspondent to be. He gave orders for my arrest. It was the second time I had been arrested in the Balkans, but I was let off again.

I bought something like a horse. It had not been broken in, and had thrown three Frenchmen who recommended it to me as a nice quiet beast, concealing their own discomfiture. When it was led out of the stable it threw back its ears, showed the whites of its eyes, and lashed out with its hoofs. Being no horseman, I regarded it with apprehension but as the three Frenchmen were onlookers I had to do something about it. I mounted successfully, and, by some miracle, kept my seat while it reared and flung itself about. Then it darted like an arrow through the stable yard and galloped madly down the road leading to Adrianople. One rein broke and I was powerless to control my steed. Fortunately it tired itself out, slowed down, and gave me the chance of dismounting. I led it back to Mustafa Pasha.

Some time later I hired a *droshky* with a driver, and three horses, so lean that I could hang my hat on their ribs. The *droshky* had a chime of bells which were very musical. In this equipage I took two or three companions and we drove in stately style towards the hills looking over Adrianople, saluted on the way by Bulgarian soldiers who thought, maybe, that some prince was on his way to win the war. Some time later my driver, my *droshky* with its three lean horses, and my animal which looked like a horse, were all stolen by the Bulgarian army.

From the hills looking to Adrianople we saw that city with the

minarets of its mosques pencilled against the clear blue sky, as beautiful
as a dream city. There were the four tall towers of the great mosque of
Sultan Selim. But there was no beauty in the life of Adrianople during
that siege. From people who escaped through the lines we heard
stories of what was happening, and they were grim.

The Turkish garrison numbered about 50,000 men, mostly picked
troops. The normal population of the city had been increased enormously by masses of refugees from surrounding villages, unwashed,
verminous, diseased, and starving. Rations were running out when they
were ringed round by the Bulgarians. The Bulgarian siege guns,
smashing into the outer ring of fortifications but not destroying the city
itself, made the earth quake. At night all hell reigned when the Turks
made sorties against the Bulgarian lines under cover of great gunfire. The cowering peasants with their women knew nothing of what the
military situation might be, and expected that any night the Bulgarians
might smash through, killing them all in an orgy of blood and fury.
They were swept by an epidemic of typhus and there was the stench of
death within the walls. So fugitives told us.

There was one night I remember when the sky above Adrianople was
as though infernal powers were at war. Great flashes rent the heavens,
the earth vomited up red flame and smoke. Thousands of shells were
bursting, and the eternal hills trembled with the fury of this artillery.
It was on a night when the Turks made their most desperate effort to
break out and smash the ring of their enemies, in vain, though there
were frightful casualties on both sides, as I saw when streams of
wounded were carried back.

Adrianople never fell, and held out until the armistice between the
Turks and their conquerors.

There were strange scenes in Mustafa Kemal. One night a Servian
division of cavalry passed through with every man asleep on his horse,
all led forward by an old man with a lantern, and to this day I remember the strange, uncanny, vision of those sleeping men with
drooping heads over their horses' necks.

I remember now also, as though it were yesterday, some words
spoken by a friend of mine as we were staring from a line of hills at the
besieged city. He was an Austrian named von Zifferer, of the *Neue
Freie Presse*, and one of the most charming men I have ever met,
chivalrous, kind, unselfish.

"Gibbs," he said, suddenly, "you and I, one day, will be war correspondents on different sides of the line. This is only the prelude of
another war which will drag in all Europe."

His prophecy came true in less than two years.

7

PUSHED OUT

In that Balkan war the correspondents were dealt with as harshly as though they were spies. Censorship was iron in its severity. We were treated with ignominy, and at last the Bulgarian High Command decided to expel the lot of us, of all nationalities, thirty-three in number. When this message reached me I said that nothing would budge me except armed force. It was a rash saying. One night when Horace Grant, Console and myself were about to have a miserable meal in our farmhouse there was a heavy clump at the door by the butt end of a rifle. Console, who had been dozing on one of the divans, sat up and grabbed at a heavy Browning as the door was burst open and a police officer entered with two soldiers carrying rifles with fixed bayonets. The police officer spoke rapidly in Bulgarian. Then seeing that we did not understand a word produced from his cap a document in French. It was very brief and to the point, and ordered us to pack our baggage and accompany the soldiers in a military wagon to the railway station, where a train would be waiting to take us back to Stara Zagora.

The game was up. This was the last insult, and behind it were two hairy men with long bayonets. We packed up our things, abandoned our poor meal, and took our places in an open wagon covered only by a canvas hood. The wagon lurched over the deep ruts, and we became mixed up in a convoy of oxen dragging guns and supplies. As we drove through the darkness lanterns gleamed on naked bayonets, on white hoods and cloaks, on the faces of bearded men. Eyeballs flashed up at us; thousands of eyes stared through the blackness into the depths of our cart.

They were the eyes of a column of Servian soldiers marching on their way to the front.

One of their officers called "Halt!", and we were surrounded by armed men. He spoke to me in German and was surprised when I told him that we were English correspondents sent away from Mustafa Pasha.

"Come with us!" he called out. "We'll show you some good fighting. You will have plenty to write about."

I sometimes regret that I did not accept his offer but it would have led to grave trouble with the Bulgarians.

We went on through the rain and the mud, and at last reached the station where we found that the train for Stara Zagora, which ought to have left ten hours before, had been shunted into a side line. Inside it, to our amazement, were our thirty comrades of the British and foreign Press. They had been expelled like ourselves and were furious at this ignominious treatment.

We spent thirty-six more hours in that train without food or drink. Among our companions was that extraordinary fellow Marinetti, the founder of the Futurists, and the father, or at least the forerunner, of Italian Fascism. He had led a campaign advocating violence of action in Italy, intellectually, artistically, and politically. He had climbed to the top of the Campanile in Venice and dropped down leaflets cursing the Venetians for allowing their city to become a show place of mouldering antiquity. He tried to inspire Italian youth with the spirit of modernity, dynamic vigour, and passionate hostility to a slumbrous and ineffective past. He painted grotesque pictures, using bits of tin and matchsticks and any old thing. He wrote poetry in futuristic style, making up onomatopoeic words to represent the sounds of guns, engines, drums, and the noises of men and beasts. On this journey to Stara Zagora he recited with tremendous spirit a long poem entitled "L'automobile", and made such a row about it that at a wayside station soldiers advanced upon our carriage believing that a massacre was taking place therein. Marinetti was a brilliant talker and a good companion, in spite of his crazy ideas.

Owing to wires pulled at the Foreign Office in London by my friend Pryor—my little red-headed editor of the *Tribune*—who had gone home some weeks previously, I and my two companions Grant and Console were allowed to return with honour to Mustafa Kemal. But it was in vain, because of the continued severity of the censorship.

The war ended with the utter defeat of the Turks, who, beyond the lines of Tchachalja, died in heaps of cholera and typhus, and owing to bad generalship, lack of equipment, and supplies by fraudulent ministers and contractors, could not stand up against the superior weight and fighting quality of their adversaries.

As a war correspondent I was utterly frustrated, though my articles and sketches—rough sketches redrawn by famous artists—had filled the pages of the *Graphic*. With Bernard Grant, who was on the Turkish side and saw the horror and tragedy of the Turkish retreat, I wrote a book called *Adventures of War with Cross and Crescent*; descriptive of those scenes I have now retold.

PART IV

BEFORE THE STORM

1

ADVENTURE IN LISBON

THERE was a revolution in Portugal, and young King Manuel, who had succeeded to the throne on the assassination of his father and brother, had to escape from Lisbon and take refuge in England.

I had seen him when he had come over here as King, merry-eyed and debonair. He was entertained with royal honours at the Guildhall. He wore the Ribbon of the Garter and many medals on his breast. During that lunch time he was in a schoolboy mood, and grinned over his glass of Waterloo port and made little jokes to his Portuguese friends, before rising to make a speech in English, hardly intelligible because of its terrific accent. Now he was in exile with us and many of his friends were in Portuguese prisons.

News came that they were being treated with great cruelty in horrible conditions—these aristocrats who had been loyal to the young King and had put up a bit of a fight for him. A strange little lady in England who was in touch with their families and agonised over their sufferings received this news constantly and resolved to attempt their rescue. For some reason, which I have completely forgotten, I was chosen by her and a group of friends, among whom were the Duchess of Bedford and Lord Lytton, to play the part of the *Scarlet Pimpernel* in Portugal, or at least to get into the prisons, if possible, and unlock their doors by revealing their misery to the world.

I went down to see the little lady. She lived in a country house far from the madding crowd, and I found her obsessed by romance and pity for these Portuguese gentlemen, and especially for one noble and gallant fellow who, according to her, was a kind of Portuguese D'Artagnan, or even like Bayard *sans peur et sans reproche*. She did not seem to belong to modern England. She was pre-Elizabethan, I thought, and looked like the pale ghost of a Plantagenet lady looking out upon the world from a castle turret, and waiting for a "very parfit gentil knyghte", who was long in coming.

The Duchess of Bedford, a very dominating old lady with all the tradition of the 18th century, assured me that there was nothing political in my mission. It was humanitarian. Lord Lytton also took this line, and anyhow I thought it would be an interesting adventure. I went out to Lisbon with a bag of gold sovereigns concealed beneath my shirt and a list of addresses, mostly of Portuguese ladies of high rank, upon whom I had to call.

On my first evening in Lisbon, when I was dining alone in a hotel off Black Horse Square, I noticed that I was being watched by a handsome fellow who looked like a Spaniard. He left the room presently and after a few minutes came back and crossed to my table.

"Are you Philip Gibbs of the *Daily Mail?*" he asked, in perfect English, without an accent.

"No," I answered guardedly. I belonged at that time to the *Daily Chronicle.*

"Oh, sorry!" he said.

He left the room again and returned a little later, and again came to my table.

"Philip Gibbs of the *Daily Chronicle?*" he said. "I made a mistake. May I have a chat with you? I'm rather lonely here. I'm a wandering Englishman."

He had wandered all over the world, he told me, ranching in South America, mining in South Africa, and having many strange adventures, some of which he told me, in other countries. He spoke well and was entertaining. I found him agreeable, and accepted his suggestion that we should have a drink at one of the open air cafés in Black Horse Square.

While sitting there on a warm evening I noticed that several men, obviously Portuguese, were edging their chairs closer to ours and watching us with lynx eyes. I felt uneasy and spoke to my new found friend.

"Are those fellows watching you or watching me?" I asked. "I don't like the look of them."

"Nor do I," he answered, but not answering the first part of my question. "I propose we give them the slip. When I leave this chair follow me and keep close."

Suddenly he rose and strode off at a great pace towards an alley leading off Black Horse Square. I kept close to him and we went down the alley swiftly. It was nearly night, but as we were approaching the end of the alley I saw two dark figures standing there under a street lamp.

"Two of those fellows have outflanked us," I said. "What's the game?"

"A dangerous one," he answered. "Come in here."

He pushed open the door of a wine tavern and I followed him through.

"We had better order a drink here," he said, flipping his fingers to a serving wench.

No sooner had the wine been brought than two men came in and sat at a table opposite. I thought I recognised them as two of the men who had edged their chairs close to ours in Black Horse Square.

"Not too good," said my Spanish-looking friend. "Fortunately I know this neighbourhood. We shall have to make a dash for it."

Suddenly he rose and went quickly into the kitchen of the wine tavern and out at the back door. I was close on his heels. We were in another alley between high walls.

"Better do a sprint," said my man.

I ran after him. He knew his way like a rat behind the wainscot, turning and twisting through narrow ways. In a few minutes we were in the hotel in Black Horse Square.

"Quite amusing!" said this strange fellow.

Like Queen Victoria when she was told an improper story I was not amused.

"I want to ask you a straight question," I told him. "Were those fellows out for you or out for me?"

"For me," he answered. "But I'm quite all right as long as I'm with you."

"In that case," I said, "I am not at all right in your company. I shall be glad if you will keep away from me. I have my own work to do."

He laughed and did not look offended.

"I have an idea what work it is, but that's not my business. I shall be sorry if I don't see more of you. Anyhow, good night, and thanks for a pleasant evening which I have much enjoyed."

The first prison I visited was the Forte Mon Santo outside Lisbon. I drove there in one of the new taxi cabs which had recently taken the place of horse-drawn cabs, and my driver went like a madman and a murderer, deliberately killing any dogs on the road. He knocked out three and was astonished at my anger.

We came to the top of a hill where, according to my map, there was a fort and prison. But I could see no building. On examination I saw a circle of ventilators, and then discovered that the fort was underground and surrounded by a deep walled ditch. The sentry on guard was suspicious and could not make out what I wanted. He spoke no English and I spoke no Portuguese, but by signs I made him aware that I wanted to get into the prison. I had an 'Open Sesame'. It was one of my gold pieces which I held out to him. He was willing to give me the prison for this bit of gold and became obsequious.

I went down with him to damp dark dungeons. No light reached the prisoners directly but only as it was reflected from the walled ditch. In the very centre of this frightful prison, in utter darkness, was a cell like a tomb, invisible from without and with only one aperture. In there were two human beings who had gone mad. They were fed by bread being pushed through the hole. I was horrified by this medieval treatment of human beings, among whom were political prisoners.

It was not the place where the Portuguese aristocrats were imprisoned, and I had to wait a few days in Lisbon before trying to reach them. I established contact with some of their relatives, among whom were an elderly Duchess and a little Contessa. I went at night, according to my instructions, and gave a secret signal when knocking at the closed doors of their mansions. It was all very much in the style of the French Revolution. When I called on one of these ladies there was a drawing of bolts and unfastening of chains, and an old servant came with a lantern which he flashed in my face with a trembling hand. I was expected, however, and having waited for some time in a salon furnished in the style of Louis XV, with heavy candelabra and painted ceilings, the door opened and a white-faced lady entered and held out her hand.

"It is good of you to come," she said in English.

She told me that so far the revolutionary government had not arrested her or seized her house. But she dared not go out and lived from day to day, expecting every minute to hear the arrival of soldiers or police, or the shouts of a mob outside. From her and others I learnt the names of their men who were being treated like criminals and convicts, having their heads shaved and fed on filthy rations—young men of the noblest families in Portugal.

I was able to get into their prison and talk with them, though I could not see how they looked. Their faces and shaven heads were hidden under cowls, which they were forced to wear, with only holes for their eyes.

Most of them spoke English and French. Their guards, bribed by gold, allowed me to have conversation with them, and they spoke of their anger and humiliation and despair. My visit gave them new hope. If only I would tell the English people they would be rescued from this living death, they said.

Between my visits to the prisons I came into touch again with that strange fellow who looked like a Spaniard and talked like an Englishman. One morning I strolled into the main street with him and was quickly aware that we were being followed.

"I have already told you," I said, "that I don't like your company. We're being shadowed again. You go your way and I'll go mine."

"Come into this shop," he answered. "I want to buy you something."

It was a shop which sold sticks and he chose one which was more than it looked. It was a very beautiful sword-stick with a sharp and narrow blade.

"Allow me to give you this," he said. "You may find it useful. I shall buy one for myself."

I declined his offer. It has always been my belief that the safest defence in any company is to be unarmed. He bought his own sword-stick, and outside in the street two men waited for us at a distance of ten yards or so. He accompanied me back to the hotel.

Next morning he approached me with a peculiar request.

"I want you to do me a favour. It sounds absurd, but it's important for me, and easy for you."

"What is it?" I asked curiously. I must admit that this man interested me, and was very likable with a certain charm of manner.

He wanted me to go down to the sea shore outside Lisbon and bring back a handful of small pebbles.

"Nothing doing!" I told him. "I should like to know why you want those pebbles. But in any case I'm not going to fetch them for you. Why not get them yourself?"

"For me it is too dangerous," he answered.

I had an idea that it might be too dangerous for me. Perhaps he wanted to lure me into a solitary place and run me through the ribs with his beautiful sword-stick.

Another prison I visited was the Limoero. I know now what the Fleet prison was like in the bad old days. It was insanitary, over-crowded, utterly squalid, but with a touch of humanity in it which was not so soul-destroying or maddening as others I saw, like the Penitenciaria.

The prisoners were allowed to live in open cells. They could visit each other. They had their wives and babies with them. They could buy things from outside, if they had money, and the poorest were allowed to beg for alms through a grating in the prison wall. They suffered from jail fever which is the same as typhus. Their cells were verminous, but at least they could talk, and quarrel, and smoke cigarettes, and read and write, and play cards on their beds. I had an idea that I would not mind much being among these people in this prison for a month or so.

I talked with many of them, political and other prisoners, in French or English and found some of them highly educated men. They were like caged birds. No charge had been made against them. They had no idea whether they were in for a few months or for years. Their women wept. Their children whimpered. Some of them lay ill and fever-stricken.

But the worst place I saw was that Penitenciaria. It was a model prison. The prison authorities were proud of it. It filled me with a cold horror.

It was a diamond-shaped building, with long corridors down which were little cells. It was all spotlessly clean. It was, I was told, very up to date, on the best and most modern system. In each little cell was a human being. Some of them were serving life sentences. One old man I saw there had lost the power of speech, for this was a prison for solitary confinement, and when once a man went into one of those cells he never saw another human being or talked with his fellow men. At exercise time a steel plate was raised and he could go out into a yard a few feet long—a whitewashed yard between high walls. I could conceive of nothing more calculated to break down the mind of a man than this solitary confinement, nothing more devilish in psychological cruelty—of which its architects were proud. We used to have the same system in England for long-term convicts. Even now prisoners in England are shut up in their cells each day for many hours.

After getting into the Lisbon prisons I went to Oporto.

The night before I started on that journey my Spanish-looking friend came to say goodbye. He told me he was going to Vigo in the morning, but on that morning I found him on the platform where the Oporto train was waiting. He told me he had changed his mind, and was coming my way. By this time I was almost convinced that he was shadowing me so long as I stayed in Portugal. I still think that may be the explanation, but I am mystified by that quest of pebbles from the sea shore. He returned to that in Oporto and one day came to see me with a little cedarwood box which he had bought in that city.

"I make a last request for a great favour," he said. "If you will fill this small box with pebbles from the beach I shall be deeply grateful to you, and as a small return will buy you anything you may fancy in the shops of Oporto."

I refused again and he was dejected. On the night before my return to England I asked him to tell me frankly what his game had been and why he wanted those ridiculous pebbles. He said that one day he would tell me, but not then. Meanwhile would I send off two telegrams for him when I arrived in England? They were already written out and foolishly, perhaps, I agreed to see that they went off. One was in code. The other, to an address in Kensington, was in English. It said

Cannot get pebbles.

I have never solved that mystery. I never met the man again. But in the train I was able to read a paragraph of news in a Portuguese paper. It said that a sentry guarding the palace, left empty after the flight of the ex-King Manuel, had fired at three men, one of whom was an Englishman, who had entered the grounds at night, apparently in search of some of the Royal jewels supposed to have been buried at the time of the Revolution. One of the men had been wounded but they managed to escape. I wondered if that Englishman might be my mysterious acquaintance, and whether those much desired pebbles had anything to do with the Royal jewels. But the theory is weak and without evidence.

2

THE LADY WITH A BIG APPETITE

On the way back to England by way of Lisbon I was delayed by a
railway accident which caused me some embarrassment. A railway
tunnel collapsed on a train ahead of us, blocking our way. We were
crossing a bit of northern Spain and all the passengers turned out
excitedly. Among them was a family of Brazilian girls, elegant and
alluring young creatures, with their father and mother. They were
desperately anxious to get to Lisbon, where they had berths in a ship
bound for Brazil. There was also a German business man with his stout
lady. Everyone talked at once. The Spanish stationmaster made
voluble orations which I could not understand. There seemed to be a
train arriving which would reach Lisbon by a circuitous route, but I was
not sure of that. Certainly a train arrived. It looked like a local slow-
going train and I doubted whether it would go as far as Lisbon, on a
loop line avoiding the tunnel. Suddenly a number of passengers
boarded it just as it was about to start. The family of Brazilians rushed
into a carriage, leaving on the platform a mass of luggage, mostly large-
sized band-boxes for hats and feminine garments. The German business
man shouted to his wife and jumped on the train as it was moving. His
gnadige Frau gave a cry of despair, and was left behind. The Brazilian
girls screamed to me in bad English, imploring me to bring the band-
boxes to a hotel in Lisbon. The train departed and was lost to sight.
The German lady came up to me and burst into tears after asking me to
help her. I found myself in a lonely station in charge of a stout lady
who spoke only German and many large sized band-boxes filled with
female attire. The German woman had a big appetite but no money.
I fed her from time to time in the railway buffet. I have forgotten how
long we had to wait before the tunnel was cleared but it seemed like
three weeks. My German lady put her trust in me. I went on feeding
her every three hours. When at last we reached Lisbon she became
sentimental and thanked me a thousand times for my company and
sustenance. She would never forget it, she said. But her husband was
sulky, and gave me no word of thanks. I dumped the band-boxes at the
Lisbon hotel, cursing those girls for the trouble they had given me, but
they had already departed in the boat for Brazil.

So ended this adventure in Portugal. But it had its happy conclusion
in Holland Street, Kensington, where for months afterwards Portuguese
gentlemen and ladies called to kiss my hand, much to the amusement of
Agnes. My articles in the *Daily Chronicle* on the harsh treatment of

political prisoners in those terrible prisons had alarmed the new Republican government of Portugal. They were anxious to keep on friendly terms with England—Portugal's oldest ally. They desired to raise a loan. The prison doors were unlocked, the aristocrats were liberated, and they regarded me favourably, until they forgot all about me. The Queen Mother pinned an enamelled cross to my breast and it lies to this day in a small box in my study as a souvenir of this episode.

3

DEATH OF A KING

King Edward was gravely ill and crowds assembled outside Buckingham Palace to read the bulletins posted on the gate. It was the second time that the nation had been anxious about him and his Coronation had had to be postponed because of an attack of appendicitis. The publishers of magazines had been caught by that. Imaginative writers had prepared descriptive accounts in advance. Artists had drawn elaborate illustrations in colour and black-and-white. More than one magazine appeared with these highly detailed narratives, describing the King's looks and gestures before the event happened. It had been too late to stop the printing and publishing.

Now after an all too short reign the King was desperately ill, it seemed, and there was distress about him, high and low, because of his widespread popularity which had reached its peak—how very English! —when his horse Minoru had won the Derby.

I was sent to Buckingham Palace to get the latest news from time to time before the bulletins were posted up. It was about nine o'clock one evening, I think, when Lord Knollys informed us that the King was sleeping quietly and that no further bulletin would be issued until the following morning. I told this to Ernest Perris, my news editor, but he was not satisfied.

"Better spend the night outside the Palace," he said.

I was tired. I wanted to go home where my wife was waiting for me. But I had to obey orders and agreed to do so on one condition. It was that I should have someone to keep me company. Young Eddy, now K.C., was chosen for this night vigil with me.

As old campaigners together we decided to do it as comfortably as possible, and after a little dinner with a bottle of wine we hired a four-wheeler and told the cabby to drive to Buckingham Palace and park himself inside the gates.

"Not a chance!" he said. "There's a big crowd there."

There was a strange heterogeneous crowd outside the gates of the Palace. Men and women in evening clothes sat in their cars, having decided to wait all night for the next news. Costers and coster girls, clerks and labourers, men in top hats and tail coats with smart-looking women, actors and actresses after theatre hours, all sorts and types of London life were packed outside the iron gates where sentries paced up and down and policemen stood motionless. Some sense of drama— tragic drama—had called them here to abandon their beds and a night's rest.

On the previous night I had heard one voice in the crowd. It said a curious thing which I have never forgotten.

"If King Edward dies," said a well dressed man, "there will be no more peace in Europe."

Eddy and I drove through the gates after a word with one of the King's detectives whom we knew. Our old four-wheeler was the only vehicle allowed inside—such is the power of the Press.

Eddy thought this night vigil was nonsense, and said he proposed to go to sleep. He began to untie his bootlaces. Being then, as now, a victim of the nicotine drug I decided to have a last cigarette and, lighting one, smoked it as I stood outside the cab watching the people on the other side of the railings. There was plenty of light from the tall lamps but a shadow world in the Palace courtyards.

Presently a carriage and pair came through one of the archways, and as it passed by one of the lamp-posts I saw by its light two faces. They were very pale and very grave, and one was weeping. Their names were George and Mary. They passed through one of the gates.

I went quickly to the cab.

"Eddy!" I said urgently, "I believe the King is dead. Let's go up to the Palace."

Eddy put on his boots again. We hurried on to the equerry's entrance. A visitor had just arrived. It was the Belgian Ambassador.

Before a fireplace in the hall was a gentleman porter in a red tail coat. The Belgian Ambassador asked him how the King was.

"Sir," he answered, glancing at the clock, "the King died one minute ago."

Eddy and I had that news confirmed by him, and then hurried out, and ran as fast as we could out of the gates, and as far as the Grosvenor Hotel where we telephoned to the office.

A voice crossed us on the wires.

It was the voice of Winston Churchill. "The King is dead," he said. At our end of the telephone Ernest Perris answered.

"The King is dead," I told him.

By the time Eddy and I left the office that night, after we had gone back, the *Daily Chronicle* was on the streets with "The Life and Death of King Edward". It was not until two hours later that the news was posted on the gates of the Palace.

I thought I was one of the very few to hear that news so soon but when I reached my little house in Holland Street and crept up to the bedroom Agnes was awake and said: "The King is dead. He died just before midnight."

"How did you know?" I asked, utterly astounded.

No one had telephoned to her. No one had called. She had been in bed some hours. How did she know?

It happened that Princess Louise was at her brother's death-bed. When he died she left the room and telephoned to her husband, the Duke of Argyll—my old friend—in Kensington Palace. He was sitting up with the Vicar of St. Mary Abbots who telephoned to his bell ringers who were standing by. They tolled the big bell for King Edward. Agnes heard the tolling and knew the King was dead almost as soon as I did, though I was inside Buckingham Palace.

I was allowed to stand for a few minutes in the bedroom of the King where his body lay. He looked calm and handsome in death. Afterwards I saw his funeral in St. George's Chapel, Windsor.

It was the end of another era—the Edwardian era—much shorter than the Victorian but with its own character and quality, less inhibited than the Victorian, but with a spirit of gaiety for those who could afford the fun of life, and with an intellectual optimism in human progress.

The Fabians were still leading the way to social reform. Bernard Shaw was its prophet—a little too wild for most of them. H. G. Wells in his masterpieces—*Kipps, Tono Bungay* and many others—was the historian in fiction of the "lower middle class" as Dickens had been in his time, with a special eye on the young thinker who went to night classes and grappled with the problems of the universe and his own place therein. Elementary education was beginning to reap its first fruits, in a higher average of intelligence and manners. Everything promised well for the future of civilisation if one did not dig too deep, or have apocalyptic visions. But all was not well, as now we know. The Edwardian era was the last of the comfortable old world for those who had the means to buy comfort, the last phase of aristocracy and landed gentry in their security of tenure, the last brilliance shining over a world whose crust was cracking with ominous rumblings of underground fires for those who had the ears to hear.

4

CORONATION

No shadow seemed to darken the splendour of King George's Coronation at which I was present in the Abbey. I described the colour and pageantry of this ceremony rooted in medieval chivalry—the dedication of a knight—and in the old faith of Catholic England, when Kings were also priests anointed by the holy oil on head and hands and breast, and pledged to the service of the people. The most dramatic moment was when the King was disrobed and stood a simple man, almost undressed, before being arrayed in cloth of gold, and girt about with his sword belt, and draped in his purple mantle, and led to the old chair—a thousand years old—above the old stone of crowning.

There was a moment when the Duke of Norfolk—that old black-bearded Duke who was Garter King-of-Arms—had some trouble in untying shoulder knots and took out a clasp knife which flashed about the King's throat while he cut them. He had a busy time—this black-bearded Duke—rehearsing the Coronation and getting bad tempered with great ladies.

"Duchesses!" he had shouted, "for Heaven's sake pull yourselves together and behave as though you had the intelligence of fishwives!"

It was a long ordeal for those of us privileged to be in the Abbey. We had to be in our seats early in the morning and some of us had had the forethought to bring some refreshment. Agnes had provided me with a packet of sandwiches, which I put on the stone parapet in front of my place. Next to me was a silent lady whom I had never met though I had had some correspondence with her, as I have told. It was Marie Corelli. I left my seat for a time to see the entry of the peers and peeresses. When I returned the pangs of hunger assailed me. "Now for the sandwiches!" I thought. But my sandwiches had disappeared. Who took them, I know not to this day. At the time I had a dark suspicion about Marie Corelli, but I may have maligned the lady. I went hungry until five o'clock that afternoon.

I was also one of four journalists chosen to accompany King George V on his coronation tour through Scotland. It was a very pleasant and picturesque experience. Scotland turned out in strength, and in the glory of youth, and with the pageantry of old tradition.

There was some difficulty I remember in getting into Edinburgh Castle. There always is when a King arrives across the border. The battlements suddenly bristled with bayonets, grasped by Royal Scots called to arms at this approach. The drawbridge was up, the gates barred. Considerable converation ensued between the King's Herald and the Governor of the Castle. It was mostly in archaic English written in a book of words.

Trumpets were blown. Bugles sounded. Then all suspicion was relieved, the drawbridge was lowered, the gates flung open. The King was received by his loyal and loving Scots. We had a banquet within the Castle walls and old ghosts walked.

King George was attended throughout this tour by the great gentlemen of Scotland, guarded by Scottish archers, played to on the pipes down hundreds of miles of roads and in many cities. Lord Rosebery was the historical guide and in Perth Castle made a speech evoking the past and linking it with the present. He was the finest orator of his time, as often I had heard him with his silver eloquence, his perfect and polished phrases, his scholarly thought, and his great charm of manner. Strange unhappy man, so restless that often he would go on a journey as far, say, as Paris, and then would order the baggage to remain unpacked because he had decided to return. So I was told by Harry Graham who was once his secretary.

The roads of Scotland were lined all the way by Territorials, splendid types of youth, magnificent in their kilts and bonnets. Scotland seemed like an armed camp, but this was the pageantry of peace. Not one of us —not I—dreamed for a moment that in a few years great numbers of these young men would be lying dead in the fields of Flanders, and that the villages with their cheering crowds through which we passed would be silent and desolate because their young manhood had gone down like grass under the scythe of machine-gun fire and the flails of flying steel. I don't know whether the King had any such thought in his mind. As far as I know it never passed his lips.

We four journalists travelled in the King's procession which had four Daimler cars, each with a little golden crown in front. The crowds were curious about us. In the first car were the King and the Prince of Wales and two others. In the second and third were the nobles and gentlemen in attendance. But the occupants of the fourth car were puzzling. Who could these four young men be? We overheard various theories. Some thought we were foreign ambassadors. Others that we were detectives. But the most striking guess I heard was on the outskirts of Perth where the King stopped to receive a loyal address. Outside our car with its golden crown were two old Jocks in the forefront of the crowd. One of them had a reddish fringe of beard under his chin. The other scrutinised us with steel-blue eyes in a freckled face.

"Who mun they be?" asked one of them.

The other gazed at us thoughtfully and answered after this careful scrutiny:

"Eh, they mun be the King's barstards," he said.

I wanted to pass that story up to the King but I hadn't the courage. It kept us laughing at intervals for half a day. It is still remembered by at least two of us four. When the Germans were coming down hard on Paris in the second World War I called at the office of the *New York Times*. The man in charge—a Scot named Percy Philip—rose and laughed.

"Hullo!" he said. "Two of the King's barstards meet again!"

5

THE LAST OF THE BOURBONS

There was a romantic episode at Wood Norton near Evesham, the English home of the Duc d'Orléans, nearest heir to the throne of France. I had gone to see the Duke at the time of the revolution in Portugal, and had found him remarkably like Henry IV of France with his spade beard and rather gallant look. He was insulting in one remark he made, though perhaps it was justified by faked accounts of the revolution written by one correspondent who gave a lurid narrative, entirely false in its details, of bloody fighting which had never happened.

When I questioned him about the Revolution he said:

"I am not a liar. I am not a journalist."

That was very hurtful to me, but he made amends by showing me some of his hunting trophies—he had hunted big game in Africa—and by being courteous after that one dagger-thrust.

Now he was going to "throw a party" to all his Bourbon relatives, from many countries, to celebrate the marriage of Princess Louise of France with a Bourbon prince. A special chapel was being built and the wedding was to be of great magnificence, bringing back the tradition of the French monarchy in the time of its splendour.

A big crowd of special correspondents, from this and other countries, assembled in Evesham to describe the marriage and its preparation, and the rendezvous of the guests, among whom were to be the King and Queen of Spain. We were, however, thwarted in our attempts to see the Chapel Royal, or anything else, before the actual wedding and our papers were greedy for descriptive accounts. No journalist, by order of the Duc d'Orléans, was to be allowed near Wood Norton until the wedding service. The way was barred to us by police and detectives.

I thought I would try to break through this cordon by strategy, and ordered a carriage from a livery stable in Evesham. The King and Queen of Spain were expected to arrive that afternoon when they would

E

drive from the station to Wood Norton. I thought it would be a good idea to drive with them.

So it happened with the greatest ease and no questions. My carriage with a nice-looking horse fell in behind the Royal party, which filled several carriages, and away we went cheered by groups of Worcestershire yokels through the great open gates of the Duke's country house. The King of Spain was accompanied by many of his gentlemen, and the detectives had no suspicion that I was not one of them. The Duc d'Orléans was waiting to receive his guests and afterwards one of his own gentlemen showed us round the Chapel Royal. Workmen were still busy hammering and sawing, and others were draping the chapel with silken hangings spangled with golden fleurs-de-lys. I saw all I wanted, and was able to write a very full account of my observations, including portrait studies of Alfonso and other Bourbons who had already arrived. One of them was a most astonishing-looking man from Russia. He had a heavy figure in a long fur coat, and flat cheeks, much rouged, fringed by a sandy-coloured beard. He wore many rings, including one on his thumb, and after the wedding, next day, he became very tight on champagne, which flowed like water, and did a little dance in the courtyard.

Looking back on this episode of which I made use in my novel *The Street of Adventure*, I am startled and slightly shocked by my own temerity, not to say cool cheek, as a young journalist, in breaking into Wood Norton against all orders. It does not seem in line with my own character, which then was full of timidity, as shy as a fawn in ordinary life, and by no means pushful. But when a journalist is out on a "story" he is spurred on by a kind of professional passion to get there at all costs. I was pricked on by this goad. I acquired temporary boldness, which led me into many scrapes for which I cursed myself afterwards. I think my boyish enthusiasm for *The Three Musketeers* had something to do with it. The lure of romantic adventure overcame my diffidence now and then.

So I saw the marriage of Princess Louise of France with her Bourbon prince. Her face was very white beneath her bridal veil. She seemed to have come from the France of the Valois to this village in Worcestershire. Many of those Bourbon princes belonged to the past and it was all make-believe. Even Alfonso of Spain was soon to join them in their gallery of ghosts, with only old memories of former power and the Blood Royal, and the *Ancien Régime*. Now they mean nothing.

6

THE GOLDEN YEARS

The years before 1914 seem, to those of us who remember them, a happy time in history, though now, in writing this, I doubt whether they were as happy as we think they were. Underneath the fair surface of our national life there was grim poverty, undernourishment of men, women and children, overcrowding in the slums, the insecurity of casual labour and much human tragedy. But much of that was hidden and unrevealed to the well-do-do classes, and to the rich who were having their last innings before crushing taxation bore down on them.

Even to me, who had glimpses of the underworld and apprehensions of international conflict, that time before August 1914 seems rosecoloured, and gay, and glittering. There was an epidemic of pageantry in England. An ex-schoolmaster named Louis Parker started the idea, and this revival of history in living counterfeit became popular all over the country. Dressing up in the costumes of their ancestors was an amusing pastime for the inhabitants of country towns, and local records were searched for historical episodes.

The Oxford pageant was most splendid and sumptuous, and a great deal of money was spent upon it. The pageant master was a young man named Frank Lascelles who enlisted the aid of Beerbohm Tree. Its living pictures of the Court of Charles I were extraordinarily beautiful with masses of lovely ladies in silken frocks and ringlets, and with crowds of undergraduates in Stuart dress. I have forgotten the name of the man who played Charles, riding at the head of his Cavaliers, but he was astoundingly like the portrait by Vandyke.

I went to a pageant in Norfolk where one of the scenes was the homage paid to Mary Tudor by twenty-two Norfolk gentlemen. The men who played those parts bore the same names and held the same land as their ancestors, showing the unbroken continuity of our landed gentry.

At St. Albans the Romans walked again in English meadows, and in a later scene the bowmen of England let loose their arrows in thick flight which screamed through the air, because each arrow had a shrill-sounding whistle for dramatic effect. I was keen on all that, and wandered about those pageant grounds talking with young knights in armour, with monks and nuns, and Chaucer's pilgrims, and Plantagenet ladies, and Danish vikings, and Saxon kings. Was it some unconscious awareness of the great ordeal to come which made us look back to the long roll call of English history, and to our saints, and heroes, and martyrs, and men-at-arms? These pageants brought back the spirit of old times and the beauty and loveliness of England at its best.

This enthusiasm for the past, and for dressing up in old costumes, was revealed also in fancy dress balls at the Albert Hall, Covent Garden and elsewhere. To one of them I went as Dick Sheridan in a white peruke and knee breeches of green silk below a square-tailed coat of the same colour and embroidered waistcoat. To the Albert Hall that night went ladies in sedan chairs, and Beau Brummels in hansom cabs, and every kind of character from the pages of history and romance. Haroun al Raschid and all the people of the *Arabian Nights* came to Kensington that evening, and the Albert Hall was thronged with beauty and blazed with colour, and its air was heavy with scent.

Many famous people were there, and gilded youth, in strange disguise, enjoyed itself before hearing a call from Kitchener for the first hundred thousand to die in storms of high explosives on the fields of the Somme.

7

THE BUTTERFLY BALL

Late one night London seemed asleep. The theatre crowds had gone home. The Guards had said goodbye to their girls outside the barracks and the coffee stalls. The down-and-outs had gone into the dosshouses and their coffin-like beds. A Bobby in Bond Street was flashing his lantern on to the locks of the shuttered shops. He was startled when life began again. Gilded youth, and the pretty ladies of the stage and halls, had no intention of going to sleep that night. Officers of the Guards and others had invited masses of little ladies to join them in a Butterfly Ball at one of the galleries in Bond Street. Sporting celebrities, dramatic critics and others had also been invited and I, strangely enough, was among them. A tall figure in magnificent evening clothes and with ginger side whiskers came down the stairway to the dance room where many guests had assembled. Everybody seemed to know him—the dancing girls and little actresses, the young gentlemen of the Guards. It was Lord Lonsdale, patron of the Turf and the Ring, friend of the London cabbies, lover of life high and low. He led off with a girl dressed, but not heavily clad, as a tee-to-tum. The Butterfly Ball was a great success, it seemed. Champagne flowed into thin stemmed glasses, many of which were broken. Golden slippers twinkled on the polished boards. Laughter shrilled from pretty lips. A gay scene before many of the young men here were sitting in verminous dugouts, listening to heavy crumps outside, or staring across No Man's Land and watching Very lights go up to gleam for a few seconds on the enemy's barbed wire and broken sandbags and things lying still between the lines.

8

LABOUR TROUBLE

Underneath our gay social life with its pleasure and pageantry and sport—the Boat Race, the Epsom races, Henley, Ascot, Cowes, cricket at Lord's, the massed mobs at professional football matches, tennis tournaments, music and mirth at the White City—to all of which I went, not for fun, but as an observer and recorder of contemporary life with critical but not hostile eyes—there were signs and sudden outbreaks of ugly conflict. Labour for millions of men and women by whom the wealth of the nation is made was underpaid, overworked, and insecure. The Welsh miners rioted at Tonypandy. I saw them marching down the Rhondda Valley. I saw baton charges not pleasant to see. My sympathies were with these men, knowing something about the miserable conditions in which they worked, underpaid and housed worse than cattle, in such foul slums as Merthyr Tydfil.

There was a general strike in Liverpool to which I was sent. It was as near to revolution as anything I had seen in England. It started with a strike of the transport workers, and spread to other unions who declared sympathetic strikes. For many weeks—nearly three months—nothing moved in Liverpool. The dockers did not handle any cargoes. The railway porters came out. The tramway men went idle. Even the road sweepers declined to work. Some troops were sent into the city to maintain order but increased disorder because they were stoned by the strikers and were not allowed to fire in self-defence. They had to retreat under showers of kidney stones with which the mob armed themselves. The situation was alarming·and not without brutality among the strikers, whose passions were aroused.

A number of men denounced as "scabs", or blacklegs, by the strikers were found to run the trams but were stoned on their journeys. On a Sunday morning I saw many trams brought to a standstill and then set on fire. In one tramcar were passengers, including women and children, who became panic stricken as stones came hurtling through the glass. One woman with a baby in her arms came on to the step, hesitating to jump out. The car was travelling at a furious speed. The driver had lost his nerve, as well he might, under that fusillade of stones. The woman on the step was paralysed with fear and suddenly dropped her baby. It fell into the roadway, and not a man on the side walk moved to pick it up. I tried to break through the crowd in front of me to do so but a woman dashed forward and lifted up the babe which was badly stunned. It was not a pleasant episode for a Sunday afternoon.

Some other journalists and I were staying at a small hotel in one of the squares in Liverpool which had become very insanitary—stinking indeed—because there had been no scavenging for weeks. Dead rats lay about with rotting cabbage-stalks and other ill-smelling refuse. This stench came through the windows and someone suggested that we should form a scavenging party and clean up the square. The idea was adopted and a party of us, armed with brooms from the hotel, went out on this job, clapped by maidservants who watched from the windows. The square had been almost empty of life, but, presently, while we worked, a crowd gathered and booed us and shouted out: "Scabs! . . . Scabs!" They were very hostile, regarding us as strike-breakers, but they did not attack and we did some pretty good work with the dead rats and the garbage.

One evening I rang up the news editor of the *Daily Chronicle* and told him that I had a good deal to send over the telephone. The Riot Act had been read out and the troops were ordered to fire above the heads of the crowds.

The news editor did not seem eager to have this story.

"Something worse is happening," he told me. "The German Fleet has put out into the North Sea. The British Fleet is cleared for action. It looks bad."

"Good God!" I said, down the telephone.

Not a line about this appeared in the papers next day. Nothing ever was published about it, but it was true, as I heard afterwards from naval officers. The German Fleet had tried to take us unawares, but the British Navy was ready for them, and they turned back. It was a warning that war was menacing the peace of the world, and ours. The English people were mostly unaware of this dark terror lurking behind their sunshine. They were playing cricket on village greens, and tennis in English gardens. The golf courses were crowded for week-ends. Youth was lying in canoes down the reaches of the Thames. The tourist crowds were taking their tickets for Belgium, France, and Germany. There was no fear of war in their minds. Why war, anyhow? Hadn't we become civilised? Who wanted war?

9

THE SUFFRAGETTES

During the early years of King George's reign the campaign of Votes for Women grew in intensity under the leadership of Mrs. Pankhurst with her daughters Christabel and Sylvia, and the strong support of Mr. and Mrs. Pethick Lawrence. From the first I was on their side, though I was shocked and distressed by some of the desperate and violent acts of these militant women. Their plea for political equality seemed to me elementary justice, though most men of my time hated the idea of it, poured ridicule and contempt upon its advocates, and worked themselves up to fury when the Suffragettes developed their aggressive tactics. Most of this type of men based their opposition upon the argument that equality of political rights would destroy the beautiful ideal of womanhood, and the old chivalry of men to women, and would lead to an effeminate and hag-ridden nation. But it was apparent that those who prated about ideal womanhood and men's chivalry were often those who advocated coarse and brutal treatment to the Suffragettes, made lewd jokes about them, and did not hesitate to knock them about when they were stewards at public meetings. Those meetings were interrupted by cries of "Votes for Women!" from little old ladies and young girls who dared to make this demonstration knowing that they would have rough treatment.

They certainly made a terrible nuisance of themselves. During debates in the House of Commons leaflets would be scattered over the heads of the members and the cry of "Votes for Women" would come from the Strangers' Gallery, until the police covered the mouths of offending women with their hands and carried them out. Political meetings by any member of the Government could not be held without these interruptions and struggles. The slogan of "Votes for Women" was printed by rubber stamps on walls and pavements and could not be erased. Presently violence increased—they were dared to it by Herbert Gladstone and others. Letterboxes were set on fire and plate-glass windows were broken in many of the great stores and shops. A woman flung herself in front of the favourite for the Derby and was killed instantly.

At first the police handled these women as gently as possible, with a certain amount of class consciousness. They were "ladies" after all, thought the London Bobby who was a bit of a snob. Barred away from the precincts of the House by police cordons women tilted against them and, now and then, by stratagem, or the swift feet of Atalanta, broke through. The police laughed and carried them away in their arms until they chained themselves to the railings and could not be removed. I remember seeing a crippled old lady charge the police cordon repeatedly in an invalid chair which she manœuvred at great speed.

The class consciousness of the police was revealed to me by a scene one day when a crowd of mill girls came down from Lancashire to assist their London sisters in the campaign for women's rights. They tried to make a demonstration in Downing Street, but the police drove them back and isolated them behind the War Office. I followed them there and was a witness of real brutality. The police tore down the girls' hair, wound it round their throats, and hurled them about the open place. Chivalry to women was not remembered then.

The Government passed the Cat-and-Mouse Act which, also, was not remarkable for chivalry or justice. They sentenced women for breaking the law by public disturbance, fed them forcibly when they went on hunger strike, and let them out for a brief period with power to imprison them again without further trial. It was a disgrace to the Law. One woman, aware of the inherent snobbishness of the English nation, even among police and jailers, disguised herself as a working woman, had herself arrested, and went on hunger strike. She was forcibly fed many times until she nearly died, being of delicate and frail physique. When she was let out, at death's door, it became known that she was Lady Constance Lytton, the sister of Lord Lytton. The Government was somewhat embarrased by this revelation, though there would have been no embarrassment if Lady Constance Lytton had been a mill girl or a sempstress.

My friend Henry W. Nevinson, always the defender of liberty, always a man of fearless courage, allied himself with the women's cause and marched with them when they advanced to the House of Commons, or spoke for them when they held meetings at Caxton Hall. Woe betide him if he fell into the hands of the stewards at any meeting interrupted by his female friends. Once he jumped into the midst of them. It was at the Albert Hall where the Suffragettes kept up constant interruptions of a big meeting where Cabinet Ministers were present. Nevinson's blood boiled when he saw one of the stewards clench his fist and give a knock-out blow on the chin to one of the militant women. Other women were being roughly handled. Nevinson jumped from the stage box, and fought half a dozen stewards at once until they overpowered him and flung him out.

I was present at the trial of Mrs. Pankhurst and her daughter Christabel for conspiracy against public order. It was a most remarkable trial and not altogether reassuring as a demonstration of British Justice. Mrs. Pankhurst, who knew her law, was aware of the right, as affirmed in the reign of Charles II, for citizens to present a petition to the House of Commons if no more than seven approached the House for that purpose. Seven Suffragettes, including Mrs. Pankhurst and her daughter, endeavoured to do so, but were barred by the police, and, after persisting in their attempt, were arrested and taken to prison. This civic right, never repealed, was waived by the Judge, who paid no attention to it.

The Court was crowded to hear Mrs. Pankhurt's defence. Christabel was not in good form and cried when she questioned the witnesses against her, but her mother was magnificent. Her speech, as many barristers agreed, was one of the most brilliant and masterly orations ever heard in Court. She expounded the whole case for the right of women to vote, with a passionate sincerity and eloquence which was very moving. Her argument was closely knit and she never hesitated for a word or phrase. She was not dramatic nor hysterical, but her whole speech seemed to burn with a spiritual and intellectual fire. The galleries were crowded. The Court was filled with men of the Bar and men of the Press. They were all spellbound by this woman's genius as a special pleader.

During the trial I had a talk with Christabel Pankhurst behind the Court. She looked ill and distressed. She had gone beyond the limit of her endurance, in which she had proved her courage so many times. She had suffered the misery and squalor of prison life. The thought of a long sentence was dreadful to her. She asked me if I thought the verdict would go against them, and when I told her that I thought it would she wept again, and I was deeply sorry for her. She and her mother were sentenced to four years imprisonment.

10

TROUBLE IN IRELAND

There was trouble in Ireland. It was not for the first time. Sir Edward Carson was raising a private army to defend the Ulster loyalists against an invasion from the south. Winston Churchill took the side of the South against this recruitment in Ulster which he said was a rebellion against the Crown. There was a threat of mutiny in the Army, led at the Curragh camp by Sir Hubert Gough who made it known that his officers would refuse to coerce Ulster, on whose side they stood in case of civil war.

I was sent out to Ireland by the *Daily Chronicle* to enquire into the smuggling of arms by the Ulstermen. In Belfast I found plenty of evidence that arms were pouring in. In the cellars of the Royal Avenue Hotel I saw hundreds of cases of rifles—German rifles mostly, I was told. There was very little secrecy about it. Wooden cases arrived in Belfast labelled "Firearms". There was gun-running in lone creeks on the coast. Every young Ulsterman was drilling with Carson's volunteers. Shopkeepers kept their rifles behind the counters. One of them told me with pride that he could shoot the King's head on a penny at twenty yards. It seemed to me an odd way of proving his loyalty to the King. I heard Carson make speeches to thousands of stalwart young men, who cheered him hoarsely. With his tall figure and long, lean, powerful face—the terror of criminals when he was prosecuting counsel—he was impressive and impassioned. He had the old tricks of oratory, and with clenched fist hammered the air and spoke with fire in a strong, Irish brogue.

It all seemed to me very dangerous, with civil war round the corner.

I made a report on all this to Robert Donald, my editor, who did not publish it but sent it to Winston Churchill. He wrote a line of comment across it when he sent it back.

"Gibbs has had his leg pulled."

But I was right and he was wrong, as history quickly proved.

One day Churchill came out to Belfast to make a speech at the Celtic Football ground outside the city, where he would meet a crowd of southern Irish, hostile to Carson and his volunteers. It was a brave act, but it was rash of him, I thought, to bring his beautiful wife with him, and brave of her to come. There was no secret about the time of his arrival in Belfast. An immense crowd lined Royal Avenue waiting for him, not with loving enthusiasm. Hundreds of young men had packed the station yard, looking grim and dangerous with their hands in their jacket pockets. I spoke to a police inspector.

"Don't you think these fellows ought to be cleared further back. Won't they attack Churchill when he arrives?"

"Ah, sure," said the inspector, "they're good lads and won't raise a finger against him, especially as his wife will be coming with him."

Winston Churchill arrived. He wore a bowler hat and a blue overcoat. Mrs. Churchill had touched her cheeks with a little colour. The crowd of young men were silent and did not move. Churchill looked them straight in the eyes and the line of his lips hardened.

Nothing happened in the station yard but as Mr. and Mrs. Churchill drove to the Royal Avenue Hotel for lunch—they drove in a blue car—the mob surged close, booing and shouting, and tried to upset them. Mounted police charged among them, beating off their hands from the sides of the car.

I followed them in another car which was also blue, and it happened that I also was wearing a bowler hat and a dark blue overcoat. This was the cause of an incident which for a few moments was distinctly unpleasant. It happened late that afternoon when Churchill had spoken at the Celtic Football ground. I had been there with my friend Randal Charlton, who shared the car with me. We drove back at dusk having seen Churchill off at a railway station outside Belfast. But the crowds in Belfast expected him to return to the Royal Avenue Hotel, outside which they were densely packed.

"Here he comes!" they shouted, when they saw my blue car. Inside was a man—myself—in a dark blue overcoat and bowler hat.

In the dusk they took me for Winston Churchill, to whom I bear no great resemblance—God wot! It was good enough for them. When we jumped out of the hired car they made a rush for us and we had a hard struggle to get into the hotel. Randal Charlton who put up a fight came off worse than I did. His collar was torn off and he was very crumpled when he got inside. I was pulled about but escaped without bodily injury, though my clothes were disordered. For two hours afterwards the crowd hooted in the street below while I wrote my account of the day.

I never told Winston Churchill that I was mistaken for him. He wouldn't have believed it!

11

THE MENACE OF GERMANY

Foreign countries were watching these troubles in England, and the menace of civil war in Ireland, with interest which was not always friendly. German agents were over here sending back reports about all this. German correspondents were writing critical and contemptuous articles in their newspapers. Old England, they thought, was revealing her inner weakness. It was, they said, demoralised and effete. The Suffragette movement was a sign of lack of virility. The young men were effeminate, pleasure-loving, undisciplined. Unlike continental nations they shirked military service, and had developed pacifist and cowardly ideals. Their Empire, wrote the German correspondents, was beginning to crack and was showing signs of disintegration and revolt. The working classes in England were getting out of hand and defying law and order by frequent strikes, especially in the coal mines. The riots at Tonypandy had been proof of this. The general strike at Liverpool was a preliminary skirmish to civil war in England. So wrote the German journalists.

One of them attracted the notice of my friend Eddy and myself. He was the Baron von Zeidlitz and we noticed that wherever trouble was in England there he was also, watching and reporting. We read some of his articles. They were venomous in their hatred and hostility. He had been down to Portsmouth when there was a strike in the dock-yards, and his account was not that of a friend of England but that of an enemy.

"That fellow ought to be hoofed out of this country," said Eddy. "I propose that we go and tell him so."

We had no instructions from our paper, as far as I can recollect, and Eddy and I took it upon ourselves to call on the Baron von Zeidlitz at a suburban house where he was living. He was surprised at our call, but was coldly polite until we charged him with being a German spy. At first he blustered and adopted an arrogant and bullying manner, but he was frightened when we told him that we should give information about him to Scotland Yard. He thought it best to leave England for a time.

In this country public opinion was becoming uneasy about the intentions of Germany. Robert Blatchford, an old Socialist, wrote a series of sensational articles in the *Daily Mail* entitled "*Der Tag*". They maintained that the German Navy had a regular toast and drank to "The Day" when they would send the British Navy to the bottom of the sea, and that the German war lords were preparing to attack this country.

For some time the Kaiser had been making unfriendly speeches in private and public. He bitterly resented our efforts to prevent an expansion of the German Navy by a naval agreement. "Germany's future is on the sea," he proclaimed.

Robert Donald, my editor, spoke to me one day about all this.

"You had better go to Germany," he said, "and try to find out the truth of things. What is the mood of the German people? Is there any real menace of war? Would the German Socialists obey the call to the Colours in the event of a European war? Take your time about it. I'll give you some introductions to German friends of mine—men of liberal minds and international outlook."

I went over to Germany, and the first introduction I used from Robert Donald was not a success. I presented it to a gentleman in Düsseldorf who was a well-known writer on economic conditions and international affairs. He had been a frequent visitor to England where he had been entertained by liberal-minded groups. He had the re-putation of being one of our best friends in Germany.

He seemed a little embarrassed when he greeted me. He was obviously fussed by my visit. Doubtless I had called at an inconvenient time. He asked me to excuse him for a little while and suggested that I should read one of his articles just published in a German weekly.

During his absence I read this as well as I could, though it was difficult stuff, and was astonished to find that it was a most hostile criticism of Great Britain and its foreign policy.

Presently its author returned and said: "Well now, let us have a talk."

I told him I had read his article and did not find it friendly. I had understood from Robert Donald that he was a friend of England.

He laughed uneasily.

"I must confess," he said, "that I am not so friendly as I used to be. British foreign policy has been consistently hostile to Germany for some time past. The *Entente Cordiale* between England and France is directed against us. It ties up England with Russia. For Germany that is a policy of encirclement. Beyond that, the speeches of many of your public men, and the articles in your newspapers, are unfriendly and impertinent towards Germany. They are becoming unendurable."

As far as I can remember that was the gist and meaning of what he told me. I went away disconcerted. If this was the attitude of Germans who knew England well and had been friends of ours the outlook for peace was not too good.

I had another experience of the same kind. Someone had given me an introduction to a Roman Catholic Bishop in Berlin. He was a close friend of the Kaiser and, I was told, a man of great quality and character. He received me in his study in a house not far from the Kaiser's Palace and I was relieved to find he spoke very good English. But as soon as I began to question him about Anglo-German relations he became angry and spoke harshly. His grievance was the same as that of the writer in Düsseldorf. Germany was encircled. Great Britain, France, and Russia had formed an alliance to strangle Germany's legitimate power and influence in Europe. France and Russia were preparing for war against Germany. Great Britain was ruthless in her economic rivalry and playing a dangerous game with the usual hypocrisy. "If this goes on," he said, harshly, "war will be inevitable."

I ventured to say something about the duty of the Church to prevent war. Surely as a Christian he would use his influence for peace?

They were mild words, but he took them as an insult and rang his bell sharply. I was dismissed. This Bishop did not behave in the Spirit of his Master. In a conversation on foreign affairs he did not like to be reminded of Jesus Christ. I had made a *faux pas!*

I made a tour of Germany and talked to people of many types and professions. The middle classes were reassuring. They wanted peace, and were aghast at the idea that there should be a war between Germany and England. "It is unbelievable," they told me. At that time the possibility of such a thing had not entered their heads. War between our two peoples, they said, would not only be horrible, but it would be a crime. There was room for both of us in the world, they thought. They admired England and did not believe what they read in their newspapers about British decadence. "All that is political nonsense!" they said. "The newspapers must have something to write about."

Over and over again I heard words like that from manufacturers and shop keepers and ordinary folk with whom I came in contact. It was only when I touched the official class and the political writers that I found hostility and exasperation.

I had a talk with Edward Bernstein, the leader of the Social Democrats, then very strong in Germany. I have forgotten the line of our conversation but I remember that he was depressed and pessimistic. He stood for international peace, but he had no faith in the pacifist conviction of his followers. "If once the drums beat and the bugles blow for war," he told me, "my beautiful Socialists, who have proclaimed their hatred of war, will march like one man when they are called to the Colours."

I wrote all this in a series of articles which were not conclusive one way or the other but reported fairly the conversations I had had and the differing views expressed in them.

I was not at all convinced that war was inevitable. Its inevitability seemed to me too horrible, and there was a lot of peace-mindedness in Germany, as far as I had been able to see.

The great mass of the middle classes seemed to be against it, but as now we know after two wars, German public opinion is slavishly subservient to authority and leadership.

Part V

THE FIRST WORLD WAR

1

ACROSS THE CHANNEL

AT the end of July, 1914, when I stood on the deck of the Channel
boat in Dover Harbour looking back on England, whose white
cliffs gleamed faintly through the darkness, a sense of tragic certainty
came to me suddenly that a summons of war would come to England
demanding all her strength and all her manhood. Perhaps it would
come to-night. The second mate of the boat came to the side of the
steamer and stared across the inky waters, on which there were shifting
pathways of white radiance, as the searchlights of distant warships swept
the sea.

"God!" he said, in a low voice.

"Do you think it will come to-night?" I asked in the same tone of
voice. We spoke as though our words were dangerous.

"It's likely. The German Fleet won't wait for any declaration, I
should say, if they thought they could catch us napping. . . . But they
won't! I fancy we're ready for them—here, anyway."

He jerked his thumb at some black masses looming through the
darkness in the harbour, caught here and there by a glint of metal
reflected in the water. They were destroyers and submarines nosing
towards the harbour mouth.

"There's a crowd of 'em," said the second mate, "and they stretch
across the Channel . . . The Reserve men have been called out—taken
off the trams in Dover to-night. But the public hasn't yet woken up to
the meaning of it."

He stared out to sea and it was some minutes before he spoke again.

"Queer, isn't it? They all sleep in their beds to-night as though
nothing out of the way were happening. And yet, in a few hours maybe,
there'll be hell. That's what it's going to be—hell and damnation, if I
know anything about war."

In the saloon were about a dozen men, drinking at the bar. They
were noisy and had already drunk too much. By their accent it was easy
to guess they had come from Manchester, and by their knapsacks,
which contained all their baggage, it was obvious that they were on a
short trip to Paris. A man from a travel agency promised them a "good
time". There were plenty of pretty girls in Paris. The men slapped him
on the back and called him "old chap".

A quiet gentleman seated opposite to me on a leather lounge—I met him afterwards at the British Embassy in Paris—caught my eye and smiled.

"They don't seem to worry about the international situation. Perhaps it will be easier to get to Paris than to get back again."

"And now drinks all around, lads," said one of the trippers.

On deck there were voices singing. It was the hymn of the "Marseillaise". I went up towards the sound and found a party of young Frenchmen standing aft, waving farewells to England as the siren hooted above a rattle of chains and the crash of the gangway which dropped to the quayside. They had been called back to their country to defend its soil, and unlike the Englishmen, drinking themselves fuddled, were intoxicated by a patriotic excitement.

"*Vive l'Angleterre!*"

An answer came back from the quayside:

"*Vive la France!*"

It was to this shout that we warped away from the jetty and made for the open sea. A yacht with white sails, all agleam as it crossed the bar of a searchlight, so that it seemed like a fairy ship in the vision of a dream, crept into the harbour and then fluttered into the darkness below the Admiralty pier.

"That's a queer kind of craft to meet to-night," I said to the second mate. "What's she doing?"

"I'd like to know. She's got a German skipper and crew. Spies, all of them, I guess. But nobody seems to bother."[1]

2

THE CALL TO ARMS

Paris was beautiful in those last days of July under a hot sun. Outwardly its life seemed peaceful. In the Champs Elysées I heard the shrill squeak of Punch as the children laughed round the *Petit Guignol*. Down the rue de Rivoli strolled American tourists in panama hats, and English tourists in summer clothes, staring in the shop windows at the latest studies of nude women, and at night went in pursuit of adventure to Montmartre, where the orchestras of the Bal Tabarin were still fiddling mad tangos in a competition of shrieking melody, and where troops of painted ladies in the Folies Bergères still paraded in the *promenoir*, with languorous eyes, through wafts of sickly scent . . . Then suddenly the thunderbolt fell with the signal of war, and in a few

[1] From *The Soul of the War*, by Philip Gibbs, 1915.

hours Paris was changed as though by a wizard's spell. Most of the children vanished from the Tuileries gardens with their white-capped nurses. Punch gave a final squawk of dismay and disappeared when the *Petit Guignol* packed up to make way for a more tragic drama. A hush fell upon Montmartre, and the musicians in the orchestra packed up their instruments and scurried with scared faces to Berlin, Vienna, and Budapest.

To millions of French homes, to thousands of apartments in Paris, a little card was delivered. It was the call to the Colours. It was the signal of general mobilisation. Young men stared at it and went white.

To many of them it was a message of death, as they guessed. Husbands and wives looked into each other's eyes and then gave a cry. So it was to be war. Why? In God's name, why?

Why, they asked, as I heard some of them ask, should France be forced into a war for which she was not prepared—those dirty politicians —and for which she had no desire, because Austria had issued an ultimatum to Servia, demanding the punishment of a nation of cut-throats for the murder of an unnecessary archduke. They had been tied up with Russia, that was the trouble, the Press had been subsidised by Russia to promote the French loan and persuade every peasant and small shopkeeper to invest his money in Russian bonds. And Germany was behind this business, forcing the pace, rattling the sword so that it resounded through Europe.

The French people were stupefied by this summons to war—a war they didn't want. Who wanted war? Not the English people who had no great army and hated war. Not the German peasants, the small people whose sons would be slaughtered.

Did the Russian folk want war, those shaggy *moujiks* in the Russian farmsteads, or the young students risking Siberia for the word Liberty, or the factory workers in St. Petersburg, underpaid and underfed? Who among all the peoples in Europe wanted this war which would devastate their lands, and destroy their cities, and pile up the bodies of youth on many battlefields? None of them wanted war. It was being thrust upon them by their leaders, by secret treaties signed between the Foreign Offices, by the crooked ways of diplomacy and power politics, by small groups of sycophants surrounding a King or an Emperor, by a few sinister brains playing with human lives as counters in a game of international poker. The peoples wanted only peace, and better con-ditions of life with more security. They would be the victims and the dupes. As soon as war started the old instinct of patriotism would be irresistible. All men would fight for their Fatherland—"my country right or wrong"—and this time, right. They would catch the war fever. They would cheer on their way to death. They would die for their Flag. . . .

There was no cheering in Paris, no flag-wagging. Crowds of mobilised men went to the railway stations with their womenfolk, silently. They shirked the emotion of the last farewell, and said quietly: *"Eh bien! Au revoir et bonne chance!"*, or held a woman tightly for a long moment, and put lips to lips in one last passionate kiss before thrusting her away and walking off white-faced, as often I saw.

On the first day of August people waited with stupefaction for the fateful decision which, if it were for war, would arrest all the activities of a nation's normal life and demand a dreadful sacrifice in blood and tears. A hundred times I heard the word *"Incroyable!"* as I walked along the boulevards. It was the answer I had from men with whom I talked, *"C'est incroyable!"*. They found it hard to believe—they would not believe—that, without any provocation from France, without any challenge, Germany would force this war upon the *Triple Entente* and make a bloody shambles of European civilisation. With this incredulity and stupefaction there was among most of the Frenchmen I met a secret dread that France was unready for the great ordeal of war, and that its outbreak would find her divided by political parties, inefficient in organisation, and corrupt in some of her government departments. They were haunted by the memory of 1870—*L'année terrible*. The Socialists and Syndicalists who had fought against the three years' service might refuse to march.

On that night of August 1st, Jaurès was killed in the café of Le Croissant by a young man who called himself a patriot. The news sent a shudder through the minds of men afraid of disunion in France in this hour of danger. But that fear passed after the funeral of the Socialist leader when all parties followed his coffin to the grave, as I saw.

3

MOBILISED

In Paris I met my old colleague Henri Bourdin, of the *Daily Chronicle* office, and many special correspondents from Fleet Street. Among them were Alphonse Courlander, the young novelist and journalist, excited and unnerved, I thought, by this menace of war.—He was in the Paris office of the *Daily Express*. There were also Hamilton Fyfe of the *Daily Mail*, Massey of the *Telegraph*, and H. M. Tomlinson, who wrote his newspaper articles in a masterly style of prose—his own style—and who as I came to know him through the years of war had a wisdom, and a humour, and a philosophy Christian in tradition, Cockney in colloquial expression, and Greek in its sense of truth and human folly and the agony of man, and the mystery of the Unknown God.

In the Paris office of the *Daily Chronicle* the telephone bell rang constantly. Bourdin was being questioned by his French comrades of the Press.

"Is England coming in? . . . Has England declared war? Are those people going to play their old role of *perfide Albion?* It would be unbelievable. It would be the last dishonour."

"Sir Edward Grey is prevaricating," said one of my colleagues. "He won't give a plain answer to the question whether we have a military pact with France. If we don't come in some of us will have our throats cut down the Boulevard des Italiens."

I went down to Nancy with the first batch of mobilised men. Before the train started the carriage in which I had taken a seat was crowded with young men who, excepting one cavalry officer in the corner, seemed to belong to the poorest classes of Paris. In the corner opposite was a boy of eighteen or so in the working clothes of a *terrassier,* or labourer. No one had come to see him off to the war and he was stupefied with drink. Several times he staggered up and vomited out of the window with an awful violence of nausea, and then fell back with his head lolling sideways on the cushions of the first-class carriage. None of the other men, except the cavalry officer who drew in his legs slightly, took the slightest interest in this poor wretch—a handsome lad with square-cut features and fair tousled hair, who had tried to get courage out of absinthe before leaving for the war.

In the corner opposite my own seat was a thin, pallid young man also a little drunk, but with an excited brain in which a multitude of strange and tragic thoughts chased each other. He recognised me as an Englishman at once, and with a shout of "Camarade!" shook hands with me, not once, but scores of times, during the first part of our journey.

He entered upon a monologue that seemed interminable, his voice rising into a shrill excitement and then sinking into a hoarse whisper. He belonged to the *apache* type and had come out of one of those foul lairs which hide behind the white beauty of Paris—yet he spoke with a terrible eloquence which kept me fascinated. I recorded some of his words in my book *The Soul of the War,* though I could not give them his white heat of passion nor the infinite pathos of his self-pity.

"I have left a wife behind, the woman who loves me and sees something more in me than vileness. Shall I tell you how I left her, Monsieur? Dying—in a hospital at Charenton. I shall never see her again. I shall never again take her thin white face in my dirty hands and say—'You and I have tasted the goodness of life, my little one, while we have starved together.' For life is good, Monsieur, but in a little while I shall be dead in one place and my woman in another. That is certain. I left a child behind me—a little girl. What will happen to her when I am killed? I left her with the concierge, who promised to take care of her—not for money, you understand, because I had none to give. My little girl will never see me again, and I shall never see her grow into a woman, because I am going to be killed. Perhaps in a day or two there will be no more life for me. This hand of mine—you see I can grasp things with it, move it this way and that, shake hands with you—*camarade!*—salute the Spirit of France with it, *comme ça!* But to-morrow or the next day it will be quite still. A dead thing—like my dead body. It is queer. Here I sit talking to you alive. But to-morrow or the next day my body will lie out on the battlefield like a bit of earth. I can see that corpse of mine, with its white face and staring eyes. Ugh! It is a dirty sight, a man's corpse. Here in my heart something tells me that I shall be killed quite soon—perhaps at the first shot. But do you know, I shall not be sorry to die. I shall be glad, Monsieur. And why glad, you ask? Because I love France and hate the Germans who have put this war on to us. I am going to fight—I, a Socialist and Syndicalist—so that we shall make an end of war, so that the little ones of France will sleep in peace, and the women go without fear. This war will have to be the last war. It is a war of Justice against Injustice. When they have finished this time the people will have no more of it. We who go out to die shall be remembered, because we gave the world peace. That will be our reward, though we shall know nothing of it, but lie rotting in the earth—dead. It is sad that to-morrow or the next day I shall be dead. I see my corpse there."[1]

A neurotic type, a poor weed of life who had been reared in the dark lairs of civilisation. But he was willing to die for France and the ending of all wars. Tragic words now that we know his sacrifice, and that of millions of other men, did nothing to prevent a second and worse war, to which youth went with the same faith.

There was a change of company in the carriage, the democrats being turned into a third-class carriage to make way for half a dozen officers of various grades and branches. The attitude of England was questioned and I was called upon to assure them of our friendship and co-operation. They seemed satisfied with my statements and expressed their belief that the British Fleet would make short work of the enemy at sea.

One of the officers took no part in the conversation. He was a handsome man of about forty years of age, in the uniform of an infantry regiment, and he sat in the corner of the carriage stroking his brown moustache in a thoughtful way. He had a fine gravity of face and once or twice when his eyes turned my way I saw an immense

[1] From *The Soul of the War,* by Philip Gibbs, 1915.

sadness in them. He fell asleep, but restlessly, awaking every now and
then with a deep sigh.

All through the night, at every station where we stopped, the platforms were crowded with mobilised men saying farewell to their
families, and all through the night, from wayside stations and villages,
there came one song sung by men's voices—the "Marseillaise" . . .

In Nancy I saw a number of German and Italian waiters carrying
bundles and saying farewell to their womenfolk. Many of them had
married French girls. Now they were going to their own countries and
they wept as they went away.

I had an interview with Colonel Duchesne, the Chief of Staff of a
French general named Foch, whose fame was not great at that time.
The Chief of Staff was charming and eloquent.

"The mobilisation of the French armies is going marvellously," he
said. "It is a wonderful demonstration of French national union—
L'Union Sacrée—in spite of all political differences. I could almost
weep at the thought of it. We who were so much divided in peace have
now closed our ranks in time of danger. The old spirit of France has
come back."

Some such words I noted down at the time.

He advised me to go back to Paris as it would require sanction from
headquarters for a foreign newspaper man to move about without
danger of arrest. It was, I guessed, a command, which I obeyed.

The British declaration of war was made after the invasion of
Belgium and the violation of "a scrap of paper", as the German Ambassador called the solemn pact to respect Belgian neutrality.

Sir Edward Grey, after desperate efforts to prevent war, abandoned
his last hope, and Mr. Asquith, Prime Minister, presented the ultimatum
to Germany which expired at midnight on August 2nd in the year of
fate 1914.

4

TOUT VA BIEN!

For a little while I stayed in Paris with other correspondents who were
awaiting their credentials as war correspondents with the British or
French Armies. Undoubtedly there would be a British Expeditionary
Force and our ambition was to be attached to it. But Lord Kitchener
at the War Office was resisting pressure from Fleet Street to grant these
credentials. He was hostile to war correspondents and thought them a
great nuisance. So did the French War Office. It was, it seemed, to be a

secret war, and the peoples who had given their sons and husbands were to know nothing about it, except by brief bulletins which told them nothing, or very little.

Four times a day we went to the French War Office on the left bank of the Seine for the official communiqués. In a big *salon* with gilded chairs and Empire mirrors, groups of French journalists sat about smoking cigarettes interminably, waiting for the next news with nervous impatience. In the room were three iron bedsteads and now and then a man would lie at full stretch on one of them as though exhausted by this nervous tension. When the news came it needed a map to make any sense of it, and then not much.

"*Tout va bien!*" said a French official cheerfully, and with obvious insincerity. What news leaked through in those days was not encouraging to France.

At the Ministry of Foreign Affairs on the Quai d'Orsay I had the honour of meeting M. Doumergue, Minister of War and for a time Prime Minister of France. It was here in this house, a few days before, that the German Ambassador spoke a few quiet words before asking for some papers which hurled millions of men against each other in mortal combat. I waited for a while in an antechamber, and presently a footman came through the velvet curtains and said: "*Monsieur le Président vous attend.*" I was taken into another room, a little *cabinet* overlooking a garden under old trees through which the sunlight filtered. A stone goddess smiled at me through the open windows. I saw her out of the corner of my eye as I bowed to M. Doumergue, who stretched out his hand to me with that expression of "*tout va bien!*" which masked the anxiety of every French statesman.

He made a set speech to which I listened politely.

"Civilisation itself depends upon the success of our arms. For years Germany has played the part of a bully, basing her policy upon brute force and thrusting her sword before the eyes of man."

After some rhetoric he said that German prisoners of war were in a bad way, starving when they fought. Where is Germany's boasted organisation? he asked. "*Ils ont bluffé tout le temps!*"

These last words were utter nonsense. Germany was already thrusting deep into France and Belgium. There was no bluff about the power, organisation, and professional training of the German Army.

"I am perfectly satisfied," he assured me, and his optimism cheered me, in spite of a little devil of doubt lurking in my brain.

5

BEHIND THE VEIL

It was hopeless, it seemed, waiting for official permission to see something of the war, and some of us decided to go in search of it during those early days, without permission. Massey, Tomlinson and I were nicknamed "The Three Musketeers" by some of our friends, and a very odd trio we made.

We had astonishing adventures which I wrote in detail in my book called *The Soul of the War*, published by Heinemann in 1915, having by some miracle passed the censor or slipped by him. After the war Tomlinson wrote his own reminiscences of those days in a wonderful book called *All Our Yesterdays*. Our trouble was to know where, and how far, to go to avoid falling into the hands of the enemy. The Uhlan cavalry were pushing into France and no one could tell us their where-abouts. We had some narrow escapes. French stationmasters were just as ignorant as we were, and issued tickets for trains which departed according to the time-table for stations where, suddenly, there would be a clatter of hoofs and a sputter of shooting, before French *cuirassiers* blew up a bridge, or the train travelled backwards with curses from the engine driver.

Hamilton Fyfe, who was on the roads with a Rolls-Royce, was actually caught by a patrol of Uhlans. The young officer who inter-rogated him ordered him to go down the road. But on the advice of a peasant he drove across a ploughed field and took cover in a wood before a considerable body of German cavalry came along. We met him that evening in some place I have forgotten.

Not all the severity of the French censorship, nor the rose-coloured communiqués issued by the French War Office in those days of August, could hide certain frightful facts. They were told by tides of refugees pouring down from the north, whom I and my two companions met on the roads and in the ports. They came with the news that Lille had surrendered, that the German tide was rolling upon Roubaix, Tourco-ing, and Cambrai, that the French were in hard retreat. The enemy's cavalry was spreading out in a great fan, with outposts of Uhlans riding into villages where old French peasants had not dreamed of being near the line of battle, until raising their heads from potato fields, or staring across the stacked corn, they had seen the pointed *casques* and the flash of sun on German carbines.

Tomlinson, Massey, and I, saw all the tragedy of the refugees in those first weeks of war. They were Belgians and French. It was as though a nation was in flight, as indeed it was, in the case of Belgium. Women of good class and of all classes, now tousled and unwashed, fought and struggled to get places on the trains going south with their families of children. Hundreds of thousands of peasants were crawling along the roads with their farm carts, or walking with perambulators and hand-carts piled high with household chattels. All that is recent and familiar in our minds during a second World War. Did it not all happen again? But this was the first time any eyes had seen it in Europe, and my eyes were stricken by the sight of those immense tides of human misery, the exhaustion of delicate women, the anguish of old people, the filth and hardships of these derelicts who had to sleep in the fields of the country-side or on the pavements of towns, who had lost their homes and knew not where to go with the enemy following close behind. They were parched in the hot sun of those August days. They were covered with white dust. They trudged on until the weakest and the oldest fell, and could go no farther. I saw it all happen again in 1940—Great God!, I saw it all happen again!

Our memory of these things is deadened to emotion now because of that second time of happening. The agony of the first World War, all its immense sum of human misery, all its courage and sacrifice, all its death, have been blotted out by the same scenes all over Europe, the even more appalling abominations which happened year after year, with piled up horror during these six recent years of war.

6

Retreat From Mons

There was as yet no news of the crossing of the British Expeditionary Force to France. In the French newspapers no word was said about the arrival of British troops on French soil. A hundred times or more in conversation with any French soldier the same question was asked—"*Vos soldats, où sont-ils, camarade?*"

Where were the English soldiers? It was always that question which sprang to their lips, and we could not answer until one day we came unexpectedly upon khaki-clad battalions marching and singing along the country roads near Boulogne. For the first time there rang out under the sky of France that foolish ballad which became, by a queer freak, the war song of the British army—"It's a long way to Tipperary", learnt with comical accent by French peasants and French girls who, in those early days, in the first fine thrill of enthusiasm, sang it emotion-ally as though it were a hymn. And because it was sung by those men of

ours in the Great War, as we called it, it carried over to their sons in the
second World War, and was sung in the factories by their daughters,
bending over their benches for six long years, cheered for half an hour or
so by "Music While You Work".

A trainload of Royal Engineers came into one of the stations where I
happened to be waiting (my memory of those days is filled with weary
hours on station platforms) and it was the first time I was able to talk
with British Tommies in France and to shout out "Good luck!" to
them. They were a gay, high-spirited crowd and my heart went out to
them with a kind of jingo emotion. Tomlinson found some fellows
from Limehouse and Wapping—old haunts of his—and talked to them
on the level. Massey had met their crowd many times in Aldershot.
While we talked to those on the platform others were shaving and
washing in the railway trucks, and chaffing the French civilians who
swarmed around, speaking excitedly in their own tongue shouting:
"*Vive l'Angleterre!*" and "*Bonne chance, camarades!*"

"Funny lingo, Bill!" said one of our Tommies. "But they mean well
with their Parley-voo."

When we left them Massey turned his head away to hide his emotion,
which I shared. Those boys meant England to us, and all its tradition,
and all its spirit, and we knew that in a little while they would have to
face gunfire and machine gunfire with, perhaps, heavy odds against
them.

Along the roads of France and in the port of Boulogne, the B.E.F.
was greeted with ecstasy by the French civilians who went mad at the
sight of them. In every village girls threw flowers at them, ran alongside
with gifts of fruit, and flung kisses at them in wayside stations when they
leaned out of the railway trucks. They had come to help save France,
these Tommies. Nothing in those first weeks was too good for them.
Afterwards ecstasy died down, when the British Army sprawled over
northern France, was billeted in a thousand villages, holding long lines
of communication. Ecstasy does not last, and French peasants and
farmers and shopkeepers thought how much money they could make
out of this swarming khaki-clad army. Quarrels arose about billeting.
Claims were presented for damage to crops or barns.

That was inevitable, but from first to last with few exceptions the
people of France paid tribute to the good behaviour of "Tommy", to his
unfailing good nature, and to his dogged courage during the frightful
years of ordeal.

Not many mornings after we had seen the arrival of the B.E.F.,
Tomlinson, Massey, and I, who were trying to pierce the veil of silence
behind which the war was hidden in those August days, came across
our first wounded. At a French junction there was a shout of command

in English, and I saw a body of men in khaki with Red Cross armlets run across a platform to an incoming train from the north, with stretchers and drinking bottles. I saw a number of Tommies with bandaged heads and limbs descending from the troop train. Some of them hung limp between their nurses. Their faces, so fresh when I had first seen them on their way, had become grey and muddy and streaked with blood. Their uniforms were torn and ragged.

I spoke to a sergeant in the R.F.A.

"We got it in the neck," he told me, and repeated those words as if they held all truth.

"Where?" I asked. He waved his wounded hand northwards and said: "Mons."

"Mons?" It was the first time I had heard of fighting there.

"You had to retreat?" I asked. The sergeant of the R.F.A. shrugged his shoulders.

"We gave 'em what for. Oh yes, they had to pay right enough, but they were too much for us. Came on like lice . . . swarming. . . . Couldn't kill enough. . . . Then we got it in the neck . . . Gord! I've never seen such work. South Africa?—No more than child's play to this 'ere game."

We were in retreat. Was it a rout?

Tomlinson, humourist and mystic, made an affirmation of faith.

"You always get the gloomy view from wounded men. I daresay it's not an easy thing to stop those blighters, but I've faith in the Justice of God. The Great Power ain't going to let Prussian militarism win out. It's going to be smashed because of its essential rottenness. It's all right, laddie!"

Massey with his leathery face and steel blue eyes was studying his map and working out military possibilities.

"Mons! I expect our next line of defence will be Le Cateau. If we're hard pressed we shall hear something about St. Quentin."

For the next fortnight we three comrades lived in a kind of nightmare which took us into the vortex of the French and British retreat, into the midst of confused movements of troops rushed up to various points of menace, and into the tide of wounded men who came streaming back from the fighting lines. French officers and men with bandaged heads and limbs told us their stories while their wounds were still wet. Women who had fled from little châteaux on the hillsides of France described to me the scenes which still made them pant like wild animals caught after a chase. We saw the unforgettable drama of the French army in retreat, blowing up bridges on the way. Out of a wild confusion of impressions, the tumult of these scenes, the inevitable contradictions and inconsistencies of men and women, drunk with the excitement of this time, we sorted out some of the clear threads of fact and saw the main outline of a grim picture.

With the help of Massey who spread out his maps on wayside banks, or on marble-topped tables outside fly-blown estaminets in village streets, we tracked out the line of the German advances and saw the peril of the French. Everywhere from east to west they were yielding before the terrific onslaught of the German legions, who came up in close formation, reckless of their losses, but always advancing over the bodies of the dead, with masses of light artillery against which the French gunners, in spite of their wonderful *soixante-quinze*—that quick-firing gun whose drum beat I heard so often in later years—could not hold their ground.

7

THE GERMAN TIDE

One night we saw the retreat of a French army through Amiens. Afterwards I was billeted in this city when I became an official correspondent of the British Armies. It was the last place of civilisation for masses of officers and men during the battles of the Somme. That night it was silent and full of fear. There had been a battle at Bapaume after a French retreat from Cambrai. It was announced as a French victory by the French Ministry of War. I did not see any sign of victory but only the retreat of the French forces engaged in the battle. It was a few minutes before midnight when they came back along the road to Amiens, crawling back slowly in a long dismal trail, with ambulance wagons loaded with wounded and dying, with many carts piled high with saddles and accoutrements upon which there lay, immobile, like men already dead, spent and exhausted soldiers.

They passed through crowds of silent people—the citizens of Amiens—who only whispered as they stared at this procession in the darkness. A *cuirassier* with his head bent upon his chest stumbled forward, leading a horse too weak and tired to bear him. There were many other men leading their poor beasts in this way: and infantry soldiers with bandaged heads clung to the back of carts and wagons, and seemed to be asleep as they shuffled by. The light from the roadside lamps gleamed upon blanched faces and glazed eyes, and flashed now and then into the caverns of canvas-covered carts where bandaged men lay huddled in the straw. Not a groan came from them. There was no shout of "*Vive la France!*" from the crowd of citizens. Everyone knew it was a retreat, and the knowledge was colder than the mist of night.

8

PARIS IN DANGER

As recorded in my book *The Soul of the War*, written shortly after this phase, I clung on at this time to a kind of hope that the German advance might be checked and turned. I think Tomlinson's mystical faith and Massey's level-headedness must have held me up, for as a rule I see the darker side of things and fear the worst. But I had come in touch also with many French soldiers who had a "hunch" and even more than that—a blind belief that all was well. They were retreating, yes, but they were leading the enemy into a death trap.

"We shall win," they said a thousand times. "In a little while they will get a hard knock. You will see."

"This spirit," I wrote in a newspaper despatch, "must win in the end. It is impossible that it should be beaten in the long run. And the splendour of this French courage, in the face of what looks like defeat, is equalled at least by the calm and dogged assurance of our English troops."

Nevertheless the enemy was bearing hard down on Paris and the British retreat from Mons was hard pressed. Tomlinson, Massey and I —three watchful ants in an upturned world—had an idea that Beauvais, lying directly between Amiens and Paris, would be the right place for us to get into touch with the French and British Armies barring the way to the capital. As a matter of fact it looked like the wrong place from all points of view when we arrived there, for the enemy's outposts were on the hills above and the noise of their guns was close.

As we approached the town we saw small parties of peasants coming down the road away from Beauvais. Some of them were in farm carts and they shouted to tired horses and put them to a stumbling gallop. They were driven on by fear. There were not many of them, and when they had passed the countryside was strangely and ominously quiet except for bursts of gunfire on the hills. The birds were singing and the fields were flooded with the golden light of the setting sun.

When we came into the town an intense silence brooded there among the narrow little streets below the Norman cathedral, a white jewel on the rising ground beyond. It was an abandoned town emptied of all its people. But presently I saw a human form. It was the figure of a French dragoon with his carbine slung behind his back. He was standing by the side of a number of bags. A little farther away were groups of soldiers at work by two bridges—one over a stream and one over a road. They were working very calmly and I could see what they were doing. They were mining the bridges to blow them up at a given signal. As I went farther I saw that the streets were strewn with broken bottles and littered with wire entanglements.

It was obvious that a very grim business was being done in Beauvais, and that the soldiers were waiting for something to happen.

At the railway station we quickly learnt the truth. The Germans under von Kluck were only a few miles away in great force. At any moment they might come down, smashing everything on their way. The stationmaster—brave old type—with two porters had decided to stay on to the last. "*Nous sommes ici*," he said, as though the Germans would have to reckon with them.

Massey, Tomlinson, and I, were also there, and we felt very lonely and unheroic. We should look silly when the Germans entered Beauvais.

Now the interest of this story is—if there is any interest in it—that von Kluck's army never entered Beauvais because of something which was happening elsewhere—the Miracle of the Marne—when Foch struck at the German centre and sent it reeling back, so that instead of taking Paris, which was within his grasp, von Kluck fell back to straighten his line, with British gunners harrying his flank. We three men alone in Beauvais, except for the stationmaster and his porters, escaped because of that turn of the tide which had come as far as the hills above Beauvais. But we knew nothing of that at the time.

The engine driver of a train which had been shunted into a siding decided to make a dash for it, and we were his only passengers, with the sound of German guns in our ears as we left Beauvais. Sitting in darkness, and shaken like peas in a pod because of defective brakes, we skirted the German Army, and by a twist in the line almost ran into enemy country, but we rushed through the night, and the engine driver laughed and put his oily hand to the salute when we stepped out to the platform of an unknown station.

"The Germans won't have us for dinner after all!" he said. "But it was a little risky all the same."

9

STRAGGLERS

The station was Creil, then the headquarters of Sir John French, our Commander-in-Chief. But they did not stay there long. News came that the Germans were drawing an iron net tighter round our men who were exhausted after Le Cateaux where their rifle fire had held up the enemy for a time. They had been without sleep for many nights. Many of them were like drunken men for the need of it.

I heard from one officer that he could not rally up his men for a step farther when they lay down for a rest. They lay like logs. It was in a French village and the officer saw a toy shop and went in and bought some toy drums and penny whistles. He gave them to a few of his men who were still standing, and told them to play the "British Grenadiers" or any old tune. This toy music roused the others. They formed up again and marched on again.

It was supposed to be a retirement in good order, this retreat from Mons, but it developed into a surging mass with many stragglers. Down the roads came a struggling tide of motor cars, motor cycles, and army wagons, carrying engineers, telegraphists and men of the Army Service Corps. Ambulances crammed with wounded joined this tide, while reports came in of a great encircling movement of German cavalry. The footsloggers had the worst of it, and there were times when German infantry were marching on parallel roads to them. Fortunately at this stage the enemy was almost as exhausted as we were, and were stumbling blindly on in the heat and dust of those August days.

In Creil the Commander-in-Chief had put up with his staff in a château. The Adjutant General, Macready, was in another château some distance away. Macready himself told me what happened to him.

"I was dictating a report," he said, "when one of my officers—Childs —looked up and said: 'It's rather quiet, isn't it?'

" 'All the better for getting on with the job,' I told him.

"Presently he looked up again and said: 'It's damn quiet!'

"This time I took notice. We went over to French's château to see what was happening. The place was deserted except for a sergeant who was scooping out a jam jar with his thumb. He said he had been left behind to clear up. The Commander-in-Chief had gone hours ago and had forgotten to notify me. . . . Everyone was damned sorry when I turned up again! They thought they had lost me for ever."

It was only by a near shave that the Adjutant General and his small staff escaped. They had only one rifle between them and when they drove away the Germans were in the woods all round them.

On the night of September 2nd, Tomlinson, Massey and I reached Paris and saw extraordinary scenes. It had become known during the day that German outposts had come as near as Senlis and Chantilly, and that Paris was no longer the seat of government. The French Ministries had stolen away, after a cabinet meeting in which there were both rage and tears. A wild exodus was made by the Parisians and the railway stations were great camps of fugitives, waiting to get out on any train leaving Paris for the South or the coast. Among the civilians were soldiers of many regiments who had lost touch with their units—Turcos and Zouaves, Chasseurs and infantry, English regulars and High-landers. Many of them were wounded and lay on the floor among crying babies and weary-eyed women. Many of them were drinking and drunk. They clinked glasses and pledged each other in French and English and broad Scots with a "Hell to the Kaiser!" and "*A bas Guillaume!*"

A Tommy with the accent of the Fulham Road stood on a chair, steadying himself by a firm grasp on the shoulder of a French *dragon* and made an incoherent speech in which he reviled the French troops as 'dirty dogs who ran away like mongrels', vowed that he would never have left England for such a bloody game if he had known the rights of it, and hoped Kitchener would break his blooming neck down the area of Buckingham Palace. The French soldiers greeted these sentiments with a "*Bravo, camarade!*" not understanding a word of them, and the drunkard swayed and fell across the marble topped table amid a crash of broken glass.

"Serves him damn well right!" said a sergeant to whom I had been talking. Like many other English soldiers who had been fighting for ten days in retreat, he had kept his head.

"We've been at it night and day," he said. "The only rest from fighting was when we were marching with the beggars after us."

He spoke of the German army as "a blighted nation on the move".

"You can't mow that down. We kill 'em and kill 'em and they still come on."

This man, severely wounded, was so much master of himself, so strong in commonsense that he was able to get the right perspective about the general situation.

"It's not right to say we've met with disaster. Truth's truth. We've suffered pretty badly, perhaps twelve per cent of a battalion knocked out. But what's that? You've got to expect it nowadays. 'Tain't a picnic! Besides, what if a battalion was cut up—wiped clean out if you like? That don't mean defeat. While one battalion suffered another got off light."

And by the words of that sergeant of the Essex regiment among others I was helped to see the truth of what had happened. He took the same view as many officers and men to whom I had spoken during the retreat and by weighing up the evidence, in the light of all I had seen and heard, and with the assistance of Tomlinson, whose wisdom shone right after a glass of *Dubonnet*, and of Massey, whose brain was never blurred by doubt, I was able to send a despatch, with theirs, to England which cheered it after a day of anguish amd dreadful rumours.

The B.E.F. was still in being, and still a formidable fighting force, after recovering from exhaustion, as von Kluck found to his cost when he fell back.

10

A Silent City

Paris was deserted when we entered it on September 2nd, that day when Foch turned the tide of battle on the Marne. A million and a half people had fled. It was so quiet that morning in Paris that the heels of my two companions and myself were loud on the deserted pavements. It was a city of shuttered shops, and barred windows, and deserted avenues.

A very old cab crawled into view with a knock-kneed horse which staggered aimlessly down the street, and with an old *cocher* who looked about him as though lost in this abandoned city. He started violently when we hailed him and stared at us as nightmare creatures in a bad dream after an absinthe orgy. I had to repeat an address three times before he came out of his coma.

"*Hôtel St. James et d'Albany. Ecoutez donc, mon vieux !*"

He clacked his whip with an awakening to life.

"Allez!" he shouted to his bag of bones.

Our arrival at the Hôtel St. James et d'Albany was a sensation. The concierge and his wife believed the Germans had come, when they heard the noise of our horse's hoofs clattering into the silence of their courtyard. The manager, and the assistant manager, and the head waiter, and the head waiter's wife, and the cook, greeted us with the surprise of people who behold an apparition.

"The hotel is shut up. Everybody has fled. We were expecting the Boches."

We had added a little item of history to that old mansion where the Duc de Noailles lived, where Lafayette was married, and where Marie Antoinette saw the faces of her friends when she passed on the way to the scaffold.

That day we had a deep emotion in our hearts because Paris was still untouched, and because, by some miracle, the enemy, so very close, had not yet tramped into its streets. How sharp and clear were all the buildings under that cloudless sky! Spears of light flashed from the brazen winged horses above Alexander's bridge, and the dome of the Invalides was a golden crown above a snow-white palace. The Seine poured in a burnished stream beneath the bridges, and far away the towers of Notre Dame were faintly pencilled on the blue screen of sky.

Tomlinson was silent, thinking tremendous things. It was when we passed the Palais des Beaux Arts that he stood still and raised two fingers, like a priest blessing a kneeling multitude, though it was lonely about us and we met only one human soul—a policeman on a bicycle along the whole way to the Arc de Triomphe.

"Thanks be to the Great Power," said Tomlinson, solemnly.

He was uplifted by a faith that Paris would never be entered by the heavy tramp of German legions, and his faith was justified that time. We did not have the gift of clairvoyance and see that twenty-six years later Paris would be entered and held for a long time by the same enemy, after the same kind of scenes that we had been witnessing—the flight of the French government, the wild stampede of refugees, the same agony and the same terror. If such a vision had come to us neither Tomlinson, nor I, nor Massey would have had the spirit to go through the years which lay ahead of us in that first World War, to see the enormous sacrifice of youth, to record the endurance of our men under ceaseless shell fire, with the daily toil of death—all wasted, all in vain, all for nothing, because the victory then was spoilt and betrayed.

We should have wept in Paris that day if we had known that.

11

DEAD AND WOUNDED

I had other adventures with Tomlinson and Massey which are still burnt into our minds. We followed up the retreat of von Kluck and saw the punishment inflicted on his flank by our British gunners and their French comrades.

We went into the little towns like Meaux and Crépy en Valois—so close to Paris!—and saw the damage done by the Germans and heard stories of their brutalities. Along the trail of retreat we saw the bodies of the dead being burnt like autumn leaves, because there was no time for burial and few men for the job.

Then we went to Dunkirk and watched the retreat of the Belgian Army from Antwerp, straggling back with hundreds of thousands of fugitives. They were broken regiments, marching disorderly for the most part, but here and there were little bodies of men keeping step with shouldered rifles. The municipal guards came by, shoulder to shoulder as on parade. They were followed by long convoys of mounted men on stumbling horses, with heaps of salvage piled on to dusty wagons; and

F

upon the top of them lay men exhausted to the point of death so that their heads flopped and lolled as the carts came jolting through the streets. Armoured cars with *mitrailleuses*, motor cars plugged by German bullets, forage carts and ambulances, struggled by in a tide of traffic between bodies of foot soldiers slouching along without any pride. Many of them were wounded and spattered with blood. It was a tragic sight and signified the downfall of the Belgian nation.

The people of Dunkirk were getting nervous. Would it be their turn next? Many of them asked me this question. An old woman who kept a little place where I lodged glanced at two pretty daughters who were having a flirtation with a young Belgian officer.

She grabbed me by the arm, closing the door of the kitchen with her other hand.

"Monsieur," she said, "I am an old fool of a woman and a coward, because I have those two beauties there. It is not of myself that I am afraid. If I could strangle a German and wring his neck I would let the rest of them cut me to pieces. But those girls of mine—those two roses —I can't let them take risks, you understand? Those Germans are a dirty race. Tell me, is it time for us to go?"

I advised her to go, though I had seen the strong fortifications round Dunkirk. But there was only a thin screen of men along the frontier and it looked as though the Belgian Army was doomed.

A few days later I saw that Belgians were still fighting on, on their own soil, miserable but heroic—the last and the best of them.

It was the chance meeting of a girl I knew which led me into the red-hot furnace of the war in Belgium, and separated me from my two comrades for a time. I saw her in Calais to which we had travelled down from Dunkirk and she raised her hand and said: "Hullo!" It was Lady Dorothy Feilding in whose big house at Newnham Paddox I had stayed with her family, as I have told. She had a gravity in her eyes which I had not seen in England, and yet afterwards I heard her laughter ring out when shells were bursting not far away. She was a dark-haired, dark-eyed girl, with a high-spirited look, which was borne out by all she did that time in Belgium, fearlessly, with a wonderful courage. She belonged, she told me, to a convoy of ambulances led by Dr. Munro. They were stationed in Furnes in an old convent where a hospital was just settling in. They would be looking after the wounded in the fighting zone which was pretty hot. She had a car with her and was just going back to Furnes.

"I should like to come with you," I told her.

She gave me a straight look and a smile.

"Hop in!" she said.

I had just time to grasp the hands of Tomlinson and Massey, to whom I was bound for ever in comradeship, and to grab at my kit stuffed into a suitcase, and then by the side of Dorothy Feilding drove towards a new adventure.

In Furnes, an old Flemish town with a medieval Town Hall, and old houses with overhanging gables, the staff of an English hospital with its nurses and its mobile column of ambulances had just arrived and were trying to sort themselves out. They had been in Antwerp, and following the line of the Belgian retreat, evacuating the wounded from towns and villages. I lent a hand with the unloading of packing cases, mattresses, and heaps of lint, helped by a golden-haired boy who had a preposterous sense of humour which kept me laughing. He turned out to be one of the surgeons and in the days that followed I saw him hard at work in the operating theatre from which he emerged hungry, tired, but still joking. That first evening darkness crept on, and as there was no gas in Furnes the old convent was unlighted. I made an expedition into the town and brought back, by extraordinary luck, a large number of tallow candles which I lit and stuck in their own grease on window ledges and tables. Many of them blew out, and in the corridors nurses rushing about to get some order out of chaos bumped into each other with little squeals of laughter. By some miracle a dinner was produced and served in the convent refectory, where the light of the candles gleamed on pictures of the Sacred Heart and the Madonna and Child. Among the company of doctors, and nurses, and ambulance drivers, was a young Belgian lieutenant named de Brocqueville, the son of the Belgian Prime Minister and the leader of the mobile column. He was a tall, thin, grave young man, with very courteous manners and, as I knew afterwards, great courage. There also was Dr. Munro—a fair-haired, blue-eyed man with whom afterwards I went into hot places in which he looked quite unperturbed, though always a little dreamy and absent-minded, as though thinking of some philosophical problem beyond this insanity of war.

Two girls in khaki were among us—Miss Chisholm and Mrs. Knocke. They were the companions of Dorothy Feilding, doing the same job and taking the same risks with the ambulance column.

From a window in the old convent I looked out that night upon the surrounding countryside. A few miles away was the line of battle. Shells were bursting, and rockets went up along the lines, and the darkness quivered with these lights and flashes. The noise of gunfire seemed very close. Before dawn some Belgian ambulances arrived loaded with wounded, and I helped to carry them out, straining my stomach by the weight of the stretchers. Some of them could stagger in on their feet with some aid, and for the first time I had round my neck the arm of a man who finds each footstep a torturing effort, and then suddenly sags with all his weight upon one. Several times I nearly let these soldiers fall. It was only by a kind of prayer that I could hold them up and guide them to the great room where stretchers were laid out for lack of beds. Already it was filled with that stench of blood and dirt and iodoform which afterwards used to sicken me as I helped to carry in the wounded or carry out the dead.

12

THE FLAMES OF DIXMUDE

I made many journeys with the flying column under the leadership of Lieutenant de Brocqueville and Dr. Munro. We went into Dixmude, sixteen kilometers away from Furnes. There were many wounded there, we were told. As we drove nearer to it, over a flat landscape through which went the Yser canal, we saw a line of villages and small towns. From each one of them rose separate columns of smoke, meeting in a pall overhead, and through the smoke came stabbing flashes of fire as German shells burst with thudding shocks of sound. This was the front line of battle.

I remember, as vividly as though it had happened yesterday, that scene in Dixmude into which we crawled at a slow pace with our ambulances. Outside the town we had been brought to a halt by a frightful barrier of dead horses and dead bodies. A German shell had burst into an ammunition convoy and blown it to bits. One Belgian soldier had been cut in half by a scythe of flying steel. Our tyres were splashed by pools of blood. Dixmude itself was being destroyed as we entered. Shells were smashing into its streets, and the cobble pavements were whipped by shrapnel bullets. A shop collapsed like a house of cards as we went down one of the narrow streets. A roof fell in, with a noise of falling tiles and masonry. Great gashes opened in the walls of skeleton houses which then toppled and fell. Many of the houses were burning and there was an acrid smell in our nostrils. Further in the town human figures appeared, rushing across a street and disappearing like rabbits fleeing to their burrows. They were Belgian soldiers.

We had been directed to the Town Hall, but that seemed impossible to reach owing to the débris.

"Try to take it," said Dr. Munro.

We took it, mounting over piles of rubble, and then getting to a spacious square, on one side of which was the Hôtel de Ville. It had already been gutted and was only the skeleton of a once splendid building. Even as we drew up to it I saw a great pillar lean forward and then topple down. A mass of masonry fell from the portico.

When we got down from the ambulances there were sharp cracks about us as bursts of shrapnel splashed down upon the Town Hall square. Dead soldiers lay outside and I glanced at them coldly. We were in search of the living.

Inside the ruined building were three living men, unwounded still, but expecting death at any moment.

A French officer stood there with two of his men. The officer's face was deadly white, and he told us in an unsteady voice that there were dead and wounded in a cellar below. A yard or so away from him lay a young French soldier of the Fusiliers Marins, a handsome young man with clear-cut features turned upwards to the gaping roof.

I wrote down my own sensations at that time. I did not expect to get out of this place alive. I felt rather numb and cold. I am sure that I was very frightened, but my hand was steady when I lit a cigarette. Here comes death, I thought. We shall all be blown to bits. It's very unpleasant. Death is horrible. . . . But I mustn't show that I'm afraid.

One of the men with me was an American journalist named Gleeson, who had given up journalism for this work of rescue with the ambulance column. I remember the clear-cut image of his face, calm and grave. It gave me more courage.

Presently when there was work to do, getting up the wounded and packing them into the ambulances—it took from fifteen to twenty minutes in the open square, with shells bursting close and that shrapnel whipping the cobblestones—I lost consciousness of myself.

I was in the first ambulance with Gleeson. We had a full load of wounded and it was time to get away. I put my head out and gave the order to the driver. As I did so a shrapnel bullet came past my head, struck a bit of iron work, and fell at my feet. I picked it up, and for some queer reason put it in my pocket, though God knows I was not looking for souvenirs.

So we started back through the blazing streets and out into the flat countryside.

"Very hot!" said the driver of the ambulance.

By an unfortunate accident Lieutenant de Brocqueville was left behind. Everybody thought he had gone with one of the ambulances, and we only discovered his absence when we returned to Furnes. Dr. Munro and I volunteered to go in search of him but we could not get into Dixmude again that night, and could not have found him if he had been there. It was burning fiercely. As it happened he turned up safely, having made his way out and found some means of transport back to Furnes.

We went into Dixmude again and rescued some more wounded.

The Germans were in one side of it and the Fusiliers Marins were holding out in the other half. On the way back one of the wounded—a French officer—groaned loudly and implored us not to jolt him. The driver of the ambulance said: "Poor devil!" and drove very slowly, though we went through shellfire.

Then there were Nieuport, and Pervyse, and other hot spots, as the German guns ranged out to many villages along an arc of twenty kilometers or so from Furnes where our ambulances searched for wounded. Lady Dorothy Feilding always had some morphia handy to give them a shot to ease their agony. We had picnic lunches on the wayside, and in spite of this close neighbourhood of war, and all the horror of mutilation and death as our daily harvest, there were always jokes and laughter over these *al fresco* meals. Strange that!—but very fortunate as one of the qualities of human nature, and particularly of English human nature, which will have its little joke even if Old Man Death is sweeping near with his scythe. At Nieuport-les-Bains—one of those little Belgian seaside places with coquettish little villas—my ambulance was parked one day. The Germans were shelling the place intermittently and all its inhabitants had fled—all but the proprietor of the Grand Hotel.

"I have no guests," he told me with grim humour. "In a little while I shall have no hotel." While we spoke a heavy shell came over and cut one of the coquettish little villas in half like a piece of cake.

13

NUNS AND NURSES

There was always some help wanted in the old convent at Furnes, especially after another convoy of wounded had arrived.

"Anybody lend a hand?" said one of the nurses. "I want a body carried away."

Another man and I volunteered.

"Be careful!" said the nurse. "He may break in half."

"Anyone care to bury an arm?" asked another nurse.

I buried the arm.

It was an ordeal for a man who once had felt faint at the sight of a cut finger. Leading in wounded men with their arms about my neck, or at one end of a stretcher, I had the greatest difficulty in not vomiting when I entered the great hall which had been turned into a hospital ward. The stench was frightful—the stench of gangrened wounds, and unwashed bodies, and iodoform, and dead bodies which had left a reek behind. Some of the wounded men vomited blood as they clung on to me, and my clothes were stained by it. But pity for them sustained me and I had a kind of pride in doing this job.

But it did not last very long as far as I was concerned. News came that the enemy had broken through the Belgian line and we were ordered to evacuate Furnes. It had to be done quickly and was a heavy task. I helped to pack up, and load the cars and ambulances with mattresses and hospital stores. Helped by the blue-eyed surgeon who refused to be flurried—he had done this kind of thing before—I lifted packing cases which would have paralysed me in time of peace, and became as black as a sweep after helping to lift the big stoves. The nuns of this old convent which had become a hospital pleaded to be taken with the nurses and doctors. They would help in the wards, they said, and do any kind of work if only they could escape falling into the hands of the Germans. I was put in charge of the nuns and nurses, and off we set for a town called Poperinghe which had no meaning for me then, though afterwards it was one of our bases and railheads in Flanders to which often I went in the years that followed. It was our great casualty clearing station during the battles round Ypres—too close to the railroad, so that the Germans reached out to it with their long-range guns and seldom gave it peace.

No arrangements had been made for billeting us, though the Queen of the Belgians had sent through a message. The mayor could not find a roof for our heads and I was commissioned to find some temporary abode for my nuns and nurses who were becoming ravenous with hunger. I discovered a low-class beer tavern into which I led my flock—or those who had not strayed away—and disposed the nuns round the bar with the Reverend Mother in the centre of them with a background of pewter pots and bottles of Dubonnet. The others crowded in anyhow and cried in a dreadful chorus, like Katharina in *The Taming of the Shrew*, "We want our supper!" Some of the nurses were getting out of hand and went on private adventures. One of them, a buxom and jolly creature who, as she confided to me, "didn't care a damn" had established friendly relations with a young naval officer and I had trouble in dragging her away from his engaging conversation.

Food! How could I get food for these hungry ladies? I had a brain wave. There were British troops in Poperinghe and therefore there would be rations for them somewhere. Out into the darkness I went, enquiring of passing Tommies where I could find the quartermaster, or some other officer in charge of supplies. None of them knew, but at last I found an officer who actually was in charge of the supply depot. Exaggerating my importance and authority I informed him that I was in charge of a hospital unit, which had had to evacuate Furnes because the enemy had broken through part of the Belgian line. Could he oblige me by providing rations for fifty-five doctors and nurses who were all devilish hungry? After some hesitation this young man turned to a sergeant and said: "Take this officer to the depot and see that he gets everything he wants." My car was loaded up with fifty-five army rations, enough to feed fifty-five starving persons for a week. I returned in triumph to the beer tavern and was received with cheers.

14

UNDER ARREST

During those early months of the war in 1914, over which I have lingered because they were my first impressions of war's agony and chaos, correspondents like myself who had gone out without credentials and, to be quite frank, against military orders laid down by Lord Kitchener himself, were liable to arrest at any moment and at any port. It was extraordinarily difficult to get our stuff back to Fleet Street, and in most cases it meant getting down to Boulogne or Calais, and asking a perfectly unknown person who was going to England to carry it with him. Several times, with an effrontery at which I am now abashed, I approached one of our King's Messengers, generally an elderly General, and after giving him a cheerful "Good morning!" asked him whether he would be good enough to take a letter addressed to the War Office. As a matter of fact it was addressed to the Editor of the *Daily Chronicle*, care of the War Office.

"Certainly, my dear fellow!" said these cheery old gentlemen.

This worked remarkably well, until I heard from Robert Donald, of the *Daily Chronicle*, that if I did it again very great trouble would ensue. Several times I had to make a dash for England myself returning the next day if possible, and always afraid that I should be put under arrest and forbidden to return.

There was, at this time, a conflict of opinion between the War Office and the Foreign Office regarding news from the Front. The War Office wanted to black out all but the official communiqués, and some innocuous articles by an official eye-witness. F. E. Smith at the Foreign Office, in charge of relations with the Press, was not at all in favour of this Secret War. I saw him several times during this period and he congratulated me on the stuff I was writing.

"We want more of it," he said. "I shan't cut out a word you've written. Those fellows at the War Office want a nice private war of their own, while our people are clamouring for news."

Lord Tyrell took the same line and asked me to come and see him whenever I came back from France and Belgium.

After one of these brief visits I missed the boat train upon which were Tomlinson and Massey. I missed it by a split second and my two friends, leaning out of a carriage window, saw the gates shut against me.

"This is horrible," I said to Agnes who had come, with my young son Anthony, to see me off.

She thought for a moment and then made a suggestion which startled me.

"Hire a special train!"

Such an idea would never have occurred to me. It was beyond my range of audacity.

It was Agnes who spoke to the stationmaster.

"How long would it take to get a special train?"

"No longer than the time it would take to pay over the money," he answered.

I ordered a special train, for the first and last time of my life. It was surprisingly cheap—£25, to the best of my recollection. In less than five minutes I was sitting in the carriage of a coach behind an engine which pulled out instantly and went in chase of the boat express. I was signalled all down the line. Men put their heads out of signal boxes to have a look at the fellow who was going to win the war. I arrived at Folkestone only a few seconds after the train I had missed. Tomlinson and Massey were walking down the platform. Suddenly they caught sight of me when I said "Hullo!" They could not believe their eyes. They had seen the gates shut against me. How had I worked this miracle?

It was a miracle in vain. There was no sea passage that morning owing to enemy submarines in the Channel. I had wasted my £25 which I had paid out of my own pocket. But years later when I told this story to Robert Donald he insisted upon my charging it to the office. He was filled with admiration for my audacity and zeal. But it was my wife's idea.

A friend in the War Office warned Donald that I was on Kitchener's black books, and that orders had been given for my arrest next time I appeared in France. I was desperate to get back, and to safeguard myself accepted an offer made to me by Sir Robert Hudson, to be his special representative in connexion with Red Cross work in France and Belgium. This would give me an opportunity of getting to the Front again, in a most respectable position with full credentials. I could still write articles on the war. A very impressive document was drawn up by Sir Robert Hudson. Big red seals were attached to it. No one, I thought, would challenge it. A sentry would present arms at the sight of it. I stepped on board the boat for Le Havre without anxiety. All was well now that I had these credentials.

All was well, until I reached the port of Havre. Three officers with the rank of lieutenant, whom afterwards I knew to be Scotland Yard men, came aboard and demanded to see my papers which they took away from me. The document from Sir Robert Hudson seemed to amuse them and they were not impressed.

I was arrested and taken into the presence of General Bruce Williams in command of the base at Havre. He was very violent in his language, and said harsh things about newspaper fellows who defied all orders, and wandered about the war zone smuggling back uncensored nonsense. He had already rounded up some of them and he had a good mind to have us all shot against a white wall. He refused to accept the document signed and sealed by Sir Robert Hudson. He put me under house arrest in the Hôtel Tortoni, in charge of six Scotland Yard men who had their headquarters there. Meanwhile, before receiving instructions what to do with me, General Bruce Williams forbade me all communication with Fleet Street or my family. This was pretty hot, and inwardly I cursed the distinguished General. For nearly a fortnight I kicked my heels about in the Hôtel Tortoni, standing drinks to the Scotland Yard men, who were very decent fellows, mostly Irish. One of them became quite a friend of mine and it was due to him that I succeeded in getting a letter to Robert Donald, explaining my plight. He took instant action and, by the influence of Lord Tyrell at the Foreign Office, I was liberated and allowed to return to England. The game was up, I thought. I had committed every crime against War Office orders. I should be barred as a war correspondent when Kitchener made up his mind to allow them out. So I believed, but in the early part of 1915 I was appointed one of the five men accredited as official war correspondents with the British Armies in the Field. All was forgiven.

15

COMRADES ALL

There were five of us at first, afterwards joined by Frederick Palmer of the Associated Press of America, who kept at bay all other American correspondents on the Western Front until the United States came into the war in 1917, when two others took his place and he became Chief Censor of the American Armies. Percival Phillips and I were permanent, but the others changed from time to time. Perry Robinson of *The Times* alternated every six months or so with the comrade of my first adventures in the war zone, H. M. Tomlinson, who also represented the *Daily News*. Captain Battersby of the *Morning Post* came out at first, but the nose-cap of a shell caught him in the stomach and later on caused his death. Two brothers who had been friends of my boyhood days—Valentine and Douglas Williams—were with us until some little time after the Battle of Loos, when they joined the Army as fighting soldiers—Valentine with a commission in the Irish Guards, Douglas in the artillery. Valentine was succeeded by Beach Thomas, who had been one of the wandering correspondents "on his own" in the early months of the war, and then was one of our crowd for three years or so. Douglas Williams, representing Reuters, of which his father had been Chief, was succeeded by Herbert Russell.

My fellow war correspondents were all remarkable characters. Valentine Williams had been correspondent in Berlin for a number of years—one of the best correspondents that Fleet Street had produced—and was full of knowledge about European affairs before the war when he had met all the big people and had learnt secret history behind the scenes. He is now better known for his novels.

Percival Phillips was of American birth and upbringing—his family were in Pittsburg where afterwards I met some of them—but he was the most English type one could imagine. He was tall, blue-eyed, and with pale gold hair, so good-looking with his charming smile that young women wilted away at the sight of him. He was so shy that he blushed in strange company, and always when he talked had a little nervous cough and laugh. He was a master journalist and had no ambition to be anything else. The noise of his typewriter was like machine gunfire. After a long day in the battle line he would come back to our head-quarters and write a couple of columns with incredible speed, every fact presented in an orderly way, perfectly fitted into his story, and meticulously accurate. He never made a mistake. He never exaggerated his impressions, or overcoloured his picture. That was crystal clear in his own mind and he reproduced it in his writing. I lived with him, worked with him, journeyed with him into many "unhealthy" places— that is to say into this hell of war—and I knew his integrity, his love of England—he had adopted England in his bones and blood—and his generosity as a fellow journalist. He never let a friend down.

I only had one quarrel with him. It was over a triviality in which I was to blame. For a few days we were not on speaking terms. For a few moments he desired to kill me, and I fingered my stick ready to strike him when he attacked. It was due to nerves on both sides—the nerve strain of two men so long together as daily recorders of enormous battles and daily witnesses of ruin, filth, heroism, and agony.

Of Tomlinson I have written before, but no one will ever write enough about Tomlinson, who should have had his Boswell. He is not one of the world's beauties. Unlike Percival Phillips he did not draw the fair sex towards him as by a magnet. He had the face of an ancient mariner, as indeed he should, having sailed the five seas in all manner of craft, and having gone to the upper reaches of the Amazon and heard the chatter of monkeys in primeval jungles. But no ancient mariner looked out of such eyes. In those brown eyes, during those years of war and afterwards, was an infinite sadness, because of world insanity and the martyrdom of man—the common helpless man caught in the machine—those boys in our armies who were being flung into the furnace fires. Tomlinson in his heart and soul was an Early Christian, but in his brain there was a grim yet ribald humour, which found expression either in Bible language or in the English of Stratford-atte-Bow.

He had dug deep into English prose and poetry. He used words like jewels, even in his newspaper articles. His books like *Sea and the Jungle* belong to the masterpieces of English literature. It was queer to find him a war correspondent. He looked odd in a front-line trench. At least he looked very odd to a sergeant of artillery, when one night he stood by a battery of field guns. It was before he was in uniform, and he wore a dirty old raincoat and a nondescript cap with a peak. The sergeant eyed him through the darkness.

" 'Oo the 'ell are you?" he asked.

Tomlinson told him that he was the correspondent of *The Times*.

"Bloody likely!" said the sergeant. "You come along with me."

Tomlinson was deaf. It gave him an advantage on a battlefield. He did not hear all the unpleasant noises. Once when we were going into Bapaume on the day of its capture he heard a shrill whistle which was that of a high velocity shell or other messenger of death.

Tomlinson put his hand to his ear and turned to Beach Thomas. "What bird is that?" he asked.

It was natural that he should turn to Beach Thomas, because that very tall man, whose puttees were always coming down, and who walked with a quick short step, was very knowledgeable about birds, and flowers, and trees, and all growing things, and the ways of nature day by day in English fields. This would come out like King Charles's head, in the work of Mr. Dick. It would come out even in the description of a battle scene when he would add a little colour to his picture by the vivid yellow of some weed which grew in the fields of Flanders or the Somme, or he would mention that he had heard some bird singing above the roar of guns. This was very disconcerting to our Tommies who read the *Daily Mail* and Beach Thomas's descriptions of battles in which they were fighting.

Beach Thomas, as I knew him in those days, was the sweetest-natured man—a scholar, once an athlete, a naturalist, and a lover of beauty and the game of life. He told me that he had wasted a terrible lot of time with little round balls, on tennis courts and golf courses and billiard tables. He hated the war and bled at the heart over the sacrifice of youth.

It was curious how many men we had in our little crowd who were very knowledgeable about birds and flowers and small beasts, and even big beasts. Perry Robinson of *The Times* was one of them. He was the oldest among us, a man getting on for sixty, with a remarkable resemblance to Rudyard Kipling.

He had a sturdy and dogged courage, but was a bit troublesome to his companions because of his dogmatic assertions on almost everything, which led to heated argument or exasperation. He disliked me cordially at first, but afterwards we became very good friends, and he said generous things about my writing for which I was grateful because he was never gentle in his criticism nor lavish in his praise.

We lived in billets or small châteaux behind the lines.

We lived with our censors and went about with them to dirty places. We always had to be with one of these officers when we visited brigade or battalion headquarters, or went into the trenches. It might have been intolerable and humiliating. It was at times humiliating, but not intolerable, because they were men of quality, with whom we became the best of friends. Three of them in the early days were Indian Civil Servants of the best type—Faunthorpe, Reynolds and Coldstream. Colonel Champion Faunthorpe was the most picturesque, and a Frenchman, or an American, would have rejoiced in him as the perfect Englishman in the romance of adventure, almost unbelievably perfect in the stage tradition. He was very tall, though he walked with a stoop. He had a hawklike profile, very finely cut, and wore a monocle in his right eye. He talked with a drawl—when he talked—though mostly he was silent, except when he delivered a sentence or two of cynical amusement at all the damn nonsense of the censorship and other idiocies. Beneath this mask he was a man of cool courage, fine intelligence—he had been a Judge in India—and what Jane Austen would have called "sensibility". He had shot eighty-two tigers and written several sonnets.

Sir Leonard Reynolds is still my friend, and we lunch together now and then and talk of those days. He has had a distinguished career in India where he used to ride out on elephants in Rajputana and receive a salute of guns at his appearance outside the gates, and had of course many native servants to do his bidding. In this last war when he retired to a manor house in Sussex he had to make his own bed and do the household chores. He and I walked into unpleasant places together during that first World War, and always he was a good companion.

Coldstream was a younger man, and, as once I wrote about him, "as neat as a new pin". But he had a hot temper and some fire of resentment burnt in him because of the restrictions and childishness of the censorship rules imposed upon him. He was glad to give it up shortly before the Battle of the Somme and go back to a job in India.

One of the censors who joined us later was C. E. Montague, the most brilliant leader writer and essayist on the *Manchester Guardian* before the war. Prematurely white-haired, he had dyed it when the war began and had enlisted in the ranks. He became a sergeant and then was dragged out of his battalion, made a captain, and appointed as censor to our little group. Always, or nearly always in those days when he was with us, he had a film over his eyes and a seal upon his lips. Extremely courteous, abominably brave—he liked being under shell fire!—and a ready smile in his very blue eyes, he seemed unguarded and open. But he was in hiding. Very rarely was it possible to get behind those blue eyes to the inner passion of the man—a smouldering fire—or to his philosophy of life. He was, as his writings prove, a man of fine and subtle humour, an idealist with a spiritual outlook on life, a severe critic of all sham and imposture, a realist in his revelation and loathing of war and its human degradation. All that comes out in his great book *Rough Justice* written after the war. But none of it, or very little, was revealed in his conversation with us. Only once or twice did he let me, who was often with him on the battlefields, get a glimpse of what was working deep below his surface manner. Once he told me that he had declared a kind of moratorium on Christian ethics during the war. It was impossible, he said, to reconcile war with the Christian ideal, but it was necessary to get on with its killing. One could get back to first principles afterwards, and resume one's ideals when the job had been done. I do not think I misinterpret him. Anyhow I think that is exactly what he did, conscientiously and sternly.

I remember his telling me once that when he was a sergeant in the front line he used to steal up at night to see if any sentry were asleep at his post, coming suddenly on a man from behind. It was a crime punishable by the death penalty, and it was at a time when his men were so exhausted that sleep crept over them as an almost irresistible narcotic. There was something rather horrible in this stealthy creeping up on men like that, however necessary it might be.

I remember being with him one day when we were watching an attack by our men on a line of trenches. We were close enough to see Germans running out of their dugouts and being shot as they emerged. Bunches of them were caught in the open by our shells, which plugged into the midst of them, blowing them to bits; and every time this happened Montague, sitting on a pile of sandbags above a captured trench, laughed in a goblin way.

"Montague," I said, turning to him, "you're ghoulish! Why do you laugh like that?"

"I laugh," he answered, "because every shell that bursts on the enemy brings the end of the war nearer."

That was a perfectly good answer, and yet somehow it seemed to me out of character—that goblin laughter—with a man of his high standard. I do not write this as a criticism of Montague who was a better and a wiser man than I have ever been, but as a glimpse of some oddity in him, some conflict within him, almost a touch of dual personality. His short stories, written after the war, are little masterpieces of satire and irony rather grim beneath their humour. *Rough Justice* to me is too painful in its description of a human soul dragged down to the depths by an inner weakness which could not stand the strain and horror of war. But it's a great book.

Closely associated with Montague in the organisation of our unit was a young officer named Captain Cadge. He had a curiously sulky way of speech which was entirely opposed to his real character, gentle, shy, and kind. To him we owed a great debt for his efficiency in running our mess, our cars, our batmen, and our way of life. It is to him, I think— because of his youth, perhaps—that Montague was most charming and revealing.

Certainly, at first, the military censorship and restrictions put upon us by General Macdonagh, Chief of Intelligence, were maddening. There was also hostility and suspicion about us in the minds of Generals, staff officers, and officers of the regular army, during the early period of our service. They thought we might be, and probably were, dirty dogs, who would give away their positions and write slush about them, and hand information to the enemy. Gradually we broke this down and won their confidence and their friendship, so that they were anxious for us to visit their battalions in the line and gave us the fullest possible in- formation during the course of a battle.

Our worst enemy for a time was Sir Douglas Haig. He had the old cavalry officers' prejudice against war correspondents and "writing fellows", and made no secret of it. When he became Commander-in- Chief he sent for us and said things which rankled. One of them was that "after all you are only writing for Mary Ann in the kitchen." The others remained silent in the presence of this tall, handsome, smiling man who could not see why we wanted more facilities to record the progress of the war.

I would not let him get away with that, and told him that it was not only for Mary Ann that we were writing, but for the whole nation and Empire, and that he could not conduct his war in secret, as though the people at home, whose sons and husbands were fighting and dying, had no concern in the matter. The spirit of the fighting men, and the driving power behind the armies, depended upon the support of the whole people and their continuing loyalties. I spoke hotly, as afterwards I was told by my companions, and I must have spoken with an intensity and sincerity because, strange as it seemed, Sir Douglas Haig's attitude entirely changed. He gave us everything we wanted, and more access to information than any war correspondents have had, even, I believe, in this last war when they have done so well and had the privilege of a war of movement and enormous drama. We were not only allowed to go to any part of the front at any time, wearing the green arm band of the Intelligence Corps, but orders were given to Army, Corps, Brigade, and battalion headquarters to show us the latest reports of any battle in progress coming in from all sources.

Haig did not regret his *volte face*. We won his confidence to such a degree that at his request Beach Thomas and I wrote for some time his weekly report on the progress of the war. When victory was won and he came riding with a bodyguard of Lancers to the Hohenzollern bridge across the Rhine it was to us that he made a speech after dismounting. In the course of it he thanked us for our long service and said: "Gentlemen you have behaved like men, and day by day have been the chroniclers of this war's history from first to last."

There was an idea, still lingering, that we war correspondents of the first World War were "spoon fed", and just wrote what we were told. That was partly due to an arrangement we made among ourselves. We decided that we would cut out all competition between ourselves. The war was too big for that, and we were too few. We decided to pool all our information, in order to give the fullest record of any action, reserving only to ourselves our personal impressions and experiences. We remained loyal to this self-imposed observance, and the nation gained by it, because instead of reading bits and pieces about a great battle they had before them a fairly full narrative from one end of the line to the other. We divided up, and one man went to one part of the line and another man to another, getting the reports from Corps or Brigade, personal narratives from officers and men, and the broad picture. Coming back, after an exhausting day, each man read out his notes as well as a great deal of vivid detail. Inevitably we told the same stories, though in very different style, and with our own personality stamped upon them. "Spoon fed!" said our critics. But it was the only workable system, and in my opinion was a good one, because our despatches, running sometimes into several columns, were not mere snippets of

"A LONG, LONG WAY TO TIPPERARY"

(By Edgar Lander)

PHILIP GIBBS WRITING HIS DESPATCHES DURING
THE BATTLES OF THE SOMME
(By Sir Muirhead Bone)

individual adventure or impressionism (though they contained all that) but were, with reasonable limitations of censorship—mostly self-imposed—accurate and detailed narratives of the day's fighting or the day's deadly routine of trench warfare.

The limitations of censorship were of course irritating. We could not give the figures of our losses—the immense sum of our casualties, as on the first day of the Somme battle. That was inevitable because that was what the enemy would have liked to know. But the worst handicap we had was the prohibition of naming individual units who had done the fighting. In many cases it was necessary, because to mention them would have been to give away our line of battle, and to let the enemy know what reserves we had called up. But time after time the enemy knew exactly what battalions he had in front of him. Had they not taken prisoners? Had they not seen their rush across No Man's Land? Had they not identified the badges on dead bodies caught on their wire? It was no satisfaction for the mothers of these boys or their wives and sisters to read of "North country troops" or "Lancashire lads" or men of our "Home County regiments". They wanted to know whether they were the 2nd Lancashire Fusiliers or the 8/10th Gordons, or the Londoners of the 56th Division. It was only after some time—months afterwards—that we could name the battalions. It created ill feeling against us, and because we were always allowed to mention Canadians and Australians when they were in action, people imagined that we were showing preference, and ignoring the poor old British Tommy who was doing by far the greatest share of fighting and the greatest share of dying. Over 80 per cent of the armies in the field were composed of English regiments who had the least credit, though not by our fault.

16

No Health Resorts

When we first went out as official correspondents Sir John French was Commander-in-Chief—a stocky, heavy-jowled, man who had his headquarters at St. Omer which for some reason he always called St. Omar. He had handled the retreat from Mons as well as might be. As a cavalry leader he was probably first class, but he was not a heaven-born Commander-in-Chief, especially when the war became fixed in trench lines. In his book *Liaison*, General Spears has given a tragic narrative of Sir John French's prejudice against our French allies and his complete lack of liaison with them during the most critical days.

That was now past history, and for a time after the first battle of

Ypres, when the Germans failed to get the Channel ports and break through our thin line, holding on desperately, the war on the Western Front settled down for a time in trenches and dugouts with a daily toll of casualties from guns, mortars, and hand-grenades.

We war correspondents studied the geography of our battle line, and became familiar with all its "unhealthy" places. We came to know the smell of the trenches with chloride of lime, and wet earth, and rats, and sodden sandbags. We saw how our men lived and died. We came to know the sound of the different shells. There was one at that time called "Whistling Percy"—a high velocity shell. Battersby of the *Morning Post* was hit in the stomach by its nose-cap and afterwards died. We walked through "Plug Street" wood, and learnt not to duck our heads when bullets came snapping through the trees. I had first been into Ypres before it became a heap of ruins, and when our men were buying picture postcards from the few civilians who remained. Now I came to know its ruins. The Cloth Hall was still standing, though already gutted, and the Cathedral had fallen into a mass of rubble, churned up over and over again by heavy shell fire which never ceased for three years. Once I took back with me a tiny leaded window with greenish glass from the Cloth Hall and an old key, which I still have in a cabinet as I write these words thirty years later.

To one small château on the edge of the Ypres salient, afterwards to be wiped off the map, I went with Reynolds one day. It was a summer day of 1915, and there were sheep browsing in the fields, and it all looked very peaceful under a blue sky with fleecy clouds. But peace was not there.

Suddenly shells plugged over among the sheep, searching obviously for the small château which we were approaching.

One shell hit it and there was a clatter of bricks and timber, and we saw two men running across the yard, scared but laughing. The officers of a battalion of Grenadiers were in the château. They were not too civil to us. It was before we had broken down prejudice.

Perhaps they thought our visit was ill timed, because the château was the target for a sudden *strafe* from German guns and they were taking cover—quite useless—under the heavy staircase. They regarded me as a strange and dangerous guest. The youngest subaltern, who was just a boy, grinned sheepishly. He didn't like being a target for German guns, as I could see. Nor did I, but had little comfort from this company. Suddenly after twenty minutes or so the gunfire switched off and one of the officers rode out on a beautiful mare, which certainly he ought not to have kept in such a place. He spoke to me coldly.

"I understand you want to see something of this neighbourhood?"

"Yes, sir."

"You may see more than you like," he said, icily. "Good day."

Much more friendly were some officers of the battalion with whom we took tea in a small house down the high street of a French village which was sinister and quiet. There was an unexploded shell in one of the walls of the room where we sat.

"This place is very unhealthy," said one of the officers. "I can't say I like being here. We expect to be blown to bits at any moment. Very unnerving. Have some more of that jam?"

Occasionally, in those early days, we went to the French Front on the Somme and the Marne, and up in Arras and other places held by our allies before we extended our line. I went with Valentine Williams to Neuville St. Vaast and Souchez, below the Vimy Ridge, when the French were there—places horrible in their menace and beastliness, and tragic in recent history. French youth, led by young cadets, had been mown down like grass at Souchez, which was now just a huddle of ruin. Valentine Williams and I went there with a French colonel, and met the very men whose martyrdom was recorded by their comrade Barbusse in his wonderful novel *Le Feu*. There was an outpost, four hundred yards or so along the road, lying directly under the Vimy Ridge.

"It is dangerous," said the French colonel, "because that road is under full observation of the enemy. Shall we go there, do you think?"

"Risk it." said Williams.

We risked it and nothing happened along that road. The outpost was commanded by a very young officer—a boy of eighteen or nineteen.

"How goes it?" asked the colonel.

The boy burst into tears.

"*Ce n'est pas bon, du tout, du tout,*" he sobbed.

No, it wasn't good at all. This little unit lay on wet straw. They were forbidden to light a fire because smoke instantly caused enemy action, and the guns were taped on them. They were wet through and miserable, and every day had heavy losses in dead and wounded.

The colonel was sympathetic and tried to comfort the young officer whose nerve had gone to pieces because of this horror about him.

I walked through the woods of Notre Dame de Lorette, running diagonally from the Vimy Ridge, and held by the French. It was spring, and but for bursts of gunfire these woods seemed enchanting because of the fresh green foliage glinting with sunlight. The French troops there were a good crowd, gay and gallant, and very comradely. With them under the greenwood tree we had lunch of beans followed by black coffee. One of their officers took me to the front line where trenches had been dug through the woods. As we talked late in the afternoon stabs of red light came through the glades as German guns fired, but a bird sang, regardless of this menace and that noise of guns. It was a nightingale, singing to its mate on Notre Dame de Lorette. I have never forgotten it.

I went down to the Marne and lunched at the headquarters of General Gouraud, the idol of his army and one of the heroes of France. He stood to receive us in the *salon* of an ancient château. One of the sleeves of his black tunic was empty and pinned across his chest. At his side gleamed a silver star. He had a spade beard and upturned moustache and looked like Henri IV of France, though his features were more finely cut. He took me to the threshold of the château from which we could see the line of the hills above the valley of the Marne.

"Here," he said, "a thousand years ago, and at this very spot, Charlemagne defeated the Huns, and here at this very place, a thousand years later, we have defeated them again."

17

Loos

There was no great action on the British Front for some months of 1915 until the Battle of Loos. We were building up our strength, sending out new divisions, "hardening" them in the forward trenches with rats and lice and filth and fire. The Battle of Loos was to be a big affair, with our best divisions engaged and two fresh ones—the twenty-first and twenty-fourth—in reserve. It was a dead secret that we were to use gas for the first time, as a retaliation for the German use of gas in the Ypres salient, when it had taken our men by surprise and sent them back reeling, choking and blinded.

The Black Watch and the Gordon Highlanders were among the first assault troops. The Brigade of Guards was put in later. It was an ugly stretch of landscape in the mining country of Lens. Slag heaps, and winching gear, called "*puits*", rose in black cones above the flat earth. They were all strongly fortified by the enemy. *Puit* 14 *bis* was a tough nut to crack, and beyond the village of Loos lay other mining villages and pits.

During the battle I went as far as the Loos Redoubt, and that was quite far enough, I thought. It was going into the heart of hell. I went with a distinguished companion. This was John Buchan, who was not a regular war correspondent but had come out for a short spell. We went up the communication trenches through which our men had advanced and from the Redoubt looked around upon a scene of desolation and death. The 8/10th Highlanders had already gone through the village of Loos, capturing many prisoners. A friend of mine was one of their officers, by name John Wood. He was one of the bravest men I have ever met, and was entirely regardless of shell fire and all such terrors, walking about a battlefield as though it were a field of buttercups and daisies, as more than once I saw in the fields of the Somme. On this day he commanded a company of Gordons and told me afterwards that he won the M.C. "for saving the lives of a bunch of German prisoners". That was his way of putting it. His men had their blood up. When the enemy emerged from cellars and machine-gun posts with their hands held high, the Gordons wanted to bayonet the lot. John Wood stood in front of them, and held his revolver, and threatened to shoot the first man who bayoneted these Germans who had surrendered. If he had lived through this war he might have regretted his act of mercy—though I don't think so, because in his heart was mercy and chivalry, though he was what his men called "a bonny fighter".

The Battle of Loos was a ghastly failure after the first smash through. The reserves—the two fresh divisions—were held too far back and came up too late. When they did arrive they were unprovided with maps, knew nothing about the ground, and made an awful mess of things, through no fault of their own. Our forward line, very thin now, received no support at the right time and was in no strength to resist enemy counterattacks. At the beginning of the battle a disaster occurred, because the gas we were using was blown back on to the Black Watch by a veering wind.

While this stage of the battle was in progress Valentine Williams and I went into the village of Choques which was crowded with prisoners and wounded soldiers. Suddenly a General came riding by on a white horse. He was unaccompanied, and we were startled to see Sir John French, the Commander-in-Chief. Every now and then he leant over his horse and questioned men who had come back lightly wounded from the battle.

Two of them were Highlanders and I heard his question to them: "How did it go with you, my men?"

"We could have gone straight through," answered one of them, "if we had had guid support, but it didna come!"

In Choques I saw the German prisoners. The officers were by no means downcast, and were arrogant young devils who mocked at my accent when I spoke to them in German. They taunted us for copying their own ideas—the one about gas, for example.—We always imitated them a bit too late, they said. The men were not like this. They lay about exhausted and cowed.

"How the devil can I handle these men?" asked one of our officers in charge of them. "I want to march them off to get their rations but I don't speak a word of German. Do any of you fellows know that horrible language?"

Valentine Williams spoke fluent German and came to the aid of this bewildered officer. I shall never forget the effect of his first harsh shout. "*Achtung!*"

Hundreds of men who had been lying on the ground sprang to their feet as though galvanised. Williams made a good job of it.

There was trouble about Sir John French. The Battle of Loos had resulted in heavy casualties. The Guards, among other battalions, had lost many of their best. It had not achieved anything, though even if perfectly handled it could not have achieved much at that stage of the war, and the over-optimism of our Generals and staff officers had been grotesque in view of the German strength against us at that time. High powers now were asking questions about this battle. Sir John French's own despatches were not forwarded by the War Office to the Press. One night an extraordinary incident happened at our small château. A young staff officer arrived and we were sworn to secrecy. He wanted one of us to go to England instantly and take the Commander-in-Chief's despatches direct to Fleet Street, cutting out Whitehall.

It was Valentine Williams who went.

A strange thing happened to me. I was invited to breakfast in Downing Street by Lloyd George. I had never had that honour before and wondered what it was about. Over the breakfast table with Mrs. Lloyd George at the coffee pot, the little great man was very genial, and it was not until the end of the meal that he turned to me gravely and said: "Tell me what you know about the Battle of Loos. I am a Cabinet Minister but we know nothing. Everything is held back from us by the military chiefs, and we have a right to know. How can we conduct this war if we are kept in ignorance?"

I told him what I knew, and he was distressed by my account.

Soon afterwards Sir John French was succeeded by Sir Douglas Haig.

18

LLOYD GEORGE IN FRANCE

The next time I saw Lloyd George was in Paris, and it led me into trouble.

I had gone to Paris on three days' leave before the Battles of the Somme when I met him in the Place de la Concorde, outside the Hôtel Crillon where he was staying.

"How are things going, sir?" I asked him.

He laughed and tapped me on the shoulder with a roll of papers which he had been carrying under his arm.

"I can tell you something that's going. Our wealth. Great Britain is the milch cow of Europe."

We were lending thousands of millions to our allies, none of whom ever paid us back, and the cost of the war was mounting to figures then fantastic, though we outdid them in the World War II, as everybody now knows to his own cost.

I dined with him that evening in the Hôtel Crillon and he asked me to do a small favour for him. It was to call on Monsieur Sembat, French Finance Minister, and invite him to breakfast at the Crillon on the following morning at nine o'clock. This seemed to me a fairly simple mission, though it was already getting late.

"I want to see him without fail," said Lloyd George. "Tell him it's important."

It was, I suppose, about ten o'clock that evening when I arrived outside Monsieur Sembat's door in a little square off Montmartre—an odd address, I thought, for a Finance Minister of France.

I rang the bell and waited. There was no answer.

A man in a neighbouring house put his head out of the window.

"Monsieur Sembat lives here?" I asked.

The man nodded.

I rang again and could hear the bell jangling. There was no answer. A woman put her head out a neighbouring window.

"It is the house of Monsieur Sembat!" she cried.

I rang again with a tug at the bell.

Two men came into the courtyard and stood staring at me.

I daresay I rang the bell six times. After all I was on an important mission. It might affect the course of the war. It might be an important date in history for England and France. But I could not go on ringing the bell and arousing Montmartre. Other people had come into the courtyard. Other windows were opened. A dog was barking.

I decided that Monsieur Sembat was not at home and that I had better call again early next morning.

So I did and after the first ring the door was opened with some violence by an old woman. She was furious.

"Was it you who kept ringing the bell last night?"

"I could get no answer," I told her. "It was very important."

"Monsieur Sembat was in bed," she said. "It was disgraceful to disturb him like that. It was an outrage."

"I wish to see him now," I said meekly. "I have a message from the Prime Minister of England."

"Monsieur Sembat is in his bath!" she said angrily. "He will not be disturbed. It is no time to call upon him."

"I will wait until he has finished his bath," I answered.

Reluctantly she led me into the house. A few minutes later, he appeared greatly to my relief, for time was creeping on to nine o'clock, when Lloyd George's breakfast appointment would begin.

Monsieur Sembat was in his dressing gown. He was also in a bad temper. When I gave him the Prime Minister's invitation he said it was an insult. Monsieur Lloyd George—he pronounced it "*Loyzhorzhe*"— had not called upon him and presented cards. Now Monsieur "*Loyzhorzhe*" invited him to breakfast at nine o'clock in the morning. It was outrageous. It was insulting. He utterly refused to accept such a slight.

I could not prevail upon him to ignore etiquette and to accept an invitation which might be of vital importance to France and to England.

"I refuse!" he answered raising his hand as though he would rather die than accept an invitation from a man who had not first presented cards upon him.

I returned to the Hôtel Crillon crestfallen. My diplomatic mission had been a failure. But after a word of regret Lloyd George was in the best of humour at the breakfast table.

I next met Lloyd George when he came up to General Headquarters and afterwards visited the Front.

There had been considerable hostility against him on the part of our Generals. They had called him "that damned little Welshman", and other epithets even more abusive. Now some of them almost fell over their swords to get near him. His talk, his wit, his candour, his range of knowledge, his marvellous gift of words, and the spirit in him, like a flame, fascinated them and held them spellbound. Once when a group surrounded him I was on the outside edge but he beckoned to me and made me sit next to him, though there were few chairs for the Generals. I felt abashed, but gratified by this friendly gesture. Lloyd George was generous to his friends.

During the Battles of the Somme he saw something of the war zone and once I saw him emerge from a dugout with a steel helmet on his head and his whitening hair curling underneath it. Two Tommies happened to be near, and one spoke to the other.

"Who's that old geyser, Bill?"

Bill stared over at Lloyd George.

"Gord!" he exclaimed. "That must be the Archbishop of Canterbury!"

19

STRANGE ENCOUNTERS

When we were weak in man-power—on the Western Front, before Kitchener's men were trained and sent out, Indian troops held part of our line about Givenchy and Estaires. It was a most unpleasant region of flat, ugly, country intersected by canals, and the Sikhs, and Gurkhas, and other Indian battalions, and cavalry, fought fiercely and heroically when the enemy tried to break their line. In this part of Flanders the winter climate was atrocious and, but for our dire need, the Indian troops ought never to have been sent there. Many times I met them looking dejected and ill in the dank mists and the waterlogged ground. Sometimes going about with Colonel Faunthorpe we would meet some of the Indian cavalry led by one of their princes. Colonel Faunthorpe would call out to them in Hindustani and greet one of the princes, who was, perhaps, an old friend with whom he had gone pig-sticking or tiger hunting.

Ranjitsinhji, whose bat at the Oval, and on other pitches, had been a flashing and conquering blade, and the wonder and delight of every man or boy who played the game, came out to France, and one afternoon visited our own mess in a small château. Someone suggested a game of cricket. We had no stumps and no bat, but by some miracle a ball was obtained. Three sticks made the wicket. A stout club served as a bat. "Ranji" went in and, marvel of marvels, was bowled first ball by Tomlinson, whose only cricket had been on a village green or on the brown grass of a London Common. It was a great moment in the life of Tomlinson. But after that in his second innings "Ranji" used his club like a sword. He had the eye of a hawk and by a touch of his club sent the ball in any direction he liked.

I have another memory of the Indians in France and Flanders. I went up to see the Ghurkas and the Commanding Officer thought it would be a good idea if I reviewed them.

When I reminded him that I was only a war correspondent, without military rank, he said that his men would take me for a prince and would be well pleased. So with stiff knees I walked down the ranks of those sturdy little men, who were ferocious fighters and the terror of the German troops into whose trenches they crept with curved knives.

In the late Spring of 1916 we could already see portents of things to come—battles on a bigger scale than anything that had yet happened. The new battalions were pouring out with the fine flower of our youth, full of high hopes for the "Great Push". New batteries of field guns were camouflaged behind the lines. Heavy guns—nine-point-twos and fifteen inches—poked their snouts out of barns, or were hidden like black monsters behind trees and hedges. Ammunition dumps were piled up along the roads from the coast. Casualty clearing stations were being prepared and enlarged in Poperinghe, and other places away back to Etaples—a grim reminder that there would be a tide of blood in those coming battles. But the "Great Push" was still some months ahead and the routine of trench warfare went on.

We had come to know all the peep-shows, and young officers took us up to their observation posts from which we could look across No Man's Land to the enemy's barbed wire and sandbagged trenches. A friend of ours who had been with our little crowd for a while—a tall moody man named Hesketh Prichard, the author of some good books and one of the finest shots in England, had become chief sniper of the British Army, and trained many men in that form of Red Indian warfare. He showed us all his tricks to induce a German to show himself for a second, just long enough for Hesketh Prichard or one of his merry men, with a telescopic sight on his rifle, to plug him through the head.

A grim game played on both sides and giving no joy to Prichard who hated the whole war as a dirty business.

I went into a strange village at the southern end of our line on the Somme which we had taken over from the French near Frise. We had taken over also for a time the French tradition of live-and-let-live between big battles.

The village of Curlu was actually beyond our front line, and was a kind of outpost in No Man's Land, within five hundred yards or so of another village held by the Germans in advance of their own front line. Between these two villages was a thicket of silver birches and willows, half of which belonged to us and half to the enemy. By tacit understanding on both sides neither of these villages was shelled.

Our officers—they were Loyal North Lancashires—used to go to bed every night in their pyjamas. I had a meal with them there, and they told me of this strange truce inherited from the French. They were all for it. One of them took me into the thicket, telling me not to speak or cough. Stealing through the trees, we came on two men dressed in green, with green veils over their faces, and green gloves. Beyond them if we had walked a few yards we should have bumped into German sentries. Occasionally there was an exchange of shots in the thicket, and sometimes a real fight, but as a rule there was peace and as a token of *pax* each side retired behind a wicket gate which was then shut. From the front line behind I looked into both villages and saw German soldiers moving about in theirs and—fantastically strange!—a woman wheeling a perambulator.

This state of things lasted until the Battles of the Somme when both villages were blown off the map.

20

NEAR TO ENEMY

I went to Arras for the first time when the French were holding it. Afterwards when we took this town over I came to know the Grand' Place and the Petite Place, and all its narrow streets, and churches, and inns, and shops, as though I had been born there, and I went there again, twenty-four years after, in World War II.

The French did not ask for trouble in Arras. It had a peaceful aspect when I saw it then. French soldiers were fishing in the canal as though they were on the banks of the Seine. French officers actually drove about in old one-horse *voitures*, still standing for hire outside a railway station where grass grew between the lines and where no train ever came.

Yet the Germans were very close—very near neighbours indeed. There was a house called the Maison Rouge into which I went with a French officer. It still stood at the beginning of the second World War. It was a red brick villa at the end of a street of little suburban-looking houses. It was furnished with plush-covered chairs, and there was an upright piano in the little *salon*. The only sign of enemy proximity was that the windows were heavily sandbagged.

My French officer spoke in whispers.

"We are now in the front line. The German line is exactly four and a half yards away. It runs through the little back gardens.

Four and a half yards seemed to be too close to be healthy. I looked through a chink between the sandbags, and saw the German wire and breast works—four and a half yards away!

"Doesn't anything happen?" I asked.

"Nothing much," I was told by the French officers. "Our lines are so close that the guns don't shell us, and the Germans only throw over stink-bombs, and other unpleasant things, just to show they are there. We don't believe in stirring up the hornet's nest."

When we took over Arras we stirred up all the hornets' nests. Our Generals did not believe in these gentlemanly agreements, and we pushed the enemy lines away from the back gardens and the surrounding fields long before the Battle of Arras which was a big and grim affair.

When we went to any part of the line the battalion commanders put our courage to the test by taking us into their most unhealthy spots, and if we felt afraid we had to wear a mask of courage, which is about the same thing as courage itself. For it is not easy to wear a valiant mask when enemy machine-guns are chattering across the road, or when one is a target for German gunfire.

I remember one General who played a grim jest with us. He was sitting outside his brigade headquarters when two of us arrived, and at that moment he received a flimsy with a message taken down by telephone.

"You're just in time, gentlemen," he said. "We're doing a lot of mining underneath the front line, and it's just a race between the German tunnellers and our own. We expect to fire a mine at any moment as the Germans are very near one of our galleries. You're just in time to see the fun."

I saw no fun in it whatever, but again we knew that our quality was being tested, and it was impossible to refuse this charming invitation. Down we went into the tunnels. It was in the neighbourhood of Hulluch, and the Canadian tunnellers showed us the works.

"You can hear the Germans," said one of them. "Like to listen to the swine?" I put on two ear phones and listened. I could hear Germans coughing and spitting and knocking out their pipes. I could hear them picking away on their side of the tunnel.

"It's just a question who blows up first," said the officer. "We've had most of the luck lately."

"How do you stand it?" I asked. "Isn't it a bit unnerving?"

He shrugged his shoulders.

"It's not really amusing!"

We spent an hour or so down those dark tunnels and were glad to get up top again before anything happened. But the tunnelling men had to stay down.

"Had a good time?" asked the General, smiling at us.

"Quite interesting, sir."

We hadn't shown the white feather and he was quite genial with us. We were breaking down the prejudice of the old tradition against "writing fellows". From the New Army, as it was called, we had no hostility from the beginning. They were glad to see us wherever they were. They were keen for us to give them a line. Some of them were "writing fellows" like ourselves. Some of them were poets, and playwrights, and artists, and Fleet Street men, and now were trained soldiers ready for the great attack. If they were officers they were proud of their men who were always a "topping crowd" and "the finest ever".

That was true of all of them. The New Army which assembled behind the Somme before July 1, 1916, was glorious in quality and spirit, and the best we had in youth. They had come from the public

schools and grammar schools of England and Scotland, from farmsteads where their forefathers had tilled the same fields through many
centuries, from old Cathedral towns so quiet round their closes, from
the highlands and lowlands beyond the border, from Welsh hills and
Irish counties, from the slums and mean streets of great cities. By
training and discipline they had become fit and strong—even the weedy
fellows from the slums. Many of the young officers had been in the
O.T.C. of Eton, and Harrow, and Winchester, and Rugby, and Marlborough, and Beaumont, and Stonyhurst, and Charterhouse. Many of
them were the sons of the "Old Quality", with names deep rooted in
English history and English soil. Most of them, from middle-class
homes, had the tradition which seeps into the English mind from
Shakespeare and Dickens, and the long roll call of history which
somehow enters the spirit of a nation. The Cockney, that sharp-witted
humourist of London, was in many battalions besides his own London
divisions—the 47th and 56th—and was always the salt of his crowd.
I once asked General Haldane—Scot of the Scots—which type made the
best soldier. Without hesitation he said: "The Cockney. You can't beat
him." The men of World War I were perhaps less educated than their
sons of World War II. Among them were rougher types, but they had, I
think, more gaiety from first to last, in spite of frightful hardship and
agonies and losses. Anyhow at the beginning they went forward to
battle with a spirit which was like a white flame, almost visible. So it
was with them at dawn on that day of July 1, when the Battles of the
Somme began.

21

ON THE SOMME

Before dawn, in the darkness, I stood with a mass of cavalry opposite
Fricourt. Haig as a cavalry man was obsessed with the idea that he
would break the German line and send his cavalry through. It was a
fantastic hope, ridiculed by the German High Command in their
report on the Battles of the Somme which afterwards we captured.

In front of us was not a line but a fortress position, twenty miles
deep, entrenched and fortified, defended by masses of machine-gun
posts and thousands of guns in a wide arc. No chance for cavalry!
But on that night they were massed behind the infantry. Among them
were the Indian cavalry, whose dark faces were illumined now and then
for a moment, when someone struck a match to light a cigarette. Before
dawn there was a great silence. We spoke to each other in whispers, if

we spoke. Then suddenly our guns opened out in a barrage of fire of colossal intensity. Never before, and I think never since, even in the second World War, had so many guns been massed behind any battle front. It was a rolling thunder of shell fire, and the earth vomited flame, and the sky was alight with bursting shells. It seemed as though nothing could live, not an ant, under that stupendous artillery storm. But Germans in their deep dugouts lived, and when our waves of men went over they were met by deadly machine-gun and mortar fire.

On that first day we took Fricourt and Montauban and made a loop round Mametz Wood, and broke through German fortified positions, but at terrible cost. I went into Fricourt soon after it had been taken and saw the dead lying there. Many Germans had been bayoneted in the first rush but even as they lay dead they had their hands slightly raised. I went down into their dugouts, marvellously built and strengthened with timber. In one a candle was still burning. In others German bodies lay huddled. Above ground I saw the fury of battle, and the sweep of German gunfire, and the ground vomiting up great columns of black earth and smoke. Prisoners, and walking wounded, were coming back and the stretcher bearers were busy. Our shells were screaming overhead, and far away on the right was the drum fire, the *rafale de la mort*, of the French *soixante-quinzes*. It was my first walk on the Somme battlefields, and for five months, on many days, I walked that way from Albert onwards towards Bapaume where every yard of soil had to be fought for by our men, from trench to trench, from one machine-gun post to another, from one underground redoubt to another, over barbed wire and sandbags, under storms of high explosives.

On the left up by Gommecourt, on the way to Thiépval, our men had got nowhere on the first day. They had been mown down like grass by German machine-gunners who, after our barrage had lifted, rushed out to meet our men in the open. Many of our best battalions were almost annihilated, and our casualties were terrible. But I remember that our young wounded officers could still find words of admiration for their enemy.

"The German machine-gunners were great," said one of them. "Came slap out into the open to meet us."

That was the sporting spirit of our youth *in excelsis*, and not yet dead before all chivalry died. It was not dead on the German side. The German General commanding at Gommecourt ordered a "cease fire" so that our wounded might be brought back, and their stretcher bearers helped.

A German doctor taken prisoner near La Boiselle stayed behind to look after our wounded in a dugout instead of going down to safety. I met him coming back across the battlefield next morning. One of our men was carrying his bag and I had a talk with him. He was a tall, heavy, man with a black beard, and he spoke good English.

"This war!" he said. "We go on killing each other to no purpose. It is a war against religion and against civilisation and I see no end to it."

A strange conversation on a battlefield, with the ruin of villages burning like torches, and shells bursting not far from where we stood!

Before those battles the landscape of the Somme had been that of a sweet and pleasant country, with wooded hills and little valleys along the river-beds up the Ancre and the Somme. Through field glasses one could see the German side of the picture—villages with little churches were still intact. I saw the château of Contalmaison when it still had a roof and chimney stacks. Then one morning I saw something happen to it. One of our gunner officers was going to open fire for the first time with a large-sized gun which he called "Grandma". It was a fifteen inch monster.

"My target is the château of Contalmaison," he told me. "You might see some good shooting if you go up that way."

I went up that way and heard a shell come travelling with the sound of an express train roaring through a tunnel. That little château of Contalmaison crumpled like a house of cards and flames burst from its wreckage.

I went into the village when it was still burning, and when the enemy was all around it. My companion that day was Muirhead Bone who had been sent out as a war artist with the rank of lieutenant. This was his first experience of standing in the flaming heart of war and it was heroic of him to bring out his sketch book and make rapid notes of the scene around him. Once when a shell burst near him his pencil went clean through his paper, but he carried on while our men were taking cover under bits of wall, and wounded were being carried off.

I spoke to one of the badly wounded German prisoners. He had been a cabinet maker in the Tottenham Court Road, and he told me of the appalling time he had had with his comrades under our bombard- ment. His company had only one dugout and they took turns in its shelter—twenty men at a time.

"Those who went outside were killed or wounded. Some of them had their heads blown off, and some of them had both legs torn off, and some of them their arms. But we went on taking turns in the hole, and those who went outside knew it was their turn to die, very likely. Then last night we knew the end was coming. Your guns began to fire all together—the dreadful *trommelfeuer*, as we call it, and the shells burst and smashed the earth about us. Then we heard your soldiers shouting. Presently two of them came down into our hole. They were two boys, and they had their pockets full of bombs. They had bombs in their hands also, and they seemed to wonder whether they would kill us. But we were all wounded and we cried 'Kamaraden!' and now we are prisoners—and I am thirsty!"

That was a story—one of hundreds—I heard from the German side during the Battles of the Somme, but there was no difference in that picture of hell on either side. Day after day, month after month, our men lay under shell fire directed against them by German batteries on a forty mile arc, and were sent forward to positions upon which the full fury of this artillery was switched. They went into the woods of death—Mametz Wood, Trones Wood, Delville Wood, and High Wood.

It was a total mistake of our generalship to attack these woods as isolated points. After our concentrated barrage fire our men could clear them of the enemy and hold them until they in turn suffered the heaviest casualties under the German bombardment. Delville Wood changed hands several times and earned the name of Devil's Wood from men who had endured its horror. I stood one day by the side of a Brigadier whose men were being relieved by another battalion in Delville Wood. They were Scots, and had gone in at battalion strength. Now they came out a small group, having lost most of their comrades. A piper played them out. He played the old lament "The Flowers o' the Forest", and the Brigadier had tears in his eyes, but raised his cap and cheered them as they marched by, haggard and weary.

By flinging human flesh—the flesh of our best youth—against flying steel—as the Russians did at Stalingrad in future history—by the sacrificial slaughter of our men who went "over the top" time and again to face the sweep of German fire, the enemy was forced back mile by mile. They smashed their way into German trenches and attacked machine-gun posts with Mills bombs, and stayed steady under German counterattacks and then crawled forward again. We broke his second fortress line up by the Bazentins, and took the Pozières Ridge, and High Ridge, and then stormed forward to Bapaume. The Germans fought with extreme courage and tenacity, especially the Prussians and Bavarians, but they could not hold up this massed assault behind tremendous barrage fire, and their losses in man-power were almost as high as ours.

In the end their High Command decided to retreat to the Hindenburg Line which had been prepared.

22

FEAR AND COURAGE

I came to know the geography, and the stench and the litter, and the landscape of the Somme battlefields during all that time. I listened to a thousand stories of individual heroism by men who had no heroics in their speech, no conceit about their own valour, and mostly spoke with humour even of the grimmest things.

It was always astonishing to me how quickly they recovered from exhaustion and the most harrowing ordeals of war. When they were taken out of the line, and brought back to billets beyond gun range, they smartened themselves up, after baths and delousing, and did not seem any the worse for their experience. One heard them singing and laughing and playing mouth organs. They kicked a football about, and played cards or dominoes in village estaminets. They did not look the same men who came out of the line with dragging feet, covered with mud, lousy and 'baked'. In twenty-four hours they were their old selves again, to all appearances, though in their minds something had happened. They knew that in a few days, or a few weeks, they would have to do it all over again, and that their chances of life were dwindling. They had four chances to one when they first went over the bags. Next time the odds would shorten.

The shell-shock cases were the worst to see and the worst to cure. At first shell-shock was regarded as damn nonsense and sheer cowardice by Generals who had not themselves witnessed its effects. They had not seen, as I did, strong, sturdy, men shaking with ague, mouthing like madmen, figures of dreadful terror, speechless and uncontrollable. It was a physical as well as a moral shock which had reduced them to this quivering state.

The concussion of heavy shells bursting close had torn their nervous system to rags and tatters. Curiously enough the bad cases of shell-shock were not among the nervy crowd, the thin, weedy, highly strung Cockneys, but among the stolid-looking countrymen who had come from the plough or the cowshed. But there were varying degrees of shell-shock and in some cases, no doubt, it was a case of blue funk. But blue funk itself is subject to psychological analysis. Who can say when the strain of ordeal by fire is at breaking point in one brain or another, or what is the dividing line between courage and cowardice? Courage, as I found myself, depends a good deal on physical fitness and unaccountable states of mind and body. One could be very brave one day and very nervous or "windy", as we used to say, the next. Discipline and self-

G

discipline helped one to wear the right kind of mask, to beat down the little devil of fear threatening to clutch at one, and to go through with the necessary amount of self-control. Only once, I think, did I give myself away. It was during those Battles of the Somme when I went up to a forward position. On the way I passed six boys of ours who had had their heads cut off by a shell bursting among them. "They've copped it all right!" remarked a young corporal, glancing at them carelessly. I don't know why that particular sight should have got hold of me so much. I had walked through heaps of dead. I had fallen and grasped bits of dead bodies in the mud. But when that day I reached a forward observation post, and listened to one of our gunner observers pointing out the German positions, I could feel my heart beating like a sledge-hammer and I was breathing with a strange rapidity. The gunner officer turned his head suddenly and looked at me.

"Feeling queer?" he asked. "Are you ill?"

"Quite all right," I told him, though I felt quite all wrong.

For a few seconds I had lost self-control, and had allowed horror to get the upper hand. God knows I had been frightened often enough. I knew the approach of fear. It generally arrived at the end of a road beyond which no transport was allowed in daylight, and when no men showed themselves above ground, and there was a sinister quietude until the enemy's guns opened up. A slight moisture came into the palms of one's hands. One's bodily heat dropped. One had, literally, cold feet. It did not happen always like this. Sometimes one didn't care a damn about shell fire however close, and the companionship of a crowd was very helpful. I always felt astonishingly safe in the trenches, though that was an illusion. It was the country behind the trenches, taped by enemy guns, that was most difficult to get through—Happy Valley on the Somme, the road from Dickebusch to Ypres, the way out of Albert with the golden Virgin and her Babe hanging upside down from the church tower, the road from Arras to Monchy, the ground below the Vimy Ridge, the way through the Menin Gate during the battle of Flanders.

Our officers were not afraid of saying they were afraid.

"I had the wind up to the nth degree." "It was all very alarming." "I was scared stiff." They said such things with a laugh, as though having said something funny.

I went into a town beyond Lillers (I have forgotten its name) on which a long range gun was being fired at intervals of two minutes. A sergeant-major stood outside the little Town Hall. I said "Good morning" to him, but he ignored the usual courtesies and spoke with a kind of anger.

"If anyone says he ain't afraid of shell fire he's a damn liar!"

I didn't contradict him. But it wasn't an absolute truth or a perfect platitude. Men were at least able to ignore that menace of death and mutilation, shutting off one part of their brain against it, and developing a fatalistic attitude which gave them a kind of indifference to "noises off", and the vomiting of black earth in their neighbourhood. When I went up to see my friends in the 8/10th Gordons, during the Battles of the Somme, I found a group of men playing cards in the open as calmly as though they were having a picnic on a Surrey Common or a Scottish heath.

A few yards away from them lay dead comrades not yet buried. Stray shells were bursting on their left and right and heavy long range shells came overhead with a noise like the rush of express trains. One of their officers, a handsome friend of mine named Captain Thom, afterwards in command of another battalion, had just been buried alive and dug out again. He was smoking a cigarette and greeted me with a laugh. "It's grand to see you up here!" he said. "Sorry I'm in such a mess."

Another friend of mine—it was John Wood who had been first into Loos—took me for a stroll over the battlefield. He was completely and utterly indifferent to chunks of flying steel whining about us, and to the columns of black earth raised by heavy crumps. In his company I felt strangely and admirably unafraid, so strong is the contagion of one man's courage—or one man's fear. If he had been nervy I should have been nervy. But he was as calm, and humorous, and talkative as though we were strolling across his golf course in Edinburgh.

These Gordons had nerves of steel, and I was glad to be with them that day though they were holding the front line with nothing between them and the enemy but some half dug trenches and machine-gun outposts. They were not frightened men, though they were cheek by jowl with old man Death.

"What is death?" asked a friend of mine, who came down to the Hôtel du Rhin in Amiens after a long spell in the line. He had been a journalist and was now with the 56th London Division. "One doesn't care a damn about death. It's the damned stupidity of our Generals that gets me down, and the damned discomfort, and the lack of sleep, and the general filth of things. I would like to kill a few staff officers. They just massacre our men by sending them against barbed wire which hasn't been cut, and into positions quite untenable when we've taken them at murderous cost."

He was very bitter with the High Command and all staff officers. So were most of our battalion officers. They blamed everything on the unfortunate Staff, even the weather, and I heard a thousand tales of inefficiency, bad organisation, lack of information about the enemy, unjustifiable attacks against positions which were death traps, troops ordered to hold trenches which were useless when held, lack of artillery support, confused orders which led to the wiping out of a company or battalion, no relief for men too long in the line—like the Irish, poor devils—and deliberate bloody murder by ferocious old gentlemen who had bacon and eggs for breakfast in far off châteaux, and ordered an attack over the telephone, between bites of buttered toast, at afternoon tea with young gentlemen in red tabs.

Some of this hostility of the battalion officers against the staff and the High Command seeped into my own mind. Doubtless many of those stories were true. Doubtless horrible mistakes were made. Beyond all doubt the first phase of the battles on the Somme taught many lessons, at fearful human cost, to generals and staffs, who lacked experience and always underestimated the enemy's strength, and the formidable power of his defence. In my book *Realities of War* (called *Now it May be Told* in the United States) I wrote harsh and critical things about staff officers and their generals. I am not going to withdraw them now; but time effaces much, including bitterness, and I find myself more tolerant, perhaps because I have forgotten or blurred the sharp edge of tragic things.

23

SOME OF OUR GENERALS

Few of our generals had a personality which was inspiring to the men. They were too far removed from the men who fought and died under their command. Sir Douglas Haig, as he was then, meant nothing to them as an individual, and they seldom or never saw him. He was always working at Headquarters. Occasionally he rode out with an escort of Lancers with fluttering pennons, extraordinarily handsome and noble-looking, but impassive and inexpressive, like his own wax effigy in Madame Tussaud's. I am sure that he was a shy man with a sensitive mind behind his handsome mask. After the war he devoted himself to the interests of the ex-service men, and he was anxious for a just and enduring peace.

The strain of the war killed him. There was, I believe, a nobility in him, but it was never revealed to the armies, and no man felt like dying for him, as the Old Guard did for Napoleon, or our men did for Wellington. To them he was a ghost beyond their reach or interest, and there was no thrill among them at the sight of him.

Very seldom, I think, he went to the forward positions, but once towards the end of the war I met him not far from the battle line at a place called Fontaine-Notre-Dame which was a bit of a mess.

"I should like the Guards to attack," he said.

It was in the old style of generalship, when Marlborough or Welling-ton watched the progress of a battle and gave orders on the field. For the kind of war he had to fight—that static trench war which had no room for strategy, and no chance for cavalry or sweeping movement—he was without genius. It was a question only of blasting a way through, and flinging human flesh against underground fortresses. He blasted his way through, but the cost was terrific to the lives of our youth; terrific also to the enemy in the blood bath of the Somme as they called it and the bogs of Passchendaele, the worst of all.

The only general who had some personal affection from the men was old Plumer commanding the Second Army. He was like a stage general played by Cyril Maude—a stout little old man, with a walrus moustache and a plump little belly below his belt. He was very active and went about his lines looking after the comfort of the men and talking to them in trenches and billets. I saw him once at a disadvantage when he had been dragged by his A.D.C. out of a shell hole full of mud into which he had stumbled. He took it with the greatest good humour. His Chief of Staff was General Harington, probably the best staff officer produced by us in the first World War. It was due to his brain that the Second Army obtained a reputation, well deserved, for good staff work during the big battles, and always he gave the credit to Plumer, with modesty and loyalty. The old Field Marshal had a tenderness of heart, not noticeable in some of the other generals, who did not turn a hair, or lose their appetite because of the fearful casualties which they regarded as part of "the game" of war. But once when my friend E. W. Hornung went to see him, after the death of his son, young Oscar Hornung of the Coldstream Guards, Plumer shook him by the hand silently, and turned away with tears in his eyes.

I always thought the most intellectual general we had was Haldane who commanded the Third Division—the Iron Division as it was called—and afterwards the Fourth Corps. He came quite often to our mess and we dined with him at his Headquarters. He was very critical of his fellow generals, and thereby was heartily disliked by them. But he was a man who had studied the history of war, who was a first-class commander in the field—though a hard one—and who raised his Division to the first rank of fighting quality. He was an intellectual soldier, and in conversation he was brilliant and amusing. He took a great fancy to old Tomlinson, philosopher, humourist, and master of English prose. Once when Tomlinson was ill, General Haldane, a haughty man of aristocratic type and mind, came and sat by his bedside. He had a fondness for children, and during the Battle of Arras I saw him surrounded by French boys and girls, explaining to them the progress of the battle with a map which he drew in the mud with his stick.

General Hunter Weston, known to the army as Hunter-Bunter, was a great character. As a Member of Parliament he had a flamboyant kind of oratory which overtook him in conversation in his mess, and I heard him giving tongue in this style on more than one occasion. He was, to the annoyance of his staff officers, a prodigious walker at a rapid pace, and I remember going for a walk with him and several of his officers when he set off as though for a wager. Being a fast walker myself I managed to keep up with him, but the others were left breathless. One story about him went the round of the army and is now a classic. Word reached the front line that he was coming along on a visit of inspection. It happened that one of the men was almost dead drunk, though how he succeeded in getting into this state in a front line trench, history does not relate. He had to be got out of the way, and was put on to a stretcher and covered with a blanket. While he was being carried down the trench Hunter-Bunter met him and, raising his hand to his brass hat, said in a solemn voice: "I salute the honoured dead."

The stretcher bearers passed on, while the 'honoured dead' poked his head up and asked in a loud voice: "What does the old geyser say?"

General Birdwood was successful in handling the Australians who were under his command. They took some handling, but this dapper general with a long record of service in India (quite the wrong type for them, one would have imagined), gained their confidence by his tact and good humour. When the first of them came to France from the Dardanelles they wore their big slouch hats, even in the front line until Birdwood issued an order for them to wear their steel helmets. I happened to go round the trenches with him when he came to see that this order had been obeyed. All the men we passed, save one, wore the regulation "tin hat". The exception emerged from a dugout. He also had a tin hat on his head but not of regulation type. It was a French chamber-pot of blue enamel. The General turned a blind eye to it until we had passed, when he gave a quiet laugh.

In the same line of trenches we came to a man outside a dugout who was stripped to the waist and washing himself from a billycan about the size of a pewter pot.

"Having a good wash, my man?" asked General Birdwood, genially.

"Yes," answered the man, "and I wish I was a blinking canary."

A very strong-willed and awkward-tempered old gentleman was General Harper, commanding the 51st Highland Division, and known as "Uncle Harper" by all his officers. He had white hair, and a ruddy face, and a fighting spirit, and was harshly intolerant of G.H.Q. and the orders that came down to him. He was bitterly critical among other

things of the attention and time given to bayonet practice, under the
blood-curdling training of Colonel Ronald Campbell, who tried to
inspire our unsadistic army with blood lust and red-eyed ferocity when
attacking sandbags in lieu of Germans. (Later he was put in charge of
restoring the *morale* and health of shell-shocked cases, whom he
treated with great humanity and imagination, getting them back from the
dark pit by teaching them games, and making them look after rabbits
and other animals.)

"Uncle Harper" thought this bayonet training was the damndest kind
of nonsense.

"No one has been killed by a bayonet in this war," he told me, "unless
he had his hands up first."

I fell into trouble by quoting that remark, which greatly annoyed
G.H.Q.

I often went to the Headquarters at Querrieux of General Rawlinson,
commanding the Fourth Army. He was always genial, amusing, and
quick in judgment. Generally in riding breeches, he would slap his
gaiters with his crop, and seemed to be enjoying the war in spite of its
appalling casualties and daily routine of death for masses of men.
Somehow I had a grudge against him for always being so cheerful, but I
admit now that generals cannot go about weeping and wailing because
of heavy losses to their men. But some of the losses might have been
avoided, and battalion officers who survived attacks, which they
thought were bloody and unnecessary murder, were very bitter against
these cheerful "old gentlemen"—they were younger than I am now—
who had sent another battalion to its doom for some bit of filthy trench
which could not be held when taken.

I came in touch with most of our generals of Army, Corps, Divisions,
and Brigades. They belonged, I thought, to a definite type and tradition.
Many of them were of the same physical mould, stolidly built, with grey-
blue eyes, square jaws, grey hair and clipped moustaches. They were
men of honour, courage, and ability, within a certain framework of
training and intelligence. Few of them stepped out of the frame
fastened upon them by Sandhurst and the Staff College, service in India,
and the professional interests of their Army career. They were not
arrogant, nor ill mannered. At their mess they were charming hosts.
They had nerves of steel and good digestions. There was a quality in
them, and a strength, which I admired and envied. But, with few
exceptions, they did not reveal any spark of genius, or any imagination,
or any touch of spirituality, or any eccentricity of mind. Faced by this
appalling trench warfare—it was really siege war—blasting a way
through fortress positions, they just slogged ahead, sending up more
guns, more human gun fodder, and more supplies, whatever the cost.

The Dominion generals were of a different type. They were not professional soldiers. They were ex-schoolmasters, or architects, or engineers. General Currie, commanding the Canadians, whom I saw many times, was undoubtedly a great general, cold, ruthless at times, but with unusual quality of brain and character. He reminded me of Oliver Cromwell—a heavily built, massive-faced man. I compared him to Cromwell in one of my despatches, and I think he was rather flattered by that comparison for he received me always after that with friendliness, and went out of his way to give me full information without reserve. During the battle for Cambrai in November of 1917 I sat with him for a time in his tent.

General Monash was another great general without professional training. He was an Australian Jew—tall, heavily built, big-nosed. It was to him, and to his acute brain and quick decision, that we owed the surprise attack by the Australians at Villers Bretonneux which saved Amiens, and perhaps the Channel ports, after the retreat of 1918, when disaster was very near and but little stood in the enemy's way that night. Some years after the war I met General Monash at a luncheon in the Guildhall. We came out together and I walked beside this tall hook-nosed man whose uniform was dangling with orders and decorations.

"Shall I fetch you a taxi-cab, sir?" I asked.

"No, my boy," he answered. "I shall go on the twopenny tube. I never waste money on taxis unless I can't help it."

In the twopenny tube we went, and this general who had helped to save an Empire sat among shop-girls, and labourers in corduroys, and city clerks, between the Mansion House and Victoria.

24

THE COMING OF THE TANKS

On September 15th during the Battles of the Somme, when we broke the enemy's third line of defence before Bapaume, the troops had a surprise which sent them forward cheering and laughing.

It was the greatest surprise of the war, and for once imagination came to the rescue of our flesh and blood. Many men claimed the honour of it. General Swinton established his claim and Winston Churchill was one of those to whom honour is due as patron if not part author.

It was the coming of the tanks which helped us to victory in the first World War and to a much greater degree in the second World War, though for a time we forgot and abandoned our original invention, and let the enemy—the same enemy—get away with it, and smash through Europe and North Africa before we put it into mass production.

It is impossible to revive the extraordinary thrill and amazement, the hilarious exultation with which these things were first seen on the fields of the Somme. It had been a secret, marvellously hidden. We war correspondents, who came to hear of most things in one way or another, had not heard a whisper about it until a few days before these strange things went into action. In my book *The Battles of the Somme* I record a conversation I had with an officer who first told me about them, and I reproduce it here because it brings back the mood, the astonishment, the wildly exaggerated hopes which this new invention caused in our minds in those first days.

"Like prehistoric monsters," said the officer. "You know, the old ichthyosaurus."

I told him he was pulling my leg.

"But it's a fact, man!"

He breathed hard and laughed in a queer way at some enormous comicality.

"They eat up houses and put the refuse under their bellies! Walk right over 'em!"

I knew this man to be a truthful and simple soul, and yet could not believe.

"They knock down trees like matchsticks," he said, staring at me with shining eyes. "They go clean through a wood."

"And anything else?" I asked, enjoying what I thought was a new sense of humour.

"Everything else," he said, earnestly. "They take ditches like kangaroos. They simply love shell craters. Laugh at 'em!"

It appeared also that they were proof against rifle bullets, machine-gun bullets, bombs and splinters. Just shrugged their shoulders and passed on. Nothing but a direct hit from a fair-sized shell could do them any harm.

"But what's the name of these mythical monsters?" I asked.

He said "Hush!"

Other people said "Hush!, Hush!" when the subject was alluded to in a remote way.

I came across a herd of them in a field, and like the countryman who first saw a giraffe, said "Hell! I don't believe it!" Then I sat down on the grass and laughed until the tears came into my eyes. (In war one has a funny sense of humour.) For they were monstrously comical, like toads of vast size emerging from the primeval slime in the twilight of the world's dawn.

When our soldiers first saw these strange creatures lolloping along the roads and over old battlefields, taking trenches on the way, they shouted and cheered wildly, and laughed for a day afterwards.

On that morning of September 15th, 1916, the front-line troops got out of their trenches laughing, and cheering, and shouting again because the tanks had gone ahead, and were scaring the Germans dreadfully while they moved over the enemy's trenches and poured out fire on every side. One of them called 'Crème de Menthe' had great adventures that day, capturing hundreds of prisoners, and treading down machine-gun posts, and striking terror into the enemy. A message came back: "Crème de Menthe is walking down the High Street of Flers with the British Army cheering behind."

We thought these tanks were going to win the war, and certainly they helped to do so, but there were too few of them, and the secret was let out before they were produced in large numbers. Nor were they so invulnerable as we had believed. A direct hit from a field gun would knock them out, and in our battle for Cambrai in November of 1917 I saw many of them destroyed and burnt out. But after the German retreat from the Somme battlefields it was the tanks who broke the Hindenburg Line, which the enemy had believed impregnable. They had dug a wide anti-tank ditch too broad for any tank to cross. But the commander of tanks, General Hugh Elles, had thought that out. He ordered the gathering of vast quantities of twigs and small branches of trees. They were tied into bundles like the Italian *fasces*. He called them '*fascines*'. Each tank advanced upon the Hindenburg Line with one of those bundles on its nose. By working a pulley the skipper could drop it into the ditch, then by nosing forward he could get the front part of the tank on to the bundle and so reach across. I followed up our troops that day across the Hindenburg Line.

The Germans had drawn their guns back and they had a big scare. I saw our tanks cruising about like a fleet in action, and was in one of them myself for the first but not the last time. The last time was when I took rides in our cavalry tanks during the first part of World War II when my skipper was a Lancer who had never driven much in tanks and did a bit of steeplechasing over ditches and hedges.

It was a very terrible and scandalous thing that at the beginning of World War II we only had old types and very few of them, while the Germans had been mass-producing them on modern lines.

25

BERNARD SHAW LOOKS AT WAR

Now and again visitors came to our mess from England. They were put up in a small château under the direction of a colonel who was a humorous fellow, though wisely he disguised his humour in their presence. They were trade union officials who came out to see the work behind the lines with a few glimpses of front-line conditions, foreign journalists and diplomats, now and again a prince or two, distinguished writers—including Mrs. Humphry Ward who wept at the sight of the soldiers—and people of high importance in one way or another. The humorous colonel had a small staff of conducting officers, who took these visitors as near the front line as advisable for their safety, and among them for a time was my friend Theodore Holland, self-entitled "Theo the Flower" who was a great source of joy to us because he played the piano like an angel and kept us laughing by his mordant and wicked wit.   The colonel treated all the visitors on the same level—princes, north country trade unionists, Spanish or Russian journalists, bishops, Japanese attachés—and sent them to bed punctually at ten o'clock so that he might settle down to a good game of bridge with his officers.

Among the visitors to our own mess one day was a little melancholy man, who was so shy when he appeared that he had his hands in his pockets and whistled like a schoolboy to keep up his courage. It was J. M. Barrie whom we were delighted and honoured to see. We anticipated a great evening with him, but he hardly uttered a word and we could not draw him out at all. Gloom settled upon us because of this disappointment, but Herbert Russell, of Reuter's, greatly daring, asked him to write something in an autograph album. Barrie thought long and earnestly and then wrote a cryptic sentence as follows:
Beware of a dark woman with a big appetite.
That was a pretty good effort in the middle of a world war!

Another distinguished man who came out was George Bernard Shaw. I had something to do with his coming because General Charteris, Chief of Intelligence, asked me one day if I could suggest some famous writer who would do a series of articles likely to be of value from a propaganda point of view. In a moment of wild inspiration I ventured to suggest Bernard Shaw, never thinking that the idea would be accepted, because he had written things about the war which were very shocking to traditional minds. To my deep surprise he arrived in due course, and I was appointed as his companion during his visit to the front. I enjoyed the experience, and every hour I spent with him increased my admiration for him as a man of genius, charm of personality, and high distinction. He said many wise and witty things, and I regret that I did not note them down. Of course he could not deny his instinctive urge to shock the conventional and rigid minds by remarks which seemed like blasphemy to their humourless way of thinking. I remember going with him to lunch with one of our generals, who hated having him as his guest and regarded him as next door to a traitor. Courtesy, however, overcame his ill-temper and he turned to Shaw, who was having a lively conversation with his A.D.C.'s and asked a polite question.

"Well, Mr. Shaw, when do you think this war will be over?"

"Well, General," said Bernard Shaw, "we are all anxious for an early and dishonourable peace."

This reduced the General to silence for quite a time but the A.D.C.'s set up a howl of mirth.

I discovered one well-kept secret of Bernard Shaw's. He was a lover of England, and deeply anxious for our victory. He gave this away one day when we were going up to the Vimy Ridge.

"Gibbs," he said, "one's thoughts about this war run on parallel lines which can never meet. The first is that all this is a degradation of humanity, a great insanity, and a crime against civilisation. It ought never to have happened. It's a dirty business for which we all ought to be ashamed. That's the first line of thought: and the second is that *We've got to beat the Boche!*"

Going into Arras one morning, when the enemy was sending over some shells into that city as usual, Bernard Shaw adjusted his steel hat and glanced at me humorously under his spidery eyebrows.

"If the Germans kill me to-day," he said, "they'll be a very ungrateful people."

He had in his mind, no doubt, all the plays which had been produced in Germany to the delight of their audiences, who were more enthusiastic in their admiration for Shaw than, for a long time, anyhow, the theatre-goers of England.

G.B.S. was very easy in his way with officers and men, and it was surprising what a lot of knowledge he had about the technical side of war, especially about aviation. He could talk to young pilots about planes, and wind pressure, and other technical subjects, in a way that astonished them and me. To whatever subject he turned his fine brain he became its master, or at least seized upon the essential facts and principles in a penetrating way. Upon his return to England he wrote a series of articles about his experiences in the war zone which maddened his critics even by his title which was "Joy riding at the Front".

They were, as I must admit, utterly useless as propaganda, and written with a flippancy which was not in the best of taste in the middle of a war which was taking a frightful toll of youth. But Shaw wanted again to shock people out of the slush and sentiment which had taken possession of many minds who evaded the grim realities. He shocked them all right.

26

GERMAN RETREAT

During the German retreat to the Hindenburg Line we followed up the enemy and liberated many villages. In some of them were civilians who came out of their cellars to greet us. Some of them rushed out to welcome a French battery on our right. The French sergeant-gunner was a black bearded man, and when some women tried to embrace him he put up his hand and said: "No embraces, if you please! I am the Abbé of Besançon." Then he lowered his hand and said: "After all I can forget that for the moment. Embrassez-moi, mesdemoiselles!"

I went over the liberated region with C. E. Montague. I remember one morning that we were ignorant of the enemy's whereabouts when we halted outside a bit of ruin where a solitary Tommy was smoking a cigarette.

"Can you tell me where the front line is?" asked Montague.

The Tommy took the cigarette from his mouth and straightened himself up.

"Well, sir," he answered, "I have an idea that I'm the front line."

The Germans had left behind them all sorts of booby traps and delayed-action shells, hidden in buildings like the Town Hall at Bapaume. There were ingenious booby traps in the abandoned dugouts, and one had to go down into any of these with great caution avoiding any trip wire, and not touching any innocent-looking thing such as a beer bottle, or an old tin of tobacco, until the experts had dealt with them. Ruthlessly they had cut down every fruit tree in little French orchards and blown up old churches in villages where they had long been billeted.

Once again as on the Somme we found that they were our masters in the building of dugouts. The cheery optimism of our generals always thought we were going forward, and therefore it was not worth while making ourselves comfortable and safe. We never made a dugout worthy of the name. But the Germans worked like beavers, and after their retreat I went down into dugouts, forty feet deep, connected with passages and with separate exits. Many of them were panelled, and had excellent bathrooms for the officers with a little gadget where the gentleman in the bath might place his cigar during his ablutions—a very German idea. They had a beer garden outside a nest of dugouts near Bray-sur-Somme, with "rustic" tables and chairs. It had long been the headquarters of a group of field artillery and they had made life very comfortable for themselves with some touch of art, like the carved and painted panels in the officers' mess, deep below the chalk hill.

That was at the end of 1916 and the beginning of 1917. Our losses since July 1st had been colossal, but the enemy's losses had also been terrific, and they had suffered infernal agonies under our barrage fire. I wrote a long account of the battle from the German point of view as I had pieced the picture together by talks with prisoners and by reading extracts from great numbers of letters found by our intelligence officers, and now and then by myself, in these abandoned dugouts. The German soldiers had described their agonies in letters to their families. All of them wrote about the blood bath of the Somme. There were terrible descriptions of their losses going up to the line and shelled all the way, and then in the front-line trenches and dugouts where they waited for death among the other dead. Thousands of them called the war the "Great Swindle". It is astonishing that such letters could pass the German field censors, as doubtless they would have done if we had not made them miss the post.

27

VIMY AND ARRAS

1917 was a year of terrific battles on the Western Front. On April 9th, after the retreat of the enemy to the Hindenburg Line, we began the Battle of Arras and the Vimy Ridge—the high ridge which for years had dominated our positions in the flat mining country below, where every road and ruined village was visible from the German observation posts, so that our troops and transport were always under heavy fire. Now that morning the Canadians and the Highland Brigade captured that sinister hill.

The preliminary bombardment had lasted for several days and I watched it on the night before the infantry attacked. It was a bitterly cold night with rain and sleet, and I was chilled to the marrow of my bones, but I was not too cold to be awed by the hellish vision I watched. Here is a bit of my description of it written at the time:

"The bombardment was now in full blast. It was a beautiful and devilish thing, and the beauty of it and not the evil of it put a spell upon one's senses. All our batteries, too many to count, were firing, and thousands of gun-flashes were winking and blinking from the hollows and hiding places, and all their shells were rushing through the sky as though flocks of great birds were in flight, and all were bursting over German positions, with long flames which rent the darkness and waved sword-blades of quivering light along the ridges. The earth opened and pools of red fire gushed out. Star shells burst magnificently, pouring down golden rain. Mines exploded east and west of Arras, and in a wide sweep from Vimy Ridge to Blangy southwards, and voluminous clouds, all bright with a glory of infernal fire, rolled up to the sky. The wind blew strongly across, beating back the noise of guns, but the air was all filled with the roar and the slamming knocks of single heavies and the drum fire of field-guns."

The Canadians took the main part of the Vimy Ridge starting from trenches (still preserved) only a few yards from those of the enemy. The Highlanders had stormed up from Arras to Tilloy and Telegraph Hill, with the English county regiments and the Royal Welsh Fusiliers of the 12th and 3rd Divisions. Among them were the Norfolks, Suffolks, Essex, Yorkshires, Sussex, Queen's, Buffs, and Royal West Kents. That morning early there were already three thousand prisoners coming down to the cages already prepared for them. They were glad to be captured and out of it, and were cheerful in spite of being numbed by the cold and snow. I talked with some of them, and they described the horrors of our bombardment. Some of them had been without food for four days, because our gunfire had boxed them in. The United States had come into the war that very day and I asked a German officer what he thought about it.

He shrugged his shoulders and said: "It is bad for us, but after all America can't send an army across the seas because of our submarines."

At this statement Canadian soldiers standing around laughed loudly.

"Don't you believe it, old sport!" said one of them. "We have come along to fight you and the Yankees will do the same!"

Next day I went up to see what was happening east of Arras, where our men were attacking towards the Scarpe. It was the ground where D'Artagnan and his Musketeers had fought in another battle for Arras against the Spaniards.

Many of our battalions had advanced upon the German positions from tunnels below ground. The city of Arras had been built out of the chalk below, and there were deep galleries and caverns right under the squares and streets, and reaching out, with the aid of our engineers, to the enemy's front line. I went with a battalion going up to the line and the scene in this underground world made a vivid impression on my mind so that I still remember it as though it were yesterday, though another war has happened since then. Lightly wounded men were coming down the narrow tunnels as the others were going up, and their steel helmets clinked as they passed each other. Along the way, lit by electricity, the tunnels opened out into high vaults, and masses of our men, held in reserve, were crowded in them, some of them sleeping, some of them playing cards in the light of candles stuck into beer bottles.

A few mornings later I stood under a hill called Monchy, not far beyond Arras, and saw something which few men have seen—a cavalry charge against a fortified position. It was not a pleasant sight and it is a black mark against Sir Douglas Haig who had ordered it, and against the cavalry generals who were glad to take this chance. It was magnificent but it was not war—in a war of machine-guns, aeroplanes and artillery. There were masses of horses and dismounted men in the fields below the hill, and I stood among them astonished, and wondering what was going to happen. The dead bodies of young troopers lay about on the ground over which I walked. One of our cavalry generals had been killed by a shell and his body was being brought back slowly, raised high above the heads of the stretcher bearers, as though a Roman officer were being carried back dead on his shield. The Headquarters staff of the cavalry with whom I talked for a few minutes, was in a shallow trench in the centre of the battlefield, sheltered by a few planks, useless against shell fire but keeping off the snow which fell in heavy wet flakes. They were studying their maps, and directing the action while reports were called down the funnel of a chimney by an officer who had been out on reconnaissance.

"It's villainously unhealthy round here," said this officer, who spoke to me after he had given his news to the cavalry general. He looked across to Monchy and said: "Old Fritz is putting up a stiff fight." At that moment a German crump fell close and we did not continue the conversation.

Some lightly wounded were coming back from the direction of Monchy with a slow dragging gait.

"How are things going?" I asked one of them, who was a young officer.

"Pretty hot!" he said, and then shivered and said: "But now I feel as cold as ice!"

Standing among the dismounted men, and that massed cavalry, I saw a speck in the sky which grew bigger.

A young cavalry officer was looking at it too and made a comment on it: "German. That fellow's eyes must be popping out of his head at the sight of us. He'll signal back to the guns, of course."

He was right and a few minutes later shells fell among us, killing men and horses.

Then the cavalry charged—they were the 10th Hussars, the Essex Yeomanry and the Blues.

I saw them riding at the gallop over Observation Ridge in a snow-storm which covered them with white mantles and crowned their steel helmets. They were slashed by machine-gun fire and men and horses fell, but they took the north side of Monchy and held it until they were relieved by English and Scottish troops who were shelled fiercely by German five-point-nines. The charge was an heroic adventure but very foolish.

28

GORDON HIGHLANDERS

During this Battle of Arras I kept in touch with my old friends of the 15th Scottish Division, and especially with the 8/10th Gordon High-landers who had adopted me as their particular scribe. (I believe I am the only Sassenach who has been made a member of the Gordon Highlanders' Association.) For the first time in our military history five battalions of the Gordon Highlanders had come together, and Captain (afterwards Colonel) Thom, whom I called the "Georgian gentleman" because of his side whiskers and eighteenth century look, was very keen to get their five pipers' bands to parade in the Grand' Place of Arras during the battle when they were relieved for a time from the fighting outside. I was an eye-witness of this picturesque scene and wished that some artist had been there to record it. The battle was still on. Arras was being shelled by long range guns. There were ruins in the Grand' Place, and recent shell holes through the roofs of these Spanish-built houses, but the five pipers' bands marched up and down, in full dress with pipeclayed gaiters, playing their wild music. From the deep cellars and vaults below the city some of the civilians, who had clung to this underground life, came up and watched with astonished eyes. The pipers wore steel helmets crowned with snow and the noise of gunfire mingled with their music.

The officers of the Gordons were billeted in an old mansion of Arras with panelled walls. I dined in their mess now and then, and one evening took with me a French officer who was a great friend of mine. In his honour they called in their pipers after dinner and the pipe-major and his men marched round the table of a smallish low-ceilinged room playing strenuously. My French friend Ruffin looked distressed, I noticed. Glancing at him to see how he was enjoying this music I saw

that he was very pale. A moment or two later he turned green, and then
went into a kind of swoon and had to be carried out. Afterwards he
described his agony as waves of frightful sound swept over him,
drowning his senses. "*C'était horrible!*" he cried. "*Epouvantable!*"
The Gordon Highlanders thought this faintness of a French officer was
a great tribute to the power of their pipes.

The Battle of Arras petered out into close and horrible fighting along
the Scarpe, but the capture of the Vimy Ridge was of high value
because it rid us at last of that enemy observation which had made life
intolerable for our men in the desolate mining region which reached up
to Lens.

29

THE MINES GO UP

The next big battle of the year was for another ridge which had been
held by the enemy with the same horrible vision upon all movements
below, for miles around places like Dickebusch and Vlamertinghe. It was
the model battle of the Western Front, with few casualties on our side and
overwhelming defeat for the enemy. For months we had been tunnelling
under their lines and had put immense stacks of high explosives into
their hillsides. I remember standing all night on a hill near by waiting
for those mines to go up just before dawn. It was a quiet night while
masses of our men were hidden in the folds of the earth for the big
attack, and for miles back our batteries were ready to protect them by
tremendous barrage fire. I stood near some of our forward batteries.
The enemy was sending over, in a desultory way, a lot of gas shells,
searching for these gun positions, and trying to stifle our gunners.
These shells made very little sound and exploded with a faint hiss. The
wind was blowing away from us and I did not trouble to put on my gas
mask. This night of June was warm and the wind was soft. Just before
dawn I heard cocks crowing in villages behind the lines. A glimmer
stole through the darkness. A faint imperceptible light crept into the
sky. It was 4.30 a.m.

Suddenly the earth quaked. A roaring noise rose up from it with tall
pillars of earth and flame. Men who had been standing up fell flat.
The earth tremor lasted for many seconds. Eleven mines had gone up
under the German trenches and fortified positions. Enormous craters
gaped open and in them were buried many German soldiers. It was
infernal, as though hell had been opened up. Then our batteries began
their drum fire and under cover of it our men moved forward. The
living enemy was stupefied and stunned. That morning with very light

losses we held the whole of the Wyghtschaete Ridge (we called it 'White-sheet') and the Messines Heights. With our troops I stood on the ridge looking back to our own country. It was startling to see how much the enemy had had observation of us. It was impossible to believe that we had been able to live, to move, to send up transport, to put men into billets, to conceal our batteries for three years, in that ghastly region of the low-lying ground, where we had put screens along the roads and notices saying: "Dust draws fire". A hundred times or more I had been one of the human ants in this army of ants passing through Dickebusch, and lucky to pass in daylight, with every cross-road taped by German guns, and every bit of rubble, which was once a village, shelled as a daily routine by German gunners.

30

THE KING AT THE FRONT

Not long after this battle the King came out and went to the summit of the 'Whitesheet' Ridge. I was one of those who went with Sir Douglas Haig and his generals. The Prince of Wales was in attendance on his father, and looked bored with the scene of war which was familiar to him. I had seen him many times in France and Flanders since he came out as a young lieutenant, and was with him on the Scherpenberg, the old Windmill Hill, when a miserable attack was made on the enemy trenches after they had been shelled by shrapnel—about as much use as spraying them with a watering can. In those days the young Prince had no definite job and used to go around on a "push-bike", hating to be recognised and saluted by officers of higher rank than himself. Afterwards he was attached to the Guards' Division and was always causing anxiety by joy-riding in dangerous places where death was near at hand.

To the King all this muck of war—the shell holes and craters and blown-in trenches and litter of battle—was new and interesting.

On his first visit he had been kept back from the Front, but now he insisted on seeing everything. To this day I don't know whether the enemy knew of his arrival and his visit to 'Whitesheet' Ridge. Probably the bunch of generals with him had been spotted by a reconnaissance aeroplane. Be that as it may, it was alarming when shells began to burst not far from where he stood. He was asked by his anxious guides to get back a bit, and when he was standing by one of the immense craters blown by the mines, the enemy guns lengthened their range. Three times this happened before the King, who was quite unperturbed, could be persuaded to leave the ridge.

He went up to the most northerly part of our line in Flanders and I was one of those who joined the party out of doors. The King was very chatty with the Guards' officers, but some of us turned cold when three German planes flew very low. Would they drop anything? If so the King might be killed as he raised his tea cup. We waited with intensity of apprehension while those black bats skimmed overhead. Nothing was dropped.

I was within a few yards of the King when he had his accident by his horse falling under him. It was outside Béthune where he was reviewing the Royal Flying Corps, drawn up in three bodies along the road. It was a soggy day and the ground was greasy. The King's horse had been rehearsed to stand steady under odd noises, but when, at the call of an officer, the R.F.C. raised their caps and cheered tremendously the horse was scared and reared three times. The King kept his seat perfectly, but at the third time the frightened horse slipped on the greasy ground and rolled right over on top of him. The generals were frightened. They dismounted and ran to the King's assistance but he lay there still for a few moments, until they lifted him up and carried him to his big motor car. A senior officer shouted to me: "Tell the men along the road not to cheer." The men further down the road had no notion that anything had happened to the King, and when his car passed them they cheered wildly before I could pass on the order. Inside the car lay the gravely injured man with his eyes shut, looking very ill.

Next day I was passing through the little town of Lillers when an ambulance came slowly by. None of the soldiers coming out of the *estaminets* gave a glance at it. Ambulances carrying wounded Tommies, with muddy boots turned up towards the tail, were too common a sight in Lillers behind the line in Flanders. In that ambulance lay George V, King and Emperor. The Prince of Wales was very scared, I was told.

On one of his visits to France, the King received us war correspondents. It was the first time I had shaken hands with him, and I was astonished by the small size of the hand he held out to me. He said a few words to each of us, and Beach Thomas, who was rather nervous, dropped a brick in answer to one of his questions by saying how long he had been in what he called "this fancy dress", meaning his uniform. At that time it had no badges, and no Sam Browne belt which afterwards we wore. The King looked puzzled at this description but made no comment. I think he was shy of us and did not quite know what manner of men we were.

31

THE HELL OF FLANDERS

After the Battle of Messines and 'Whitesheet' we came to the awful battles of Flanders in July when our armies fought their way to Passchendaele through mud and blood.

The original plan of attack had been made in conjunction with the French who, under General Nivelle, the new Commander-in-Chief, were about to launch a general offensive in the Champagne. The idea was that the French would smash through the Germans, drawing in their reserves, and that we should then strike in Flanders against a weakened enemy. We had had a good deal of trouble with the French, who complained that we were not pulling our weight and not holding an adequate length of line. They did not take into consideration the enormous numbers of men required by the British Navy and those fighting on other fronts.

Under political pressure Sir Douglas Haig had lengthened his line north and south of St. Quentin, and now agreed to make the big attack on Passchendaele. But the Nivelle offensive, much advertised in advance, openly talked about for months in French restaurants and *estaminets*, and perfectly well known to the enemy, was a complete and disastrous failure.

The German High Command had made full preparations to meet this attack, and they withdrew all their heavy guns beyond the range of the French artillery. When the French troops advanced, including many Senegalese and other coloured regiments, they found only a thin screen of rearguards, who fell back before them until the French lost the protection of their guns and were out in the blue. Then the German artillery opened up and massacred the human waves of assault. It was a tragic blow to French hopes and French morale. Their losses since the beginning of the war had been stupendous. French youth had been mown down. Verdun had been an heroic holocaust. 400,000 Frenchmen had died in that shambles. Now after Nivelle's failure they were sick unto death of this endless drain of blood. There was trouble not only behind the political scene but also in the Army itself. Some of the French divisions mutinied. The combined plan upon which Sir Douglas Haig had reckoned had broken down, but he decided to go forward with the battles in Flanders, into which the Germans were now able to fling their reserves. Instead of meeting a weakened enemy we had to meet, during the next five months, the main strength of the German Army on the Western Front, reinforced by divisions withdrawn from Russia after the collapse of the Russian Armies.

Every man of ours who fought on the way to Passchendaele agreed that those battles in Flanders were the most awful, the most bloody, and the most hellish. The condition of the ground, out from Ypres and beyond the Menin Gate, was partly the cause of the misery and the filth. Heavy rains fell, and made one great bog in which every shell crater was a deep pool. There were thousands of shell craters. Our guns had made them, and German gunfire, slashing our troops, made thousands more, linking them together so that they were like lakes in some places, filled with slimy water and dead bodies. Our batteries, as often I saw them, were stuck in the mud up to the axles of the wheels. Our infantry had to advance heavily laden with their kit, and with arms and hand-grenades and entrenching tools—like pack animals—along slimy duckboards on which it was hard to keep a footing, especially at night when the battalions were moved under cover of darkness. If a man were wounded and fell off a duckboard into one of those water-logged craters, he drowned in it.

The line of the attack was out from the ghost city of Ypres—now a vast heap of rubble, with a few rags and tatters of towers and churches —from the river Lys to Bosignhe. It was the country beyond the Ypres Salient which we had held for three years. The enemy had all the rising ground, not very steep in this flat landscape but high enough to give him observation from the Pilkem Ridge and St. Julien, and further on at Stirling Castle and the Frezenberg Redoubt, west of Zonnebeke, and Inverness Copse and Glencorse Wood—terrible names in English history because so many of our best were killed in taking them. Little rivers—tributaries of the Lys—intersected this country until shell fire spread their waters and made new quagmires. On August 1st the heavy rainstorms began after our men had advanced to the Pilkem Ridge and the northern curve of the Ypres Salient, and it veiled the battlefields in a dense mist, keeping our airmen down and making artillery co-operation with the infantry very difficult. It continued like this for several days and this August was like the foulest weather of a Flemish winter.

I wrote at the time: "It is all rain and mud and blood and beastliness." Nevertheless, somehow or other, our wonderful men—English, Scottish, Irish, and my old friends the Gordons among them—captured important ground, and crawled forward, and smashed their way through German pill-boxes and machine-gun posts and breastworks, under the flail of enemy shell fire. Wounded men struggled back yard by yard, plastered with mud, so that they looked like the dead who had crawled out of their graves, until the stretcher bearers carried them back, sometimes falling with their burdens in the bogs. They even took great numbers of prisoners, dazed by our barrage fire, cold to the bones, many of them with cramp in the stomach and very miserable. I talked with some of them and they were utterly downcast, saying that the German victories in Russia only lengthened the time of misery and that in the end Germany was bound to be beaten.

I told this story, day by day, in great detail, filled with the anecdotes and narratives of men who had such stuff in them that they defied all these horrors of hell and did heroic things, without knowing their heroism or making any fuss about it. I heard those men talk in field dressing stations where they warmed their cold bodies by the braziers, and on the way to Glencorse Wood and Passchendaele, where I saw that hideous landscape like Dante's vision of the Inferno, and met German prisoners coming back—some of them carrying our wounded—and stood by the side of our field batteries talking to young gunner officers, and met the remnants of battalions and friends of mine, just relieved from forward positions, and heard how things had gone with them. I heard some of these narratives when I myself was cold and had to steel my courage, such as it was, against the noise of heavy shells round about, and against the sight of dead bodies and bits of dead bodies, and the menace and stench of death in that countryside which war had blasted and made hideous.

Reading my own chronicles of these battles—I have glanced at them recently while writing this book—I am staggered by the stuff that is in them. It is the real stuff as told to me at the time by these men of ours—their own authentic words, their own spirit coming through them. It is a record and revelation of those terrible days, and of those wonderful men, and of all their agony and endurance, and of all their courage and quality. I say so not because I wrote it—God forbid—but because here is the raw material of history, told by the men who made it whilst their wounds were still open and while the mud and blood were still upon them. Such stories could never be recaptured.

32

FORGOTTEN HEROES

It is astonishing to me, now that I have reread these despatches, that the censors passed them. They hide nothing of the horror and nothing of the agony.

Sir Douglas Haig, when he was Field Marshal Lord Haig after the war, told a friend of mine that I had exaggerated these things and that conditions were not so bad as all that. He had not seen the things that I had seen. But another man said in a book that the war correspondents had slurred over all this. "Gibbs," he wrote in his memoirs, "lied merrily like the rest of them." That man was David Lloyd George, then Prime Minister.

It was grossly untrue, as my printed words prove in page after page of my book *The Struggle in Flanders* which is a reprint of my newspaper despatches. And it was very unjust of Lloyd George of all men to make this accusation against me.

I remember an evening I spent with him at the end of 1917 when he listened to a speech I made at a private table, and was profoundly distressed by it. Robert Donald, my editor, arranged a dinner for me at which the Prime Minister and General Smuts and perhaps a dozen other men were guests. I had made no preparation or notes for a speech, but when I was called upon I was determined that I would tell this company about the ordeal and sufferings of our men, without any glorification of war and without any false heroics. I spoke that evening for the men who had crawled out of the mud. I spoke for our young battalion officers who went forward in these frightful battles. I told the naked truth that night, and it had such an effect upon the Prime Minister that he wept and had to leave the room for a little while. It was a proof of his humanity and his sensitive heart and mind, not smothered by power and politics. But he never forgave anyone who attacked him, as afterwards he told me, and after the war I attacked him about his support of the Black and Tans.

My account of Passchendaele is one long narrative of gallant men flung into the Slough of Despond.

"In these recent battles," I wrote at the time, "home troops and overseas troops have been mixed together in the mud of the battlefields, and they come down together out of the shell fire to field dressing stations, waiting to have their wounds dressed and telling their tales of the fighting. There is no difference there between them. They are all figures carved out of the same clay, with faces and hands of the tint of clay, like men risen out of wet graves. A moist steam rises from them as they group round the braziers and they know each other—Australian and English lads, Scot and Welsh, Irish, New Zealanders—as comrades who have taken the same risks, suffered the same things, escaped death by the same kind of miracle. They talk in low voices. There is no bragging among them, no wailing, no excited talk. Quietly they tell each other of the things that happened to them, and of the things they saw, and it is the naked truth."

It was the naked truth of what that kind of war meant to the individual man, with his individual mind and body, and his secret solitary fears and agony.

I heard men talk of these things after an attack round Poelcapelle when they had hardly been able to drag their limbs forward because of the quagmire. I met them when they came back with holes in their legs, and mangled arms, and bloody heads. They had been fit and well in going up. How they managed to get back was a mystery to themselves. They crawled through the slime and then fell into deep pits of water with slippery sides so that they could hardly get out. They lay down in the mud and believed they must die, but some spark of vitality kept alive in them and a great desire for life goaded them to make another effort to go another hundred yards. They cried out to one another, and heard other cries around them, but were alone in some mud track of these battlefields with a great loneliness of soul.

One man told me of his night like that, told me with strange smiling eyes that lightened up the mud mask of his face under a steel hat which was like an earthenware pot on his head. All the time he opened and shut his hands, very slowly and carefully, and looked at them as things separate from himself. They had become quite dead and white in the night, and were now getting back to life and touch from the warmth of a brazier over which he crouched.

"I crawled a thousand yards or so," he said, "and thought I was finished. I had no more strength than a boy, and my head was all queer and dizzy like, so that I had uncommon strange thoughts, and saw things that weren't there. The shells kept coming near me, and the noise of them shook inside my head so that it went funny. For a long time while I lay there I thought I had my chums all round me, and that made me feel kind of comfortable. I thought I could see them in the mud all round, with just their shoulders showing humped up, and the tops of their packs covered in mud. I spoke to them sometimes and said 'Is that you, Alf?', or 'Come a bit nearer, mate.' It didn't worry me at first because they didn't answer. I thought they were tired. But presently something told me I was all wrong. Those were mud heaps, not men. Then I felt frightened because I was alone. It was a great queer kind of fear that got hold of me, and I sat up and then began to crawl again, just to get into touch with company, and I went on till daylight came, and I saw other men crawling out of shell holes, and some of them walking and holding on to each other. So we got back together."

That is only one tale from many hundreds I heard, as recorded in my despatches; and with my own eyes I saw the terror, and the misery, and the human endurance of our men on that ghastly road to Passchendaele, through Glencorse Wood and Inverness Copse.

33

Private Conversation

I was sent for by Lord Milner at the Foreign Office, and wondered why he wanted to see me. It appeared that he would be glad of my views about the morale of the British armies on the Western Front. What was going on in the minds of the officers and men? Were they getting tired of the war after such fearful casualties? Did I think they would stand for a negotiated peace?

That last question staggered me. I dared not answer it. How could I speak for the whole British Army? I knew how tired they were, how desperate many of them were for an ending of this war. I knew the padre of a London division who had had to lie to them to keep them from despair. He had heard, he told them, "on the highest authority" that the war would be over in three months. Three months passed three times, and he had to invent new reasons why the war would come to an end very quickly. I had heard the bitterness of battalion officers against the generals who had sent their men into the slaughter fields, not caring a damn, they thought, about their losses. I had seen the horror of Passchendaele, and knew the exhaustion of the men who had gone that way. To Lord Milner I told some of this but did not care to generalise or make inaccurate deductions from individual minds. I did not allow my own feelings to colour my report, but balanced it, as I was bound to, by other things I had heard from officers and men. "We've got to finish the job whatever the cost." "We'll have to beat the Boche somehow." The Dominion troops were, I thought, resolute to go on until Jerry was down.

When I returned to France I was sent for by a British general in liaison with the French. Colonel Neville Lytton went with me, and was astonished and peeved when he was asked to leave me alone with the general, outside whose door a sentry was placed so that our conversation should not be interrupted.

I was asked almost exactly the same questions as those put to me by Lord Milner. Would the British Army stand for a negotiated peace? That was the gist of it. Again I was cautious and non-committal. I gave this general careful answers desiring to keep to the strict line of truth as far as I knew it. An enormous responsibility was being given to me as an interpreter of men's minds. I did not wish to interpret them falsely, or go beyond my own experience and knowledge. We talked for something like an hour.

"Thank you," said the general, rising at last.

I rejoined Neville Lytton and when we had left the Headquarters he asked me what was the subject of our conversation.

"I'm very sorry," I said, "but I am pledged to secrecy."

"But my dear fellow," answered Lytton, "I am your superior officer. I have a right to ask you."

I kept mum. These conversations seemed to show that the Government and our Supreme Command were thinking of the possibility of a negotiated peace, after so much slaughter, and mutinies in the French Army. They had more knowledge than I had about German strength and the reserves of our man-power. I only knew that I would have thanked God at that time for any kind of peace which would stop the slaughter of our young men, provided the Germans would clear out of Belgium and France and get back to their own frontiers. That for them would be defeat. That for us would be victory enough. What was the use of a victory, I thought, which would be over the graves of our noblest and best? The German soldiers called this war the "Great Swindle". They had more sense of comradeship with our own men, who were killing them and whom they killed, than with their war lords and generals. In the first Christmas of the war they had come out into No Man's Land, fraternising with our men as ours with them, until both sides were sternly ordered back. But supposing they had not obeyed the order? Supposing all along the lines men had met each other in No Man's Land and said: "This killing of each other is senseless. Let's stop it. Let's all go home." It might have stopped war for ever in Europe and created a new comradeship across the frontiers. Now after this second World War, and all the cruelties and atrocities of Nazi-trained thugs, no such ideas are within bounds of ordinary imagination, but in the first World War it was still possible to believe that the mass of German people were human like ourselves, that their men could be our friends as well as our enemies, and that they might revolt against the militarism of their war lords and establish a comradeship with us.

But the military caste, and the Junkers, and the German Foreign Office, and Big Industry, would have seen to it that no such ideas would prevail, and would have crushed such a revolution from below with bloody ruthlessness, unless they had been overwhelmed by it and strung up to the lamp-posts. But the Germans have no genius for revolution, and prefer obedience, and order, and authority, even if it leads to their doom, as now it has.

34

MILITARY HOSPITAL

An epidemic called trench fever (it was a near relation, I believe, of typhus), spread through the army in 1917 and attacked great numbers of men. It came on with extreme suddenness. Gunners riding along on their hairies fell off their saddles. Men in the trenches suddenly felt "queer" and then staggered and collapsed in a state of high fever.

I fell a victim to this disease, and alarmed my friends one night by giving deep sepulchral groans and calling out all sorts of nonsense in bad French and worse German. In the morning I was taken to the Canadian hospital in Amiens. When I was carried in on a stretcher an orderly felt my pulse and seemed to be baffled.

"Gee!" he exclaimed, "you haven't got a pulse at all. You're going to die all right!"

I was put to bed in a long ward with many young officers, some of whom were wounded and others slightly shell-shocked. Those who were convalescent looked very young indeed—just schoolboys in their pyjamas—and I remember one good-looking lad who flirted with the prettiest nurse, denounced the war as a bloody business which had no sense in it, and proclaimed his dislike of having to die when he next went back to the front line, as of course all second lieutenants had to do, like little gentlemen, for King and Country. He desired, he said, to live, surrounded by his children and his children's children. He didn't live, poor child, on his return to the trenches.

Hospital discipline was severe. We were roused at six o'clock in the morning, and were given blanket baths, with all windows open, by stalwart Canadian nurses. After that we had to shave. When I remonstrated with my nurse she laughed and said: "There's no mercy in this hospital."

In the next bed to me on my right was a General named Johnson who was waited upon by the same nurse, and had a daily duel of verbiage with her, in which he abused her as a woman devoid of all tenderness and charm. She retaliated by describing him as an arrogant old stick, who thought he could get away with murder because he had two crossed swords on his shoulder when he was properly dressed.

Now that he was in his pyjamas she wouldn't stand any nonsense from him. It all began because he utterly refused to be roused at six o'clock in the morning or to shave himself before 11 p.m.

"I'm a general," he told her. "Kindly don't forget that."

"I'm a nurse," she answered, "and I've got the upper hand of you."

So they went on at each other, hammer and tongs, and doubtless enjoyed this daily duel of wit.

On my left was a young officer of the Coldstream Guards, by name of Bootle Wilbraham. He was a very handsome young man, with a fine and delicate profile. He was also a very intellectual young man, and had at his bedside a pile of books by Anatole France. He handed some of them over to me and we read them alternately, discussing them afterwards. We also discussed the ethics of the war, criticised generals and were critical and bitter about the Battles of the Somme and other actions. Or perhaps it was I who was bitter while he listened politely. He must have repeated our conversation for I got into hot water about it, and was rebuked in a letter from E. W. Hornung who was running a trench library in Arras. Twenty-five years afterwards, or thereabouts, I met Bootle Wilbraham again. He was now commanding the 2nd battalion, Coldstream Guards, in the second World War.

We were bombed quite a bit in Amiens while I lay in hospital, and many of the officers in my ward were nervy. I remember a Lancashire fellow among them who used to dream horribly and call out in his sleep. During an air raid he suffered mental agony. "If there is another raid I shall go mad," he cried one night. The night nurses were very brave and came round the ward to comfort those who felt anxious. There was one pretty little New Zealand nurse who had the face of a saint and the heart of a mother to all these boys, as mostly they were. They desired to be comforted by her. The boy who wished to live to a ripe old age was particularly anxious to be comforted. She knelt down by their bedsides, one by one, whispering to each of them, little whispered conversations full of tenderness, and if a boy wanted a kiss I think she gave it to him, though I wouldn't swear to that. I wanted a kiss but never had the pluck to ask her. I wonder if she remembers those nights of charity and pity?

Some little time after I had left the hospital—the orderly was wrong about my dying—I was sorry to see in an illustrated paper a photograph of General Johnson who had been in the bed at my right hand and with whom I had become friendly. "Killed in action." But I met him face to face on a duckboard in the neighbourhood of Bapaume.

"Hullo, General!" I exclaimed. "I thought you were dead!"

"They put in the wrong photograph," he said cheerfully. "It was another General Johnson. I'm still walking around!"

35

GRIM FOREBODING

In February of 1918 the Intelligence reports which we received every morning, with maps showing the German order of battle, were alarming. The enemy was moving up big reserves behind their front facing the Fifth Army on our right. It was obvious that they were going to try to make a smash through, and we were given permission by G.H.Q. to warn the British public that a heavy ordeal was facing us in the near future. Our articles were very ominous indeed, but they only seemed to amuse certain divisional generals holding the line opposed to this menace.

"G.H.Q. has the wind up," said more than one of them whom I visited at this time. "We can hold this line till the crack o' doom."

I remember only a few days before March 21st going up to see the 47th London Division. They were putting up an excellent show behind the lines. It was a gymkhana and all very merry and bright. There were races on hairies of the field artillery. One man had dressed himself up as a comic general with a big black moustache and a monocle and a red nose. No one laughed more heartily than the general himself.

"G.H.Q. has the wind up," he told me in a moment of aside.

But one morning two of us war correspondents were summoned to the Headquarters of General Sir Hubert Gough, commanding the Fifth Army. He spread out his maps before us, showing us his line with which we were familiar, and the strength with which it was held.

"Gentlemen," he said, "you know as well as I do that the situation is serious. We're holding this line very thinly in comparison with the great strength the enemy has massed against us."

Other words he spoke, in a quiet amiable way, made me feel the touch of an icy finger down my spine.

"We may have to give ground. We may have to fall back on our main battle zone. That won't matter very much. It is possible that we may have to go further back. Our real line of defence is the Somme. It will be nothing like a tragedy if we hold that. If we lose the Somme crossings it will, of course, be serious. But not a tragedy even then. It will only be a tragedy if we lose Amiens, and we mustn't do that."

The Somme crossings! . . . Amiens! . . . Such a possibility had never crept into our minds. It was a terrible thought after all the years of sacrifice and bloody fighting to push back the enemy to his present positions.

The line was held thinly. Sir Douglas Haig had called for more men

from England, but Lloyd George was loth to send them after the
slaughter on the way to Passchendaele. Sir Hubert Gough had called
urgently to Haig for more reserves to meet the coming threat, but Haig
told him he would have to do with what he had. There had been very
little digging for lack of labour, and no strong lines of defence in depth
had been prepared. The situation was perilous, as we knew, though not
to the extent which Sir Hubert had revealed to us. We left his Headquarters silently and deeply anxious.

From captured prisoners we learnt the exact date of the coming
attack—March 21st. A few days before that morning I went to the
extreme right of the line, opposite St. Quentin, to see my brother Arthur
who was commanding a battery of field guns. They were within 1,200
yards of the German front line. I did not dare tell him the date of the
coming attack, and I don't think he knew how formidable it would be.
He was quite cheerful as we sat eating a bit of lunch on a little knoll
from which we could see across the German lines. It was all very quiet
there. Nothing moved. No gun fired, though Arthur, my "kid brother"
as I called him, told me there had been a certain amount of gunfire for
ranging purposes.

"They've been damn quiet lately apart from that," he told me. "You
wouldn't think there was a war on. But my battery is uncomfortably
near the German line. If anything happens I shall have to pull back and
it won't be easy." When I said goodbye to him I thought I had seen
him for the last time.

36

THE GREAT ATTACK

The Germans launched their great offensive in a dense fog on the
morning of March 21st. They had a heavy superiority in men and guns.
They had an overwhelming power of artillery. Opposite three of our
divisions they had 1,000 guns, and in most parts of the line one gun to
every twelve or fifteen yards of front. They concentrated heavy fire
upon our battery positions, ammunition dumps, roads of communication, and villages in back areas. They had brought up a number of long
range naval guns, and their shell fire was scattered as far back as
twenty-eight miles behind the lines.

Their infantry had been trained to a new system of attack which was
called "infiltration". It was done by small units, led by non-commissioned officers, who acted like molecules of the larger masses and,

with great skill and courage, took advantage of the gaps in our lines when a break-through had been made. The fog helped them. Our forward troops found themselves isolated, with the enemy beyond them and around them, before they had become aware of their danger. Many of our outposts were cut off like this, and fought to the last. So it was in the Manchester Redoubt, near St. Quentin, where the 16th Manchesters of the 30th division held out with their machine-guns for ten hours after being surrounded. By means of a buried cable they were able to send messages. The last words came from the commanding officer at about 3.30 in the afternoon when he was wounded. He spoke calmly, even cheerily; but said they could not hold out much longer, as practically every man was hit. "The Manchesters will defend this Redoubt to the last moment," he said. No other words came from him and the Redoubt was overwhelmed.

The Germans smashed through our lines in many places, and advanced rapidly, in spite of heavy losses inflicted upon them by our rearguard actions. Some of their divisions lost between 30 and 50 per cent of their man-power, but their reserves still came on over their dead bodies, and our battalions, losing touch with each other, because all telephone wires had been put out of action by shell fire, fell back and fought desperate rearguard actions, with the enemy cutting in between them and behind them. They came back over the old battlefields for which we had fought in the Battles of the Somme at stupendous cost, and back again over the ground from which they had retreated to the Hindenburg Line. After five days and nights our men were utterly exhausted and drugged with lack of sleep. "Nothing could keep them awake," said one officer, "except another attack." There were only small bodies and groups of men standing between the enemy and the Channel ports when they had fallen back through Albert and through Bapaume where the Germans got very drunk on our stores at the Officers' Club, and almost to the outskirts of Amiens.

General Sir Hubert Gough's Fifth Army had been almost annihilated.

I was an eye-witness of many scenes in this disaster and realised its bitterness and tragedy. It was a dreadful thing to see the enemy coming back to the old fields of the Somme and to see places which had been quiet, far behind our lines, under shell fire again. I saw, without field glasses, the German guns and transport coming through Fricourt and Montauban which we had captured on July 1st, 1916. Having the use of a car I could reach positions not yet captured, and I remember going up to High Ridge when it was still held by the Naval division. An officer spoke to me cheerfully.

"We can hold this position till the crack of doom."

"The enemy is cutting in behind you," I said. "They are already driving through the ruins of Mametz. You have hardly time to get out."

They had to make a forced march back to escape from the trap closing upon them.

The Germans came as near to Amiens as Villers-Bretonneux on the low hills outside. Their guns had smashed the railway station of Longeau, which to Amiens is like Clapham Junction to Waterloo. Across the road was a tangle of telephone wires, shot down from their posts. For one night nothing—or next to nothing—barred the way, and Amiens could have been entered by a few armoured cars. Only small groups of tired men, the remnants of strong battalions, were able to stand on their feet, and hardly that.

That evening, having seen the worst, our small bunch of war correspondents, seven of them, I think, because we had been joined by two Americans—Philip Sims of the United Press and De Witt Mackenzie of the Associated Press of America—sat down to get a scratch meal in the old Hôtel du Rhin, where many times we had been billeted during the Battles of the Somme. In the room were officers on lines of communication which had been cut by the enemy, and Town Majors who had lost their towns, and other administrative officers. Behind the cash desk sat the lady to whom we paid our bills. Her face was pallid beneath the dabs of rouge on her cheeks. Gaston, the head waiter, a boastful fellow like Tartarin de Tarascon, was subdued by the imminent peril and looked as though death were near, as indeed it was.

The first bomb fell during dinner. It was a colossal crash, very near, and many of the officers at table went to the floor. We heard a splintering of glass. Many windows had broken but we were all undamaged. Captain Cadge, in charge of our cars and general organisation, raised the question whether we should go or stay that night. The enemy might come into Amiens at any hour and we might all be captured. Was there any sense in that? There seemed to be a diversity of opinion among us. Cadge wrote out seven ballot papers and suggested that we should put a X against the alternative Stay or Go. I voted for staying. So did a majority of the others. We stayed the night in Amiens.

It was not an amusing night. Until 4.30 in the morning the enemy sent over squadrons of aeroplanes and bombed this small city mercilessly.

"We had better go down into the cellar," said Montague. "There's no sense in staying upstairs." There were good cellars below the Hôtel du Rhin, full of wine casks and crates. The Town Majors who had lost their towns, and the officers on lines of communication which no longer communicated, bedded themselves down in straw. So did our Colonel Faunthorpe. At intervals through the night I saw

H

him stretched out, sleeping as peacefully as a babe, with the flickering light of candles on his hawk-like profile.

The candles had been lit by the two Americans, Philip Sims and De Witt Mackenzie. They had settled down to a game of cards, using a wine cask as their table. So they played all through the night.

I did not like that cellar. I was restless and sleepless and kept going upstairs to my bedroom, lying down on the bed awhile, and then getting up when the sound of exploding bombs and crashing buildings, like avalanches of masonry, shook the bed and the floors and the walls as though by earthquake shocks. I smoked innumerable cigarettes, and wondered what it would feel like if the floor suddenly yawned beneath my feet and I was hurled to death amidst the ruins of the Hôtel du Rhin. Should I feel anything? Should I have time to know anything? I wondered what would happen after death. Should I retain my personal consciousness and awareness? Would my brain go on working after its physical mechanism was destroyed? Would something in me— the soul—be liberated and continued? Or was death just nothingness? I crossed myself several times, I remember. But I was not afraid, I think. And looking back on that night now I see that it was no worse than hundreds of nights in London and other cities where millions of citizens—women and girls—went through such hours with a kind of fatalism and were still unnervous at dawn.

Through the broken windows on the big staircase I could see brilliant moonlight shining on roofs and walls, and somewhere nearby great fires were raging with scarlet flames. I could feel the heat of them, and smell the acrid smoke. A part of Amiens was a roaring furnace.

Before dawn I went downstairs again. Suddenly the aerial bombardment had ceased. Broken glass crunched beneath my feet on the stairs. In the hall I met Montague. "Let's go outside," he said.

We went outside and walked a little way down the *rue des Trois Calloux*—the Street of the Three Pebbles—which was the main street of Amiens, trodden by hundreds of thousands of our men, and by Australians, and New Zealanders, and South Africans, and Scots and Irish, during and after the Battles of the Somme. Muddy soldiers in dripping capes had pressed their noses against the window panes of small shops, and moved from one *bistro* to another for glasses of *porto blanc*. At night little torches had flashed into the eyes of young officers, and the voices of little sluts had lured them in French or English. "*Une nuit d'amour, mon petit.*" . . . "Come with me, leetle English officer." Soft hands had grabbed at their Sam Browne belts. In the Godebert restaurant little Marguerite, as saucy as a *vivandière*, had made eyes at all the pretty boys, who craved for a kiss after the lousy trenches . . . Amiens!

Now that night part of it was on fire. All the Arcade was a glowing furnace. Over 2,000 houses had been hit. In the Street of the Three Pebbles lay the bodies of dead horses and dead men. The body of a British officer lay at the entrance of the Hôtel du Rhin. He had been killed as he banged at the door. The street under the moonlight was like burnished silver. The old Cathedral still stood, every pinnacle and bit of tracery shining like quicksilver, with magical beauty.

That morning all the living inhabitants—many were killed that night—fled from Amiens, which presently was under shell fire, with the enemy outside.

Many times afterwards I went through that deserted city in which I had made many friends—Mademoiselle Carpentier of the book shop, an old printer with his three pretty daughters, one of whom—the most beautiful—fell in love with an English officer who was already married, and other pleasant *bourgeois* people. It was very sinister then in Amiens, with only a few soldiers walking single file close to the walls and shells coming over intermittently. But, while it was deserted like that by all civilians, I had lunch one day in a cellar beneath the Hôtel de Ville as the guest of a French general. It was the 14th of July and he had decided to give a little banquet. Among his guests was a young American officer, representing the American Army now fighting round the Chemin des Dames and Château Thierry. With me went Colonel Neville Lytton who had joined our staff, to our great pleasure because of his wit, gallantry, and artistic temperament. (He played Bach on an eighteenth century flute and spoke French like a Parisian, and was beloved by French correspondents of whom he had been in charge.)

Down in the cellar of the Hôtel de Ville the tables were decorated with roses from the little gardens of Amiens, now abandoned and neglected. Each of us had a *menu* by the side of his plate. There were speeches. The French general, a fierce-looking old man, but a fine type, drank to the health of the glorious British Armies. It was Neville Lytton who returned thanks, in perfect and humorous French. The French general drank a toast to the glorious American Army. The young American officer had to respond. He rose, uttered the one word "merçi" and sat down again, not knowing any more French. A year or so later I found myself in New York. An invitation to lunch with the young American officer had been delivered on board before we landed. I accepted it, and by my plate in an American apartment was one of the *menus* from the cellar in Amiens, and we had the same things for lunch, and the same French wine, and the table was decorated with little red roses. Only an American would have thought out this idea, which I found charming.

37

RESCUE OF AMIENS

Foch said "I guarantee Amiens". French cavalry, hard pressed, had come up to the northern part of our line. I saw them riding by, squadron after squadron, their horses wet with sweat. To some of them I shouted out "*Vivent les poilus!*" emotionally, but they turned and gave me ugly looks. They were cursing the English, I was told afterwards, for the German break-through. "*Ces sacrés Anglais!* Why couldn't they hold their lines?" It was different when the French line broke by the Chemin des Dames.

I was with a French regiment which took over in the neighbourhood of Bailleul when this old city, which for years had been well behind our lines, suddenly became one great torch, and when hamlets and farmhouses around it came into the line of fire. That was when the Germans extended their attack northwards. "Where are the trenches?" I was asked by French officers, and they were disgusted when I told them there were no trenches. The German offensive had swept beyond our trench lines.

Amiens was saved by the counterattacks of the Australians, and especially by the brilliant surprise attack at night on Villers-Bretonneux under the generalship of Monash which I have mentioned before. The Australians had been having a rest cure behind the lines for quite a time and were untouched by the exhaustion of retreat. They came up fresh and confident, and we were lucky in having them in reserve. They were great fighters who had developed a marvellous team-work of their own, differing from our English discipline—they were bad boys behind the lines—but magnificent and grim in action.

Amiens did not fall into the hands of the enemy, though he came very near and held Albert not far away. In a village further south I met some light artillery passing through, and a voice shouted out: "Hello!" It was my brother Arthur bringing up his field guns. I had never expected to see him alive again, but there he was looking as fresh as if he had just had a holiday at Brighton. He had had strange adventures since that morning when I had last seen him. He was on the extreme left—our right—of the German attack and succeeded in pulling back his guns below the knoll where we had lunch together. The British Army had disappeared from him. The Germans passed and passed for three days. He fired at them with open sights, but never once did they debouch to deal with this single battery. He decided to get on the move and found himself defending a French division in retreat. So he had come to the place where I found him a few kilometers from Amiens. The French general had embraced him and gave him a flag from his own car. But he was reprimanded for having lost touch with the British Army. Such is the injustice of war, at times.

38

THE NORTHERN ATTACK

The enemy's northern attack, which opened on April 9th of 1918, struck most heavily against a line held by the Portuguese between Neuve Chapelle and Fleurbaix—that flat country, intersected by the River Lye and many little canals, which had been held in the early days of the war, as I have told, by our Indian troops and for ever haunted by their ghosts.

I had seen the arrival of the Portuguese, ill clad for a Flemish winter and not very impressive. One of our colonels, who was a humourist, introduced me to their Chief of Staff, a burly man with his breast covered with decorations.

"Gibbs," said the colonel, "let me introduce you to the Portuguese Chief of Staff. We call him Old Bumface."

Fortunately the Portuguese Chief of Staff knew no English and shook hands with me solemnly.

Many of the Portuguese soldiers brought with them big baskets of fancy-coloured straw, quite empty. When enquiries were made as to the purpose of these baskets we found that they were for loot from German cities. I was sorry for them. In the trenches they were always getting the wind up and sounding their gas alarms, to the great annoyance of British troops on the right and left of them. The conditions of war on the Western Front were unknown to them, and they were raw and untrained when the terrible storm broke upon them, backwards and forwards in waves of high explosives, from the trench line opposite Neuve Chapelle to the second line opposite Fauquissurt and Richebourg St. Vaast. Both lines were broken and the Portuguese, after heavy casualties, retreated—all except their gunners who held out very gallantly by the side of our own batteries.

I have always said, with some seriousness, that the Portuguese won the war. The Germans had some twenty-five fresh divisions in reserve, and if they had hurled them into the Amiens Front they could have smashed through to the coast. But they could not resist the lure of the open hole left by the Portuguese, and switched their fresh divisions up there. Now the 55th division of Lancashire men had held fast at

Givenchy on our right flank, and they wiped out wave after wave of German storm troops, while the 34th and 50th Divisions were giving equal punishment before they fell back south of Armentières—for ever famous—into which they poured gas and high explosives. In the end the German attacks were held—it was touch and go—and they suffered such heavy casualties that they had no great reserves to fling into the line when our own turn came for the counter-offensive, which turned the tide and never ebbed until journey's end on November 11th, 1918. In the end it happened so, but while it lasted it was very terrible and deeply depressing to those of us who had been with our armies in France and Flanders and seen the cost of their advance across the battlefields. My spirits sank to zero when I watched the enemy's come-back to Wytschaete and Messines, to the woods round Hazebrouck, to the villages about Bailleul, to Laventie and Merville and Estaires, to Mametz and Montauban and Albert. Much of this country had been beyond reach of enemy guns for years. The inhabitants had lived behind the lines with a sense of security because we were there. Our troops had been billeted in their farmsteads and cottages. Now they found themselves in the heart of flaming war. Their villages were shelled and gassed and burnt while they were fleeing down the roads, or before they fled, while they were grabbing a few household treasures. Our batteries took up position in their orchards. German guns ranged upon them. There were heartbreaking scenes again as the women and children and old people took to the roads. I remember one old woman who watched her cottage burning and then cried suddenly: "I must go back! . . . I must go back!" Very likely she wanted to find an old silver teapot, or a wallet stuffed with paper money. Her cottage was burning like a torch, and I put my arms about her and held her back in spite of her struggle to get free.

39

BACKS TO THE WALL

Sir Douglas Haig sent his famous message to the troops asking them to fight with their backs to the wall. They were the same troops mostly who had sustained the first attack on March 21st, and had been fighting ever since, like the 51st Scottish Division (to whom the enemy dropped a message: "Good old 51st. Still sticking it. Cheerio!") and like the 25th, 34th, 50th and 55th Divisions and many others of England, Scotland, Ireland and Wales.

I found our officers and men dog-weary, but full of confidence. If they were forced back they were glad to know that they had made the enemy pay heavy prices and that our line was still unbroken. I was among them in villages just being evacuated, and in back gardens where our guns were limbering up. I went into Flemish farmhouses where our officers were studying their maps, and fell asleep for a few seconds on kitchen chairs until they jerked themselves up again, before sending orders to their men. I went into the Forest of Nieppe, when the enemy was nearby, and it was from villages there among the woods, and between Hazebrouck and St. Venant—old familiar places behind our lines where I had eaten many a pleasant lunch—that I saw the flight of many families, while German shrapnel was overhead and the tumult of the guns came louder and closer. I saw many tragic scenes which I recorded at the time, and I saw them with tragic eyes because my own mind was full of distress, and pity, and deep anxiety at that time. Were we going to lose the war after all? Could we hold our line before the enemy reached the coast?

I quote one passage only from the long despatches I was writing in those anxious days.

"The scene to-day along the line of battle was most tragic, because all the cruelty of war was surrounded by a beauty so intense that the contrast was horrible. The sky was of summer blue, with sunshine glittering on the red-tiled roofs of cottages, and on their whitewashed walls, and on their little window panes. All the hedges were clothed with green and flaked by the snow-white thorn-blossom. In a night, as it seemed, all the orchards of France have flowered, and cherry and apple trees are in the full splendour of bloom; the fields are powdered with close-growing daisies, and the shadows of the trees are long across the grass as the sun is setting. But over all this, and in the midst of all this, is agony and blood. On the roads are fugitives, wounded soldiers, dead horses, guns and transport. There are fires burning on the hillsides. I saw their flames and their great rolling clouds of smoke rise this morning from places where, the day before, I had seen French peasants ploughing, as though no war were near, and young girls scattering grain over fields harrowed by small brothers, and old women tending to the soil in small farmsteads where all their life was centred, until a frightful truth touched them, and they had to leave. Sometimes to-day I wished the sun would not shine like this, nor nature mock at one with its thrilling beauty of life."

Well, that agony passed. The frightful menace was frustrated. The great German offensive wilted and failed and stopped. By the courage of the common soldier, by his tenacity and refusal to be beaten, by sticking it out in ditches, behind hedges, in farmsteads and bits of ruins, by the magnificence of our gunners firing at short range and always on the move, by the dogged, obstinate, grim and unbelievable valour of dirty, dusty men, drunk with sleeplessness, parched in the heat, standing up among their dead, wounded but still carrying on, the German onslaught was halted after bloody losses which used up their last reserves. My eyes saw those things, and it is now like a dream, and I am like a ghost remembering an ancient past in another life.

40

THE LAST RESERVES

I have described how Foch sent his cavalry up to our relief in hours of crisis. After them came many of his picked divisions. By doing so he weakened his own front and exposed it to the extreme peril of the attack which the Germans had waiting for him. That happened, and the enemy smashed their way across the Chemin des Dames, thrust down through Fismes in a rapid drive, and reached the Marne. The German High Command thought they were "sitting pretty", and that Foch had no reserves with which he could make anything like a big counter-attack. But Foch rose to the supreme moment of his genius and risked everything to gain everything. He had but little time to act—a few short days—but he made lightning decisions. He withdrew all the men who had gone rushing up behind the British lines—I shall never forget the sight of that tide of men pouring back along the roads in dense clouds of dust, all through those days and nights—and borrowed some of our best divisions, and then sent forward the American trained divisions who had been fighting in the Argonne and in Lorraine. Those American divisions were Marshal Foch's trump card. He held them back until the psychological moment and then played them for all they were worth. They responded to his call with supreme spirit and courage on the Château Thierry side of the German salient, as the British and French troops did on the other side. The trump card was played and won the game there on the Marne. The Crown Prince's armies were sent reeling back. Ludendorff choked when the news reached him and he had an apoplectic seizure. He knew the German Army was doomed.

Our turn was at hand. The swift and far-reaching success of Foch's counter-offensive led quickly to the possibility of a British advance north and south of Amiens against the armies of Ruprecht of Bavaria. His reserves had been called for by the Crown Prince. Against our own front there were no longer great odds in man-power, and in the battles that opened on August 8th the enemy was hard pressed to support and relieve his fighting troops.

41

ENGLAND IN WAR TIME

By the worst kind of luck I was on sick leave in England when our great counterattack began on August 8th of 1918 which turned the tide of the war and drove on to victory. My place for a time was taken by H. W. Nevinson, veteran war correspondent, paladin of them all, *sans peur et sans reproche*.

England . . . I had seen little of it during the war. I knew nothing, or very little, of its spirit, its suffering, or its toil. I had had seven days leave every six months or so, and those days seemed to pass like one day, and I was being seen off again by my wife outside the boat-train platform in Victoria station, where wives said goodbye to their returning husbands and did not weep until they were gone. Often when I go to Victoria station now I remember, not the scenes of the second World War, but of that first one when there was great slaughter of young officers and men, and when a man going back said goodbye, in so many thousands of cases, to life itself, and knew that the odds were heavy against him. Nearly always it seemed foggy and wet on those days of farewell. A wind was blowing hard in the Channel. Men would be sick all over the decks. The gates to the platforms were shut against the women and children, standing there to get the last glimpse of a man with sad eyes who called out: "Cheerio!" So it was always, as I remember. Another dream!

My wife had moved from Holland Street half way through the war. She had taken a big old house—once belonging to a rich city merchant of the Georgian era—in Finsbury Park, beyond a slum part of London. It had painted ceilings and carved mantelpieces and big cellars. There was a garden of two and a half acres—big for London—with a mulberry tree centuries old, on the lawn, upon which it scattered its juicy fruit in harvest time. There were many outhouses and sheds.

But we did not have this house to ourselves during the war, and when I came home I found it filled with contingents of boys of the Cockney type from London slums and suburbs. It was Agnes's war work, and it had a spiritual as well as a social purpose which I respected, grudgingly. The idea was to give three-day "retreats" to Catholic boys whose fathers were mostly at the war, and who lacked parental discipline, and were in moral danger because of wartime wildness. They were a tough crowd, always changing—boys of 14 or 15 years old, mostly. I was shy of them and could not have handled them, but Agnes had a way with her—a laughing way yet strict—which kept them tame and well behaved. Never once did she have any rowdiness among them, though some of them were very tough indeed. They behaved like angels —or at least like little gentlemen—in her presence, and adored her. I found them a damn nuisance in my house, where the drawing-room was turned into a chapel, and in my garden, but for Agnes's sake I bore it meekly. Catholic priests were in attendance, giving these retreats. Two or three of them were even harder to bear than the boys, for they had fallen in love with Agnes, without evil intent—poor gentlemen!— and I didn't like it, though I understood and was sorry for them. Agnes teased them unmercifully, because that was the only way to handle a situation which, anyhow, she thought absurd.

I noticed a change in her. She looked worn and thin. The war, so unending it seemed, was a horror to her, with all its casualties of youth. She saw no sense in it—nothing but massacre and misery on both sides. And she felt that she had lost me. I had been away so long. She had said so many prayers for me. Now she was tired of it all—very tired of it all, like millions of other women. She hated all the fierce hatred which kept some women going by an inner flame of ferocity.

"Dilly, dilly, come and be killed," she said about the recruitment of new classes of boys.

She hated the despatches of war correspondents always holding out a hope which was never fulfilled, always describing the heroic valour of boys who, of course, were sentenced to death. In the end she hated mine, for the same reasons, and I didn't blame her, because that was the truth. She hated the calm way in which many people—her own friends, the priests, and the women—took the monstrous casualties of the Somme and Flanders as a matter of course, as though boys were only born to be killed for King and Country, as though they ought to like being killed. She wanted it to end, somehow and anyhow, and there seemed no end.

Even in that war bombs fell over London, and Agnes had listened at night to the coming of the Zeppelins, and had seen them touched by our searchlights, and had heard the crash of high explosives not far away— so close that bits of jagged metal lay about our garden. German aeroplanes made night and daylight raids, and they had flown above our chimney-pots while she lay alone. I saw a tragic look in her eyes when I came back. She found a stranger in me because the war had changed me, she thought, and I was no longer the delicate boy she had loved—her shy fawn. I found her a little cold, a little distant, with some invisible barrier between us, though I came back to her with passionate longing, and left her again with tears in my heart. The war had hurt her horribly.

I found England drab, weary, and bored with the war. Tragedy had

stalked into millions of little homes, and the civilian population were
not keyed up to the same pitch of moral strength as in the second World
War when their own lives and liberties were more directly threatened,
and when they were under prolonged bombardment. There was a
greater gap between the people at home and the men at the front.
The wounded who came back, and the men on leave, spoke very little
about their own way of life. They put it away from their own minds, or
could not find words to tell the tale. People didn't understand anyhow.
Imagination could not cross the Channel or get as far as the trenches.
One had to have been there to understand.

So it was that when Sheriff wrote his *Journey's End* after the war it
came as a revelation and a shock to those who had pictured the war in
terms of conventional heroism. I remember seeing it with a man who had
been through all that, and had shirked seeing the play because it might
be too painful and bring back hideous memories. But he sat very quiet
and afterwards said: "I was back there again. The illusion was complete.
That is how I saw the war." But a young girl, not more than nineteen
or twenty, was furious. She made a little speech in the foyer, raising her
voice so that people could hear. "It's a libel on our officers and men. It
ought to be suppressed!" It was because she had believed that all
officers, like her father perhaps, were noble and perfect, and ready to die
with simple heroism and fine words. She did not believe that fear broke
any of them down, or that the horror of a dugout under bombardment
was like that, shaking our men with shell-shock or straining their
nerves until sometimes they snapped. It deromanticised the war and
she thought it abominable. Many elderly women held the same view
and many old gentlemen who had sat in London clubs, or done their
"bit" by helping with the harvest, and cracking little jokes while other
harvest fields were littered with dead youth. One doesn't blame them.
They just didn't understand a war which was not quite the same thing as
the Boer War, but very much like Hell.

The men who came from that hell were silent about what they had
seen, and went to *Chu Chin Chow* with their mothers and sisters (as I
did with my son Tony) or took young women to night clubs and cabarets
where there was the thump-thump of jazz bands and the twinkle of
dancing girls' legs. Many of them went to other places, less respectable,
with little sluts whom they had picked up in the Strand, or the Euston
Road, or at the corner of Shaftesbury Avenue. "What did anything
matter?" they asked. Why not grab at a little pleasure when they could
get it? In another week or two they would be dead, most likely, and
they were starved of life and women.

The Strand was crowded with soldiers from all the Dominions,
hanging about outside the Y.M.C.A., or the beer taverns and cheap

restaurants and the A.B.C.'s. In Piccadilly, at night, officious little
A.P.M.'s who had never been near the war took the names of officers
improperly dressed (that is to say not wearing gloves) some of whom
said "Go to hell!" aggravating the offence. So it happened to me.
There was a fierce and feverish gaiety, underneath which were frayed
nerves and despair, because the war had lasted so long with such
unaccountable sacrifice and so many wounded souls. That was how
England seemed to me on seven days' leave or sick leave. It was better
at the front, in spite of war's hell. There was more comradeship, a
cleaner spirit, a finer morale, taking it all in all.

42

THE WAY TO VICTORY

I was desperate to get back. I had been in at the beginning, I wanted
to be in at the end.

By the time I went back in the third week of August the tide of war
had definitely turned. The enemy was in general retreat, fighting only
strong rearguard actions. Since August 8th, "the black day of the
German Army" as Ludendorff called it, we had taken 50,000 prisoners
and 500 guns. But, as I wrote at the time, the change had been greater
in the minds of men than in the taking of territory. On our side our
army was buoyed up with the enormous hope of getting on with this
business quickly. They were fighting for quick victory and quick peace,
so that they might get back to normal life, and wipe this thing clean
from the map of Europe, and restore the world to sane purposes. The
change was also in the enemy's mind. The German soldiers and
officers were different men since they had launched their offensive on
March 21st. They no longer had a dim hope of victory on the Western
Front. All they hoped for now was to defend themselves long enough
to gain peace by negotiation.

On August 28th I saw a scene which made me think for the first time
that the war would soon be over. It was around Monchy beyond Arras
—the scene of that cavalry charge in April which I have described.
The Canadians fighting here had taken 2,000 prisoners, many of them
belonging to the 2nd German Guards. When those who had been first
taken saw batches of their comrades coming down they shouted:
"Bravo! . . . Bravo! . . . The war will soon be over!" They were
sullen with their officers and no longer saluted them. Some of these
prisoners told me that they had been sacrificed too often by a brutal
command. All they wanted was peace.

I followed up with our advance and it was like the lifting of an evil spell to see the old battlefields of the Somme cleared again, to walk up the Albert-Bapaume road again, to go for the second time on a day of victory into Bapaume itself, just a rubble of red brick, from which rosy clouds of dust rose when shells fell into it from the retreating enemy, but a symbol of all the sacrifice which had gone to its taking in 1916. Roaming about its ruins I was accosted by a New Zealand soldier.

"Who are you?" he asked.

When I told him he shook hands and said: "I'm a literary man myself. I'm the editor of the *Waranooroo News*." (It sounded something like that.) "I never expected to find myself in Bapaume." We talked about war and life until a shell exploded near us and we were choked with red dust.

For nearly three months I went with our advancing armies across old battlefields and beyond them into country we had never held, and into cities long in German hands.

Peronne was ours, and burning when I entered it with a blind man named Arthur Pearson, as I have written. We cleared the enemy off the old ridges, and went over ground littered with their dead and the wreckage of their war machine. We passed our old cemeteries, with their rows and rows of white crosses. The Germans had respected them, and not far away were new cemeteries, their own, with German steel helmets above other crosses of brown unpainted wood.

I saw the fighting round Cambrai, very stiff and bloody, and on October 10th went into the city taken by our troops that morning. I went towards it too early to know whether it was ours, and even after I had been into its streets and out again some machine-gunners on the outskirts did not know, and were amazed when I told them that I had come out of the place and that it was filled with our troops. Along the straight road going to the entrance of the city on the western side lay dead bodies, killed a few hours before by shell fire, and in one place a pile of dead horses which some of our men had covered with brushwood to hide their blood and mangled bodies.

Further on by some ruined cottages two dead Germans lay, their field-grey uniforms stained red in patches. They seemed like two last guards of the city gates. There was no living German to bar our way in. We crossed the Scheldt Canal by a wooden bridge and got into the streets of the city. In the heart of it fires were smouldering, by the *Place du Théâtre* and every now and then there was the noise of explosion and falling masonry. These sounds gave us a sense of alertness to danger as we walked, as men who knew that there was no safety on the way. For we knew that Cambrai had been mined, and we had had warnings of booby traps, so laid that if one tripped on a wire or touched any innocent-looking object in a deserted house, sudden things might happen which would end all further interest in war or life.

All the civilians had been evacuated. Before going the Germans had looted all the houses and shops. There were many fine houses in Cambrai owned by wealthy people and on the walls there still hung gilt-framed mirrors, and pictures; and torn tapestry hung at the windows, and books and papers were scattered about the upturned furniture which was in the style of Louis Quatorze. These houses and *salons* into which I looked suggested scenes in the French Revolution which must have happened like this in Cambrai. But what touched one most was the abandonment of the smaller houses and little shops. I looked into houses where women's sewing machines still stood on the tables, as they had done their work with their babes around them. Perambulators stood on the thresholds or in the passage way, and children's dolls lay on the floors as they had been dropped, because of the terror that had followed a proclamation pasted on the walls by the German *Kommandantur* ordering the civilians to leave Cambrai.

I remember one queer object which stood in the middle of a street. It was a dressmaker's mannikin, wearing a straw hat with a necklace of sham pearls round its wooden shoulders; and in another street nearby there was something more queer. At first I thought it was a mask of the Kaiser's face fastened to a drain-spout, but going nearer I saw it was a human skull staring at me with sightless eyes.

I went into Douai with a young officer. We were the only human beings in that fair-sized city, for our troops had not yet entered. Before leaving, the Germans had sent the population behind their lines perhaps to save them from bombardment, or to use them as labourers for digging trenches. As we walked through deserted streets delayed-action mines went up here and there, and we trod warily. It was an uncanny experience. The doors of the houses were open and we went inside some of them. Their former inhabitants had fled in a hurry. Some of the tables had been laid for a meal which was never eaten. Clothes lay strewn on the floors as they had been pulled out of cupboards and drawers.

The only living things we met were a few lean cats prowling about heaps of refuse. We went into the famous library of Douai and saw its books scattered about the floors. I picked up one and put it in my pocket. It was the only looting of which I was guilty in the war. It was a little history of Douai, and I think I have it still. One day I will send it back.

43

LIBERATION

I have unforgettable memories of the liberation of great cities and the ecstasy of their inhabitants at the first sight of British uniforms. To me those memories are vivid and precious, but they have taken a second place in history now because of more recent deliverances in another war. Yet our entry into Lille will always find a little corner in historical records and the story of great days. For more than four years the inhabitants of Lille had been under German rule, which had been harsh and intolerable. Everything had been taken from them—the mattresses off their beds, their linen, their brass pots and candlesticks, their silver and pewter, the machinery out of their factories. The greatest outrage against them was the forcible levy of young girls sent behind the German line for slave labour, and the seizure of able-bodied young men for the same purpose. They had suffered, these people of Lille, and for years they had heard the guns, and the noise of great battles, as the British Army fought towards Lens and the Vimy Ridge. They had seen the flash of our gunfire and had lived on hope, year after year, that one day we should come. At last we had come! Their joy was delirious. The war correspondents and a few officers were the first to enter across broken bridges. At the sight of our khaki uniforms there were wild scenes when we were nearly torn to pieces by surging crowds. They flung themselves upon us, grabbing at our shoulder straps, embracing us, holding our hands, kissing us. I was kissed a thousand times in Lille by young women and old, by grizzled men with tears running down their leathery cheeks, by old women in black bonnets. Baldheaded babies were pressed against my face. Everyone wept, laughed, shouted, and sang. They sang "It's a long long way to Tipperary" as though it were a hymn, and then wept again and laughed again.

So it was in Bruges. After the last battles in Flanders I edged my way to Bruges, and Beach Thomas and I, taking a chance, went into that lovely old city before we were quite sure the Germans had left it. But they had gone that morning and the people of Bruges stormed around us. Again we heard the song of Tipperary. It was sung to us by a number of old burghers in top hats and frock coats. It was sung to us by the crowds who swarmed like bees about our car.

I had a special reason for getting into Bruges. I had a sister-in-law—my wife's sister Beryl—who was a nun in a convent there. We had heard nothing from her during the years of war. We did not know whether she was alive or dead. I found the way to the convent of St.

André and opened the garden gate. I saw a nun walking down the path, and recognised her.

"Hullo, Beryl!" I called out.

She looked at me as though she saw a ghost. Then she gave a cry and ran towards me and flung her arms round my neck. To her it was like a miracle from Heaven. She did not even know that the Germans had left Bruges. That very morning they had been in the convent grounds.

She led me up the path to the lawn in front of the house and called out in French. Suddenly there was a swarm of nuns, like black and white birds fluttering out of an aviary. I was embraced by all those ladies, who were uttering shrill cries of joy, and my friend Beach Thomas was astonished at the scene, not knowing that nuns are human and emotional.

They were wonderful days. Victory was in the air and in our hearts. Our men pressed on and on, never giving the enemy a rest, smashing through his rearguard lines. They could not hold a line. Their war machine had disintegrated. They could not bring up fresh reserves. We entered Valenciennes and Liége. For the last time I saw a dead German. It was the body of a young man lying outside the station of Valenciennes. He lay in a pool of blood with his arms outstretched as though crucified.

44

ARMISTICE

On the morning of November 11th, 1918, I was on the way to Mons, where for us the war had begun. Our guns and transport were still moving forward along the roads. Bodies of our men—the poor old foot-sloggers—were trudging on, with wet capes and muddy boots, and sweat dripping below their tin hats. It was a dank morning with white mist lying on the fields. At an advanced headquarters an officer came out and spoke to us.

"Hostilities will cease at eleven o'clock."

A young staff officer was excited.

"The end of the war!" he cried. "And not too soon for me."

He did a little dance in the road.

We knew it was coming. For several days there had been talk of a German surrender. They had asked for terms. Now it had come, and it seemed unbelievable. Peace? Could it be possible? No more blood! No more casualties! No more mutilated, blinded, and shell-shocked men. No more sacrifice of boys, too young to die. Peace! . . . How marvellous! How incredible! How miraculous!

Civilians were coming back our way already, mostly young men. They carried little flags, though Heaven alone knows how they found them. They were some of the young men who had been sent behind the German lines, and now were straggling homewards to Liége and Lille.

I followed behind our transport wagons on the way to Mons. We looked at our wrist-watches—11 a.m.

Through the white woolly mist a bugle sounded. It was the Cease Fire to a world war. The transport went on. The guns went on. The infantry slogged on with wet capes and sweat under their steel hats.

I went as far as Mons where the Canadian cavalry had been fighting the night before. . . . The Retreat from Mons. . . . How long ago it seemed—like a lifetime ago. Now we were back again, and it was the end of the war after rivers of blood. It was—at last—Peace!

"Last night" (I wrote in my last despatch from the war zone) "for the first time since August in the first year of the war, there was no light of gunfire in the sky, no sudden stabs of flame through the darkness, no long spreading glow above the black trees, where, for four years of nights, human beings were being smashed to death. The fires of hell had been put out. It was silent all along the front, with the beautiful silence of the nights of peace . . . On the way back from Mons I listened to this silence which followed the going down of the sun, and heard the rustling of the russet leaves, and the little sounds of night in peace, and it seemed as though God gave a benediction to the wounded soul of the world.

"Other sounds rose from the towns and fields in the yellowing twilight and in the deepening shadow world of the day of Armistice. They were sounds of human joy. Men were singing somewhere on the roads, and their voices rang out gladly. Bands were playing. Bugles were blowing. In the villages from which the enemy had gone out that morning, round about Mons, crowds of figures surged in the narrow streets and English laughter rose above the silvery chatter of women and children.

"The British soldiers were still on the march, with their guns and their transport, and their old field cookers, and all along their lines I heard these men talking to each other gaily, as though something had loosened their tongues and made them garrulous. Motor cars streaked through the Belgian streets dodging the traffic, and now and then, when night fell, rockets were fired from them, and there were gusts of laughter from young officers shooting off Very pistols into the darkness, to celebrate the end of hostilities by this symbol of rising stars, which did not soar so high as their spirits.

"From dark towns like Tournai and Lille these rockets rose and burned a little while, with white light. Our aviators flew like bats in the dusk, skimming the tree-tops and gables, doing Puck-like gambols above the tawny sunset, looping and spiralling and falling in steep dives which looked like death for them, until they flattened out and rose again.

"Late into the night there were sounds of singing and laughter from open windows in the towns which had been all shuttered, with the people hiding in their cellars, a week ago or less; and British officers sat down to French pianos and romped about the keys, and crashed out chords, and led the chorus of men who wanted to sing any old song. In the officers' clubs glasses were raised, and someone called a toast, and no one heard more than the names of England, Scotland, and France, with Victory as the loudest word. Men had risen from all the tables and boys were standing on their chairs and there was the beginning of cheers which lasted five minutes, ten minutes, longer than that. And some of those who cheered had moist eyes, and were not ashamed of that, because of the memories in their hearts of old pals who had gone missing on the night of the Armistice. Perhaps the old pals heard these cheers and joined in the toasts, for the noise of all this gladness of living men rose into the night sky along the length and breadth of all our armies. And in the midst of all this sound of exultation men had sudden silences, thinking back to the things which have passed."

45

Dancing Mania

After the Armistice, in towns which had been in German occupation —Ghent, Brussels, Tournai, Bruges—the lights went up again. No more darkness because of air raids. Soldiers and civilians danced down the streets all through the nights to the tune of town bands or any kind of music. I was caught up in these dances, held hands with strangers in a jig which stretched through many streets. It was the beginning of that dancing mania which overtook the world after the war—the beginning of Jazz.

They danced in Verviers one night, led by a brass band of old men in "pot" hats, who puffed down their trombones to the unending tune of "Madelon".

They danced on the dyke at Knocke, close to Zeebrugge, where once there had been hell, to the tune of a piano organ.

They danced in the Grand' Place at Brussels, below the gilded houses of the merchant princes; and soldiers who had been starved of love grabbed a kiss or two from girls whom they met in the crowd and laughed in their eyes. . . . It was youth demanding its rights. It was the pagan spirit breaking bounds in the heart of the world after so much sacrifice. The music of the saxophone was Pan playing his pipes again, to the wild beat of the satyrs' hoofs, to the laughter of his maenads—while in quiet rooms women wept for sons or lovers who would never come back again though Peace had been declared.

In Ghent and other towns there was another kind of dance now and then, as I saw. Belgian soldiers and civilians danced round the flames of furniture thrown out of windows and doors and set alight to make a bonfire. Sometimes they set the houses on fire with great laughter. They were the houses of people called *Flamagands*, accused of being pro-German during the time of occupation. In the public hall there in Ghent I heard that shout of "Flamagand!" It rose suddenly from the floor of the dancing hall where hundreds of young men and women had linked arms. In the gallery where I stood was a tall, handsome young man who turned dead white at this shout which seemed directed at him. He fought like a tiger against a group of men who tried to seize him. He was bleeding about the head before they kicked him to death in the street outside.

In a restaurant in Ghent a pretty woman, well dressed, with a fur tippet round her neck, until she hung it on a peg, sat down at a table near my own. Suddenly the waiter spoke to her, and his voice rang out sharply with passion.

"A week ago you were sitting here with a German officer!"

He called her a frightful name, and I saw the colour leave her face, and a look of terror come into her eyes as she rose and fumbled for that fur, when a Belgian officer strode towards her wolfishly.

That night in Ghent I heard the screams of women—blood-curdling— and a man told me the meaning of it, though I guessed.

"They are cutting off some ladies' hair. . . . They were too friendly with the Germans, you understand. Now they are being stripped for shame. There are others, monsieur. Many, many, if one only knew. Hark at their howling!"

He laughed heartily at this merry sport with hunted women.

46

INTO GERMANY

I went with the first cavalry patrol—the Dragoon Guards—across the Belgian frontier into Germany. The young lieutenant in charge of the troops was slightly nervous. "We shall probably get sniped," he said.

Our way to Malmédy was down winding roads through dark pine woods. Nothing stirred on either side. For mile after mile there was no sign of human life. It was silent, and we had a sense of something uncanny in the utter loneliness and quietude of this advance into the enemy's country. Presently a mongrel dog came out of a farmhouse and barked at us.

"First signs of hostility," said the young lieutenant.

Then as the troop rode down a steep road to Malmédy, some girls standing on a bank waved handkerchiefs at us in the friendliest way.

"Very queer," said Percival Phillips who was with me.

It was a Sunday morning. When we came into the town of Malmédy the people were coming out of church. They were mostly old people and young girls, and when the troopers dismounted the girls came round them and patted the horses' necks and cried out *"Wunderschön!"*

"They seem to like us," said one of the cavalry men. "We might be their long lost brothers. Nice-looking wenches, some of them."

A young man in the crowd, in black civilian clothes, spoke in perfect English to the sergeant-major.

"Your horses are looking fine. Ours are skin and bone. When will the infantry be here?"

"Haven't an idea," said the sergeant-major gruffly.

A young man spoke to me in French, explaining that in Malmédy the people were bilingual, being so close to the frontier. He had had a Belgian wife and when he was mobilised she said: "You are going to kill my brothers," and wept her heart out. She died in 1916. He had been in the first and second Battles of Ypres and was badly wounded, so that he was sent down to the base for two years as a clerk. Then when German man-power was running short he was pushed into the ranks again and fought in Flanders, Cambrai and Valenciennes. Now he had demobilised himself, as all the others were doing.

"I am very glad the war is over, monsieur. It was a great stupidity from the beginning. Now Germany is ruined."

He spoke in a simple matter-of-fact way, as though describing natural disturbances of life, regrettable but inevitable, owing to human stupidity.

I asked him whether people further from the frontier would be hostile to the British troops, and he seemed surprised at my question.

"Hostile? Why, sir? . . . The war is over and we can be friends again. Besides, the respectable people and the middle-classes will be glad of your coming as a protection against the evil elements who are destroying property and behaving in an evil way—the sailors of the Fleet and low ruffians."

"The war is over and now we can be friends again!" That sentence in the young man's speech astonished me by its directness and simplicity. Was that the mental attitude of the German people? Did they not understand the passion of hatred that existed in England because of many things they had done—the early atrocity stories (many of them false though some of them true), the submarine war, the execution of Nurse Cavell, the sinking of the *Lusitania*, the air raids over London?

Then I looked at these troopers in the market place. One of them had given a cigarette to a boy who spoke to him in schoolboy English. Another was in conversation with two German girls who were patting his horse. We had been in this German village ten minutes. There was no sign of hatred here on one side or the other. Already something was happening here which in England, if they knew, would seem monstrous and incredible.

So it was in other places on the way to the Rhine. At Mürren I stood by while a number of trench mortars and machine-guns were being handed over by German officers according to the terms of the Armistice. The officers were mostly young men, extremely polite, marvellous in their concealment of any humiliation they may have felt—must have felt—in this surrender of arms. They were confused only for one moment when a wheelbarrow trundled by with a load of German swords —elaborate parade swords with gold hilts.

One of them laughed and passed it off with a few words in English. "There goes the old pomp and glory—to the rubbish heap!"

A non-commissioned officer talked to me. He had been a hairdresser in Bayswater and a machine-gunner in Hell. He was a little fellow with a queer Cockney accent.

"Germany is *kaput*. . . . We shall have a bad time in front of us. No money. No trade. All the same it will be better in the long run. No more conscription. No more filthy war. We're all looking forward to President Wilson and his fourteen points. That is the hope of the world. We can look forward to a good peace—fair all round. Of course we shall have to pay, but we shall get liberty—like the English."[1]

A few days later we drove with another body of cavalry into Cologne and parked our car outside the Cathedral. The city was untouched by any sign of war and we came to know its old gabled houses, and its market squares, and its old churches, and its bun shops and beer halls, and the view across the Rhine. None of us had a vision then of what would happen to Cologne in a second World War. None of us believed that these people, so utterly defeated, would ever fight us again. Wasn't it the war to end war?

We put up in the Domhof Hotel. Most of the waiters including the

[1] From *Since Then* by Philip Gibbs. Published by Heinemann, 1930.

head waiter, who had been a *Feldwebel*, that is to say a non-commissioned officer, had only just taken off their uniforms. Not many weeks previously they had been in rearguard actions against us, and by an odd chance two or three of them, as they discovered, had actually fought against this very cavalry brigade, whom now they were serving at table. It was at Fontaine Notre Dame and our cavalry officers were amused and interested by this encounter.

"Good Lord! I was behind that line of busted sandbags on the left!"

With knives and forks they reconstructed the battle. The head waiter, a tall heavily built man with a ruddy complexion who spoke excellent English, declared that he had been only a few yards away from one of our own officers who was talking to him. A few months, even a few weeks ago, these men had been trying to kill each other. Now they were talking and laughing together, and did not use the knives on the white tablecloth to cut each other's throats. There was certainly no hatred on either side.

That evening after dinner a German girl came into the lounge, opened the piano, and played some melodies by Chopin. The English officers sitting around were somewhat surprised at this entertainment, but quite liked it as an accompaniment to coffee and cigarettes and the buzz of their conversation.

"Astonishing people!" I thought. "We shouldn't do this kind of thing if the Germans had defeated us, and were drinking coffee in a hotel at Winchester or Oxford, or one of our historic cities.

An old French colonel in liaison with the British Army was in the lounge. While the German girl was playing he paced up and down angrily and said several times in a perfectly audible voice: "*Sales Boches!* . . . *Sales Boches!*"

The German girl heard, turned a little pale, folded up her music and slipped out of the room.

Remembering that little scene now it seems to me characteristic of the mentality of three peoples—English, French, German. Our young officers had no hatred against these young Germans now that the war was over, and, anyhow, they believed in good manners having been brought up as little gentlemen. The French colonel could neither forget nor forgive the destruction of northern France, the deportation of the girls in Lille, the massacre of French youth at Verdun. *Sales Boches!* . . . *Sales Boches!* . . . The German girl, like millions of other Germans, at that time accepted their defeat almost with gladness because it put an end to blood baths and other miseries, and saw no reason (not believing themselves guilty of any crime against civilisation) why the English should not like them. In any case it was best to make friends with their victors, who were very nicely behaved on the whole.

There was one reason why the people of the Rhineland were glad to see the entry of British troops who came in before the appointed time at the invitation of the *Burgemeister*. German marines and bluejackets had mutinied, and gone Communist, and marched into Cologne and other cities, looting the shops and stores, opening the prisons, letting loose all the ruffians who joined them and committed many brutalities. The British Army would restore law and order. They were, in the opinion of shopkeepers and middle-class folk, deliverers rather than conquerors.

On the morning of our arrival a British Tommy walked on to the Hohenzollern Bridge and drew a line across it half way with a bit of white chalk. It was the line and limit of our military occupation of the German Fatherland. Sir Douglas Haig came riding on to the bridge with an escort of lancers. He dismounted and spoke to a small group of men standing there in the dank mist of a November day. They were the little group of war correspondents whom he had summoned to meet him.

"Gentlemen," he said, "you know as well as I do all the sacrifices, and all the losses, and all the valour of our men on the way to the Rhine which now we have reached. I hope we shall make a just peace and not a peace of vengeance which will lead to new wars."

He thanked us for our own services.

"You have been the chroniclers of this war," he said. "You have done fine work."

Years had passed since he had pooh-poohed our work and said that we, after all, only wrote for Mary Ann in the kitchen.

He gave us each a little flag which we thought very childish though in his mind it was a symbol of victory and a personal tribute from himself, but we were glad of his good words.

So the occupation of the Rhineland began under British, French, and American command in different zones. In our zones there was immediate fraternisation to which commanding officers and the civil administration turned a blind eye. It all sounds very shocking now, because of another war and German cruelties in concentration camps and in the majority of the captured countries, but I should be writing falsely if I left that out. Our men liked the Germans and the German way of life. They liked them far better than the French among whom they had lived.

"When one turned on a tap in France no water came out," I was told by one of them. "In Germany, when one turns on a tap water comes out. They're a civilised people."

Many went further than that.

"We've been fighting the wrong people," they said.

Our men lived in German billets. The *Hausfrau* brought them up an early cup of tea. They were as snug as bugs in a rug after the filth and muck of war. They went out with German families for picnics and fell in love with German girls. They gave so many of their own rations to German children before the blockade was lifted that the general commanding the Army of Occupation wired to Whitehall that he could not answer for the health of his men unless food were sent to Cologne and the rest of our zone.

It was by the order of Winston Churchill that food was sent.

Every evening in the Germania tavern down the Hohestrasse, and in many other beer halls, British soldiers clinked mugs with Germans who had torn off their shoulder straps and gone back to civil life.

"Have another beer, Ma," said a sergeant to a German woman with two young daughters. "Tell the Mädchen to have another cake. *Noch ein Bier*. Isn't that how it's said? *Jawohl und Bitte schön*."

Very soon they had established a *lingua franca* and Germans learnt English with a Cockney accent or a Lancashire burr.

So it was among the rank and file on both sides.

Years afterwards our men who had been on the Rhine still kept friendly memories of the German people. "They're nice folk", said ex-soldiers, who were now gardeners or bricklayers or carpenters. So said a man working in my own garden. When the second World War happened and stories of foul atrocities were published in the newspapers they did not believe them. It was impossible for them to believe that the decent people they had met belonged to a race of sadists and torturers. So it was with thousands of English people who had spent their holidays in Germany and found nothing but civility and good nature. It was incredible, they thought, that these Germans should have so changed in twenty years or so, and that they would lend themselves to foul cruelties, inhuman and subhuman in their beastlike brutality. "Newspaper stuff!" . . . "Propaganda!" said men who had been in the Army of Occupation, and young people who had gone hiking through German villages or had stayed with German families—until they were forced to believe in the ghastly revelations of the concentration camps and the torture-chambers. But even then they could not link up these horrors with the ordinary German folk whom they had met and liked after the last war, in the tea-shops of Cologne, or the beer halls of Munich. Nor indeed could I, though my knowledge of German psychology went deeper than that, and I had had glimpses of the dark forest filled with goblins and satyrs and pagan gods in the racial mind of many Germans.

In the old mansions of Cologne where our officers were billeted during the time of occupation the German owners were less cordial and more aloof, though as a rule courteous. I dined in some of these houses

and talked with Germans of good class. It was there that I first became
aware of a myth which persisted in the minds of most Germans, and
which nothing would alter.

"Our armies, of course, were never defeated in the field", I heard.
"It was a stab in the back which betrayed them. Revolution from
behind by Communists and Jews."

They had set their faith on Wilson's Fourteen Points, which promised
a just peace with no bartering of populations like chattels from one
frontier to another.

When the Treaty of Versailles was published they were stunned by its
severity, and regarded it from the first as a violation of President
Wilson's pledges.

In the French zone of occupation there was more trouble. The French
authorities were instigating a movement for a Rhineland Republic. Its
nominal leader was a plausible and smooth tongued man named Dr.
Dorten whom I met several times. He was in the pay of the French who
provided him with motor cars and money. They recruited a riff-raff
from the prisons and stood by while German policemen were shot in
cold blood. A friend of mine named Gedye, a distinguished correspondent, wrote a book about it called *The Revolver Republic*. At that
time he hated the French with a passionate and excited hatred. But
afterwards he hated the Germans, or at least Nazi Germany, with even
more hatred.

I returned many times to the Rhine during our period of occupation
but I went further afield year after year in search of something which I
never found. I went in search of peace.

Part VI

IN QUEST OF PEACE

1

THE FUTURE HOPE

I WAS alive after a war which had killed so many. It seemed to me—it was a very deep and abiding conviction in me—that we who had survived and had seen those things had a sacred duty to do in this world. Such a war must never happen again, we thought, and it was for us to prevent it so that the next generation of youth would be saved from its agonies and sacrifice. I dedicated myself to peace, and made a vow in my heart that I would work for it above all other motives and interests.

I made this dedication of myself not in any set form of words, not with any self-consciousness or self-conceit, but with a passionate emotion which soaked right through me and lay deep in my sub-conscious mind. For that war to me had been a long torture, not because of my own ordeal—nothing compared with that of the fighting men—but because I had been the eye-witness of the enormous tragedy, an onlooker of blinded boys, shell-shocked men, men gasping with poison gas in their lungs, maimed men without legs and arms, and had seen the splendour of youth slashed to death year after year. Now in peace time the survivors—many of them—had secret wounds for which no pension was given. They were wounded souls. Something had broken in them. Not all the courage, nor all the comradeship, nor all the jokes of Cockney humourists, nor the quick revival of those who forgot the horrors and remembered only their laughter in billets and the spirit of their crowd, could efface in my mind the abomination of a war between civilised peoples whose scientists had invented a machinery of slaughter unknown before in its annihilating power.

We writing men, especially we war correspondents, had something to say after our last despatches had been written. It was to put in all that the censor, or our self-imposed censorship, had omitted. Now we were the critics and the judges. It was our bounden duty to tell all the truth, however terrible. Out of this dreadful history of which we had been the chroniclers we must try to find a different way of life for the common man who had been its victim and its hero. In any case, our mission, surely, was to remind people everywhere, not let them ever forget, the armies of the dead—the young dead—not let the younger crowd believe that war had any glamour or romance.

National pride, the old jingoism, the glory of Empire, the thrill of marching men, the rush to the Colours when war was declared, were no longer the noblest motives which could be taught in public schools. War had become too infernal for all that, engulfing civilian populations as well as the fighting men, and spreading ruin and destruction in its devouring flames.

Before her death Nurse Cavell had spoken words true as death itself—"Patriotism is not enough."

There would be no peace unless there were a deeper sense of human comradeship across the frontiers; unless people of different nations and races could understand each other and be tolerant; unless international justice and good will took the place of the old rivalries and the secret game of diplomacy played by men of cynical minds, or narrow tradition. So millions of us believed after the day of Armistice, and we had the hope—a hope constantly frustrated but always renewed—that such a peace would be made with justice and security for all nations.

2

MAN OF PEACE

One man who, many of us believed, was the greatest man in the world, promised these things. The words of President Wilson, before and after the ending of the war, had been noble and thrilling. His Fourteen Points seemed to be the blue print of a better world, based on justice with liberty and self-determination for the smaller nations. As Sir Douglas Haig had hoped it was not to be a peace of vengeance, but a peace which would give humanity a chance of building a better way of life beyond the ruins of war. No people, said Wilson, would be transferred like chattels behind other frontiers. He was going to found a League of Nations. General Smuts and others had worked out its plan which would be a Parliament of the World for the maintenance of peace and the remedy of grievances, and the reign of law. They were promises which seemed to lift us all out of the dark pit into which we had fallen. After all, we thought, it had been a war to end war. The sacrifice and agony might not have been in vain. So we hoped.

I was in London when President Wilson drove through. Millions of Londoners came out to see this man pass—a new Messiah he seemed to them—a Messiah in a top hat. I stood wedged in a crowd at the end of Old Bond Street when he drove down Piccadilly. There were many people ahead of us. We only had a distant view of that American President, and then for a second. But the people around me had wet eyes when they cheered him, and I found that my own eyes were moist because of a sudden and profound emotion. This was the man who was going to make the good peace. His name would live for ever as the architect of the League of Nations which would secure us against future wars. Wilson was going to turn back the old pages of history written in blood, and on a new leaf write the beginning of a new chapter which would change human history. We believed in him.

3

THE ACCOLADE

Soon after the war I and three of my fellow war correspondents were knighted by the King. I spoke to Beach Thomas about it after we had been playing chess together in Groom's café, in Fleet Street.

"What do you think about this knighthood idea? I should like to get out of it."

"I wouldn't mind refusing it," said Beach Thomas. "But it's too late now, I imagine."

He didn't think it mattered much, either way.

I felt that other men deserved the honour far more, and in any case what did a title mean after all that death, and in this new unhappy world?

I remembered being cross-questioned on the subject by a young woman behind the cash desk of an American coffee shop. The girl who had served me had written my name on top of the bill having seen my portrait and announcement of a lecture in the local paper.

The girl behind the cash desk looked at it and raised her eyebrows slightly.

"*Sir* Philip Gibbs?" she asked with emphasis on the first word.

"Yes," I answered.

"Why *Sir*?"

"I am a knight. I was knighted by King George V."

"Yes, but why?"

"I suppose he thought I had done a good job of work!"

"And had you?"

I "hoped I had".

King George V had been eating his breakfast and was wiping the morning egg off his moustache when I arrived at the Palace for the Investiture. I was in a tall hat and a tail coat, and on the side of my coat, according to instructions, a little loop had been sewn. There was a queue of naval and army officers, airmen, military nurses and others.

We were coached in the procedure, which was simple. When my turn came I knelt down on one knee on a velvet cushion—it would be frightful I thought if I had a touch of cramp—held my top hat in one hand and saw the King take a step in my direction. He touched me on the shoulder with a sword, hung a silver star on the loop of my tail coat, and put a cross and ribbon round my neck.

"I am very glad to give you this," he said.

The cross dangled on its ribbon as I stepped down.

I was a Knight Commander of the British Empire.

"Your food will cost you more," said a friend of mine.

I also became a Chevalier of the Légion d'Honneur. Only my son and I were present when this was conferred on me by the French Ambassador, Monsieur Cambon. He made quite a little speech about it, and then pinned the cross to my breast and kissed me on both cheeks. I was glad of the honour, having a romantic affection for France and her historical traditions, and her poets and saints and heroes. As a boy, d'Artagnan had been my greatest hero. But I seldom wore the little bit of red in my buttonhole, and I had forgotten to do so one evening at a French reception in London. I apologised for this omission to a young Frenchman I knew.

"You are distinguished in being undistinguished," he told me.

All the men present wore the ribbon of the Légion d'Honneur.

4

BERLIN AFTER THE WAR

I went to Berlin soon after the Armistice and many times afterwards. Outwardly, the capital of the Reich seemed untouched by the war and life under the Weimar Republic seemed to be returning to normal conditions.

I heard a debate in the Reichstag and stood in the lobby talking to some of the deputies, among whom was Count von Bernsdorff who had played a tricky game in the United States before they came into the war, but now was talking glibly and smoothly to American journalists. When I looked down upon that scene in the Reichstag I had a queer feeling. If I had been there, I thought, a few months before, and had been discovered as an Englishman, I should have been killed like a rat. These men had been our enemies, organising the German war machine for our destruction. Now they were all very civil, if one happened to be introduced to them.

In the Adlon Hotel, where there was still a bust of the Kaiser with upturned moustaches, elegant ladies wearing rich furs sat in the lounge eating cream buns, with ex-officers who clicked their heels and kissed hands before sitting down. Several of these ladies were English women, wives of German aristocrats, who had been in Berlin all through the war. They had suffered. They had heard the bells clash out for German victories. They had put their fingers in their ears to stop that sound, or lain face down on their pillows weeping because their brothers had been killed on the Somme or in Flanders. But the Germans—their husbands' families and friends—had been kind to them, they told me.

The swing doors of the Adlon opened constantly, and into the lounge came youngish men who had flung off their uniforms and put on civilian clothes not long ago. They all carried black attaché cases filled with papers, diagrams, and blue prints. Over the tea tables in the Adlon they talked business in low voices with other men who had come in with black attaché cases. They were getting back to business much more quickly than our officers were doing in England. It was before the time of inflation.

In the streets the crowds looked shabby, but not stricken by defeat. For years they had lived on *Ersatz* food, *Ersatz* clothes, *Ersatz* everything. Coffee was still being made out of acorns and other substitutes. Some of the people looked puffed and pallid but not starved. Numbers of men still wore their old field-grey tunics from which they had torn the buttons and shoulder straps. At street corners stood blinded men licensed by the police, motionless, with match-boxes on trays. Cripples without legs wheeled themselves about on bits of board. They were the men who had fought in Flanders and on the Somme. This was their reward—to stand sightless listening to the passing crowds, or showing their limbless bodies to passers-by who turned their heads away. The Glory of War!

There was a hectic night life down the Friedrichstrasse. Ex-officers crowded the night clubs and cabarets, drinking cheap champagne and watching naked girls, but looking bored and nervy and—some of them—very evil. For years they had been in the trenches. They had had the luck to come through with life. Was it luck? Wouldn't it have been better to fall with their comrades, instead of sitting here with little sluts, drinking bad champagne and watching naked girls, and falling into deep silences because of the uncertainty of life ahead and the futility of those haunts of vice? Inflation was coming presently. Unemployment was going to sweep up like a tide. Germany had lost the war. The price of defeat would have to be paid. Everything had broken down, even in men's minds. Another bottle of champagne? Another dance with a painted woman?

5

SPARTACISTS

I went to the poorest districts and visited the *Nachtasyl*—the biggest dosshouse of Berlin.

It was crowded at night by the down-and-outs, among whom were ex-officers and at least one *Freiherr*, or nobleman, brought low by drink and dope. They lay in rows in coffin-like beds, coughing, snoring, or lying awake with staring eyes, as I passed between them. So it was in room after room filled always with the same stench of unwashed bodies. There was an enormous wing for women of the lowest class but I was advised not to enter it as so many were hysterical.

In between these two extremes of vicious luxury and social degradation was the great majority of respectable middle-class Berliners trying to carry on in the old way, but anxious about the future which lay behind a dark veil. Most families had lost a son in the war; many of them two or more sons. Only the youngest and the children had escaped the blood bath. What would happen to them?

They were afraid of Communism on the Russian model. They were afraid of secret murder societies already forming and killing their chosen victims. For a few days groups of young men who called themselves Spartacists—they were really Communists—had tried to seize power by force of arms. It was a little Jew named Sklarz (whom I happened to meet) who helped to crush this attempt at revolution. He was a millionaire, living in the Privatstrasse, off the Thiergarten, in a big house filled with art treasures and early printed books. He was afraid that something might happen to his treasures and his million of marks if the Spartacists got the upper hand. At his own expense he had hired a number of ex-officers, paying them twenty marks a day, to put up a fight against these revolutionaries.

They strewed the streets of Berlin with the bodies of the Spartacists, he told me, as a pleasurable reminiscence. "I directed them from the steps of the Reichstag." But it was Comrade Noske who smashed the *Spartacusbund*. It was he who had led the revolt of the Fleet in Kiel, but he came over, or was bought over, to the side of law and order and laid siege to the offices of *Vorwärts* and other buildings in the hands of the Spartacists, who defended themselves with rifle and machine-gun fire, until each stronghold became a shambles under the fire of Noske's Guards.

The Spartacist risings in Saxony, where for a time they did seize power, were put down with merciless brutality. Dr.Liebknecht and Rosa

Luxemburg, who had been the leaders of this movement, were arrested and murdered on their way to prison.

The Socialist leaders of Germany who formed the Provisional Government were men of moderate views and not men of revolution. Ebert the saddler, who became the first Chancellor of the Weimar Republic, was very mild in his democratic theories. Philip Scheidemann who helped to draw up the new Constitution would have been called a moderate Liberal in England.

I had a talk with him and was interested by his personality. He looked more like a Frenchman than a German with a little pointed beard and moustache. In the white jacket he wore when I saw him he might have been a painter, or sculptor, in a studio near the Luxembourg in Paris. I cannot remember much now of what he said, but it was not startling. He hoped there would be a just peace and that Wilson's Fourteen Points would be upheld at the Peace Conference. He spoke of the difficulties ahead for the new Republic in Germany. There were many reactionaries hostile to it behind the scenes. He hoped for the support of British democracy, and that the peace conference would not thrust Germany into the abyss, but would give the people a chance of renewing their economic life with a new and peaceful spirit. I cannot quote him literally, but that, I think, was the gist of our conversation. I left him with the opinion that he was a *poseur* and a man of weak character. Some people regarded him as the German counterpart of Ramsay MacDonald.

6

VIENNESE TRAGEDY

Vienna after the war was more stricken than Berlin. It was utterly stricken. I remember arriving there one evening and seeing the tragic plight of a city which had been renowned for its gaiety and charm. There was no gaiety now but only misery. Along the Kärntnerstrasse emaciated people passed, and in the days that followed thin hands clawed at me and begged for charity.

There was in Vienna, at that time of winter, no fuel in the houses, and no lighting because there was no fuel, and very little food anywhere, even for foreigners like myself who had the means to pay for it. A terribly high percentage of the Viennese children—more than sixty per cent—were suffering from advanced rickets, which in German is called "the English disease". I went into some of the hospitals and saw these little victims of the war. They had no bones in their bodies, but only gristle. They looked like starved monkeys.

A friend of mine named Sir William Goode (he had once been a journalist) was sent to Vienna on the Reparations Commission but he soon found that the idea of reparations in Austria was just a cynical illusion. What they needed was a Relief Commission, and that indeed was what his office became.

A little group of scientists from the Lister Institute in London had arrived to do something about the cure of rickets. One of them was a lady named Mary Chick—now Dame Mary—whom I had known for many years as one of Agnes's friends. With her colleagues she discovered that ultra violet rays and cod liver oil were the best cure for ricketty children, and her work in Vienna was amazingly successful. Years afterwards when I used to go to Vienna I looked at the young people passing and wondered whether as children they had been victims of undernourishment, as indeed they must have been. But there was no sign of that. They looked healthy and sturdy, and something of the old gaiety had returned to them, though other menaces, leading perhaps to a new generation of rickety children, and another chapter of human misery were threatening them from across the German frontier, and from strife between themselves.

I met another English woman in Vienna who brought relief. She was a saint named Eglantine Jebb. In her spirit was a white flame, in her heart great pity for suffering childhood. It was she, among others, who founded a society called "The Save the Children Fund". At that time, even in England, there was so much hatred against the Germans and the Austrians (though less against the Austrians) and so much indifference to the sufferings of many peoples that it seemed hopeless to call for charity. The Government refused all pleas to abandon its blockade of enemy countries until the actual signing of peace, and those who made the pleas were written down as weak sentimentalists by the newspaper Press, with few exceptions. But the call from Eglantine Jebb and her friends to save the children was the first little lamp of charity which was lit in this darkness, and presently it became a bright light. I am thankful now that I was one of the first to link up with it, there in Vienna, when the lamp was first lit, because of the spiritual appeal of that lady whom I called "The White Flame", and I have never lost touch with it in the years that have passed. Eglantine Jebb worked herself to death for the world's children, using the money that began to flow in to provide them with food and clothes and medicine. Her work reached out to Russia in time of famine, which also I saw, and in due time to many stricken countries. It was she who drew up the Children's Charter, which became adopted by the League of Nations, but for a time was lost in the darkness of another war and another peace.

I was cold in Vienna on that first visit after the war. There was no

I

comfort for anyone. I think I must have looked ill, for Miss Chick, as she then was, and one or two of her friends, used to invite me round to their rooms and thrust a little food at me from their own rations.

Vienna had been the capital of a great Empire. Now it was swarming with Austrian refugees of the old aristocratic class who could no longer administer the Czechs, or the Slovaks, or the Slovenes; who had broken away from them. After the Treaty of Trianon when the old Austro-Hungarian Empire was cut to pieces, Vienna became like a bulbous head without a body, and the Hofburg and government departments swarmed with officials on small salaries or pensions with no work to do. Because of new frontiers and new tariffs, trade and industry could not flourish, and Austria tumbled into bankruptcy, and remained for many years impoverished and hopeless.

That was the main cause of an Austrian movement towards an *Anschluss* or union, with Germany, forbidden by the High Powers which now controlled her destiny. Within the German Reich they might, they thought, find new markets, new jobs, and new strength.

The Jews and many intellectuals were hostile to this idea, and terrified of it when Hitler came, but it had a strong support from the business classes and peasants, and from a body of men—the first Fascists—who formed themselves after the peace treaties into battalions with the *Hackenkreuz* or *Swastika* on their armlets.

Standing at a lamp-post in Vienna on another visit I watched thousands of these men pass, and asked a man next to me what was the meaning of this procession.

"They will make trouble one day," he told me. "They have no sense in their heads. They want to kill all Jews—I am a Jew—and they want an *Anschluss* with Germany, and they hate our Social Democrats more than they do Monsieur Poincaré!"

7

The Spirit of Hungary

In Hungary, to which I went a number of times after the peace treaties, there was a bitterness beyond words. Many millions of Hungarians had been put on the wrong side of new frontiers, contrary to the pledge of President Wilson who had weakened at the council table in Versailles, bewildered and deceived because of his ignorance of European geography and conditions, and the passionate propaganda of the Czechs, the Servians, the Rumanians and others.

Hungary had been amputated, and had lost many of her own people, much of her agricultural land, many forests and waterways. A proud race, they smarted under a sense of injustice and humiliation. They would never accept this amputation, they declared. The Czechs, who had been formed into a new state by the gentlemen of Versailles in the sacred name of liberty, with masses of Austrians and other races like a patchwork quilt, without the slightest homogeneity of race, language or friendship—what idiotic statesmanship!—were already violating every law of liberty and democratic idealism by deporting Hungarians—professors, doctors, lawyers, business men, and respectable civilians from places where they had lived all their lives. They had closed the schools and universities. They forced the Czech rule and language upon their minorities, and especially upon the Hungarians. So Hungarians told me, until I was tired of hearing it, because one gets tired so soon of other people's grievances, and because these people brought it into every conversation.

In Budapest there was a propaganda department which worked skilfully and cleverly. Any visiting Englishman, who they thought might be useful to them, was introduced to charming women, entertained over tea tables and dinner tables. Their beautiful eyes looked into his until he wilted and was melted into pity and partisanship for the woes of Hungary. I met many of these ladies and found them charming, but kept my head knowing that underneath this social life in Budapest—pleasant dinners in the Duna Palota on the banks of the Danube—the state of Hungary, the poverty of the peasants was not all the fault of the peace treaties. It was still in a state of feudalism, and the peasants were living in miserable conditions.

Terrible things had happened here in Budapest. Count Karolyi, whom I met in London—he was a great talker but difficult to understand because of a cleft palate—had formed the first government after the war, but had yielded and fled during a Communist uprising led by a Galician Jew named Bela Kun, who had been a tool of Trotsky and the editor of a paper in Moscow. They had seized the city for a time, committing many atrocities, hanging and looting.

After a reign of terror they fled when the Rumanian Army entered Budapest, but the Rumanians were robbers on the grand scale and looted everything before they too departed. A bloody vengeance was taken against the Jews because of Bela Kun when Hungarian cavalry and artillery led by Admiral Horthy gathered in force and marched upon the capital. Outside the Duna Pelota many Jews were shot in cold blood.

The Duna Pelota, sometimes called the Ritz, was a fine hotel—one of the *hôtels de luxe* of Europe. Geoffrey Moss made it the scene of his novel *Sweet Pepper*, and often coming down the grand stairway I used to pass beyond the heavy curtain which his little heroine pulled on one side to watch the scene below. A fat old Turk, in baggy trousers and short jacket of scarlet cloth, served coffee to the guests. A Hungarian band played Gypsy music and the new Jazz. Young naval officers of ours from the Danube Commission danced with Hungarian girls who were all Countesses, or Russian girls who were Princesses, or English girls working with the Reparations Commission and looking prim among these exotic beauties. Unlike Vienna, Budapest was not without fuel and light and food, not even without luxury.

I saw Admiral Horthy open Parliament in the noble buildings—not unlike our own Houses of Parliament—down the Danube, beyond the Iron Bridge, with old Buda on the heights above the opposite bank. It was like a pageant, with Hungarian cavalry officers in the brilliant uniforms of the old Empire, and crowds of young girls in Hungarian costumes, singing and strewing flowers. All very strange after a world war which these people had lost!

They advertised their losses in tramcars, and restaurants, and post offices, but with defiance. They had picture postcards which pulled out, showing the parts of Hungary cut off from them, and underneath, and on the posters pasted up in the tramcars, was the question: "Can it remain like this?" And the answer was given in black letters.— "No, No. Never!"

This conviction that one day all that would be changed was passionate in every Hungarian mind, as far as my own experience went. It flamed out over dinner tables with intellectuals. Pretty women whispered it to one even at the Opera, where one night I went with our Ambassador and his beautiful wife who wore vine-leaves in her hair. It was told to me one day by a Hungarian farmer who spoke German. They were peace-loving folk he said—knowing too much about war. But there was something worse than war, and that was robbery and the loss of one's kinsfolk, and injustice to a whole race.

"There is not a lasting peace in Europe," he told me simply, as though saying that the sun would rise next morning. "The Balkan countries are restless. There will be war again. And when things like that begin Hungary will be there. The old women from the farms will march with our men and sharpen their scissors to cut the throats of our enemies, who have stolen our land, our property, and our kinsmen."

On that day when Horthy opened Parliament and bands were playing Hungarian marches a little lady by my side—she was of course a countess—suddenly seized my hand and spoke burning words.

"We shall never forget! . . . Never! . . . There are things we can never forgive. Never! . . . We belong to a fighting race. This peace cannot last. We shall get our people back, and our lands, if we have to fight with our fingernails!"

The prospect of Peace, so soon after a world war, did not look serene. The peacemakers had sown dragons' teeth in many fields.

8

THE PEACEMAKERS

In Paris the peacemakers with their innumerable staffs and advisers and secretaries had been working at the task of imposing terms upon Germany and reshaping the structure of Europe.

I went to Paris during the Peace Conference and heard with some apprehension of the intrigues and lobbyings behind the scenes, and of the passionate propaganda from the delegates of many nations, or would-be nations, seeking for a revision of frontiers in their own favour. Dr. Benes was very active on behalf of the Czechs, Venizelos on behalf of the Greeks.

I met a little grey-headed man named Colonel House—friends of mine nicknamed him Colonel 'Mouse'—who went about among these delegations, listening and feeling the pulse of passion, on behalf of his chief, the American President, to whom he reported. He was very tactful and diplomatic to all who believed him to be the President's most influential adviser, and therefore were eager to press their points of view upon him, and so reach the ear of the President himself. He over-did his tactfulness and, by trying to smooth out all differences and difficulties, misled everybody, including the President himself. To those like the Czechs and the Greeks and the French who objected to various clauses of the Fourteen Points he gave them interpretations of his own which whittled them down and made them mean almost anything. Meanwhile the propagandists were drawing maps and printing statistics to prove that the Poles had a racial predominance in Silesia, or that the Czechs had historic rights in the Sudetenland, or that Rumania should be given Transylvania. Young gentlemen from Whitehall lay on their tummies studying these maps and making their own. Mr. Harold Nicholson had something to do with the shaping of the new state of Czechoslovakia, and once described his handiwork over the wireless. It was shaped at first like a very thin emaciated crocodile without a tail. It was given a tail by putting in Slovenes and others. Its stomach wanted filling out, so some other minorities were cut off from their own people and used as padding. Its back was too flat, so a bit of Hungary was added. The Austrians of the Sudetenland were of course necessarily incorporated because of their mountains which would give a military barrier to the new nation. None of this could be reconciled with President Wilson's Fourteen Points, none with his pledge about the self-determination of small peoples.

Dragons' teeth for future wars were strewn about the map of Europe by these eager young gentlemen, and by the old men to whom they sent their memoranda.

At the peace table in the Hall of Mirrors, Clemenceau sat there in his black skull cap, saying "No!" to everything if it conflicted by a hair's breadth from what he thought were the vital interests of France. Lloyd George tried hard and valiantly to make a fair and just peace, and showed great wisdom in many of his recommendations and arguments. But always he had his ear to the ground for vibrations in Westminster. He could not go beyond the mood and passion of his own people. He would not jeopardise his own political power even for justice and fair play. Telegrams reached him from the House of Commons urging him to enforce strong penalties on the defeated enemy. He had to take note of that, even if it meant putting Germany into the mud by unpayable reparations.

President Wilson sat there a troubled man. How could he deal with these cauldrons of human passion in Europe? How could he unravel all these tangled races on the border lines? Who was telling him the truth, or who was lying? Fortunately he would establish the League of Nations. That would be his gift to humanity. The League would remedy any injustices which might lurk in the peace treaties. There would be a chance of revision afterwards. The League would prevent future wars and all nations would be able to voice their grievances.

Looking back on all that after a second World War, with Germany as the aggressor and Germans guilty of atrocious crimes, public opinion in its present mood will say: "Clemenceau was right!" "The four hundred M.P.'s were right. The fault of the peacemakers was not their severity but their lenience to Germany and her allies. They ought to have been put in the mud, deeper even than they were. They ought to have been given no chance whatever of economic revival. Lloyd George was soft with them. We were all soft!"

That is one point of view, interesting and arguable, but not valid. It was not at that time accepted by the common folk of the world, nor by the quiet thinkers, nor by millions of people who believed that after the frightful lessons of that war humanity might take a forward step, with a closer comradeship among those who had been the victims and whose sons would be the next, if war came again. They were looking for something better than a war of vengeance. Had not Haig warned them against that? They were looking for a new era, based upon justice and collective security, and inspired by good will. Millions of Germans at that time—those who had fought against us, those who had lost two, three, or four sons, those who had eaten the bread of misery—were eager for admittance into this new ideal of unity and comradeship.

The leaders of Europe, the politicians, the diplomatists, the propagandists, the jingoes, and the corrupt, let down the decent-minded common folk everywhere in all countries, not only by a badly made peace, but, worse still, afterwards, by their betrayal of the League. If they had made a better peace, if they had been sincere in their lip-service to the League, the second World War would not have happened. They missed one of the great opportunities in history, in a time of deep human emotion, caused by the long agony of war and by the sense of relief when peace came, to rise above national egotism and narrow patriotism. For years, for long years, the proof of this was the support of the League ideal in millions of little homes in this country and others, long after its weakness was apparent to most of us, until the last hope and the last illusion faded and war was inevitable.

Would Hitler have had his chance if Germany had not gone down into the abyss in the time of inflation, followed by a tidal wave of unemployment?

9

DANSE MACABRE

Paris during the Peace Conference was abnormal, feverish, and a little mad. Like all cities in Europe it had St. Vitus' dance and was possessed by the Jazz mania. They danced all night long in halls and cabarets, the *midinettes* and the men who had been the *poilus*—the hairy ones—of Verdun, and the Champagne, and the Somme, as well as the women of many nations who were in the secretariats of foreign delegations, and the young gentlemen of the Foreign Offices and commissions. Old Clemenceau watched this jigging up and down the polished floors to the beat of drums and the wails of saxophones. Beneath his shaggy old eyebrows his steely eyes glinted and he made a *bon mot*.

"Je n'ai jamais vu les visages si tristes ni les derrières si gaies!"—"I have never seen such sad faces nor such gay backsides!"

It was a *danse macabre*.

It was a false and fevered gaiety. Beneath all this chase of joy there were innumerable tragedies. French youth had been mown down and this was a dancing on their graves. In the Palais des Beaux Arts, to which I went one day, maimed and mutilated men were trying to get some life back into paralysed limbs by exercises with strange-looking machines. In military hospitals were men without noses or jaws or any human-looking face. There were thousands of blinded men. They did not dance.

And already there was the beginning of a greed and corruption associated with the devastated regions of the north which, I am convinced, led to a general lowering of morality among French politicans and individuals, followed by a complete cynicism of the people regarding their political leaders, accountable in part for the weakness and defeat of France in 1940. Those devastated regions, the long track of ruin—forty miles deep—from one end of the fighting line to the other, where the most heroic youth of England and France and the United States had fought and died in masses, the terrible place names of the war—Souchez, Vimy, St. Quentin, Verdun, Château Thierry—became the happy hunting ground of those contractors, builders, engineers, lawyers, sharks, who had claims, or bought up other people's claims, for reconstruction. Many claims were faked and their values multiplied by cooked arithmetic. Local deputies passed them with a nod and a wink for a share of the plunder. I heard fantastic stories of small contractors and members of business syndicates who suddenly blossomed out into great style, rushed about in enormous cars, flinging money about with wild prodigality, moved into fine apartments down the Avenue des Champs Elysées, and lived with expensive mistresses— all out of some rubble heap in the bombarded areas upon which they had built up a claim for millions of francs. Little contractors, makers of cement and tiles, timber merchants, sanitary engineers, were finding the devastated areas an inexhaustible mine of wealth, and in the *bistros* where ex-soldiers who had been through the fiery furnace of the war sat with their women or their old comrades, these things were known and discussed with exceeding bitterness and foul oaths.

10

THE LITTLE GENTLEMAN IN ROME

I went to Rome. In a lighthearted moment the news editor of the *Daily Chronicle*, my friend Ernest Perris, said: "Go and interview the Pope." "Not a chance!" I told him, but I was glad to go to Rome.

Little Italian officers with grey-blue cloaks flung over their shoulders —the tradition of the *toga*—walked up and down the Pincio Gardens, or the Piazza di Venezia, talking, talking. I overheard one word always. It came as a kind of chant from every group of Italians in the cafés or in the streets. Fiume . . . Fiume . . . Fiume. D'Annunzio, the bald-

THE FIRST JOURNALIST TO INTERVIEW THE POPE
(By F. Matania)

BERLIN CATHEDRAL
(A drawing by the Author)

headed poet, had raised a force of volunteers and seized this port on the Adriatic, to the great displeasure of the peacemakers who were shocked by this grabbing of territory before the peace treaties had been signed, or before the ink was dry upon them.

The Italians were furious about the Peace Conference. Italian claims had been utterly disregarded they said. England had gone back on all her promises and the secret treaty she had made with Italy. President Wilson, that "sham Messiah" (as they called him) had ruled out the secret treaties. Orlando had sat at the table muttering four words: "Il Tratta di Londra". No one had paid attention to his claims or protests. Italy had been betrayed, they said.

So I was told by an Italian officer in Rome who became very passionate on the subject.

"Next time," he said, "we shall know what to do. We shall not be so trustful of the British word of honour. We will drive a harder bargain."

I hoped there would be no 'next time'. Why were people talking about another war while the wounds of the last were still unhealed?

I was not in a hurry to do anything about an interview with the Pope, which I knew was a fantastic and impossible idea. No journalist had ever interviewed a Pope. I went to see St. Peter's and walked up its mighty pavement and looked at the fat cherubs on the great columns, and stood at the altar with its marble *baldachino*, and thought of all the history of the Catholic Church since the time of Peter. I had friends in Rome with whom I lunched and dined. One was a merry little man named Emanuele, the editor of the *Corriere della Sera*. He had been with me at Sangatte near Calais when Blériot was preparing to cross the Channel. He was always laughing at life and its absurdities. He thought the making of peace ought to have been left to us journalists. We knew where the places were. We should have made a better peace than the politicians and the young men in the Foreign Offices.

"What are you doing here in Rome?" asked some of my friends.

I laughed and told them.

"I have come to interview the Pope!"

They thought that very amusing. No journalist was allowed inside the Vatican.

So I was told also by a cardinal who had been in the United States for some years and spoke perfect English with a slight American accent. I had an introduction to him and he received me very cordially. He was a tall heavily built man with good-natured eyes and an informal manner. He raised his hands and laughed when I told him of my mission in Rome.

"My dear Sir! No Pope has ever been interviewed by a newspaper man. No journalist is even allowed into a public audience because now and then one of them has abused this privilege. It is quite impossible!"

I agreed. I told him that I would return to England at once.

"Well, not at once," he said. "Have a look round Rome. There are many things to see. Where are you staying?"

I told him the Hotel Bristol, and he made a note of it.

"Don't go until you have come to see me again," he said.

Three mornings later when I was shaving in my bedroom at the Hotel Bristol, a little envelope was brought to me. Inside it was a card on which a few words were written. His Holiness would receive me at 12 o'clock the following morning.

I was astonished. I also felt alarmed and nervous. What was the meaning of this? I could not believe that there was any chance of getting an interview with the Pope for the purposes of publication. Probably my friendly cardinal had arranged a private audience, or an audience with a group of others who would go down on their knees to get his blessing and hear a few words addressed to them. Not for a moment did I believe that I should be allowed to question him and publish his answers. But in any case it was embarrassing. One had to put on evening clothes, I knew. One had to go down on one's knee and kiss his ring. I should probably knock my nose against his hand. I should make a fool of myself because of my nervousness.

On the morning when I was to be received I put on evening clothes in full daylight and spoilt two perfectly good ties. That was a disaster and time was getting on. I rang the bell and sent for a waiter.

"I want you to lend me a white tie," I told him, "I'm going to see the Pope."

He was willing to oblige and lent me a white tie, which would not lie straight. I am hopeless at making a good bow. I was late in getting a *vettura* and had to urge the driver to go faster. "Presto! Presto!"

He whipped up his lean nag, but it was a long way from the Hotel Bristol to St. Peter's and I kept glancing at my watch. I had cut it rather fine. It would be frightful if I arrived late. I had only a few minutes to spare when I arrived at the flight of steps leading into the Vatican from the great square of St. Peter's. An officer of the Swiss Guard examined my card and then saluted elaborately and pointed the way upstairs with his sword.

On the next flight I had to pass through a long chamber in which other guards were pacing about. They looked magnificent in their costumes of the sixteenth century shouldering long pikes which they grounded in salute as I passed. My knees felt weak. I was conscious that my evening tie was working up at the back of my collar. It was an ordeal to face these guards and those in other rooms, as I walked alone across polished floors on which it would be easy to come a cropper.

I was shown into an antechamber in which a bearded monk was sitting. A little door was opened by an ecclesiastic in black with a touch of red. He beckoned to the monk who passed through the little door. Presently, when the monk came out, it was my turn. The door was opened for me. The chamberlain beckoned with a smile. A very little man in a snow-white habit stood there. It was Benedict XV called *il Gobbo*, or the dwarf, by the Roman populace. Yet his small size did not rob him of great dignity and he had a saint-like face with dark, luminous, lively eyes, behind his spectacles. I went down on one knee but he grasped my wrist, and raised me up, and led me to a gilded chair beside his own in which he sat.

"Now we can talk," he said, in French with a strong Italian accent.

My nervousness left me. The Pope was not frightening.

He spoke simply and directly, asking many questions about the state of Europe and the feeling in England and America. Then he spoke about the war and its results. He alluded to the abuse he had received from both sides because of his neutrality. The French had called him pro-German. The Germans had called him pro-French and pro-English. Stories of atrocity had poured in from all sides. French stories of German atrocities, German stories of Russian atrocities. He had condemned this war as a sin against God. Many times he had called upon the peoples to stop their fratricidal strife, but his speeches had been suppressed. He had tried to alleviate the cruelties of war through the Red Cross and other agencies. They had done a good deal for prisoners of war. Then he brushed that on one side, and entered into a discussion on the economic results of the war. He could see no quick way of escape from ruin, no rapid means of recovery.

"We must steel ourselves to poverty," he said, and alluded to the great illusions of masses of people, duped by their leaders, that after the destruction of the world's wealth there could be the same prosperity. He spoke sternly of the profiteers and in a pitying way of the poverty-stricken peoples.

"Those who profited out of the war must pay most," he said.

He spoke of the lust for money of many employers of labour, and used a gesture familiar in Italy to denote the money grabbers. It was a little gesture of rubbing the thumb against the forefinger which I had seen Italian peasants do. He hoped that there would be more widespread recognition of the rights of the working classes, their fundamental rights of wages sufficient to support their families in decency and health, to educate their children, to have a good roof over their heads without overcrowding in foul conditions. That, he said, is the first charge on employers and those are the natural and legitimate rights of all men, denied at this time to millions of them everywhere.

He reminded me of the Encyclicals on Labour by his predecessor Leo XIII, and described them as more liberal and progressive than any social policy yet fulfilled. He hoped I would try to make them better known by ordinary folk and political leaders who were anxious to improve the status of the working classes, for Pope Leo XIII had set out and analysed in great detail the principles of social justice, and laid down the foundations of economic welfare.

He spoke very movingly, I thought, about the horror and tragedy of the war and of the heritage of hatred which it had left behind. A good peace and a lasting peace could not be built upon hatred or revenge. Humanity must first learn charity, and comradeship, and a new brotherhood of men across the frontiers. If another war were to be avoided there must be charity and peace in the hearts of peoples.

All the time he was talking I was troubled by the uneasy doubt as to whether I might publish this conversation, and whether indeed he knew my profession and purpose. I could not leave him with that uncertainty in my mind, and with some timidity I asked him if I might publish the words he had spoken to me. He smiled through his spectacles and said: "That is the purpose of this conversation!"

I went back to my hotel and wrote down the interview in detail and at considerable length. Then I paid another visit to the cardinal who had obtained this great favour for me and asked him whether he would read and pass what I had written.

"No, no!" he answered. "Not a word! You can write what you like and publish what you like provided it is the truth. We trust you."

I did not abuse this trust, and my interview with Benedict XV was quoted in all the great newspapers of the world. The comments upon it were favourable. It had a "good Press" far outside the domain of Catholic journalism, and many people of liberal views were surprised and impressed by the ardent desire of the Pope for justice to the common man, and by his condemnation of the money grabbers and profiteers.

His plea for charity and peace in the heart of the world in order to avoid a new war was read, no doubt, by the world's statesmen and politicians, and by the younger intellectuals over café tables, and by fathers of sons who would be old enough for the next war if it came. But it had no effect whatever on the course of history. Its warning and its wisdom were utterly ignored, and those people of power who may have read it did exactly the contrary of the Pope's emotional and noble pleading. He had pointed the way to peace. They took the other road to war by selfish economic policies throttling trade, by hostile combinations, by betraying the League, and by political hatred and corruption, until out of all that there was the devil to pay.

11

VICTORY MARCH

I was in London for the Victory March. I had a place on a stand outside Buckingham Palace not far from the King's saluting point where the war correspondents and other newspaper men were assembled.

It was a magnificent pageant of the fighting men of all branches in the Army, and of naval men from the Grand Fleet, and airmen and merchant seamen, and women from the services. One forgot for a little while the troubled state of Europe, the low-grade morality of European statesmen, the land-grabbing already happening, the failure to make "homes for heroes", or to redeem any of the promises held out to the nation. This was our Victory Day, and a tribute by vast crowds to those who had saved us in time of war. There were many men in the crowd who still wore hospital blue, and many—given front places—who had wheeled themselves here in chairs for cripples. One watched the passing of this pageant with emotion. These men marching by were those whom I had seen covered with the clay of Flanders and the white chalk of the Somme. Now for an hour or two they had their reward. They were the heroes. They deserved the roaring cheers of the crowd, rising louder, as I was glad to hear, when our merchant seamen—neglected before the war and forgotten afterwards—went by with unmartial step. We owed our victory, our liberty, our lives, to all of these. The old, old Past walked with them—all our history and all our ghosts.

That night London went mad, but the most part of it was a decent joyous madness without vice in it. I was caught up in the surging crowds who linked arms and were cheering and singing. Outside Buckingham Palace they called for the King time and time again, and he had come out to his balcony, with the Queen and his family, smiling down on this vast multitude, raising his hand to them. At night I found myself in Pall Mall, with sore feet which had been trodden on many times. A soldier, just a little drunk, was on the pedestal of Florence Nightingale's statue, with his arm round the figure of that lady. He was making a speech to which no one listened except myself. Over and over again he assured the crowds that the bloody war wouldn't have been won without the help of women like good old Florence. "It's the women of England who won the war," he shouted, "and that's the bloody truth of it!" No one challenged this statement.

No one listened except me, curious to know what he was saying with such fervour and passion. I never pass the statue of Florence Nightingale now without thinking of that champion of womanhood who was a little drunk.

After the Victory March, what then?—There had been riots among the men even on the parade ground of Whitehall because of delay in demobilisation. They had done their bit. They were fed up with Army discipline. They wanted to fling off their uniforms and get back to Civvy Street. Millions of them did before long, but Civvy Street was not strewn with roses nor paved with gold. It was difficult to find jobs. Women had taken many of the places for lower wages than men and employers were loth to let them go.

Employers in city offices received the personal applications of young officers somewhat coldly. "What do you know?" they asked of young men who had left their public schools to join the New Armies, who had been very fine machine-gunners, or pilots of aircraft, or tank officers, or with the P.B.I. which was the "Poor Bloody Infantry". Many of them had been captains and majors before the age of twenty-five. But they couldn't answer that question: "What do you know?" very satisfactorily. They had had no training in office work. They had not been trained for anything except war, which was now at an end. Some of them bought little farms and lost their money. Some of them went in for chickens, and lost their money. Some of them became agents for vacuum cleaners, or cosmetics, or women's underwear, and hated ringing the door bells to ask for the lady of the house, and could not make a go of it.

So it was with the men during this transition from war to peace and afterwards—for years afterwards—during the tides of unemployment.

The streets of London were put to ransom by groups of crippled or able-bodied men playing the old war songs or the new Jazz. Their scouts stood on either side to catch the passers-by. Pianos mounted on carts were played by young men attended by six or seven others who rattled their collecting boxes. They were, perhaps, rogues and vagabonds by instinct, and made a fairly good living out of the compassion of the public. I asked one of such a team—about eight of them—how it worked out financially. "Not too bad", he said frankly. "About thirty bob a week for each of us. Better than starvation."

But there were hundred of thousands of ex-soldiers who wanted better work than that and could not find it. They became bitter and ugly tempered. I heard them talking and holding meetings in public places. I had an idea then that we might be on the edge of revolution, or of riots and uprisings. The "dole" saved the situation in that way, but it was a demoralising and wretched substitute for work. The weaklings made the best of it, preferring the dole without work, to work on wages not much better. The men with pride in them—craftsmen, and mechanics, and factory workers—hated this enforced idleness. It got them down in the end.

I visited the London dosshouses at this time and found them crowded with young men—not the old tramps and lags and down-and-outs. There was a new class here—ex-service men who still washed themselves and kept their clothes clean if they could. Somehow they scraped up a shilling a night for a doss down in a Salvation Army shelter. No "Homes for Heroes" after all!

12
COUNTRY LIFE

My private life at this time after the war was peaceful in its surroundings, though there was no sense of peace in my mind. We gave up the old Georgian house in Finsbury Park and built a bungalow at Dorking in Surrey on the edge of Deepdene House which was being run as an hotel by a Russian princess—or if she wasn't a princess she ought to have been. It was at the top of a winding lane called Punchbowl Lane and Agnes called the bungalow 'Ladygate'. My cynical and romantic-looking friend Colonel Champion Faunthorpe—the man who had killed eighty-two tigers and written several sonnets—was amused by these names and sent me a postcard addressed to "The Boozing Ken, Dorking". It came to me as straight as an arrow! We had several acres of ground surrounded by beautiful meadows and clumps of noble trees. It was, we thought, a little Paradise—until one day we observed an alert and sharp-eyed young man making marks on the trees and measuring up the ground. Then to our horror we found that we were to be on the edge of a new housing estate. The trees were cut down, small houses were built, and new roads marked out before we fled further afield, outside a village called Puttenham, south of the Hog's Back.

There I came to know a charming old gentleman by name of Henry Howard, a descendant of those who once held the high places in England. Standing outside his little old manor house one day he said: "My dear sir, I tremble to think of what will happen to this countryside in three hundred years!" Remembering my experience at Dorking I was startled by that long look ahead. "My dear sir," I answered him, "I tremble to think of what will happen to this countryside in three years." So far the countryside thereabouts has escaped the advance of the jerry builder, and nightingales still sing in the holly trees, rabbits still scuttle in the meadows, the cuckoo calls in the great park of Peper Harrow, as it did to Saxon ears before Domesday Book was written.

The cattle browse on the short turf of the heath where a Roman legion pitched its camp and left a tesselated pavement, still buried a foot or so below the soil. The thrushes still pipe out "Pretty Dick, Pretty Dick!" as when the Normans built the little old church. The blackbird chuckles in the hedge along the Pilgrim's Way through Compton, where those on the road to Canterbury scratched their crosses on the pillars, as one may see. But one fears for the safety of this beauty and its peace so near to London, so easily grabbed by the jerry-building men.

We had a pleasant house called 'Overponds' in Puttenham, with a fair garden in which Agnes worked and made roses grow.

One day, not long after the war, two men came down from Harrods, and brought a big box, and set up an aerial and turned a switch. Suddenly out of it came loud music followed by the voice of an announcer from Savoy Hill—a pleasant, friendly, voice which afterwards we came to know. It was the beginning of "Wireless", one of the greatest miracles of the new world, and one of the greatest boons to lonely men and women and blind men and women, and lovers of music —sometimes frightful with its modern cacophanies—or delirious Jazz— and to nurseries of small people listening on winter's evenings to the Children's Hour, and to clerks and farmers and seamen and all sorts everywhere, tuning in to the news or a symphony concert, or Myra Hess playing Mozart, or Kreisler's magic bow, or to some loveliness of words, and sometimes, but not often, to some wisdom which went deep to the root of things. The pleasant voice announced the news of the world, year after year, smoothly, and blandly, and unalarmingly, though it was a story of disillusion, fading hopes, betrayals, economic catastrophe, political idiocy, international strife; and then one day the announcement of the second World War, still in that suave and cheerful tone, as though nothing alarming were on hand.

My son Anthony was at Oxford after his Stonyhurst days, and then for a time became assistant editor of a magazine produced by the Harmsworth Press until he asked for a year to try his hand at novel writing. His first novel was *Little Peter Vacuum* which went through eleven editions.

Our house and garden became a rendezvous at week-ends for old friends and new. The old friends came down from London in a variety of cars. The new friends belonged to the neighbourhood of the Hog's Back who had called upon us. Many pretty young women were attracted by Tony's good looks, though he was curiously indifferent to their charms. His Stonyhurst friends came down for week-ends and played tennis on our lawn, or a wild Oxford version of croquet which was called "madders" because it made the players get madder and madder. I still teach it to young friends and sometimes beat them. Old colonels with their lady wives, rich city men who had gone rustic and become local squires, dames of the old quality devoted to gardening like Miss Jekyll, American editors and literary men (including Sinclair Lewis) passed across my lawn and sat in my sunny rooms. One of these Americans named John Tunis, a well known writer on international sport, attended one of our tea parties and had to leave the room from time to time to laugh outside the door. The English accent was too much for him, with the "zwah-zwah" of the military gentlemen, and the high pitched cries of the Surrey ladies, and the Oxford accent of the younger men. He told me that it was like a Somerset Maugham play. He couldn't believe it was real. It struck him as being incredibly comical. My old friend, Edgar Lander, did a caricature of one of these Saturday afternoons at Overponds, which still hangs on one of my walls and makes me laugh every time I look at it.

It all sounds gay and peaceful, and so it was in sunny hours now and then, but we were not happy. It was mostly my fault. I was incapable of being happy at that time, because the war had left me with frayed nerves and a painful obsession. I could not forget the tragedy of the war and the slaughter of youth. I was obsessed with its horror, and felt guilty of having a car, of living in comfort in this good house and lovely garden when so many men who had been the heroes of the war were trudging about the streets looking for jobs. I agonised foolishly—what could I do about it?—over the state of the world, the interminable delays and disappointment of the League, the ghastly happenings in Russia, the misery of Germany and Austria in time of inflation, the economic madness of tariffs and exchange barriers throughout Europe, the Black and Tan brutalities in Ireland. I was in search of peace when there was no peace, and I must have been a trying fellow to live with. Perhaps also I was searching for personal happiness and couldn't find it, lacking serenity. A friend of mine described me at the time as a man waiting at a junction of life for a train that never came. And underneath Agnes's social gaiety, her wit which always raised a laugh, her incessant work in house and garden, she was not happy. She had been very ill, after serious operations. Twice her life had been saved at great hazard by Dame Mary Scharlieb, that wonderful old woman who, at eighty years of age, was still performing miracles of surgery. But it was in her mind that Agnes suffered. She too had agonised horribly in the war. Now this country life seemed to her foolish and futile, in spite of its loveliness. Some bigger ambition of work was taking shape in her mind. It was to become a scientist, possibly a doctor. But how could she set about that when she had to keep house and entertain guests, and look after the household bills, and the maidservants, and the gardeners? She still had to look after me, and that job held her back and was very worrying.

For I was always worrying. Every time I wrote a book I announced in a sepulchral tone: "This is the last book I shall ever write. I've used up all my ideas. I'm finished!" They had heard that so often that it only raised a laugh and a sigh. It was the boy who cried: "Wolf! Wolf!" But one day, as I reminded them, the wolf really came.

It was necessary to write books, for now that was my means of livelihood. I was no longer a journalist, except for special missions abroad, having resigned my position on the *Daily Chronicle* and the best salary I had ever earned in Fleet Street, because of the Black and Tans in Ireland. It sounds absurd now.

The *Daily Chronicle* had been bought by Lloyd George and a group of friends, and their Irish policy in this paper which I had served so long, was to suppress the demand for Irish independence and liberty, by putting in the young ruffians of the Black and Tans with *carte blanche* for reprisals in towns and villages. I felt very hot about it—too hot perhaps—because the young Sinn Feiners who ambushed our troops and burned down fine old mansions belonging to the Irish gentry, and who did worse things than that on a Sunday morning in Dublin, were not angels. Many of them were just young murderers, backed by their priests who called it a holy war for the old faith and the old dream of an Irish nation. But it seemed to me shameful, and it does so still, that after a war which was supposed to be for liberty and the self-determination of peoples, we should hire a lot of young thugs and let them loose upon the Irish. I heard horrible stories of their drunken orgies and their shooting up of Irish villages, and their killing of boys—some of whom at least had the old dream of Ireland in their souls. I resigned—on a postcard—to the regret of Ernest Perris who had become editor, and the deep annoyance of Lloyd George.

I was now a novelist, once again with nothing between me and penury but a wad of typewriting paper, the click of a machine, and the hope of a plot for a new story which often would not come, while I racked my brain, had restless nights, and went for long nervous walks at a great pace in search of ideas, which played hide-and-seek over heaths and commons.

But I went further afield than that. I went on my first visit to the United States of America.

Part VII

AMERICAN JOURNEYS

1

STAGE FRIGHT

It was in the early months of 1919 that I made my first American lecture tour, to be followed by the same exhausting adventure in 1920 and 21, and, after a long gap, 1941. On my first visit, the American people were racked by a nation-wide feud between those who stood for President Wilson and his ideal of the League of Nations, and those who were bitterly, passionately, and fiercely against him—as very quickly I discovered.

In an article written for the *New York Times* I slipped in the phrase that I was "all for Wilson", and in answer to that I had hundreds of letters from unknown correspondents "putting me wise", as they said, to the bitterness in their breasts because Wilson, in their view, had played a party game, not taking Republicans into his counsels for the Peace Conference, and was busy dragging the United States deeper into the European jungle which had already cost them one war, and from which they were eager to escape. He was, they told me, a hypocrite, an egoist, and a man of low moral character. In fact there was nothing too bad they could say about this man whose passing through the streets of London had brought tears to the eyes of thousands.

Ignorant at first of this intensity of political feeling I made a *gaffe* of the first order a few days after my arrival. Chief Justice Hughes, afterwards Secretary of State for Foreign Affairs, was my Chairman at a talk I gave in the Union Club, and, sitting next to him at lunch, I asked him what he thought of President Wilson, not knowing—God help me!—that he had been the Republican candidate for the Presidency against Wilson himself. It was the last question I should have asked him, but Mr. Hughes was a great gentleman and he gave a character study of Wilson free from personal prejudice or any touch of malice.

When I landed in New York I was astonished to find that I was not unknown to the American people. It was a pleasant and, I must say, an alarming fact. During the war my work as a correspondent had been published year after year (without any payment to me) in the *New York Times*, and syndicated throughout America. My articles appeared on millions of American breakfast tables with the grape fruit and the Post-toasties. By this great good luck I had made, unknown to myself, innumerable friends.

One of these unknown friends was the first to greet me when I reached the Vanderbilt Hotel and found a stack of cables awaiting me. I was rung up on the telephone and a girl's voice spoke to me in the friendliest way. "Welcome to our city, Philip Gibbs—and here's another call for you." It was the telephone operator.

She spoke to a frightened man. I found New York, and the welcome given to me, and the first lecture for which I was booked at the Carnegie Hall, more terrifying than war. I was a bundle of nerves and timidity. My first impression of driving through the streets of New York up from the docks convinced me that I had left the old world which I knew and had stepped on to another planet. Those towering skyscrapers, through which the narrow streets seemed tunnelled, the roar of motor traffic, the seething crowds rushing about like ants from an upturned ant-heap, and presently the hundreds of telephone calls, the thousands of hands I had to shake, the crowded receptions with innumerable new faces, and that audience in the Carnegie Hall on my first appearance, filled me with terror, though I had to keep smiling and hiding this blue funk. I wrote a sentence in the *New York Times*—they had lagged me for a series of impressions on America—which described my first sensations with poignant truth, though it greatly amused my readers. It was a phrase which came from my nerve ganglia, all quivering after a first walk through Broadway at night. I wrote that I felt "like a trench cootie under the fire of 10,000 guns". Now a cootie is a louse, as I had lately learnt, and this simile tickled them to death, as I was told, though it expressed in utter truthfulness my impressions as a traffic dodger down the Great White Way.

During those first days and nights in New York I became dazed and bewildered, especially by the parties "thrown" in my honour. There were so many new faces, and so many new names to remember or forget, so many hands to shake, so many friendly words and questions to answer. A baldheaded, dark-eyed, blue-chinned man in evening clothes came up to me half way through one of these parties and spoke as though he knew me well.

"How are you getting on, Gibbs? Hard going, eh?"

I didn't know him from Adam and he saw that I didn't.

"That's all right," he said. "I'm the guy who was having tea with you this afternoon for two and a half hours."

It was Tom Wells, editor of *Harper's Magazine*, and afterwards a great friend of mine in London, and then in Paris where he went to live in a charming apartment overlooking a garden near the Ministry of War on the Left Bank.

My brother, 'Cosmo Hamilton' as he called himself, and his American wife, Julie, met me at the docks and took me in hand as though I were a timid and tired child—as indeed I was! I went to their home in Greenwich (not Greenwich Village) forty miles or so from New York to which I had to keep returning. My brother was in the heyday of fame and fortune. He was writing with untiring industry and zeal, plays, serial stories, short stories, film stories and novels, earning what seemed to me astronomical numbers of dollars, all of which were required to pay for his house, his car, his English clothes, his flat in New York and his wife's frocks and parties. My brother would arrive home when he was in New York to find masses of hats and coats in the hall, and to hear the chatter and laughter and shrill screams of women guests. His wife was giving another party. He would creep away into his study, heave a sigh or a curse, and settle down to work on a new play or film story, while Julie in the drawing room was having a gay time and keeping her friends laughing by her audacious wit and her exuberant vitality. On that first visit she mothered me and I was grateful to her.

"What's the matter with your arm?" asked my brother soon after my arrival.

I could not raise my right arm without pain beyond elbow height. It had been like that since a day or two after the Armistice when I was travelling in a car at sixty miles an hour through a triumphal arch beyond the field of Waterloo. On the other side of the arch I saw an old woman throw an apron over her head and I knew that something unpleasant was going to happen. It did, and my car was knocked to bits by a military lorry travelling with equal speed. It caught my arm a glancing blow, and Cecil Roberts who happened to be there sat up all night massaging it. But it had remained stiff, as I told my brother.

"Little old Dr. Cook will put that right," he told me. "Let's go and see him."

'Little old Dr. Cook' was a wonder worker in New York, to whom my brother went repeatedly for advice on diet—no meat, no eggs—and get what he called 'a touch of the juice'. The 'juice' was a form of electrical massage which made my brother feel, he said, like a two-year-old, and step down Fifth Avenue as though he owned it.

Dr. Cook was a remarkable little man, the soul of kindness and charity, with many odd and unorthodox theories on the human body and the cure of disease which had given him the reputation of being a quack and a charlatan. Nevertheless he cured people of cataract by electrical vibrations—I met an old lady in his rooms who had been blind for fifteen years and now could read small print without glasses—and of all manner of illness due, he said, to wrong diet, and especially to eggs which he regarded as deadly poison to many people. Anyhow he had a look at my arm, laughed merrily, and said: "We'll soon put that all right! Step into that box for a few minutes." I went into a little cabinet and heard the whirr of electricity. A slight sweat came into the palms of my hands.

A few minutes later I came out and he said: "Now raise your arm."

I raised it.

"Any pain?"

"Not a twinge!"

Then he took a glass tube and rubbed my arms and legs with it. Sparks and crackles came from it. It was the 'juice' which my brother had mentioned.

It seemed to tone me up. I had a dose of it now and then before lecturing and it braced me, I felt, for that unpleasant ordeal, though its effect only lasted an hour or so.

I was without its aid when I stepped on to the platform for my first lecture in Carnegie Hall in evening clothes with a beautiful white tie, looking like an English gentleman, I hoped, but feeling like a mouse in a trap, or a frightened rabbit.

My chairman on that occasion was Frederick Palmer, the famous war correspondent who had been with me during the Battles of the Somme. He made a very fine speech, I am told, but I did not hear a word of it, and wondered whether I could get through the first sentences of my own speech without being sick. Then I was aware somehow that I had to begin. There were 10,000 people in that hall, and suddenly they all rose, and it was like a wave with the sound of a wave. I was startled and did not understand for a moment, but it was, as I was told afterwards, the highest compliment which an American audience can pay to any speaker. Does that sound like bragging? Well, I am not a bragger, but I like to remember that great and kindly courtesy to a writer whose words through the first World War had reached out to them.

I had a tragic tale to tell. It was about the war and the effects of war in Europe, but twice I made the audience laugh when I didn't mean to. I had been going for about thirty-five minutes and it seemed like an hour. I glanced at my wrist-watch and could not believe that such a short time had passed. Ten minutes later I looked at it again, and thinking to myself: "Good heavens! My watch has stopped!" raised it to my ear. The whole audience laughed, guessing my trouble. Then at the end when I made my bow and breathed a silent prayer of thanks that somehow I had got through this ordeal I tried to get off the stage by way of the door through which I had come in. But I could not find the door in the panelled back scene. I pressed one of the panels. It did not yield so I returned and bowed to the audience again. Three times I did this, and at the third time the audience laughed very heartily.

Nothing I ever did in the way of lecturing was so bad as that first ordeal, but I never overcame my nervousness before standing on a platform and talking for an hour and a quarter. It was the stage fright from which so many actors suffer. There does not seem to be a cure for it and it attacks some of the greatest orators, of whom I am not one. I remember dining next to Lord Reading when he was making his farewell to the Bar before going as Viceroy to India.

"You are not eating your dinner," I said to him after a while. "No," he said, "I have to make an after dinner speech." Yet as Rufus Isaacs he had earned his living by making speeches every day in court.

And once my brother Cosmo stood behind Lord Balfour, when he came to America during the war and spoke to a great American audience in New York. He had a serene smile. His words flowed like a silver stream. His phrases were perfect. His voice was mellow. But behind his back his hands were shaking like aspen leaves in a stiff breeze.

2

ODD HAPPENINGS

On this first visit of mine I had to talk to the City Club of New York, but it was arranged by my agent that I should break off halfway, allowing my audience to have a little drink and stretch their limbs. I should be transported to the Forty-fourth Street Theatre to make a speech on behalf of funds for American soldiers and sailors. So it happened. I was thrust into a taxi-cab, hurried off to the theatre, received by a tremendous explosion (a flashlight photo) in the dressing room of Al Jolson, the funny man, thrust on to the stage in the middle of a harem scene (scores of beautiful maidens) and told to make my speech while the audience raffled for an original letter from Lloyd George to the American nation.

Surprised by my rapid transmigration from the City Club, and by my presence in an oriental harem, feeling very hot, rather flustered, and not knowing what to do with my hands, I kept screwing up a bit of paper which had been given to me at the wings. By the time I had finished my three minutes speech it was a bit of wet mushy pulp. When I left the stage a white-faced man in the wings who had been making frantic signs to me, informed me coldly that I had utterly destroyed Lloyd George's letter to the American nation which had just been raffled for many hundreds of dollars. . . . After that I went back to finish my speech at the City Club.

3

LECTURE TOURS

I came to know all the horrors of a lecture tour in the United States, mitigated, but not abolished, by the abounding and generous hospitality of the American people, by the friendliness and alertness of American audiences—quick to laugh at any little joke or amusing anecdote—and by the many pleasant people one meets on the way. The horrors are made up of long journeys in overheated trains whose coaches jerk one out of a nightmare sleep when the train is shunted or brought to a standstill; then staggering to one's hotel after a lecture, taking a bite of food and catching a midnight train to the next destination; then the early arrival on platforms in the depth of winter, with the temperature twenty below zero (maybe) where one is received by a deputation from the lecture committee who have a full programme for that day's schedule—a talk at 10.30 to a gathering of journalists. An interview with the Press and flashlight photographs at 2 p.m.; lunch and speech at the Rotary Club; a tour of the city to see its art collections and historical treasures; tea and speech at the Women's Country Club; dinner with Mrs. Blank, the most important social leader, to meet her most charming and influential friends; a short speech expected; a lecture at 8 p.m.

After the lecture, a reception by the Governor and his lady wife; or by Judge So-and-so, a very cultured gentleman and his good lady who entertain all the literary folk passing through their city.

To an Englishman the overheating of the American trains is a torture. Having with great difficulty taken off my boots, my trousers and upper garments, in a top or lower berth concealed by heavy green curtains, behind which the black thumb of a coloured man would fumble from time to time, I tried to sleep and thought I should suffocate. Always I had one dream, from which I awoke in a sweat. It was that I had dried up in my lecture, having forgotten the thread of it. But it is only the Englishman who suffers. Well do I remember the voice of a genial old fellow rasping down the corridor when I was wet with sweat and had a hammering headache.

"Say!" he called out to the darkey bed-maker, "can't you get any heat into this train?"

On my third visit to the States in 1921 I took my son Anthony, cutting short his career at Oxford because I thought this experience would be of greater value to him, as I think it was. We were in Lynchburg, Virginia, one night and after my lecture, when we were both dog-tired, we had exactly an hour to rest before catching the midnight train to New York, a very long journey away. In New York I had an important lecture date, only to be made if I took that train.

"Time for an hour's sleep," said Tony.

Before going up to the bedroom I had arranged that the hall porter should call me at twenty minutes to midnight and have a taxi-cab waiting at the hotel door. That would give us ten minutes to spare before boarding the train.

We had a room with two beds. Tony took off his evening clothes.

So did I, letting them drop to the floor. In a few moments we were both sleeping after an exhausting day ending before the lecture with a dinner attended by Virginians who still hugged the old tradition of love for England and hostility to the Northerners who had ruined them after the Civil War.

Suddenly after what seemed like a minute of sleep, I sat upright as though awakened by a sudden shot. I glanced at the clock. It was ten minutes to midnight.

"Tony!" I shouted.

Our bags were unpacked. We had to scramble round the room ramming in things we had left about.

"We shall have to make a dash for it," I told my son, "leave everything else."

We stumbled down to the hall. The hall porter was sleeping like a babe with his arms on his desk and his head on his arms. He had forgotten to call us. Fortunately there was a taxi waiting outside.

"Drive like hell!" I shouted to the man. "The midnight train to New York!"

"Sure, I'll make it," he said.

He drove like hell. We stopped within one inch of the station wall, and a miss is as good as a mile.

There were no Red Caps about. I shoved a wad of notes into our driver's hand.

"Great work!" I told him.

"The train is pulling out," he answered with a grin.

Tony and I boarded it with our bags while it was beginning to move. We had made it with not a second to spare. Wonderful!—and enough to take a year off one's life. Tony had left his waistcoat behind and other odds and ends. I had lost my dinner jacket and bought a Tuxedo, which is the same thing, in New York, before my lecture.

Tony had an advanced 'Oxford accent'. It made him completely unintelligible to most Americans, and I had to act as his interpreter. In the dining coach a darkey waiter asked what he would drink.

"Cocoa," said Tony.

"How?" asked the waiter.

"Cocoa," said Tony.

"Say, mister, I can't get that!"

"Cocoa," I said.

"Oh. Cocoa! Sure!"

Between my first and second visits to the United States, Wilson's tragedy had happened and the American people by a great majority had refused to enter the League of Nations. The Republican Party had swept the country for a variety of reasons not all connected with the policy and personality of Wilson. There was a general desire to get rid of a government associated with all the restrictions, annoyances, petty injustices, military controls, and a war fever which had left the nation cynical and disillusioned. As a friend of mine said: "The question put to the electors was not 'Are you in favour of the League of Nations?' but 'Are you sick and tired of the present administration?' The answer was 'By God, we are!' "

President Harding reigned in the place of Wilson.

4

PRESIDENT HARDING

In Washington I went to see my friend Lowell Mellett who was one of the distinguished team of journalists in the capital. After preliminary conversation he asked: "Is there anything I can do for you? Are there any people you would like to see?"

"Certainly," I told him. "Is it possible to have a talk with one or two of the big men? Senator Lodge, for instance."

"That's easy," he told me. "I'll put you through to a bunch of the big boys. Anyone else? The President?"

I laughed. "I'm only here for one night. I can't expect to see the President at a moment's notice."

"Why not? I'll fix it for you."

He did some rapid telephoning, at the end of which I had appointments with half a dozen Senators and the President of the United States. I wondered how long it would take for a literary man to get appointments with half a dozen members of the House of Lords and the King.

"You're a miracle worker!" I told Mellett, but he thought I exaggerated his powers.

I had some interesting conversation, mostly about the state of Europe after the war and the attitude of the United States towards the League of Nations, which was one of benevolent neutrality after their repudiation of Wilson.

Then I was taken to see the President. There was already a whispering campaign about his moral character and the corruption of his friends who closed round him—"The boys" as he called them—and blackmailed him. I found him a big, genial, kindly man, ready to talk, and talking with great good humour. He spoke with warm affection for England and actually called it "our old Mother Country" which I thought was a remarkable phrase from an American President. He assured me that the American people and his own Government were deeply anxious to co-operate with us in establishing peace and justice in Europe and supporting an international code of law. He even spoke hopefully about the work of the League, and seemed to forget that the United States had left that baby on the doorstep. Perhaps he was talking with the utmost insincerity, though he seemed honest and straight, with human sympathies for the sufferings of poverty-stricken peoples. Or perhaps—as I am inclined to believe—this was the real man speaking and expressing genuine ideals at which his friends would jeer. They would see him in hell before he put any of them into action as President of the United States. He came to a tragic end and escaped from "the boys" by the back door of death.

The morning following my talk with the President I had an extraordinary experience in Washington which was an ordeal as well as an unusual honour to a foreign journalist. I was summoned to give evidence before the Naval Committee of Congress dealing with the possibility of a naval agreement between the United States, Great Britain and Japan before the Washington Conference on that subject. I had no time to prepare notes, and found myself sitting like a mouse in a hole in the centre of a horseshoe of raised seats, occupied by about twenty-five of the Committee. I was in a state of high tension masked by a supreme effort of nerve control. I knew I should be speaking on behalf of Great Britain and taking upon myself the responsibility of expressing the views of my own people and their desire for international peace. I knew I should be asked some tough questions, and that in answering them I should have to be accurate and truthful, while avoiding any offence to American opinion. I was asked to make a preliminary statement regarding British foreign policy and I spoke for ten minutes, during which the Committee remained absolutely silent. Then I was asked a number of searching and difficult questions, some of them rather sinister in their suggestion of British Imperialism and power politics. It was one of my lucky mornings. I came through the ordeal without having made any horrible *gaffe*, or said anything which might be challenged as inaccurate or offensive. I was warmly congratulated afterwards by our naval attaché and members of the British Embassy who had come to hear my evidence, and told me I had said the right things in the right way. The *New York Times* published a verbatim report and it went on to the records of Congress. At the time I was warmed by the thought that I had done a little bit of service to England and the world. Now the best I can say about it is that I did no harm that day, and in that time, and in the mood of that time, stood for Anglo-American friendship, and co-operation in world affairs, and international peace.

5

IRISH AMERICANS

It was on my second visit that I had a most exciting time. It was just after I had resigned my position on the *Daily Chronicle* because I felt hot about the Black and Tans in Ireland. But the Irish Americans at that time, feeling even hotter than I did on that subject, made a dead set against any visiting Englishman if he appeared on a public platform—and I was booked again for the Carnegie Hall.

Not so dreadfully frightened this time, I stood on the platform facing a great audience. The hall was filled to the topmost galleries. Down below in the front seats I could see the rows of people in evening dress, with the lights gleaming on the bare arms of elderly women and on the white shirts and waistcoats of baldheaded gentlemen. I got going on the subject of stricken Europe, with my own experiences and impressions, and was just telling a story about an Austrian doctor when something very odd happened in the front row of seats below me. I saw one of the dames in evening dress suddenly rise and very deliberately smite a younger woman over the head with her fan. It seemed to be a kind of signal for a general fight. In the main body of the hall everybody was standing up and taking part in some kind of scrimmage. Shouts and shrill cries came from the galleries and suddenly there was a display of flags. They were green flags with the Iriih harp thereon. Other people were trying to grab them and tear them up. Arms were whirling about. There were dogfights in all parts of the hall.

I hadn't the faintest idea what it was all about. Nobody had warned me. The Irish conflict had not occurred to me. It was no use proceeding with my talk. My voice was drowned in the general hubbub and the conflicting shouts and cries. I stooped at the edge of the platform and made a mild enquiry as to the meaning of all this. Several people answered, but I could not hear them. A stentorian voice in the gallery shouted out a question.

"Who sent the English to Ireland anyhow?"

An answer came from another loud voice.

"The Pope of Rome!"

"This is all very curious," I thought. "Everybody has forgotten me. But it's a pleasant relief from lecturing. No need to say anything. I've just got to go on standing here until the storm passes. I wonder what it's all about?"

The storm lasted for about three quarters of an hour and was quelled at last by the police throwing out the most noisy demonstrators.

Then I continued my speech, interrupted frequently but not overwhelmed. Everything I said was applauded tremendously. Some reference I made to England's place in the world brought the audience to its feet, cheering, waving handkerchiefs and fans, and when I finished there was a surge up to the platform, and thousands of hands grasped mine and generous, excited, splendid things were said which I found good to hear. When I left the hall surrounded by a bodyguard I saw my brother Cosmo. He was greatly excited and had thoroughly enjoyed himself in hand to hand fights with the Irish. His knuckles were bleeding and there was the light of battle in his eyes. "There was one big Irish fellow," he told me, "who was out for your blood. I knocked him down. Then he came at me and I knocked him down again. Finally I flung him down a flight of steps where he lay quiet."

In my brother's flat that night there was an excited group of friends who shook my hand warmly, patted me on the shoulder, and greeted me as a hero. "You were marvellous!" they cried. "You were wonderful!"

"How?" I asked, having done nothing at all but stand watching the affray.

"You were perfectly calm," they said. "You didn't turn a hair! You even looked bored."

They thought this look of boredom was in the best tradition of the English character. They loved it. But as a matter of fact I had not been the least bit bored. I was only interested and bewildered.

My lecture agent Lee Keedick—a most humorous and charming man—was greatly pleased. He had been in one of the galleries and was full of amusing stories about the back-chat he had heard and the running fights.

"It was grand!" he said. "If we can keep this up your lecture tour will be a great success."

It was. In other cities I had no sooner appeared on the platform than —Crash!—The Irish were at it again. I had no need to lecture. I just had to stand there while the audience did the rest, because it was a fight between the Irish and those Americans—mostly in the majority—who were enraged by this discourtesy to an English visitor and this political outrage, as they thought it, against the American tradition of free speech and good manners. The Press entitled my lectures "*Philip Gibbs's Sinn*

Fein Tea Parties". Many people bought tickets just to see the fun.

I suggested to my agent, Lee Keedick, that it might be a good idea to give a special lecture, giving my views on the Irish problem so that Irish Americans would know that I was not a hard-boiled Englishman wishing to tread on the neck of Ireland. He thought it was a grand idea and hired a theatre for the next available date. But the Irish in New York had no intention of listening to my views, as soon I learned, and the anti-Irish were arranging for organised counteraction. Shortly before the lecture I was rung up in my bedroom at the Hotel Plaza by a young woman who spoke excitedly. She told me that she was leading a squad of patriotic American girls to the theatre that night. They would carry a large banner of the Stars and Stripes. She and her girl friends would be delighted if I would head the procession and lead them into battle. Suppressing my laughter at this alarming idea, I told her firmly that I would do no such thing on any account whatever, I was going to give an impartial talk about Ireland, and anyhow I was a visiting Englishman who could not get mixed up in American conflicts. She was gravely disappointed at my lack of the sporting spirit.

I anticipated trouble that evening and I got it. The Irish turned up in force. So did their political opponents. There were fights and scuffles outside the theatre where rival flags were captured. Inside the theatre the row began almost as soon as I appeared on the platform. I could not make myself heard. Irish banners floated down from the galleries and there was continual booing and shouting. My friendly supporters used their fists on my behalf. The Irish, who love a fight, were enjoying themselves thoroughly and making a rough house. After this had gone on for nearly an hour I saw a tall man in black coming towards me down the central aisle and make a leap on to the stage. The idea came to my mind instantly that he was an Irishman who desired my blood. He turned out to be an Irishman, but so far from wanting my blood he put his hand on my shoulder and reassured me.

"I'm Father Murphy," he said. "I was Chaplain in the New York Division. The boys will be as quiet as lambs when I talk to them."

He raised his hand and his voice, expecting to calm the storm. On the contrary. The storm broke out with renewed fury. The boys were not to be appeased even by Father Murphy, though he was one of their heroes and well beloved. They refused to behave like little lambs when their shepherd tried to round them up. They would not listen to one word and were more excited than ever by this intervention. Finally the police arrived and cleared the theatre. It was a great evening, and as the country reporters say "a good time was had by all".

My lecture date in Chicago coincided with St. Patrick's Night. I arrived a day or two beforehand, and somewhat to my surprise and amusement was confided to the care of two big detectives who accompanied me everywhere when I left the hotel. It was the first time I had ever had a personal bodyguard.

The humorous thing was that they were both Irishmen and regarded me as one of the enemies of dear old Ireland. On the afternoon of my lecture one of them desired to make his position clear. It was when we were in a taxi-cab.

"Sir Gibbs," he said in a strong Irish broque. "It's not your life we're worrying about at all, at all. No, sir! It's our reputation."

I told them that this was very satisfactory to me, if he would cling on to his reputation.

Ten minutes before the lecture I was smoking a cigarette in the green room behind the stage, when a very tall and powerful-looking gentleman in uniform announced himself. He was one of the police inspectors of Chicago. He was putting on a pair of white kid gloves, a bit too tight for him.

"Sir Gibbs," he said as he pressed them on, "before you start on your talk I propose to make a speech of my own. Yes, sir! I'm going to tell them that I have a bunch of my boys behind the scenes stripped to their jerkins, and that if there's any trouble they'll use their cudgels without mercy."

"Now, look here, Inspector," I said firmly. "I can't allow you to make that speech. It would be the worst kind of introduction to an English lecturer."

He was very insistent but I flatly refused to allow him to appear.

"Well, I guess you must take the consequences," he said at last. "There's a very ugly crowd in the theatre, quite a few of the bad boys. They're out for your blood to-night."

When I faced that audience in Chicago I was conscious for the first time that I was in personal danger. At other times the audience had scrapped between themselves, leaving me out of it. But there in Chicago there was a new note in the storm that broke out on my appearance. It was really hostile. There was a grim menace in it. It was like the old nursery rhyme "Fee-Fo-Fi-Fum! I smell the blood of an Englishman!" Those Irish boys were in a murderous mood. They hated my 'guts' to use an American expression.

My local lecture agent—or perhaps the manager of the theatre, I have forgotten exactly—stood by my side and said: "Keep cool. Don't lose your nerve. Jolly them up!"

I was perfectly cool and my nerve was all right, though I knew I wouldn't have a chance if those Chicago boys stormed the platform. But I didn't like the noises coming up to the stage where I stood with that little man by my side. The booing was deep and low and rather beastlike. Harsh and angry shouts were coming from the galleries. Fighting had already started. I was glad to see that I had some friendly support in the house. Everybody was standing up and the whole audience, which I could only see dimly looking across the footlights, was swaying and surging. Suddenly after what seemed to me a long time my police inspector's 'bunch of boys stripped to their jerkins' surged in and got busy. I could hear whacks and thuds. Many an Irishman left my lecture with a broken head that night. Did I say "my lecture"? I hadn't spoken a word of it.

"I'm afraid you're going to have a hot time in Boston," said Lee Keedick. "It's an Irish stronghold."

Other friends warned me that I might expect the worst in Boston. My brother Cos was anxious about me. He overdramatised the situation—as usual! Still after all these warnings I faced a big audience in Boston with some trepidation. Politically the Irish had taken possession of Boston. This would be the climax, I thought, to my 'Sinn Fein Tea Parties'.

I was startled by the silence of the audience when I stepped on to the platform. Not a murmur!

"That's funny," I thought. "The hush before the storm. Let's see— What was my lecture about?"

I had to pull myself together to get going. I hadn't delivered my lecture on the state of Europe after the war for quite a time. At the back of my mind was the thought that I should be interrupted at any moment now. But no, I went on and on. A quarter of an hour passed. Half an hour. Not a sound! Perhaps the whole audience had gone to sleep. Perhaps there was no audience there at all. "Good heavens!" I thought, "am I speaking to a perfectly empty house?" No, I could see the people in the stalls, row after row of them, and vague faces staring down at me from the upper seats. I went right through my lecture. There was no laughter at my comic anecdotes, no applause for my stories of heroism, no murmur of pity for my tales of tragedy. It was a most deadly business, that lecture and I missed the excitement of former experiences.

"What happened?" I asked afterwards. "What has happened to the Boston Irish?"

"Most astonishing!" I was told. "Some big boy—the Cardinal—must have told his flock to behave themselves under pain of hell fire or excommunication."

My Boston audience, mostly Irish, behaved like angels, silent, calm and cold in the presence of a foul fiend. It was a great disappointment to me.

The end of that chapter came when I was given a dinner at the Waldorf Astor by a group of friends before I sailed back to England

It was a very great honour, the best that has ever been given to me. A thousand people were present, including many of the most distinguished people in America. They were eager to show how utterly they repudiated the Irish hostility to England, how fiercely angry they were that a friendly visitor to the United States should be howled down as I had been. It was un-American. It was, they thought, an insult to the American reputation for courtesy and good manners, and they were there to testify their friendship to England. They were there also, if I may dare say so (as I wrote in my book *Adventures in Journalism*) to testify their friendship to me as a man who had tried to serve England, and America too, in speaking and writing. All of them wrote their names for me in a book which I keep as a treasure of good will across the Atlantic.

There were some handsome speeches made, generous about England, very generous about my own work. The Americans have a great gift for that kind of thing, and that night there was some fine oratory and excellent wit. But while the speeches were going on messages kept reaching me from a crowd outside. They were not flattering. "You are a dirty English rat." "You ought to be deported." Another informed me that I was a paid agent of the British Government. Another was a general indictment, informing all American citizens that it was a disgrace to dine with me, and an act of treachery to their own nation. Another little missive described me as a typical blackguard in a nation of cut-throats. So they followed each other to the high table, while speaker after speaker rose to say kind words. It was the '*sauce piquante*' to this memorable banquet.

6

IMPORTANT PEOPLE

Before leaving the States on that second visit I was asked to make a speech on the economic conditions of Europe to a group of about sixty of the leading financiers of the United States. Looking back upon that occasion I am startled by my own audacity in accepting that invitation, for in private life I never count my change and have a very poor head for figures. But after listening to my address, and putting me under a fire of questions, these American financiers agreed warmly with what I had said.

"The truth is," as I wrote at the time, "that a very few simple laws underlie the whole complicated system of international trade and finance. As long as one held on to those laws, which I did like grim death, one could not go wrong in one's analysis of the European

K

situation, and all facts and figures adjusted themselves to these elementary principles.

Money, for instance, is only a symbol for the reality of values behind it—in grain, cattle, mineral wealth, labour and credit.

When paper money is issued in advance of a nation's real values it is merely a promissory note on future industry and production.

France, Germany, and most European nations were at that time issuing vast quantities of these promissory notes which were not supported, for the most part, by actual wealth, that is to say by exchange of goods.

The prosperity of a country like Germany increases the prosperity of all countries. Its poverty leads to less prosperity in all countries.

Commercial prosperity depends upon the interchange of goods between one country and another. No prosperity could be established if the interchange of goods were thwarted by high tariffs, customs barriers, exchange restrictions.

I even ventured to declare that the payment of the American debt by Great Britain and other countries would do the United States no good at all, and, in the long run, could not be paid, so long as the United States exported her own goods but, by a high tariff system, prevented the entry of goods from her debtors.

By keeping these facts firmly in mind I was able to talk on a straight line of commonsense in the wild labyrinth of our European problems after the great war. But I had also seen the actual life and conditions of many countries in Europe and could tell what I had seen in a simple straight way to the business men of the United States. It was what they wanted to know before all other things, and I think they believed my accounts more than those of more important men, because I was not a government official or propagandist, but a literary man without any axe to grind, and an eye-witness of the conditions I described.

They agreed with me—theoretically—and went on doing the very opposite, year after year until the great crash came.

7

PEOPLE OF DESTINY

One evening when I had returned from one of my lecture engagements there was a tap at the door of my bedroom in the Lotus Club in New York. I had just unpacked, and my bedroom was in a state of high disorder, with shirts and socks strewn around. It was embarrassing when a friend of mine named Barr Baker opened the door and said: "Mr. Herbert Hoover would like to have a talk with you. May he come in?"

"Not here!" I exclaimed. "My bedroom is like a battlefield."

A quiet voice said: "That's all right," and in came Mr. Herbert Hoover, afterwards Republican President of the United States. He wanted to have a talk with me on European affairs. I was surprised that he should want to do so, for he knew far more than I did about conditions in Europe, having administered the American Relief to stricken countries. But he sat down in an armchair regardless of socks and shirts and stayed for a long talk. I had a great respect for this heavily built, quiet, undemonstrative, man whose brown eyes were thoughtful and brooding. He was pessimistic about the state of Europe, and thought European Statesmen were all doing the wrong things and adopting narrow nationalistic views. Once he spoke emotionally about his own ambition to help the world forward to commonsense for the sake of the common man.

"It's the only thing that keeps me inside the political arena," he told me. "It would be easier and pleasanter to retire to my yacht."

Here is a man, I thought, who has a fine vision of life, and deep knowledge behind it. But when he became President he failed to fulfil that vision, and was overtaken by the typhoon of economic disaster which swept around the world and plunged the United States into financial chaos.

During these visits I came to know and like the American people with warm sympathy and admiration. I had met all types and classes. I had "commuted" for a time from Greenwich, Connecticut, where my brother had a house, to New York City, and had met the people who corresponded to our suburban folk. I had established friendly contacts with University professors and their students, literary men and women, judges and lawyers and journalists, the leading citizens of many cities from New York to San Francisco, the ladies of the women's clubs, coffee shop girls, taxi-drivers and garage hands, the newspaper boys at street corners, the ordinary fellow sitting on a high stool in the drug store of any Main Street. I had found them friendly and frank in their way of speech, glad to meet an Englishman however critical of England, apart from the Irish hostility which was not long lived in its intensity. I saw much to admire in the American way of life, in its dynamic vitality, in its democratic approach to life, in its material standards of living—high compared with Europe except in black patches here and there. I was deeply impressed by the educational opportunities for all classes and by no uncertain signs that the results of this system were being revealed in fair measure over a wide area of social life.

I did not go about with blind eyes, or with uncritical vision. I had glimpses of dark problems here and there, and of evil things lurking beneath the glittering surface of this noisy and cheerful mass-produced civilisation. I sensed the presence of intolerance and ruthlessness against those who do not conform to the ordinary conventions of American life. I had been "put wise" to the activities of the Ku Klux Klan—a horrible sect of fanatics and Fascists. I had seen something of Babbitry in the great hotels, with their seething mobs of men and women attending conventions or social receptions. I had visited towns where race riots had just happened. I had seen the American urge "to keep up with the Jones's". I knew that this civilisation in the United States was not a heaven on earth, and that it included criminal and corrupt types, hidden cruelties, political tyrannies among local Bosses, and lots of human misery, as in other civilisations, but more intense here and there—more dramatic and violent, because of the mixture of races in a Melting Pot which hadn't yet melted. Something still carried over from the pioneer days when fingers were quick on the trigger and the loud-mouthed bully lorded it in Roaring Camp. And yet without turning a blind eye to all that, not looking at American life through rose-coloured glasses, I saw them as a great people, not yet sure of their own destiny but certain some day to throw their weight, with enormous power, their terrific driving energy, into the scales of fate which would decide the future course of human history. I believed they would be on the side of liberty against tyranny, on the side of spiritual ideals against evil powers, on the side of the common folk of the world against the black reaction of political dictators. I spoke of these things once to General Swinton, the inventor of the tanks, who also knew the United States.

"The Americans," he said, "are the only idealists left in the world. The rest of us have become cynical and selfish."

It was an exaggeration, because we have seen in recent years that our own people were neither cynical nor selfish and faced the ordeal of war because of some high faith beyond their own lives and egotism. But it was true that the Americans also, in the mass and at their best, are idealists, recognising values beyond the immediate chance of prosperity for themselves or the safety of their skins. They have proved it in recent history, as God knows.

I saw the bigness of the United States, and the bigness of some fate awaiting them without their knowledge. They were finding themselves in a groping uncertain way. That was the summing up in a book called *People of Destiny* which I wrote after my first visit.

8

CROSSING THE ATLANTIC

My comings and goings across the Atlantic were in the big ships, the

Adriatic, the *Olympic*, the *Aquitania* and others. The big ships met big storms once or twice when I was in them, and I saw the full fury of Atlantic gales when the seas seemed mountains high and the great waves advanced upon us like Surrey hills on the move. It was awe-inspiring and, to say the least of it, uncomfortable. But generally I had the luck of the weather and enjoyed these Atlantic crossings. One loses touch for a while with the earth and its troubles and one's own anxieties. It is like an interregnum between two periods of time. People became liberated a little from their own moorings. Some of them become a little mad, I have noticed, and lose their moral and social restraints. Elderly men and women play childish deck games with the enthusiasm of youth. Love affairs spring up after two days, becoming emotional for six more, until they cool down when the Statue of Liberty has been sighted. Ship friendships are notoriously ephemeral.

I had pleasant company on all these voyages. On one of them was John Galsworthy and his wife who kept aloof from most of their fellow passengers but were friendly to me. Galsworthy and I had long talks pacing the decks and I found him a good companion, sensitive, gracious, with a noble mind. There was nothing common or mean in him. He was an intellectual aristocrat, but never arrogant, and without a touch of affectation. Because of other people's agonies and other people's brutalities he was never happy I think. He hated all cruelty, and there was a lot of that in life, he found. He hated loud-mouthed vulgarity, but loved the common folk who are never "vulgar". He shrank from anyone who tried to invade his privacy and for that reason shut himself up in his cabin a good deal. Our friendship did not stop at the dockside and we met sometimes in London.

I came to know Myra Hess, that enchanting pianist, and one evening was her partner at a fancy dress dance in one of these ships—was it the *Adriatic?*—when she was a bandit with a big moustache and I was a romantic-looking villain of uncertain race and period. She was generous enough one evening to accompany my son in a few songs.

A lovely lady—I think the most beautiful girl in England at that time —was on one of these Atlantic crossings. It was Blossom Forbes-Robertson, the eldest daughter of the old actor to whose house I went once a week or so in the years that followed. And at the captain's table I sat next to a fascinating little lady named Lydia Lopokova. She was the life and soul of the company, with a wit and gaiety which were spiced by her Russian accent. She made all sorts of animals out of her table napkins but, alas, she never danced to us.

Ernest Shackleton crossed with me once. It was his last trip across the Atlantic before he died in the Antarctic. I had known him in the old Fleet Street days when he came often to see Ernest Perris at the *Daily*

Chronicle office. He gave a lecture on board ship one night and for some extraordinary reason a group of Americans showed hostility to him and openly jeered while he was speaking, though he was a born lecturer with a genius for words and had a fine heroic story to tell with the greatest modesty. Everybody felt outraged by this breach of good manners and I was asked to write a tribute to Shackleton which was printed on the ship's printing press and put beside everybody's plate at dinner. Shackleton was much touched by this and I was embarrassed by his thanks for such a small service to one of the world's great explorers and real heroes, in line with Frobisher and Franklin.

That remarkable lady Clare Sheridan was on this voyage when Shackleton was with us. She had her little son Richard with her. She had big blue eyes and hair of spun gold, and the ship's officers gave her their homage. But Shackleton was cold in her company. He did not approve, I think, of her visit to Soviet Russia when she had made portrait busts of men like Trotsky and Radek and Tchicherin. A great hostess in New York—Mrs. Cornelius Vanderbilt—invited her to lunch one day and then started cross-examining her about that Russian visit. Had she been paid by those Bolsheviks? Did she accept money from them for her work? Of course she did, she was a professional sculptor. Mrs. Cornelius Vanderbilt did not approve. Clare Sheridan did not like the disapproval, and rising white-faced from the table left the house. I was told the story by both ladies and my sympathy was with Clare Sheridan who was Mrs. Cornelius Vanderbilt's guest.

I met many pleasant people on those voyages, and in ten days or less made good friends with some of them, having tremendous talks on the boat deck and playing innumerable games of chess with some of them, including David Davies then known to all of us as D.D. He was one of the best chess players in the House of Commons so that nearly always he beat me. With him chess had become a vice, he told me, and used to interfere so much with his work in the House that he offered to give his valet a guinea every time the man caught him out in having played. Coming into his room in the morning the man used to ask now and then: "Did you play chess in the House yesterday, sir?" "Certainly not!" said D.D. "I told you I had given it up." But very often he would sneak in a few games before having to pay his self-inflicted fine.

It is more fun to cross the Atlantic in a ship than in an aeroplane. One has more time for pleasant conversation, and making friends, and forgetting the troubles of the world while on the great grey sea.

PART VIII

THE NEAR EAST

1

THE SEA OF ENCHANTMENT

IN the Spring of 1921 I lay on the deck of the steamship *Gratz* of 7,000 tons, once Austrian and now flying the Italian flag, bound from Brindisi to Constantinople. With me was my son Anthony.

It was a lovely voyage through the sea of enchantment where every little isle is haunted by the fairy tales of ancient Greece—if one remembers them—and through which all European history has passed and passes. The sea was blue under a blue sky, so deeply blue that it seemed as though one's hand might be dyed to this colour if one dipped it in, and so smooth that it was like cleaving our way through jelly. At night when the stars came out they were like bright jewels on the dark blue velvet of this sky over the Mediterranean.

Not so beautiful was the human nature aboard. Our fellow passengers were an unattractive crowd—fat women of uncertain nationality who ogled the men of equally uncertain origin, except for some Jews and a few Turks who wore the fez. Our table companion was an American Jew of German, or perhaps, Russian, ancestry. He spoke many languages, including English, badly, pronouncing King as 'kink', and ring as 'rink'. His table manners were shocking and he bullied the Austrian stewards now in service under the Italian flag and had two helpings of everything. But he was very friendly to us, and apart from one other was the only person on board who showed any friendliness at all. The other exception was a young British officer of the Great War, as we still called it, now "demobbed" and resuming his career as a commercial traveller in woollen underwear. Before the war he had made as much as £3,000 in one year as commission on business with Turkish merchants in Constantinople. Being a simple-minded fellow without much knowledge of European conditions, and having the usual English optimism, he believed that trade was reviving and that there would be a quick recovery from the effects of war.

Others did not think so. Our table companion did not think so. Lying on the sun-baked decks I listened to conversations by these students of international business, as I had been listening for two years or more since the war to the talk of men and women in Belgium, France, Holland, Italy, Austria, Hungary, Germany, Canada and the United States. It was always the same, as I wrote in my book *Adventures*

287

in Journalism which narrates some of these experiences. They had no certainty of peace, no sense of security, but rather an apprehension of new conflicts in Europe and outside Europe, a fear of revolution, anarchy, and an upheaval of forces beyond the control of men like themselves of international mind and business commonsense. But here in this boat going down the Mediterranean there was talk of peoples and forces not generally discussed in those other conversations to which I had listened in wayside taverns, in railway trains, in wooden huts on the old battlefields, in the drawing rooms of London, Paris, Rome, Vienna, Budapest, Berlin and New York.

"The Angora Turks have got to be reckoned with. Mustapha Kemal is getting powerful. Greece is making a big gamble. Venizelos grabbed too much. . . . The Armenians have not all been massacred. . . . The East is seething like a cauldron. . . . The Arabs have been betrayed and won't submit to French domination. . . . It's the oil that will put all the fat on the fire. . . . Russia is not dead yet, and make no mistake. My God! This peace is just a breathing space before another bloody war. . . . It's a world gone mad. . . . What we want is business." I noted down those scraps of conversation in 1921. Those low-class international traders on their way to Constantinople knew the smell of things. They smelt the smouldering of fires under the thin crust of this peace in Europe. I listened to them with gloomy apprehensions, for I was a traveller in search of peace, and had no other mission.

The Near East was in their minds with now and then a casual anxious glance towards the Far East and its mystery. The Turkish Nationalists under Mustapha Kemal, a cavalry general, were not sitting down under the peace imposed upon them. Smyrna and its hinterland in Asia Minor had gone to the Greeks because Venizelos had put a spell upon Lloyd George and President Wilson. The Turkish Nationalists would never submit to that, and supplies and funds were going to Ankara from Istanbul.

The French were asking for trouble, and finding it, in Syria. Had not the British under Colonel Lawrence promised the independence of the Arab States? The French bombardment of Damascus, which presently happened, was not exactly the way to make the Syrians love their French "protectors". What would happen in Red Russia? They were smashing General Wrangel's army out of the Crimea. Then all Russia would be Red. What would come out of that bloody civil war between the Reds and the Whites without mercy on either side, and what would this new faith of Communism with its apostles everywhere in the Red International—"The Comintern"—bring forth in Western Europe, in Soviet cells, in factories and workshops, wherever men were bitter and unsatisfied, or half starved, or starved? Those were some of the questions discussed in veiled language, or with sudden flashes of candour, and with sideway glances at me by young Turks and Levantine Jews, and those fat women of unknown nationality on board the *Gratz* bound for Constantinople.

We passed through the Corinth Canal, so narrow that one could throw a stone across it. Small Greek boys ran along a footpath, clamouring for pennies like gutter urchins round an English char-a-banc. Then we lay off Athens but in spite of a special Greek *visa* from the Consulate in London, for which I had paid, I was not allowed to land. Through my glasses I saw with a thrill of emotion the tall columns of the Parthenon. At our ship's side was a crowd of small craft rowed by brown skinned boatmen who kept up a chant of "Kyrie! Kyrie!" ("Lord! Lord!") touting for the custom of passengers, as they did three thousand years ago, with these same shouts, and waving of brown arms, and curses to each other, and raising of oars, when ships came in from Crete and the Mediterranean ports with merchandise and travellers.

We came into the Aegean Sea and saw on our port side like low lying clouds the Greek islands in which the gods once dwelt and the old heroes. We drew close to Gallipoli and I thought of heroes more modern, lying there in graves that were not old. They had done deeds needing more courage than that of Ulysses and his men and had faced monsters of artillery more dreadful than dragons and many-headed dogs and the Medusa head. The trenches were plainly visible, British and Turkish, and the old gun emplacements, and the Lone Tree, and the barren slopes of Achi Baba where the flower of Australian and New Zealand youth had fallen, and many Irish and English boys.

As I leaned over the side of the ship a fellow passenger spoke to me in a soft-mouthed way.

"Quite a good landing place!"

I looked at him, aware of irony, and remembering the landing of the Twenty-ninth Division and the Australian troops under withering fire. This elderly man said again in a cheerful way: "A nice cove for a boat to land in!"

He was gloating over the remembrance of British losses at the hands of his fellow Turks.

Many of the men on board, of whose nationality I had been uncertain—there was no facial distinction which gave them away—suddenly revealed themselves by putting on the red Fez of Islam, and paced the decks restlessly with their eyes strained towards the city of the Sultan.

The fat American Jew touched me on the arm and spoke solemnly, with a kind of warning.

"For those who don't wear a fez Constantinople won't be a safe place, I guess. They say there are bodies floating every morning off the Golden Horn—stabbed in the back. I'm keeping close to Pera."

2

CONSTANTINOPLE

As I wrote in my *Adventures in Journalism* the first view of the Golden Horn was as beautiful as I had hoped and more than I had imagined, as we rounded the old Seraglio Point and saw in the early sunlight of a May morning the glittering panorama of Constantinople. The domes of San Sophia lay like rose-coloured clouds above the cypress trees. Beyond was the great mosque of Suleiman, its minarets, white and slender, cutting the blue sky like lances. Further back, rising above a huddle of brown old houses, was the mosque of Mohammed, the conqueror who, five hundred years ago, rode into San Sophia on a day of victory, over the piled corpses there, and left the imprint of a bloody hand on one of the pillars, where it is now sculptured in marble. White in the sun on the water's edge were the long walls of the Sultan's palace. One could see Galata, and the old bridge which crosses from Stamboul, and above, on the hill of Pera, with its Grand' Rue, its night clubs, its cabarets, its Christian churches, and its haunts of vice.

Before we anchored, our ship was surrounded by a swarm of boats, as at Athens, but these were the narrow caïques of the Golden Horn rowed by Turks, who hung on to us by thrusting grapnel hooks through our portholes and by clinging on to ropes. They were old sun-baked Turks with white beards, and young Turks with only down on their faces and roving eyes for the unveiled women on our decks, and together they raised a wild chant as they called: "Effendi! Effendi!" and invited us to go ashore. Other ships passed us, crowded with Russian refugees fleeing from the Bolshevik pursuit of Wrangel in the Crimea. There were British destroyers, sailing ships with leg o' mutton sails billowing white above the blue water, and many of the little caïques where, on Turkish rugs, sat Turkish ladies like bundles of black silk, deeply veiled so that one had no glimpse of a face.

My son Anthony and I shared a caïque with the fat American Jew who, apart from the English ex-officer, had been the only friendly soul on board as far as we were concerned. The caïque was deeply laden with his cases of samples—he was a traveller in boots and shoes—and our frail craft nearly sank. On reaching the Customs we were held up until our papers were examined by very arrogant young Turkish officers who smoked cigarettes incessantly, and refused to pass the American boots and shoes until they had chosen and taken a few pairs for themselves. This bit of graft was done with the utmost nonchalance, as a matter of course. After that we drove in a smart carriage with two horses to the Pera Palace Hotel in the Grand' Rue of Pera.

Here I was delighted to find my old comrade-in-arms Percival Phillips with a few other British, French, Italian, and American journalists who had come to this city to watch its international drama and to await further and dangerous developments in the Near East.

As I have written in another book (*Adventures in Journalism*) it was Phillips, as well as the High Commissioner, Admiral Webber, and various Intelligence Officers, who put me wise to the situation which had its secret plot in Constantinople but its fighting centre in Asia Minor.

Here in "Constant", as our naval men called it, there was a mask of peaceful obedience to the decrees of the International occupation. It was called "International", and there were French and Italian troops and police on both sides of the Galata Bridge, but the real command was in the hands of the British Fleet. The French were "huffy" because of that, and Général Franchet de l'Esperey had left in a temper because he would not take orders from the British, and was up to his eyes in political intrigue.

The Sultan was a puppet in the hands of the British, ready to sign any document we put before him, provided his personal safety was assured. But all the Turks in his palace, and in the back streets of Galata and Stamboul, were rebels against his submission, and spies and agents on behalf of the Nationalist Turks in Angora. Those were the dangerous fellows. They refused to recognise the Allied terms of peace, or any peace. They were contemptuous of the Sultan's enforced decrees. They even denied his religious authority. They had raised the old flag of Islam and were stirring up fanaticism through the whole Mohammedan world as far as India. But they were modern in their ideas and methods, "Nationalist" and not religious in their faith. They were raising levies of Turkish peasants, drilling them, arming them (with French weapons), teaching them that if they wanted to keep their land they must fight for it.

There was a man named Mustapha Kemal. He would be heard of later in history as a great leader. He was raiding up the coast as far as Ismid, and little companies of British Tommies had to fall back before his irregulars. Not good for our prestige! But what could we do on the Asiatic side with only a few battalions of boys? Meanwhile the Turks in Constantinople were sending men and money and munitions to the Nationalists, and there was precious little we could do to stop them, in spite of our troops and police. There was gun running under the Galata Bridge almost as open as daylight.

Mustapha's strength was growing. Nobody knew how strong it was.

Perhaps it was underestimated.   Perhaps one day the Greeks, holding a long line across Asia Minor for the protection of Smyrna would get an unpleasant surprise.

What, I was asked by young British officers, was the British Government—that beggar Lloyd George—doing with all this pro-Greek policy? It was doing us no good, they thought, in the Mohammedan world. Even India was getting restless because their political agitators were pretending that the Sultan was a prisoner and the Prophet insulted. Not that the Indian Mohammedans, I was told, cared a curse about the Sultan, belonging to a different sect. But it was all propaganda and dangerous. The whole situation was full of danger, and Constantinople was a very interesting city in this time of history.

All that I heard, from men who knew, through a blue haze of cigarette smoke over Turkish coffee in the Pera Palace.

To my son Anthony who had just left Oxford it was a romantic episode like a novel by Seton Merriman, or by his own father.

I was nervous about him sometimes when we crossed the Galata Bridge into old Stamboul, or wandered about lonely places where there were no troops or police. We heard many stories of bodies floating in the Bosphorus, and of men being stabbed in the back by fanatical young Turks. Often when we passed groups of Turks squatting in the market places or squares of Stamboul I saw them spit furtively and sullenly. They were angered when our young naval officers from the Fleet went into the bazaars very breezily and gave the glad eye to Turkish ladies whose black eyes they caught for a moment until the curtains were closed with little giggles. A French band played in one of the squares every afternoon and their audience was almost entirely made up of Turkish ladies whose faces were hidden behind their veils.

We saw the Sultan drive in state out from his palace on the way to one of the mosques, and Tony and I were almost the last Englishmen to see this procession, for in a little while after the coming of Mustapha Kemal the Sultan and his harem and his janissaries had fled with all that belonged to the ghosts of history. So too we were among the last to see the Turkish women veiled. When I next went to Constantinople a year or so later the women were unveiled, the fez had gone, and Turks, like a Lancashire football crowd, were wearing a hideous cloth cap. Mustapha Kemal was a revolutionary who swept away the old code of Turkish religion and custom with a clean sword-cut between the past and present.

3

THE ENCHANTED GARDEN

When we were there the Pera Palace Hotel was like a musical comedy with tragedy well hidden behind the scenes. Two nights a week there was a dance attended by our young naval officers who found it all very amusing. Here, awaiting their invitations to the dance were Italian, Greek, Armenian, Jewish and Russian women of considerable allurement, though all but the Russians were on the plump side with their white shoulders billowing from low-cut frocks in the Parisian style by way of the stores in the Grand' Rue de Pera.

Our young naval officers walked them around the polished boards with great vivacity, but awareness of danger. They winked at each other as they passed and said: "Hot stuff, my little one! Beware!" They stood their ladies drinks between the dances and one overheard laughing conversations in broken English and worse French, while here and there Turkish officers and merchants watched the scene with disapproving (or perhaps envious) eyes.

One night Tony danced with a lovely lady in her own house. It was a little palace overlooking the Bosphorus where the British Fleet with the *Iron Duke* lay with all its lights gleaming. It was a magical scene under the dark blue canopy of the night sky, spangled with stars. We stepped out of a pleasant room on to a flat roof overlooking a garden with tall spearheaded cypresses. In the garden was a tiny mosque with a slender minaret, and at sunset, before the sky darkened, an old Turkish *muezzin* in white robes climbed up the little tower and chanted the evening prayers, his voice rising and falling on the oriental scale which brought all the East into this garden. Faintly from the shadow land and through the warm scented air came other voices as other *imams* in the city of mosques gave praise to Allah and to Mohammed his Prophet.

"Let's have a dance," said the beautiful lady. A gramophone was turned on and Tony moved round the flat roof with her to the rhythm of a ragtime melody, and I envied him.

Her husband, who was head of a great English trading company in Constantinople, stepped out on the roof leaving in the room a group of young naval officers who were drinking his wines.

He stood by my side and spoke quietly, as the *muezzin* ended his wailing chant.

"The Turks aren't finished yet. . . . And behind the Turk is Russia —and the East."

A chill made me shiver a little. The sun had gone down.

Twenty years after, or nearly that, when the second World War had brought a British Army to France again, I was walking past some mining cottages in the city of Lens, beyond the Vimy Ridge, when an officer in battledress came out of one of those small houses, and after giving me a searching glance said: "You're Philip Gibbs, aren't you?"

"Yes", I answered.

"Who am I", he asked with a smile.

I stared at him but could not give him a name.

"Cast your mind back to a little palace overlooking the Bosphorus with a *muezzin* chanting on that tower and afterwards a lady dancing round the roof."

"You're Baker of Constantinople," I said. "I remember."

He nodded and laughed.

"Quite right! Now I'm a Security policeman in this dirty mining cottage in Lens. Queer, isn't it?"

4

RUSSIAN REFUGEES

In Constantinople at that time there were hunger, and disease, and despair, and many people who laughed a while and then wept a while and said—if they had a jewel or two left in some hidden place—"Let's eat, drink and be merry for to-morrow we die".

They were the last remnants of the Russian army, and the last refugees from Red Terror after the defeat of Wrangel in the Crimea. I saw them arriving from the Black Sea after their escape from Sebastopol and Novorossiisk. Many of them had been taken off by British battleships. Others had crowded on to merchant ships and small tugs with their babies and their bundles. Now the last of them camped on the dockside of Constantinople below the Galata Bridge. Tens of thousands were herded together in relief camps where typhus caught them. The luckier ones—were they lucky?—had found some kind of lodging and some means of earning money in this international caravanserai by opening little restaurants, or playing the *balalaika* in music halls, or dancing in low haunts. I often saw Wrangel himself in the Pera Palace Hotel, a very tall man in Cossack uniform.

The happiest, for a time, were those who had been taken to the island of Prinkipo within sight of Stamboul where they were fed on British rations and billeted in villas once belonging to rich Turks.

Tony and I used to go with Percival Phillips to one of these Russian restaurants. The cook had once been the admiral of the Czar's yacht.

The waitresses were little Russian princesses, very dainty and charming. Cossack officers, in their long black coats and astrakhan caps, and cartridge belts across their chests, came in for food and kissed the hands of these little ladies before taking their place at table.

Phillips liked this place. It appealed to his sense of romance. Also his little shy smile and his blue eyes found favour with one of the pretty princesses and he was having a pleasant flirtation with her when she could spare a few moments from other tables. Phillips was like that. His shyness, his little nervous cough, his blue eyes and his smile were very attractive to women and he had love affairs, of a mild kind mostly, in many cities of the world where he sipped golden liquids of infinite variety while he watched the world and recorded its drama, until one day, alas, before his time, the curtain fell for him.

I talked to some of the Russian officers, and soon discovered that they regarded Great Britain as the real cause of their defeats. In spite of all the British arms and gold sent to Denikin and Kolchak, in spite of all the stores we gave them, and the expeditionary forces sent out by Winston Churchill, there was no gratitude among the White officers for our aid. On the contrary. It was the former admiral of the Czar, then handing me a pork chop, who said to me: "England has betrayed us!"

By English officers who had served in Russia that feeling was reciprocated. Sitting one night in the Pera Palace with one of them, while a group of Russian officers were entertaining their ladies, I heard him speak some bitter words.

"I'm not blood-thirsty," he said, "but it would give me the greatest pleasure in the world to cut one of those fellow's throats."

He told me a long tale about the vanity, inefficiency, jealousy and damned selfishness of many White officers. Many of the stores we sent them never got to the front. Crowds of these fellows never went near their men in the trenches or holding the lines, and were hundreds of miles behind, gambling, and drinking, and pursuing amorous adventures. Some of the women were just as bad as the men and perhaps worse. We had sent out consignments of clothes for the Russian nurses who were in rags at the front, looking after the wounded. That underclothing, with stockings and boots and raincoats, never reached them. They were seized by harpies, hundreds of miles behind. The young officer had more respect for the Reds than for this White rabble, as he called them. One day the British tax-payer, he said would want to know why we were feeding thousands of them in the Isle of Prinkipo and elsewhere.

One day the British tax-payer did want to know, and no more rations went to Prinkipo. They had to fend for themselves and it was a rough and stony way ahead in a world that became tired of them.

Some of these Russian refugees had brought their jewels with them, hidden in their boots or tied up in their bundles. In the Pera Palace Hotel two Jews sat outside the dining room ready to change a diamond or a pearl into Turkish money. For to the Pera Palace Hotel they came to give a little banquet to their friends, to drink good wine, to smoke expensive cigarettes, to kiss each other's hands, to pretend, just for an hour or two, that they were still the spoilt children of Imperial Russia. Behind them was the horror of civil war, most murderous and pitiless, and sudden flights from houses and villas where they had known luxury, and frightful hardships on roads crowded with fugitives like themselves, dirty, verminous, typhus-stricken. Before them was the unknown future in a world where they had no place, and where, as they moved from country to country, the foundations of life broke beneath their feet, because money went bad and ruin crept on them again. They talked and talked, with sudden silences in which they saw the ghosts of the past. They laughed a little, and wept a little, and now and again a man would leave the table and kiss the hands of the ladies, and go out to shoot himself in some foul lodging.

With Percival Phillips Tony and I visited the mosques, and explored Turkish street life on the Stamboul side, and went up to Eyoub and the Sweet Waters of Europe, and wandered among the charred ruins of a quarter of the city where a great fire had raged. Once, with the young commercial traveller in vests and pants we walked to lonely districts where Indian cavalry had pitched their camps beyond the city, and where, in a little Turkish coffee shop, remote and solitary, some wild Gypsy women in tattered robes of many colours, through which could be seen their bare brown limbs, danced and sang to us. No need to ask the origin of the Gypsy folk after seeing these. They were people of the Far East, and their songs had the harsh and ancient melody of oriental nomads. How strange that their language is still spoken by Gypsy girls in Surrey, with one of whom I walked behind a caravan through my own village one day while she told me the Gypsy words for 'smoke' and 'fire' and 'bread' and 'water', and other things which I named.

"Not particularly safe to wander far afield like this," said the young commercial traveller. He told stories of Turkish robbers and assassins on the outskirts of the city. But it was just as dangerous at night in Constantinople. In fact there were battles almost every night between British and American bluejackets. The Americans got drunk first, liking alcohol better than beer, and that was a disadvantage to them. Their Admiral, on excellent terms with ours, said the sooner the military police knocked them out and sent them back to ship the better for them.

In narrow alleys up from the Galata Bridge I saw the poorest of the

Russian refugees, ragged, dirty, undernourished. Some of them had lived in good homes once—in Petrograd, Moscow, Odessa, Kieff. I remember one young man, very handsome but haggard, who swayed for a moment as I passed and steadied himself with his hand against a wall.

"Are you ill?" I asked in French. "Can I help you?"

He smiled and shook his head.

"It is nothing! I am a Russian refugee, you understand? It is not amusing to be a Russian refugee."

But over in Prinkipo, an enchanted isle, it was amusing—for a time. I went there by boat with my son. They were living a Gypsy kind of life, those Russians, many of whom belonged to the old aristocratic families. They were billeted in the Turkish villas and their washing was hanging up to dry in the gardens. They had got rid of lice—at last. They had organised a *balalaika* orchestra and all day long one heard the tinkle of this music. They had laid down boards on the grass and used them as a dancing floor. Russian officers and ladies were practising the new fox-trots under the blue sky and within sight of the blue sea around them. Far away on the horizon one could see, faintly pencilled, the minarets and cloud-like domes of the mosques in Constantinople.

There were donkeys on the island, hired out by Turkish boys, and Cossack officers and their womenfolk had donkey races, shouting and laughing as they rode. After all, the sun was shining. They were still alive. They had lost everything but nothing was lost while they laughed, and sang, and danced, forgetful of the past and careless of the future. They were Russians of the old régime. They were like that. But the women, especially, had courage and spirit, and some fine quality which they did not lose in Vienna, or Berlin, or Paris, or London, or New York, where they served in restaurants, or danced in ballets, or sat as sempstresses in milliner's shops, or served tea to English visitors along the Côte d'Azur where afterwards I met them.

There was a cabaret called the *Petits Champs* in Constantinople. It was a show put up by the Russians. They were all amateurs, and Russian girls of well-to-do families in the old régime came here to dance in very scanty clothing for the delectation of British and American sailors, Turks, Greeks, Armenians and Jews. The dancing was not very good, but the girls had white and beautiful bodies. The orchestra played wild Russian music, badly. But the *Petits Champs* was always crowded, and Tony and I sat at the tables many times, watching the scene around us through a haze of cigarette smoke, and in an atmosphere which reeked of beer, coffee, unwashed bodies, and women's scent. I remember one young Yankee seaman who sat with his petty officer at the same table as ours. The boy was silly with drink and put his watch in a glass of iced water and smiled at it. Later, after a few more drinks, he went mad and seizing a tray beat it like a gong and danced the *hula-hula* with Hawaiian cries. No one paid the slightest attention to him. The Russian orchestra drowned his noise. The thump thump of its drums, the gurgle of the saxophones, dazed one's senses. It went on until the small hours of the morning when Tony and I lay in our beds in the Pera Palace Hotel trying to sleep. One tune they played over and over again. It ends with the rapid Russian rhythm, like wild horses galloping over the Steppes. Once or twice Tony and I have heard it in Paris or elsewhere, and instantly we look at each other and smile.

"Reminds you of anything?"

"The *Petits Champs* in Constantinople. Those awful nights!"

5

A SHIP GOES TO SMYRNA

It was a British ship which took us from Constantinople to Smyrna, and it gave me a thrill of patriotic pleasure to get porridge for breakfast and ham and eggs with buttered toast.

Apart from the officers and crew there were few British folk aboard. I can only remember one—a good-looking and good-humoured major, who was bound for Alexandria with a pretty Greek woman, who seemed to be under his chivalrous protection. The other first-class passengers were Greeks, Armenians and Jews. On the lower decks were groups of Italian soldiers who sang and danced continuously, a few Turks, an old Arab woman in a dirty white robe—who gazed all day long over the side of the ship as though reading some spell of Fate in the lacework patterns of froth woven by our passage through the dead calm sea—and families of Israelites lying among their bundles.

It was good to be on the boat deck in the full glare of the sun, pouring its warmth down from a cloudless sky, and to watch with half-shut eyes the golden glitter of the sea, and its change of colour and light, from deepest blue to palest green, as the currents crossed our track, and white clouds passed overhead, and the sun sank low as evening came.

Fairy islands, dream-like and unsubstantial, appeared on the far horizon, and then seemed to sink below its golden bar. At night the sky was crowded with stars, shining with a piercing brightness, and it seemed no wonder then that to each of them the Greeks had given a name and god-like attributes. They seemed closer to the world than in an English sky, heaven's brilliant train, and on this ship in a lonely sea— no other boat passed us—the company of the stars was friendly and benign.

From the lower deck came the singing of the Italian soldiers with liquid words and open notes, in which I heard something very old in the melody of life. The Greeks were singing too, in a separate group, softly to themselves and with a melancholy cadence. Tiny sparks of fire like glow-worms, flitted to and fro on the lower deck. It was the glow of cigarette ends, as the Italian soldiers danced the fox-trot and the one-step. Now and then a match was lighted, and one saw it held in the hollow of brown hands, illumining a dark Italian face.

Tony and I sat on coils of rope, up on the boat deck, with a Greek girl with whom we had made friends. She talked and talked, and held us spellbound by her philosophy of life, her gaiety, her bitter wisdom, her fearlessness and wit. It was a short voyage and we have never seen her again, but we shall not forget that laughing Greek girl who spoke half the languages of Europe, and English, perfectly, and American with such intimate acquaintance that she could sing little old negro melodies with a perfect accent, as it seemed to us. Yet she had never been in England or America, and had spent nearly all her life in Constantinople, with brief visits to Greece, and two frightful years in Russia. She had learnt English and her negro songs in the American college at Constantinople, to which she looked back with adoration, though she had been a naughty rebel against all its discipline.

As a governess to a German family in Russia she had learnt another language and had been thoroughly amused with life, until the Red Revolution broke in Moscow. Her Germans fled, leaving her alone in their empty flat, and then she learnt more than ever she had guessed about the cruelties of life. She was saved by her gaiety and "cheek" as she called it.

When a crowd of Red soldiers threatened to cut her throat she jeered at them, and then made them roar with laughter by playing comic songs on the piano and singing them with merry pantomime. That was all right, but she starved and went in expectation of death, month after month. Her Russian friends, students and intellectuals, were mostly shot or hanged. She recognised some of them as they hung from lamp-posts in the streets, and she gave us a vivid imitation of how they looked, with their necks cricked and their tongues hanging out. She became used to that sort of thing. . . . After wandering adventures, abominable hardships, in dirt and rags, she got through at last to Constantinople, and lived for a time on a Greek gunboat, as one of the crew, wearing a naval cap and a sailor's jersey.

She was tremendously amused with all this experience. She wouldn't have missed it for the world! It was the adventure of life and the great game.

There was nothing in life but that—and what did death matter after this adventure, whenever it came? We spoke of war and the chance of world peace, and she scoffed at the chance. War, she said, was inevitable—the greatest adventure of all. Cruelty? Yes! That was part of the adventure. Men were heartless, but amusing, even in their cruelties. It was no good looking at life seriously, she said, breaking one's heart over impossible ideals. It was best to laugh, and take things as they came, and shrug one's shoulders, whatever happened. It was Life. . . . So we talked under the stars.

There was another girl on board who talked to us. She belonged to a different type and race—a tragic type, an Armenian. She had some frightful photographs in a satchel which she wore always round her waist. They were photographs of Turkish atrocities in Asia Minor. There was one of a Turkish officer sitting on a pile of skulls and smoking a cigarette. Those skulls had once held the living brains of this girl's family and townsfolk at Samsun.

She told me of the death march of the Armenians when the Turks drove them from the coast into the interior. The women and children had been separated from their men, who were then massacred. Her father and brother had been killed like that. They passed their bodies on the roadside. The women and children had been driven forward until many dropped and died, until all were barefoot and exhausted to the point of death. Kurdish brigands had robbed them of the little money they had and their rings. Some of the younger girls were carried off. Their screams were heard for a long way. There were not many who reached journey's end. . . . A terrible tale, told with a white passion of hatred against the Turk, but without tears, and coldly, so that it made me shiver.

In that ship, sailing under the stars in the Aegean Sea, I learnt more than I had known about the infernal history of mankind during war and revolution. I had seen it in the West. These were stories of the East, unknown and unrecorded, as primitive in their horror as when Assyrians fought Egyptians, or the Israelites were put to the sword in the time of Judas Maccabæus.

6

The Doomed City

Our ship put in at Mitylene, and with the Greek girl we explored the port, and walked up the hillside to an old fort built by the Venetians in the great days when Venice was the strongest sea power in that part of the world

On the way the Greek girl chatted to shopkeepers and peasants in

their own tongue and then climbed to the top of the fort, sitting fearlessly on the edge of the wall and looking back to the sea over which we
had travelled, and down to our ship, so small as we saw it from this
height.

In the valley, Greek peasants of better type and stock than those at
Athens, and true descendants of the people whose tools and gods and
jewels they turned up sometimes with their spades, were leading their
sheep and goats.

Some of them were singing, and the sound rose clear up the hillside,
with a tinkling of goat bells and the baa-ing of sheep. Wild flowers
were growing in the old walls of the fort, and the hillside was silvered
with daisies. We seemed very close to the blue canopy of the sky above
us, as we sat on the edge of the wall, and in the warm sunshine, and
above that calm crystal-clear sea, mirroring our ship, we seemed to be
touched by the immortality of the gods, and to be invested with the
beauty of the springtime of the world.

"It would be good to stay here," said the Greek girl. "We would
keep goats and sing old Greek songs."

However, presently she was hungry and scrambled off the wall and
cried: "The ship, and supper!"

So we went down to the little port again, and rowed away from
Mitylene to the ship which was sounding its siren for our return.

We reached Smyrna next morning, and I was astonished by the
modern aspect of its sea frontage upon which the sun poured down.
Beyond the broad quays it swept in a wide curve of white houses, faced
with marble, and very handsome in the quarter inhabited, I was told, by
rich Armenian merchants.

"The Turks will never rest until they get Smyrna back", said the
English major by my side, and his words came as a sharp reminder
of the lines away beyond the hills, where a Greek Army lay entrenched
against the Turkish Nationalists under Mustapha Kemal. But no
shadow of gloom crept through the sunlight that lay glittering upon
those white-fronted houses, nor did I guess that one day, not far ahead,
Englishmen, like myself, looking over the side of this ship, would see the
beauty of this city devoured by an infernal fury of flame, and listen to
the screams of panic-stricken crowds on those broad quaysides, hidden
behind rolling clouds of smoke. . . .

That grim secret of fate lay hidden in the future when Tony and I
booked our rooms at the Grand Hotel Splendid Palace—what more
noble name?—and entertained our little Greek lady to breakfast, and
then at midday waved towels out of the bedroom window in answer
to her signals from the ship which took her on her way to Alexandria
and another adventure of life. The English major brought a bucket to

the upper deck, as we could see distinctly, and wrung a towel over it as a sign of tears. We made the countersign.

7

GREEK FAITH

I was anxious to get the latest information about the military situation away to the back of Smyrna, and for that purpose called upon the British Military Mission, represented by a General Hamilton and his staff. A charming and courteous man he was obviously embarrassed by my visit, not knowing how much to tell me of a situation which was extremely delicate in a political as well as a military way. He decided to tell me nothing, and I did not press him, seeing his trouble.

I obtained all the information I wanted, and even more than I had bargained for, from the Greek authorities. The fact that I represented the *Daily Chronicle*, known for its pro-Greek sympathies, and for its official connexion with Lloyd George's Government, gave me an almost embarrassing importance. No sooner had I revealed my mission than I received a visit from a Greek staff officer—Lieutenant Casimatas —who put the entire city of Smyrna at my feet, as it were, and as one small token of my right to fulfil the slightest wish, sent round a powerful military car with two tall soldiers under orders to obey my commands. Tony was pleased with this attention and other courtesies which were showered upon us. It was he, rather than myself, who interviewed the Commander-in-Chief of the Greek Army, and received the salutes of the soldiers as we drove magnificently to General Headquarters.

A military band was playing outside—selections from "*Patience*", doubtless in our honour—and in the antechamber of the General's room Greek staff officers, waisted, highly polished, scented, came in and out. The Commander-in-Chief was a very fat old gentleman, uncomfortable in his tight belt, and perspiring freely on that hot day. The windows of his room were open, and the merry music floated in, with the scent of flowers and the aroma of the warm sea.

"He received us most politely," as Fragson used to sing in one of my brother's plays, and with his fat fingers moving about a big map explained the military situation. It was excellent, he said. The Greek Army was splendid, in training and morale, and longing to advance against the Turk who was utterly demoralised. Those poor Turkish peasants, forcibly enlisted by Mustapha Kemal, wanted nothing but leave to go home, he told me. The Greek advance would be a parade. The Commander-in-Chief, speaking in French, repeated his words with relish and pride—"a parade, sir."

Unfortunately, he said, Greece was hampered by differences among the Allies. The French were certainly intriguing with the Turkish Nationalists of Angora—supplying them with arms and ammunition. The Italians were no better, and very jealous of Greek claims in Asia Minor. Greece trusted however in the noble friendship of England, in the sympathy and aid of that great statesman Lloyd George. The Greek Army would astonish the world.

So the old gentleman talked, and I listened politely and kept my doubts to myself.

It was Lieutenant Casimatas who had introduced us to the Commander-in-Chief, and he devoted himself to the task of presenting us to all the people of importance in Smyrna, and taking us to schools, hospitals, museums, and other institutions which would prove to us the benevolence and high culture of Greek rule in Asia Minor. He was a cheery stout little man, speaking English, which he had learnt in India, and almost bursting with good nature and the desire to pump us with Greek propaganda.

He took us to the Greek Metropolitan of Smyrna, a black-bearded, broad-shouldered, loud-laughing, excitable Bishop of the Orthodox Church, wearing the high black hat and long black robe of his priestly office, and reminding us of one of those Princes of the Church in the Middle Ages, who led their armies to battle and sometimes wielded a battle-axe or a sword in the Name of the Lord. "An old ruffian," I heard him called by an English merchant of Bournabat, whose sympathies, however, were decidedly pro-Turk. A picture representing the martyrdom of St. Polycarp at Smyrna, in the early days of the Christian era, adorned the wall, opposite his desk, and he waved his hand towards it and spoke of the martyrdom of the Christian people, not so long ago as that, but only a year or two ago, when they were driven from the coast, as that Armenian girl had told me.

"The spirit of St. Polycarp," he said in barbarous French, "animates the Greek Christians to-day, and nothing would give me greater joy than to die for the Faith, as he did."

His wish was fulfilled. I heard that he was flung to death when the Turkish irregulars came down into Smyrna after smashing the Greek line.

For a long time he talked of the sufferings of the Greeks and Armenians, calling upon various men in the room—his secretaries and priests—to bear witness to the truth of his tales. Presently, with some ceremony, servants came round with silver trays laden with glasses of iced water and some little plates containing a white glutinous substance. As the guest of ceremony it was my privilege to be served first which did not give me the chance of watching what others might do.

I took a spoonful of the white substance and swallowed it, hoping for the best. But it was the worst that I had done. I discovered afterwards that it was a resinous substance called *mastica*, something in the nature of chewing gum. The mouthful I had swallowed had a most disturbing effect upon my system, and even the Metropolitan was alarmed. Tony, served second, was in the same trouble.

In the Greek schools in Smyrna all the scholars were kept in during luncheon hour, while we went from class to class inspecting their work and making polite bows and speeches to the teachers. The scholars, ranging from all ages of childhood, did not seem to bear us any grudge for their long wait for lunch, and we were much impressed by their discipline, their pretty manners, their beautiful eyes. Tony felt like the Prince of Wales, and was conscious of the "glad eyes" of the older girls. . . . When Smyrna was reported to be a city of fire and massacre I thought with dreadful pity of those little ones.

We touched with our very hands the spirit of this ancient race in the time of its glory, when we went into the museum and handled the pottery, the gods, the household ornaments, the memorials—found by peasants with their picks not far below the soil—of that time when Homer was born (it is claimed) in this city of the Ægean, when the Ionians held it, when Lysimachus made it great and beautiful, until it was one of the most prosperous ports in the world, crowded with Greek and Roman and Syrian ships trading between the West and East.

Lieutenant Casimatas took us to his little home away on a lonely road beyond the Turkish quarter, and we spent an evening with his family, a lovely wife and three beautiful children, who sang little songs to us in French and Greek. The poor lady was nervous. Some shadow of fear was upon her because of that Turkish Army beyond the Greek trenches. I hope with all my heart that she escaped from Smyrna with her babes before the horror came. . . . I drank to the welfare of Greece in the sweet resinous wine which Lieutenant Casimatas poured out for us. It was a sincere wish, but at the back of my mind was some foreboding.

8

ENGLISH RESIDENTS

We drove out one day to Boudja and Bournabat, past the slopes of Mount Pagus and away in the hills. Turkish peasants riding on donkeys or in ox wagons, jogged along the dusty tracks. We passed Turkish cemeteries with tombstones leaning at every angle below tall black cypress trees, and looking back saw the brown roofs of Smyrna, as in a panorama under the hot sun which made the Gulf look like molten metal.

In the country we lost touch with the Western world. It was Asia, with the smell and colour and silence of the East. A camel caravan moved slowly in the valley, like a picture in the *Arabian Nights*. But at Boudja, and later at Bournabat, we were astonished to see English-looking girls in summer frocks carrying tennis rackets and appearing as though they had just left Surbiton.

These two villages were inhabited by British merchants who had been long settled there as traders in oriental carpets, spices, raisins, dates, and all the merchandise of the East. We called on one of them at Bournabat, and I rubbed my eyes when, with Asia Minor at the gate, we drove up to a house that might have been transplanted from Clapham Park in the early Victorian period, when Cubitt was building for a rich middle class.

The house was furnished like that, except for some bear-skins and hunting trophies, and the two old ladies and one old gentleman who gave us tea might have been transported on a magic carpet from a tea party in the time of the *"Newcomes"*. We had toasted muffins, and the stouter of the two old ladies (who wore a little lace cap and sat stiffly against an antimacassar, in a chintz-covered chair) asked whether we would take one or two lumps of sugar. Tony, who was beginning to feel an exile from civilisation, beamed with happiness at this English life again.

The old gentleman had been the greatest trader in Asia Minor, and in his younger days had hunted with Turkish peasants in the mountains. He loved the Turk still, though he deplored the cruelties they had done to the Christian populations in the war. For the Greeks he had pity and dreadful forebodings. He knew something of what was happening behind the Turkish lines, with Mustapha Kemal. There would be no peace, he said, until they had Smyrna back again. The Greeks had claimed too much. Venizelos had lost his head. Lloyd George . . . The old man sighed, and fell into gloomy silence.

"I'm afraid of the future," he said presently. "Nobody will listen to my advice. The Greeks think I am pro-Turk. What I want is a just peace, and above all, peace. This is only an armed truce." He told me many things about the situation which filled me with uneasiness. I promised to see him again, but after a few days we left Smyrna for Athens.

9

BEAUTY OF ATHENS

We travelled in a little steam yacht which had once been Vanderbilt's, and now was a Greek passenger ship called *Polikos*. It was crowded

with Greek officers, in elegant uniforms and looking very martial until a
certain hour of the evening.The passage began in a wonderful calm,
and after darkness there were groups of singing folk of various
nationalities, as on that other ship, but presently a terrific storm broke
upon us, and the singing ceased and the *Polikos* was a ship of sick and
sorry people. Tony and I crept into our bunks in a big crowded cabin,
and the Greek officers in the other bunks were frightfully and out-
rageously ill. Early next morning their martial appearance had gone,
and they were the dishevelled wrecks of men. Tony, with extreme
heroism, staggered to the saloon and ordered ham and eggs, but
thought better of it before they came, and took to his bunk again, which
I, less brave, had never left. We were glad to reach Athens without
shipwreck.

We had a week of joy there, in dazzling sunshine, and wandered
about the ruins of the Acropolis, and touched old stones with reverence,
and sipped rose-tinted ices in the King's Gardens, and saw Greek boys
throwing the discus in the very arena where the games were played in the
Golden Age, and tried to remember old scraps of classical knowledge, to
recall the beauty of the gods and the wisdom of the poets. We saw
Venizelos looking as wise as Socrates, and the young King Alexander
who died soon afterwards from a bite when trying to rescue a dog from
the attack of a monkey in his gardens.

It was as pro-Greeks that we returned to England, with memories
which made us understand more sharply the tragedy of that defeat
when the Cross went down before the Crescent, and the horror happened in Smyrna, and all the world held its breath when Constantinople
was threatened with the same fate.

10

THE COMING OF KEMAL

By good luck we had a man in Constantinople who saved the situation
from becoming a bloody tragedy. This was Sir Charles Harington,
generally called "Tim" Harington by his friends. I had come very
closely in touch with him during the war, when he was the Chief of Staff
of the Second Army under General Plumer. He was, without doubt, the
best staff officer produced in that war, and the correspondents had a
great respect and liking for him because, before and during the big
battles, he always invited us to his headquarters, spread out his maps
and told us all his plans in great detail.

I remember still those conferences in a big conservatory on the edge o the Ypres Salient when rain came slashing down upon the window panes as this tall quiet-voiced man expounded, like a scientist, plans which however successful would involve the slaughter of a great number of our men. Now in Constantinople he had to be a statesman as well as a soldier and to handle a situation which was delicate and dangerous.

Lloyd George under the spell of Venizelos had given the Greeks too much, and more than they could hold. Now he wished to fulfil his pledges, and when the Greek lines were broken in Asia Minor he was eager to raise the fiery Cross on their behalf throughout the Dominions and in the homeland. But our people and those of the Dominions were having none of that. They were utterly sick of war. They were exhausted by it. They had no enthusiasm for a war with the Turks on behalf of Greece. They wanted peace and nothing but peace. Messages came from the Dominions turning down this appeal for a new Crusade.

Lloyd George had been warned. It was Winston Churchill his own War Minister who had warned him.

When Lloyd George was exhilarated by a Greek advance in Asia Minor before Mustapha Kemal had organised his forces of resistance, Churchill wrote to him grave words:

"It is a fearful responsibility to let loose the Greeks and reopen the war."

In his *World Crisis* he quotes one of the memoranda he wrote at this time to the Prime Minister.

"With military resources which the Cabinet have cut to the most weak and slender proportions, we are leading the Allies in an attempt to enforce a peace in Turkey which would require great and powerful armies and long and costly operations and occupations. On this world so torn with strife I dread to see you let loose the Greek Armies—for all sakes and certainly for their sakes. Yet the Greek Armies are your only effective fighting forces."

Later he advocated the evacuation of Smyrna.

"If the Greeks go off in another half-cock offensive the last card will have been played and lost, and we shall have neither a Turkish peace nor a Greek Army."

It was a most uncanny foreboding of what happened, and one must pay a tribute to Churchill's far-seeing judgment.

Mustapha Kemal was biding his time and gathering his strength with the secret aid of France. They had as their French agent and most ardent champion a French deputy named Franklin Bouillon whom I had met several times in Paris. He spoke English with great fluency and was an excitable, emotional, and flamboyant fellow. Now he was intriguing with the Turks up to his neck and was passionately hostile to

Lloyd George's pro-Greek policy. So were all Frenchmen at that time. They had been shocked by the return of King Constantine to Greece, utterly pro-German as they believed, though he denied it strenuously. They were also embittered against the British, so recently their Allies in the great war, by troubles in Syria which they believed were entirely due to British intrigues against them with the Arab race. As far as Syria was concerned it was the same situation then as repeated itself in 1945 after another World War. Now in 1921 and 1922 they were selling arms and ammunition to the Turks by every possible means of transport, knowing full well that they might be used against British troops who had fought by their side through those tragic and heroic years. Such is the frailty of international loyalty—God help us all!

After the Greeks had made an offensive which petered out, Mustapha Kemal struck back on August 22nd, 1922, and smashed through the Greek line south of Karahissar. The Greeks retreated in disorder which became a panic. They abandoned their guns and fled to the coast.

In the Gulf of Smyrna close to the front lay some British and American battleships awaiting orders. No orders came to open fire against the Turks and rescue the Christian population. On the quaysides panic-stricken crowds struggled to get on any boat that would take them away from Smyrna. They abandoned their chests and bundles. Many of them waded into the sea with outstretched arms towards the ships. Forty thousand of them got away before the first lines of Turkish cavalry entered the city. Fifty thousand of them could not get away.

Naval officers, staring through their glasses, heard a wail from thousands of voices which came out to sea like the despair of lost souls to freeze the blood of simple naval men who had liked these people in Smyrna, who had danced with some of their girls and taken many a drink in the Grand Hotel Splendid Palace. Presently flames rose from the Armenian quarter and a veil of smoke spread across the whole front. When darkness fell the flames rose like torches. The Grand Hotel Splendid Palace was a smouldering ruin. The marble-fronted houses were gutted by fire, and in the distance across the strip of sea there was the sound of shots and screaming.

A shudder went through the world at these screams from Smyrna, and then, for most people, there were other things to think about, closer at home, and more personal in anxiety. There were two million unemployed in England. France was threatening to enter the Ruhr to get a stranglehold on German industry. Italy was in the throes of a political revolution. What did Greece matter? Tragic and terrible was this abandonment of Greece.

The Turks advanced to the coast opposite Constantinople. There was a line at Chanak held by the British and French. It was defended by barbed wire behind which our British Tommies stood, wondering what was going to happen and whether they would be ordered to fire on Turkish soldiers, who came to grin at them. One morning early, the French were no longer there. Our Allies had left us in the lurch. Franklin Bouillon and his pro-Turk friends had prevailed. General Harington walked about with a slip of paper in his pocket authorising him to take military action if necessary but he did not want to use it except as a last resort. He had weak forces—six battalions—under his command and France had gone over to the Turkish side. He opened negotiations with the Turkish leaders at Mudania on the Sea of Marmora. There were protracted discussions and Mustapha Kemal hesitated to declare war on the British. They wished to be reasonable, these Turks. Harington handled this situation with infinite patience and tact and at last a new treaty—the Treaty of Lausanne—was signed. It was favourable to the Turks. They had Constantinople again and the country of Thrace up to the Maritza river, where I had stood on the bridge with Fox Ferdinand after the Bulgarian victories against the Turk. One clause of the treaty was dreadful in its inhumanity. The Greek population of Asia Minor—descendants of those who had settled there 2,000 years ago—was to be deported to Greece in exchange for a small number of Turks in Greek territory. So it happened and nobody cared for this beginning of a frightful precedent—nobody but idealists and "sentimentalists" as they were called.

I was in Greece again when that chapter of history was being written. I saw the arrival of hundreds of thousands of those poor Greeks from Asia Minor. The League of Nations helped in their resettlement and the mainland Greeks and their government did their best to feed and house these people and find places for them in national life. I thought the job was well done, this incredible job of dealing with nearly a million people uprooted, penniless, and workless, suddenly dumped down upon the shores of Greece. In a year or two they had been absorbed somehow or other into the economic life of Greece. Lately, talking to some Greek diplomats, I said: "That was well done." One of them looked at me and answered: "It was badly done. Square pegs were put into round holes. It was handled with stupidity." I still think that this tragedy of the uprooted was dealt with wisely on the whole and with remarkable success, though doubtless there were mistakes as in most human undertakings. And out of tragedy came some kind of value. The mainland Greeks were strengthened by this good stock which came to them. When Italy attacked them in another war they were heroic in defence, as all the world agreed.

I went to Constantinople again, and saw the social revolution effected by that astonishing man Mustapha Kemal. By the stroke of a pen and an iron will he abolished a thousand years of tradition. The last of the Sultans had fled under British protection before his coming. Women were unveiled. The fez was forbidden. He modernised religion and social life. By clever diplomacy, taking great risks, or at least skating on thin ice, the Turks under their new leadership succeeded in maintaining their neutrality in the second World War. But the future still veils their destiny. What will Russia do about it? I ask this question as I write these words at the end of 1945. It may be answered before this book is published.

PART IX

SOVIET RUSSIA

1

JOURNEY TO MOSCOW

TOWARDS the end of 1921 I went to Russia at the invitation of the Imperial Famine Relief Fund, who asked me to make a report on a famine in that country.

Was there a famine? The *Daily Mail* and other papers said that it was just Red propaganda to obtain economic aid. But stories were coming in, mostly from Riga, about terrible starvation along the Volga. It was my job to find out the truth, as far as possible.

I was accompanied by a friend of mine named Leonard Spray who was a correspondent in Berlin where I joined him. Here we were advised to buy blankets, medicines, cooking utensils, and as much food as we could carry. Travelling in Russia was likely to be rough.

I was helped in my shopping by a kind lady who afterwards became the wife of my friend Daniels, correspondent of *The Times* in Berlin and afterwards in Paris. I could not entertain the idea of carrying enough food for a longish spell in Russia—the human animal requires a lot of nourishment in bulk for any length of time—and I restricted my supplies to some tins of soup and an enormous Dutch cheese which I regarded as a kind of life insurance which would carry me through lean days, if necessary.

After hanging about some time in Berlin, for a Soviet *visa* to our passports and other necessary papers, Spray and I set forth on our journey. It took us through East Prussia where we saw something of the desolation which had been caused by the Cossack cavalry who had swept over it at the beginning of the war of 1914 onwards. Then we had four days or so in Riga where it looked as though we might spend four months before getting into Russia. The British Consulate were pessimistic about our prospects which they regarded as almost hopeless. So we had time to explore the capital of Lithuania with its narrow streets and medieval houses and ancient churches, and the old castle of the Knights of the Sword, built in the fifteenth century, as well as modern restaurants and cafés. One thing we discovered very soon. The people of Riga seemed to turn their night into day. It was hopeless to expect dinner at seven o'clock. Ten o'clock was about the time when things began to brighten up. At midnight they were in full swing. At two in the morning when Spray and I were in bed we could hear laughing and talking and dancing feet in the streets. It seemed a gay little city in those days when Lithuania was rejoicing in its independence after being long under Russian rule. Now it is under Russian rule again and I doubt whether there is much laughter or dancing now.

Depressed by the inactivity of the British Consulate regarding facilities for getting into Russia, Spray and I went round to the American Consul and put our case to him.

"That's all right," he told us, "there's a train going to-morrow night with a bunch of our boys on it belonging to the A.R.A., the American Relief Administration. Is there a famine? Yes sir, with a capital 'F'. Millions dying of starvation along the Volga."

The next night Spray and I went to the railway station which was in absolute darkness. An unlighted train stood at the end of a long track down which we stumbled. It was surrounded by a crowd of Lettish porters quarrelling and cursing and fighting for the baggage. Chaos was reduced to something like order mainly by a young American giant whom we came to know afterwards as the Milk-fed Boy. He was an American courier who had done this journey many times and knew all its difficulties and horrors. By a mixture of jocularity, laughter, and bullying, he managed to sort out the baggage and get it carried on to the train. He knew half a dozen words of Russian and those were enough. "*Kraseva*" (Fine). "*Tavarish*" (Comrade). "*Seichas*" (Immediately). He punched the porters, embraced the guard and the engine driver, roared with laughter in the midst of a scrimmage. He was a grand fellow by name of Fink. Spray and I obtained an empty carriage and spread our blankets on its bare boards which were the only seats. That night an army of lice came out of their lairs and attacked Leonard Spray who suffered tortures. They left me alone for some reason, which I suspect was my lifelong devotion to Virginia cigarettes. The stores we had bought in Berlin were now called for and we fixed up a pot slung across the carriage by a strap and heated up tinned soup, with only a fifty per cent chance of setting the bunks on fire from candles stuck in their own grease on the window sills.

A group of young Americans who were on their way to join the staff of the A.R.A. spent their night cursing the filth and darkness, and singing rag-time.

Every twenty miles or so during that long journey to Moscow the train stopped and the *provodniks*, or guards, left it on expeditions to get food for the engine. At these times we would all get out, pacing up and down to ease our limbs and keep ourselves warm. A light snow lay on the ground and the bare trees were black against its whiteness.

In the train was a King's Messenger named Wilton with whom we made friends. He was a delicate-looking man, and a great gentleman of the old school, with charming manners, but when he spoke of Russia a curious red glint came into his eyes as though some inward fire were burning him.

It was the fire of a suppressed passion and agony. He had Russian relatives who had suffered terrible things in the Red Revolution. To him, Communism under Lenin was reeking with cruelty, torture, murder, and all evil, covered by fine phrases and theoretical ideals. But he dared not say these things openly, and only hinted at them with that suppressed fire in his eyes. I used to meet him afterwards in London.

We arrived at last at Sebesh on the Russian frontier, and saw Red soldiers for the first time. They wore their winter coats with pointed hoods over their heads. They were mostly very young soldiers—boys of seventeen or eighteen—and, I thought, they looked a pasty-faced lot, unhealthy and undernourished.

Here at Sebesh we saw a trainload of refugees from the famine districts of Russia. They were mostly Letts and were in bad shape after their long journey. Many of them were stricken with typhus and I saw young girls carried out on to the platform and laid in the snow. They had flushed cheeks and were in a high state of fever.

An elderly man in a sheepskin coat spoke to me in English with an American accent. He looked like a farmer.

"It has taken me a year to reach this frontier," he told me. "I did it on foot, mostly."

"Where do you come from?" I asked.

He waved his thin hand as though to the far distance. "Ufa. Three thousand miles."

He wanted to go to America and asked if I could exchange Russian money into American dollars or English pounds.

"What's it like in Russia?" I asked.

He looked at me with tragic eyes.

"Everybody starves," he said.

Our train crawled forward through flat desolate country. Here and there we saw people in the railway stations. There was no cheerfulness among them. At last we came to Moscow and I saw for the first time that beautiful and fantastic city, very oriental in its aspect, surrounded by big walls with fan-shaped battlements, and with an inner city—the Kremlin—with palaces and government offices and churches, also surrounded by high walls like a medieval fortress. Here and there, at each gate, outside the Kremlin there were long stone stairways leading to the battlements and little towers for the guards.

In a droshky drawn by a lean-ribbed horse we drove through the gate leading into the city. On one side, deeply cut into the wall were the

L

words in Russian (as afterwards I learnt): "Religion is the opium of the people", but on the other side was a little chamber, the shrine of the Iberian Virgin, before which the Czars of Russia used to halt, and I noticed that our driver pulled off his fur cap and crossed himself furtively.

2

FORGOTTEN TRAGEDY

Spray and I were put up at a place called the Guest House, on the other side of the river and looking towards the Kremlin. It had belonged in the old days to a monopolist in sugar, one of the richest men, and had remained in its old style throughout the revolution, though most of the big houses in Moscow had been turned into tenements and their furniture had been burnt for fuel. On the walls of spacious rooms in the Louis XV style, with gilded chairs, were pictures by well known French artists. I remember there was one by Greuze.

When we entered this house bolts were drawn by the house *kommissar* to let us in, and after our entry chains rattled and the bolts were fastened again.

I glanced at Spray and raised my eyebrows.

It looked rather as though we were prisoners.

We were led up a noble stairway, richly carved, and then down a long corridor where strange people passed us. They were six Chinese mandarins, walking with their hands in their sleeves. A curtain was pulled on one side and behind it stood a coal-black negro with a red fez. Further down the corridor a man came out of a room with his braces hanging down and a grey flannel shirt tucked into his trousers. He carried a sponge and as he passed us he squeezed it and said in English: "The Devil is dead."

"All this is very odd," I said to Spray.

We were taken into a big *salon* richly furnished.

"Here is your bedroom," said the Swedish housekeeper.

But there was no bed. This defect was remedied by two soldiers who staggered up with the bits and pieces of a great four-poster which they fixed up. Spray took possession of this and I made use of a broad divan. It was bitterly cold during those Moscow nights and I shall always remember how Spray wrapped himself up head and all in his blankets and disappeared from sight.

We had arrived in Moscow at an interesting time. Lenin, still alive though nearing his death, had just promulgated his new Economic

Laws. They were a reversal of his former creed of Communism in its economic policy, which had utterly broken down. The idea had been that all citizens should be servants of the State and in return for their service should receive food, shelter, clothing, education, and other essentials of life on equal terms. It hadn't worked. On October 17th, 1921 I was there when Lenin made an historic speech in which he admitted with amazing frankness the complete breakdown of the Communistic way of life which he had imposed upon the people. He explained, with a kind of vigorous brutality, that owing to the hostility and ignorance of the peasants, who resisted the requisitioning of their foodstuffs, and the failure of world revolution which prevented any international trade with Russia, industry had disintegrated, factories were abandoned, transport had broken down, and the system of rationing, which had been in force in the cities, could no longer be maintained.

"We have suffered a severe defeat on the economic front," said Lenin; "our only safety lies in a rapid retreat upon prepared positions."

He then outlined the new economic laws (called *Nep*) which abolished the rationing system, re-established the use of money, permitted private trading, which had been the unpardonable crime, and even invited the introduction of foreign capital.

I saw the immediate, though gradual and tentative effect, of this reverse of policy. Spray and I went into the market places of Moscow and saw crowds of peasants bringing in their produce for sale, under the watchful eyes of Red soldiers who, a week or two before, would have dragged them off to prison. Among the peasants stood men and women who obviously had belonged once to the old régime. The men wore black overcoats, green now, and stained, and creased. The women, with dirty hands (there was no soap in Moscow), and much worn clothes, could not disguise their old gentility. They had been ladies of Imperial Russia. Now they stood among the peasant women with little trays on which they had put bits of jewellery, their wedding rings, babies' shoes, silk scarves, trinkets, and bits of fur which some-how they had saved. The men, mostly elderly, were trying to sell pipes, slippers, books, socks, and odd things. The peasant women fingered them, shrugged their shoulders, and passed by. I did not see anything bought.

I spoke in French to one of these ladies. I guessed her age to be thirty or thereabouts. Once she had been beautiful.

"Tell me something about your life," I said. "I know all this is tragic for you."

Her face went dead white. She looked terrified. She would not answer.

When I spoke a few words more she answered me in French in a whisper.

"Do not speak to me. It is very dangerous. I beg of you. We are already watched."

A Red soldier moved towards us and I turned away and went to another part of the market.

I spoke to other women who had been ladies of the old régime, but took care that no Red soldier was near. They were all terrified and would say nothing about their way of life. One of them wept. I remember one woman who seemed to be dying. She was standing near the shrine of the Iberian Virgin selling sunflower seeds, which the Russians split between their teeth, and eat all day long. She was emaciated and her face was like a tragic mask. When I spoke to her in French she answered in that language.

"Why do you speak to me?" she asked. "You are English, are you not? Once I spoke English."

She spoke English now.

"I beg of you to go away!"

I went away deeply pitiful for these last derelicts of the old order which had been "liquidated" *en masse*—those who had never escaped to Constantinople or made their way out of Russia before the Red trap closed. Nobody bothers about them now. Their misery, their agony, their courage, are all forgotten.

3

BEHIND THE SCENES

I saw the first little restaurants open in Moscow and went to one of them. Spray and I seemed to be the only customers, except for a Red Army officer now and then, and a member of the *Cheka*, or the *Ogpu*, as the secret police were afterwards called. It was opened timorously by a distinguished man of early middle age who had been famous in his time. Even now I dare not mention his name lest trouble might befall him if he is still alive, which is very doubtful. When we were left alone in his restaurant he spoke to us in German but was always afraid.

"It is very dangerous!" he said many times.

He introduced us to his mother, a charming old lady who spoke English, and one day eight or nine ladies were waiting to see us and came out from the back premises when there was no one about but ourselves. They had brought bits of jewellery among which were some diamonds, and wanted us to buy them for a few English notes. Perhaps if they could get those, they told me, they might be able to escape from

Russia. I bought a few for their sake though I was nervous of doing so. When I returned to England I gave them to my wife who sold them to buy platinum dishes for scientific work which she was now doing.

These Russian ladies, mostly young, gathered round us, whispering, while our host kept a sharp ear on the door and listened for any footstep coming down the street. To all of them the presence of two Englishmen was exciting. They had been shut off from the outer world since the revolution. There were many things they wanted to know, but they dared not talk too long and presently we took our leave. I wonder if any of them are still alive, poor dears.

Our diplomatic representative in Moscow—he was not called ambassador—was Mr. Hodgson, and we became very friendly with him. He employed a number of Russian secretaries and typists, mostly young women of the old régime, partly because they knew foreign languages and partly, no doubt, because of pity for them. To them, this employment was like entry into Paradise. Once a week or so there were little dances with the members of Mr. Hodgson's staff, and these Russian girls had to take turns in going because they had to lend each other frocks and shoes for evening wear. Our own young men were not great exponents of the new form of dancing and some of them went round the room with chairs as their partners, practising the fox-trot and the one-step before they dared to dance with one of those Russian girls. But it was all very pleasant and amusing—while it lasted. Afterwards when Mr. Hodgson left things were not so pleasant, I heard . . .

I went into several Russian homes mostly kept by old ladies who had survived the revolution in spite of their bourgeois or aristocratic antecedents. One family I met was of very noble name. The old man was living in a cellar with his wife and two daughters. He had been familiar with foreign courts and still had a fine house in Paris. Now he slept in a little room about the size of an English bathroom on a truckle bed above a pile of wood which he had dragged in for winter fuel. There was no door to the living room but a bit of old carpet tacked up. The two girls were highly educated and very attractive, with a gaiety which I found heroic. One of them had escaped from Russia. She had reached Paris and had gone to her father's mansion. The door was opened by an old servant who had stayed on there through the war years and the revolution. The girl stayed there a few days and then was conscience-stricken at having left her parents and sisters in that Moscow cellar. Her psychology was very Russian. Perhaps only a Russian would have gone back again to that cold cellar. She went back after the greatest difficulties and I met her in the cellar.

Before I left Russia and when I returned to Moscow after a journey down the Volga I went to see these people again and was surprised to find a young officer of the Red Army with them. He was a distant relative of theirs as I discovered when I became friendly with him.

"How is it that you are a Red officer?" I asked.

He shrugged his shoulders.

"There are two reasons. If I were not an officer of the Red Army I should be dead. But I am a Russian and there is a new order in Russia. I am a young man and it is best for me to take part in the new order of things."

They seemed to me very good reasons. Before I met him for the last time he asked me whether I would take a letter from him to England. It was to his mother whom he had not seen for seven years. He had an idea that she was in England or France. I might be able to find her.

Somewhat reluctantly I agreed to take the letter. It might be dangerous to do so, if I were searched at the frontier. When I reached England I was quick in finding the whereabouts of the lady. She kept a hat shop in the neighbourhood of Kensington. I went to the shop one morning with her son's letter in my pocket and felt emotional on this mission. There were two or three women in the shop buying hats, and taking a long time about it. The Russian lady who was serving them glanced at me once or twice as I stood on one side. When her customers had gone she asked what she might do for me.

"I have just come back from Russia," I told her.

She raised her eyebrows and said: "Yes."

"I was in Moscow," I said. "I met some relatives of yours. I bring a letter for you."

"From my son?" she asked.

"Yes. I am very glad to do so."

She took the letter and looked at it for a moment.

"Is he as fat as he used to be?" she asked.

I laughed.

"Not very fat when I saw him. There is not much food in Russia."

She glanced at the letter again, and then tore it into pieces and let it fall to the floor.

"He is an officer in the Red Army!" she said with cold passion. "I do not wish to read a letter from him."

4

GLIMPSES OF LIFE

In Moscow Spray and I wandered about by day and night and saw something of its life. It was vastly overcrowded, we were told. Different families were living in the same room divided by a curtain. Some of them in the streets were respectably dressed, though very shabby. Through the Red Square all day long came peasants pushing hand carts or drawing little sledges through the snow. Their feet were tied up with straw or rags. The only people with good boots, and they looked very smart, were Red Army officers or *kommissars* in well-cut uniforms. They were obviously well fed, and had privileges denied to the peasant and labouring class. Communism had not established anything like equality, as far as we could see. The old aristocracy and bourgeoisie had been eliminated by Soviet officials and Red Army officers had taken their places and formed a higher social stratum above the proletariat.

Behind the scenes the revolution was still at work. The *Ogpu* was busy. One morning I saw a group of young men being led through the Red Square under guard of Red soldiers with fixed bayonets.

"Who are they?" I asked my droshky driver.

I understood from him that they were Social Democrats.

He made a sign with his hands as though holding a pistol to the back of his head. Those young men were going to be shot.

So far I had seen nothing of famine in Russia. Here in Moscow there was food, according to the old Russian saying that "All things roll down to Moscow". The American Relief Administration opened soup kitchens for the children and I went to see them. The children turned up in great numbers but did not look starved, though some of them were undernourished.

"What about this famine?" I asked one of the officials.

"Not here," he answered. "Wait until you get to the Volga. It's there all right!"

It was a long way to the Volga and hard to get there. Few trains were running—only one now and again with a patched up engine which generally broke down. We had to wait in Moscow for some time.

Spray and I went to the old Imperial Opera House one night. It was packed from floor to ceiling, and the audience was made up mostly of factory hands and mechanics in Russian shirts or leather jackets. Some of the women wore scarves over their heads but others were hatless and looked clean and tidy. In the old Royal box where the Czar and his family had often sat the balcony was draped with the Red Flag, and behind it sat a group of working men and women who had happened to draw these seats. Here, anyhow, was the Russian proletariat having a good time. They put on *Madame Butterfly* and it was magnificently done with superb *décor* and acting. The singing seemed to me rather harsh but the Russians like that. Between the scenes we walked about the *foyer* and were observed with curious looks because we were foreigners. One young Jew came up to me and spoke in English with an American accent.

"What has happened about the revolution in England?" he asked.

He would not believe me when I told him there had been no revolution in England. He had read all about it in *Pravda*.

"In the United States," he told me, "things seem very bad. Men are selling themselves as slave labourers in New York."

I smiled at him.

"No truth in that," I told him.

He knew nothing about what was happening outside Russia. His mind was full of fantastic nonsense in which he himself hardly believed.

"What do you think of Russian Communism?" he asked.

I was very cautious in my answer. He might have been a police spy.

On this anniversary night Lunacharski, the Minister for Education, made a long speech on the education of the Russian masses and the marvellous things that were being done by the Soviet Republic to raise the standard of culture in Russia. I remember him as a handsome refined-looking man with a little pointed beard and moustache and I felt sympathetic towards him because he had saved the golden eagles of Russia from being smashed off the domes and towers of Moscow and Petrograd. He was a genuine enthusiast for education, and though I could not understand his speech I read a translation of it afterwards.

This enthusiasm for education had not yet made much headway in Russia. Masses of pamphlets had poured out of the Government offices, laying down rules for a nation-wide educational system which so far was not functioning. I went to the University in Moscow and talked with some of the professors. They were oldish men—some of them very old—who had been kept on from prerevolutionary days. But speaking privately to me they complained that life was harder for them and that education in Russia was at a standstill because of economic conditions. They themselves were half starved and just dying slowly on their feet. There were no books, no paper. The students were too ill fed to study.

Afterwards on the Volga I went into a village and met two schoolmistresses. I was with an American who spoke Russian. They told us that the school was not open. What was the use of opening it when the children were starving and could not learn?

But in Moscow there was a zest for knowledge and evening classes for young people who were working during the daytime.

5

IN THE KREMLIN

Several times I had interviews in Moscow with Tchicherin, the Minister of Foreign Affairs. I found him in his room at the Foreign

Office which was guarded by Red soldiers, pasty-faced and sleepy-looking, who sat about with rifles and fixed bayonets across their knees. Tchicherin lived all his time in one room where he cooked his own food, and made his own bed. He was a thin pallid man, with delicate transparent hands, and a consumptive cough. He had been born an aristocrat but had given up his land and wealth for his ideals of revolution. His chief enemy at that time when I talked with him seemed to be Lord Curzon for whose foreign policy he had no good word to say. They were carrying on an argumentative duel, the details of which I have forgotten. Tchicherin spoke I thought very reasonably and mildly, and had a gift of irony touched with acid. He struck me as being an idealist out of touch with the realities of the Russian situation, or at least utterly aloof from its cruelties and agony. He condemned the peasants for selfishness in resisting communal methods and said that their ignorance and greed were the cause of a temporary breakdown of Communism. They were very crafty, those peasants. They hid their produce. They resisted requisitioning. The *kulaks* or peasant farmers were hostile to the ideals of the revolution. . . . He could not understand why Curzon refused political recognition to the Soviet Republic.

There was no sense in that, he said. Russia was prepared to make a treaty of friendship with Great Britain in return for economic aid. But what could one do with a man like Curzon, rooted in prejudice, ignorant of world changes, narrow-minded and autocratic?

That was the kind of thing he said to me though I have forgotten his exact words. We discussed the possibility of Germany's being made the instrument of industrial reconstruction in Russia with the backing of Great Britain, France, and the United States, who would be able to recover from Germany, by this means, the reparations which otherwise that country could never pay. It was an idea I carried back to England.

I had a talk also with another Russian leader in those early days after the revolution. This was Radek, one of the Old Guard who afterwards were liquidated by Stalin, though Radek himself was one of the few, almost the only one, to escape execution. I had a pass to see him in the Kremlin and advanced one afternoon to that inner city behind its high walls and fan-shaped battlements. I was halted for twenty minutes at the first guard-house and put in charge of Red soldiers while one of them telephoned for orders to let me through if my credentials were in order. Twice more I was taken in charge on my way to the office in which Radek was waiting to receive me. Then an officer of the Red Army led me into a big building like one of our Government offices in Whitehall, and I was handed over to an official who led me down many corridors. Doors opened here and there and I had a glimpse of life within. In one room a bearded man in a Russian shirt over his trousers was playing the concertina, while a woman rocked up and down with a baby in her arms. Another door opened and a short-haired young woman came out with a teapot emptying the leaves into a garbage can. Life in the Kremlin seemed to me like that of a Gypsy camp.

Somewhere in one of these rooms Lenin lay dying—that extra-ordinary little man who had been the leader and the autocrat, and from whose brain there came the ideas and the technique of a revolution which was world-wide in its influence, destructive of old systems, and old creeds, and old moralities. Bitter, sardonic, blunt and brutal in his power of words, he lashed the inefficiency of his own followers and was a realist as well as a visionary—not afraid of admitting failure or altering his system when it did not work. I saw him only once, and then from some distance. It was when he was driven out of the Kremlin in an open car to the Red Square. He was huddled up in a big overcoat with an astrakhan collar and I had a glimpse of his wizened face and little pointed beard.

Radek whose name means "scoundrel"—he had taken it for his pseudonym—was a big man with a great round flat face fringed by a reddish beard, and with brown eyes behind big horn-rimmed glasses. He spoke English fluently and appeared to be a genial laughter-loving man. He was at that time the chief of international intelligence and propaganda, and there was nothing he did not know about political workings behind the scenes in most of the countries of the world. He had his agents everywhere. By secret ways Russian money was at work in Paris, Berlin, London and other capitals. His knowledge of the political situation in England was better than mine. He knew far more about the debates in the House of Commons and about political personalities who meant very little to me. We had a long talk and gradually approached the subject of a possible treaty of friendship between Great Britain and Soviet Russia, which at that time seemed out of the question because of our fear and hatred of Bolshevism.

"The British Empire and Soviet Russia," said Radek, "are the greatest oriental powers in the world. Why should we act as enemies? Why not come to a friendly understanding which would be helpful to both of us?"

I remember telling him that the most active hostility in anti-British propaganda was coming from Russia and that we could not be friendly with a power which was stirring up trouble everywhere including India and China.

He was quite frank in his answers.

"Yes," he said, "the Third International is busy at all that. I admit the difficulty. But after all the Union of the Soviet Republics is not dominated by the Third International. I confess that I am far more interested in the old Imperial tradition of Russia than I am in economic Communism. That is outside my department really. I leave that to others. But I'm very keen to get an agreement with Great Britain, especially in the Far East."

"Could you call back your little lads of the Third International?" I asked him. "Would they come if you called?"

He laughed and quoted a line from Shakespeare:

"You may call up spirits from the vasty deep, but will they come?"

He confessed that many of them would not come. They were missionaries of a new creed and had all the fervour of religious crusaders.

At the present time he was encouraging them. That was his job. That was the game now being played. So long as England was un-friendly Soviet Russia would retaliate. But it was silly, really, this international game of poker. It would lead nowhere. If Great Britain would recognise Soviet Russia and help her to become industrialised and reconstructed he certainly would do his best to call off anti-British propaganda, but as an honest man he couldn't promise that it would cease entirely. The Third International had an independent existence. It was not under control of the central Government. And anyhow, the ideals of Communism were seething below the surface of many countries. Russia or no Russia, that leaven would go on working. England would have to realise that and face it as a natural evolution of the human mind and the human experiment. But speaking in all sincerity (so he said) he would do his level best to fulfil any obligations desired by the British Government in return for a pact of peace and economic aid.

That was the gist of our conversation which went on for a long time.

I must say that I was impressed by this man Radek. He seemed to me to have a powerful intelligence and a not unpleasing character, despite his grotesque ugliness. Anyhow, he had a sense of humour, an unceasing flow of eloquence spiced by wit, and a friendly smile behind those horn-rimmed glasses. But as I talked to him I remembered the frightful cruelties of the revolution, the stories I had heard about *Ogpu* tortures, and the misery then extending over wide areas of Russia which afterwards I was to see. These men like Radek and Tchicherin who had held themselves aloof from all that were nevertheless promoting the system which produced such things and shared the guilt. Their own defence would have been that these were the only means to an end and that the end justified the means. That seems to me a descent into moral hell, but it is an argument now accepted by the majority, even in this country, who are thankful to Russia for the defeat of Germany, and think that Soviet methods were justified by stupendous victory.

6

PETROGRAD

Spray and I went to Petrograd while waiting for some means of transport to the Volga. It was, I thought, a magnificent and tragic city. The domes of its great cathedrals and churches gleamed with gold under the blue winter sky. Its palaces, and bridges, and great public buildings, were widely spaced on both sides of the river. Down there, formidable in its mass, was the great fortress of Peter and Paul. The Winter Palace of the former Emperors looked magnificent and grim with snow on its roofs and an untrodden carpet of snow around it. I remembered how a young priest had led a crowd of people here not many years before to make a petition to the Czar and how they were shot down by the police. We walked down the Nevski Prospekt and saw the grandeur of a city which once was full of life and wealth and magnificence—and misery. Now it seemed deserted. The Government offices were empty. The palaces were abandoned. A population of three million had been re-reduced we were told to something like seven hundred and fifty thousand.

Here and there in the streets we saw men sweeping away the snow, which lay deep during this Russian winter. Some of them wore bowler hats and old black coats with bits of astrakhan round the collars. They were the last of the bourgeoisie of Petrograd, sweeping the snow to earn their rations.

At every street corner, and in a cold wind which cut like a knife, and in a hard grim frost, were men and women selling cigarettes and sunflower seeds. They too had belonged to the bourgeoisie—the most hated class by the Bolsheviks and to this day I remember one woman, ill clad and pinched with cold who made me shiver in my soul at the look of her.

We went to see one of the refugee homes established for people who had fled from the famine. There were hundreds of thousands of them in camps round the city and four thousand in the old Imperial barracks to which we went. In these bare whitewashed rooms there was no heat for lack of fuel, and men and women and children lay about huddled together for warmth. Many of them were fever-stricken. Some of them were too weak even to stagger up to fetch their ration of potato soup. Many were stricken with typhus.

The doctor who took us round pointed to these and said: "There's no hope for them. They'll be dead to-morrow or the next day."

He took us across a courtyard and stopped a moment to thrust open a heavy door.

"Our morgue," he said. "Three days' dead." Inside was a great pile of dead bodies, men, women and children flung on top of each other. Hands and legs obtruded from this mass of corruption. For them it was journey's end.

How did they live, these people in Petrograd and Moscow? I never could find out in actual detail. Russian money was a mystery. When I changed ten pounds in Moscow I received four big bundles of notes containing three million roubles. My first experience of the purchasing power of the money was when I wanted to buy a pair of boots in the market place. They were good top boots for snow and mud but when I was asked one million roubles for them I was abashed. Yet after all it was not much in English money. But what did it mean to those Russians?

"What do you think of Bolshevism?" asked Spray one night in the Sugar King's palace. We lay in bed with only our mouths and noses out.

I asked him three questions in return. Was there liberty in Russia? Was there equality? Was there a higher type of civilisation and human happiness here than in Western Europe, or any chance of it? I asked the questions without prejudice, and we discussed them between the low divan and the four-poster bed in that great gilded *salon* opposite the Kremlin, where in some secret room Lenin sat that night scheming out some way of saving Russia from the fate into which he had led her, to test his theory of the Communistic state.

We could find no liberty. The official papers—*Pravda* and *Izvestia*—were propaganda sheets under Government control. There was no freedom of speech or opinion. There was no equality, even of misery, surely the first step of the Communistic state? Between the Soviet *kommissars*, even the "trade union" audience of the Marinsky Theatre, and the peasants, and the workers, and the underfed masses, there was a gulf wider than between the profiteers and the unemployed in England, wider, though lower down the scale of life for everyone. Civilisation?—Human happiness?—Well, there was the Marinsky Theatre and those laughing boys and girls walking through the snow after a performance. Human nature adapted itself marvellously to the hardest conditions of life. Perhaps there were happy people in Russia, but for the most part Spray and I had met only those who told us tragic tales of imprisonments, executions, death and misery.

7

THE ROAD TO FAMINE

In Petrograd I met a man who saved eleven million Russians from death, and had very few thanks and no gratitude from the Soviet Government for this tremendous rescue.

It was Colonel Haskell, who was directing the work of the A.R.A. in Russia. He was a tall, lean, silent man of the soldierly type, and I came to have a great respect and admiration for him. Under him was a first rate staff of enthusiastic, efficient, and brave men—it needed courage to face typhus in the famine districts—who carried out this enormous work of relief under heavy handicaps, because transport had broken down in Russia and they had to organise everything from scratch.

It was with the colonel and some of his staff that Spray and I travelled to the Volga and were able to report upon the famine as eye-witnesses of its dreadfulness. Without their help and comradeship we could not have gone.

We went from Moscow to Kazan in a train which panted, slowed down, and stopped after every twenty miles or so. Before we had been in it long one of the coaches caught fire and had to be left behind. Among our travelling companions was a white-haired old gentleman with blue eyes and the complexion of a new born babe, and the spirit of a Christian knight, or even of a Christian saint, with a sense of humour. It was Governor Goodrich of Indiana who had come to make a report on the famine conditions to the American Government. All through our journey he lived entirely on bread and apples and seemed to thrive on that diet. With us also was a young American doctor and one day he spoke grave words to a group of us sitting in his carriage.

"The adventure ahead," he said, "is not without peril. You fellows ought to realise that. Some of us are going to die of typhus."

It was curious and tragic that he was the only one among us who died of typhus.

After four days in that train we came to Kazan which lay under a heavy mantle of snow. It was now the capital of the Tartar Republic— a province of Soviet Russia—and was at the head of the richest grain growing district of the Volga valley. Now there was no grain because it had been burnt in its seed time by a terrible drought, leaving the peasants without food because their reserves had been taken up to feed the Red Army.

With deep snow on its roofs and lying thick on the ground so that no passing footsteps sounded it was like a city in a Russian fairy tale. Here in the old Czarist days nobles had built villas and laid out fine gardens for their pleasure in summer months. Now those houses were filled with refugees from famine, dying of hunger and disease, and across the snow came small children, hand in hand, who had walked a long way from starving villages where their parents were already dead. Like frozen birds many of them died in the snow. There were forty homes here for abandoned or wandering children. I went into a number of them and they were all alike in general character. In big, bare, rooms the children were naked and huddled together like little monkeys for warmth. There was no other warmth as there was no fuel. Their clothes had been burnt because of the lice which spread typhus among them. There were no other clothes to replace their ragged old sheepskins and woollen garments. Often it was too late to check the epidemic of typhus and thousands died and now were dying.

We went into the hospitals and they were dreadful. Because there was no fuel the patients, stricken with typhus, dysentery, and all kinds of diseases, lay together in unventilated wards. Many of the beds had been burnt for fuel, and most of the inmates lay on bare boards. Those who had beds lay four together, two one way and two the other. There were no medicines, no anæsthetics, no soap, no dressings.

In one of these hospitals, where I went with the American doctor, the nurses came rushing at us like wild animals. They were crying and wailing, and were fierce in their clutchings at us. They were crying out for food. They were starving. Some of them had caught the fever and their faces were flushed. They were dying of the diseases they could not cure.

"This is very terrible," said the young American doctor. "There is nothing we can do about it now. Somehow we must get them food and medicine."

He was deeply distressed and I felt sick, and nearly vomited in the yard outside because of the stench and the awful misery.

But there was a good opera even in Kazan. We went to hear it one night, and afterwards when we returned to our billet which we shared with some of the Americans we heard voices coming across the snow. There was a bang at the door and about a dozen members of the opera company including the Persian *prima donna* who had played the part of Carmen, surged into our room. Could we spare them any food? They were all starving, they told us in French and German and broken English. Our American friends brought out some of their rations. I looked at Spray and he nodded. The time had come to sacrifice that enormous Dutch cheese which we had bought in Berlin. At the sight of it the Persian *prima donna* gave a cry and leapt at it. Others shared her enthusiasm. Nothing was left of it but a little bit of rind which I kept as a relic.

We talked all night. I wish I had made notes of that talk. One of the men spoke French fluently and told me a thousand things about life in Russia during and after the revolution. He was philosophic and detached as an observer of this life. He was always hungry like the other players, though they were pampered children compared with the mass of people. Hour after hour he talked and the others were all talking together though now and then one of them slept. The Persian *prima donna* laughed, sang, wept, and went on talking. Outside in Kazan it was very quiet under the snow.

8

DOWN THE VOLGA

The A.R.A. chartered a steamer to go down the Volga and Spray and I were among its passengers who included two or three Americans on Colonel Haskell's staff, the colonel himself, and an ex-journalist—an Irish American—named Murphy, who became my very good friend. Murphy had learnt quite a bit of Russian—marvellous man!—and acted as our interpreter. It was a ship of horror. It crawled with vermin of all species. It stank horribly. At night we dare not sleep in any of the bunks and I laid down on a table in the dining saloon—there quite good quarters—hoping that insects would not crawl up its legs. They crawled up its legs, and I had restless nights. How any of us escaped typhus I do not know to this day.

There was ice on the Volga and we were the last boat to get through, having to break our way. I shall never forget that voyage—the flat mud banks of the great river lying white under snow, the Russian villages, deep in snow within their stockades, all with whitewashed churches with pear-shaped domes, the landing stages where little groups of gaunt hunger-stricken men and women waited to see us, and tell their tales, and beg for help. Now and then a man would come on board and our interpreter would question him. Always he told of the famine which was threatening twenty-five million people with death in the broad valley of the Volga.

We went into some of those villages and saw tragic things. There was no food in the market places and money was useless, even if there were any money. At one stage of the journey we found a *troika*—a sledge with three horses—waiting for us. It had been ordered by the Commune of the district who had been notified by Moscow. The driver was excited by our presence and drove his *troika* like a Roman chariot at a great pace, with his long whip curling above the horses' heads.

They seemed to be the only horses in the district. The others were dead and their skeletons lay on the roads, their flesh having been eaten. The villages were as quiet as death. No one stirred from the little wooden houses, though now and again we saw faces at the windows—pallid faces with dark eyes staring at us. In one village I remember we had as our guide a tall, middle-aged peasant who had blue eyes and a straw coloured beard. When he spoke of the famine in all those villages hereabouts he struck his breast and tears came into his eyes. He led us into timbered houses where Russian families were hibernating and waiting for death. In some of them they had no food of any kind. There was one family I saw who left an indelible mark on my mind. The father and mother were lying on the floor when we entered and were almost too weak to rise. Some young children were on a bed above the stove, dying of hunger. A boy of eighteen lay back in a wooden settle against the window sill in a kind of coma. These people had nothing to eat—nothing at all.

In other houses they were still keeping themselves alive by a kind of brownish powder made of leaves ground up and mixed with the husks of grain. Others were eating some stuff which looked like lead.

It was a clay of some kind, dug from a hillside named Bitarjisk, and had some nutritive quality, though for young children it was harmful, making their stomachs swell. Everywhere we went in these villages peasant women, weeping quietly, showed us their naked children with distended stomachs the sign of starvation at its last stage. From other cottages they came to where we stood, crossing themselves at the door-ways in the old Russian way and then lamenting. Only once did we meet with a wild desperation which made the women fierce and frightening. They seemed to think we had brought food and they came shrieking and clawing at us like starving animals, as indeed they were! Mostly they were quiet, even in their weeping, and we went into homes where the little ones looked like fairy tale children but with the wolf outside the door waiting for them. Spray and I saw the famine. . . .

It was the report of Governor Goodrich of Indiana, which he let me read on the journey back, which brought vast supplies of food into the Volga valley from the base in New York. It was handled by only sixty American officers of the A.R.A. They organised committees of Russian men and women. They organised teams of men to drag the sledges from the landing places because there were no horses. At first only the children were fed but the Americans saw quickly that this was a wrong policy. The children were helpless without their parents. They fed eleven million people every day for a year. My report to the Famine Relief Committee did something to help. We used the old war stocks and fed about four million. The "Save the Children" Fund, the Red Cross, and other societies became active. According to Nansen's figure two million died in the famine stricken areas. Twenty odd million were saved in the nick of time. As I wrote in my book *Adventures in Journalism* which tells some of these things: "It was work well and nobly done in the spirit of Christianity, kept alight in a dark and cruel world, which is this jungle of Europe."

This tale of the time of misery and famine in Russia which I have told carries with it an astonishing postscript, amounting indeed to something which has never happened before in world history. That is the recovery and transformation of Russia in twenty years or so after that break-down of economic life. In those twenty years starting from that Slough of Despond, Soviet Russia has risen to be the greatest military power in Europe, and the second greatest in the world. Its factories have turned out enormous numbers of guns, and all weapons of war, made by workers who mostly had to be taught and trained and had no technical tradition behind them. Over a vast area this nation of peasants—serfs in Czarist times—were industrialised and mechanised. Machines were made for mass production. Generals, staff officers, commanders in the field, gunners, pilots, quartermasters, had to be raised from the raw human material of a nation with a population of a hundred and sixty millions, which, when I saw it, was at a low level, almost the lowest level of civilisation compared with the Western powers. Their people were illiterate, their educated classes had been "liquidated". Great numbers of their people were oriental or half oriental. Yet in twenty years they not only produced one of the most formidable war machines in the world, but men who outfought and outgeneralled the professional army of Germany with its long tradition of military discipline and military science. How was it done, this miracle, as it seems? How was it done in so short a time? The answer must be incomplete for there is much in it beyond facts and figures, but it was done partly by the iron will power of the Soviet leaders, ruthless in discipline, all powerful in command, demanding the utter obedience of the masses, and inspired with a demoniacal energy and genius. By intensive propaganda directed day and night through loudspeakers, by picture posters, by Government officials they inspired the masses with something of their own determination and schooled them in endurance of long hours, hard work, and a low standard of living which they were made to believe was high in comparison with other countries.

The younger generation responded with enthusiasm to the Soviet system, and those who did not respond found themselves in the hands of the *Ogpu*. There was only one punishment for disobedience, inefficiency, failure even by accident, or political resistance of any kind. It was a shot in the back of the head. Factory managers who did not get ahead with their work and come up to schedule were shot as saboteurs. If a machine broke down because of technical mistakes, those responsible were charged with sabotage. Abandoning all Communistic ideals of equality of reward, high wages were paid to those who proved themselves most efficient. There was a propaganda of hero worship for those who could put in most hours at a bench or speed up production at the highest rate. When the Ukrainian peasant farmers resisted orders to work under a communal system as field labourers for the State, Stalin withdrew their reserves of grain and two million of them at least were starved to death in 1933.

The old egalitarian ideals of Communism were abandoned, and its former leaders executed. The wage-scale had greater differences between the lowest and the highest than in Great Britain. Military rank was restored. A new bureaucracy took the place of the old bourgeoisie, and had privileges far beyond the reach of the proletariat. But the young Russians went to the technical colleges and evening classes and undoubtedly had a sense of high adventure in absorbing knowledge which would make them mechanics, engineers, draughtsmen, and experts in some way or other. Labour was conscripted for the mines, the timber forests, and the rough toil of unskilled hands. They were the slaves of the system and any disobedience brought them the punishment of slaves. In every factory, in every collective farm, in every school and village, secret police watched, listened and reported. Woe to those who fell into the hands of the *Ogpu*, according to all reports which have come out of Russia. But to her workers, to enthusiastic youth, to young men and women with keen and ardent brains, eager for knowledge, inflamed with faith in the Soviet State, there was reward and—I do not doubt it— happiness.

The questions Spray asked me one night in Moscow more than twenty years ago still demand the same answers. There is no liberty, as we know it, in Russia, no liberty of speech, no liberty for the unorthodox. There is no equality. In the army, the old badges of rank are worn. In civil life there are rich men, living in luxury compared with the masses who live at a low grade.

The Totalitarian State is supreme in its control over individual life, allowing no dissenters, but within its framework there are high rewards for service.

Now that Russia is one of the greatest powers in the world after stupendous victories over Germany, one is forced to the conclusion that only by ruthless methods, only by an iron system of control, could such miracles have been achieved—miracles to which this country owes its life and liberties, because without them we should have been invaded and destroyed. But has that conclusion any moral justification? If we think so we abandon all our own moralities, all the Christian tradition, all our faith in individual rights and liberties, all our old hatred of cruelty and torture, all our belief in justice.

If we do not deny that, we deny all our own history and tradition and all virtue, and all pity, and the qualities of the civilised mind.

After my return from Russia I recorded my own experiences in various articles and books. One night when I was giving a little dinner party one of my guests—a pretty woman named Peggy Grippenberg—the wife of the Finnish Minister, suggested brightly that we should go on to a reception at the Russian Embassy. In any case her husband would have to go. I resisted the suggestion but yielded to her persuasion, as I yield everything to a pretty woman—or even to an ugly one! So we went and were received by Mr. Maisky, the Soviet Ambassador.

When my name was announced that little black-bearded man gave me a sharp glance and said: "I have a dossier about you."

I knew that I had been barred out of Russia and that I was on their black list for describing the things I had seen, though my mission had helped to rescue the starving children.

PART X

THE POST-WAR YEARS

1

THE DEFEATED

IN October of 1922 I was walking down Unter den Linden in Berlin when I stopped in front of a shop window and stared with incredulous eyes at a Press bulletin pasted up in the window.

"The Black Watch," it said, "are being carried shoulder-high by German crowds in Upper Silesia."

It was only three years since the Black Watch had been called the "Ladies from Hell" by German soldiers who feared them greatly. Now they were being cheered and hoisted up by the German workers in Upper Silesia, where they had been sent to police that region from a forcible occupation by Polish troops. The Poles under Pilsudski, first of the Dictators, demanded the possession of this industrial area with its rich mining districts, and were impatient to grab it without awaiting the decision of a committee (presided over by a Japanese) appointed by the League of Nations.

I met a friend of mine in the street and discussed the situation with him. It was Raymond Gram Swing, afterwards famous for his American broadcasts.

"You ought to see Stresemann," he said. "He is the leader of the Volkspartei and likely to be Chancellor one day. I should be glad to introduce you."

He took me that evening to the headquarters of the Volkspartei where the members were sitting at tables, drinking beer, and all talking excitedly. Stresemann himself, whom I saw for the first time, was at one of the tables with two or three friends and a flagon of beer by his elbow. He invited us to join him. He was at that time not so overloaded with flesh as he became afterwards by a disease which killed him, but he was a stout genial-looking man with pale gold hair and fair skin. Afterwards I met him a number of times at the British Embassy where he came to lunch and seek the advice of Lord D'Abernon, who had a great influence over him.

He spoke excitedly, and at times with a passion which reddened his smooth baby-like skin.

"If we lose Upper Silesia," he said in a loud voice, "or any considerable part of it, we shall be unable to pay the indemnities. There lie our main sources of raw material for manufactures. German capital, labour, and organisation have built up the prosperity of the Reich. Take that away from us and we are crippled."

I remember only part of the conversation now but I know that I was startled when this leader of the Popular Party in Germany announced in a loud voice as he put down his beer mug:

"I am a Monarchist. This Republic does not carry the support of the German people. We need the Monarchy again."

Yet afterwards he became Chancellor of the German Republic, and was the part author with Sir Austen Chamberlain of the Locarno Pact which for a time seemed to promise peace.

At this time there were two men in Germany, who, with great courage, were endeavouring, by what they called a Policy of Fulfilment, to lead their country out of the abyss into which it had fallen. They believed that if Germany put her shoulder to the wheel and showed an honest endeavour to pay reparations, however impossible, the Allies would modify their demands and scale them down to a reasonable level, so that Germany could be liberated from slave labour and regain her own economic prosperity, and link up on equal terms with her former enemies. These two men were Rathenau and Dr. Wirth.

I heard Dr. Wirth, then Chancellor, make an historic speech in the Reichstag, explaining the principles and possibilities of "Fulfilment" and the need of intense industry, economy, and sacrifice on the part of the whole nation. The Reichstag was crowded. They listened with grim silence, broken every now and then by cries of "Amnestie! . . . Amnestie!" from a group of Left wing deputies who demanded the release of Communist prisoners, and by harsh laughter at times from the extreme Right who hated and derided this policy of "Fulfilment".

It was Walther Rathenau, Minister of Reconstruction in the Wirth Government, who inspired this policy. He was a man of remarkable character. Of Jewish race, he had a kind of dual personality, one part of his mind being intensely practical and realistic—he was the Director of 84 industrial companies and the head of the enormous electrical combine known as the A.E.G.—and the other part of his mind being idealistic and mystical. He was the author of two remarkable books which I read—*The Mechanisation of the Mind* and *In Days to Come* in which he denounced the soul-destroying influence of industrialism and the danger to humanity of being mastered by the machines which its intelligence had created. Above all he urged the need of liberation from the standardisation of the modern mind and from the narrow intolerance of nationalism.

His programme had five points.

To improve relations with France.

To modify the peace terms.

To effect a reduction of the indemnities.

To establish better conditions in Germany.

To restore Germany's moral strength.

Rathenau created a favourable impression on Lloyd George, whom he visited in London, and with whom he discussed the subject of German reparations in a conference at Wiesbaden, and afterwards at Cannes.

At Wiesbaden he proposed that payments in gold should be replaced by deliveries in kind, and that German material and labour should rebuild the devastated districts of France. Loucheur, who represented the French Government, agreed. He was the only man in France who had the courage to face and tell the facts. He made a speech, not reported in the French Press, pointing out that Germany could only pay enormous sums in cash by a terrific increase in exports which would undermine French trade and capture all the markets of the world by under-selling at cut-throat prices. But French industrialists refused to employ German labour and material. What would become of their contracts? Raymond Poincaré, French Premier, turned down the idea flatly.

It was from this point that a kind of political duel arose between Lloyd George and the French Prime Minister. Lloyd George had come to believe that peace and prosperity in Europe could only be regained in the long run by giving the German Republic a fair chance of recovery and reasonable prosperity. Was he wrong? It was my own deep conviction. But it infuriated the French.

"Europe will only get peace when she has vomited out Lloyd George" wrote a distinguished French journalist. On his side Lloyd George believed that Europe would never get peace while Poincaré insulted and strangled Germany beyond the limits of endurance.

2

CONFERENCE IN CANNES

There was a conference at Cannes dealing again with the subjects of German reparations. Aristide Briand attended for France and showed himself conciliatory to a moderate view. But he played a game of golf with Lloyd George, or rather was initiated into the mysteries of that game. It was his undoing. The French Press regarded this game of golf as high treason. The caricaturists made it the subject of their most bitter satires, and Poincaré recalled Briand.

Next there was a conference at Genoa. Curiously enough I had something to do with it in an indirect way. I had come back from Russia—God help me!—with a "Plan". I had discussed it with Tchicherin who approved, and it seemed to me a very fine plan indeed by which to save the world from its economic misery. I sent a memorandum on the subject to Lloyd George who also thought it good. The idea was just this: if France, Germany, England and the United States would form a kind of international syndicate for the reconstruction of Russia on certain strict conditions of control, the workshops of Europe might get busy again, the starving people of Russia might be fed, and last but not least, the Red Army which menaced the peace of Europe might be demobilised in return for guarantees regarding the Polish frontier and demobilisation of Poland. Tchicherin had consented to these conditions. He told me that Russia would acknowledge her war debts to the Allies in return for political recognition and economic aid. He agreed that Soviet Russia must look mainly to Germany for the technical equipment of a revival of industry.

At that time I became friends with Mr. Harvey, the United States Ambassador in England. A most eccentric personality with a scarifying wit, and a style of journalese hardly caricatured by Dickens in *Martin Chuzzlewit*, he had been the chief force in securing the Presidency of the United States for Harding, with whom therefore he had great influence. He was always extraordinarily hospitable to me and invited me to some of his dinners at the American Embassy. When I put up to him this plan for Russia he was vastly interested in it and arranged a dinner party at which the idea might be discussed. He had invited a distinguished group of people including Herr Stahmer, the German Ambassador in London—with whom I had discussed this idea. After dinner he rose and said: "I would like to hear from Philip Gibbs, who has just come back from Russia. He has something to say to us."

I said my stuff and outlined my plan. It certainly interested the company, and, as far as I can recollect, there was very little criticism against it from those at table called upon to speak by Ambassador Harvey. Anyhow, the idea got through to Lloyd George, and it was the plan he had up his sleeve when he went to the Genoa conference in April 1922.

As I wrote in my book *Since Then* the conference took place in the sombre grandeur of an old Italian *palazzo*, where Lloyd George, genial, persuasive, vital, humorous and eloquent, presided over this strange company of delegates, among whom were the Russian Bolsheviks who sat in public conference for the first time since the revolution. There was an air of melodrama about the meetings staged in that old palace, gloomy and dimly lit, though the hot sun of Italy shone without. Mussolini, new in his dictatorship, passed through the corridors and spoke a few ironical words to the English journalists to whose profession he had belonged. Secret police and Italian soldiers guarded the hotel where Russian delegates were strictly confined. There was a nervous apprehension of assassination, not only among the Bolsheviks. Rathenau had a conviction that he was marked down for death, as truly he was.

Even Lloyd George knew instinctively that his own political career was at stake upon this conference. The Greek Army had broken in Asia Minor. His support of the counter-revolutionary armies in Russia had failed. His star was waning at home.

The conference was sabotaged from the start by Poincaré. He refused to allow any discussion of German reparations. Barthou, his Foreign Minister, made a violent protest against Tchicherin's offer to disarm the Red Army as soon as the other nations disarmed. The French delegate speaking for his Government refused any discussion of disarmament, though Lloyd George reminded him that a pledge had been made to that effect in the Treaty of Versailles. The economic proposals of Russia were also obstructed by Barthou. He hated that idea of making Germany the instrument of Russian reconstruction, whatever the controls.

Behind the scenes were many intrigues, and a bombshell burst when it was revealed that Rathenau, seeing no hope in this conference, had signed a separate treaty with Russia at a private meeting in Rapallo. He himself was nervous of what he had done. "*Le vin est tiré,*" he said to his friends in French, which he spoke perfectly, "*il faut le boire!*"— "*The wine is drawn, one must drink it.*"

So the Genoa conference broke up with a few pious resolutions to hide its failure which was apparent to the world. Looking back on it, I think a great opportunity for a peaceful Europe was deliberately sabotaged by France. It would have prevented the horrors of inflation which awaited Germany and out of which Hitler drew the poison of his creed. Russia would have been brought back to co-operation with the Western Powers, and not thrust back into isolation. Germany would have been linked up with the general disarmament of Europe. At least it was a chance of moving towards peace in the spirit of the League of Nations instead of moving surely and inevitably towards another war. We forget those days now. We do not think of Germany before the coming of the Nazis. Lord Vansittart believes that nothing would have made any difference.

Anyhow, my beautiful plan—I was only the Mercury, or messenger boy, of the gods—was washed out, and my attempt at peacemaking failed at the starting post.

3

OCCUPATION OF THE RUHR

In 1923 French forces occupied the Ruhr and I went to Essen, the headquarters of Krupps, to see what was happening.

It was an acute crisis in European affairs and the cause of a painful and irreconcilable divergence of views between France and Great Britain.

It arose out of the failure of Germany to pay the vast and fantastic amount in reparations which France and other countries, including, for a time, ourselves, hoped to get out of that defeated nation. The peace treaty had not settled on a definite sum. Germany was to be drained of all wealth for a generation to come, for the payment of war damage in all countries which had suffered the wounds of war, for the military occupation, and for war pensions of wounded men. With an extraordinary defiance of all the laws of arithmetic and economic commonsense, as pointed out by Keynes in his *Economic Consequences of the Peace*, the peacemakers expected a defeated and ruined Germany to pay in gold values enormously more than the richest among the victor nations —namely the United States—could possibly have raised. None of them seemed to realise that the only way in which Germany could pay substantial sums in gold values was by selling vast quantities of manufactured goods in world markets, which would undermine the trade and industry of other nations. This plain and simple fact was acknowledged first by public opinion, and especially by the opinion of hard-headed business men, in this country. Gradually, indeed quickly, here and there after the Treaty of Versailles they veered to the opinion that the Reparation clauses had been a mistake, and that if Europe were to regain economic stability they ought to be scaled down to more reasonable levels, and that Germany should be allowed a chance of recovery.

Not so in France. The French Press, subsidised by the Government and political groups, had duped their people into the belief that Germany could pay astronomical sums, and that she was wilfully in default in not doing so. Monsieur Poincaré, that formidable and stubborn man, maintained two views which in terms of logic and commonsense were in direct conflict. One was that Germany must be kept weak, the other that Germany must pay. The sum fixed by the Reparations Commission in his mind was £6,600,000,000, afterwards acknowledged by the Dawes Commission as utterly beyond the bounds of possibility.

It was, curiously enough, Aristide Briand—for he was converted later to a different point of view—who first advocated the invasion and occupation of the Ruhr. He called it "putting the bailiff in" and tried to persuade Lloyd George to join France in this expedition. Lloyd George utterly refused. "Not a man, not a gun!" he said, to the great indignation of the French Press who accused him of being the best friend of Germany and the worst enemy of France. So to give this enterprise an international sanction France persuaded Belgium to join her and sent a great force of troops into the Ruhr.

I had been to Essen once before. That was soon after the Armistice when the German workers in the great armament factories were busy, under the supervision of British officers, smashing all the delicate and complicated machines which had been used for the production of guns and other weapons. I saw that work of destruction, which, I was told by the officer in charge (I have forgotten his name) was carried out ruthlessly and completely. Then Krupps had turned over to the manufacture of ploughs, reapers-and-binders, and a thousand things for peace-time needs.

Now when I went into the Ruhr during the French occupation I found silence and desolation. Lloyd George had told Briand that he could not imagine German factory hands working with enthusiasm under the stimulus of French bayonets. He was right. They refused to work at all and went on strike.

I saw and talked with these crowds of idle men. They looked worn and underfed and pallid. They vowed that they would starve to death rather than work for the French. I had a talk with Herr Krupp and some of his managers. Krupp himself spoke mildly (in perfect English) and said that the French action was a mistake from their own point of view for it would lead to nothing but chaos and the economic downfall of Europe. Later during the occupation he and his managers were all arrested and imprisoned.

French officers and engineers were having a troublesome time and disliked their job. They could not disentangle this riddle of the Ruhr network of rails and turn-tables and points and signal boxes. They tried to move trains about but they ran off the lines, or got hopelessly jammed in sidings from which it was difficult to shunt them. French soldiers on these trains became nervy. At night German saboteurs were busy. At any moment a train might be blown up or derailed. French officers lost their tempers and used their whip on German civilians. "A good thing too!" I can hear my readers saying, after a second World War and horrors unspeakable in German concentration camps, but at that time we thought otherwise, not sympathising with this French action and believing, as I still believe, that it was sowing the dragon's teeth for a new war. The occupation of the Ruhr and its consequences created a bitterness in the German mind which played into the hands of Hitler when he began his political campaign.

And yet it was in Krupp's private hotel in Essen during the French occupation that I listened to some extraordinary words from a man named Paul Schaeffer, the most brilliant German journalist at that time.

He spoke at first of the situation in the Ruhr.

"In the end," he said, "these fellows will have to submit to work under French coercion. They are poor dumb dogs. They will submit in order to live."

Then he talked a lot about the future of Europe and Germany's place in it.

"There is only one reasonable combination in Europe," he said. "That is an economic, political, and military alliance between France and Germany. When that happens England will have to look out for herself."

It was a startling theory to hear at a time when the whole of Germany was enraged against France. But afterwards I met the same view in Paris among business men and representatives of the Right.

"France," they said, "can never afford to fight Germany again. Win or lose, the drain of blood would destroy France for ever. We ought to make a military and economic alliance with Germany. Then we could dominate the rest of Europe. It wouldn't be a happy day for England!"

That was as far back as 1923. People who said those things were not thinking in terms of peace guaranteed by collective security under the League of Nations. They were thinking on the old lines of force and combinations of power, and international rivalry. Representatives of the extreme Right were already advancing along the road which led to the weakness and defeat of France in 1940.

Before the end of the Ruhr occupation the catastrophic inflation of German money had begun. The Government printing presses were turning out paper money and sending wads of it into the Ruhr to support the passive resisters, but it had no real value behind it, either in gold backing or industrial wealth, and its purchasing power dropped every week, and finally every hour. Wages were raised after strikes and riots to get more of this paper money to buy the essential needs of life, and that meant more work for the printing presses and a further drop in the value of the mark. It was what is known as the spiral of inflation, and has since become the terror of all those in charge of national finance.

It was a terror then to the German housewife and all Germans. Potatoes, bread, meat, milk, soared up in price beyond the reach of the weekly wage, and when that was raised the prices had soared again. At first this did not happen with terrifying velocity. It was gradual. In Berlin, great numbers of Jews had time to gamble on the downfall of the

mark and make money—which withered away later on—out of the
financial ruin of Germany. It was remembrance of that, among other
things, which inflamed the hatred of Hitler against them. But as the
weeks and the months passed the velocity of inflation accelerated, until
it became a maddening nightmare.

I remember going into the great store of Wertheim in Berlin at this
time, and seeing the girls marking up the prices behind the counters
early in the morning. By the time I had gone round and bought a few
things they were marking them up again. In exchange value for English
pounds or American dollars the mark was almost meaningless.
British and American journalists were living like princes in the Adlon
Hotel, and some of them drinking heavily in the Adlon bar, for next to
nothing. I remember giving a dinner party in one of the restaurants in
Berlin to about a dozen people. I ordered good wine. The food was
excellent. We had coffee and cigarettes and my younger guests danced
to a good band. In the end when my bill was presented to me it came to
thousands of marks, but translated into English money it cost me something like 7s. 6d. That was at the beginning of inflation. Later on that
dinner would have cost millions of marks and then hundreds of millions,
and in English money would have been a few shillings.

Many people now believe that this inflation was deliberately engineered by men like Schacht and the heads of the Reichsbank, as a
well-thought-out plan to avoid reparations and wipe out all internal
debts. I had that suspicion myself for a time, and still think that when
once it had started down the slippery slope the leaders of German
finance said: "Let it rip!" "We can't stop it, anyhow." But I don't
think it was planned at the beginning and I remember interviewing two
of the heads of the Reichsbank and becoming very much embarrassed
when they burst into tears and put their heads in their hands and
looked like stricken men. I never thought I should see bankers weep.
But those men wept, and I cannot think that they were play-acting.
They saw the collapse of the financial structure of Germany. They were
men who felt themselves caught in a typhoon over which they had no
control, and which was sweeping across Germany destroying all known
values and creating widespread ruin.

4

GERMAN EPISODES

There was at least one honest German at this time to whom I must
pay a tribute for heroic honesty when something like a fortune fell into

his hands—out of mine. I went into a tobacconist's shop in Bonn to buy a packet of cigarettes. (All my life I have been going into little shops up and down the world to obtain nicotine poison.)

I passed a few words with an old man behind the counter and noticed in those few moments that he had a bust of old Hindenburg in his window. I lit a cigarette and left his shop, and also my wallet, which contained eighty English pounds and a thick wad of German notes. Eighty English pounds to a German in time of inflation was a prodigious sum of money.

It meant something to me also, being necessary for my expenses and travel.

Bonn was then a pleasant city. I passed several hours in it, and then wished to get the tram back to Cologne. It was at the tram stop that I discovered the loss of my wallet. I remembered that the only shop I had entered was the little tobacconist's with a bust of Hindenburg in the window, but I had forgotten its whereabouts. All I could remember was that it was in a little narrow street not far from the market place. I ran round about the market place searching for the street, the shop, and the bust of Hindenburg. If I could only see the grim old face of that whiskered old gentleman! But as I ran the shops were closing. Down came their shutters, and down went my spirits. I was on a hopeless quest which finally I abandoned. I had sufficient small change to get back to Cologne.

Two months later when I was in Rome again, I received a packet. It came from the A.P.M. in Cologne. It contained my wallet with eighty English pounds and a heavy wad of German marks. The old German tobacconist had taken great trouble to discover my identity and had not subtracted one mark. Needless to say I sent him my thanks and an adequate reward.

The name of Hindenburg comes into another story I remember of this time. It cropped up at that dinner party I have mentioned. One of my guests was a young actor named Malcolm Todd, who was playing the part of a young English naval officer in a film they were making of one of my stories at Starken near Berlin. Young Todd had been in the Flying Corps during the war. One day his squadron received orders to fly as low as fifty feet above the chimney-pots of a small château in France and drop a load of bombs on it. It was the headquarters of Field Marshal von Hindenburg. They were to blow it to blazes. Malcolm Todd obeyed orders, dropped as low as fifty feet above the château, but was knocked out by a bit of flak.

Now it happened that one of my other guests was a lady named Marie von Hindenburg, well known in the literary world of Germany and England.

When young Todd had finished his story I said: "Let me introduce you to a lady who, I am sure, would like to talk with you.—Frau von Hindenburg." Malcolm Todd looked stupefied for a moment at this extraordinary coincidence, but pulled himself together and made his bow to the lady.

I went out to Starken several times to have a look at the film production of my story *The City of Temptation* which had its scene in Constantinople. It was an American production with a cosmopolitan caste. That included a talented little actress who played the part of my Russian heroine, and a crowd of American, English, Russian and German film actors and actresses. The Russians were refugees from the old régime. Among them was the Countess Tolstoy with whom I had many conversations, and pretty little Russian princesses who surrounded her. It was like one of my own short stories, played in an enormous studio which had once housed the Zeppelins which came over to bomb London. At great cost they had built up a scene in Constantinople, so real in its effect that it seemed like walking into it from the Galata Bridge. Donkeys were going up the steep steps between the old houses, the minaret of a mosque rose above them. Greeks, Turks, Russians, wandered up and down as I had seen them in the city.

One day when I went there the American producer was worried. He said: "A bunch of Turks have come down from the Embassy in Berlin. They're making trouble."

They made a lot of trouble. The plot of my story led inevitably, and in a predestined way, to the death of a young Turk who was the villain of the story. Unless he were killed the whole of the preceding plot was pointless. At least it was the inevitable fate for a dramatic end. The gentlemen from the Turkish Embassy in Berlin refused to let that young Turk die. They brought diplomatic pressure on the German Foreign Office and won their point. When the film was produced in London and New York people remained seated thinking there was more to come. The end was a complete anticlimax, and the film was a failure.

5

SURREY GARDENS

Soon after the war we fled further afield to the village of Puttenham, south of the Hog's Back, where many nice people like to live.

My wife laid out a lovely garden and in it on summer days I sat, with a typewriter on a little table, and a box of cigarettes very handy. At another little table nearby, with another typewriter and another box of cigarettes (superior to mine) sat my son Tony, also writing novels after a brief career in Fleet Street which he hated like hell. And sometimes for a week or two we had a visit from my brother Cos who was half-way through a novel or play, or just beginning another. He scorned a type-writer and wrote beautiful-looking manuscript with a steel nib. He too loved to sit in the sun, when there was sun, and had irregular times of work, not getting down to it seriously until the evening when he would go on to the small wee hours.

Pleasant and interesting people came into my garden from time to time. *Remembering my Friends*—to use the title of Molly Hamilton's book—I have nothing but good recollections of them. "Why don't you write a book about bad people?" asked a girl friend of mine. "Why don't you write about the evil side of life? Your people are all so good!" The answer is, as I told her, that I have not come in touch with many bad people except among the "higher-ups" who led the world to ruin. Even some of them were quite pleasant to meet across a dining table and disarmed one by their personal charm, being quite unconscious of their own misdeeds, and mistaking them for the noblest form of patriotism or public service.

South of the Hog's Back I found people kind to their dogs, fond of gardens, without murder in their hearts. A little snobbish, some of them perhaps, oldfashioned or narrow-minded in their views, now and then, a little laughable to foreigners who like my friend John Tunis had to leave my room from time to time to laugh outside the door.

My next-door neighbour for a time was an old lady named Lady Violet Greville. She was the daughter of the Duke of Montrose, but as a young woman had scandalised her family by breaking away from its tradition and becoming one of the first, if not the very first, woman journalist, writing weekly articles for the old *World* which afterwards my brother Cos edited. Her stories of childhood were vastly amusing and almost unbelievable because of their medievalism. I made use of them in a novel I wrote called *The Golden Years* but offended her, alas, by so doing. When, as a child, she was driven out in a governess cart and came too close to the "common people", she was made to gargle on her return home. When her family went to Holy Communion they were preceded up the church by liveried footmen, carrying their prayer books on velvet cushions while the congregation stood respectfully. What courage for a young girl to run away from all that and take a job in Fleet Street!

The Irish family of Verners were charming neighbours coming over from a village called Seale close to the Pilgrim's Way. Sir Edward Verner had had to leave Ireland in the time of the "trouble", though he was Irish of the Irish, with a delightful touch of the brogue. Fortunately he had saved his family treasures—a lovely portrait of Marie Antoinette to whom his great aunt had been a lady-in-waiting, chairs tapestried by that poor lady before she went to the guillotine, a diamond necklace worn round her neck, and other relics. The house at Seale was hung with beautiful portraits of Sir Edward Verner's own family in the eighteenth century of whom he told the most amusing anecdotes, and I read his great grandfather's diary, written during the Peninsular War and Waterloo. Wellington seemed to like this young officer, and it was he who passed on to his fellow cavalry officers the Duke's invitations to the Waterloo Ball. Two of the Verner girls came often to our garden and it was more beautiful for their presence and their laughter.

Near to us was an old house and an old garden which I think was haunted if any house is haunted. Two remarkable people lived in it and we became close friends, in spite of a preliminary misfortune which happened to me when they first called. I have a very carrying voice, and standing in the porch when this husband and wife had, I thought, driven beyond the gate I remarked to my wife: "That lady is old enough to be his mother." At that moment their car reappeared backwards as they had forgotten something, and my words rang into their ears. They forgave me, though the little lady told me afterwards that she had heard what I said. She was a little lady remarkably like Marie Tempest, and her husband, many years younger had been a cavalry officer in a crack regiment until he had put his colonel on the fire in a moment of annoyance. He had had the most astounding adventures, some of them very terrible among savage tribes in Abyssinia, and he had brought home from his travels a collection of native weapons, masks, jujus, and sacrificial relics, which cluttered up his walls. They could not have done much good to the spirit of the house which always seemed to me rather sinister, as it did to the lady of the house who would never walk beyond a certain line in the garden because she was afraid of invisible things on the other side.

She gave entertaining dinner parties to which were invited singers, pianists, and, once, a great lady of Spain—Alfonso's aunt—who sat on a kind of dais and received the homage of the guests—which was all very odd.

Among our week-end visitors was a red-headed volcano named Sinclair Lewis. He was more like a genius, as he is, than any writer I have known, for his conversation was ceaselessly exhilarating, and his imagination took wild flights from breakfast time till bed time which was very late. He dramatised his stories and I remember he committed an imaginary murder with sensational effects.

M

6

THE GREAT ACTOR

It was at this time that I established a warm friendship with a young publisher named Hamish Hamilton, and through him, with Forbes-Robertson and his family to whom I was devoted. Forbes-Robertson himself, with his delicate and noble profile—the greatest Hamlet of all time—was a man of exquisite charm and graciousness, and told enchanting stories of his life and experience, first as a painter and then as an actor. As a boy he had known Swinburne and used to guide him past the pubs into which he was tempted after an evening with the Robertson family when he had arrived slightly fuddled. Forbes-Robertson had known and worshipped Ellen Terry in the glory of her beauty, and when he spoke of her his eyes lighted up and her spell came back to him. He had met many lovely women in his time and told charming anecdotes about them, but in his old age was forgetful of names. At his tea table in his old Georgian house in Bedford Square, where the walls were hung with portraits of Ellen Terry and others which he had painted as a young man, he would be baffled for a moment about one of these names.

"I remember her when she first played. She was an enchanting creature then. I fell deeply in love with her. . . . Let me see, now. What was her name?"

The name of this "enchanting creature" was provided instantly by his daughters Jean or Blossom or Chloe or Daphne. They had heard these stories many times and knew them by heart, but always listened to their father with smiling attention, as though they heard them for the first time. They were a pretty crowd round the tea table—Jean with her elfin look and Blossom, truly, I think, the most beautiful girl in England, and Chloe and Daphne and their young-looking mother who was like an elder sister.

I once went with Forbes-Robertson to a play called *Berkeley Square* in which Jean was acting. It was a good play though ghostly, and its theme was that of a young man who gets on to the wave length of those who lived in this Georgian house and finds himself back in the eighteenth century. I went from the play to the house in Bedford Square and here were the same vibrations and atmosphere.

Ian Forbes-Robertson lived within reach of Puttenham and used to come into our garden. He was devoted to his brother of whom he talked with loving admiration, and another Robertson, not related to them, came over now and then. This was Graham Robertson, a painter

and friend of painters, and of all artists, including in his youth the great
Sarah. Sargent painted a famous portrait of him in a long black coat.

He wrote one of the most delightful books of reminiscence called
Time Was, and once, when I sat at his table in a charming house near
Witley in Surrey, I made a good discovery about him. We were talking
of pageants, and I said the best pageant I ever saw was one at Guildford
after the war. It made me weep like a babe not because of tragedy, but
because of its beauty, and some touch of magic bringing back the
springtime of England.

Graham Robertson was silent for a moment and I saw a little flush of
colour creep into his face.

"I wrote it," he said with humility. "I'm glad you liked it."

So at Puttenham we had pleasant friends and agreeable visitors,
including many young people who had been to Stonyhurst and Oxford
with Tony.

7

GLORIOUS EDITOR

But all the time I was a hard worker, pursued by that haunting
thought that having dealt with one idea I should never find another.

In addition to my novels I wrote a number of short stories which had
their best success in America and helped to butter my bread and even
provide a little jam. This was due to the enthusiasm of a little American
named Ray Long, who was the editor of the *Cosmopolitan* and liked my
stories to an almost embarrassing degree. Exciting cables arrived from
him. "*Your last short story is marvellous. I insist on paying you an
additional sum. Ten thousand thanks.*"

He paid me far too much, but then he paid almost everybody far too
much, being overtaken by megalomania in a most agreeable way, and
delighting to fling dollars about like a medieval lord scattering largesse
as he passed in glory and beneficence. In appearance he reminded me of
d'Artagnan, with his brown eyes and little moustache and gay look.
Once a year or so he held court at the Savoy Hotel where he gave
banquets to his authors.

To one such banquet my wife and I went one night, finding ourselves
at table with almost all the famous writers of the day. My wife sat next
to Ray Long and noticed that he was rather odd in his manner—a little
excited, she thought. A beautiful lady next to me said: "Poor Ray is
very, very drunk!" That was at the beginning of the dinner. Wine
flowed, after preliminary cocktails. The entire company was lit up, and

when called upon by Ray Long to make a speech—they were all called upon in turn—spoke with surprising wit and eloquence. One of our most distinguished women writers, with a distinct resemblance to Queen Victoria, fell fast asleep for a considerable time and awoke with a start, wondering where she was. It was a very successful dinner party, and it seemed to go on for weeks and weeks, like all American parties.

Next day I returned to the country to begin another short story for Ray Long. Now the poor little man is dead, having been brought low at the end by an excess of megalomania and riotous prodigality. Since then I have written no more short stories.

A shadow touched me towards the end of those days in Puttenham. There was something a little wrong with my eyes, I thought, and I was advised to see an oculist. I went to one of the most distinguished men of the profession in London, recommended by a friend. He had a look at my eyes and his voice softened with a kind of gentle pity.

"You are going blind," he said. "You have advanced diabetes. That is incurable in its effect on the eyes. I can do nothing for you."

I left his consulting room like a man condemned to death, or worse than death. I had always had a horror of blindness. Now I was told that I was going blind. It seemed to me unbelievable and after an hour of mental agony I rang up the distinguished oculist on the telephone.

"Did I understand you to say that I was going blind and that the disease is incurable?" I asked.

He answered impatiently.

"I told you so. I don't like being rung up on the telephone."

He switched off.

When I went home I told Agnes.

"I don't believe it!" she said. "Diabetes?—Nonsense!"

Rather late that evening she drove me over to Godalming and brought a doctor out of his bed.

"It seems to me rather extraordinary," he said. "Well, I'll test him for diabetes."

I was stuffed with sugar. My doctor's report was that I had an almost unnatural resistance to sugar. There was not a trace of diabetes.

"That man ought to be shot!" said Agnes, referring to the distinguished oculist. He wasn't shot, but a year or two later he died.

Nevertheless there was something a little wrong with my eyes—just a faint dimness of vision, just a shadow. Nothing much. I still went on looking at life.

8

EGYPT

Between my spasms of work we went abroad a good deal, year after year, to Egypt, Palestine, Germany, France, Hungary, Italy and Switzerland. Agnes loved travel and foreign scenes and languages.

My brother Arthur and his American wife joined us in a voyage down the Mediterranean as far as Alexandria and then to Cairo and Palestine. Once again I saw the beauty of Athens and for the first time the enchantment of Egypt. In the ship going down the Mediterranean—that sea of ghosts and gods—was one of the most distinguished Egyptologists of our time—Professor Breasted—an American scholar whose books on ancient Egypt are illuminating. He gave us a few lectures at which I presided, and I found him a good companion and a fervent friend of England. I had mugged up a bit of ancient Egyptian before making this journey and was able to read some of the inscriptions on the tombs, thereby greatly impressing our dragoman, Abdul Arti, son of the Sheik of Mena, who called me the "Seer". He fell in love with us, I think, and afterwards wrote to us every year. With him we camped in the desert with an American husband and wife as our companions, and under the stars by the white tents, while the camels and their leaders were sleeping, Abdul Arti and I talked of life and its meaning. He was a thoughtful man who spoke a kind of Bible English and looked very handsome in his white robe and black cloak.

One night he spoke of the desire of the Egyptians for independence.

"England has been the old Mother," he said. "We are grateful to her, owing her many things. But it is like all children with their mothers. There comes a time when they grow up, when they need to break away from this mothering, when they want to be free and do things themselves which may be wrong but are the signs of escape to freedom. So it is with us Egyptians. We feel the need of liberty for our young manhood."

It was a pity that they were murdering some of our officers even in Cairo.

We rode over the desert on camels and I felt easy on mine as though I had been born on a camel. Under the white moonlight flooding the desert we saw the tombs of the Kings and the old Sphinx, commonplace by day but magical by night. And there was something in the desert which caught hold of me—a sense of being etherealised and being drenched through even to the spirit by this sunlight and this translucent atmosphere.

In Cairo we went into the mosques and the old quarters and sat with

Abdul Arti in the shops and parlours of his friends. His uncle had an antique shop in which he served us coffee and cigarettes. Probably he was a dealer in faked antiques, but before I left Cairo he put a gift into my hands.

"It is good," he said. "I give it to you because you are a friend. One gives one's best to a friend. One does not cheat him."

He gave me a little bronze of Rameses. There was a glint of gold round its eyes. When I got back to England I scraped it with a knife and found a thin layer of gold where I scratched.

We had only a glimpse of Palestine, but that was unforgettable. Everywhere the flowers of the field spangled the earth. Blue was the water in the Sea of Galilee by which I stood with emotion. We went to Nazareth and the life there seemed unchanged since Mary and her Son were there, except that Ford cars took us through the village.

In Cana we went into a house which had been excavated by monks. It had been the house of a man of substance in the time of Christ and they had found tall wine jars. Was it possible—the monks thought it quite likely—that this was the house of the marriage feast when water was changed into wine?

At Haifa there were men making a new road, stripped to the waist.

I heard them talking and their language was that of the Bowery in New York. They were American Jews who had come out to Palestine with all those other Jews who were building the new city of Telaviv and buying Arab land and creating a new problem full of future danger, and conflict, and murder between the Jewish and Arab races. I had divided sympathies, remembering all the persecution of the Jews—less terrible than those to come in Germany and Poland—and their ideal of founding a new home in Palestine. They were irrigating the land and raising good harvests where the Arab had only scratched the earth. But the Arabs had been here for a thousand years. It was their land. They resented with extreme bitterness this invasion, and accused us of betraying them and our own pledges made by a young man named Colonel Lawrence and by the British Government.

Most of our soldiers and officers in Palestine were pro-Arab but tried to keep the peace between the two races and failed, because Arab leaders had formed a secret resistance movement with assassination as its method. Arrest and imprisonment of these men only checked for a time this racial vendetta.

Some of the Arab leaders fled into Syria and other countries and I met most of them in London to which they were called under safe-conduct. They were the "bad men". I was introduced to them by a girl brought up in Egypt by her father who had edited an Egyptian paper—a relative of my wife. This girl was ardently pro-Arab and became their unofficial hostess, enjoying herself vastly. These "bad men"—the Arabs called them heroes—were highly educated, spoke several languages, dressed in European style, and were witty, cynical and elegant. They pumped Arab propaganda into me, and I thought they had a strong case when they reminded me, and gave the text, of solemn promises made to them by us during the great war in which they had fought on our side. But we had made solemn promises also to the Jews under the Balfour Agreement, and they could not be reconciled so that now, as I write, the situation in Palestine and the Arab world is full of high explosives.

In Cairo one night I woke up with a fierce pain in my right eye. It was as though someone was driving a red hot poker into it. It was caused by poisoned dust and I have sometimes thought that the trouble in my eyes, about which I have written—that faint shadow creeping over my vision—dated from this time.

9

THE PLEASURE HUNTERS

But it did not prevent me from becoming a passionate painter in oils, after making innumerable sketches with a sharp pointed pencil. It gave me an additional interest on foreign journeys. I went on sketching holidays with Edgar Lander, my old friend from Fleet Street days. He had had his left arm broken to bits in the war and it was with his left hand that he had always worked. But now he learned to draw and paint with his right hand and took out sketching parties to France. He was a born teacher and a good companion. His pupils were mostly people of talent and very keen on the job. I went with them to La Rochelle, and Lander shoved us into a little hotel of the most primitive nature down by the port. But the *patron* had been a sea cook and produced good food from his kitchen, and his wife, who slaved with him in this third-class old house, was a woman of some beauty and elegance when she emerged now and then to join us in the evening at the Casino. She might have been *Madame la Comtesse*. Our *patron*, dressed in a neat black suit, revealed himself then as a man of natural culture, who had brought back from his voyages vivid impressions of what he had seen which he was able to describe with a real gift of words. That is characteristic of the French people, as I have found them. They have an inherited and traditional culture which lies deep in their minds of whatever class, and their elementary education is far higher than our own. A rough fellow with a three days' growth of beard on his chin, coming out of a factory or a tramp steamer knows something of classical history and quite a bit about Corneille, Racine, Victor Hugo, and other masters of French literature.

Above all, even in the lowest class, they have an interest in art. I remember when Lander and I were sketching outside La Rochelle three tough guys looking like stevedores came across to have a look at our work. They became enthusiastic about Lander's drawing, and were loud in their admiration of his technique.

"Quels coups de crayon!" cried one of them.

That would never have happened in England where an artist is regarded by men of that type as something comic and ridiculous.

An old woman emerged from a cottage behind Mentone where Lander and I were painting.

She gazed at my effort.

"Is that for sale?" she asked.

She offered me five francs for my work and I was much touched by this tribute from this old peasant woman with a pippin face creased into a thousand wrinkles. No one in England—or, now I come to think of it, only one—has offered to buy one of my pictures even for a shilling.

La Rochelle is a city for artists, magnificently picturesque and drenched in colour, where the ships move out from port with sails of all colours and the very slops of the seamen look as though they have been washed in wine. There is a constant movement as the ships get ready to depart or come back to harbour at a great pace. The towers and churches and sea walls, are drenched in an all-pervading light, golden and glowing as the sun sinks low. It was here that George Villiers Duke of Buckingham, about whom I wrote a book, fought his unsuccessful siege against a French Army under Richelieu, and it was here in the second World War that the Germans held on when the British and Americans had chased the *Wehrmacht* out of France.

Year after year, Agnes, Tony and I used to spend some time on the Côte d'Azur where my brother Arthur rented a little villa in the grounds of the Hôtel Cap d'Antibes.

It was the paradise and playground of English and Americans, especially when the franc had fallen low in relation to the English pound. Elderly colonels and their wives lived cheap in the little second-class hotels of Mentone and Nice. Spinsters from South Kensington put up in the little *pensions*, and chattered brightly in the English tea rooms. Literary men who sold their wares to Ray Long of the *Cosmopolitan* before the American slump, or whose novels were in great demand, had enchanting villas in the hills. Rich Americans had taken over medieval châteaux, or picturesque farmhouses in the hill towns of Vence and St. Pol, with their narrow streets, and colourwashed walls, and orange trees and olive groves. Poor American artists and literary men had found little dwelling places above Nice, remote from the sophisticated life below, but within reach of a second-hand Citroën when they became very bored with paradise, or cast an eye upon their own art and said: "Hell! What's the good of it, anyhow?"

H. G. Wells had a villa at Grasse. W. J. Locke, the "Beloved Vagabond", had another behind Monte Carlo. He gave luncheon parties to his friends, at which wine flowed very freely with good conversation round his board, and with blue shadows cast by the awning over his verandah. Old brandy of priceless bouquet—a few drops at the bottom of enormous glasses—was the last touch of his Lucullan feasts, from which his guests rose stupefied at three in the afternoon. Locke was the most charming of hosts, and never seemed to do any work. But he worked at night, and he told me that if, during a long night, he had written five hundred words he was well satisfied with his progress. In that time, I confess, I might have written five thousand, but not such good words.

The Baroness Orczy, of *Scarlet Pimpernel* fame, had a villa at Monte Carlo and invited us there sometimes. She was a good-natured lady with many friends, among whom were the young Prince and Princess of Monaco. The Prince asked me up to his palace and I was saluted by his army (of six soldiers or so) and received in audience in a painted *salon* where he sat on a gilded chair rather higher than the one to which he bid me. It was very much like Ruritania. The Baroness Orczy gave little dances, and one night I found a lady in my arms as light as gossamer and was astonished to find myself going round a room with Vesta Tilley, then Lady de Frece.

At the tables of Monte Carlo I watched the gamblers, at first with interest and then with boredom. Many of them had mask-like faces and were well known by the croupiers. *"Faites vos jeux!"* . . . *"Rien ne va plus!"* These were the old regulars who had their little systems, which in the end ruined them, or brought them low. The amateurs showed more excitement, especially when they won, and sometimes with beginners' luck—the old Devil tempting them—raked in a lot of chips, which they exchanged for French money.

An American publisher whom I happened to know came into Monte Carlo for a night, flung down high stakes, and went away with his pockets stuffed with thousand franc notes, which paid for his voyage from the United States, and all his expenses in Paris where he had had a good time with his wife.

At Cap Martin and Beaulieu there were gala nights in which elderly couples put on false noses and threw little balloons and squeakers at each other, and jigged up and down polished boards to the thump-

thump of jazz bands. Old ladies with frocks up to their knees swayed about in the arms of oily-haired young gigolos, who were well paid for this service. The healthiest crowd in these places were the tennis champions, who had to keep fit for the tournaments which had brought them here. I came to know Suzanne Lenglen with her eagle face, supreme above all others. Film stars descended upon the Côte d'Azur and lay about sun-bathing on the edge of the swimming pools, looking very lovely, but not so glamorous as on the screen.

It was the playground of those who lived in a world of make-believe cut off from realities, utterly artificial, and resulting for many of them in a dreadful boredom and sense of futility. Here was beauty, sunshine, music, luxury, but somehow no happiness. They were the lotus-eaters in a world which was slipping down the slopes of ruin, with a morass of unemployment, with money going bad behind tariff walls, with international trade at a low ebb because of artificial barriers and restrictions between one country and another, and with misery spreading among many peoples, undernourished or starving.

I was glad to get away from that coast of pleasure hunters into the mountains and their high-perched villages, where the life of the peasants was real, and nature was unspoilt by luxury hotels and jazz bands. Putting on old jeans my brother Arthur and I would go there with our paints and canvasses and have a good time trying to capture some of this loveliness. We covered ourselves, as well as our canvasses, in oils. We forgot our food. We became tanned by the hot sun. We were excited by this pursuit of beauty beyond the reach of our brushes. But for me these sketching holidays were only brief interludes between hard spells of work and the anxious study of a world going from bad to worse, with an occasional gleam of hope and a mirage of peace ahead.

10

GENERAL STRIKE

There was trouble in England in the year 1926. It began with the dockers who demanded better wages for a hard job. The transport workers came out in sympathy. The Trade Union Council backed them up and declared a general strike, which was obeyed by the railway men, the printers, the engineers at power stations, and many other workers. No newspapers appeared and Winston Churchill as Home Secretary issued an official Gazette with a page or two of type, while there was a rush for wireless sets as the only means of hearing the world's news.

My sympathies have always been on the side of the underdogs and the underpaid, but they were not in favour of this general strike which was an attempt by the T.U.C. to coerce the Government of the country and take over its power. It was an attack on our Parliamentary system and tradition, and, if successful, would have been the tyranny of a minority over the commonweal.

The Government called for volunteers to carry on the essential services of the country and to maintain order. It was answered by the "plus-four boys" as they were called—young gentlemen from the Universities and the public schools, the sons of the Middle Class, who at week-ends wore the baggy breeches and tasselled stockings which gave them their nickname. It all looked very serious. Foreign correspondents came to England anticipating riots and bloodshed in a social revolution. But they were astonished by the good nature of both sides. The police played football matches with the strikers in Wales. The "plus-four boys" did their jobs on the busses and tramcars with a great sense of humour.

"This bus goes anywhere you like," was chalked up on one of them. . . . "No fares and kind treatment." . . . "Joy rides to the East End."

One young gentleman, diverting his bus from its normal route, stopped outside his house in Eaton Square to call for his morning letters.

Boy and girl drivers handled great lorries full of milk churns, and drove them all through the night to bring milk to London where there was a dump in Hyde Park. Elderly ladies established canteens for the volunteers who had long hours and little food.

I had a look at all this, and one morning went down to the docks which were supposed to be hot spots and very dangerous because of the temper of the men. At the approach to the East India Docks I enquired my way to the dock gates.

"Better not go there!" said a man. "You might not get as far as that."

"Why not?" I asked.

The man spat on the pavement.

"I'm just telling you," he said, with an ugly look.

I went on further and saw a group of dockers lounging about, and went up to them.

"How do I get into the Docks?" I asked.

One man answered me.

"You don't! They're in the hands of the military. Nobody's allowed in."

"I bet you I'll get in," I told him.

There was a general laugh.

"Not you! Sentries with loaded rifles at the gates."

They came as far as the gate with me to see what happened and we had a talk on the way. I found them very decent fellows, with no desire to declare war on the nation or any class of it. What they wanted was a bit more pay and regular work, instead of being turned off for long spells because trade was bad and few ships were coming in.

"We've a right to live, haven't we?" said one of them.

I agreed with him.

At the dock gates I was questioned by a tall policeman who looked suspicious.

"No one allowed in here," he said grimly. "What do you want? What's your name?"

When I told him my name he stared at me and then laughed and grabbed my hand.

"Good God!" he exclaimed. "I knew you in Flanders and on the Somme. Come in. I'll get a chit for you from the O.C."

The group of dockers outside the gate were impressed. They thought I must be a hell of a fellow—the Home Secretary or somebody big.

The docks were deserted. Nothing moved. Only here and there a Guardsman marched up and down on sentry-go.

From one great shed came the sound of merry music. It was playing "Dear Little Buttercup". It seemed to me very odd, and I went into the shed and found a Guards' band playing a selection from Gilbert and Sullivan, without an audience.

"Doing their bit," said the officer who led me round.

Only in England I think could such a thing have happened. Truly we are a very amusing people.

Towards the end of the strike I decided to go North to have a look at things up there. I was told that a train was running now and again, with amateur engine drivers. With luck one might get to Manchester. I decided to try my luck and went to Euston early one morning. A train with steam up was waiting at one of the platforms and a small group of people, mostly business men, assembled to make the journey. After a long wait a cheery young gentleman advanced along the platform and raised a bowler hat.

"Good morning everybody!" he said. "I'm the engine driver. I hope to get you as far as Manchester, and I'll certainly do my best for you."

He put on a pair of gloves and smiled at the small crowd.

"Very nice of you to come!" he said. "It shows great faith in me."

Somehow or other I didn't have much faith in him. He was too good-looking. He was too damn cheery.

I took my seat in one of the carriages with three or four others. One of them was a young woman who wanted to join her husband and children in Manchester. She had come to London on a visit to an aunt, and had been cut off by the General Strike. She didn't know how her man was getting on with the children. They were regular pickles and not old enough to look after themselves.

The engine was throbbing and presently it gave a jerk which knocked the backs of our heads against the carriage. It did this three times and then made a start on that journey to Manchester. We got nearly as far as Harrow. Before then I felt a little sweat in the palms of my hands and on my forehead. Our train was lurching in a most alarming way. Suddenly there was a grinding of brakes, a tearing of rails, and the whole train ran off the lines and came to a standstill.

We all jumped out. Our gentleman driver alighted and raised his bowler hat again with a cheery smile.

"That's torn it!" he said. "So sorry! Some little thing went wrong."

We had torn up quite a bit of the permanent way.

No train went to Manchester that day.

On the following day I decided to get up North by car and learnt from some source of information that a motor car was starting for Manchester with room for one other passenger. The starting place was a small pub in a mean street and when I presented myself the driver invited me to a cup of tea while his assistant was loading up his packing cases.

"You'll be a little uncomfortable," he warned me. "Not much space. But I drive like a demon."

He spoke with a foreign accent and I discovered later that he was a Greek salesman of oriental carpets. He was taking some of his stock up to Manchester.

He had laden his car heavily. It was an open car and many large packages were piled behind the back seat. I had a back seat. After ten miles or so the packages slipped and I had to support them on my shoulders. Our Greek drove undoubtedly like a demon, but a very humorous and excitable demon with a great gift of eloquence. He talked all the time, turning his head to tell a funny story, and then laughing explosively. Being a Greek and needing gesture to accompany an anecdote he took both hands off the wheel from time to time. I said a few prayers.

We got as far as Coventry after several breakdowns. In Coventry I saw a notice, handwritten in large characters, pasted up in a window.

"STRIKE ENDED".

It turned out to be true. Ramsay MacDonald and his colleagues had hated this strike from the beginning and had sat up night after night with representatives of the T.U.C. urging an ending to this business. The "plus-four boys" had beaten it. They were carrying on the essential services fairly well, apart from the railways. The nation as a whole would not stand for it, and if it came to civil war——

The T.U.C. called it off.

11

THE DREAM OF GENEVA

During the first ten years after the first World War I went several times to Geneva as an observer of the proceedings of the League of Nations, and for a long time had the hope that in spite of all its delays and disappointments, its critics and intriguers, its hypocrites and saboteurs, it would succeed in maintaining peace and establishing international justice.

It is well to remember those hopes and efforts which were shared by millions of the common folk of the world and by all liberal-minded men and women in this and other countries, for they created an attitude towards life, and policy, and passing events, which is now forgotten. One must judge history not by one's knowledge and mental state when writing it, but by what was the mood and mind of the people who made it. We know now that the League failed. We know now that all the idealism, the emotion, the faith, which supported it ended in disillusion and war.

People talk and write now as though the period between the two wars was one of blindness and stupidity, and total lack of foresight amounting to treason. There are many who scoff at the League and write history or comment on that time from the date when Hitler showed the cloven hoof. They leave out all that went before and jeer at the peacemakers whose work ended in disaster and a general conflagration. That is bad history.

It was a blow when the United States Senate refused to support President Wilson and the League which was part of the peace treaty. But at the time it did not seem like a mortal blow. Forty-three nations were members of the League, and in the General Assembly gave their support to the principles of international justice. They had behind them an immense force of public opinion, and for a time at least statesmen and politicians had to reckon with that mass opinion and emotion which they knew could not be ignored or openly opposed. The peoples of the world, or nearly all of them, wanted peace. They thought the League would give it to them by a system of collective security and by revision of grievances which might lead to war. They wanted general disarmament, to which the League was pledged. They wanted a world at peace and sure of peace.

There were many critics and sceptics. The world at that time was divided between those who believed that ideals of international justice could prevail and those who believed only in force, naked and unashamed. All the old reactionaries, those of the Junker mind in this country and others, belonged to the second group, the believers in force and nothing but force. Because of fear and hatred of Germany, which now seems justified because of the second World War, French leaders like Poincaré had no faith at all in this way of peace, and did everything to sabotage it, as did some of our own Right Wing statesmen.

"They were right!" many people say now. "Were they not proved right? Was not Poincaré a wiser man than these League enthusiasts, because he refused to disarm and surrounded himself by a *cordon sanitaire* of states like Poland, to which he sent credits for the purchase of arms and ammunition on a heavy scale?"

The answer is "No!" He was not right. His policy did not succeed any more than the League. It ended in the surrender of France. If France had backed the League, if Laval, Foreign Secretary of France, had not made a secret pact with Mussolini, giving him a free hand in Abyssinia and "ratting" against Anthony Eden at the time of Sanctions, and if there had been general disarmament and control of national munitions before the coming of Hitler, there would have been no second World War.

In any case, the failure of an ideal does not mean that it was wrong. The idealists of the League, as they were called with contempt by its opponents, and all that massed strength of human emotion and hope behind them, were working to enforce some better system of argument and justice than the abominable arbitrament of war. They failed not because their ideal was wrong but because they were betrayed. After the second World War, which was the price of betrayal, the same ideal is to be tried out again, as the one last hope of civilisation against the forces of destruction—without the same faith behind it and with, alas, less chance of success, because one cannot impose justice upon injustice which is already established over a wide area of Europe.

As far as my own poor pen could reach I was one of the advocates of the League idea, and I was heart and soul for its success, though often doubtful and anxious, because I knew the insincerities, the double-crossings, the intrigues behind the scenes.

I went to Geneva now and then with a friend of mine who was always called by his friends "D.D." It was David Davies, afterwards Lord Davies. He was a rich man who devoted most of his wealth to the cause of International Law and Justice and he gave an enormous sum of money to the League of Nations Union.

He had several bees in his bonnet which made him a bore to some of his friends, though they were very honest and admirable bees. He believed in an international police force to carry out the rulings of a Court of Equity. He was for a time very keen to have the meeting place of the League at Constantinople.

I didn't find him a bore. On the contrary, I found him a most entertaining man, brimming over with good humour. He had been an ardent huntsman in Wales, keeping his own pack of hounds, and on the way to Geneva, between conversations about the League, he would sing Welsh hymns and croon to his favourite hounds, with gusts of hearty laughter. Afterwards when I met him in London or in New York he would hail me with a "Yoicks!" and a "Tally-ho!" like an eighteenth century squire. He was a tremendous worker for peace, writing many books and innumerable pamphlets, and presently founding the New Commonwealth with a membership from all parties, creeds, and many nations, which has for its purpose international justice with an International Police Force to enforce the law if need be. (Not to be confused with Sir Richard Acland's Common Wealth, which is a form of Communism in the economic sphere.)

"During the assembly of the League Geneva was a city of international activity and a rendezvous of many types of humanity. On the terrace of the Hôtel Beau Rivage, facing the lake, one saw them in earnest conversation over the little tea tables. Among them came the tall stooping figure of Lord Cecil with his falcon face, with Gilbert Murray whose ideas of democracy went back to Plato, and Sir Eric Drummond, afterwards Lord Perth, Secretary General of the League, relying upon Lord Cecil and his own gift of diplomacy to steer the League through one crisis after another. There was nearly always a crisis.

I described the early scenes at Geneva in a book called *Since Then* (a history of Europe after the war).

"The representatives of all the earth were there, even if they were not on the League. By the waters of Lake Leman they swarmed, speaking all tongues, and those unceasingly, in anger, in agony, in pleading, in ridicule and in contempt, in all human passion. While the Council of the League sat behind closed doors, knowing their own weakness, there were intrigues in the corridors, in the cafés, in the bedrooms of hotels, in the gardens of outdoor restaurants. Journalists of all nations jabbered at each other, buttonholed their favourite big men, and sent off telegrams at urgent rates announcing that 'The League is dead', or other rumours more alarming. Frenchmen shrugged their shoulders and said 'Foch rules. Why all this talk?' Italians flung their arms into the air and cried

'We have been betrayed!' Germans drank more beer and said 'There is no justice, and therefore there can be no peace'. There was a lot of other conversation. Few people believed that the League of Nations could fulfil any of its objects and ideals in a world of national antagonism and economic madness."

Nevertheless it made many converts. Sceptics and cynics who came to scoff remained to pray. I saw this happen with French journalists, the most cynical and the most sceptical. After long discussions and arguments at *al fresco* dinner tables on the other side of the lake, and after recording the work of the Assembly, some of them became ardent advocates of the League and criticised the obstinate hostility of Raymond Poincaré. When Briand came and stood up as its champion many of them supported him with enthusiasm.

Several blows struck the League in its early years. One was in 1920 when Poland seized Vilna from Lithuania. Another was in 1923 when Mussolini bombarded Corfu and killed a number of children in revenge for the killing of some Italian officers who were fixing the frontier between Greece and Albania. The League did nothing about either of these things except to express disapproval. How could they do anything at the time when action was in the hands of the Supreme Council of the Allies to whom idealism was ridiculous? It was not a good precedent when Spain withdrew because she was not admitted as a permanent member of the Council.

Yet the League had its victories now forgotten. By its threat of an economic blockade it stopped a conflict between Jugoslavia and Albania in 1927, thus preventing another Balkan War which would have been a spreading fire. The Council stopped an almost certain conflict between Turkey and Great Britain by persuading the Turks to accept a provisional frontier line around Mosul and an impartial commission of enquiry. In 1925 they prevented war between Greece and Bulgaria. There were other frontier disputes, as between Hungary and Czechoslovakia settled by the machinery of the League.

12

BRIAND AND STRESEMANN

But peace in Europe, the prevention of another great war, depended mainly upon the relations between France and Germany.

Could Germany be brought back to the family of nations on equal footing and as a good neighbour? Could the legitimate fears of France be relieved—thus bringing a sense of peace to Europe still feverishly

arming—by a new era of conciliation and international law? Lord
Vansittart and his followers would say: "NEVER!" That was an
illusion as recent history has proved. Perhaps so, but there were many
Germans at that time—the mass of the German people, I truly believe—
who were eager for their country to be admitted to the League of
Nations and sincere in their desire for peace. There was one great and
patriotic Frenchman—Aristide Briand—who believed this possible.
There was one great Englishman, not a Labour nor Left Wing man—
Austen Chamberlain—who worked with untiring devotion to bring this
about. In Germany there was another Englishman, our Ambassador
Lord D'Abernon, with whom I had had many talks in his Embassy at
Berlin, who persuaded Stresemann to adopt this policy of conciliation.
There are some now who believe that Stresemann was utterly insincere
and that he had the Junker spirit. They quote from his letters and
diaries. But I believe that he risked his life for this policy of a pact of
friendship with France, and he told his friends in Geneva that he was
doing so.

I sat sometimes on the terrace of the Beau Rivage with Sir Austen
Chamberlain, who had his young son with him. He told me of his
anxieties and his hopes. He had adopted the D'Abernon scheme which
afterwards took shape in the Treaty of Locarno between France,
Germany and England, guaranteeing the Western frontier between the
two first countries. In the event of German aggression British forces
would go to the aid of France. If France invaded Germany Britain
would go to the side of Germany. The plan had many critics in France
and some in England, in spite of a good Press which gave it a paean of
praise, and many speeches over the radio when the spirit of Locar-r-r-no
was hailed as a new era in world history. As I wrote at the time the
French hated that clause mentioning British aid to Germany, and
people in England did not like the thought that if war broke out again
between the old antagonists another generation of youth would have to
go into the furnace fires on one side or the other because of other
people's passions. But Briand and Stresemann stifled these doubts.
Curiously enough for such different types they got on well together and
came to an understanding.

"The spirit of Locarno," said Briand, "denotes the beginning of a
new era of trust and co-operation."

"We have assumed responsibility for the treaty," said Stresemann,
"because we believe that only by a peaceful and neighbourly life can we
secure the development of states and peoples."

Germany was to be admitted as one of the Great Powers on the
Council of the League, and Stresemann had set his heart on this when
he came to Geneva in March of 1926. But Spain and Brazil raised prior

claims to seats on the Council, and so postponed the entry of Germany. Stresemann was bitterly disappointed. His enemies at home were violent and dangerous, and he needed this success to keep them in check. On his return to Germany he became very ill, but in September of that year he came back to Geneva with renewed hope.

Even then there were intrigues behind the scenes to prevent the entry of Germany. To the last moment Sir Austen Chamberlain was on tenterhooks, as I saw, and as he told me, lest some technical rule raised by Germany's enemies should frustrate this great act of reconciliation, as it seemed at the time.

It was not allowed to happen, and I was present at the historic scene on September 10th, 1926, when in a great hall in Geneva, before a crowded assembly, representing the whole world except the United States and Russia—important exceptions!—with all the galleries thronged, the President of the League summoned the German delegation to take their places.

I was in one of the galleries. Next to me was Wickham Steed of *The Times*. Around us were journalists of many nations. We had been talking together during a long wait. Then there was tense silence for several seconds. A curtain was drawn and we saw Stresemann enter with the other Germans. The German Foreign Secretary was very pale and his emotion was visible. Away in Germany, as he knew, were people who would want to kill him for this act. But for him and for all the rest this moment was the reappearance of Germany among the Great Powers of the world after defeat and agony and despair. We thought it good at that time. Everyone in the public galleries rose and cheered, and although such demonstrations were against the rules of the League the President made no protest.

Now who were these men and women in the public galleries? Were they all fools? Were they all dupes and dolts? They belonged to nearly all the nations. Among them were hard-headed journalists, apt to be cynical, and men of quality and distinction from all parts of the world. It is well to remember that, when reviewing history between the two wars. It is well to remember that the efforts of the peacemakers, now derided, were supported by public opinion still horror-stricken by the last war, and uplifted that day by the tremendous hope that this act of reconciliation between hereditary enemies would lead at last to peace. They cheered and cheered again, and this emotion was like a flame. Who shall jeer at them now for their ideals and their hopes? Who shall condemn them, though their hopes were blasted and their ideals went down into mud and murder? I was one of those who cheered and had tears in my heart if not in my eyes.

The President of the League called upon the representative of France.

The representative of France was Aristide Briand. I had been watching
him down below. He had sat hunched up, looking like an old-clothes-
man with scurf on his collar, shabby and shaggy. Now he mounted the
platform, pulled himself up and flung out his hand, and was no longer
like an old-clothes-man but like an old lion. He was the greatest orator
of France. His voice was wonderful, marvellous in tone, in musical
resonance, in exquisite elocution. He paced up and down. We listened
to his words spellbound. They were golden words, sometimes sinking
to a whisper which all could hear. He was a great old actor, with all the
tricks of oratory, but one believed that day in his sincerity and his
emotion. He pledged the soul of France to peace and good will with the
soul of Germany. He turned his back, as the French people would turn
their backs, upon the Way of Blood, that long road of flaming war and
monstrous death, which both nations had traversed, and he faced a
future when Germany and France would work together for the peace of
humanity, the safety of women, and the rescue of the world's young
manhood. He held out both hands to Stresemann in the name of
France. It was a speech which those of us who heard it will never
forget, and it is made more poignant now by the terrible fact that both
those nations went back again along the Way of Blood. Stresemann
died. Briand died. The world economic crisis swept all nations into
financial ruin. The League was betrayed. . . . Hitler came.

PART XI

EUROPEAN JOURNEY

1

PARIS IN FERMENT

IN the Spring and Summer of 1934 I made a journey through Europe with two friends for the purpose of writing a book commissioned by Charles Evans of Heinemann. Priestley had written a book called *English Journey* which was brilliantly successful and Evans wanted me to follow it with *European Journey*. My two companions were my old friend Edgar Lander who was to do a number of sketches for the American edition—Evans did not want illustrations—and Cecil Roberts, the novelist, who came for his personal interest and pleasure.

We hired a Daimler car in Paris. Our driver was a tall Russian—now a naturalised Frenchman—who called himself Gaston, and wore a chauffeur's livery. Once he had been a naval officer under the Czar, but all that was to him like the dream of another life, and now he behaved respectfully to his clients whom he drove about France, mostly English and Americans. Never once would he join our wayside meals, but always ate his own some little distance apart. But in the evenings when off duty he would take off his chauffeur's uniform, put on a lounge suit and a felt hat, and walk down the street with a stride and air of an ex-naval officer. At the wheel, where I sat next to him, he was amusing and talkative, and very shrewd in his comments about French life and politics.

In Paris we put up at a modest hotel behind the Madeleine and I was soon made aware of the political passions stirring in the French capital. It was not long after a riot which had led to shooting in the Place de la Concorde. We took a glass of vermouth at the Weber in the rue Royale and one of the waiters told me what had happened there on the fatal night.

"This restaurant was a field dressing station. The wounded were carried in constantly. It was a tragic affair, and the politicians—those dirty dogs—will have to pay for it. It was a massacre of honest folk—the *anciens combattants de guerre*—who were protesting against corruption. You have heard of the Stavisky scandal?"

Certainly I had heard of it. It was one of those financial scandals which seem to belong to French melodrama, with murder and suicide behind its political ramifications. Many highly placed people—even members of the Government—were involved in it. It was a proof of deep corruption in French official life.

It had also aroused violent demonstrations from the parties of the Left and Right, and particularly of a Royalist and Fascist group called the 'Croix de Feu' under the leadership of Colonel de la Rocque, supported by the venomous and vitriolic pen of Léon Daudet in his paper L'Action Française.

It was the young men of the 'Croix de Feu' who had made most of the trouble in the Place de la Concorde where the mass of people, moving towards the Chamber of Deputies, were made up of clerks, business men, and the veterans of the last war. The Royalists marched down from the boulevards, smashing newspaper kiosks and tearing up the railings round the trees to use as weapons. The police were overwhelmed. The Gardes Mobiles had been unseated from their horses and badly mauled. Then somebody lost his nerve and gave the order to fire. Thirty people had been killed and a thousand wounded, including a little maidservant who was killed while watching the scene from a window in the Hôtel Crillon.

This shooting had aroused a storm of fury in public opinion. The French Government under Daladier had yielded to this demonstration of rage and indignation and to the panic of the deputies, some of whom were chased like rats when they dared to show themselves. A brave old man—Doumergue—formerly President of the Republic—had been summoned to form a National Government, but I was told that he could not hold the situation very long, and that there were all the symptoms of revolution in the mind and temper of the people. Young men belonging to many political groups of the Right and Left were buying cheap revolvers. Underneath the surface of French life there were, said my friends, smouldering fires.

I talked with French people in Paris at that time and heard all the views from the extreme Left to the extreme Right—among them a Royalist who believed that the only thing which could save France was a return to the Monarchy under the Duc de Guise. But down by the Seine I talked with a wiser man who was selling books at one of the stalls along the quais.

"Ninety-nine per cent of the French people are moderate," he told me. "The danger comes from the two extremes who are in a small minority but make a lot of trouble."

He spoke about the young men—the boys—who were among the trouble-makers. "Youth wants to take charge," he said. "It wants to wrest power from the older men. It's impatient. Can you wonder? It's a hard time for youth nowadays. There is much unemployment. The high cost of living keeps them without much margin for amusement. They have many anxieties, and sometimes a sense of anger. Over there" (he pointed to the Latin Quarter), "there are many young men who have to study hard without much hope. They do not always eat enough. I know. I talk to them."

2

FEAR IN FRANCE

As we motored through France, taking our time about it, stopping to make sketches, giving me an opportunity of talking to farmers and peasants and all manner of folk, I deepened my knowledge of what was working in the minds of these people. They were exasperated by the dishonesty of their politicians. They were bitter because of the high cost of living—that was on every tongue—and they were under the shadow of a great fear. It was the fear of a new war with Germany.

I had a talk about that with the sacristan of the Treasury in Sens Cathedral. He had been showing me the vestments once worn by St. Thomas à Becket who stayed there during his exile from England. We stood in the dusk—the evening light was fading among the old tapestries, and cloth of gold, and ivories—marvellously carved—which had been brought back from the Crusades by St. Louis of France and his knights.

"It is terrible," said the sacristan, "this talk of a new war with Germany! It is inconceivable that such a horror should come again. The newspapers fill me with despair. Are we all mad? Have our politicians no sanity? No! I cannot think that it will happen. We are not unreasonable. The French people have an instinctive intelligence and commonsense. We must make an arrangement with Germany. Why can't we live in peace with these people? They are Europeans like ourselves. There is no cause for a new conflict between us. The Saar will certainly go back to Germany. They are German folk there. That is undeniable. After that what do they want from us? We must make an arrangement to live on terms of peace. It is necessary for the future of civilisation. Nobody wants war—none of the working people who remember the last. The next war, if it happens, would destroy everything that is meant by civilisation. . . . If only we could get rid of fear between ourselves and Germany! Hitler says he wants peace with us. He has said it several times. I want to believe that he means it."

I recorded that conversation in my book *European Journey*. Now reading it again it has a new poignancy. What that thin sad-eyed sacristan said to me in the glory of Sens Cathedral I heard from many other people in France—the workers, the humble folk. They wanted peace with Germany. They hated the idea of another war. But the shadow of the fear was upon them.

Yet it was a pleasant journey through France. We sat on the edge of flower-spangled fields and watched little rivers flowing under old bridges, and I wandered away from Lander and Roberts to talk to carpenters, sawing wood at their benches, and blacksmiths at their forges, and French peasants who had been bending over the earth and now straightened themselves to say "Bonjour!" and have a friendly conversation. They were good honest folk and I renewed my love for France and the French people of the working classes, so much better than their politicians and financiers.

The middle classes of France, and especially the little *rentiers*, living on small pensions, were having a hard time.

On the quayside of Mâcon—a fine old town with six bridges across its broad river—I caught the eyes of one of its citizens, a respectable little man of the white collar class, though a little shabby.

"A charming evening, M'sieur," I ventured to say.

"It is a fine evening," he agreed.

"All goes well in Mâcon?" I asked.

He looked at me with moody eyes.

"All does not go well", he answered. "On the contrary. All goes badly."

"That is deplorable," I said.

"*Yes*, it is deplorable," he agreed.

"Business is bad?" I suggested. "You are no doubt a business man?"

He hesitated for a moment and then sighed.

"I am not a business man, monsieur. I am what they call a *rentier*. That is to say I am trying to live on the interest of savings put by after a life of hard work. That is to say I am not succeeding to live, because it is impossible, you understand."

I did not understand. At least I desired more information. He gave it me with great candour.

"It is simple. It is a matter of simple arithmetic. Since the war the cost of living has increased six times. Salaries have only increased three times. Make your own reckoning. It is impossible, as I say, to live.

"Take my own case," said this new acquaintance, with a frankness which was surprising. "I have six thousand francs a year."

I made a sum in mental arithmetic. Six thousand francs translated into English money would be seventy-five pounds a year.

"You may see for yourself that such an income is ridiculous," said this gentleman of France. "Everything is taxed. Prices increase. Rents are abominable. Clothes are expensive. One does not amuse oneself on an income of six thousand francs. Yet I do not pretend that I am worse off than others. Certainly not. In France there are hundreds of thousands like myself, or with less than myself, after serving the state faithfully for forty years. I am not complaining even of the Government. I am a reasonable man. It is necessary to balance the Budget. The Government would much like to decrease taxation but is unable to do so. It is no use urging it to lower taxation. Then the Budget would not be balanced. Then the financial state of the country would be worse than now, which is, of course, deplorable. I do not see any solution."

After further conversation which I found illuminating we took off our hats to each other, and my *rentier* friend walked slowly away—homeward perhaps for a meal with strict economy. I doubt whether he could afford to drink the wine of Mâcon.

After further wanderings in France and many wayside conversations we went along a straight road above the Rhone leading through a French fort with a double drawbridge, and, then a little farther, we came to a barrier where Customs Officers surrounded us. After various formalities we were allowed to go on and passed through another barrier.

"We are now", said Gaston, our driver, "in the land of the picture postcard." We were in Switzerland!

3

THE BUILDING OF A PALACE

We made for Geneva, and put up at the Hôtel d'Angleterre, facing Lake Leman, and not far from the Beau Rivage which was reserved during the League Assemblies for Foreign Ministers and their secretaries. When we arrived some of their juniors had been sent in advance and were occupying the second-best bedrooms.

They were preparing the ground for what might be the last Disarmament Conference, which, after many years, many plans, and many hopes—the hopes of all peace-loving peoples in the world—had reached an *impasse*, no longer to be concealed or circumvented by any face-saving formula. Germany claimed equality of rights in the matter of disarmament. It had, as a matter of fact, been acknowledged as a theoretical justice by France, Great Britain, Italy and other Powers. But the advent of Mr. Hitler and his Nazis had, said the French, created a new situation. They declined to admit the right of Germany to rearm up to their own level until France was assured of security against German aggression.

That was the situation when we came to Geneva, and the Disarmament Conference failed before we left Switzerland to arrive at any agreement, or even to adopt any face-saving formula which might deceive a schoolgirl.

My friends Edgar Lander and Cecil Roberts were scornful of me because I still had—still tried to have—some lingering faith in the League of Nations.

"How," asked Lander, "could you expect any good to come out of an assembly just making eye-wash for long-haired pacifists, and old women who subscribe to the League of Nations Union?"

"The failure to deal with Japan when it attacked China," said Cecil Roberts, "was the League's confession to the world that it was impotent to enforce decisions. It died then. It's no use pretending that it has any power or life. Definitely the international idea has failed. Every nation has been forced back to self-defence. England must realise this before it's too late. We're utterly defenceless in the air. We have weakened our Navy. All our pacifists are undermining the spirit of the nation. . . . A touch of Fascism wouldn't do us any harm."

I was challenged in everything I believed and hoped as we walked along the lakeside of Geneva, green in the hot sunlight under a blue sky. And reading again the record of that conversation I have to admit that both Lander and Roberts were right and that my last lingering hopes in the League were in vain. But those who worked for the ideals of the League need not regret their labour, need not be ashamed of their advocacy, need not haul down their flag.

They were the civilised minds trying to convert the world to civilised ideas. They failed because the world or part of it, had uncivilised minds, and because the world's leaders, or some of them, were half-hearted or deliberate traitors to the idea of international law and collective security. The peace-lovers failed. So did Christianity fail.

After a second World War—what now? Another one? Have those who jeered at the League made a beautiful success? Do they enjoy the ruin they made?

We went to look at the new Palace of the League, then being built.

"I'd like to do a drawing of this 'House of Dreams' ", said Lander, grimly and with sinister intent.

I talked with some of the workmen, making cement blocks, and said something about the new building.

One of them looked up and grinned.

"No," he said, "we're not building a new Palace for the League."

"What then?" I asked.

"A new hospital for the wounded of the next war", he answered.

He spat on the ground, and looked at me with blue laughing eyes, but he raised the hair on my scalp. It was a bitter and frightful phrase.

When I repeated it to Cecil Roberts it excited him.

"What an epigram! It's worth coming all this way to hear it. Terrible, all the same!"

There was one wise woman in Geneva, with whom I had a talk. She sat in a little newspaper kiosk and after preliminary remarks about bad business, due to the lack of tourists, I asked her what would happen next week when the League of Nations would be meeting again.

This thin worn-looking woman, sitting in her little box behind a pile of papers she could not sell, repeated my words with a kind of mockery.

"The League of Nations! . . . Ah, monsieur, what a downfall is there! What a tragic affair! What dreadful failure to confess to all those millions of people who have been hoping against hope that they could give peace to Europe!"

"They will arrange nothing?"

"They will arrange nothing except to increase their military strength. Year after year I have hoped that we had finished with bloodshed and the sacrifice of young manhood. Now I do not hope so much. The world is too wicked."

"It is wickedness you think?"

"Greed and egotism, monsieur. That is what prevents peace among the nations. Everybody drags the eiderdown over his own head. If you are a married man you will understand that that is selfishness."

I was much struck with that phrase about the eiderdown. The elderly woman continued in that line of thought for some time. Capitalism, she thought, was the enemy of civilisation. The rich wanted to get more rich.

Presently she spoke again about the danger to world peace.

"If war comes it will be from Germany. But how extraordinary are those people! What will they obtain from war except corpses? They are, of course, mad. That is self evident. Hitler is a madman. General Goering is also a madman. It is a country inhabited by madmen. They put the poison of their madness into young brains, and those gentlemen in the League of Nations, what are they doing? How can they face their peoples? How can they go on talking insincerities, with disaster creeping nearer? Is it impossible for them to get above all this insanity and lead the peoples back to peace and happiness? If that is impossible then war will come again and plunge us into the blackest ruin. Because, monsieur, we cannot stand the strain of another war. It will let loose the beast in mankind. It will take us back to the beginning of things, before civilisation. I am very much afraid when I think of these things!"

I put my hand into her little house and she clasped it tightly. We were two souls on the roadside of life, very much afraid when we thought of these things, not because of any fear for ourselves—we were both elderly—but because we hated the thought of another massacre of youth, and the letting loose of the beast.

I recorded her conversation in that book of mine and reading it again I see how true, and how tragically prophetic, was this humble old woman in that little kiosk by the lake of Geneva. . . . The beast was let loose.

Our journey came to an abrupt halt for a time in the picturesque old town of Sion, perched on a high hill. We had secured rooms in a good hostelry and then went out to have an *apéritif* before dinner. Sitting outside a café in the main street I fell into conversation with a young man at my side, and remarked to him that the people passing did not look like Swiss.

"They're Romans, really", he said. "Descendants of a Roman legion up there on the hills, more than a thousand years ago. Many of them speak the Roman language—very much like Latin."

I had an interesting conversation, but suddenly felt hot and then cold. "A bit of a chill," I thought. "I must have caught it when a cold wind swept down to Lake Leman from the mountains."

That night I was in a high fever. I became delirious and babbled in French and German. I was aware of doing this. One half of my mind seemed perfectly conscious of what was happening to the other half which had lost control. I went on talking nonsense, to the distress of Edgar Lander and Cecil Roberts who came into my room. They sat up with me all night, and I knew they were there. Next morning I had a fierce pain in my left lung as though someone were stabbing it. "Pleurisy," said a doctor who was called in. It was a great nuisance. It kept us all hanging about for three weeks in that little hill top town, where I stayed in bed very weak and ill. Lander did many sketches of Sion while I listened to the sounds outside—the baa-ing of the sheep, the moo-ing of the cattle, the clucking of hens, in the market place near by. One morning a lady stood by my bed. It was Agnes, to whom Lander had sent a telegram. She was rather frightened. Lander had taken a serious view of things. He thought it might be my last journey.

"What have you been doing?" asked Agnes. "How did you get into this state?"

I could not plead guilty to any folly. It was just bad luck.

It was wonderful to have Agnes there, and when I was fairly well—"you are not cured," said the doctor—she joined us on the next stages of the journey through Italy and Germany.

With Gaston still driving us we crossed the Simplon Pass, and I lay in the short grass, flaked with snow under a blue sky and a warm sun, by the side of that high mountain road over which Napoleon had come with his men dragging their guns. I could hardly walk more than a few yards without feeling exhausted, but that air on the Simplon cured my lung more rapidly than if I had lain in bed in Sion.

4

FASCIST ITALY

We arrived with a broken spring at the frontier town of Gondar. Gaston was gloomy and feared the worst, but was recommended to a garage proprietor at Domo d'Ossola, near by. While he was examining the car I had a talk with an elderly Italian who seemed to have no work to do and spoke very good French.

"How are things going in Italy?" I asked.

"They are not brilliant", he told me. "Business is bad. There is much unemployment. Taxation is heavy. There is a terrible deficit in the Budget.

"It is difficult to know what will happen," he said gloomily.

I was surprised at those candid remarks by a man behind whose head was the portrait of one who did not encourage criticism of his régime.

We drove on slowly to Domo d'Ossola and Gaston was in a despondent mood. "It is most unlucky," he said, "about that broken spring. One can do nothing against ill luck."

We were slowed down to a crawl by a funeral procession and Gaston became even more gloomy.

"It only needs this!" he said. "The corpse in that coffin is probably the proprietor of the garage to which I have been recommended."

For some reason that remark made me laugh indecorously behind the funeral procession.

The broken spring was mended. We drove on to Baveno on Lake Maggiore, sparkling in the golden sunlight which gleamed on the white houses of the Borromean Islands.

"This," said Lander, "is a good spot. I can't imagine anything better on earth."

Next morning was a Sunday and from the windows of the Hôtel Suisse we could hear bugles blowing, and the marching of feet, and young voices singing *Giovenezza*, which is the song of youth. When we sat in the garden of the hotel we saw youth passing for a parade, masses of young men and girls, troops of children with flags. They all looked healthy and happy. Mussolini had denied them free speech, he was contemptuous of liberty, but his young people seemed to like his discipline, and one was bound to admit, I thought, that he had raised the standard of life in Italy. But that morning I read one of his speeches in an Italian newspaper.

"I absolutely disbelieve in perpetual peace. It is detrimental and negative to the fundamental virtues of men, which only by struggle reveal themselves to the light of the sun. Whatever happens the Italian people will face the future with complete discipline."

After the parade the Italian youth and the small children came marching back with songs and laughter. What will happen to them one day, I thought, if Mussolini thinks the time is good for a beautiful war?

I spoke to an Italian who had greeted me before when I came to sit under one of his umbrellas with blue and white stripes. He was the proprietor of the hotel and spoke very good English.

"Those young Fascists look happy," I remarked, as another body of them marched past with their flags.

He shrugged his shoulders and flicked the ash off his cigarette.

"It's all wrong", he said. "It's just Bolshevism."

I looked over my shoulder to see if anyone were listening. My Italian friend did not seem to mind.

"The whole system is wrong," he said; "Italy is marching steadily towards disaster."

It was difficult to believe that, with the sun shining on the Lago Maggiore, and in this garden where pretty women were under the blue shadows of the striped umbrellas in an earthly paradise.

"The Government," said my Italian friend, careless of being overhead, "makes roads to create work. It distributes money and food to those who are unemployed. It gives the people cheap trips to Rome and back. All very nice for them, of course! But who helps the Italian manufacturers and business men, who are being ruined—who indeed are already ruined, like me?"

"As bad as that?" I asked.

"Worse than that", he answered.

He gave me a gloomy picture of business life in Italy. Everyone was taxed for unproductive public works, for an army of officials, for an army of police. It was just Bolshevism under another name.

A group of little girls in black frocks and white blouses marched along the esplanade. The Italian looked at them with a benign smile.

"I have a little niece", he told me. "She is six years old. When she went to school for the first time she was asked to bring fifteen lira. She brought them. She became enrolled in the Balilla, and was taught to hold up her right hand at the name of Il Duce. Every baby born in Italy, and they keep on being born—poor infants—becomes *ipso facto* a Fascist. No question about it. No case of conscientious conviction. There you are, my little one—Fascismo for you, and don't squeal about it! Wonderful, isn't it?"

He regretted the old days of liberal thought and free speech when a man might say anything he liked, even if it were nonsense.

He said too much and too openly, that little man in the garden of the

Hôtel Suisse on Lake Maggiore. I had a message from his wife some time later. He was in grave danger and in hiding. Could I procure an English *visa* so that he could bring his family to England? I wrote to Sir John Simon, the Home Secretary, and other friends helped him. He came to England and set up a little restaurant in the Brompton Road, and his wife used to kiss my hand every time I went there. Later on when the second World War began and Mussolini went over to Hitler after the fall of France, thousands of Italians were rounded up in London under 18b of the Civil Defence Act. Among them was this Italian friend of mine. Again I heard from his wife. Her husband had been in prison for some time. Would I help to get him out? I wrote to Mr. Herbert Morrison, and said that I thought it strange that an Italian hostile to Fascism, who had come over here by the help of one Home Secretary, should be kept in prison by another Home Secretary. I don't know whether it was this letter which unlocked his cell, but shortly afterwards he was liberated. And in my garden now there is a little model of the Simplon tunnel with stones and pebbles from Lago Maggiore. It was sent to me as a souvenir by the former proprietor of the Hôtel Suisse, on that lovely lake.

In Milan I talked with our British Consul and he gave me a gloomy picture of trade and finance in Italy.

"All the people in Milan are looking very well-to-do," I said. "I can't understand it."

We had, indeed, remarked on the well-dressed crowds in the Galleria —that rendezvous of clerks and typists and business men after office hours. They all looked smart, and better dressed than a similar crowd in London.

The Consul smiled, and admitted the difficulty of finding the truth.

"One has to get down to essential facts," he said. "They're all living on a very thin margin."

He gave me many essential facts, and they revealed Italy's bad financial state, with drastic cuts in wages, and rising prices, while trade languished. And yet, looking back on that conversation the mystery is that Mussolini was able to finance a war and keep his fleet in being, and supply his armies, and feed his people. How is it done by a bankrupt state? That is one of the mysteries.

As we travelled through Lombardy, stopping at Bergamo, and Brescia, and Verona, and in many small towns and villages drenched in sun, old in beauty, I heard the same story from people with whom I talked. Taxes were terrible. Prices were mounting. There was no business. Italy was on the edge of ruin. Yet because of the sun, perhaps, which is worth more than gold, the peasants and the working classes looked happy enough under this Fascist régime. In the fields the peasants sang at their work. In the little market places the barbers were doing a good trade. There was no outward sign of misery. But in Verona I heard a fact which was revealing of things beneath the surface.

An unemployed man, as I was told by an Italian, gets three lira fifty a day for a period of three months. I had paid as much as three lira fifty for a cup of coffee.

5

The Wisdom of the Old

We did not go to Rome on this European journey but I had been there shortly before and had had a conversation, among many others, with a remarkable old man which I now repeat because it was a prophecy of things to come, partly fulfilled, and partly unfulfilled, but interesting now to read again in the light of what has happened since then.

It was an old gentleman named Cardinal Gasparri who, for many years had been in the Vatican closely in touch with foreign affairs. I had a letter of introduction to him which I took to his villa where he was living in retirement. At the gate was a man in livery who shook his head when I asked to see the Cardinal.

"His Eminence is not receiving to-day," he said in Italian.

I spoke a few words in that tongue—

"*E molto importante.*"

He shrugged his shoulders slightly but condescended to take the letter. Presently he returned from the courtyard and was deferential.

"His Eminence will see you."

I waited in an antechamber which led into an immense drawing room with a painted ceiling, and heavy candelabra, and long curtains which kept out the sunlight. There was a faint scent of polished wood and old furniture. An unseen hand touched some electric switches and the candelabra were lighted one by one until their cascades of crystal were all glittering. There was a shuffle of feet along a corridor. The man in livery appeared and said "His Eminence" and bowed before retiring with a sign that I should enter the great drawing room.

An old man in a black gown with a red sash and a red skull cap stood peering at me.

"Why have you come to see me?" he asked in French. "I do not understand."

I tried to make him understand. I was travelling in Europe, I told him, trying to find out what was happening below the surface of an uneasy peace, the new groupings of powers, fears and dangers of some new catastrophe. I knew his Eminence was in retirement, but doubtless he was still interested in all these things. Something of the sort I said in French.

He shook his head and a faint smile twisted his thin old lips.

"There is nothing I can say," he told me. "I am in retirement. I have no first-hand information."

He made a sign to me to be seated, and then sat down himself, wearily, on an uncomfortable couch of the Empire period, very stiff for an old man's bones. I think I must have disturbed his afternoon nap. He gaped behind his transparent hand several times, and once or twice while he talked, seemed to doze off for a moment, pulling himself back to wakefulness with an effort. But he talked, and I listened attentively.

"The situation is no doubt grave. There is no real peace in the minds of nations, no sense of security. Everybody speaks of the need for disarmament, but everybody increases armaments—even England now. It is all very unwise. It is all very dangerous."

He sighed deeply and pushed his red skull cap—a cardinal's cap—on one side.

"We were very near war not long ago," he told me. "If German Nazis had invaded Austria, Italy would have taken action with her army. It was a delicate situation. Some accident may happen like that, any day, to light the fires of war again in Europe. One never knows. One reads the headlines of the morning papers with apprehension, because anything may happen to stir up the fires of war again. . . . There is Germany, of course. Germany cannot be ignored. She has a hundred thousand officers fully trained—the *cadre* of her Army Staff. All her young men are drilling as soldiers. There are evil minds in Germany, though the mass of the people are good and honest. So far they are not sufficiently armed. Herr Hitler is sincere in saying he wants peace—for some time! The internal situation inside Germany is not good. It is far from good. They may have another revolution. There will be a struggle for power among the leaders."

Not long after he spoke those words to me there was a struggle for power among the German leaders followed by Hitler's blood purge of Röhm and his confederates.

It was at this moment that the old Cardinal seemed to doze off—pulling himself back to consciousness with a start.

"Excuse me," he said, "were we talking about Signor Mussolini?"

I was very glad that he should talk about Signor Mussolini.

"He has a strong will power and a considerable genius," said His Eminence. "His word is law. The people obey him and believe in him."

He seemed to think that Mussolini also wanted peace—for a time.

He had something to say about the general spread of Fascism in Europe.

N

"It is the impatience of youth and their need of leadership. But there is, of course, always the danger of a revolutionary movement against dictatorship. The only way of criticism must be revolutionary. England will never become Fascist. With France it is different. There is much corruption in high places in France. French youth is roused against the Government. Their political groups are arming against each other. I foresee much trouble in that country."

He was silent for a few moments and struggled again with the desire for sleep.

"Shall I tell you what is the real danger for Europe?" he asked after this interval.

I begged him to tell me.

He shifted forward a little and peered at me.

"Japan has captured Manchuria. Next she will dominate China. There will be six hundred million Asiatics under discipline. As a Japanese gentleman said to me the other day: 'When that happens Europe will have to be careful.' That is true. Europe will have to be careful. It is better for the European nations to stand together. It is indeed urgently necessary. Japanese competition is becoming irresistible in the world's markets. The Japanese labourer works ten hours a day for six *sous* a day. In Switzerland the Japanese are selling cheap watches by weight—like potatoes!—at thirty francs the kilo. What can we do against that? This cheap production has already destroyed England's cotton industry in the East. Meanwhile European nations are quarrelling and rearming for another war. That is the way of suicide. It is very unwise, don't you think?"

I agreed, and when I left the presence of this very old gentleman I felt that I had been talking with one so near to the other world that he could look upon the world in which we live with the vision of Eternity. Not all of what he said has come true, but it was very near the truth. Japan made that effort to dominate China. But for Pearl Harbour his prophecy would have been fulfilled.

6

POWDER MAGAZINE

When we resumed our journey we crossed the Brenner Pass into Austria. In the town of Bolzano on the frontier we talked with Austrians who had been taken over by Italy. They were very bitter about it. And one young Austrian, an ex-soldier like all of them, was bitter about the general state of Europe.

"There is talk of a new war," he said. "If any officer comes to me and says: 'You are wanted for a new war' I shall shoot him dead on the spot. The last war was enough. What madmen will make another?"

But in Austria we found great conflict and trouble in the minds of people with whom we talked. Many thought that the Government of Dr. Dollfuss was in danger. Many thought that the only solution for Austria was union with Germany.

In a café in Innsbruck I had a talk with a young man who glanced over his shoulder now and then. But there were only two other people in the café. One was a young girl writing a love letter with a soft look in her eyes and a little secret smile.

"Outwardly," said the young man, "Austria is peaceful. Underneath it is a powder magazine."

Many of the young men, he said, were desperate, and ready to resort to any kind of violence. They were already making bombs and setting them off. If they were Social Democrats they hated the Government for the bombardment of Vienna and the suppression of their party. If they were Nazis they hated the Government for playing into the hands of Italy and preventing their union with Hitler's Germany.

This young man himself thought that perhaps the Dollfuss régime was the best for Austria. But he didn't see how the situation could last. So much passion must lead to an explosion.

The situation did not last. Six weeks later the Hofburg in Vienna was attacked by a group of men, while another group seized the wireless station. Little Dr. Dollfuss was dragged from his room in the chancellery and then shot, but took some time to bleed to death.

7

MARCHING YOUTH

I was in Berlin in the early part of 1934, a year after Hitler had come to power. Although I had been to Germany several times since the war my visits had been at a time when the German people were hag-ridden by inflation, when there was an immense amount of unemployment, and when German youth seemed to be without hope, as well as without work. Now I noticed that a great change had come over the scene. Youth was marching about in endless parades, carrying banners, playing bands, singing martial songs, and these boys, I must say, looked in fine health and high spirit. But what did it all mean, this discipline and parade of youth, and this worship of Adolf Hitler by the younger people—though not, I found, by the middle-aged and the elderly?

There was an exhibition in Berlin called *Der Front*. All day long German boys had their noses glued to the window panes. German students with their girls paid a mark to go inside. Now and again, but rarely, a middle-aged German with his wife stared at the windows, hesitated for a moment, and then went in. It was a war exhibition, devoted to the instruments of slaughter—trench mortars, machine-guns, aerial torpedoes, large-sized shells, lurid pictures of battle by sea, land, and air. A guide showed a young German girl how to work a machine-gun. She was very much amused by this demonstration. "*Ausgezeichnet!*" she exclaimed, as though a machine-gun were a charming piece of mechanism suitable for the home.

Why all this revival of interest in things which the rest of the world—England, anyhow—was trying to forget?

I asked this question of a young Nazi I encountered, as I have recorded in my book *European Journey*.

"It's difficult to explain," he answered, "but it's not at all what foreigners think. You see, in England and France you were proud of your soldiers after the war. It was your victory. You put up your memorials. You had your two minutes silence. But in Germany it was all too painful at first, and our returning soldiers were insulted by Communists and Social Democrats. They had their badges torn from their shoulders, and their Iron Crosses were grabbed. No one remembers the heroism of the German troops and all their victories and sufferings. Now at last, under Hitler, we wish to remember. We're proud to remember the courage of our fathers and all they went through during those frightful years. It's a revival of German pride in heroic achievement, but not a revival of the war spirit, or the wish for another war, which we all know would be the end of European civilisation. You won't find a single Nazi who has war in his mind—except perhaps as a menace of war against Germany itself. I assure you that is true."

He believed it was true at that time, and much later I found that great numbers of Germans, including the young Nazis, believed that Hitler was sincere when he said—as almost always he said (—in spite of *Mein Kampf*—) that he desired peace in Europe and was working to preserve the peace. Over a tea table in the Fürstenhof Hotel I had a talk with an American lady who had long been married to a German. When I expressed to her my fears that this militarism of German youth would lead to a new war, she was startled and shocked.

"What makes you say so?" she asked.

"Most people in England, and everybody in France," I told her, "believe that Germany is preparing to fight again."

"But that is impossible!" she cried. "It's ridiculous! Why should they believe such an absurdity?"

I gave her some of the reasons. (I quote again from my book written at that time.)

Every news-reel in every cinema, I told her, showed German youth drilling, marching, parading. There was a conviction that Germany was rearming secretly, and that every German was a soldier. Hitler's book *Mein Kampf* was not exactly reassuring. All that stuff about absorbing the Nordic people, and extending German Kultur over Holland, Denmark, Sweden, parts of Hungary, Austria and Czechoslovakia, was alarming.

The Hitler régime had begun with brutality against the Jews. The spirit of the bully was exalted by the Nazi creed. Men like Rosenberg, with his mystical nonsense about the Germanic race and the old paganism, was preaching a cult against intellectualism, and proclaiming the right of instinct and biological force. It was a denial of all civilised ideals. It was a hark-back to barbarism. There was a book by a man called Banse, a professor with an official appointment, as a University instructor. It was written in the spirit of blood lust. It exalted war. It called upon the German people to smash France and England in the fulfilment of a divine destiny. There was a lot of rubbish like that.

So I spoke and the American lady, who had lived many years of married life in Germany, listened to my words attentively. She was very much surprised.

"My German friends laugh at Rosenberg's nonsense," she said. "Do you think they take it seriously? As for that man Banse I have never heard of him, and I doubt whether the people I know have ever heard of him."

She said the German boys liked marching about just as English boys loved cricket or football. It gave them a sense of comradeship which is a great need, she said, in the minds of young Germans.

"I know so many of these young Nazis," she told me. "They talk very freely to me because I am the wife of a German and therefore a German. They never talk of wanting war. On the contrary they hate the idea of it. If ever they speak of war it is because they have a fear that France and her Allies will force it upon them. Naturally they feel they must defend the Fatherland. Wouldn't any other nation feel the same? Wouldn't England, if it were threatened with invasion?"

It was then that I became aware of several young waiters of the Fürstenhof listening with their ears cocked.

"We had better get into a quiet corner," I suggested. "We are having an audience."

We retired and continued our talk. She was a very knowledgeable lady, I thought. She knew Hitler and admired him.

"He is all for peace," she assured me. "Foreigners don't believe in his sincerity. But I am certain that he wants to make a friendship with France. It is his strongest wish. And you must admit that he has said so publicly many times. Why doesn't France accept the offer?"

I repeat this conversation because now that we know what Hitler did and how he led his people into war and to the uttermost ruin, it is interesting, I think, to remember that people who knew him believed quite honestly that he stood for peace. I met others in Berlin who believed in his sincerity—some of them English people who met him often. They sized him up as a fanatic with the obstinacy of a fanatic, but sentimental, emotional, and honest. His head, they said, had not been turned by power. On the contrary he had abandoned some of his wild ideas, and the verbal fury of the demagogue. He was anxious to preserve peace in Europe, they told me. His claim to equality in arms down to any level, or up to any level, was, they thought, just. Its justice had been admitted—and then repudiated—by England and France. He was, they told me, a very pleasant person to meet, perfectly modest and unassuming, rather gentle even . . .

It was before the thirtieth of June, 1934, when he was not so gentle with those who had been his comrades.

8

AN AMBASSADOR TALKS

I had an introduction from a member of his family to Monsieur François-Poncet, the French Ambassador in Berlin. In my book *European Journey* I had to disguise his identity as a "French business man", but there is no reason now for that camouflage. When I was shown into his room in the French Embassy he glanced at his wrist-watch and said: "I can give you half an hour. What do you want to know?"

I told him I wanted to know his views about Germany under Hitler's régime.

"Let me divide my enquiries and conclusions," he said, "into eight chapters. . . . Chapter I."

The gist of Chapter I was that 35 per cent of the German people were ready to die for Hitler.

"And that," said the French Ambassador, "is a lot in a people of sixty million and more."

They were willing to die for Hitler, he said, because he promised them all the things they most desired—employment of youth, freedom from foreign restraint, pride of race, hero worship, with Hitler as hero.

"The mass of people outside that 35 per cent," said the French Ambassador, "are indifferent and waiting to see what is going to happen, hoping for the best but fearing the worst.

"Then there is a minority—but an important and large minority—of bitter critics who think that Hitler is a low-class adventurer, surrounded by men of evil character, bent upon the destruction of property, religion, and the old tradition of German character. They hate him because he is so powerful against the Junker spirit. They hate him because he threatens the industrialists. They hate him for a hundred different reasons, some of them intelligent and some of them passionate.

"Chapter II. Germany rearms. It's half accomplished. There is no doubt of that. I have the facts. Thousands of men have been taken on by Krupps and other armament factories. Their imports of steel and iron have been enormously increased. What are they making? Safety razors? Steel nibs? They are making guns, and rifles, and every kind of weapon. In two years they will have rearmed. We must regard it as a *fait accompli*. We cannot stop it now. What then is France—I speak from my own point of view—what then are we French people going to do about it?"

I was interested to know, and he continued his idea in Chapter III.

"We must accept the *fait accompli* and exert control. France, England, Italy, Czechoslovakia, Poland and other countries must—or should, if they have any sense—agree to act in case of German aggression. That is the only policy. There is no alternative by which European civilisation may be saved. A preventive war is not possible. The people wouldn't stand for it. It is out of the picture . . .

"Let us then proceed to Chapter IV. That must penetrate more deeply into German psychology. Why, for instance, is Germany a danger to the European system? Why should we be afraid of granting her equality, even without control? . . . Chapter V."

Before he reached the end of his analysis his time was up, but he went to a cabinet and unlocked a drawer and took out a typewritten document.

"You may care to read this," he said. "It sums up my ideas about Germany after much research and reading. You will be the only one to read it, if you read it. I am sending it to the French Foreign Office. There, no one will read it. It will go into a pigeon-hole. Let me have it back within two hours."

I thanked him very much and took the document. In a taxi-cab to the Adlon I glanced at it and felt my back hair rising slightly on my scalp. I am an absent-minded man and lose things all over the place—cigarette-holders, letters, pocket-books, almost everything that I carry loose about me. Supposing I were to leave this document in a German taxi-cab? It was very private. Pinned to the first sheet was a letter signed by the French Ambassador to his Foreign Office.

I clung on to that document as though it were part of my own flesh until I reached my bedroom in the Adlon Hotel. Then I locked the door and read it with intense interest. It was an historical and psychological analysis of German mentality.

The French Ambassador had been reading a lot of German literature. He had soaked himself in the German *mythus* as interpreted by Alfred Rosenberg and others. It was, he wrote, a hark-back to paganism and the German tribal system. That system was essentially different from the European and Christian culture, as developed by the Romans and the Catholic Church. It did not recognise a nation. It did not acknowledge the value of constitutional government under a monarchy supported by a Parliament and by free discussion. It did not even acknowledge the limitation of frontiers. It was racial and tribal. Germanic tribes would be governed by chieftains, under one supreme chief whose word would be law, and whose person would be half divine, like one of the old pagan deities, half god and half warrior. The tribal system would extend beyond the frontiers of nations. Blood would call to blood. There would be a loose confederation of the Germanic race with its roots deep in the primeval forests. Scandinavians, groups in Poland, Hungary and Russia would come within the tribal confederation. They too belonged to the German forest with its deep roots in the pagan past. The old gods were not dead. They were only sleeping. They had been dispossessed by the Christian myth, weakening, hostile to instinct and nature, devitalising, dehumanising. Strength, courage, vitality, would be the virtues of manhood again, instead of introspection, intellectualism, and morbid consciousness. The pagan gods, the pagan spirit, would stride back into life.

Monsieur François-Poncet devoted many typewritten sheets to this analysis of the stuff written by men like Rosenberg, and taught to young minds in Germany. It was not taken seriously enough, he thought, by those outside Germany. In his judgment it was very serious. It was a challenge to European civilisation and Christianity. Frenchmen and others were apt to dismiss it, and say it was just the ravings of a few lunatics. But it was a definite philosophy held by men who had the destiny of a nation in their hands. It was the education being given to young minds, plastic in the hands of those who moulded them. One could not understand what was happening in Germany—Hitler's advent, the spread of the Nazi cult, the attack on Jews and Catholics, and the Protestant dogma—without taking all this into account. It was not an accessory of the Nazi faith. It was fundamental. It was the mainspring of German energy. It was the reason why we could not regard them as equals and partners in the European progress.

That was the gist, as far as I could remember it, of the French Ambassador's document addressed to the French Foreign Office, who would not read it. It was, in my opinion, masterly, and I was deeply impressed by it. I was also anxious to get rid ot it. I dared not copy it out, as I should have liked to do, and at the end of two hours I drove back with it to the French Embassy, and delivered it with my very deep thanks.

9

Those Who Were Bored

This report by François-Poncet, one of the most brilliant of French Ambassadors, left its mark on my mind, but afterwards I talked with many Germans who ridiculed the philosophy of paganism and had no use for the writings of Alfred Rosenberg. My own experience then and afterwards, in watching the life of Germany and talking to its people in all walks of life, led me to the same conclusion as the French Ambassador's regarding the numbers of Hitler's fanatics. But I put it in a different way. It seemed to me that, roughly every German under thirty was a hero-worshipper of the Führer. Between those of thirty and forty there was an uncertain and doubtful allegiance to him. Those over forty—again roughly—were against him, secretly and furtively or, now and again in private conversation, passionately.

I remember being in a big Berlin café when Hitler was announced to speak over the microphone. The loud speaker was turned on and before Hitler's speech there blared out the old tune of 'Heil Dir im Siegeskranz'. Next to me was a group of German business men. They went on talking in low voices. At another table was a woman writing a letter. She went on writing. The only man who stood up was a little fellow with his tie creeping over his collar at the back of his neck. No one in this crowded café listened to Adolf Hitler. They were nearly all middle-aged people. So it was on a morning when many officials and Gauleiter were required to take a new oath of allegiance to Hitler swearing obedience to his orders. Loud speakers boomed down Unter den Linden. A tremendous parade of youth had marched off to the assembly ground. But in Unter den Linden the passers-by paid no attention to Dr. Goebbels' oratory over the loud speakers. It seemed to me very queer.

10

THE EVIL SPELL

On this European journey, with Agnes now with me, we motored through Bavaria, stopping at many little towns and villages, and talking to the people, all of whom went out of their way to be friendly because we were English. Looking back upon what has happened since —all the bombing, all the German atrocities, all the slaughter of civilians on both sides, and now the utter ruin of Germany—one can only denounce again those men who led those people, those friendly folk, as certainly they were, along the road to war, by poisonous propaganda and by the old irresistible call to patriotism when once war is started.

But recent and frightful history has proved that many Germans under the evil spell of Hitler and by some racial and primitive strain were capable of foul cruelties and mass murders and human degradation to a hellish depth. None of that was revealed to us, nor was it in the minds I am certain of the decent folk we met.

We went to Munich and stayed awhile. It was a city to which my wife and I had been several times since the first World War and the old head waiter at the Vierjahreszeiten greeted us as old friends, but confessed to us one day in a low voice that he was deeply anxious about the future of Germany under this Nazi system.

"It is very dangerous," he said. "Where are we going to? Down what road does it lead?"

One morning I went to the Brown House to find a young man named Hoffmann to whom I had been recommended. It was the headquarters of Hitler's storm troopers. There was no guard at the door and I went in unchallenged. Several young storm troopers were in the hall, and when I enquired after Herr Hoffmann one of them pointed to a house opposite and said I would find him there. On my way out I peered through some hoardings and saw deep excavations. I was told that an air-raid shelter was being built with gas proof chambers capable of holding four thousand people.

"But why?" I asked a German friend. "Who is going to bomb Munich?"

"Frankly, I don't understand it," he said; "Hitler promises us peace, and I believe him."

Mr. Hoffmann, who was a handsome young man with brown hair dyed by liquid gold, believed that Hitler wanted peace.

He laughed when I told him that the French people and many English believed that Hitler was preparing for a new war.

"Germany doesn't want to attack anybody," he answered. "Hitler knows what war means. He was blinded for half a year. He went through the horrors. He knows, as we all know, that another war would end European civilisation."

He hoped that there would be a friendly agreement with France. It would be greatly welcomed by all Germans who had no quarrel with France.

I spoke frankly and told him the cause of French fears—this re-arming, this marching about, this aggressive national spirit preached by Hitler.

He thought all that was a misreading of Germany by superficial observers.

"Anybody who stays long enough in Germany to get at the truth must admit, if he is honest, that we have no aggressive plans or purpose. We are rearming for self-defence."

"Against whom?" I asked him. "Who is likely to attack you?"

He looked at me with very blue luminous eyes.

"We may be invaded. We know that there is real danger. Germany is a corridor between France and Russia. If Russia has a war with Japan other nations may be involved. France may want to march through Germany, to link up with Russia."

It seemed to me a fantastic idea, but this young man believed it. Other men I met believed it.

We became friendly with a German Baron of youngish middle age who spoke English perfectly and was a talented artist. My friend Edgar Lander thought his water-colour drawings were good. He had no liking for Nazi officers, but because of his position was chief of the Labour Camps in Bavaria. With him we went to visit some of these camps and were much impressed by them. The boys looked healthy and fit. They had good food and plenty of rest. They were of all classes and types, from German Universities downwards, and according to the new law every young man in Germany had to put in six months of this training before resuming his studies.

Lander thought the idea ought to be carried out in England. It would do our young toughs a lot of good, he thought—all those boys on the dole.

I talked with some of these German lads, and made them laugh. They all seemed to be in high spirits. One of them was stripped to the waist, sitting in the sun and polishing his boots.

"How do you like this kind of life?" I asked.

"Not bad," he said. "A fine open air life on the land. But it interrupts one's academic studies."

He told me that he got on very well with the other fellows, whatever their class or type. It was *Kameradschaft*. But naturally he drifted towards men of University education.

In the evenings they had lectures. I wondered what was taught in those lectures, and thought back to the analysis of Nazi philosophy by the French Ambassador in Berlin—the poisoning of the mind of youth, an education in brutality, a revival of paganism. That was a side of those Labour Camps which we did not see or hear.

11

WHAT FOR?

On our way out of Germany on that tour we came to Stuttgart, and as we sat in a beer garden young officers in the German Air Force were shaking collecting boxes under the noses of the passers-by. All the way on the roads we had seen streamers carrying the same slogans.

Lift Up Your Eyes.

Germany's Future is in the Air.

The German Folk must become Air-Minded.

Who helps the German Air Force helps Germany.

I spoke to the waitress who served us with tea.

She was a pleasant woman with smiling eyes, and after handing me some strawberries was very willing to talk.

"You are English?" she asked.

"Yes. I'm English."

"Englishmen are very polite," she told me, and I liked her compliment. I enquired into the state of things in Stuttgart.

She laughed and then gave a deep sigh with her hand on her bosom.

"It is hard on working women, especially if their men have been out of a job for three years like my husband. He is in work again now, *Gott sei dank!*"

She told me about wages and prices and general poverty.

"Everybody seems well dressed," I remarked.

She laughed again and then lowered her voice until some girls passed.

"Germans make a good show in the streets," she told me. "But go into their homes. You will find a lot of poverty there. Everybody has to stint. Every *pfennig* has to be counted. Every rag of underclothing has to be patched up. Food has to be served out carefully, by spoonfuls. The father of a family grows white at the thought of his rent and taxes."

She hastened to say that she was not complaining for her own sake. She agreed with Hitler that women ought not to take the men's places.

"So you are all for Hitler and the Nazis?" I suggested.

She looked at me with honest smiling eyes.

"Did I say that?"

She lowered her voice again.

"I'm not sure about this Nazi government. The boys and girls go marching about with flags. Well, if it keeps them happy that's good. But it doesn't bring in bread and butter. And we working people have collecting boxes under our noses every day of the week and put in a few coins. But where does all the money go? Some people think it goes to buy nice uniforms and big motor cars for the smart young officers. That's not quite right. Now there's the collection for the Air Force."

"Yes," I said, "what's it all about?"

"It might be dangerous", she said. "What are they for, all those aeroplanes? That's what I ask myself sometimes. What do we want them for? What is the meaning of all this propaganda about a danger creeping close to us?"

"That's what I've been asking", I told her.

She breathed hard, with her hand to her bosom.

"If war comes again I shall die! I know the meaning of war. I was in Strasburg when it happened. My husband was in the Württemberg regiment. His letters told me all about the horrors. And now he's anxious, and says it might happen again. No one wants war. I'm certain of that. Germany suffered too much in the last to want another war. But it may happen. Wars happen without people wanting them."

I saw that for a moment tears had come into her eyes. She blinked them away and spoke a few words which touched me.

"I do not complain for myself. I am only afraid for the young people who do not understand. And it is no use talking unless one tells the truth."

I believed that she was telling me the truth as far as she could see it in her simple soul. I am sure the things she told me—those hopes and those fears—were in the minds of millions of German women of her class and age. "Wars happen without people wanting them", she said. Another war happened and, in my belief, still the great majority of German people did not want it to happen. But now they are starving amidst their ruins, and women like that one in Stuttgart see their children getting weak and dying of disease, and the innocent are suffering for the guilty, as always happens. But few people have any pity for them.

Three weeks after I had left Stuttgart—on the thirtieth of June—there was a purge of high Nazi officers—Hitler's closest friends and collaborators, and many others including Röhm, Chief of the Staff of the S.A.—the Brown Shirts. Old Cardinal Gasparri in Rome had been right when he told me that there would be a struggle for power among the German leaders. In Berlin, General Goering—that fat man whom I had seen sometimes in the streets of the capital, joking with the people on the sidewalks as he drove past them—had been busy. He summoned a meeting of Press men and told them there had been a plot against Hitler's life. He had not worn mittens, he told them, and, as he spoke, pulled off a pair of soiled white gloves. The plotters were dead. General Schleicher was dead, and his wife was dead having flung herself across the body of her husband when the Blackshirts fired at him. No evidence was given of the plot. The bodies of the dead men, who had been the heroes of the Nazis, proclaimed by Dr. Goebbels, had been cremated. Dead men tell no tales.

I listened to Hitler's speech in the Reichstag as it came over the wireless to a little old house where then I lived in Ewhurst, Surrey. His voice was harsh and hysterical at times.

"I gave the order to shoot," he screamed. "Only ruthlessness and bloody intervention could have averted revolution. For twenty-four hours I myself was the Supreme Court for the German people." . . .

It was from a high German officer, a year later, that I heard many details of the plot, and he put his life into my hands in telling me. He had first heard that something was going to happen when a young friend of his called upon him one day and said: "I am finished." He was in a desperate state of mind, and confessed that he had become involved in a plot against Hitler on behalf of Röhm. A group of officers in the Brown Army had been selected to kill Hitler, and he was one of them.

"Why don't you get out of it?" asked his friend. "It means certain death for you."

"Too late," the young man answered. "I am up to my neck in it. My name is on the list."

That night he shot himself. Two of the other officers gave away the plot. Hitler flew to Munich before Röhm and the others were ready for him. It was they who died.

We went into rural Germany again on the way back to France. Agnes parted from us in Stuttgart and went back to England. She had work to do. We came to one of the last towns in Germany called Pirmasens. We had midday dinner there and fell into conversation with the company gathered round the table. They were very friendly to us, finding we were English, as all the Germans we had met had been friendly. When we left we had an ovation. Our hostess came out into the street with her husband. She was a buxom woman and good humour danced in her eyes. She shook hands with each one of us as though we were parting after a long stay in Pirmasens. The other people in the inn waved hands to us from the windows.

"The Germans are friendly folk," said Lander. "They seem to like us—and one can't help liking them."

Some years later he wished the entire German race to be exterminated. And some years later—only five—I stood beyond the Maginot Line looking over No Man's Land which was wide hereabouts. There were some deserted villages and towns beyond the German front line— the Siegfried Line which had been built by hundreds of thousands of those boys in Labour Camps. The French soldiers had come across to meet them. "Nix bombe-bombe!" said the French soldiers in sham German. The Maginot Line was stuffed with artillery pointing towards Germany. The second World War had already been going for six months, but without much fighting. But no Frenchman now went far into that No Man's Land, except at night in scouting parties. And at night men of ours in the Guards, and other regiments sent down by Lord Gort, lay out there freezing to death, almost, in a hard winter. I looked through a pair of field glasses at those abandoned villages.

"What's the name of that place?" I asked an officer who was with me.

"Pirmasens," he said. "A sizable place without a living soul there."

12

INVASION OF AUSTRIA

I was in Vienna several times during the régime of little Dr. Dollfuss, the 'pocket dictator' as his enemies called him. Even his friends made jokes about this miniature man, who had dissolved the Austrian Parliament when its parties were so hopelessly divided that no stable government could be formed with any majority behind it. "Dr. Dollfuss," said one story, "is walking up and down under his bed thinking out a new Constitution." He wished to found a kind of Christian Commonwealth, but there was a touch of Fascism in his plans, and young Prince Starhemberg, who supported him with a volunteer army paid for by Signor Mussolini, was not remarkable as a Christian when he ordered his artillery to bombard the working men's dwellings in Vienna.

I sat one evening in the room of one of Dr. Dollfuss's heads of departments. He was a cripple with a fine delicate face and long thin hands, and he gave me a seat by his side.

"This is a grave day for Austria", he said. "We may be invaded at any moment by battalions of Nazis. For months they have been assembling on our frontier and gathering strength. Now they are marching. If they cross the frontier to-night there will be great bloodshed, for we shall defend ourselves. Excuse me while I get the latest reports."

He was busy on the telephone. While we talked the telephone kept ringing and he listened to messages coming in which he interpreted for me. Austrian troops were moving to the frontier. . . . The Nazi groups were assembling at different points. . . . The situation was very threatening.

"What is Italy going to do?" I asked.

He looked at me with anxious eyes. His long thin hands touched some papers on his desk, the flimsies of cable messages.

"We are waiting to know," he said. "That is the great question. Signor Mussolini has promised us support, but has not yet moved his troops."

He moved his troops that night. Hitler ordered back his Nazis. He was biding his time and put a black mark against the name of Dollfuss. It was a sentence of death.

The main object of my visit had been to get an interview with Dr. Dollfuss, and this little Austrian baron whose name I have forgotten promised that he would arrange this for me in a week or two. At the moment the little doctor was heavily engaged and deeply anxious. Would I give him time?

I never had that interview. All doors had been open to me in Vienna, but after a brief visit to Budapest all doors were closed. I could not understand it. When I rang up Austrian officials I found they all had bad colds or were otherwise stricken in health. I knew I was being frozen out, and I had no notion why, until after my return to England when I had a letter from a friend in the British Embassy. He told me that several articles had appeared in the *News Chronicle* unsigned except by "our special correspondent", strongly hostile to the Dollfuss régime. The British Embassy in Berlin knew the author of those articles—the wife of John Gunther, the American journalist—but they were unable to say so, and their denial that I had written them was not accepted by the Austrian Foreign Office. Knowing that I was an old *Daily Chronicle* man they were convinced that I was the author of this hostile criticism and shut all doors in my face. I bear no grudge against the Gunthers for this misfortune, of which they were entirely ignorant and which I have never mentioned to them.

I was in Vienna again within a few hours of the tragic episode which led to the bombardment of the working class settlements—those big and beautiful blocks of buildings on the outer Ring which had been built by the Socialist municipality out of money raised by special bonds bought by the workers themselves. They were inhabited by ordinary working folk, but among them were groups of ardent young Social Democrats,

LYON
(By Edgar Lander)

Bolzano
may 1914

BOLZANO
(By Edgar Lander)

GREEK REFUGEES FROM ASIA MINOR
(By Edgar Lander)

Corpus Christi night.
Innsbruck 30th May

INNSBRUCK
(By Edgar Lander)

deeply hostile to the Fascist forces under Prince Starhemberg. Starhemberg, I was told, was ordered to wipe out these nests of Democrats as the price of Mussolini's military support and financial aid to Austria. I cannot vouch for that, but in Austria it was generally believed.

He advanced towards Vienna by way of Linz, and the Social Democrats in Vienna, mostly young men and boys, seized their rifles, took up position on the roofs of the Goethe Haus, and the other big blocks of working class dwellings, and prepared to defend these positions. Their leaders declared a general strike, but something misfired and the response was only partial. The leaders themselves fled, leaving the boys to do the fighting and the dying.

They hadn't a chance against Prince Starhemberg's artillery, firing at short range against these blocks of apartments, swarming with women and children. Some of the boys fought to the end, and their dead or wounded bodies lay in the courtyards. Others were captured and hanged.

I went to see the results of that bombardment. No journalist was allowed near, but some Austrian friends made a plan to get me in. I was to go to the Goethe Haus at a certain time. There I should see a working woman and a small girl struggling to carry in a big washing basket. I would help them carry it and go in with it. Of course I mustn't be too well dressed.

According to plan I met the woman with the washing basket and took one handle of it. But my way was instantly barred by an enormous policeman with a rifle slung over his shoulder.

"What do you want?" he asked in German, very grimly. "What are you doing here?"

I was aware that I did not resemble an Austrian working man and that I could not get away with anything like that.

"I am an English journalist," I told him. "I wish to see the bombarded dwellings."

He was a giant of a man and looked ferocious.

"Come with me," he said.

"I'm for it!" I thought. "I shall certainly be arrested and put into some unpleasant cell."

But he took me through the courtyard, entered the great block of buildings, and led me into a flat which had been smashed up by gunfire. Then this giant wept, with big tears dropping down his cheeks.

"It is terrible!" he said. "It is tragic! You see what they have done? These poor people here paid for these buildings out of their own money. They were not political, these mothers and children. They were honest, simple folk. Suddenly they found themselves under artillery fire. They were very frightened. All their belongings have been blown to bits. It is terrible!"

My heart went out to this big man with pity in his heart and tears blubbering down his cheeks. I put my arm round his shoulder and agreed with him that it was terrible. When he had pulled himself together he took me into other apartments where there were groups of people, searching among the ruins of their rooms for small treasures which might have escaped the effects of shell fire. They stopped their search and told me their tales of what had happened to them during the bombardment. They were tales of panic-stricken women and terrified children, and working men who were their husbands and fathers caught in this trap. Many of them took refuge in the cellars but others could not get down because of shell and machine-gun fire coming through the windows or the walls.

I went to several of these bombarded dwellings, one at Floridsdorf where the worst fighting had happened. One of my guides was a young bank clerk who had a nice flat where he lived with his young wife. Their little place had escaped the wreckage. There was a piano in one corner of the room, and good etchings on the walls. It was the home of a cultured young couple. They had escaped from death and high explosives, but the young man had been dismissed from his employment, and he told me that thousands of others, employed by the municipality and therefore suspected of being Socialists, had also lost employment.

"It is a very gloomy outlook," he said gravely. "My wife and I had a happy little home here. Now we are, perhaps, ruined, like so many others."

I still think that the bombardment of these houses was a crime of which little Dr. Dollfuss must share the guilt, though he did not give the orders. Such action did not seem beautifully in accord with his idea of a Christian state. Later in history Dr. Schuschnigg, his successor—when Dollfuss had been murdered by Nazi agents—returned from a bullying talk with Hitler and prepared for a plebiscite to decide the fate of Austria. He called upon the support of the Social Democrats in the sacred name of liberty. But not long before great numbers of them had been in concentration camps. It was rather late to rally up those who had been treated as enemies, and by that time Austrian youth, especially in the country districts, greeted each other with the words "*Heil Hitler!*" and gave the Nazi salute, and were eager to welcome their German comrades.

During the Dollfuss régime I came to know a woman at whose house I met many interesting people—some of them Jews of good class. Her name was Schwarzenwald, and she was headmistress of a well-known school—her own—in Vienna. She was a woman of flamboyant speech and dynamic quality of character, an egoist like so many successful people, but not without a healthy sense of humour and strong human sympathies. I visited her school and was impressed by her young ladies, one of whom—a pretty Austrian girl of eighteen or so —helped to show us round.

"I hope your discipline is not too severe?" I said to her. "I have seen that film called *Mädchen in Uniform*."

"Nothing of that kind here!" said the girl, with a laugh. "We are Austrians, and Frau Schwarzenwald does not believe in that kind of thing, thank heaven!"

Frau Schwarzenwald believed in the freedom of the soul, as once she told me over her own dinner table with most passionate words about the poisoning of German youth by the Nazi creed:

"It is their greatest crime", she cried. "They are inflicting terrible sufferings upon German Jews, they have a creed of brutality and cruelty, but their most evil crime is the debauchery of young minds, the deliberate infection of German youth with falsehood, lies and abomination. It is their worst crime against humanity."

Round the table where we sat more than one evening there were young women who spoke perfect English, having been educated in England, and an Austrian doctor, a lawyer, and an old man who had been a professor in the University. I listened to their talk. They were dismayed by the political passions seething in Austria.

"Austria is a volcano", said the young doctor, who was a Jew.

One extremely pretty young woman, fair-haired and blue-eyed, justified with warmth the defence of the working class dwellings by the Social Democrats, which others at table had deplored.

"They were the defenders of the Constitution," she cried. "They belonged to the *Schutzbund* which was organised to defend it. They were not cowards. They did not run away like so many others. They are martyrs for liberty."

"It would have been better if they had not taken to arms", said one of those at table. "After all we must support Dr. Dollfuss. Only he stands between us and a German invasion. If that happens . . ."

Everybody was silent. Some of them here, as I have said, were intellectual Jews. In that moment of silence they were thinking of the Nüremberg laws and the dreadful treatment of Jews down the Kurfürstendam in Berlin. If Hitler came to Austria it would be for them a sentence of death.

There was another family I came to know in Vienna. The father was a distinguished historian whose books were known in England. It was Professor Herz who had studied at the British Museum and the other

English libraries, and who had many English friends. His wife was a doctor with a good practice, especially for children, and they had a daughter who was also studying medicine. They invited distinguished people to meet me, and I heard many things about the Austrian situation and its past and present history. Professor Herz himself spoke always without passion and in a calm philosophical way, but he did not disguise from me the gravity of the situation nor his own peril. He was fortunate in leaving Vienna before the entry of the Nazis, and I met them again in London. It was hard on his wife that her Austrian degrees in medicine were not recognised in England so that she had to pass examinations all over again.

Vienna had lost its old tradition of gaiety and lightheartedness. Dead was the spirit of the Prater with its little restaurants and innumerable orchestras. Young people still went there, and I went with them, but it was impossible for them to be carefree again. There were too many dangers lurking round the corner, too many passions, even among the students. Brutality and cruelty took possession of youth, even in Austria. I was there again with my wife after the German invasion and the arrest of Schuschnigg. We gave lunch to a husband and wife whom we had come to know very well. The old man had been an official of the Hofburg and a director of the art galleries in Vienna. His wife, when we had first known her, had been intensely anti-Hitler. Now we found a change in her. All her ideas had changed, as she told us over the luncheon table.

"When the Germans came in," she said, "something happened to me. I went a little mad, if you like to think so. I found myself screaming out '*Heil Hitler!*' with thousands of others. I found myself marching about, hour after hour, waving a little flag in the midst of the crowds who had flung flowers at the German troops. It was the old German spirit which caught hold of me and all of us. We are, after all, German. Our spirit was united with our German brothers. Hitler has worked this miracle for unity. I know I thought otherwise when you were here before. But I have changed. Suddenly that night I changed."

So she talked with a flame in her eyes. . . . After she had gone I spoke to the young waiter who had been serving us. He was an intelligent and good-looking young man who had always done his best for us in the hotel of the Meisel und Schaden.

"How do you feel about the German occupation?" I asked.

He smiled and lowered his voice slightly.

"It has made a little difference", he said. "The *tempo* of life has been speeded up. We work harder, with longer hours, and we shall die quicker!"

On the night of the German invasion, and afterwards, the Austrian

Nazis—young ruffians and toughs wearing the sign of the *Swastika*—
had gone Jew-hunting, beating up harmless and defenceless people,
looting Jewish shops, robbing old Jewish women. They made educated
Jews and Jewesses scrub out anti-Nazi slogans which had been stamped
on the pavements. They stood round and jeered while this was being
done. I was told by many Austrians that German officers behaved
better than these young brutes and prevented some of their outrages.
One Jewish girl was accosted by a group of these Austrian Nazi youths.

"Why don't you carry a flag?" they asked. "Why aren't you wearing
flowers?"

She looked them straight in the eyes and raised her chin bravely.

"I am a Jewess," she told them; "I am against Hitler and all his
works."

"Is that so?—Well then . . ."

They caught hold of her and dragged her off and made her wash out
the latrines in their barracks. There were brutalities worse than that.

There will always be a difference of opinion about what would have
been the result of Dr. Schuschnigg's plebiscite if Hitler had not prevented
it by sending in his troops. I have heard Austrians declare that ninety
per cent or more would have voted for Austrian independence. That is
not my own impression, from all that I saw and heard during those
times when I was in Austria. The Nazi creed, and the desire for the
Anschluss which had long preceded it, had won over great numbers of
young men and women. A friend of mine in the British Embassy at
Budapest told me that he had to drive from that city to Vienna on the
very day the Germans entered Austria. He knew nothing about that
until he crossed the Austrian frontier, when he found that all the people
had 'gone mad' in the villages and towns through which he passed.

"I hate Hitler and the Nazi régime worse than anything," he told
me, "but as an honest observer I am bound to say that I never saw such
demonstrations of joy in every place I passed. All the young people,
and many of the old, were out flag-wagging, dancing, singing, holding
hands as though at some deliverance."

Be that as it may. The facts will always be disputed, but I remember
conversations I had with a little Hungarian lady at that time. She was an
attractive young creature though she suffered she said from "anguish"
which was an undefined malàdy.

"You English", she said, turning to me, "do not understand that
Fascism is the new pattern of life."

"I profoundly hope that is not true", I told her, and she smiled into
my eyes and said: "I am telling you. You will see. We are all advancing
towards the ant system of life. Call it what you will—Communism,
Fascism, Nazi-ism, Socialism. It is all the same thing. Youth likes to

have it that way. They want to worship the State. It is the new religion."

"Do you agree with it?" I asked.

"I hate it," she told me. "but I see the truth of things. I am not English. I am Hungarian. We are realists. The English see only what they wish to see, and believe only what they wish to believe. I have an English husband."

Going back to Austria I had an interview with Seyss-Inquart who had been leader of the Austrian Nazis, and now had been put in as civil head of Austria by his German master. Agnes came with me and helped out my bad German when we had passed many guards who saluted us impressively. Seyss-Inquart did not help me out. He was sullen, ill-tempered, and rude, not answering the questions I put to him about the future of Austria and the effect of the German occupation on the international situation. He was, I thought, the most unpleasant type of man I had ever met, with shifty eyes and a cruel mouth. History has proved him to be so.

PART XII

THE FOUR HORSEMEN PREPARE TO RIDE

1

MY SCIENTIST

AGNES had returned to England because she was heavily engaged in scientific research. That was her astonishing and gallant adventure towards the Autumn of life. She had begun from scratch, passing her matriculation and studying for a science degree at King's College.

She looked so young and was so gay that her fellow students had no idea of her age and treated her as one of themselves. At first her idea was to get a medical degree, but she found that her eyes were not good enough for anatomy, and she switched off to other branches of science, specialising in geology and obtaining a B.Sc. in due course. It was heroic of her, and when one thinks of all the memorising required it is astonishing that at her age she was able to absorb all this new knowledge in great detail. She fascinated her professors because of her wit and audacious comments, and only they knew that she was my wife and the mother of Anthony who was writing novels. She went on geological expeditions with her fellow students, and her hours were long at the College so that I felt I had lost her for a time. But I did not grouse about it, being filled with admiration for her achievement.

In addition to our country house—a little old farm called Bildens, at Ewhurst, afterwards damaged in the blitz, we had for a time a charming old house in Clievden Place, near Sloane Square, and then moved round the corner to "Little House" in D'Oyley Street, which was, I believe, once a farmhouse belonging to the Duke of Westminster when Eaton Square was a market garden. It was old and low-ceilinged but fitted up with electric lights and gadgets of all kinds. Its chief drawback was that it was rather dark because of its lattice windows. We spent most of the week here and only went down to Ewhurst for week-ends, except when Agnes had her vacations from the Imperial College of Science where now she was doing research work in minerals. It was mostly chemical analysis to ascertain their composition for practical and theoretical purposes, the last having to do with the age of the primeval rocks. Very few people were doing this and the results of my wife's work were published in scientific papers both here and in Germany—remarkable for a woman who had entered the scientific world so late, but who had a brilliant flair for this study.

It is my deep regreat that she did not embark on this adventure much earlier in life. In that work she was happy and used to tell me amusing anecdotes of those who worked at benches near to hers, including an Indian student, and an Egyptian who used to ask her advice upon all manner of things and discussed the philosophy of life with her. She looked so young in a black frock with a little white collar, and in whatever company she was she kept them laughing by her jokes. In one of my books I called her "The Laughing Lady", but in her heart sometimes she wept because of the sadness of life and the shadows of another war which filled her with horror.

2

MERRIE ENGLAND

We became friends with humble people in the neighbourhood. The dustman used to rush across the road whenever I emerged from "Little House" in D'Oyley Street, and shake me warmly by the hand, and give me his latest observations on the political situation. He had fought in the last war and was a type of the old soldier whom Kipling would have known. He had a liking for the Royal Family and, leaning on his broom gave me his views on that subject.

"The Royal Family is a very respectable lot," he said.

He had a personal liking for the King.

"He's all right—a nice fellow—not like that there Hitler in Germany, who puts folk into concentration camps because they don't see eye to eye with him. His Nibs does his duty like the rest of us, like I do mine, and I don't envy him his job."

Then there was a tall ruddy-faced man who sold papers outside the Court Theatre in Sloane Square. He was bitter about the Government and "Vested Interests". He thought our Statesmen were mostly crooks, and he had an idea that the people were being taken down the wrong road. All the unemployment, he said, was a scandal. The dole was demoralising thousands of men. There were fellows who would rather live on the dole than do an honest day's work.

I passed many a twenty minutes with this pessimist who handed out his papers to his customers as we talked, or, rather, as he talked. He was an out-and-out Socialist, and yet was also a patriotic man with no quarrel with the spirit of the English people during the time of King George's Jubilee.

"The crowds were as peaceable and law abiding, and good natured, as a school treat in a country park," he said; "I'm proud of England and I don't mind saying so."

I was proud of England too during that time of jubilation. Something was let loose in the spirit of the English people during that time and something surged up into it, the spirit of Merrie England, the quality and character of Shakespeare's men and women, and the England of Charles Dickens in a mood of jollity. Why this happened I don't know. There were great numbers of unemployed—there was much poverty—but King George's Jubilee called the people out into the streets and the parks where they came dancing and singing on glamorous nights.

The King himself was astonished by the ovations he had from those hundreds of thousands of his people, who surged outside Buckingham Palace all day long, shouting: "We want the King!" and cheering him with untiring enthusiasm. He had no notion until then that he had won the hearts of the people. He had been ill, and the doctors were nervous about him, but all this gave him a new lease of vitality, and greatly pleased him so that he drove out day after day without any official programme, into all parts of London, and especially into the poorest parts. In the mean streets every house and railing was beflagged, and vast crowds of Cockney urchins shouted themselves hoarse and chased the King's carriage where he sat smiling.

The weather had something to do with it, the sun-drenched days, the warm moon-lit nights, and a desire for jollity and frolic and a touch of the old pagan spirit of nature. The 'Pipes of Pan' called down the streets, and in the glades of the parks. Little shop girls became wood nymphs, and fled laughing from young satyrs in flannel trousers and sports jackets.

I came very close to the heart of England at that time, going about among these crowds, talking to many of them, overhearing their conversation on the kerbstone while we waited for the King to pass— much of which I recorded in a book called *England Speaks*.

Not for many years—two hundred, said one of the newspapers—had there been such a warm May and such sultry nights.

"You know," said a girl inside a kiosk on the Underground, from whom I bought a box of matches, "I think it was meant."

"Meant?" I asked, not getting her meaning, and hearing the approach of an Inner Circle train.

"God", she said, lowering her voice.

It was a nice idea that God should give such weather for King George's Jubilee. It was a pity that a frost came afterwards, destroying all the English orchards and ruining many fruit growers.

The girl in the tobacco kiosk had had a fine time, she told me, in such a friendly way that I let a train pass.

"We had a wonderful time down Fulham way", she told me, with laughing eyes. "You've no idea! I danced the shoes off my feet until three in the morning. Of course I felt a bit tired next day. One always has to pay the price for a bit of fun, doesn't one?"

"Nearly always," I agreed, regretfully; "but how did you get your music for the dancing?"

"Oh, it was marvellous! Down our street—Fulham, you know—there were two gentlemen with wireless sets. They put them in the front windows and the dear old B.B.C. gave us dance music till midnight. Then the people wanted the old tunes—'Dolly Grey' and all that—so we fetched a gentleman who played the concertina. He played it grand and we kept on dancing till we nearly dropped. I must say we enjoyed ourselves, though I did dance the shoes off my feet!"

There were thousands of other girls in London—hundreds of thousands of them—who danced their shoes away in the streets and, like Cinderella, forgot the chimes of midnight. Behind Curzon Street there was a party in one of the big houses with a band to play for them. A crowd gathered outside, making use of this music, and presently the pretty ladies with bare arms and silk frocks, with young gentlemen in boiled shirts and tail coats, came out and joined the street dancers, without class consciousness, or, at least, with a sense of comradeship. Extraordinarily un-English!—except when, now and then, the English take off their masks and forget their inhibitions.

I sat with the people in the parks. They had been there all night. Young women were combing their hair in the sunshine. Children were swarming over the grass. Families were having picnic meals.

"Keep away from them flowers, Tommy!" shouted a young mother.

Thousands of people had been encamped in the parks, but as I was told by one of the keepers not a single flower was broken.

There was for the first time in my experience a kind of pride, some touch of self-consciousness and self-analysis, on the subject of the English character during this time of Jubilee. Was it, I wonder, a premonition of the terrible ordeal to come, with its blitz and its menace of invasion, or was it due to a contrast between the English way of life and what was happening in Europe then? I heard quite a bit of praise for English character by men who helped to make it. One such man worked in my own garden at Ewhurst, once having served in Palestine during the great war.

"One can't help feeling proud of what England means in the world," he said, leaning on his spade. "We're not bullied about by youngsters in different coloured shirts. We're free men, as you might say. We have our liberty."

One night King George V spoke to his people all over the Empire and indeed to the whole world. It was the first time in history that one man's voice had been heard by hundreds of millions of men and women. It was, as I wrote at the time, a portent—this one voice talking to all the world. One day a man may say something to all the world which may change its destiny.

That night in England, as I wrote in *England Speaks*, in thousands of villages far from the glare and traffic of London, surrounded by quiet fields and woodlands, the rural folk gathered and tramped to their hillsides to see the lighting of bonfires, which made a chain from peak to peak, not only in England, but from Wales to the North of Scotland, as the beacons were lit in the days of Elizabeth when the Armada was sighted. The Soul of England spoke again that night, and these rustic folk remembered the war in which many of them had served and were glad of peace, and proud of a country, which, with all its faults, and troubles, and injustice, here and there, stood, they thought, for liberty.

Some of us knew that night that our peace might be threatened again. Some of us heard the stirring again of the Four Horsemen. Some of us smelt burning. But not many. The English people, and the Scots and the Welsh, were in a mood of jubilation. In London the Cockneys 'took the lid off' and let themselves go.

3

LOW AND HIGH

There was a darker side to the picture of English life at that time, and I saw something of it. I saw it in the dosshouses and below the surface of London night life, and in the farmhouses, and in the distressed areas as they were called up North.

Every night in London, before midnight struck and the theatre-goers were catching the last trains and the last busses, hordes of boys and girls, of ages ranging from sixteen to twenty-three or so, assembled in Trafalgar Square and on the Embankment to get free suppers provided by the "Silver Lady" and other misguided philanthropists.

There were about three or four thousand of those young vagabonds in London living a kind of outlaw life. Some of the boys had qualified for the dole by having had some sort of a job for twenty-six weeks. Now they were out of work and not keen to get it. On the dole they were the barons of this underworld, having a room somewhere and sharing it with four or five others. During the day they cadged sixpences from city girls and others, with which they bought a cheap meal and cigarettes. At night they were fed under the Admiralty Arch or on the Embankment. It was a training school of vice and demoralisation.

I spoke about it one night to a police-woman in St. Martin's Crypt where she was looking after derelicts of the older type—middle-aged and elderly men out of employment and down-and-out. At least she looked like a police-woman though I knew she was a saint.

She told me that the girls were worse than the boys—little sluts of the most frightful viciousness and the foulest language. The boys had no discipline, no work, no prospect in life but crime.

"We want a Hitler over here!" she said in a moment of despair. (That was before Hitler had threatened to come!) "He wouldn't stand it for five minutes. He would put them all into the Labour Camps."

It seemed to me astonishing that our own authorities could stand this kind of thing for more than five minutes—for five years. Those boys and girls ought to have been put to work on the land, willy nilly. Liberty? Yes! I am all for liberty, but this young crowd were deep in hell and ought to have been dragged out and given a chance of a healthy and disciplined life.

When I went to St. Martin's Crypt that night I had to ask my way to the entrance as it was dark, and a decent fellow of the labouring class had a touch of pity in his voice when he showed me the way down. "Good luck, mate", he said, thinking that I had need of a night's free shelter. Down there, in semi-darkness, the crypt was full of men asleep on the wooden seats. Others came down from time to time while I talked with the police-woman who was really a saint in uniform. She told me that young King Edward (it was after the death of George V and that merry Jubilee of his) had been down there a few nights before. He was in evening dress but wore an overcoat, tightly buttoned up, and a bowler hat pressed down on his forehead. He talked to many of the men as they came down and not one of them recognised him. He had come from some dinner party and stayed an hour in this stench of unwashed bodies. He had come alone. No newspaper reporter lay in wait for him.

I had other friends besides dustmen and down-and-outs. Sometimes I dined with people of high degree—the old aristocracy who came out of their ancient lairs, conscious, poor old dears, that the times were hard on them and that they belonged to the historic past. I found most of them simple and pleasant people, without a touch of arrogance.

The best dinner parties in London were given by an old lady who was good enough to invite me to her table on those occasions. Indeed I often acted as honorary host, she being a widow and needing a man friend to look after her male guests. She had a hired butler (from Harrods I believe) who had great dignity, though he was slightly familiar with me from time to time, regarding a newspaper man as being more or less on his own level.

"I often used to read your stuff in the war", he told me once, *sotto voce*, when handing me the port. When I was showing out some exalted old gentleman, with a name famous far back in English history, he would wink solemnly as though to say: "What a life! What a game!"

Lady Struthers—that was the old lady—had a real genius for gathering together a distinguished and interesting company who were pleased to dine with her and meet each other. She reminded me of one of the old ladies of the French *salons* before the Revolution, Madame de Deffand. She was no beauty, dear soul, and not in a very high order of intelligence, but she was a perfect hostess and kept things going with vivacity.

She specialised in Ambassadors and their wives. At her table I met a series of German Ambassadors, starting with Herr Stahmer who was a pleasant and thoughtful man, and ending with Herr von Diercksen who agonised over the menace of war. The French, Chinese, Japanese, and Dutch Ambassadors came to her tables, and seemed to enjoy themselves. I sat next to the wife of the Chinese Ambassador and found her a very sweet and humorous little lady. Lady Struthers's other guests, who were her personal friends, included Dean Inge, the Bishop of Durham, Sir Reginald Wingate, Marshall von Bieberstein and his beautiful wife, intensely pro-English, Mrs. Baldwin (with whom I had a passage at arms), and many of the old Quality of exalted rank.

One of these dames, of very high degree, reached out for the little card at the side of my plate and read my name.

"What do you do in the world?" she asked.

"I write books", I told her humbly.

"Well, I've never heard of them", she replied.

There was good conversation at this table. I heard many interesting things of history behind the scenes, for some of these people had been, away back in the past, the makers of history, like Sir Reginald Wingate, Sirdar of Egypt, who told me in great detail one evening the story of Fashoda when he had been Kitchener's right hand man.

Dean Inge liked talking but it had to be mainly a monologue because of his deafness. It was none the worse for that, and he was always witty as well as wise. I told him once, with sincerity, that he was the best journalist in England, and he did not resent the compliment.

There was another table in London, round the corner from Sloane Square, to which came people worth meeting. One night at dinner there I sat next to Sir Austen Chamberlain whom I had met so often in Geneva. He was a man of the most charming courtesy, and we started a conversation about foreign affairs which wrecked the dinner party, or at least gravely upset its customary ritual. All the guests listened to an argumentative duel, and then to some vastly interesting reminiscences by Sir Austen Chamberlain. No one moved for more than an hour and a half after dinner, and now and again the servants crept in to look at us, wondering what had happened and unable to clear away.

"Good heavens!" exclaimed Sir Austen at last, "this is very terrible behaviour!"

Our hostess forgave us. It had been a great evening.

One day before long there would be no more dinner parties in London, no more servants to clear away, and no more windows in this house near Sloane Square.

I took lunch one day in a Salvation Army shelter in Blackfriars. There must have been about eight hundred men feeding there. I talked with some of them across the table, and one I found had been a ship's steward and couldn't get a job. Liverpool was crowded with stewards who couldn't get a ship. Now he was getting so ragged, he told me, that he would find it hard to get a job anyhow.

"They don't give you a rig-out in these places," he said. "That's the snag."

Further down the table where I sat was a man who glanced at me once or twice. He looked to me typical of the ex-officer class, good looking with a little moustache.

Presently when other men left he shifted his seat until he was opposite.

"You're Philip Gibbs, aren't you?" he asked.

I nodded.

"How did you know?"

"I've seen your photograph many times. I've read your *Middle of the Road* and other books. Have you come down to this?"

"No," I said "I'm only a visitor."

"I have", he told me.

After the war he had got into trouble with his mess account in West Africa. Booted out, of course. Now he had been cadging off old friends. No chance of a job. He had tried everything.

I managed to find him a job, but I doubt whether he kept it. I had found jobs for other men of his type and class. Most of them let me down by heavy bouts of drinking. One of them, for whom I had obtained a free bed in a convalescent home—he was a handsome fellow who had had good positions—arrived drunk, and assaulted the matron. That kind of thing is discouraging.

But unemployment at this time had hit hundreds of thousands— getting on for two million—honest and decent men, some of whom I met in those dosshouses and shelters. Gradually it was getting them down, though many were remarkably patient about it and showed no sign of bitterness and despair—or at least not much. They seemed to think it was as inevitable as the winter rains. They were not revolutionary or wild-eyed. They talked about their social state with a kind of resignation, and sometimes with a Cockney humour. It was I who in my mind cursed the Government for a restriction of credit which was the main cause of this tidal wave of unemployment. We were struggling to keep on the gold standard and look the American dollar in the face. As my son Tony once remarked: "Winston Churchill" (then Chancellor of the Exchequer) "looks the dollar in the face but he can't look two million unemployed in the face."

One hates to bring that up against him now. He was taking the advice of Montagu Norman who ought to have known better.

4

THE STRICKEN NORTH

I went up to the distressed areas in Yorkshire, Northumberland, and Durham. It was all very tragic up there, especially in the mining villages with their rows of little houses reaching out to the slag heaps. In some of them there was complete unemployment. The mines had closed down, having become "uneconomical" to work. The men lounged about, just able to keep body and soul together on the dole. Rent took a lion's share of their dole—as much as 17s. 6d. in some districts.

Men still working on a few shifts a week were haunted by the menace of being paid off and joining the big battalions of workless men. Their women lived in the constant dread that their men would come home one evening with the news that another pit had been closed for ever.

"There's not much doing," I was told by one of the Durham miners, standing under the shadow of a slag heap in one of these villages. "Men who are working are not much better off than those on the dole. One goes down there and sweats, and take's a risk of one's life, for wages which don't give a man much of a time, especially if he's married with a family. . . . All the same it's best working. It keeps a man from fretting."

He stared away beyond the slag heap.

"These young fellows round here," he said, "haven't a chance of a day's shift. They're closing down many of the pits. And it's worse for the older men who are put off first, and won't get another week's wage as long as they live. It's a black shame when men have no kind of hope. That's what's happening in this country, but perhaps it's nobody's fault."

How tolerant was this man looking into the face of misery! It was somebody's fault. Our statesmen were children in the science of economics. They had adopted an utterly wrong policy in national finance, as their White Paper after another World War has admitted by reversing it. After the first World War they restricted credit and production. Now they put all their emphasis on expansion of credit and the speeding up of production. It took another World War, and the slaughter of civilians, and the pouring out of national treasure, and a thousand horrors, and a peril unto death, to teach them a few elementary lessons. It took that second World War to bring back men to their factories, skilled craftsmen who were losing their skill, old fellows who had never hoped to get another job in the forge or the factory, and now were wanted. It took another World War and the threat of famine to get the fields tilled again and to raise great harvests. It was somebody's fault. We are very tender to our politicians.

I made a study of conditions in the distressed areas and met many types of men. I was deeply touched by their character and courage of outlook, by their heroic endeavour to keep on the right side of that line —by an inch or two—between sanity and despair.

They were not without help though it didn't amount to very much in this far-stretching bog of unemployment.

The "lucky South" adopted some of these northern towns and sent them clothes and other supplies. Local committees in touch with the National Council of Social Service did something to bring a little brightness and some purpose to these distressed areas. They taught the jobless men to take up hobbies and learn new handicrafts. They encouraged them to build village halls and playing grounds and sports pavilions. It kept them busy. It gave them a sense of doing something worth while.

Above all in value was the allotment system. Miners, and out of work factory hands, and all manner of unemployed men, worked on the land, raising vegetables and fruit, and poultry, and rabbits, and pigs, for their own families. They worked from dawn to dusk, many of them. They loved this work in the open air and could hardly drag themselves away from it for food or family life.

Back in London after this investigation I lunched one day at a table—it was in No. 10 Downing Street—where the Minister for Agriculture, whose name was Dorman-Smith, sat next to me. I found him a most charming man but disappointing when presently I spoke to him about those unemployed miners in the North.

"Here are men," I said, "who are out of work and who love the land. And there is the land lying idle and without labour. Surely it would be possible to put those men on the land they love? Would it require a miracle to do that?"

He looked at me with a smile and shook his head.
"Very uneconomical, I'm afraid!"
In my very bones I knew he was wrong. In the second World War
we proved how wrong that was.

5

FARMING FOLK

I knew the troubles of English farmers. I had been all round England,
a few years before, enquiring into their conditions of life which at that
time were at a low ebb of fortune, to say the least of it. The year 1931
was the blackest for English farming.
I remember talking to one of the Gurneys of the banking family in
Norfolk.
"The Norfolk farmers", I said, "tell me that they're in a bad way."
He looked at me from his desk, and smiled, and raised his hands in a
tragic way.
"If they say that," he answered, "they're understating the case.
They're all bankrupt. I'm carrying them on my books."
All over England, as I wrote in *England Speaks*, the farmers were in a
desperate state, I found. A world economic crisis and a complete
dislocation of world trade had forced down agricultural prices to such
low levels that farmers were suffering heavy losses on almost every
commodity they produced.
Many foreign countries, stricken by internal poverty and loss of
markets beyond their frontiers, were using England as their dumping
ground at any prices they could get. Foreign fruit and vegetables were
pouring into Covent Garden, and English growers found their own
harvests unsalable, or bought at a rate which meant ruin to them.
When I sat in one of the old farmhouses in Oxfordshire, taking tea
with the farmer and his wife, my eyes roved to a picture on the wall. It
was a print of Watt's picture of 'Hope'—the blindfolded girl playing a
harp with broken strings. This farmer, whose ancestors had come over
with Hengist and Horsa, did not notice this allegory on his wall. He
passed me a piece of bread and butter and said: "Perhaps if we can
hang on for another few years things will brighten up a bit."
He was right in holding on to hope. The National Government under
Ramsay MacDonald made a desperate effort to raise the condition of
agriculture by all kinds of subsidies and quotas, very unsound perhaps
in the long run, but helpful to the farming community in their desperate
plight at that time. But it needed a second World War for the recovery

o

of our English land and our farming folk. Cut off from imports overseas by the action of enemy submarines and the strain on shipping, we had to grow much more of our own food or perish. The old arable farmers whom I had met in many counties, had grieved over the turning of their land to grass. Now millions of acres were under the plough again. And it was not "uneconomical" as Dorman-Smith had told me. It was our life insurance. It saved us all from starvation.

Now after the defeat of Germany and the opening of world trade to the traffic of our ships the problem of our agriculture will have to be thought out again.

I believe in Free Trade. It was the departure of the world from Free Trade, and the raising of tariff walls in the United States and everywhere, which led to economic disaster in many nations, and untold misery. But we must still grow more of our own food with guaranteed markets. That will be forced upon us, I think, in the long run, because after a temporary demand for our manufactured goods, due to world shortages, we shall find it difficult to maintain and increase our export trade by means of which we used to pay for our imported food. We must grow our own stuff or go hungry.

There is a moral as well as an economic reason for supporting our farming folk. They are our best stock. From their class and craft came much of our English genius, most of our best men and women. For out of the soil of England comes our best blood and our best spirit.

I say that without sentimentality, of which there is too much from literary men writing about the life on the land, because of the beauty of old farmsteads and a thousand associations of poetry and history. As I wrote in *England Speaks*, for the men working on the land and tending the beasts, there is none of that sentiment. They are in the front line tenches of life. Their toil is never-ending. They are deep in muck when weather is foul, and the slaughter of beasts is not pretty. Nature is a rough school of men and women. But it has its compensations, and it breeds character. All that is strong and hard and simple in our national life has its roots in the old earth which is England.

6

PRIME MINISTER

I came to know Ramsay MacDonald before he was Prime Minster, and afterwards when he held that office. I met him several times in Molly Hamilton's flat in the Adelphi, and later in other houses. Politically I was not altogether in sympathy with him, but in private life he had great charm because of his handsome face, and beautiful voice with its Scottish accent, and a gentle way with him. Listening to his conversation, which was always good until his breakdown in mind and health, I placed him as belonging to the old romantic school, of which my father was one. His mind belonged to the eighteen-eighties rather than to the nineteen-twenties. He still regarded Scott as the greatest novelist who ever lived, and I do not think he had any use for the modern realists. Although democratic in his political theories he fell under the glamour of old titles and old names which belonged to English and Scottish history. His enemies, who were once his friends, accused him of being a snob and "ratting" to the other side when he became Prime Minister of a Coalition Government, because he delighted in dining with Dukes and Duchesses. But I am sure it was not any vulgar snobbishness. It was this romantic strain in him, and no doubt also a touch of vanity, from which he was not immune. He had been one of "the people". He had been brought up in humble surroundings. He had had a hard fight for it. Now it was pleasing to him when the old aristocracy, who had been his enemies, flattered him and liked him. But always he kept his own simplicity and natural charm, and not even his enemies could call him an evil-minded, or cunning, or ruthless man, though they accused him of political disloyalty.

It was due to a chance meeting at lunch with him that he invited me to become a member of a Royal Commission on the Traffic in Arms. I was travelling about after this luncheon and at least five telegrams were sent to different addresses before one reached me. I went to see him in the House of Commons and was shown up to the Prime Minister's private room. He explained the scope of the Commission. He wanted it to be a serious enquiry but not a "fishing expedition in dirty waters". He wanted its members to hear all evidence and then report their finding as to whether the nationalisation of the arms industry was advisable or not. I had an idea from what he said that he was against nationalisation, but he did not wish to prejudice me one way or the other.

"It's an important business", he said. "It brings in something like two million a year which we can ill afford to lose these days."

He had difficulties with his papers. He could not read the list of names which he had written down.

"I'm terribly blind", he told me.

One day after another lunch at which I met him he drove me back in his car to the House of Commons. There was a detective sitting in front with the driver but we had a glass screen between us and could talk privately.

"My dear Philip," he said suddenly, "I am a broken man. I can't put two sentences together, and I can't put two ideas together. I am blind, and old, and useless."

He grasped my hand and clung to it like a small boy needing comfort, and my heart was filled with pity for him, and I was stirred by the poignancy of this tragedy. But when I left him I was disturbed by the thought that a man in this state of mind and body should be Prime Minister at such a time in our history. For it was a time when the situation in Europe was appalling in its gravity and when our own economic life and national stability were threatened by the financial collapse in many countries and a rising tide of unemployment at home.

Philip Snowden was one of those who had followed Ramsay Mac-Donald in forming a National Government and he had turned on his former colleagues in the Labour Party with a concentrated fury of denunciation. His speeches against those with whom he had worked all his life used almost to freeze my blood, not because I disagreed with him —I did not know enough of what had happened behind the scenes to agree or disagree—but because there is always something terrible in a man turning against his lifelong comrades and accusing them of criminal folly. One night I dined with a private party in the House of Commons and Philip Snowden and his wife were there.

Mr. and Mrs. Pethick-Lawrence were our host and hostess. After dinner I walked through the courtyards of the Palace of Westminster with Snowden. Because of his crippled condition he took an incredibly long time over this short walk under the archways, and I had to slow down to a funeral pace. We had been talking of the European situation, and I noticed, as I had done before, how gentle and low was his voice, and how pleasant his smile. It seemed to me astonishing that a man who in private life was so gracious could be so harsh and venomous in his political denunciations.

Suddenly he stopped and in the dim light of that summer night under an archway of this historic place I saw his eyes flash and the whole face of the man was contorted.

"Those people," he said, "my former colleagues, those Labour members!—They're incurable. Their dishonesty is deep-rooted. They would not pay any heed to my warnings. They have betrayed this country."

I listened to this crippled man—Chancellor of the Exchequer—with alarm and despondency. From what he told me we were on the edge of a financial abyss. All Europe was stricken. It was a crisis in civilisation which might lead to terrible things.

7

BILDENS

I have said that my wife and I divided our time between Bildens farm near Ewhurst and "Little House" in London. Bildens was a little old house, pre-Elizabethan, with many crooked beams and low ceilings. I turned the cow house into a study by putting down a new floor and boarding its walls with many shelves. We called it the "cow study", and between spells of writing or reading I would lean over the green door, which folded back half way, and look into the yard where a small boy named Martin—Philip Martin Gibbs—was playing with his ball or a bow and arrow. I made many bows for him and taught him to shoot them. It was so much more amusing than writing books, and while he was with me I lived in Seventh Heaven.

Tony had been married for five or six years now, and Martin was his son, afterwards joined by a sister called Frances who looked like a fairy but had the spirit and will power of Queen Bess. My son's father-in-law was Sir Charles Martin, distinguished as a bacteriologist, and for many years head of the Lister Institute, and I came to have a profound admiration for him because of his knowledge and balanced judgment on all facts of life. Lady Martin also had a fine mind, very different from her husband's, with an unfailing sense of humour even in her old age, and a spiritual outlook on life which sometimes she put into verse of unusual quality.

8

MADAM, WILL YOU WALK?

It was my wife's idea that we should give a Youth Hostel to Ewhurst. The Prince of Wales had made an appeal on behalf of youth for playing grounds and recreation centres, and the idea of a hostel for young hikers appealed to Agnes who had many devoted young friends in the London University when she was studying for her B.Sc. We bought a good ten acre field. A young man named Lobb—a good old name used by Barrie in *Dear Brutus*—designed a house with bunks and shower baths, and a central lounge with a big fireplace round which the travellers could gather on chilly evenings, and a kitchen where they could cook their food.

Soon it was much frequented by these young wanderers going from hostel to hostel, and I spent an evening with them once, and listened to their conversation. It was worth while. Here one could find what was working in the minds of young people, free and untrammelled.

We had a little opening ceremony when the hostel was built. Young King Edward had promised to come, but he was otherwise engaged at the time. It was Sir John Jarvis who made the opening speech which he did well. In reply I hoped it would be a good dosshouse for young tramps.

As I walked to it that evening there was a party of campers in an adjoining field. They had carried their own tents—'pup tents' the Americans call them—and were putting them up for the night. A girl among them was busy over a camp fire. A good smell came from her frying pan, and as I passed she stood up with the evening sun behind her, and gave me a smile of greeting which was very friendly, so that the words of an old song came singing through my mind—

> "Madam, will you walk,
> Madam, will you talk,
> Madam, will you walk and talk with me?"

In the hostel at eight o'clock that evening there was a pleasant scene. About thirty-five boys and girls of eighteen years onwards were getting ready for their evening meal. Some of them were already sitting down to it, at small tables in the big common room. Some of the girls wore breeches and strode about like young Rosalinds in the forest of Arden. The young men with them had no affectation. Most of them, I think, were medical students out for a walking tour. One of them carried a guitar on which he gave a tune now and then, accompanied by a humming chorus from his comrades.

I had a chat with the warden's wife, who prepares an evening meal for those who don't want to cook it for themselves.

"What kind of a crowd do you get?" I asked her.

She looked at her company and laughed.

"Every kind of type! They're all very intelligent and well-mannered. They think a lot about most things. You would be surprised what a lot they know about books, and art, and history, and nature study. And their minds are open. They have no use for intolerance or narrow prejudices. Most of them have an international outlook and are keen on peace. Of course they're rather bewildered, poor dears, about this strange world of to-day—who wouldn't be?—but they're not worrying."

I looked over at a young man and woman sitting at a separate table. The girl had very fair hair in neat little plaits. The young man would not have looked out of place on the Zugspitze in Bavaria.

"What nationality?" I asked.

The warden's wife thought they were Danes. The hostel had only been opened for a few weeks, but already they had had Danes, Swedes, Norwegians, Germans and Americans. A young German was taking some photographs of the hostel, but he accepted one of my cigarettes and was glad to talk.

"You English people don't realise your own happiness," he said, presently. "In Germany I found it impossible to be happy. There is always a sense of apprehension and—in my case—of fear and insecurity."

"Why in your case, particularly?" I asked.

He smiled and shrugged his shoulders.

"I am not completely Aryan. A touch of Jewish blood. Enough to make things very uncomfortable."

He spoke about life in Germany. There was much to be said, he thought, for some aspects of the Nazi régime. He approved of the Labour Camps. The Nazis had some good ideas, but they exaggerated the discipline, the rigid organisation, and the suppression of free opinion. There were vast numbers of Germans who disliked the Nazi régime intensely but didn't dare to express their views. The whole thing was held together by the personality of Hitler, who undoubtedly must possess some genius, but had the fanaticism of the man who thinks he is God, or held up by the Hand of God.

After supper we sat round the hearthside and talked. My presence among them—an elderly man—didn't seem to bother them at all. They exchanged ideas about the international situation. It was the time of Mussolini's threat to Abyssinia. They all condemned that as a violation of the League. They didn't like the look of things in Europe.

There was an extraordinarily pretty girl there. She was Irish but had spent several years in south Russia, climbing mountains and living with Russian peasants. She spoke remarkably well, describing her experiences. She had an idea that another European war was not far away—an idea which was received with groans.

"Let's forget all that," said the young man with the guitar. "Let's sing something." They sang: "There is a tavern in the town".

I had a good evening with them and walked out into a night of stars. Myriads of them twinkled above the tunnel of the lane. The dew was falling and there was a sweet smell of hay from the fields. A rabbit scuttled across the path. On such a night as this, in August, twenty-one years ago exactly, a war began which called for the service and sacrifice of English youth, and the youth of many nations. What good had it done? What problem had it settled? What happiness had come out of it for any people? Now, when I went home, there was news over the wireless that another war was brewing. Italy was sending young men to be stricken with fever and dysentery and all manner of diseases on the frontiers of Abyssinia. "We need more babies," said Mussolini, who gave a bounty for full cradles. "We must expand or burst," he said in another mood. He was sending his fleet of bombing planes by way of Egypt. Some English statesmen had expressed their sympathy with Italy's need for expansion—only to be gained by the invasion of other people's lands, but now, faced with the danger of this Abyssinian War they were working feverishly at Geneva for some kind of formula which at least would play for time. Anything might happen to touch off the powder magazine in Europe if the gates of Janus were opened wide in Rome.

9

GALLANT BROTHER

My brother Cosmo had come to Ewhurst and lived in an old cottage close to the church in order to be near me. He was a ruined man, after having been a rich man, but took it with a laugh. All his savings had been lost in the American slump, which also knocked out English authors because American editors decided, rightly, that their own authors must get any money that was going. My brother had invested in American stocks which soared high for a time and then dropped into a deep pit. By bad luck his money was in one of the banks which never opened its doors again.

When he arrived in Ewhurst he was bright-eyed and bronzed, and seemed to have no shadow on his mind.

"It's no use crying over spilt milk," he said, "I must get another cow."

He bought some penny exercise books and started all over again, with novels and plays and short stories, and never once, in my hearing, uttered one word of self-pity for his losses. That was heroic of him.

For many years—ever since he was a young man—he had lived without regard to cost. He had made masses of money in the States by his plays, novels, and film stories. In New York he had entertained heavily in his expensive apartment in Park Avenue, and in London he had, for a time, lived like a duke in Albany Courtyard, furnishing his rooms with priceless antiques. Once he had turned to me and winked and said: "This can't go on for ever, old man. It's just an illusion!"

Now he was amazingly happy in that old cottage where he lived alone. He cultivated his garden according to Voltaire's advice in *Candide*. He worked far into the night—villagers could see his light burning. Often he turned on his wireless and listened to the music he loved—all the best—conducting imaginary orchestras with his fork during his simple meals. He became devoted to a canary, and gave the glad eye to every pretty girl in Ewhurst who seemed pleased to get it, in spite of his age, because of his handsome looks as he strode down the village street, still the best-dressed man in Surrey, from a well-stocked wardrobe which he had kept out of the ruin. His plays and novels were satires on human life, sometimes bitter, but there was something very childlike in his nature and he had a great gift of enthusiasm for anything which

HIGH STREET, GUILDFORD
(By Edgar Lander)

BILDENS, EWHURST

interested him. He would get as excited over a game of garden golf as though he were playing a match on the best golf course in the United States, where often he had played. He was brilliant with his pencil and drew amusing caricatures of the world's great men and his own friends. He was a witty and brilliant talker, until deafness crept upon him just before the second World War and became a great tribulation. He and I differed about almost everything in a political way, but never once did we have a quarrel or a harsh word. He was my greatest comrade whom I found very exasperating sometimes, as doubtless he found me, but for whom I had a deep and abiding affection. He over-praised my work and was always wildly enthusiastic about my books, whereas I was critical of his and hated myself now and then for being so critical when he was so generous. Now when I pass that old cottage near the church in Ewhurst I see his gay and smiling ghost which for ever will haunt it with good vibrations, because he was such a generous-hearted man, with the spirit of a boy, and a love of birds, and flowers, and music, and pictures, and pretty women, and all pleasant things.

One afternoon over the tea table I sold Bildens farm to Charles Evans of Heinemann who coveted it. Agnes and I could no longer afford "Little House" in D'Oyley Street, and decided to put all our furniture into one house. Bildens was too small for that and after a search we found a house at Shamley Green. It was not a beautiful house when we bought it, either inside or out, having been built in the early Victorian era, but it had a beautiful garden and Agnes saw its possibilities. She had a real genius for architectural work and transformed this house called "Dibdene" so that its own builder wouldn't have known it. She had its roof-line lowered, put in large windows where there had been small windows, and revolutionised its interior. Now it is not too bad-looking. At one end of the garden is a large-sized cottage which Agnes made out of a small-sized cot. It is used as a school for young children up to the age of seven—about thirty of them who come peeping round the hedges in my garden and say: "Hullo, Philip!" and make a rush at me when I meet them in the lanes, for they know somehow that I am a friend of theirs with a soft spot in my heart for every one of them. (Since writing this the school has moved.)

My brother Cos, refusing to be separated by any great distance, let the old cottage in Ewhurst and took a small house in Wonersh Park, a mile or so away from Shamley Green and within easy walking distance. So we were situated when the shadow of another war crept over Europe and touched us in Surrey gardens.

10

ENGLISH ANXIETIES

While Mussolini was preparing for the invasion of Abyssinia and ridiculing the League, people in England of all classes were beginning to be anxious.

In my book *England Speaks* I record an authentic conversation I overheard in a third-class railway carriage from Waterloo to Guildford. It was very hot on that August afternoon, and my fellow travellers buried themselves in their newspapers, sweating their seats. There was silence as far as Surbiton. Then one of them spoke to a youngish man opposite.

"What do you think of this Abyssinian affair? Serious, isn't it?"

The youngish man withdrew his gaze from the window and stared at the questioner—a silver-haired man who looked as though he might be a writer of books, and answered after a moment of intense thought. He spoke with a kind of anger.

"I know what I would do if I had any control of the situation."

"What?" asked the silver-haired man.

"I would keep out of it. We don't want any damned nonsense like a war."

It was the beginning of a general conversation in the third-class smoking carriage. I listened from a corner seat.

"I agree!" said the silver-haired man. "All the same we ought to support the League of Nations, and the ideal of collective security."

"Damn the League of Nations!" said the youngish man. "I'm not going to be dragged out for war to support the League or its principles. I'm interested in my garden. I have two kids at home. What do I care about the Abyssinians? I don't know where they live on the map, and I don't want to know!"

A stout man on the other side of the carriage, who had been perspiring very freely, joined in the conversation. He looked like a stockbroker, I thought.

"It will be absolute madness if the Government insists on sanctions, as they call it, against Italy. That means war. Well, they won't get me again! I was in the last. Quite enough as far as I'm concerned. But all these pacifists are howling out for war! They want to take action against Italy to uphold abstract principles, and all those pacts and pledges which statesmen signed with their tongues in their cheeks. They would like to drag us into war for the sake of collective security! Lord Cecil and this crew keep writing to *The Times* about it. It's sheer lunacy."

"It's newspaper stuff," said another man whose pince-nez were askew as he looked over his *Evening Standard*. "The newspapers ought to be suppressed. They stir things up."

The silver-haired man laughed slightly.

"All the same," he said, "it's not a newspaper stunt this time. I happen to know that there's grave anxiety behind the scenes. And I don't think we ought to let Mussolini get away with his brutal policy of attacking the unfortunate Ethiopians. It's an attack on the civilised code. We're pledged too, up to the neck. We're under a solemn obligation to uphold the Covenant of the League. If Mussolini is declared an aggressor by the Council of the League we must take some action accordingly. Otherwise there is an end to law in Europe and we all go back to barbarism and anarchy. Collective security is the only way of preserving peace in Europe."

"I disagree!" said the youngish man in the corner.

He breathed hard for a moment and stared fiercely again at the silver-haired man.

"The League of Nations was supposed to be an instrument of peace," he said. "I used to think so. Now I'm convinced it's the most dangerous bit of bunk in the world. It would make every war a world war. It would drag us all into every petty dispute. What have we got to do with this quarrel between Italy and Abyssinia? Let's get on with our own job, which is to increase the prosperity of our own people and keep the peace."

"Yes," said the silver-haired man, "but what are you proposing to do if——"

"I'm getting out at Claygate," said the youngish man reaching up for a parcel on the rack.

He got out at Claygate.

That night when I went back to Bildens farm—it was before I had left Ewhurst—I had no sense of peace or security. All the nations were arming. The gates of Janus were opening wide in Rome. The German tribes were proclaiming a creed of force and might. There were smouldering fires in Europe, and terrific forces were stirring under the thin crust above the boiling lava of national passions. Upstairs in a little room with crooked beams a small boy was sleeping in my cottage. I had told him a fairy tale before he went to sleep. I was afraid for his sake. It's such a pity for the small boys of life when they find that fairy tales are untrue in a world of high explosives and bombing aeroplanes.

My gardener had something to say about all this when leaning on his spade. He is a lean fellow with a hawklike face and tanned skin.

Here are his actual words as I wrote them down at the time—

"I don't like this talk of another war," he said. "There oughtn't to be a war if the nations stick together and prevent Italy acting like a mad dog. It's what they promised to do and I don't see how they can go back on it. There's no hope for Europe if the League lies down under the heel of Mussolini. There won't be any war if we all act together and tell that Italian that he must be a good boy or he'll get it in the backside. But of course if the other fellows 'rat' we can't act alone, can we? It's not for us to play the policeman while the others look on and laugh at us. If there's no united action then I'm all for keeping out of trouble and making our own peace. I don't suppose they'd call me up again, but I'm thinking of the younger lads. It's a pity they should be called upon in the prime of life to lay down their lives because there's no sense in the world. We want to avoid that, but I don't like the look of things all the same. I can't help thinking that that there Hitler is out to make trouble. Do you think there is any chance of his being at the back of Mussolini? . . . Well I wouldn't like to fight the Germans again. But what I ask myself, when I'm working in this garden, is why mankind must always be fighting or under fear of war? Seems silly! Aren't we old enough to have learnt better?"

He spoke for his comrades in the British Legion, of which he is a member in this village. Millions of men all over England were thinking as he did. They were for peace, but they held on to the idea of collective security, and were convinced that if Mussolini were allowed to "get away with it" the League, in which they had hoped, would be proved a broken reed, and that other wars would follow.

Italian journalists jeered at our hypocrisy. They reminded us of the Boer War when the British Empire had attacked a peasant folk. They wrote of Omdurman when we mowed down the Fuzzy Wuzzies. They dragged out of the files stories of all our wars in Africa against savage tribes which stood in our way of annexation. "How can these people," they asked, "dare to sit on a high horse of morality because Italy wants more room in the sun and is anxious to bring Italian civilisation to the savages in Abyssinia?" There was something in those reminders. They nagged in my own mind. Our past history has many blots on the pages which we cover up by moral platitudes. But what these Italian journalists ignored was the change of character in England and Scotland after the experience of the first World War. They had abandoned the old jingoism. They were sincere in their new idealism. They had put their faith in the League.

11

ABYSSINIA

The Council of the League imposed sanctions upon Italy with the full votes of the Assembly behind them. Anthony Eden, on behalf of Great Britain, led the case for the prosecution of the aggressor nation. But France, or rather Laval, the Foreign Secretary of France, had "ratted", and made a secret pact with Mussolini, giving him a free hand in Abyssinia. "Sanctions" would not work if there were an open hole on the French-Italian frontier, through which all supplies could pass.

Some years later, during the second World War, when Anthony Eden came out to France I ventured to ask him a direct question about this.

"Did you know while you were putting your case against Italy that Laval had sold the pass?"

"I was told about it," he answered, "but I had no direct evidence. I wasn't sure."

If there were a war with Italy it would be the British Navy who would have to fight it. The British Navy was not in good shape, or ready for war. I happened to go to Sheffield during the crisis and the head of one of the big steel works spoke to me in a low voice.

"Things don't look good", he said. "We've just had rush orders for naval shells from the Admiralty."

No, things weren't looking good. They looked worse to many people when the Hoare-Laval proposals were published, with a map which suggested that Mussolini should get the lion's share of Ethiopia. There was a storm of protest. Letters and telegrams poured in to No. 10 Downing Street. It was like a tidal wave of popular indignation. It was one of those rare times when a Government trembles before the voice of the people themselves, surging up suddenly and passionately. I remember a line in a letter written by Lady Violet Bonham-Carter which expressed the indignation of many millions.

"It is we, and not the Abyssinians alone, who have been betrayed."

Mr. Baldwin, then Prime Minister, had been away on a holiday. He came hurrying back to Downing Street. Sir Samuel Hoare, part author of the plan, had to put on the white sheet of repentance in the House of Commons and was forced to resign. But Mussolini went on with his war, and Hitler, watching all this with an intensity of interest, must have licked his lips. It would be his turn next. Ribbentrop whispered to him "These people will not fight. They will not fight for anything."

12

WINSTON

Two R.A.F. officers with distinguished service came to my house in
Shamley Green one day, and each carried a despatch case crammed with
papers. They wanted to talk to me about something very serious.

One of them was a friend of mine whom I had met a number of times
at a big house in London where we had gone into corners to talk over
world affairs. It had been a gloomy talk because this airman was
convinced that there would be a new war for which we should be
utterly unprepared. I guessed therefore when he called with his friend
that this would be the subject of his talk. It was.

These two men had considerable knowledge of German progress in
the building up of a mighty Air Force, not only as regards the manufacture of machines but with an immense ground staff and a system,
highly developed for the training of immense numbers of pilots and
technicians.

"If war breaks out suddenly," said my friend, "and I see it coming—
we shall be lost. We have no Air Force comparable with the Germans.
They will be able to give us hell."

He gave a detailed picture of the particular form of hell which we
should suffer. They would be able to smash up our ports, and destroy
our shipping. They could concentrate on our sea routes and cut us off
from our food supplies thereby starving us to death in a very short time.
With supremacy in the air they would break up our command of the sea
and clear the way for an invasion of our island. Their bombers, which
they were building feverishly, would drop high explosives on our
industrial cities and reduce them to dust and ashes.

"It doesn't sound too good", I remarked.

The two airmen smiled grimly at this understatement.

"It's simply frightful," said one of them. "Our Air Ministry is
hopeless. The people as well as the Government are being deceived by
hot air and inaccurate figures in Parliament."

The Air Ministry . . .

They made a bitter indictment of that Ministry, staffed by men who
knew nothing about flying or the scientific development of aircraft, or
the necessity of a ground organisation on a big scale. Training, they
said, was farcical. The whole show was a disgrace and a betrayal. If
nothing were done about it this country would be doomed.

They pulled out their papers, and proved their argument by facts
and figures, and showed me secret reports they had written in the hope—
quite vain—of getting something done.

"Why do you come to me?" I asked.

One of them answered.

"The people ought to be told. The nation is being lulled to sleep while the Germans are working overtime for our destruction."

They knew, as they admitted, that they were risking their own careers, and perhaps their liberty, by revealing these facts. If I wrote about them it would be traced to them. It might be the Tower of London for both of them. They didn't care. They were out to save Britain from mortal peril. Nothing else mattered—not even their lives.

I was deeply disturbed. These two men were no scare-mongers. They were not men with a personal grievance. They were sincere and patriotic. But what could I do about it? No newspaper would dare to publish such facts. They would be lagged under the Officials Secrets Act.

I suggested that the best thing to do with the facts they had given me was to pass them on to Winston Churchill who was now out of office— the Right Honourable Gentleman below the gangway—who was already challenging the Government on its air policy and neglect. They thought this a good idea and I wrote a letter to Winston Churchill which he answered by inviting me to go and see him at his house in Westerham.

I went down there one morning with the airmen's reports, and he read them carefully.

"I know most of it," he told me. "I get good information. I don't get my facts out of the blue. But I agree with every word these fellows say."

I happened to be writing a book at that time called *Ordeal in England*, and I made use of this information, heavily camouflaged in order to conceal the identity of the two men, and leaving out actual figures which would have been of service to the Germans. It attracted a good deal of attention in the Air Ministry who must have wondered how I knew so much. But when war came, as all the world now knows, we were vastly outnumbered in the air and only the superlative heroism of our young pilots—"so few against so many", as Churchill said—saved this country and all of us in the Battle of Britain.

My visit to Winston Churchill that day was interesting apart from the particular object of it. I had a chance of getting a closer glimpse into the character of that astonishing man for whom I had a great admiration, with some secret doubts and criticisms, afterwards dispelled by his heroic leadership of the nation.

Mrs. Churchill was at lunch with us, and very charming. Years before I had met her when she was a young married woman of great beauty. Here on the other side of the table was a man named Lindeman whom I knew vaguely as a scientist. Churchill was in good form. His conversation was brilliant and amusing. After lunch he lent me a pair of goloshes and walked me about his estate at a great pace. I saw his exploits as a bricklayer, and they were prodigious. Balbus built a wall, but Churchill has built many walls, surrounding his paddocks and his fruit garden. They were noble looking walls, helped by some miserable fellow who mixed the mortar while Churchill laid the bricks. He had also built himself a studio into which he took me. As a passionate painter in oils myself I was keen to see his work and was much impressed with it. He paints in the impressionistic style, tackling subjects which would make a professional blench with terror. They were done with dash and a sure touch, each stroke of the brush laid on without fumbling or any messy effect. If Churchill had devoted himself only to painting he might have been a master painter. That reminds me of a young friend of mine named Christopher, aged seven who, gazing at some of my own work, said: "Sir Philip, if you go on until you get older you might become a great painter." But Churchill has all the talents and a vital urge which drives him on whatever he undertakes.

He turned to me after showing me his work and made a staggering remark.

"I regard a day as ill spent," he said, "if I have not painted two pictures."

"Good heavens!" I exclaimed. "A professional painter is satisfied if he produces two pictures in two months."

He had been a friendly host, but as I was leaving him that evening he laid me low by a parting remark.

"Gibbs," he said, "you are one of the goody-goodies."

If he had called me a thug or a murderer I should not have been so abashed. But a 'goody-goody'!—How frightful!

"I'm a stern realist," I told him, and he laughed.

Why 'goody-goody' I wondered when I left him? Doubtless he had read some of my writings, and had seen that they were steeped in hatred of war. I had denounced war-mongers and war-makers, and had dedicated my pen to peace. But I don't call that being a 'goody-goody'. Was it not the only realism? Churchill did not think so because in his soul was a love of the romance and heroism of war, the thrill of a cavalry charge, the call to the blood by bugle or band. He has never forgotten the South African War, though all that has gone for ever.

13

TRAFFIC IN ARMS

In the summer of 1936 I finished my part of a job which had absorbed —and wasted—a lot of my time. It was the Royal Commission on the Private Manufacture and Trading of Arms.

There had been a similar Commission in the United States, under Senator Nye, which had discovered and published evidence involving British firms. Doubtless this and our own public opinion had forced the Government under Ramsay MacDonald to make the enquiry. Those appointed to the Commission were J. H. Spender, great liberal and great journalist, Professor Gutteridge, K.C., an authority on international law, Dame Rachel Crowdy, Sir Kenneth Lee, and Sir Thomas Allen. Our Chairman was the Right Hon. Sir John Eldon Bankes once a Judge and—by all accounts—the handsomest man in England.

We were all determined that it should not be a whitewashing Commission. We wanted to get at the truth of the case—if any—against the private trading in arms, and to decide after full evidence, whether arms manufacture should be taken over by the State or left in the hands of private manufacturers. I for one resolved that I would do my best to uncover the truth about all this as far as possible.

It was an amusing experience, vastly interesting, and very novel to me. But it involved a lot of hard work, including the study of documents mostly printed in small type and very trying to the eyes.

A great number of witnesses came before us, beginning with the Peace Societies led by Lord Cecil, on account of his work with the League of Nations, and followed by Arnold Forster and others representing the National Peace Council and other allied organisations. The Communist Party had their say under Harry Pollitt, and we heard the British Movement against War and Fascism. Lord Davies spoke for "The New Commonwealth Society" and Sir William Jowitt for the Union of Democratic Control. The case against private trading was presented forcibly by peace advocates.

Mr. Harry Pollitt, the Communist, had a glorious moment. He began his evidence by reading out a list of eminent people who had investments in the manufacture of arms. Among them he gave the name of Sir John Eldon Bankes, our Chairman! The members of the Royal Commission sat back as though they had been shot. We had all given our word that we had no financial interest in any munition firms. Sir John himself went on making notes unperturbed. Being slightly deaf he had not heard his name on the list. When he was made aware of what had happened he was distressed. It appeared that some relative of his had died recently making him one of the trustees of a property which involved a few shares in one of the big armament firms, entirely without his knowledge, as he stated in the next meeting of the Court.

Sir John Eldon Bankes was at the time of the Royal Commission a man of eighty, but his brain was as clear as crystal, and he had the complexion of a new-born babe. He was a most charming and considerate man, liberal-minded and wise in his judgment. We could not have wished for a better Chairman. But he was somewhat worried by his team, and especially, I think, by myself and Dame Rachel Crowdy, whom he regarded as his "Left Wing", and likely to go farther in our examination of witnesses than he thought was necessary or advisable. When we or others asked such questions, or when witnesses were boring him, we always knew that he was getting impatient for he had a habit, quite unconsciously, at such times, of wagging a pencil with a little ring at the end which gave a faint tinkling sound.

Our toughest time was when we had to cross-examine the representatives of Vickers, of whom there were about six led by Sir Charles Craven. Before they arrived we had to study our brief carefully as it was a very long one. The Nye Committee in the United States had obtained a good deal of evidence which linked up the Vickers Company with Dupont and other international traders in arms, and we had to get down to all this in great detail.

I had something of a duel with Sir Charles Craven, the Managing Director of Vickers, who, as the Americans would say "hated my guts". Several times he appealed to the Chairman against my questions, but he received no satisfaction or sympathy from Sir John.

"I advise you to answer the questions, Sir Charles", said the old gentleman.

The atmosphere became distinctly warm, not to say hot, when Sir Charles jibbed at some of my questions and those of Dame Rachel Crowdy. I said I should demand to see the books of the Vickers firm, according to our authority as a Royal Commission. This had the effect of a bombshell. All the heads of the Vickers firm whispered together. Then Sir Charles Craven said: "We have no objection to an examination of our books."

Sir John was perturbed inwardly, I think, though he showed no outward sign of that.

"How do you propose to bring the books to this court, Sir Philip?" he asked suavely. "In a pantechnicon?"

I suggested that I should go to Vickers House to examine them with another member of the Commission. I suggested Dame Rachel Crowdy, and she looked at me and nodded.

This was arranged, and one morning Dame Rachel and I advanced upon Vickers House, behind St. James's Park Station. Office boys and clerks and typist girls bobbed out of their doors to have a look at us.

The Directors received us in a big room round which portentous looking ledgers were stacked. Sir Charles and his co-directors were most polite. They handed out cigarettes and offered their services in any way to help us. After courteous conversation on both sides, I intimated that we desired to be left alone with the books, and regretfully the heads of the firm departed.

When they were well beyond hearing distance Dame Rachel and I looked at each other and laughed. The sight of those heavy ledgers was formidable. It would need months of labour to go through them.

"Well, we may as well have a look at some of them," said Dame Rachel. "We shall get our hands dirty, anyhow!"

Now Dame Rachel Crowdy had a mind like a sword and the eyes of a lady eagle. Perhaps also we were directed to a certain ledger by some spirit hostile to the traffic in arms. Before an hour had passed we were on the track of an astonishing story which did not look good for the reputation of Vickers, and we found other entries which aroused our interest and suspicion. Now I do not want to throw mud at Vickers and company. They were selling arms to any country which might order them, and their agents were out to get such orders from Chinese generals or Japanese officials, and were good salesmen. "A nice little line in machine-guns of the very latest type—The gentlemen over the way have just put in an order for so many thousand. Doubtless you would like to strengthen your own position? May we suggest——" All that was strictly according to the law and encouraged by the British Government with Board of Trade consent. But in the case we tracked down, one of their agents—a wild and adventurous fellow—had gone further than that, and was making a Tom Tiddler's ground for himself in China. It was like a story by a writer of adventurous romance but not redounding to the credit of Messrs. Vickers. When we made a report about it to Sir John Eldon Bankes and the others they took a serious view of it. Sir John presided over a special and private enquiry on this case, calling witnesses from Vickers and other firms and after his summing up his judgment was a severe reproof.

But it was one of those cases inevitable in a system of private trading in arms when agents are bound to get out of hand now and then. What staggered me was the defence of such a system by men of honour and high moral code. One of them was Sir Maurice Hankey, afterwards Lord Hankey. No one who knew him could doubt for a second that he was not above all ignoble motives. His life had been devoted to the public services in the highest measure, and he was a man of fine intelligence and character. How then, I asked myself, was it possible that such a man should defend the traffic in arms, lock, stock and barrel? This he did. He came to the Court with a most detailed refutation of all the charges brought against the armament industry. Point by point he demolished them—to his own perfect satisfaction, though not to mine.

I will quote only one question I put to him.

"Sir Maurice, in your general argument in defence of private manufacture you have used certain phrases about the critics of that system, such as that 'they are under a delusion' and that the grave abuses of which private manufacture is accused are mostly 'figments of the imagination'. Do not you think that it is curious that some of the best brains in the world to-day should be convinced of these grave abuses? I would mention the representatives of many of the great countries, including France, at Geneva, on the disarmament committee and commissions who do accept the fact that there are grave abuses, and argue a case upon that. Do you not think that it is rather curious that this illusion should persist, if there were no grave abuses?

Sir Maurice Hankey did not think that curious at all. It was due, he thought, to intensive propaganda from one side only.

One of his chief arguments in favour of private manufacture and international trading in arms was that without it there would be no progress in design, and no skilled craftsmen ready to expand the industry in time of war. He did not see anything wrong in firms selling their weapons to any country which would buy them, even if that country were to go to war with us and kill British troops with shells manufactured in British factories. He was passionately against the nationalisation of the arms industry, and thought it would be a disaster to this country.

In the course of our enquiry a great number of witnesses came before us, many of them highly distinguished in all branches of service, and to some extent it was a pageant of English life.

We examined Admirals and Generals, very true to type and tradition, engineers from the shipyards, members of the great steel firms (who certainly played into each other's hands for maintaining a fixed price of steel against which the Government had no argument). Before us came former Ministers of Munitions, like Dr. Addison and Lloyd George, pacifists, and hard-faced business men, newspaper proprietors, and Government officials. On the whole one's respect for the public services was increased by the character of these witnesses and by the obvious integrity of most of them. We were not confronted by a morass of villainy making money out of slaughter and stirring up war in order to increase their business—"Merchants of Death" as they have been called. After hearing all this mass of evidence and looking at it in a judicial way I was bound to admit that, apart from a few cases of individual shadiness, there was little evidence that war had been engineered in that way, though I still hold, despite Lord Hankey, that the international traffic in arms is open to grave abuse, and is a dangerous and immoral form of trade. "Not so dangerous as novel writing," said Sir Charles Craven when I put it to him that it was a more dangerous form of trade than selling Christmas crackers. He got a laugh for that from the audience in Court.

Our report did not go as far as recommending complete nationalisation, not for any political reason, but because the weight of evidence was, in our opinion, against it. But we advocated a much more rigid control by the Government over the export of arms, and greater authority and direction in the manufacture of arms for the purposes of expansion in time of war. We advocated a kind of headquarters for research, design, and training, closely in liaison with the whole engineering industry and all firms, however small, which could be turned over to the manufacture of munitions and all instruments of war in case of need, with jigs and gauges ready, and with experts sent out from this headquarters establishment to give instruction in mass production. We recommended a Minister of Supplies, and in case of war, conscription of Labour as well as of men for the fighting services.

This report of ours fell with a thud between two political stools. The Government regarded it as far too revolutionary. Labour rejected it utterly because we did not report in favour of nationalisation, unable or unwilling to see that from their point of view it was the next best thing. It was, I am certain, a document of great value. There were some brilliant brains at work on it, those of Spender, Sir Kenneth Lee, Gutteridge, Dame Rachel Crowdy, Sir Thomas Allen, to say nothing of Sir John Eldon Bankes with his fine judicial mind. If it had been adopted when it was published the nation would have been saved long delays in war production and the conscription of Labour—perhaps that was what stuck in the gizzard of the Labour Party—would have saved vast sums of money.

To me it was an interesting experience, though very time-wasting. All we got out of it was a personal letter of thanks to each of us from the Prime Minister—then Ramsay MacDonald—and some free and frugal lunches at the St. Ermin's Hotel. We had to pay for our own coffee and drinks if we needed them. Never again shall I serve on a Royal Commission.

14

THE KING'S CAMP

Before young Edward came to the throne I spent a day with the present King when he was Duke of York. One of his pet hobbies was a boys' camp at Southwold which he ran at his own expense. The idea behind it was to break down class consciousness and get boys from the public schools, like Eton and Harrow, to live for a time in close comradeship with boys from industrial classes and districts.

"You will be surprised," he told me, "how well it works. There is absolutely no class consciousness. The whole camp is run on team work, and they learn a lot from each other. Anyhow, they have a jolly good time."

I was sceptical about that. It seemed to me impossible that Eton boys would get on to easy terms with those from Limehouse and Bermondsey, but I didn't say anything like that to the Duke. One doesn't try to spoil a man's dream. But after some hours in the camp I saw that he was right. The boys were getting on together marvellously well, without the slightest thought of snobbishness or class consciousness. It seemed to me a little miracle in England.

The Duke invited me into his own car, just he and I together, and talked to me about all sorts of subjects. I noticed that in private conversation his speech was easy. He was keen on industrial problems and wanted much more to be done for boys just over school age. Then he began talking with obvious admiration of his elder brother, who was Prince of Wales at that time.

"My brother," he told me, "is going to make a speech to-morrow for something like an hour. To me it would be a tremendous ordeal. But he has a gift that way, don't you think?"

He was very shy, I noticed. Whenever the car slowed down, and there was a chance of his being recognised, he drew back, and once pulled down the blinds.

"I never get used to it," he told me. Now as King he has been forced to get used to it and bears himself bravely before vast crowds.

When we reached the camp he had a tumultuous welcome from the crowd of boys who swarmed after him when he made a tour of inspection. He knew many of them by name, and stopped to talk to them, and I noticed that they were perfectly at ease with him and, what I admired more, he was perfectly at ease with them. That is not always easy with boys of that age. He was just simple, and natural, and full of good humour with them. He went down to bathe with them and they played all sorts of tricks with him, splashing water over him and then rubbing him down with towels. It was obvious that he was enjoying himself, and not just doing it with a sense of duty. At lunch time he came down from the high table and sat with one of the teams, chatting with the boys at table, and making them laugh. There were a few speeches with an excellent time-limit to them. If one of the speakers became ponderous, or boring, or exceeded three minutes, he was brought down by a pistol shot. Several of them were, but I escaped this penalty.

There were some games and a sing-song in the evening. The team spirit prevailed. The public school boys were keen that their crowd should win and coached young Bill of Bermondsey, or Peter from Peckham, and they were all on tip-toe to come out first against the other teams.

"Don't you think it's good?" asked the Duke when we started on the journey back after that sing-song round the camp fire in which he had joined heartily.

"Magnificent!" I said, with absolute sincerity. His eyes brightened.

"I'm frightfully keen on this," he said, "though it's a very expensive hobby for the limits of my purse, which has many other calls."

The next time I saw this young man was when he stood before the altar in Westminster Abbey waiting for the crown to be put upon his head.

It was filthy weather just before the coronation, wet, cold, and horrible, on that night of May before the great event. Millions of people were already taking up their places preparing to spend the night in the parks.

The porter at my club spoke to me about them as he held a dripping umbrella over my head.

"They're already beginning to line the route. Marvellous! That's what I say. What a heart! I wish I had a touch of it myself."

He had been one of the heroes of the Great War.

At five o'clock on the morning of Coronation Day, when I looked out of my windows, I saw the crowds hurrying on their way like ghosts in the grey dawn. At six o'clock I sat in a taxi-cab on the way to the Abbey in an endless procession of motor cars.

London had been barricaded as though for a siege. They had over-done all this, fearing enormous crowds, and many people had been frightened from coming, but there were crowds enough.

The Abbey itself was already filling up. It had been turned into a vast auditorium for eight thousand people. Inside it was very dim at first with lamps glimmering like stars between the grey columns. Presently the high clerestory windows brightened. Shafts of cold light struck across the great nave and touched some of the pillars. My seat was high up but I could look down on part of the scene set for the royal drama, and through my glasses I could recognise some of the people below—the nobility and gentry of this realm, and of the Dominions beyond the seas. Busy about the altar moved bishops and clergy in gorgeous copes. Hundreds of choristers in white surplices and black or crimson cassocks passed up to the choir. Presently peers and peeresses arrived. Some of them had come to Westminster by barge, others by a threepenny train in the Underground, and others by car through the massed crowds. But they looked as if they had just come from the Middle Ages. The peers wore their long robes of purple-red with capes of ermine, and held their coronets under their arms as knights used to carry their helms. Some of them were very old, and stumbled in their robes. Some of them were young, and looked jaunty and debonaire. The long velvet robes of the peeresses touched the old stones of the floorway, and one saw among them here and there pretty young faces and the grace of English beauty.

But as I waited for the coming of the King and Queen (as I wrote in a book called *Ordeal in England*) I was aware of old ghosts about me. I heard old voices from the past, as far back as the Saxon craftsmen whose stonework still stands in some of these walls. Here on that worm-eaten chair many kings and queens have been crowned. Among them were lion men and tiger men, very fierce and cruel. Norman William had stridden up to this place in chain mail. Richard with a great sword at his side had come here for his crown, though he spoke no English. The early Edwards had helped to build this Abbey as we now see it. They had held their kingdom by sword and battle axe. Henry of Agincourt, a friend of low fellows in his youth, stared down this nave with his falcon eyes. All the great figures of our story had come here for a little while, like shadows passing, saints and heroes and villains, fair women with tears in their hearts for the world's cruelty in times of passion, murder, plague, war, and the unending struggle of life by our forebears. By some spirit in them, for a thousand years, they were greatly daring in adventure. It is still unfinished, that adventure. That day another one began with the crowning of another king.

Sitting next to me was Gilbert Frankau, with whom I talked in low tones now and then. We watched the old ceremony of coronation, which combines the dedication of a knight in the age of chivalry with the old Catholic ritual of priesthood. We saw the young Queen Elizabeth, full of grace and charm, and Queen Mary whom I had watched at her own coronation, and the little princesses, peeping and whispering.

Frankau and I were anxious to escape after all this, but very rigid rules had been made for leaving the Abbey, and it took most people several hours. But we had to describe the story to the world and by good luck we were able to persuade one of the high officials in charge of our tier of seats. He let us out through a little doorway which led to a winding staircase and so outside the Abbey where a vast multitude was gathered on the stands and roofs. We were the first out. George VI was King, and in the minds of his people, in my mind, at least, there was apprehension of future history.

PART XIII

THE DARKENING SHADOW

1

THE MOOD OF ENGLAND

DURING the year or so which preceded the second World War I noticed and recorded an increase of anxiety among the people I met in London and the country; not only the "higher-ups", who were watching the international situation, but the man and woman in the street and the third-class railway carriage and Surrey gardens. A sense of inescapable war was fixed in some minds, because of the failure of the League over Abyssinia, and because of Hitler's invasion of Austria and his support of the Sudeten Germans in their claim for self-government. Yet Hitler—history's greatest liar—still proclaimed his desire for peace. After his reoccupation of the Rhineland, which at that time had seemed justified to many English minds—was not the Rhineland as German as Sussex was English?—Hitler had gone far in his declaration of pacific intentions.

"The period of so-called surprises," he said, "has come to an end. As a nation enjoying equality of rights, Germany, conscious of her European task, will loyally collaborate in solving the problems which affect us like other nations."

He had offered a limitation of armaments, an abandonment of big guns, tanks and bombing aeroplanes on the same level to which other powers would agree. That offer was never taken up, and I still think we should have done well to enter into discussions with him on that subject, pinning him down to his own proposals—if anything could have pinned down that slippery snake!

Instead, the British Government started plans for intensive re-armament, held back by Mr. Baldwin until after the election and strongly opposed by the Labour Party when they were produced.

The mood of England at that time was uneasy. Many people I met were heated by a kind of impotent rage against all the powers-that-be who were so conducting affairs that we might be involved in another war, against the will of the nation, and on behalf of people like Czechs and Poles of whom they knew very little and about whom they cared not at all. This anger, this rage, this despair, because of impending doom, was not revealed mainly by pacifists and Left-wingers. The Left indeed had been much more bellicose than the Right, against dictatorship—except Russian dictatorship—though still opposing the means to fight them. Ordinary young men in middle-class life, married perhaps and

434

with a baby or two, were afraid when suddenly they became aware that there was a real and imminent danger of being dragged out of their homes for military service, and for the murderous business of war. This fear, this anxiety, crept into the minds of young married women with two or three children and young husbands. They were old enough to remember the last war when their fathers and brothers had been killed on the Somme or in Flanders. Was it going to happen again, and worse next time? No! They refused to believe it. They could not believe it.

In my book *Ordeal in England* I recorded a conversation with a young airman on this subject. We lunched together by the side of a swimming bath in a London club, into which a portly old fellow had just flung himself from the diving board with a considerable displacement of water. My friend was a cheery-looking lad, curiously sure of himself in this world of uncertainty and doubt. Certainly he was no "long-haired pacifist", though a hater of war.

"No nation wants to go to war nowadays," he told me. "Some of us walk around a bit in Europe. We talk now and again to foreigners in their own countries. People of our generation are all against war. I'm certain of that. It's beyond all argument, in spite of the filthy nonsense, the daily spate of lies, in most of our newspapers."

"What about Germany?" I asked.

He didn't blink an eyelid about Germany.

"Perfectly sincere in saying that their rearmament is for self-defence. Don't we say the same thing? Why should we always be abusing the Germans because they don't want to be kicked in the pants by France and Russia, and take steps to regain their independence and self-respect?"

"Aren't they in a dangerous state of exaltation?" I asked. "They all seem ready to fight and die for the Fatherland and Adolf Hitler. Mightn't this spirit for self-sacrifice lead them into any kind of war if their Leader touched a button on his desk one day?"

The young airman shrugged his shoulders. I understood him to say that he didn't think Hitler would touch the button. He wouldn't be such a fool, he thought. But as far as he was concerned—and he spoke also for his friends—the desire for martyrdom was non-existent.

"We didn't join the Air Force in a sacrificial spirit," he told me firmly. "We're not panting to die for King and Country. We don't *want* to die, damn it! Why should we?"

He was wrong in his facts, as I and others were wrong. Hitler touched the button, and though they were not panting to die this young pilot and his comrades in our little Air Force fought against all odds in the Battle of Britain which saved us all.

Because Hitler touched the button and plunged the whole world into war it is easy now to say: "Of course he touched the button! It was perfectly obvious that he intended to touch the button." But, before Munich, and before he revealed himself as the world's greatest liar, it was not perfectly obvious. There were many people closely in touch with him, including his own people, who believed that his rearmament was for the defence of his own frontiers and the renewed strength of Germany as a great political power no longer to be brow-beaten or treated as an inferior. German youth believed it.

Some of my books, like *Blood Relations* had been translated into German and had had a wide sale in Germany. I used to get letters from university students and lads in Labour Camps.

"You seem to think," they wrote, "that our Führer is leading Germany towards war. But that is not so. He has promised us Peace and we believe him. No German wants war and least of all young men —my comrades and myself—who would have to do the fighting and the dying. Of course we should have to defend the Fatherland if it were attacked, but the Führer has no intention of crossing anybody's frontiers, as he has told us many times. So why, Sir Philip, do you suggest in your novels that there is a danger of this, or that there is any hatred of England in Germany? On the contrary. We admire England and like the English. I very much want to come to England myself one day."

That is a typical letter out of many I received, and they seemed to me sincere.

2

THE LAST HOPE

There was a German in England with whom I became friendly and who disliked the ending to *Blood Relations* in which I had stressed the danger of the Nazi régime and all this marching and drilling of German youth. The son of my English "heroine" who had married a German breaks his mother's heart by becoming an ardent young Nazi and regretting that he has English blood.

"I wish you hadn't ended it like that," said Marschall von Bieberstein of the German Embassy—a very tall young man, six foot three at least, with a wife who spoke such perfect English, and was so English in her ways and manner, that it was difficult to believe that she was German.

"No boy in Germany would regret having English blood," he said; "and I find the end of your novel terribly pessimistic. There must never be another war between Germany and England."

He had shirked reading my book when his wife had passed it to him.

He could not read a book which brought in the war, he said. But when he started reading it he became absorbed because he had been a Rhodes scholar, like the young German in it, and his mentality and experience had been much the same. He told me about a dinner he had been to recently. A number of German officers who had fought in the last war had been entertained by a number of English officers in London. "There wasn't a shadow between us", he said. "We all felt like comrades. When I left the table and came out I had tears in my eyes. Our two nations must never fight each other again. It would be a crime and a tragedy."

All the people at the German Embassy were pro-English and pro-Peace, but I could see their anxiety, both before and after Munich. I came to know the German Ambassador von Diercksen and his wife whom I used to meet at dinner tables. The Ambassador was a serious, delicate, overworked, and anxious man, deeply perturbed by the perils ahead. He regarded the idea of war with horror, and as its shadow crept nearer after Munich he was in despair. We had long talks together, and he was very frank, not disguising his apprehension, but believing, or trying to believe, that there was still time for an Anglo-German understanding.

Frau von Diercksen was a very different type, being a large-sized lady with a big bosom, and big arms, and a big voice. I used to meet her at the house of that old dame, Lady Struthers, of whose dinner parties I have already written. Always when she was about to leave, the Ambassador's wife would rise and say in a loud voice: "*Wo ist die Hausfrau?*" looking about for her hostess. One night on returning to the German Embassy she found a big crowd of Jewish folk who surrounded her car, booing and shouting, because of the persecution of the Jews in Germany, of which she did not approve.

She took a liking for me which was somewhat embarrassing, for towards the end of a dinner she used to become jocular and nudge me with her bare elbow, making her husband nervous at this familiarity, and the frightful indiscretion of her conversation.

She was a hundred per cent Nazi, but did not believe that Hitler contemplated war.

I met other Germans in London and became friends with some of them, hoping that by such friendship better relations between the two countries might be helped, and anyhow sharing their hopes and anxieties for peace. Among them were Wolff von Dewal and his wife, Elfa, who became devoted friends of Agnes. Dewal was the London correspondent of the *Frankfürter Zeitung*, the most liberal German newspaper even under the Nazis. He was a Prussian, and as a boy had been in one of the aristocratic cadet schools, of the old type, with frightful discipline. But he had a philosophical mind and a sense of humour and was a brilliant journalist writing "with his finger-tips," as he used to say.

We had tremendous talks together and I learnt a lot from him but always we ended with only a hope—wearing thin after Chamberlain's efforts at Munich—that peace might be maintained. Dewal laughed at the Nazis whom he called "the naughty Nazis", but believed, or tried to believe, that if the right man went to Germany at the right time an arrangement might be made with Hitler guaranteeing peace on condition that Germany should be given an economic sphere of influence in the Balkans. Hitler he regarded as a strange incalculable genius, not without a touch of madness, who was so emotional and temperamental that anything might be done with him if he were handled in the right way, especially by England. A generous gesture from England, a real offer of friendship by some outstanding personality might have a profound effect upon him, for he had respect and admiration for our country.

Anyhow Wolff von Dewal himself abhorred the idea of a war between us, and said a little prayer every night for peace, though not a religious-minded man, and making a joke of his own prayerfulness.

Elfa, his wife, many years younger, was pretty and charming and very intelligent, but deeply hurt now and then because her English friends were cold to her, or departed from her, because of suspicions about Hitler and disapproval of Jewish persecution.

During Chamberlain's visit to Munich, they made my wife a gift of a beautiful eighteenth century candelabra which had once hung in an Austrian castle. They called it the *Friedenslampe*—the Peace lamp—symbolical of their hopes. We hung it up above the stairway and they came to see it in all its glory of twinkling lights. When war came I wondered whether it would crash in an avalanche of crystal, but it still hangs there after six years of war in spite of many bombs which fell round about during the German Blitz.

One night the Dewals gave a party in their London flat. It was after Munich when Hitler was beginning to show his hand. Towards the end of dinner Dewal raised his glass and drank to the King. We honoured the toast. Then he raised his glass again, to the Chancellor of the German Reich—Adolf Hitler.

"No!" said Agnes. She pushed her glass away and there was a painful moment.

The war had been going on for six months when I received a message from Wolff von Dewal at G.H.Q. in Arras. It came over the air and was picked up by our Intelligence who listened to German broadcasts. A chit was sent to me.

"Extract from broadcast by Wolff von Dewal of the Frankfürter Zeitung.

"Whatever happens in this war it will make no difference to my friendship with Philip Gibbs."

3

THE LAST ATTEMPT FOR PEACE

Before the meetings at Munich Agnes and I went to Germany again. I was filled with the deepest apprehension but could not bring myself to believe that war was inevitable. Was it inevitable? The vast majority of the German people were as anxious for peace as we were. Of that I was convinced and am still convinced. Hitler in all his speeches was still insisting upon his peaceful intentions. He had not yet shown the cloven hoof. We might, and did, dislike the Nazi code. I hated its intolerance, its persecution of the Jews, its racial theories, its denial of free speech and free thought, and I hated the iron dictatorship in Russia, but every nation has a right to its own form of government. It was with horror that I regarded the possibility of another war. Had we not pledged ourselves, to our dead in the last war, that it should never happen again? Wasn't I—were not all my contemporaries who had survived the last war—committed in our souls and in our honour to prevent at all costs, or almost all costs, another massacre of youth? For that we had backed the League of Nations, for that we had written our books. For that we had agonised over the mistakes and lack of vision of the world's statesmen, including our own, who had failed to create a new era of peace in Europe by a spirit reaching beyond national rivalry and old hostilities, and economic barriers, ruinous to trade. I could not bring myself to believe that the enormous insanity of war, that frightful crime against humanity, was even now beyond avoidance.

"Can't you do something about it?" asked Agnes.

I shook my head and laughed gloomily.

"I can do nothing about it. None of us can do anything about it. What is one man's pen or one man's hope—unless he pulls the strings of power? The peoples of all nations have no control over their own destiny. Those fellows on top settle it for them. All the same, if there is any sense left in the world, this war won't happen. It won't happen unless we let it happen."

That was my last hope when I went to Germany for the last time before the war. It was a hope darkened by fear. In all my books that sense of drift towards war had come out almost against my will, almost against my convictions. It must have been strong in my sub-conscious-ness, for reading them again I see it emerge, not only in my novels but in my non-fiction books like *European Journey* and *Across the Frontiers* and in a new preface I wrote to *Realities of War*. I did not slur over the dangers, nor give false reports of what was happening in Germany and other countries. They were objective and realistic and faithful reporting of things seen and heard. I had been to the best of my ability and conscience a truth-teller. But now I would not let myself sink into the blackest pit of pessimism with an acceptance of war's inevitability. If all the little people, the ordinary folk, were to get together and say: "We will not have another war", there would be no war, and among them would be the majority of the German folk. If European statesmen were to say: "We will have no war", there would be no war. At that time there was no proof that Hitler was beyond all reason and all instincts of humanity.

Nevile Henderson, our Ambassador in Berlin, still thought there was a chance of peace, and he knew more about Hitler than I did, and was not a fool.

"I have staked my whole career upon preventing an 'inevitable' war", he told me. "I may fail. I get precious little help from statesmen at home. They do all the wrong things, and say all the wrong things. They don't send out the right men to talk to Hitler. The Labour Party is always taunting him and insulting him, though they are hostile to re-armament. Anyhow, I'm doing my damnedest to work for peace. I am accused of being pro-Nazi. I am not, but I don't want a war between Germany and England because of rival ideologies. I know perfectly well that if I fail all fails and the world will be in flames again. I don't care a damn about myself or my career. I'm thinking only of the boys who will die if war happens again."

I had long talks with him. I saw him at Nazi parades and listening to Hitler's public speeches. He was not popular with his colleagues. He had a stiff manner and an outward austerity. He had no illusions about Ribbentrop and Goering and the others, but did not think that they were committed to a war policy. They were playing power politics, not without some justification in their demand for a sphere of economic influence in the Balkans. He thought Goering had certain qualities of good nature and was definitely in favour of peace. He wanted to keep on good terms with them. Hitler of course was incalculable, a bundle of emotion, not without some sentimentality upon which one could work, but easily moved to rage and with occasional brain storms. A genius with a touch of madness. A queer crowd for a British Ambassador to handle. But Nevile Henderson, greatly maligned because of his failure, had at least a noble motive behind his patience and his diplomatic work.

It was to save the world from war. Should he have done otherwise? Was his failure due to blind stupidity? I knew the man and had a high respect for him. For some reason he revealed himself to me more emotionally, I think, than to his own colleagues.

4

SATAN'S RIGHT HAND

During this last visit to Berlin I had an astonishing conversation with Himmler, that devil in human form. He was not a man I wanted to meet. I had heard some grim stories about him, but as a journalist one does not refuse to interview a man unless he is strictly virtuous and full of moral nobility.

"I shall probably have to shake hands with him", I told Agnes. "Do you happen to have any carbolic soap?"

I was received by him at his headquarters of the S.S. Before reaching his room I had to pass a number of officers in the black uniforms of his police army who saluted me with almost staggering ceremonial. I was in the company of a German naval officer who was to be my interpreter if my German failed at any point, Himmler not being able to speak English.

He was in a large room with big windows. At one end of it I noticed a globe on a pedestal. He rose from his desk and came towards me, and for the first time I saw the man who was responsible, I should say, in the years to come, for more cruelty, torture, and human agony than any human being in modern times. He did not look like that. He looked like a professor at a university, or even perhaps like an artist. He wore a white tunic with brass buttons over black riding breeches and boots. He had, I thought, a slightly Mongol look and was very un-Germanic. But there was nothing repulsive about him. On the contrary, he was genial, vivid, and humorous. It was difficult to believe that I was in the presence of a most damnable villain.

He saw my searching look and laughed.

"You see", he said, "a man whom your English newspapers call 'the worst man in Germany'. Well, it is for you to judge. I shall not hide myself."

After some preliminaries he said he would like to have a good talk with me.

"Let us talk with brutal frankness," he said; "I will be frank with you and you can be frank with me. That is the best way of conversation. Is it agreeable to you?"

"Perfectly", I told him.

"Well now, let me ask you a few questions. First. Why do the English people think that Hitler is preparing a new war in Europe? Tell me exactly."

"Many people in England think", I told him, "that Hitler, after rearming, may be tempted to play the part of Napoleon and attack other people's frontiers."

Himmler laughed as though very much amused.

"That is not only not the truth," he answered, "but the very opposite of the truth. I know what is in Hitler's mind, and that is not part of it. After all we have read a little history. We know something about Mr. Napoleon. We know what happened to him. We know also that if Hitler were to attack other people's frontiers and march across Europe, as you suggest, it would be for Germany the road to ruin. That is a way we shall not go."

I made a note of these words immediately afterwards. They are exactly the words he used. And looking back upon them they seem to me astonishing. Why did he say that? If he were lying to me that would be easy to understand, but surely he would not have lied in such a phrase? He need not have prophesied that a war of aggression would be for Germany the road to ruin. Even now I find its psychology inexplicable.

He talked to me about the economic state of Europe, and the economic necessities of Germany. He seemed to think that they were thwarted by British policy. He spoke of the Ottawa agreement and said that these Imperial preferences shut out Germany from many markets.

"Why do you begrudge Germany any way of expansion?" he asked.

He referred back to my mention of Napoleon.

"You talk of Napoleon," he said, "but what about the British Empire? Come over here for a moment."

He took me over to the big globe on its pedestal and turned it swiftly, putting his hand on certain red splodges.

"Red!" he cried. "Red! Red! Red! The British have taken all that of the earth's surface, and yet they do not want Germany to have any open door for her trade, not any kind of expansion, however peaceful."

He harped on that a good deal, and coming back to his desk spoke of the real necessity for Germany to have a sphere of economic influence in the southeast of Europe. She had to import in order to feed herself. To import food she had to export manufactures. But England tried to shut her out and steal the markets. It was a dangerous policy. Germany wanted peaceful expansion, but she must have a free hand in southeast Europe. So he went on.

It was interesting but I need not repeat all of it here.

"Have I your permission to report this conversation to the British Government?" I asked.

"By all means!" he said. "I should like your Prime Minister to know exactly what I have said. I have been perfectly frank."

I departed from Himmler, and breathed more freely when I was beyond his police headquarters. It seemed to me astonishing that men of Himmler's ruthlessness—the full extent of his cruelty had not then been revealed—should show so few marks of the beast on him. In a London club he would have been regarded as a rather agreeable fellow, not good looking, but vivacious in conversation and with good manners. Astonishing, and yet true to history, for the worst of men, the murderers and the torturers have sometimes been quite pleasant in private life, like the Medici, and the Borgias, the Inquisitors, Robespierre in his home life, Henry VIII among his ladies in Whitehall on the day when the noblest man in England—Sir Thomas More—had his head lopped off.

I made a report on this talk to Lord Halifax, then Secretary of State for Foreign Affairs and he was interested. Afterwards, when Hitler violated all his pledges and invaded Czechoslovakia, *The Times* published a letter from me entitled "Herr Himmler's Prophecy", in which I repeated the words that if Hitler crossed other people's frontiers and marched across Europe it would be for Germany the road to ruin. That prophecy was fulfilled by a German ruin, complete and overwhelming, and Himmler who made it poisoned himself, and left a name of infamy never to be blotted out of history.

I heard from Germany that Himmler was furious when he read that letter, and had put me on to his Black List. In September, 1945, my name was on the list of those to be arrested after a German invasion of England in 1944.

I was in honourable company.

5

LAST CONTACTS

All that was in the future, though not the distant future, when I was in Berlin before the war. I remember a conversation I had with one of Hitler's A.D.C.'s named von Hevel, of which I took notes at the time. He was a very tall young man, slightly too stout, but good looking and easy in his manner. He spoke perfect English, and knew a great many English people. He told me a lot about Hitler which may have been true, as it had no propaganda motive. Hitler, he said, would summon some of his generals and experts and ask their views on different points.

Having received them he would retire to his own room and keep them hanging about, smoking cigarettes, fidgeting and yawning, perhaps for a couple of hours. Then he would return and say: "Gentlemen, I have been thinking about the advice you gave me, for which I thank you. I have decided to do the exact opposite."

He had a recurrent dream, said von Hevel, which was very odd. Many times he dreamed that he was driving from a London railway station to Buckingham Palace (he had never been in England) greeted by the cheers of the London crowds. It was a wish-dream!

Von Hevel liked English whiskey, which I obtained for him in the Adlon. After three whiskeys he became talkative and indiscreet. But even in his indiscretions he never hinted that Hitler intended to make war. He had a complete contempt and dislike for the Italians and I met him one morning in the full dress uniform of the German Air Force—"very beautiful", as his sister said with slight sarcasm—putting on a pair of white kid gloves.

"I am going to Italy with the Führer," he told me; "I hope I shall wear these gloves all the time. I don't want to shake hands with an Italian, unless I have my gloves on."

6

DESCENDANTS OF KINGS

Agnes and I had lunch one day at the hotel with two interesting people to whom I was introduced by my host. They were the Duke and Duchess of Brunswick. I knew that the Duke was the lineal descendant of George III, but it was only after some conversation with his wife that I realised she was the only daughter of the Kaiser. Perhaps I had been a bit too familiar with her, but she did not seem to think so and was very bright and talkative and frank. She was a gay-hearted lady, extraordinarily charming and vivacious, I thought. She took a great fancy to Agnes and told us some interesting things. When Hitler had first arrived she had fallen under his spell and had been enthusiastic for the young Nazis, but gradually she had come to see the danger of it all, and the low character of the Nazi leaders. Ribbentrop had behaved like a cad to her. One day when she had been to a Nazi rally in Nüremberg a tremendous storm had broken, and she had become wet to the skin, "like a drowned rat", she said. She had fled back to her hotel and was just going to have a bath when a message reached her that Herr von Ribbentrop wished to speak to her immediately down below. She sent down an answer.

"Tell Herr von Ribbentrop that I cannot see him just yet. I am going to have a bath."

Another message came up.

"Herr von Ribbentrop insists upon seeing the Duchess of Brunswick immediately."

The Duchess's hair was sopping wet. She tied it up in a knot and the daughter of the Kaiser obeyed this summons from a former salesman of cheap champagne.

When the crisis in the Sudetenland arose, the Duke and Duchess were in despair. One of their sons was under orders to move with his regiment. They feared the worst. Then one evening when they were at the dinner table they heard over the wireless the announcement of Chamberlain's flying trip to Godesberg, and like a *bourgeois* couple the Duke and Duchess took hands and danced round the table. It was, they thought, the certainty of peace. Chamberlain had saved the world from horror and destruction, they believed. They were still thinking so when I met them, and the Kaiser's daughter showed me a snapshot of her five sons, tall and handsome young men standing in a line with their mother.

"I don't want them killed in another war", she said.

The Duke of Brunswick and I had some conversation on our own while his wife talked to Agnes and our host.

He told me of an episode in the last war. He was with his regiment passing through a Belgian village when he was met by Prince Rupprecht of Bavaria.

"Good God! You here!" exclaimed Rupprecht. "A descendant of George III of England, fighting against the English!"

"You also, my dear Rupprecht," said the Duke of Brunswick; "what about your own ancestors?"

Prince Rupprecht of Bavaria was the legitimate heir to the Stuarts.

"Rather strange, don't you think?" said the Duke. "Two descendants of English kings meeting in a Belgian village on the wrong side of the lines!"

I told him of a memory of my own about Rupprecht of Bavaria.

During the war of 1914-18, I went down a dugout in the Somme battlefield and put into my pocket some papers and letters lying there. One of the documents was a manifesto to his troops by the Prince.

"My Bavarians," it said, "the only people who stand between us and peace are the accursed English. Slay them!"

It was signed 'Rupprecht'.

During this luncheon hour the Duke was silent for a little while when the others were talking. Presently he turned to me and said in a low voice:

"It's a dirty world, isn't it?"

It was odd that soon after meeting these two people I should be introduced in London to a young German named Friedrich who was a relative of theirs. We were in a drawing-room, and I only caught the name Friedrich when I sat next to a good looking, fair-haired, and quietly spoken young man. He spoke perfect English and had been in England for several years he told me.

"What part of Germany do you belong to?" I asked.

"Well," he answered, "I rather think I belong to every part of Germany."

"And why are you living in England?"

He glanced at me with a smile.

"Because I like living among civilised people. Germany under the Nazis is not civilised."

It was later that I was told I had been talking to Prince Friedrich of Prussia, grandson of the Kaiser. He refused to go back to Germany when war broke out and was interned in Canada by Home Office orders. A year or so before the end of the war he was allowed to return to England where he worked on a farm in Herefordshire, living simply with the farmer and his wife, and working hard. On the very morning when I wrote these lines there appeared a report of his marriage at Little Hadlam to Lady Brigid Guinness.

7

GÜRTELROSEN

I made a speech in Berlin to a big audience among whom were several Foreign Office officials. I began humorously with a study of the differences between German and English character, making them laugh, but presently revealed the dangers of the international situation as it then existed and told them plainly enough that the peace of the world depended on Hitler's keeping his pledges that the "era of surprises was over" and that he had no further territorial ambitions.

It was von Hevel who came up to me afterwards, speaking angrily.

"You have said the most terrible things about Germany as though you were handing us bouquets", he said.

It had been a great strain, and, perhaps, it was the cause of an illness which attacked me on the way from Berlin to Budapest.

My head felt on fire as though someone had seared it with red-hot irons. Agnes was alarmed, and when I reached Budapest enquired for a doctor at the Duna Pelota. I was recommended to a Jewish doctor and when I went to see him in his consulting room he examined my head.

"You have been fighting", he told me.

"No", I answered, "I am a man of peace."

"Certainly you have been fighting," he answered, firmly. "I can see the wounds."

I assured him that he was wrong but he did not believe me. He poured balm on to my head and rubbed it in softly and was full of pity for me.

"My poor man!" he said. "You have been beaten about the head. It is a cruel world. But come and see me to-morrow."

His balm did me some good—for three minutes. That night I suffered agonies and paced about the room hour after hour in real torture. It was as though my head were on fire.

Early next morning I went to see the doctor again. Again he examined my head and then laughed.

"I was wrong," he said; "they are not wounds due to being beaten. You have *Gürtelrosen*."

"Shingles", said Agnes who was with me.

It was a painful malady, and it crept all over my head and down my forehead threatening my right eye which was my good eye. Fortunately it stopped short of that but it was most unpleasant for nearly two months. I did not lie abed for it. In Budapest I had many people to see and I did not want to spoil Agnes's pleasure. So I stuck it out, and talked brightly to all sorts of Hungarians over little tea tables and dinner tables on St. Margaret's Island, and other pleasant places. Outwardly these Hungarians were gay and carefree. There was a lot of laughter among them over little glasses of golden liquids. But in their minds was fear. Now and again I had grave conversations with some of them.

"If war comes again I shall kill myself", said the mother of a young son. She and her husband, who was a professor, lived on the hills above Buda. She took me down to her garden gate when I was leaving and suddenly cried out these words. She was afraid that war was not far away. The world was going mad again. The German leaders were mad and bad. Her husband, now an invalid, had talked about war coming. She lived for her young son who was a brilliant boy. Why should he be sent into the shambles because other people had gone mad? Presently she wept and clung on to my hand, though I did not know her well.

I left her garden and walked down the hill, towards Pesth. I was alone and in the loneliness cried out aloud—

"O Christ!"

Was this war coming? Were we all drifting towards that unimaginable horror? Surely to God we could come to some settlement with Germany? Hitler still talked of wanting peace. If Great Britain took the lead there might be an agreement with him for general disarmament and a new pact of peace in Europe. There was still time, surely, to dispel this sense of doom and inevitability which had taken possession of men's minds.

A distinguished Hungarian named Ballog, editor of the *Hungarian Review*, talked to me about the political situation. He regarded it as grave, but not beyond a peaceful settlement.

"Great Britain must exercise her influence," he said; "her frontier is not on the Rhine but on the Danube. We Hungarians look to England for the pacification of Europe. But she must act quickly and with decision. Friendly overtures to Hitler guaranteeing the frontiers of Germany, giving them economic advantages in the Danubian basin."

I had talks with Count Teleki, the Hungarian Prime Minister on this and other visits. He invited me to his house for these conversations and I sat with him in his book-lined study. He thought there ought to be a Danubian Federation under a new king—one of the English princes. But when I last saw him he was depressed and anxious. He was a man of philosophical mind, a scholar and a scientist who believed in intelligence, who hated the insanity of war, and was a man of culture and charm, at his best in a study like this which he left only for the political arena because of his patriotism and sense of duty. But his belief in intelligence was betrayed by madmen. His hopes for peace were unavailing. In despair he shot himself when war began.

8

LAUGHING ITALIAN

Agnes and I went to Italy. It was almost our last journey abroad together. She was ill but I did not realise how ill. She had to be very careful about food and hardly ate anything, but her spirit rose above this distress of the body as always it had done through our married life and many illnesses, and she was gay among friends and made the waiters laugh by her little jokes in Italian. Always at eleven in the morning we sat in an open-air restaurant in the Pincio Gardens with coffee and cigarettes. Several times we saw Mussolini riding by on a big brown horse which he put to the gallop. He was always unattended and took no notice of the little groups in the gardens. He had become stout and heavy and frog-like.

One of our friends lived in an apartment in an old tower looking right down the ruins of ancient Rome. He had a little balcony with flowers in green tubs. It was Emmanuele whom first I had met when he was a young journalist sent from Italy to report the first attempt to fly the Channel, when Blériot startled the world by that achievement. We had spent the night together on a boat lying at Sungatte on the French coast. Now he had been a prisoner of the Fascists who disliked his criticisms in the *Corriere delle Sera*. All his friends had expected his health to be broken down, but he came out of prison after many months looking remarkably well and still laughing. He was always laughing and it was that gift which led to his liberation. How could you keep a man behind bars who just laughed at his judges and his gaolers and made them laugh with him? He had bribed one of his warders to buy him bottles of salts which made up for lack of exercise.

"I came out looking better than when I went in," he told us. He had lately taken up painting in oils with a kind of passion. It enabled him to forget politics, and the absurdity of Fascism, and the death of human intelligence in Italy. He forgot to eat when he was painting. He forgot his wife and his nearest and dearest in this absorbing hobby. But he did not know what to do with his pictures when they were finished. His wife refused to let him hang them up on the walls. He was delighted to hear that I had taken up the same hobby.

"That is wonderful!" he cried. "It will solve all difficulties. We will admire each other's pictures. We will praise each other. We will even exchange our work from time to time, and ignore all hostile criticism."

Agnes and I sat listening to this merry little man on his balcony near the Temple of Trajan looking down the Via Imperiale towards the Colosseum. He laughed at the absurdity of life, at the ridiculous character of dictators, at the folly of the mob who followed them. He laughed at prison cells—"Stone walls do not a prison make nor iron bars a cage"—because he kept the liberty of his mind. He laughed because otherwise he would have wept for the betrayal of free thought and the death of art, and the oppression of the Fascist régime in Italy. I do not know as I write whether he is still alive.

9

LEOPOLD OF THE BELGIANS

I had a talk with King Leopold of the Belgians. He had read some of my books, and to an American friend of mine he had expressed a wish to see me. It was a Royal Command, so my wife and I went out to Brussels and it was arranged that the King would come in for coffee and conversation after dinner at my friend's flat.

We had a day or two in Brussels before that evening and I talked with a few shopkeepers and the ordinary man in the street. They seemed to be worried about the political situation in Belgium and I became aware that there were smouldering fires of passion underneath the surface of Belgian life. One young man spoke to me about the King.

"He is no good to us."

"Why not?" I asked.

The young man shrugged his shoulders.

"He is a Flamagand. He is pro-German. He is anti-democratic."

There was a political crisis. Monsieur Pierlot was trying to form a new Government. There was a party of Fascists called the Rexists who were menacing. The Left was making trouble. But I have forgotten the details of this political storm.

We had a pleasant dinner party of about eight people and soon afterwards young King Leopold arrived accompanied by one of his gentlemen. He was in evening clothes and seemed to me an attractive young man with a very quiet way of speech and a touch of shyness. He spoke perfect English without accent, having been to Eton as a boy. He shook hands with everybody, and talked to Agnes for a little while. Then he came and sat down beside me and told me that he had read some of my books and would be glad to have a conversation with me.

I have forgotten how it started but very soon he mentioned the political crisis in Belgium.

"It's all very difficult. I am above all parties, but I am the target of criticism from all sides. I only want to be fair to all sides. The Walloons think I am favouring the Flamands, because I think they have not had a fair deal. It is rather like the situation in Ireland where there are two different races always hostile to each other."

Presently he talked about the Spanish Civil War and the hatred between the Italians and the Germans who were fighting as volunteers on the side of Franco.

"They have to be kept apart," he told me. "The Germans despise the Italians and the Italians detest the Germans. When Hitler went to Rome to see Mussolini the Italian people had to be ordered to cheer. It was all a farce."

He did not seem to like Mussolini or the Italians and I remembered that his sister was the Crown Princess of Italy, and was surprised that he spoke to me with this candour.

"The situation in Europe is very perilous", he said. "It's all boiling up to something very unpleasant."

"Do you think there will be war?" I asked.

He smiled and shrugged his shoulders slightly.

"Who knows? But I can tell you one thing for certain. There will not be a war for six months."

I raised both hands slightly.

"Six months? Can't it be six years?"

"Not before six months", he repeated.

I made a mental note of that. It was exactly six months to the very day when war was declared. That young man knew something.

The neutrality of Belgium was mentioned, and I ventured to say that I regretted it, and thought that it would be better if he made a military alliance with France, and other countries who might form a defensive *bloc* in case of German aggression.

"No!" he said. "My neutrality will be very helpful to France by giving her a left flank on the Belgian frontier. It shortens the French line. The Germans won't attack Belgium this time."

He was wrong about that, though he knew that the war would not start for six months.

He began to talk of human history in a philosophical way.

"It all moves in cycles of civilisation. If one studies history one sees that most civilisations have about five hundred years after climbing up the curve which leads to their zenith. Then they begin to decline. It seems a kind of law or destiny. England is only just beginning to climb up to the zenith."

I was astonished at that, and told the young King that I thought England had reached her peak in the Victorian era and now was on the descending curve.

"No, no!" he said. "England will have five hundred years ahead before she reaches the summit of her civilisation. I am certain of that."

"Well, that's very hopeful for us," I said, cheerfully; "I am glad to hear it."

He began to talk of his Eton days and asked after friends he had made there, some of whom I knew. He was so English in his manner and way of speech that one almost forgot that he was a Belgian.

Our conversation was interrupted by two gentlemen who brought urgent messages about the political crisis. The young King retired with them to a corner of the room where they talked long and earnestly.

Then they departed and Leopold came back to talk to the ladies of our little party and was very simple and charming with them. Not much more than a year later he surrendered with his broken army and became a prisoner of war in the hands of the Germans.

10

THE MAN OF MUNICH

Then came Munich and 'The Man with the Umbrella'. Neville Chamberlain's efforts at appeasement are now regarded by Left Wing minds as a shameful episode. The word appeasement—a very good word once belonging to Christian ethics—has taken on a new meaning and is used as a stigma or disgrace. To call a man "an appeaser" is to write him down as one lacking moral integrity. There was a time when Someone said: "Blessed are the peacemakers". But we have forgotten that. The name of Chamberlain is mentioned in certain company—the Right Wing as well as the Left of English political opinion—as though he had betrayed his country and was a man of debased character, or, at the best, cowardly, blind, and gullible. But those who abuse him now forget. How short is their memory!

When he announced that he would fly to Berchtesgarten to talk with Hitler there was a rush across the floor of the house, and amidst great cheering everyone tried to shake his hand and wish him 'Godspeed'. On that morning when he flew from Hendon the members of the German Embassy rose early and went down to the aerodrome and seized his hand also with emotion. I knew one of them named Dr. Koch. Like his Ambassador von Diercksen he was passionately on the side of peace between Germany and England. So was General Wenniger, the German Air Attaché in London, who used to come each week to a luncheon table which I joined with a group of friends. He had a charming wife and a little daughter who spoke English as well as she did German. But these people belonging to the German Embassy—all pro-English and pro-peace—were being put on one side by Ribbentrop and his friends in Berlin. They had no influence at all. They were kept in the dark and, towards the end, ignored.

"Out of this nettle, danger," said Chamberlain as he stood by the aeroplane at Hendon, quoting the words of Hotspur, "we pluck this flower, safety." He carried his umbrella to Germany, and to all Europe that 'Man with the Umbrella' stood as a symbol of commonsense. The quiet English gentleman with his code of honour and his lack of fanaticism, and his wish for peace, had a moving reception in Germany. Crowds of women, the mothers of young sons, rushed round his car waving and cheering, and, some of them, weeping. They did not want war, those young wives of German men, those mothers of young sons.

The immediate trouble with which Chamberlain had to deal was the claim of the Sudeten Germans for self-government. They were being roused to rebellion by a leader named Henlein who was instigated by Hitler. Hitler's propaganda at this time, put out by Dr. Goebbels, was utterly false in its description of the agonies and suppression under which the Sudeten Germans (who were really Austrians) were supposed to be suffering. Hitler's heart 'bled' for them. His 'patience was exhausted'. All that was damned nonsense. Nevertheless the Sudetenland should not have been put within the Czech frontier by any standard of justice or commonsense. Nor had the Czechs fulfilled their pledge to give them local autonomy.

In any case, Chamberlain had only one motive—to prevent war and save the peace. From a military point of view his policy of appeasement was forced upon him. He knew our weakness. Apart from the neglect of the Air Force we could never raise an army on the continental scale and our few divisions were, at that time, ill equipped. If there were any guilt in this all parties were equally guilty and not least the Labour Party who, as proved by many speeches, had voted constantly against re-armament while clamouring for the Government to "stand up to the Dictators". Nor was France in better shape, as Chamberlain knew. Daladier was horrified at the idea of war. The French nation, after frightful losses in the last war, were in no mind to fight another, and they were divided by political ideas and betrayed by political corruption. How could France fight against Germany with an utter lack of confidence in their own Government and political leaders, and with a deep pacifism in public opinion? France did not want to fight for the sake of Czech domination over the Sudetenland.

Collective Security had failed, but all intelligent peace-loving men and women had supported this ideal as fathered by the League of Nations. It was the hope of all civilised minds, as the one way of escape from war with all its destruction and ruin. That hope and idea must be remembered in judging the men and the mood of the time which had led to this unpreparedness for war. Who shall scoff at the idea of Collective Security, though it failed? Is it not revived in the charter of the so-called "United Nations"? Is it not still the only hope of avoiding a third World War, and the end of all things?

Hitler aroused suspicion in the mind of Chamberlain by stiffening his demands when concessions had been made, but after Chamberlain's second visit he made solemn promises which seemed sincere and worth the journey. He had no further territorial ambitions, he said. All disputes between Germany and England would be dealt with by friendly discussion.

When I asked Germans afterwards why he made these promises and then had broken them, they were abashed. "He wanted to be kind to the old gentleman", said one of them.

When Hitler revealed himself as a liar and perjurer by his invasion of Czechoslovakia I gave up all hope of peace to which I had clung desperately, with enormous doubt but holding on to that last straw. I had backed the policy of appeasement as the only one to avoid a universal conflagration in which we might all go down to ruin after tragic sacrifice. I still believe that Chamberlain was right in making those journeys with his umbrella. Supposing he had not made them?

Supposing he had failed to make those last efforts for peace? Would he have had the people so solidly behind him when war had to be declared? They knew at least that he had tried to the uttermost, and that he was a broken-hearted man when he had to make that declaration.

I met a German lady at a luncheon party after the entry into Prague. "What do you think of it?" she asked.

"I think it is damnable!" I said. "It means war between Germany and this country."

"No!" she cried. "Not that! Why do you think that?"

"Having crossed one frontier Hitler will be tempted to cross others", I told her.

She turned dead white.

"He must be mad!" she said in a low voice.

Some time passed before the trouble came over the Polish corridor. Hitler's patience was again exhausted. His voice was more strident over the microphone, to which I listened in my Surrey home. We handed a *carte blanche* to the Poles. It was for them to decide, said our Government, whether Hitler's demands constituted a threat against their independence which we would guarantee. I have always thought that it was unfortunate that we should have had to declare war over the question of the Polish corridor. For twenty years all international opinion had ridiculed that corridor dividing Germany from East Prussia. Foch, almost on his death-bed, declared that it would be the cause of the next war. But it was really a question of drawing the line against Hitler's spirit of aggression somewhere, and we drew it in Poland, though we had no strength behind our guarantee of aid to the Poles and could not reach them by land or sea.

11

A FORECAST

We were on the edge of war looking into the fiery pit. Many minds still resisted the thought even then, and would not allow themselves to think it conceivable. At the last minute, they thought, there would be a settlement, somehow. Why should we go to war about the Poles? Why should the whole of Europe be plunged into agony and death because of a frontier dispute between Germany and Poland? The Poles under Pilsudski had been aggressive and intransigent. Now they were riding a high horse and refusing not unreasonable demands. So many people argued in private houses and third-class carriages, as I overheard them. "There ain't goin' to be no war," said a friend of mine who had a shrewd and realistic mind. It was my literary agent, Curtis Brown.

Another friend of mine—a very extraordinary, brilliant, and amusing man, who edited a weekly review with great courage and audacity, was positively certain that war was out of the question. Only a few days before it was declared there were several Germans at his luncheon table, among them a good-looking fellow in the German Embassy named Fitz-Randolf with his pretty young wife, and General Wenniger, and a young German painter. They were astonished by his levity.

I spoke in a low voice to Fitz-Randolf and his wife who were sitting at a separate table in a restaurant near Victoria station, crowded at lunch time.

"Do you think this war will happen?"

"I hope not," he answered, "but I'm afraid. The situation is very serious."

A day or two later the young painter came to see me.

"I want your advice," he said; "I hate the Nazis and all their ideas. But if this war happens do you think I ought to go back to Germany and fight for the Fatherland—I'm on the reserve of officers—or stay over here in an English prison?"

What answer could I give him? It was a moral and psychological problem which he must answer for himself.

"I suppose it's one's country right or wrong!" he said. "Isn't that the English code?"

General Wenniger and I had a talk together in a Surrey garden where a game of croquet was in progress. His wife was there with a handsome young son.

"Is war coming?" I asked him.

"I pray not", he answered. "There is just a chance of peace. It depends on Hitler. We know nothing over here."

"What kind of a war will it be, if it comes?"

We were alone in that part of the garden. The August sun was warm upon us. There was the scent of garden flowers. Women's voices were laughing. They had forgotten the threat of war. They felt no trembling of the earth beneath their feet.

"It will be a strange war", said General Wenniger.

He looked down at the close mown lawn, as though thinking deeply. He knew a good deal, this Air Attaché in London. How much should he tell me?

"If it happens," he said, "the people in London will look up at the sky and say: 'When are they coming, those German bombers?' But they won't come. Months will go by, and they won't come. The armies in Europe will move up to their frontiers waiting for the German attack. But the German Army won't attack. This will go on for a long time, nearly a year perhaps. Everybody will think that it is a stalemate—a war without fighting. Then one day it will begin. The sky will be filled with bombing aeroplanes. The German tanks will move. It will be the beginning of hell on earth with every destructive weapon vomiting out steel. . . ."

"Very strange!" I said. I thought it was just his phantasy. What he told me made no deep impression on my mind. But what he told me was what happened. Looking back on that conversation I am astonished that he told me so much.

Now he is dead.

12

So It Came

One afternoon Wolff von Dewal and his wife, Elfa, sat at the tea table in the big lounge of the R.A.C. A little orchestra was playing but presently it ceased and the wireless was turned on. A series of official messages was broadcast. They were to do with the evacuation of school children from London. All arrangements had been made in case of need.

"This is terrible!" said Elfa. "I don't think I can bear it."

She turned very pale and whispered to my wife.

She and her husband were under orders to go at any moment.

A young waiter in the tea room spoke to me.

"I'm an Austrian. I suppose I shall have to go back. No doubt if I go back I shall be killed. Nevertheless I shall have to go."

"It will only be for a long week-end," said Wolff von Dewal; "I am told at the Embassy that it will only be for a long week-end."

It was the last time we saw them. He rang me up before going and repeated that phrase.

"It will only be for a long week-end. *Auf Wiedersehen!*"

In my house at Shamley Green we listened to Chamberlain's declaration of war. He spoke with the voice of a broken-hearted man.

"So it has come!" said Agnes.

We looked into each other's eyes. She was in ill health but I did not know that she was dying, my beautiful and beloved Agnes.

PART XIV

SECOND WORLD WAR

1

GHOSTS

MY son Anthony preceded me as a war correspondent with the British Expeditionary Force, owing to my private tragedy, and I was sorry to displace him. Afterwards he went to Holland and Belgium on the other side of the lines and had strange encounters which he put into a book, getting into trouble about it from the censors. There was too much truth in it, for indeed everything that he foretold, owing to his acute observation and the evidence he had obtained, came true uncannily. His prophecies were too grim, and shocked the censors profoundly, as did his light and brilliant treatment of the "phoney" war.

When I arrived at G.H.Q. in Arras, in the Autumn of 1939 I had the queerest sensation of being a ghost and walking among ghosts. For every village into which I went, and every bit of country through which I passed, every town in which I halted with the younger crowd of war correspondents, was haunted by the young officers and men of the old war. Here I was in Arras again—the Arras into which I had gone so often with a steel helmet on my head when it was being shelled, when our men went through the tunnels to the big attack, when the pipers of the Gordons played up and down the Grand' Place with snow on their helmets.

Away towards Lens was the Vimy Ridge, captured by the Canadians and Scottish through a snowstorm, after years when from its height German observation officers had seen everything of ours below and signalled to their guns if smoke curled up from Souchez or Neuville St. Vaast.

Outside Arras, only a few minutes in a car, was Monchy Hill which I had seen charged by cavalry when the bodies of young troopers lay about the ground below.

All over this countryside were the war cemeteries with their rows of crosses in crowded ranks. There below the soil lay the lads whom I had known, whom I had seen trudging up the Arras-Bapaume road, whom I had heard singing in *estaminets*, who had walked the Street of the Three Pebbles in Amiens, who had been up to their waists in the trenches sometimes, and who knew their chances were one in four when they went over the top, and less than that the second time. Those graves, those dead, the living spirit of those men had never been put out of my mind all the years between. It was the massacre of those young men—among them our very best, our future poets and painters, our finest quality in all ranks—which had made me so passionate for peace, so hard-working for it in all my books and in every line I wrote—all waste now—and made my mind resistant to the possibility of war, even when Hitler came to power. God Himself, I thought, would not allow it, if there is a God Who cares.

I was ghost-haunted. I myself was a ghost of that previous war. I went one day into Amiens and turned towards the Godebert restaurant with an officer who was with me. On many nights I had seen this place crowded with those who had come down from the Somme battlefields when their battalions were out of the line for a time. They had drunk too much wine here. They had flirted with little Marguerite. Now some of the officers of the second World War were there, but not many.

A woman came up to take my raincoat. She stared at me and then spoke to me in French.

"I remember you in the last war. I am almost certain of that."

"Yes," I said, "I was here in the last war. What were you doing then?"

"I was a young girl then," she answered. "I used to take the officers' overcoats when they arrived on rainy nights."

I remembered her. She had been a slim dark slip of a girl. Now she was a middle-aged woman, thin, and worn, and plain. Twenty-three years had passed since the Battles of the Somme, and I was elderly and haggard, and Agnes was dead, and there was another war on.

Or was it the same old war? Had I been on seven days leave and come back again? Or had I just had a dream and awakened to find the war still going on? That was another illusion. Everything looked the same. The Vimy Ridge looked the same, through dank mist or a flurry of snow. The British soldiers in Arras were just like those others—their fathers—with the same cut of the jib, the same Cockney accent if they were Londoners, the same broad Scots if they were Scotsmen. They were singing the same songs: "It's a Long Long Way to Tipperary", "The Long Long Trail", "Pack up Your Troubles in your old Kit-Bag", with a few new ones which I didn't know. The sons of the fathers were not much different, though afterwards in talking to them I found a difference. They were better educated, perhaps, and not so tough.

2

THE NEW CROWDS

I was billeted in the old Hôtel de l'Univers in Arras—a ramshackle old place which had been a convent in the eighteenth century. I had a small bedroom, plainly furnished, with bare boards and one small electric light bulb which gave a poor light for writing. In a room opposite mine was J. L. Hodson, whom I did not know before and with whom I made a firm friendship. He came into my room and said: "Hullo! I'm Hodson." He was, and is, a tall, thin, delicate man, with a long face and a long nose, melancholy-looking until his eyes light up with laughter, as often they do. He has a slight Lancashire accent, very broad when he tells Lancashire stories. After a few conversations with him I knew that I was in the company of a man of complete integrity, with a veritable passion for truth, shrewd, observant, critical and kind. Having served as a private in the last war he saw this one from the point of view of the private soldier, and was always out to remedy legitimate grievances they might have and unnecessary hardships they might be suffering—anything which might bring them a bit more comfort. He has made a great name for himself by his war diaries in France, North Africa, and on the Home Front, and by his broadcast talks. Before then he had been successful as a playwright, novelist, and journalist. Wherever one might find oneself, in whatever tight corner, one would like to have J. L. Hodson as one's comrade, and I was lucky in finding him there in Arras, and glad to keep his friendship afterwards.

I think it was Geoffrey Harmsworth, one of the new crowd of correspondents (for a paper he owned himself) who nicknamed Hodson "The Cardinal" because of some fancied resemblance to Cardinal Richelieu.

Geoffrey is the nephew of Alfred Harmsworth, Lord Northcliffe, and not unlike him in miniature. From the time of my arrival he devoted himself to me, regarding me as an Ancient and a frail thing, and we became inseparable companions. I needed his aid, for my eyes were getting bad and I was completely helpless in the darkness of Arras nights, beginning at four on winter afternoons. There was a longish walk from the Hôtel de l'Univers to the Censors' Office, and then to the post office where we had to telephone our messages to London. There was not enough light in the telephone box for me to read what I had written, but a young and highly intelligent corporal volunteered to read my script and did it perfectly.

Arras is not a good city for drunken, blind, or half-blind men.

Along the main streets steps go down from each old house across part of the pavement and on the other side the lamp-posts are a yard inside the kerbstone, so that if one avoids the steps one is apt to bump into the lamp-post, or if one steers past the lamp-post in the darkness one sprawls over a bottom step. The friendly hand of Geoffrey Harmsworth led me safely through this Scylla and Charybdis, though sometimes I ventured alone and came up against a *bec de gaz*.

I was one of the Old Brigade, and wore the ribbons of the last war on my tunic. A young officer staring at them and seeing the grey hair beneath my forage cap said: "Good God! You must be one of the original 'Angels of Mons'!" That, I suppose, was because I wore the Mons ribbon.

In the last war the number of war correspondents on the Western Front, as I have told, was seven. Now in the second World War there was more than a score at Arras and afterwards they multiplied exceedingly. Some of them were the sons of men I had known—among them young Montague carrying on the tradition of his father and writing very fine stuff as far as the censors would let him, which wasn't very far. Richard Dimbleby, who has made a great reputation for himself, was a phenomenon significant of a new era since the old war, broadcasting his despatches and doing them with great artistry, skill, and courage. It was indeed the men who spoke over the microphone who became famous in the second World War, and were beyond competition from those who wrote their stories, having a direct dramatic and intense effect through this new medium.

Richard Dimbleby was, when I knew him in Arras, a stout young man bubbling over with good nature, and wit, and, when occasion offered, with sweet strains of music. He had discovered a pleasant instrument in Arras—something resembling an accordion but with a difference. He drew heart-moving chords from it one evening, when lying on a four-poster bed in his billet. The four-poster bed was not strong enough to support his weight, and suddenly came down with a crash. Dimbleby continued to play his melody unabashed.

3

CENSORSHIP

There is a belief that the correspondents of the second World War were less heavily censored than their predecessors, but in my experience that was not so at all, nor did they have, until open movement began, anything like the facilities which we enjoyed. They were not allowed to see the intelligence reports, or the reports of Corps, Brigades, and

Battalions, during the course of an action, which had been my privilege. Up to the retreat from Dunkirk the censorship was rigid, frustrating, and ridiculous. The censors were so scared of letting anything through which might be of use to the enemy that they passed very little at all, and after writing a message so many words and sentences were deleted that often my verbs did not agree with their subjects, and the result was illiterate. Then I was writing for a paper—the *Daily Sketch*—which had but little space to spare and cut my stuff ruthlessly when it arrived, so that the result was ludicrous. Gone were the days when I spread myself over five columns in describing a battle. The only compensation was that during the "phoney" war there were no battles! But I wanted to describe the life and conditions of our men during a hard and cruel winter out there. Could I do so? No, sir! The censors prohibited any reference to the weather, and therefore one could not enlarge upon the difficulties and sufferings of our men, lying out beyond the Maginot Line or freezing almost to death, in old barns along the Belgian frontier. The Germans had only to poke their noses above the Siegfried Line to see the snow and ice. They too were having the hell of a time, but the ruling was that they were not to be told a word about it.

John Hay Beith ('Ian Hay'), a friend of mine, now Major-General, in charge of "Public Relations" under which came the war correspondents, arrived in Arras in all his glory and presided over a conference. I raised this question of the weather, and pointed out that German scientists knew enough to discover the state of the weather a few yards beyond their own frontiers, and even further than that. A depression travelling westwards did not suddenly stop and turn round.

"It is one of the rulings of the 'higher-ups'," said Major-General Beith.

I saw a glint of humour in his eyes when I suggested that the "higher-ups" ought to alter their ruling.

Once when the King came out for a visit we were not allowed to mention any village through which he had passed, but I wrote that one hamlet had a name like an old French *chanson*. It was Issy-les-Moulinaux, I believe.

The censor in charge sent for me and looked hurt.

"I can't pass that!" he said, pointing to my phrase.

"Why not?" I asked.

"The German Intelligence will know that old French *chanson*", he answered, sternly.

I assured him that this was only a figure of speech but out came that touch of imagination.

"It was all very difficult!" as we used to say in another war.

4

ALL THE WORLD'S A STAGE

The Hôtel de l'Univers was full of drama. In fact there were times when it was so like the setting of a musical comedy that it seemed unreal. Staff officers and King's Messengers used to be billeted there and Major-Generals—even Lord Gort the Commander-in-Chief himself—used to dine or take breakfast there with A.D.C.'s and G.S.O.I.'s. But it was also one of the inns frequented by ENSA entertainers led by Basil Dean. Into the courtyard when generals and staff officers were waiting for their cars would come little ladies with pink finger-tips and scarlet mouths, dressed in red trousers and yellow pullovers, or other highly coloured garments.

"Good morning, General!" would cry a famous comedy actress who probably had dined with him in pre-war days somewhere near Piccadilly.

"Good morning, Violet!" would answer the General, tapping a top-boot with a little cane.

"Good morning, Major. Any war this morning?"

"Hullo, Gertie! I didn't know you were here. No, nothing like war this morning, thank God!"

A little comedian would poke his nose into the courtyard and say: "Well, well, well, very fresh, isn't it? Not really balmy, I should say!"

He looked so exactly like himself on the stage that at the sight of him one laughed. He had made me laugh until my eyes were wet in *A Little Bit of Fluff*, when both of us were younger. It was, of course, Leslie Henson, unchanged and irresistible. He became a friend of mine and I often sat down at his table, but it was not for a light-hearted talk. Leslie Henson, comedian, preferred a really good go at world economics and the international situation. Still I remember one funny story he told me. He put it on to his son aged four who was taken to school for the first time. When asked how he liked it he said: "Not bad, Daddy. But some of the blokes come in their pwams!"

These ENSA companies used to play at the old Théâtre Royal, Arras. It was as cold as death in that winter of 39–40 and the poor players used to shiver and shake in their icy dressing rooms. It was ghost-haunted, for me, anyhow. Robespierre used to sit here listening to performances of *Racine* and *Corneille* and the comedies of Molière, before he became the Sea Green Incorruptible. I went into his house in a back street in Arras, still standing with its old shutters and hinges, as when he was a young lawyer, severe and prim. There, too, in one of the boxes had sat a villainous ex-priest Joseph Le Bon with his mistress. He was an ogre who led the Reign of Terror in Arras where the guillotine was busy, and where there was no pity for women or old nuns or young men with noble names.

The ENSA companies entertaining the troops of the British Expeditionary Force were brave and devoted. It was a frightful winter, beginning with heavy rains and going to be the hardest weather known for something like fifty years, when the roads were covered with snow and ice. Once it thawed and then froze again, putting the whole countryside under ice as smooth as glass. Cars span round like tee-to-tums. Tanks could not grip the ground. Pedestrians fell after a few steps. There were many broken pates and limbs.

But the gallant-hearted ladies of ENSA and their cavaliers set off on motor journeys to Lille and other far places along the lines and took all the hazards of the roads, escaping serious accident by a hair's breadth, or not escaping. Violet Lorraine and one of her friends were badly hurt and cut about.

During the rainy weather before the frost I was sitting and writing in my room of the Hôtel de l'Univers when I heard a cry of distress outside the door. It was a female voice. I rose from my typewriter in the middle of a sentence and opened the door. Outside was a distressed and bedraggled lady.

"Can I help at all?" I asked.

"Dear man, you can!" she cried. "For the love of Mike lend me a batman. I have been up to the line and fell in a trench, and I'm covered in mud from head to foot, as you may see. In twenty minutes I have to be on the stage and this is my only frock, and these are my only boots, my luggage having gone astray."

"Bad business!" I agreed. "Unfortunately my batman has disappeared for the day and I haven't the faintest idea how to find him."

"It's too terrible!" she cried. "What am I going to do?"

"I will be your batman," I said in a rash moment. "If you'll take off your frock."

She retired to take off her frock and flung it out of the bedroom door, followed by a pair of little fur-topped boots.

"God bless you," she cried. "I'll smoke a cigarette while you get on with the good work."

I needed her blessing. The frock was bespattered from the hem to the waistband. It was hard mud and I had no brush except a nail brush which became my instrument for this operation. But before getting down to it I shouted for Geoffrey, whose typewriter was tap-tapping in a nearby room. He answered my call and I explained to him the desperate situation of this lady in distress.

"While I get on with the frock, will you deal with the boots?"

I asked. "*Noblesse oblige!* And we have less than a quarter of an hour."

Geoffrey rose to the occasion.

"I'd better put them under the tap," he said. "It's the only way to get off that mud."

I made a good job with the nail brush. In ten minutes the mud was removed. Geoffrey brought back the boots triumphantly. They were wet through, the fur looked like a drowned kitten, but they were clean.

"Darlings!" cried the lady receiving them with ecstasy. She had no time for thanks. The stage of the Théâtre Royal was waiting for her.

But she thanked me next day. It was at luncheon time. I was sitting at table with General Nation and others. The *salle-à-manger* was crowded with high-ranking officers, including General Mason Mac-farlane, our Chief of Intelligence. Suddenly our lady of the comedy stage came into the room. She saw me from afar, and gave a cry of delight which caused everyone to look up. Swiftly she came towards me and when I rose she flung her arms around me and kissed me generously.

"A thousand million thanks!" she cried. "My Knight Errant!"

General Nation and others were surprised.

While I am telling about the old Hôtel de l'Univers, afterwards wrecked by bombs which killed one of the King's Messengers (a gallant old general) I cannot leave out the two maids who did my room, and little Yvonne downstairs who made me her *ange gardien*. Every afternoon, generally when I was in a frantic hurry to write "a piece for the paper", the two maids would come into the room with a Hoover, or some instrument of the kind, and with dusters and pails for a clean up. They had already dealt with Geoffrey's room and he had rewarded them with marvellous chocolate creams which used to arrive for him from female relatives and friends. One of these women was rather beautiful in a peasant way, with a rose-like complexion and brown smiling eyes. The other was a stocky little person, very downright and vigorous, and full of commonsense like most women of the French peasant class.

"For God's sake!" I would cry out in French, "can't you come at some other time?"

They explained that there was no other time. They had something like forty bedrooms to do and much other work.

We became good friends and had interesting conversations regarding French opinion, and the strange character of this war without fighting, and the chance of Arras being overtaken by war when the real thing began, if ever.

One day the stocky little woman, in answer to a question of mine, came close to me and lowered her voice.

"*Il faut faire un arrangement avec les Boches*", she said. "That is the only sense of all this. An arrangement with the enemy before the fighting begins. The French people have no heart in this war, and the Germans will be too strong for us. Our politicians have betrayed us. Also many of the soldiers are Communists. It is not a good outlook for France."

The woman who was rather beautiful was also friendly, and conversational, but never about the war or politics. She had a husband in the Maginot Line and I hope he was the father of the child born in my room one day when I was down at Metz, as afterwards I was told by her colleague.

"These little accidents will happen now and then", she explained.

Downstairs in the dining room Yvonne, aged about eighteen, was delighted to receive the attentions of the war correspondents and officers, particularly if they were young. But she was kind to the elderly, and, as I have said, promoted me to the rank of her guardian angel. It was a responsible position and one full of peril. She was as pretty as she was impudent and vivacious. She was, indeed, a charming and naughty child, very high spirited and aware of her prettiness, with dark eyes, and cheeks so rosy that they needed no artificial touch, and a merry tongue which she was pleased to wag. She had a never-ending feud with the *patron* who was severe with her, and with Charles, the waiter, who regarded her as an imp of mischief, and with the kitchen staff whom she exasperated to the point of fury.

"If you talk to me like that," she said one day to Charles, "I'll drop all these plates."

"You wouldn't dare!" he answered. "The *patron* would send you about your business. Never again would you see L'Hôtel de l'Univers and all the beautiful English officers."

Some words of that kind passed between them behind the swing door leading to the kitchen, as afterwards we were told. We heard a mighty crash. Yvonne had dropped her pile of plates—a yard high—to the stone floor. The *patron* sacked her. A petition from the war correspondents resulted in her being let off. As '*ange gardien*' I had no success.

5

MAGINOT LINE

"*Il faut faire un arrangement*", the bedroom maid had said, in a low voice. It was more than the expression of her own idea. Was that the kind of talk going on in the kitchens and *estaminets*, and cow-sheds and barns?

I had a sudden revelation of French opinion on the extreme Left when I went to the old mining city of Lens one day—to get to Lens in the old war had cost us hundreds of thousands of men—when Lord Gort was given a reception by the Municipality in the big Town Hall. While the official speeches were being made by the French *Commandant de Place*, and others, I talked with a group of miners, among whom I stood. There were crowds of them in their big leather hats, having come up from the galleries for this reception.

"What do you think of this strange war?" I asked them. They looked at each other and laughed and one answered—

"Do you wish to know what we think about this war?"

"I should like to know."

"It is the same old war", said the man who had first spoken.

"That is perfectly true," said the others; "it is the same old war."

"What do you mean by that?"

"We mean that it is a war made by Capitalism for the defence of Capitalism. It is a war for rival economic powers. Germany wants more power to make more money for her capitalists. France wants to defend her power so that our politicians may grow rich. The working man will again be her victims. They will die as they did in the last war, unless they decide that it is a fool's game."

"You are Communists?" I asked.

The men laughed again.

"That is the truth, comrade. We believe in Communism, as the only remedy for this kind of thing."

While they spoke to me the Mayor of Lens completed a speech in which he talked about the undying comradeship between France and Great Britain inspired by a common love for Liberty. Our Commander-in-Chief echoed his sentiments with warm sincerity. But I was hearing the opinion of the groundlings below the dais and it caused me to wonder what might happen in France if this sham war became real, as certainly it would one day.

6

OUR WEAK DEFENCES

With other correspondents, mostly with J. L. Hodson and Geoffrey Harmsworth, I went many times from one end of our lines to the other, and I was not impressed. If we had searched around for the worst kind of line anywhere we should have found it here, running along the

Belgian frontier. It was low-lying ground, without natural defences, and in many parts it was waterlogged so that trenches were impossible and there were only breastworks. A series of concrete pill-boxes, placed to give enfilading fire, were being made by the enormous labour of our men, wheeling barrow-loads of wet concrete along greasy duckboards. When finished they would constitute a fairly strong position against infantry and machine-gun fire, but with no kind of strength against heavy artillery and massed assault with tanks.

The French had left a few pill-boxes here and there, with steel doors. The Colonel of the Coldstream Guards—it was Bootle Wilbraham— the young subaltern who had lain in the bed next to mine in Amiens in the previous war, with a pile of books by Anatole France—tested one of these steel doors by taking a rifle from one of his men and firing at it point-blank. The bullet went through the steel as though it were butter. But on our left, where one French division was holding a long line, there was an open hole. The French were doing nothing about it. There was a number of old pill-boxes of the last war facing the wrong way and filled with muck. All the hard toil of our men sweating with heavy wheelbarrows, mixing masses of concrete, was made completely vain, because of that gap, unfilled between them and the coast. On the right there was no link up with the Maginot Line but an open corridor through the appendix of Holland. I could see no sense in what we were doing. Hodson, Harmsworth, and I were aghast at the condition of all this and at other weaknesses in the position and equipment of this British Expeditionary Force of seven divisions—to which two more were added later on. Our tank force was totally inadequate to hold up a German Army. Most of the tanks were of the old model and when I first went out were ill equipped. I was hurtled about the roads and fields of France by an officer of a cavalry regiment, lately mechanised, who had not even a shoulder piece to his machine-gun. He was a very amusing fellow, more used to fox-hunting than driving a tank, which he did with great spirit and recklessness. Though he made a joke of everything he was without illusions as to future peril.

"I'm one of the winkles on the pin," he told me; "a succulent morsel for the Jerry boys when they get going!"

Several times I rode with him in his iron steed down the long straight roads beyond Arras, across flooded fields, and over banks and ditches, while he talked over the wireless to his friends in other tanks, very lively and chatty conversations which kept me laughing. At journey's end I was surprised that I still had the use of my limbs, and was not just a mass of bruises, having been boxed between two plates of steel and jerked about like a pea in a pod.

But the more I saw of the military situation the less I liked it. If the

Germans struck through Belgium in heavy force how could our seven divisions hold them up, or how could the Belgians? Should we go forward into Belgium to meet them? That seemed to be the plan, as far as I could get it from generals and staff officers. In that case why all this intensive labour on pill-boxes and breastworks which would never be used? But there seemed to be a conflict of ideas about this in high quarters. When Anthony Eden came out and talked to us, very frankly, he turned to me and said: "It will be madness if we put our heads into that hornets' nest."

There was the Maginot Line. To the French Army and nation the Maginot Line was a kind of fetish. Nothing could pass the Maginot Line, they said. It was impregnable. The Germans would be wiped out in front of it. Behind it France would be securely held in a defensive war, economical in man-power.

Certainly when I went down to the Maginot Line I was impressed by it. It was marvellously constructed, in a series of underground defences like steel fortresses, equipped with the mechanism of modern battle-ships. Everything worked by machinery and electrical power. At the touch of a button great guns would turn in their turrets, and the ammunition would be brought up and loaded and fired. In addition to the main tunnels and fortress positions deep in the line of low-lying hills there was, to some extent, a defence in depth, with forts, visible only from above by their steel cupolas, providing a cross-fire. The whole line was manned by technical experts, and the best type of French officers, and men proud of this marvel of defensive and destructive power. They had worked out their field of fire in little squares, and had an apparatus which would show instantly an enemy attack in one of the squared places. All guns could be concentrated on that spot and nothing could live, they said, under the fire that would sweep it. I took their word for it, though a friend of mine named Blacker, of the Coldstream Guards, told me that he thought the available fire-power had not impressed him.

Beyond the line were frightful tank traps. If any German tanks were to get into those ditches they would be destroyed by the guns firing up and down them from either end.

"*Peu confortable!*" I remarked to a French lieutenant who took me to the edge of one of those pits of hell.

He grinned at this understatement.

There was a Gascon colonel in charge of one of the steel forts who strode with us across the countryside. He was like Porthos in *The Three Musketeers*, with a heavy stomach and a big appetite.

"If the Germans attack the Maginot Line," he said, "they will be annihilated. Their dead will be heaped up in piles. That is why they do not attack. The Maginot Line is impregnable. They know that."

It was a lovely countryside with gentle hills like the Sussex Downs and here and there a dark wood and a little valley. Over there was Germany. Through my glasses I could see German villages with their church spires. Some of them were in No Man's Land, six or seven miles in depth. It was then, on one of these visits to the Maginot Line, that I looked into Pirmasens where once I had taken lunch with friendly folk who had waved us goodbye.

I had conversations with many of the French officers and men, and had lunch with them in their underground messes, and saw all the routine of this subterranean life, with baths, and recreation rooms, and hospitals. Some of the personnel had lived down there for several years, only coming up top for short spells.

"It's not good for one's health," said one of the young officers; "it's damp down there and the air is not really good, and the absence of sunlight is regrettable."

He looked ill, I thought, and many of the men were pale and un-healthy-looking.

A French colonel spent some time with me in another section of the line and when we emerged into the open countryside through the great steel doors leading into one of the tunnels in the hillside he said:

"*Eh bien!* What do you think of our Maginot Line?"

"It's magnificent!" I answered. "But the Germans will never attack it."

He stared at me with sombre eyes in which there was a look of consternation.

"That is the most terrible thing you could say!" he exclaimed.

"They will be wise if they never attack it," I answered; "it is im-pregnable."

That was to cover up my *gaffe*. But he knew that I meant the Ger-mans would walk round it, through that open corridor opposite Sedan, and he had the same idea, no doubt, thrust away into his subconscious mind, because it was a terrible thought which would mean the doom of France.

7

ENCOUNTERS IN FRANCE

I cannot give a guess even now what was in the minds of the French High Command during this period of waiting for the German attack. Did they think it would never happen? Were they playing with the idea that before it happened they might come to terms with Germany? They were doing nothing to extend the Maginot Line and make it one continuous chain to the coast. Their main and immediate anxiety seemed to be to avoid any aggressive action against the enemy and any bloodshed on either side. Every day there was a certain amount of artillery work. German guns pounded French villages or positions where, as probably they knew, there were no French soldiers. The French answered back in the same way. Occasionally if the Germans happened to kill a few French soldiers the *soixante-quinzes* did a twenty minutes *strafe* as a sign of annoyance. But I remember an incident which was revealing of this passive form of warfare.

A group of correspondents, of whom I was one, was being shown some of the French heavies and long range guns behind the Maginot Line. A French gunner officer stood with us on a little hillside and pointed towards a wood.

"What do you see there, gentlemen?"

We stared ahead and some one said: "a line of trees".

"Nothing else?"

"Not a thing."

"Wait!" he cried with a laugh.

Out of the line of woods, rising above it, came very slowly the barrel of the biggest gun I have ever seen. It looked as long as the wood and a French soldier was astride its barrel.

The French gunner officer gave us its length. I have forgotten the figure but it was prodigious. It fired a ten ton shell.

A young New Zealander was with us in his slouch hat. He turned to the French liaison officer who spoke English.

"Has that gun ever fired at the enemy?"

"Not yet", said the officer, after a moment's hesitation.

"Well, don't you think it would be a good idea to fire it now? You're at war with Germany, aren't you?"

The French liaison officer became red in the face and he turned angrily upon his questioner.

"You civilians are so blood-thirsty!" he exclaimed.

The young New Zealander was abashed. He raised his hands several times, but could find no words. I knew what was working in his mind because I had had some talks with him. Either we were at war with Germany or we weren't. But he could not understand this holding back. If the French had good guns why didn't they fire them—or get busy in another way and make peace? All this war without a war was idiotic, he thought.

8

THOSE IN COMMAND

A distinguished visitor to G.H.Q.—Mr. Hore-Belisha, then Minister of War—seemed pleased with the general situation and with this form of warfare.

"Gentlemen," he said with extraordinary optimism, "we are winning the war comfortably."

How often after Dunkirk he must have regretted those words, but most of us have uttered words we should like to forget, and, worse still, have written them.

I had a long talk with Lord Gort, our Commander-in-Chief, and always when I met him he was very kind. But he discussed technical things rather than the general situation, and was reticent as to whether we should go into Belgium or not if the enemy attacked that way. He was always genial, high-spirited and simple in his manner. The day I saw him most pleased was when we visited a French school of interpreters and they put up a sham fight with guns popping all over the place. Every time they popped, Lord Gort seemed more delighted, and I am sure he would have liked it better if their missiles had been more dangerous. For Lord Gort was one of those men who are serene and cheerful under fire, as he proved on Dunkirk sands.

Sir John Dill was another general who was very charming to me and others. He was a brilliant talker and had a distinguished mind, I thought. Among the things he knew were Germany and the Germans. He had met most of the German generals, and they had gone out of their way to be courteous to him, and had let him see things concealed from most others.

From time to time we met most of our generals with the B.E.F. including Sir Alan Brooke, afterwards Chief of the Imperial General Staff and "Becky" Smith, Commanding the Brigade of Guards who invited me to lunch in his headquarters when the Coldstream Guards were holding the outposts of the Maginot Line. He was billeted in a château of impressive architecture, like a château on the Loire, but mostly modern. He was on terms of friendly badinage with his staff— a very whimsical and amusing personality.

One general whose name I have forgotten sent a wire through to Press Headquarters, desiring to see, at nine o'clock next morning, M. André Maurois and Sir Philip Gibbs, whom he would show round his front. We had seen his part of the front many times, and thought little of it, but this was a high command which had to be obeyed.

André Maurois and I rose at an early hour, for that general was a long way off and the roads were in a terrible state, owing to snow and frost. It was dark, with a cold mist, when we set out and we were chilled to the marrow bones when we arrived.

"Doubtless we shall have a good breakfast," said Maurois. "Porridge, ham and eggs, plenty of hot coffee. Glorious thought!"

We were saluted smartly by the sentries outside headquarters. We were shown into a nicely furnished room. On one of the tables lay a big book opened with blank pages.

The General entered and greeted us breezily.

"Good morning! Good morning! Rather cold!" He chatted a little about the weather.

"A hard winter, eh? Very unpleasant for the troops!"

Then he turned to André Maurois.

"I keep a visitors' book," he said. "I should much like to have your autograph, if I may. Here's the book."

"With pleasure," said Maurois. With a fountain pen ready for him he wrote his name in the big book.

"Will you oblige me too, Gibbs?"

"Certainly, General."

I wrote my name in the big book.

"Well now, that's fine," said the General. "Sorry you had such a long way to come. Good morning, gentlemen!"

He shook hands with each of us. We were conducted to the door. The sentries saluted smartly. We found ourselves in the road again with the snow and ice and the chilling mist.

When out of ear-shot of the sentries Maurois and I laughed loudly.

"Unbelievable!" I exclaimed.

"Is it possible?" exclaimed Maurois. "No hot coffee! No porridge! No ham and eggs!"

"One day," said Maurois somewhat later, "I shall write a short story. It shall be entitled *La signature de M. Maurois*. I will have my revenge!"

9

THE KING RECEIVES US

During the King's visit to the B.E.F. we took turns in going round with him to different units billeted in French villages and old farmhouses, where the stench of manure, and cows, and pigs holds the very spirit of rural France. It was all very picturesque with a touch of historical romance in its setting and the young King who had been so good with boys in his holiday camp, was equally simple and unaffected with officers and men.

One day he asked to receive the war correspondents and there was quite a little crowd of us. We arrived late as our leading car went astray outside Arras on its way to G.H.Q. and we had to run at the double when we arrived at the gates. The King came round and talked to each one of us, and, because I was the veteran among them, stood chatting with me quite a while.

"Back to the old job?" he said with a smile when he shook hands with me. "All this must seem familiar to you."

While he was going round Lord Gort came up with his curiously spring-like step and asked me a conundrum.

"Do you know the origin of the word '*estaminet*'?"

I had to confess that I didn't.

"It's a relic of the Spanish occupation of the Netherlands. It means '*Sta minute*', wait a minute. Rather good, eh? You never find it down south."

10

THE GRIM WINTER

During that hellish winter of 1939–40, our men of the B.E.F. suffered from the bitterness of the weather in the old barns and billets with only one blanket at night when they lay on the straw. Influenza caught hold of them, and there was quite an epidemic from which we correspondents were not immune. Almost everybody went down with what we called 'Arras throat'. It was a throat which became red and raw as though one had swallowed a knife. It caught hold of me among all the rest, but my own worst ordeal was when the roads were turned to ice after a heavy thaw. I found it impossible to keep on my feet, and every few yards went down with a crash, like most others. One evening after dark, but with a glimmer of snow by which I could find my way, I made a sprawl on the ground and excited the compassion of two French soldiers who were advancing my way. But before they could pick me up they hit the ice-bound road and lay on top of me cursing and laughing. But it was no laughing matter for those who broke their arms and legs, as many did during those months of frost. Worse still was it for the men who had to lie out at night without any kind of shelter in the outposts of the Maginot Line, which they took turns in holding. My friend Captain Blacker, of the Coldstream Guards, used every possible device to keep his men from freezing stiff at night. He made them rub their legs with oil, stuff straw into their boots and leggings, and cover their ears in Balaclava helmets, under their steel hats. In spite of all this when dawn came many men could hardly move their limbs.

Q

11

GRACIE FIELDS

Gracie Fields came to Arras and there was a rush for seats. Most of them were allotted to the men, but a number were reserved for G.H.Q., other officers, and some of the war correspondents. I was not one of the lucky ones, and when the others had left for the performance I retired to my little bed-chamber—entirely without heat—and felt like Cinderella. I lay down on the bed, and was trying to keep warm under a blanket when there was a tap at the door. It was my batman.

"A ticket for the Gracie Fields show," he said.

I arrived late, being in fact the last to come. The Commander-in-Chief had taken his seat. So had the French *Commandant de Place*, so had all the officers and men. But the French Guard of Honour was still in the *foyer* and when the Officer of the Guard saw me enter he thought no doubt: "Here is the highest bird of all. Here is the really Big Fellow!"

He shouted a command to his men and I received a royal salute to which I responded, I hope, with dignity and modesty. It greatly surprised two of my colleagues who happened to be watching. But after this grand reception there was an anticlimax. The ticket in my hand was for the topmost gallery, and to that altitude I climbed and stood among the Tommies.

It was worth it. Gracie Fields revealed the full range of her genius to that great audience of soldiers in the old Théâtre Royal of Arras. She was astonishing and inimitable in her changes from low comedy to high beauty, from the sublime to the ridiculous and back again. She put a spell of enchantment upon those men. Their shouts of laughter were followed by a hush when she sang without mockery or musical accompaniment, a rendering of the Lord's Prayer. She stirred them, uplifted them, and held them in the hollow of her hand. Next day she was seen in Arras and a vast crowd of soldiers followed her cheering, and singing her songs.

"She could have led them to the gates of hell!" said a staff officer. "They would have followed her to Berlin."

Noel Coward was one of those who entertained the troops, and put up at the Hôtel de l'Univers in this fantastic period of the war. I went with him to the Vimy Ridge one day and gave him an account of the battles there. It was a day much like the one in April 1917 when the Ridge was captured. There was snow on the slopes and the sky was grey and leaden. For some reason Noel Coward was deeply moved by what I told him, and his imagination enabled him to see and feel the history of that hill and the bloody fighting which ranged about it, at close quarters. I found him a serious and sensitive man—as sensitive as an æolian harp to every impression and every kind of atmosphere. No detail of character or scene escapes his notice, and as far as my experience went with him his wit and sense of humour were subordinated by courtesy and by simplicity of manner, which I found very pleasant.

12
CHRISTMAS PARTY

Lest there should be an idea that the B.E.F. spent its time in attending entertainments I must say that nothing of the kind happened. A man was lucky if he saw one show a month and thousands of them never saw a show at all. Though they were free from high explosives at this time, life out there was no picnic, and they endured great hardships from the weather and other conditions, especially if they were in lonely units like the anti-aircraft gunners, cut off from their fellows in muddy or ice-bound fields with a desolate landscape round them.

The war correspondents gave a Christmas party to General Macfarlane, Chief of Intelligence. He was our own Chief and always we had access to him, for he was pleased to lunch or dine at any time with us, and seemed to like our company. I had long talks with him about Germany, where I had met him first as military attaché, and he was very knowledgeable and interesting on many subjects, without thrusting forward his rank or authority. He also gave us some extremely good lectures on the whole set-up of the Intelligence Corps. But he was reticent about many things we wanted to know, perhaps for the reason that he did not know the answers. And now a glorious opportunity came to learn the inner secrets from him during our Christmas party. It took place at the Hôtel de Commerce at the other end of the town from the old Hôtel de l'Univers. Everyone was in a good mood. The Chief was highly amused by our Christmas gift of an enormous blue pencil. Songs went round the table. So did the wine. Somewhere about midnight I perceived that a group of my colleagues had entirely surrounded Mason Macfarlane and had their heads very close to his. He was answering all their questions. He was revealing, I thought, the inmost secrets of the military situation, as obtained by his beautiful system of espionage and information. I was much envious of those colleagues who had their heads so close to his, but could not break that barrier. The next morning the correspondent of *The Times* met the correspondent of the *Telegraph*.

"A great evening!"

"Marvellous!"

"Mason Macfarlane was in fine form. He told us everything."

"Yes. Wonderful! He just opened out. By the way, what exactly was it he was telling us?"

"I'm not quite sure. I knew it was frightfully interesting, but, well, as a matter of fact, I was going to ask you. I mean, just exactly what were the main points?"

No one could remember a single syllable of those priceless words uttered at a Christmas party by the Chief of Intelligence. . . . Not one among us would have prophesied that in the great political landslide of 1945 he would become a Labour Member of Parliament.

At one talk he gave us he stopped suddenly and seemed to be lost utterly in thought. That silence lasted quite a time and we were astonished. Then he seemed to pull himself back to his company and for some reason addressed me individually, perhaps because I was the senior of this crowd.

"Gibbs," he said, "you know as well as I do that when this war becomes active it will all resolve itself into relative power of men and machines. No body of men can stand against overwhelming weight."

Those may not have been his exact words. They were more veiled and cryptic, but that is the meaning I gathered from them. And they had no reference to what he had been talking about. But somehow they made me feel as though an icy finger had touched my spine. They were a warning of things to come.

I needed no such warning, though it confirmed my own dark apprehensions of what lay behind the veil. How could our seven divisions—afterwards increased to nine—with their oldfashioned tanks, and our lack of massed artillery, hold up a German Army of forty or fifty divisions? What was the good of that line of ours along the Belgian frontier? Hodson and I were so aghast at the general situation that we drafted a private memorandum to the Prime Minister and sent it to him, without result. It told the painful truth of things.

13

PRIVATE REPORT

PRIVATE AND CONFIDENTAL   *January 10th*, 1940
Memorandum prepared at the request of Lord Kemsley by Sir
Philip Gibbs and J. L. Hodson

1. In our view the Maginot Line is immensely strong (although it may not be impregnable if the Germans are willing to sacrifice enough men and material).

   Its strength is such that a major German offensive will probably be forced to the North. To that degree the attack is 'canalised'.

In the North the British hold a salient roughly from Armentières to St. Amand. The soil is clay, in winter readily waterlogged; trenches fill with water, streams widen very considerably. Our troops have done their best to strengthen the Front by trenches, improvements to wire and obstacles, and breastworks. Blockhouses are constantly manned. Fields of fire, however, are obstructed in various places by villages, woods and houses. These, it is understood, would be demolished were an attack expected. How long would demolition take? Is our Front one that could withstand a violent and powerful German attack? (By Spring the German divisions will number 176, but whether the whole of this number can be concentrated on the Western Front is not known by us.)

We are gravely doubtful if our Front could withstand the assault. It is not very strongly held in man-power. Blockhouses do not fire to their own front, but protect each other, and are at intervals of several hundred yards. The weather has not permitted the construction of a trench system which is formidable, although other trenches have been built several miles to the rear.

During the past few months British troops have worked extremely hard to strengthen the defences the French handed over to them.

Can it be said the French on our left (from Armentières to the sea) have been making similarly vigorous efforts to make their line more powerful? From what we are told by French officers and French war correspondents no digging is being done or has been done. Little exists beyond infrequent pill-boxes. When our 7th Cheshires took over a new part of the line near Armentières (and this battalion took over 15 miles in width) no digging had been done and pill-boxes (a mixture of old German and new French) were far from being in first-rate shape and were often befouled. (This was in November.)

It seems to us that while the Maginot Line is immensely strong, an extraordinary 'hole' exists in the North, inviting attack. Why the French have not done more to close it is beyond our knowledge or understanding.

The strategical plan is apparently to go forward into Belgium and meet the Germans there—perhaps on the Belgian lines of defence wherever they may be judged to be. But who can say the Allied troops will reach that place, or that the enemy will be stopped there? If we fall back, to which position shall we retreat? The Belgian Frontier where British trenches are dug? In that event, why not dig French trenches also?

But can the enemy, supposing they are advancing strongly, be held on that comparatively slender line? We seriously doubt it.

If not, whither do we next fall back? The line which suggests itself is the old German line on Vimy Ridge, held by the enemy for the best part of four years, a line which Nature has done so much to design. But are we, in fact, preparing that line or preparing it in any marked degree? So far as we know, the Allies are not.

In our view the Allied Front in the North is more vulnerable than it ought to be, or need be. Enormous numbers of workmen could be employed, diggers, concrete-makers, builders. Precious time has been lost. Every day is important. The ideal would be to construct a true Maginot Line along the whole Belgian Frontier. That is impossible now, but the nearer we get to that ideal the better.

2. *Equipment*:

Deficiencies still exist. A few examples follow:

We have only *one* Tank Battalion in France. It has 50 Infantry tanks which are Mark 1. They are not numerous enough, modern enough, or big enough. We urgently need tanks three or four times the size which will fire 2″ shells. We haven't got them. These tanks of ours (size about 30 tons) may find themselves opposing 80- or 100-ton German tanks. We have no precise knowledge of the size of German tanks.

(We possess, of course, in France other and smaller tanks than the infantry tanks, tanks manned by ex-cavalry and used mainly for reconnaissance.)

Our armoured cars will stop a bullet but not much (if anything) more. They cannot (as the French cars can) be driven backwards as easily as forwards. Ours must go into reverse. In short, ours are out of date.

At the end of December a captain in the Royal Fusiliers asked us to point out that not ten per cent of his men had battle dress and few of them when up in the Maginot Line in 20 degrees of frost had a pair of gloves.

In November the Intelligence officer of a brigade informed us that their Infantry battalions still lacked their full complement of mortars. Instead of two per platoon, they had about two per battalion and half of those lacked sights.

Of our infantrymen and gunners who now possess gum boots, the bulk have bought them out of their own pay.

Our battalion in the forward outposts in the Maginot Line is given two Tommy-guns (sawn-off machine-guns) for patrol work. Those guns are handed over to the incoming battalion (that is, from one battalion to another). Is this because we possess only two such guns? Other examples could be given.

In our view the army is overmechanised. We are now importing mules to France from India. It is high time. In the recent severe frost 60 per cent of our mechanised transport on the Maginot Line was immobilised. The French transport we have seen near the Maginot Line is almost entirely horse transport, including horsed artillery. Perhaps they have not gone far enough, but we have probably gone too far.

3. *Food*:

While food is good, any suggestion that the men have 4 meals a day is, in 90 per cent of cases, nonsense. Usually the men's last meal of the day is tea at 4 or 4.30. Nothing further is issued to them till breakfast next morning—a gulf of 15 or 16 hours. They have 3 meals within 8 hours followed by a gulf of 15 or 16 hours. Is this wise? Why not make the evening meal later or insist on cooks and quartermaster devising an issue of soup during the evening?

Why not issue the troops with a proportion of brown bread? It is more nutritious, keeps better and has more taste.

A bacon-cutting machine is needed to make the 3 ounces of breakfast bacon go as far as possible and look its best. Many battalions left their bacon-cutters at home.

4. *War Correspondents*:

After 3 months in France no British journalist has been, so far, allowed to visit our troops in their advanced posts in front of the Maginot Line although, for the most part, it is as safe there as in the Strand, W.C. (or safer). It is the French who will not permit it. Are we wise to allow them so much control over us? Several of the journalists' conducting officers have been to these advanced posts, but no journalist. One conducting officer described the Front Line the morning he was there as resembling Hampstead Heath on a Bank Holiday, so numerous were the visitors. But no journalist was among them.

If we cannot visit our troops at the only spot where they face the enemy, what are we doing in France?

PHILIP GIBBS
JAMES LANSDALE HODSON

14

A FAMILY IN FRANCE

I came to know a little family in Arras where my friend Douglas Williams had arranged a little private mess which he allowed me to join. The house was occupied by a mother and three children with whom I became good friends. They were three little girls, ranging from six to ten or thereabouts, and sometimes they would sing the little old *chansons* of France to us. One of them, the eldest, played the violin remarkably well for her age. The mother was a pleasant looking French lady of youngish middle age who provided us with most excellent dinners, marvellously well cooked, so that Douglas Williams was able to entertain distinguished guests—several generals from G.H.Q.—and to give them something good. It was a pleasant little retreat, and we were friends of the family. When I went there alone one day the mother asked whether she could speak to me in confidence.

"*Certainement, Madame!*"

"Sometimes I'm afraid for the little ones," she said. "Do you think the war will come this way, when it comes?"

"There is a chance of that," I answered.

"Do you think I ought to take the children away now? As you know my husband is an officer in the army and I do not want to let him know that I am worried. But I ask your advice as a friend."

I told her that if I had three children in Arras I should take them away down south. "I know nothing about the future course of the war but Arras might well be in the danger zone."

"It is very difficult for me," she said. "This is our home. We have no other place. But I would not like my little ones to be killed."

I do not know whether she fled in time, before Arras became a battle-ground, and before the Germans occupied it. I hope so with all my heart because of those children.

15

FRENCH DEFEAT

I went home on leave on a military plane from Rheims, known by its code word of "Panther", just before the German attack in April. It was bad luck from the point of view of a war correspondent and directly I heard of the opening of the offensive—it was the end of the "phoney" war at last—I made every effort to get back, but was held up for a few days. My friend Blacker, of the Coldstream Guards, and Geoffrey Harmsworth, were in the same case. Blacker was a neighbour of mine in Shamley Green, living in a house on a hill top which once was mine, and we talked one day of the ordeal ahead. It would not be amusing. The Germans would hurl everything against us, and there would be enormous casualties. He, as a medical officer, and I, as a war correspondent, would be under fire with the rest and there was a chance, perhaps, almost a certainty, that we should not see Shamley Green again. Neither of us said so, but that thought was in our minds, and in the minds of those who said goodbye to us and held us in their arms. Shamley Green was beautiful before we left that day with the Spring sunshine on the little hills and the first green showing in the woods where the cuckoo was calling.

"I've had a good life," said Pip Blacker. "I've enjoyed this house and garden."

We were going by different routes and said: "Well, goodbye, old man!" It was almost humiliating when we both returned alive and well a few weeks later when the Germans reached the Channel Ports.

Geoffrey Harmsworth and I were given places on a plane setting out for Paris. From there we should have to get to Amiens to rejoin our crowd at Arras. Among our fellow passengers was a large-sized lady with a beautiful face who was going to work in our Embassy in Paris. She was a heavy weight, and our pilot raised his eyebrows at the sight of her. We had to come down near Dieppe because of a German air raid in the neighbourhood, and our landing place was surrounded by ammunition dumps, which would make a fine display of fireworks if any bomb touched them off. I walked around with the large-sized lady, who was highly intelligent and very charming. But she looked wistfully at the aeroplane standing in the field.

"I don't think I shall be able to get up there again!"

"Oh, I'll lend you a hand," I said.

She laughed at this offer of help from a small-sized fellow.

"My dear man," she said, "I don't want a hand. I want a crane!"

However she went aloft and in due course we came down on Le Bourget aerodrome near Paris. It was on a day when the Germans had broken through at Sedan, just through the gap where the Maginot Line ended. Their massed tanks were driving towards Boulogne. Geoffrey and I did not know that until we were about to board a train to Amiens crowded with French soldiers. Suddenly the stationmaster cleared everybody out.

"What's the matter?" I asked.

"This train will never get to Amiens," I was told. "The Germans are already there. They are bombing every train."

The Germans in Amiens! I could not believe my ears. If that were so the British Expeditionary Force was being cut off. We should never get to Arras. What was happening to our colleagues? How could we rejoin them? Worse still, what was happening to France and the British Army? It looked like a major disaster. Paris itself was not safe if the Germans were in Amiens. These thoughts, rushing into my mind, were almost paralysing.

"We must get back somehow," I said to Geoffrey.

There was a man I knew in Paris named Lord Malise Graham. He was Military Secretary. I had once had lunch with him in Lowndes Square with his beautiful mother, the Duchess of Montrose. He might be able to put us in touch with our own crowd. Geoffrey and I went to see him and he looked worried.

"My advice to you," he said, "is to go back to England while the going is good."

"No," I said, "we must rejoin our unit. We must get orders somehow."

The next day he managed to locate our little crowd. They were on the move with a net closing on them. One message came through about us.

"We advise them to stay where they are."

There was one Scottish division and one English division south of the Seine. Geoffrey Harmsworth and I decided to get in touch with them and after hiring a car we established contact with some of them near Évreux. I remember one officer who was very civil to us. He had brought out his fishing gear, hopeful of having some good sport.

"I'm afraid fishing is likely to be disturbed," he remarked; "the situation is not beautiful in these parts. It looks as though the Boches will be over this countryside before long."

He advised us to go and see a certain colonel who was getting together a scratch force, capable of putting up a defensive fight for bridges and other vital positions. We went to see him but he didn't like the look of us.

"How am I to know that you are not spies?" he asked coldly. "Let me see your papers."

We showed him our papers but they didn't satisfy him.

"How am I to know that these are not forged?" he asked again.

Our simple demeanour finally convinced him that we were all right, and slightly repentant of his excessive caution—he was fully justified—he invited us to tea with a number of officers in his mess, established in a little old château. They were a very nice and friendly crowd but did not disguise their anxiety as to the military situation which was appalling. The Belgian Army had broken. The B.E.F. were in extreme peril. The Germans were getting near to Boulogne.

We saw the first exodus from Paris. But it was astonishing that the Parisians on the whole—the ordinary *bourgeois* folk—were calm and confident until a week or so later when panic took hold of them. They put their faith in Weygand.

"It was worse in the last war," they said, "until Foch struck at the right moment in the right place. . . . Weygand is biding his time. He will cut through that German column thrusting towards Boulogne. It is very narrow. By attacking from north and south he will cut off all the Germans in the West. You will see. Weygand is a great man. The Germans are extending their neck too far. He will lop it off."

So I heard from old fellows at the bookstalls on the quais and from men at café tables.

"We await Weygand's counterattack," they said.

So did we all. But day after day passed always bringing worse news, and the counterattack did not happen.

What in God's name was happening to the French High Command and the French Armies? The French Forces did not seem able to hold a line against the fury of that onslaught covered by swarms of dive-bombers.

They were bombing the outskirts of Paris and villages on the way to Paris. Geoffrey and I heard the crash of those bombs coming nearer and sounding heavier.

We hired a car and drove out to Pontoise and beyond. It was the road which the Germans would take on their way to Paris. The French countryside was sweet and lovely thereabouts, lyrical in its beauty, as when the old poets of France sang of these fields in Spring time. Wild flowers spangled the grass by the wayside. Little streams meandered through the meadows. The fresh green leaves of the poplars caught the sunlight like little flames. Here and there the roofs and turrets of old châteaux were visible beyond rusty wrought-iron gates. We passed through villages of ancient houses, but no one walked in them and they were abandoned.

Along the road by the side of a stream our driver got down to look at his car.

"It is beautiful here", I said.

He raised his hands and his eyes filled with tears.

"It is terrible to think", he said, "that the Germans may be swarming over this countryside like vermin."

I kept on asking one question to myself and to Geoffrey—

"Where is the French Army?"

There was no sign of a French Army along those roads which led to Dieppe. No sign of a French Army standing between the enemy and Paris. The roads were solitary. There was no French Army in this region. Now and again we saw a few French soldiers lying on the grass banks. Now and again a few more walked in single file, but they looked like stragglers without orders and without a purpose.

Not far from Pontoise we met a long column of refugees, and my mind jerked back to the early days of the first World War when I had seen an endless tide of people in flight from the same enemy. It was the same scene of heavy farm carts laden with household goods, on which were packed old women and babies. Peasant women pushed wheel-barrows and hand carts packed with bundles, and there were girls on bicycles, and elderly men and women trudging behind the carts, and young children clutching their mothers' skirts.

I talked with many of them. They had just been machine-gunned by a German aeroplane flying low. One girl had been killed and several wounded. A baby had been killed by a machine-gun bullet.

"Bandits! . . . Assassins!" cried a girl raising her clenched fist to the sky.

There were long slow columns of these fugitives along all the roads. They were white with dust and looked exhausted. Some of them camped out in the fields. They had fled from Dieppe and Boulogne and scores of villages where once our soldiers of the first World War had been billeted.

It was all happening again, the flight from the *sales Boches*, but this time there was no escaping, however far they went.

Paris was exquisite in those last days before the Germans entered it, and the last time I saw it. It was lovely at night through the Tuileries Gardens, or looking up the far vista of the Champs Elysées. But it was being abandoned, this city of enchantment and of the liberty of the mind, and of art, and genius, and corruption, and passion, and quiet hard-working lives, and of love which goes hand in hand through its streets and gardens. Cars were speeding away heavily laden. The trains to the south were packed. Weygand had not attacked. France was in mortal peril. The Germans would soon be in Paris.

There were a few English people stranded here still. One of them was a lady I knew. Her husband had been with me in Arras as a war artist, by name of de Grineau. She was getting scared because of the difficulty of getting back to England. I was able to be of some little service to her by putting her in touch with a man at the British Embassy who was helpful. Then Geoffrey and I were ordered back.

It was Lord Malise Graham who gave us this order, which had to be obeyed. We flew back and reached England before the Germans entered Paris and while our men were standing on Dunkirk sands waiting for the little ships.

England knew the worst which came with the surrender of France. We were alone.

PART XV

THE WAR AT HOME

1

THE DEADLY MENACE

WE expected invasion, and some of us knew that if the Germans landed in strength by airborne troops, or by sea passage protected from our Fleet by dive-bombers, our means of self-defence were utterly inadequate. Churchill made his heroic speech in the House of Commons, saying that we should fight on the hills and in the valleys and everywhere else, but under his breath he is said to have added that we should fight them if need be with broken bottles, for we had little else. That was true. We had little else. The Guards back from Dunkirk were standing on the coast of Lincolnshire without arms or ammunition. We had left all our equipment of guns and material of war in France. At the moment we had nothing to replace it, except flesh and blood and spirit, magnificent but helpless before the scythe of machine-gun fire, and the Tommy-guns of German parachutists, and the advance of light tanks and artillery brought on gliders.

Anthony Eden called for volunteers for an army of Home Defence, the beginning of the Home Guard, and a national response came from all classes and all ages. They were distinguished at first only by arm-bands, and they had no weapons in their hands. These young farmers and factory workers and gardeners with veterans of the last war—old buffers over sixty, who joined up for the guarding of bridges and night duty in damp fields, risking pneumonia, and getting rheumatism, were untrained and undisciplined and unarmed. What could they have done except die like heroes in the ditches if Hitler had gone all out to invade us after Dunkirk?

Many of us knew the full measure of our weakness. I knew it. The whole people were vaguely aware of it. But what astonished me on my return to England at this time was the complete lack of panic, the calmness, and a kind of fatalism with which most people faced this extreme peril. Friends came into my Surrey garden and played our family game of "madders" on the lawn, and did not seem perturbed. Now and again our eyes met, and each knew that behind this game of ours was the spectre of invasion, massacre, and death.

My gardener gave tongue on the subject.

"If any Germans drop down in Shamley Green I shall kill at least one of them with my spade."

"Then you will be a *franc-tireur*", I said. "You haven't even an armband. Shamley Green will be shot up, and the elders of the village, of whom I am one, will be led on to the Green for immediate execution."

I had an idea that this was a very likely ending for me and others, but I can honestly say that I thought it would be rather a good end, if invasion happened.

In my house there were conversations until late at night, similar to those happening in thousands of English homes. Mostly it centred round a young boy or girl—Tony's children. What would be the best thing to do about them? Shamley Green would be on the outer defence of London—not a safe place for children. Some arrangement ought to be made for immediate evacuation if the worst happened. Their mother, utterly unafraid for herself, wished to save these young people from the possible fate of being brought up under Nazi discipline and education. In her mind was working the possibility of getting them to the United States. Much argument ensued on that subject, with a thousand *pros* and *cons*, day after day, night after night, but on the whole with good humour, and always without a touch of panic.

In London, to which I went most days, there was no look of fear, but much of thoughtfulness, in people's eyes. At the Club the members discussed the chance of invasion as though they were talking about the chance of a wet summer. The balance of opinion was that it wouldn't happen because of the British Navy. But one noticed sinister signs about. Barbed wire appeared in the parks, utterly useless as a means of defence. Cement blocks suddenly obstructed one's way. Roads were mined on the way from Guildford to London. Dragons' teeth were sown in flat fields to prevent the landing of hostile aircraft. At Newlands Corner and other places, on what might be the outer defence of London, machine-gun posts, artfully camouflaged as barns or teashops, were prepared for a German Army of invasion and would have been handy little suicide posts for any brave lads defending them, if they had any weapons (which I doubt) to fire a few shots. Knowing something about war I observed these things on my way to London by car, with a smile and a laughing groan. It was just child's play. It was too ridiculous. It was enough to make a cat laugh—or an angel weep!

If the Germans were to come across in swarms of aircraft we should be at their mercy, unless they gave us time to rearm and re-equip our Army and our Home Guard. . . . Lord God! Give us Time! . . .

2

AIR ARMADAS

From my own garden I saw in the sky above many tourneys in that Battle of Britain which saved us from invasion. There were no guns around us, and this part of the sky was left to the fighters. It was marvellous weather and the sky was cloudlessly blue for many weeks. While a 'dogfight' was in progress I could watch the evolution of the machines by their vapour trails, weaving in and out as though flinging coils of white tape into the air. The sun glinted on the wings of these midges—our Spitfires and Hurricanes attacking squadrons of Messerschmitts always with heavy odds against them, sometimes one against five, one against ten, one against twenty. There were short bursts of machine-gun fire followed by something dark falling downwards, or something like a torch dropping—one of theirs, or one of ours. They did not flash across the sky like streaks of lightning, but manœuvred round and round, trying to force an enemy down, thrusting him back, flying above him for the kill. Villagers gathered on the Green to watch these high distant fights, sometimes three thousand feet above their heads, though often much lower. Women in their Surrey gardens stared up from their flower beds, and listened to the chatter of that machine-gun fire. Some of them had sons in the R.A.F. Perhaps their own boy was up there. Over the wireless each night we heard the gains and losses. Always the Germans lost more than ours, but always many of those R.A.F. boys were "missing". They were being thinned down. Our reserves were being drawn upon heavily. Our numbers of young pilots were decreasing rapidly. How long could they keep it up—this battle against tremendous odds,—this battle into which each of these young men flung himself, whatever the odds, recklessly, knowing that he was fighting for that landscape below, which was England? We hung on to the wireless for the nine o'clock news. Those quiet, bland, reassuring voices of the B.B.C. announcers gave us figures which were deciding the fate of our people for all time.

Eighty German planes shot down. . . . Ninety-two. . . . A hundred and twenty. . . . A hundred and eighty-six.

Goering's Luftwaffe could not stand the strain of those losses. We had won a great victory in the air. It was the second miracle in our favour. The first had been the evacuation from Dunkirk.

3

BLITZ

There followed the Blitz, with nine months of terror and destruction from German bombers.

I saw it in town and country. I saw with astonished admiration the valour of the English folk—old ladies and young girls, shopkeepers, taxi-drivers, dwellers in mean streets, nurses, old couples living in basement rooms, working girls in sky-high flats, clerks and factory girls —during this time of fiery ordeal. They were marvellous in their courage, in their spirit, in their endurance. Even now, remembering all that, it seems to me that it was supernatural in the sense of being beyond ordinary courage and ordinary human endurance. Some age-long tradition of pride and fortitude surged up among them. The strain of their forefathers who had endured and struggled through centuries of war, famine, plague, and grim conditions of life, stiffened them. Some faith, unspoken, in English liberty, in London pride, in scorn of all their enemy might do, held them up and would not let them wail. A sense of humour made a mockery of Hitler's devilry. They had their little jokes even in the ruins of their own houses and shops. "I'd like a nice cup of tea, dearie," was the only request of old women buried alive in their basements and dragged out from the ruins.

4

REFUGEES

The evacuation of London mothers and children was well and quickly done, and English villages became overcrowded with these refugees. Every cottage and every country house took in these children, and the billeting officers did not find many selfish people who resisted this obligation, though always some. There was an unhappy revelation of the foul conditions under which many of them had been living in London slums. Many of the children arrived verminous, and some of them were imps of Satan who had never been trained to decent ways. But in my village we were lucky and the children who arrived were mostly from respectable families, and many of their new foster parents fell in love with them.

The mothers were the most troublesome. I had two mothers and two families of small children boarded on me. One mother was an Irish woman of high spirit and ceaseless eloquence in the rich brogue of Southern Ireland. She had one small boy of seven or eight, another of four, and a third to come. The other woman was a Londoner of ample proportions, with a little girl and a baby. From the moment they were put together, with beds and bedding, in my largest room, a deep and deadly feud prevailed between them. The children joined in this family vendetta. The Irish lady's small boy hit the London lady's baby. Screams and howls resounded throughout the house. One of them was thrown out of the window—not high from the ground. The Irish lady with arms akimbo had much to say about life, including her husband who seldom sent her a part of his wages and expected the 'bloated rich' to keep her in comfort. The Cockney lady's husband came down for week-ends, sleeping in my hut at the end of the garden. He was on embarkation leave before sailing to Egypt and had come to say goodbye to his wife. When he left I slipped a bit of money into his hand, shook hands with him warmly, and wished him the best of luck. On his departure his stout wife moaned, swooned, and had to be restored by brandy. A piteous scene, but one which staled on repetition. The husband came down for several week-ends. Each time his wife wept, moaned, and swooned, requiring a further dose of brandy. They stayed with me a year or thereabouts, during which time another baby arrived. "It was all very difficult!"

I had two Swiss maids who were German-speaking and temperamental. In the evening they kept their wireless on until late hours and always it was turned on to German stations from which the voice of Hitler screamed. They were anti-Hitler but liked to hear the news in German. They gave the glad eye to my young nephew, Barry Rowland, who was living in the house with me, quarrelled with my sister, wept from time to time on my shoulder, and when the air raids were heaviest—they happened every night—came down in their dressing gowns to sit in a damp cellar which had been fixed up as an air-raid shelter.

5

THE AMAZING SUMMER

When the Blitz first began my son with his wife and two children were living with me, and when the sirens howled the two children who had been fast asleep were brought down to the shelter, while Tony, and Maisie, his wife, waited and listened above the trap door in the hall which led down to that cellar. Heavy crashes shook the house, and I thought of all the children in England whose first impressions of life would include this shrieking of the sirens those heavy thuds which shook the earth, and perhaps a look of fear in the eyes of their fathers and mothers because of this peril to them.

One small girl, as dainty as a fairy, came tripping through my garden every morning on the way to school, and stopped to have a few words with me. Her family had been killed by a bomb nearer to London and there was a scar on her neck but no look of terror in her eyes.

Fortunately the majority of children were kept away from fear, unless they saw death and mutilation around them. At the end of my garden I had a cottage used as a school for small people from four to seven years of age. Sometimes during daylight raids they were brought over to my air-raid shelter, and I went down with them and made a game of it, pretending that the beds were railway coaches, and that we were on express trains going to Manchester and other far places. There was great competition to be the engine-driver, or the ticket-collector, and screams of excitement and laughter drowned the noise of the howling sirens or the crash of distant bombs.

The bombs were not always very distant. The German bombers, beaten back from the outskirts of London by anti-aircraft fire, growing more intense, had a habit of scattering their bombs on the way back, and Shamley Green was in a direct line with Shoreham Gap which was their mark for coming and going. One evening I was playing billiards with my brother-in-law on a miniature table when the whole table lifted up from the ground, and the balls ran down to one end. The walls shivered and there were seven explosions from a stick of bombs dropped on Farley Heath above the village, but sounding as if they were in my garden.

"Rather close," said Eric Ibbetson; "and I was just making a break!"

They were lovely summer nights when the Blitz first started. It was "The Amazing Summer" (of 1940). But from the velvet sky above the flower-scented earth came these death-searching devils, and the silence of the countryside was broken by most unpleasant noises. The worst of them were almost disembowelling but I only heard it once. It happened when I was strolling round my garden with two or three ladies of the neighbourhood and my sister Helen. Suddenly there was a noise like the howling of seven devils. It had a wild shrieking, disintegrating note, growing louder and louder with frightful menace as it neared the earth.

"O Christ!" cried one of the ladies of Shamley Green, falling among the bushes in my garden.

For a moment we all thought we were dead. But we were perfectly alive.

And one night I was up on the hill in the house I had built some years before, now inhabited by my friend Blacker and his beautiful wife, Helen. They had a grandstand view of the air war over the Sussex

Downs. They could see scores of searchlights feeling through the sky with their long white fingers of light for hostile planes. They could see our coastal batteries opening fire, and the anti-aircraft batteries, concealed behind woods, sending up shells which left white puff-balls in the sky. I had dined there one evening and listened to some music of Chopin and Schubert played by a talented lady. Here was civilisation in a world delivered over to hellish things. "Let's go outside. Something funny is happening", said a commander in the Navy who was the pianist's husband, home on leave after his ship had been torpedoed.

We went outside. It was fairly late, and a velvety darkness had crept across the sky, pierced by many stars. But this darkness had suddenly been changed to a vivid greenish light coming up along the line of the Downs and spreading across the whole countryside in which we stood. It turned the grass to a bright sinister-looking green. Our faces and hands were green. Away there on the coast we could see some flares rising and falling.

"This is like the end of the world!" said the naval commander in a low voice. "It's frightening. I've never seen anything like this before." I never saw that phenomenon again, and to this day I do not know what it was.

Every night in Shamley Green we heard the German bombers on their way to London, flying low, it seemed, flying so low that one could see these black bats of death skimming the tops of the trees and flying over our chimney-pots. The searchlights were in action, criss-crossing the sky, feeling for one of those black-winged things and catching it sometimes in their white beams. The guns at Dorking, and Reigate, and Newlands Corner, and Brooklands, would open fire, turning back some, perhaps, but letting others through the outer defences of London. Presently we could see the sky redden and pulsate, as flames licked below a pall of smoke. London was on fire again. To-morrow I should drive through new ruins. To-night the Londoners would be crowding into the tube shelters or sitting below the stairs in little rows of houses, which would go down like packs of cards if bombs crashed among them. There would be more piles of charred timber and masonry, more litter of glass in the street, and in the dawn people staring at the wreckage of their homes. Men would be working feverishly to dig out dead and living bodies from the rubbish heaps. London was "taking it" again.

6

NIGHT SHELTERS

My brother Cos was in London, working with the postal censorship. He had rooms in Grays Inn which he loved. One evening he came out at the beginning of an air raid to see the bursting shells. He felt the lash of a whip across the back of his left hand.

"Who did that?" he cried instinctively.

"Hitler!" said a voice from the darkness.

He had a bit of shrapnel through his hand.

He was getting on in life, and becoming rather deaf—very deaf—before the war, and all war ended for him, but he joined the Home Guard and looked distinguished in his battle dress when this uniform was issued. Later when the Americans entered the war one of their generals came to a place he was guarding and, glancing at my brother, who was preparing to present arms in style, said in a genial way: "Say! Do you salute me, or do I salute you?"

As an anodyne against war, air raids, black-outs, and all unpleasantness my brother became a passionate painter in oils. During luncheon time he would make a pencil sketch of Grays Inn, or some other place, and at night, alone in his room, when London was rocking under another air raid and houses were falling round about, and fires were raging, this brother of mine would sit painting with a fine brush, hour after hour, absorbed in his work. But one day he had a "hunch" not to sleep that night in Grays Inn. He stayed in his office with other colleagues, playing chess with one of them. When he went to Grays Inn next morning he found his room badly damaged, with its windows and doors out, and everything covered in broken glass and plaster. He had to find other lodgings in London and twice he was bombed out again, but not while he was in them.

My brother-in-law, Eric Ibbetson, used to drive me up to town when I had work as Vice Chairman of Charing Cross Hospital, among other duties. Always it was with a sense of tragedy that we passed through more ruined streets, past more ruined houses, and churches, and theatres. So many of our historic treasures were destroyed—Chelsea Old Church, The Middle Temple Hall, The Guildhall, the old streets round Cheapside and St. Paul's. I walked over the broken glass and the litter of rubble, past the wreck of St. James's, Piccadilly and into Jermyn Street where houses were still burning. The Carlton Club was like a ruin of ancient Rome, with broken pillars and the sky showing through its roof. A daylight raid had done that damage, and by a miracle the staff escaped that avalanche of falling masonry in the cellars below. The cook, and the chambermaids, and the serving maids and the men marched over to the R.A.C. and my friend the porter of that club, a hero of the last war, was filled with admiration for their courage.

"You would have wanted to kiss every one of them, Sir Philip!" he told me. "They came marching like Guardsmen. What hearts! Marvellous!"

I made an appointment one morning for lunch with Eric Ibbetson, but when we met in Lisle Street our restaurant was only a hole in the ground. Eric named another place in a neighbouring street, but that too had disappeared overnight. So had St. Anne's, Soho, now a pitiful ruin.

On one night the bombers dropped their stuff down Queen Victoria Street, smashing up *The Times* office and many others, and raising hell-fire round St. Paul's, as in the Great Fire of 1666. Among other burnings were all the book stores of the wholesale agents and publishers. Two million books were destroyed that night, including all the cheap editions of my own and of many other authors. It was a heavy loss to some of us because they could not be reprinted. But nothing seemed to matter very much in this time of sudden death and blazing ruin. If you were alive you were lucky—if you liked life.

There was a scrubbing maid at Charing Cross Hospital. She always cleaned the steps and was generally singing at her work, with a bright "Good morning!" and a push of her pail for everybody who passed. But the matron noticed that she had been down in the dumps lately, until one morning she was singing again.

"Hullo, Molly," said the matron; "what's been the matter with you?"

"Well, matron, it was like this," said the cleaning maid; "when I married my Bert 'e made a nice little 'ome for me. Vawses on the mantelpiece, a gramophone in the corner, everything pretty. When 'e went away to the Army I kept worrying lest the Germans should come and bomb it all. Kept on worrying, you know! Then two nights ago they came and bombed it. So now there's nothing more to worry about. See?"

Many of these people developed a fatalism, which is another word for courage and resignation. I spoke to a girl in a tobacco kiosk. She had had a bad night down Clapham way. Lots of houses destroyed. Lots of people killed.

"Do you keep your nerve?" I asked.

"O Lord, yes! Why not? If one gets killed, well, that's that. I ain't worrying!"

A friendly policeman in Soho, which caught it badly, took a more cynical view.

"I can't understand the courage of these people," I said; "how do they stick it out night after night like this?"

"Can't do anything else!" he said. "No blinkin' alternative. And, bless you, they can't go to sleep now if the guns are quiet."

There was an alternative. They could have trekked out of London, slept under hedges, begged food in the villages. But no, they preferred to stay in London, to sleep in basements or tube shelters, in little shops of their own still standing amidst the ruins, though all the glass was out and the windows were pasted up with cardboard. One remembers the slogans they scrawled up when their windows were blown out.

> *"We believe in fresh air."*
> *"Hitler can break our glass but not our spirit."*
> *"This shop is more open than usual."*

They hoisted little Union Jacks over the piles of rubble which once were their homes. I never saw anyone weeping for treasures that had gone.

7

DOWN THE TUBES

I went down into the tube shelters at night and saw the life there. Every evening at dusk there was a queue outside the stations—men with mattresses on their heads for families following behind, women with babies and blankets; young girls; factory workers in trousers and pullovers; respectable-looking men and women neatly dressed; boys with books under their arms. At first conditions had been frightful. The atmosphere was stinking. Sanitary arrangements did not exist. There were scrambles for places on the platforms. But this was sorted out. Tickets were issued. Sanitary measures were taken. Fresh air was pumped down.

I went to see a number of these shelters with the matron of Charing Cross—Miss Cochrane, of nursing fame. She was going to inspect a number of first-aid posts attended by Charing Cross nurses. With us was Mr. Jones, secretary of the Hospital, whom I call "The Angelic Jones", because he is that. We were glad to have the company of the matron that night when there was a heavy raid again, for she has the spirit of Queen Victoria, the courage of Florence Nightingale, and the humour of Marie Lloyd. With all hell raging overhead she was very cheerful and jolly. As we emerged from one tube station to go to another the sky above us was scarlet, and throbbed like boiling blood, as the matron said. The streets were utterly deserted and the roofs of the houses and the pavements were like shining silver under a bright moon which looked down that night upon the scene of fire and destruction.

The tube shelters were crowded and once during the night the matron drew me on one side.

"I tremble to think", she said, "of what is going to come out of these shelters. Some frightful epidemic will sweep London like a plague!"

But by some miracle no epidemic came. That was partly due to nursing posts provided by Charing Cross and other hospitals. Doctors went the rounds watching out for flushed faces or feverish children, while the nurses did devoted work. The matron had a great reception, I noticed, when she appeared, and the nurses made a rush at her with smiling eyes. She was a disciplinarian but a human laughing soul and always on their side.

I had some strange conversations with those people in the shelters. There was one place we went to under the Adelphi Arches which was set aside for the downs-and-outs, the verminous, the drunks, and the lost souls. It was run by a group of conscientious objectors who were certainly doing a good work of Christian charity. There was an old tramp there, as merry as Falstaff, who told me he had had a good life on the open road. He knew every road, every field path, every heath in England.

"Try me out", he suggested.

I asked him how he would get to Peaslake from Shamley Green across country. He laughed and said: "That's easy!" He knew it like the lines on his hand.

"The War Office ought to employ me," he said; "I'm better than a map. For sixty years I've walked the roads and the heaths from John o' Groats to Land's End. I've had a good life, and if a bomb gets me to-night I shan't complain. A good death and a quick one!"

A strange lady was there who spoke French and knew Paris and the Riviera. She had been a lady's maid with titled people. She had interesting views about life and war—tragic views. For here in this shelter, under the Adelphi Arches, she was with the down-and-outs who were very verminous. And yet I swear that, with some exceptions, they were a cheerful, friendly, crowd, and I lingered with them.

The German bombers had passed when we went up to the fresh air again, but the sky was still throbbing with the glow of angry flames. It was another night of London agony.

8

WAR IN THE AIR

I went up North to Liverpool. My daughter-in-law was taking her children to the United States, and Tony was going with them to do newspaper work and lecturing. I went on board with them, exciting the deepest suspicion of two young officers who had heard my name and thought I was there to give away the whole show as a journalist. That is the kind of suspicion which still clings round my old profession, as though journalists were dirty dogs. Have they not proved their loyalties? Have they not as much integrity as other professions? They are not always snooping around for news like garbage-hunters.

The ship was a big cargo steamer, carrying a naval gun and gunners. She had an enormous deck-space and I shuddered at the sight of my little grand-daughter, Frances, dashing about like an elf with every risk of falling overboard. Martin, my grandson, had boarded this ship, armed with a long-bow and arrows, as though for great adventures among the Red Indians. I said goodbye to them and my heart gave a lurch. Should I ever see them again? The perils of the Atlantic crossing were not negligible. German U-boats were taking a terrible toll of our shipping.

That night I put up at the Adelphi Hotel.

Most of the visitors had gone to their rooms when the sirens howled over Liverpool and presently there was the first great crash of high explosives.

In the hotel a number of arrows at the end of passages and stairs pointed the way to the air-raid shelter. Down the stairs came a crowd of people, not hurrying, not panic-stricken, but making little jokes to each other. Quite a different crowd from those in the London tube shelters. Young women with scarlet lips came down in their dressing gowns of flowered silk, smoking cigarettes in long holders.

"What a bore all this is! What a nuisance that man Hitler makes of himself!"

"Dammit, I can't get a decent night's sleep", said an elderly colonel.

"What about a spot of bridge?" asked a young naval officer to a tall, slim, thing with straw-coloured hair.

It was all very chatty, like an interlude at a dance.

Some of these young people sat with their backs to the wall of the basement room with their hands clasped round their knees. A group of officers played gin-rummy on the floor. Outside in Liverpool the guns were firing, and every now and then the earth shook with an exploding bomb. Away there in the docks was my family on a big cargo ship. The docks were the target of the night.

So it went on for nine months. "London can take it", said the American newspapers. But so did Coventry, and Bristol, and Portsmouth, and Plymouth, and Exeter, and many other cities, and many villages with no military objective and only little old churches and thatched, or tiled, cottages and one old inn. The black demons went to

Clyst St. George in Devonshire where those of my name lie buried, and destroyed the church, and broke their tombstones, and upheaved their bones. But the loss of life was worse than the ruin of old buildings, and in Coventry men and women stood by a common grave in which many were buried. Yet by some miracle of the spirit they had the heart to cheer the King and Queen who went among them.

For the first time in human history, and in the history of war which fills so much of it, the civilians, as well as the fighting men, were the victims of attack. The old ladies, the young mothers and their babies, girls in the freshness of youth, harmless and helpless old men, were those mutilated and massacred by this aerial warfare. The time was coming when we should pay the Germans back with ten times more than they had given us; when we should blast their cities off the earth and kill hundreds of thousands of civilians who were no more guilty of the war than ours—the young mothers with their babies, and the old men who had wanted peace, and girls in the freshness of their youth. Every time our bombs grew bigger many people rejoiced, and though we had cursed the Germans for strafing refugees on the roads with machine-guns we had no mercy on three million refugees who crowded round the railway stations in Berlin towards the end of the war. We sent strong squadrons night after night to smash them into pulp, as announced with satisfaction in the wireless news. And on Sundays pious folk went to Church and thanked God for these victories in the Name of Jesus Christ. How could any of us reconcile this way of warfare with Christianity or with civilised ideals? Was it not an abandonment of all morality by all of us? That I think will be the verdict of those who come after us, if humanity survives the newest weapons of destruction, so greatly improved, and such beautiful revelations of scientific genius.

9

ACROSS THE ATLANTIC

When the Blitz had died down I made arrangements through the Ministry of Information to go for a lecture tour in the United States, and I flew out to Lisbon, and thence by Clipper to New York.

Lisbon was intensely hot, crowded with international spies, and horribly expensive. I succumbed rapidly to a microbe which attacked the tummies of all its visitors, and on the advice of a charming lady bought a big bottle of white liquid which she said would cure me in a month or two.

At tables in the hotels I saw Germans whom I had met before the war, and we carefully avoided each other's eyes. After hanging about for some time for the American Clipper, and making expeditions to Cintra and other places, feeling very weak inside, I was notified late one night that I should have to start early next morning. There next morning on the Lisbon aerodrome was the great white bird ready for its flight across the Atlantic.

I remembered the time, not long ago, when the first flight across the Atlantic was announced as a miracle. Now it was a commonplace and a routine affair. This Clipper was like a little luxury hotel, with every comfort and convenience for its passengers. One could walk about in it from one little drawing room to another, sitting on the arm of somebody's chair, taking nourishment at frequent intervals, going to bed very comfortably. Among my fellow passengers were Sir Andrew McFadyean whom I came to know afterwards on various committees, and Jessie Matthews, the famous little actress, who devoted herself to the babies on board, and who was so charming that everybody fell in love with her at once. In twenty-four hours we all came to know each other as though we had been together for twenty-four days, and it is astonishing that air travel, which is so swift, seems very long while it lasts. There is nothing to look at except cotton wool clouds far below; the minutes creep by, and one's mind is bored and impatient.

We dropped down for an hour or so in the Azores and the Bahamas; like little paradises, they seemed; and then next day we saw the high towers of New York faintly pencilled against the sky, until, presently, they seemed to lurch this way and that, drunkenly, as the Clipper banked and then, as lightly as a gossamer, skimmed to the great field of La Guardia airport. Here my son Tony was waiting for me, with a group of friends. I still had the Lisbon bug inside me and there was a heat wave in New York. I felt so weak and limp that I could not walk two blocks that evening and felt like death, but when the heat wave passed and I spent some time by a lakeside in Massachusetts, I rapidly recovered.

My brother Arthur was living here with his wife, Jeannette, in an old New England house surrounded by woods of silver birch. Across the road was another old house they owned with its woodwork painted white, and in this Maisie, my daughter-in-law, was installed with young Martin and Frances. Those two children lived a fine free life, bathing and swimming and boating on the big lake which was only a few hundred yards away. They had a perilous passage across the Atlantic. The convoy in which they sailed had been attacked by submarines and two of the ships had been sunk. Now the children—taller since I had last seen them, and as sunburnt as Red Indians—had taken happily to the American way of life. Martin had made friends with neighbouring boys, a fairly "tough" crowd, who would arrive at odd hours outside the house on red-rimmed bicycles, utter Indian war whoops, desiring his company on some adventure. Frances, aged seven, and as delicate as a fairy princess, ordered these young fellows about in their own way of speech—she liked 'em "tough". They were very chivalrous to her, greatly amused by her dominating spirit and her desperate endeavours to keep pace with them in all their games and sports. When winter came I shuddered at the risks this little creature took on skis and toboggans, hurling herself down snow-clad slopes, whizzing past trees within a few feet of her head, and getting spilt into snow-drifts from which she would emerge, panting and dauntless. They both went to a little school at Taunton, Massachusetts, and it says something for American education that when they returned to England three years later they were able to take their places among their own age-groups—Martin at Stowe and Frances at the Perse School, Cambridge.

10

THE AMERICAN IDEA

I arrived in the United States at a time when there was growing anxiety lest President Roosevelt should get them involved in the European War. There were great numbers of Americans who did not like the Lend-Lease Act, nor, later on, his "shoot-at-sight" order for American ships attacked by German submarines. The isolationists were very perturbed by his obvious bias in favour of Great Britain. They were, however, in a minority, and the vast majority of American people—most of those with whom I talked in all classes and many cities—were warmly in favour of "Aid to Britain", as far as sending us supplies of every kind, including munitions of war. They had been deeply moved by the heroism of the British people, and especially by the Londoners in the Blitz.

Over and over again I heard words of astonished admiration for the spirit of the Cockneys under that ordeal, and many times they wondered whether their own civilians could "take it" so well.

For Churchill, the embodiment of the English spirit as they took him to be, they had unbounded enthusiasm, and every time he spoke on the wireless all America listened. They were distressed when Britain had a "set-back", and at that time we were having our blackest misfortunes with hardly a gleam of light anywhere, and in their minds was the secret fear that we might go under. The Germans were advancing towards Moscow. We had fallen back into Egypt. We had failed to save

Norway or Greece. Was little old England doomed? No, never! They could not believe that. There was always applause and emotion in restaurants and dance halls when someone stood up to sing: "There will always be an England", but that song itself really held a secret doubt, by its proclamation of our survival which before had always been taken for granted.

"I suppose England can take care of this war?" asked a lady with whom I dined. Afterwards the same question was put to me. I did not understand its meaning at first. To 'take care' of a thing means in the American parlance, to handle it with success. They hated the idea that Great Britain might have to call for the help of American manhood. As I have written elsewhere there was a dead line in the American mind before Pearl Harbour. "All aid to Britain but no Expeditionary Force." I found that thought and that resolution in almost every mind I met.

I did not blame them. When I was down in Texas and Kentucky that war over in Europe—Hitler's war—seemed to belong to another planet. What had it to do with these Texan farmers, or these Kentucky horse-breeders? What menace could ever touch them from the other side of the Atlantic? No bomb would ever reach them. Had not their fore-fathers come all this way to escape from the European jungle? Why should they go back to that? Here there were peace, prosperity, liberty, and a good life. Here women and children were safe. Only by a kind of intellectual struggle could I bring myself to believe something which I knew—the grim fact that if the British Navy were lost these United States would be vulnerable, with an undefended coast line, and that, anyhow, this country could not stand aloof from a world in which all civilised ideas and human liberties were defeated. But how could men of Kentucky think that out? How could a Texan on a three thousand acre ranch see the threat approaching him? It needed an intellectual struggle not to be an isolationist, and my wonder is that American intelligence was high enough to abandon isolationism which was the traditional, and the wise, old policy of the United States, before the era of the World War.

In a book called *America Speaks* I have recorded the experiences and conversations I had on this last lecture tour of mine. Perhaps I was lucky in my contacts, but everywhere I went I was impressed by the intelligence, the friendliness, the good nature and the wit of the American people. The coffee shop girls used to come and talk to me because I was lecturing in their city that night and was newly arrived from England.

How was it going over there? How could the people stand it? How did they live when their homes were bombed?

They were able to talk very reasonably about the international situation. They had read good books. Some of them were university girls. It was one of them who spoke to me about Japan. The day before I had had a talk with the Adjutant General of the American Army who had told me that the United States had nothing to fear from Japan who was playing a game of bluff. But the coffee shop girl said to me in a low voice:

"D'you know, I sometimes think the Japs will start on us without a warning or a declaration of war. They will come with their aeroplanes before we are ready."

I had earnest conversations with the floor ladies in the hotels, and with any fellow who sat opposite at table with me on a long-distance journey, and with garage hands, and newspaper sellers, and small shop-keepers in small towns, and taxi-drivers in many cities—a shrewd and humorous crowd—and all manner of folk who came to my lectures and lined up afterwards.

11

A RARE BIRD

I was a lonely representative of England. Lord Lothian, when our Ambassador, had laid down the law "no lecturers, no propaganda". This rule had been maintained with some exceptions by the Ministry of Information. It was a grave mistake. The American people did not want, and would not tolerate, propaganda, but they wanted people from England to tell them all the things they were eager to know about English life in war-time, and the British war effort, and our purpose and our chances, and what was happening in the minds of ordinary folk in the great ordeal of the Blitz.

I had a talk with a newspaper seller—a one-armed man—in Fort Worth, Texas. He talked well and was a thoughtful fellow, quite sure that the United States would be in the war pretty soon.

"We're in it already," he told me; "that 'shoot-at-sight' order by the President means that we've started the naval war against Germany."

"Do you get many English here in Fort Worth?" I asked.

"You're the first Englishman I've ever seen", he answered.

Then he glanced at me with a smile and added: "And I must say I ain't dissatisfied."

From New York to San Francisco I had fine audiences, and somehow or other held their interest, and even aroused their emotion. I am not a good lecturer. I have no natural gifts of eloquence or oratory, but just can tell a plain straight tale of things seen. I told them about England under bombardment, and what happened in towns and villages, and in the air-raid shelters, and in the minds of our folk. Something reached out to them. I spoke, at least, with sincerity, which was what they wanted, and what I had to tell was moving enough without any oratory, which they did not want. In San Francisco there was a great audience and there were prolonged cheers for England. The platform was stormed by emotional ladies who flung their arms about me and kissed me on the cheek with tears in their eyes, greatly to my embarrassment, and the amusement of a handsome young man named Bob Keedick who was travelling around with me as a kind of A.D.C.

In spite of this being my fourth lecture tour in the United States I was still intensely nervous before facing an audience, and suffered agonies because of that. I think my worst ordeal was in Baltimore where I was to lecture at the Lyric Theatre. The Governor of Maryland was present with a small group of friends and "The Star Spangled Banner" was played on his arrival. Before going on to the stage I had to sit in a box with some friends, watching the audience come in, and there was the big stage looking a wide and empty field with one American flag on a golden staff.

"Good God!" I thought. "I have to talk to all these people. I shall have to stand like a little white mouse on that enormous stage."

Generally there was a question time after my talk, and after some lectures I came to know exactly what questions would be asked.

"What about India? Why doesn't Great Britain give India freedom and self-government?"

"What about Ireland? How do the English people feel about Irish neutrality?"

Never once, even on the Pacific coast, did anyone ask: "What about Japan?"

Some of the questions were amusing, and some difficult to answer without dropping bricks and giving offence. The most astonishing came from a young man in a hurry to get a lot in before question time closed.

"Sir Philip," he shouted, "what do you think about the balloon barrage over London, and the Duke and Duchess of Windsor?"

A roar of laughter from the audience saved me from any need of a serious answer.

I saw the beauty and the vastness of the United States, making many trips by air. The most beautiful sight which ever met my eyes was when I flew from Chicago to the Pacific coast at night. Down below, Denver and other towns on the way looked like cities of shining jewels on the black velvet of the earth, fairy-like and magical. When I soared over San Francisco I saw the most beautiful thing on earth—that great city looking as though built of diamonds and shining gems along the sweep of the Pacific coast, so marvellous and so enchanting in beauty that one had to cry out aloud in wonder.

12

I Didn't Die in Omaha

I always had an idea, partly humorous, that I should die in Omaha. It is in the Middle West, half way across the United States, and I thought that was about as far as any fellow on a lecture tour could go before he died of exhaustion. This time it was a near thing to death on the way to Omaha. With Bob Keedick, my faithful and good-looking companion, with whom all the ladies fell in love instantly, I was held up by the floods in Kansas. The Mississippi had overflowed its banks and the train in which we travelled stopped for ten hours before bridges could be strengthened in a wilderness of water.

"No lecture to-night!" I said to Bob Keedick, several times.

He was anxious about it. There was a big audience waiting for me in Omaha.

At last we pulled into Kansas City with two hundred and fifty miles to go and time running short.

A little man with a pippin face and innumerable little wrinkles about his eyes approached us as we alighted from the train.

"I'm going to fly you to Omaha," he said.

He did not inspire me with confidence. I had even less confidence when he led us to a soggy field and showed us his aeroplane. It was a very small aeroplane. At some distance it looked like a baby's perambulator with wings.

"We'll have to get there before dark," he said. "Don't want to come down in a flood."

Bob Keedick and I clambered into the plane. There was enough room for two if we squeezed up. The pippin-faced man—a hero of the last war—put on a crash helmet and a pair of goggles. We set off at a surprising speed—200 miles an hour. But when we had been going half an hour we flew into a snowstorm. Visibility was nil. We could see nothing but snowflakes. Our pilot had lost his bearings. He was flying blind. We could see him peering over the side of his machine, trying to see some feature of the landscape which might give him his direction.

"I can't say I like this", I said to Bob Keedick. I could feel a slight sweat in the palms of my hands. That was the beginning of fear.

"I guess we'll make it", said Bob Keedick; "that pilot is a wizard."

So, after all, I thought, I should end my days in Omaha.

But after twenty minutes or so, perhaps longer, our pilot saw below him a broad winding river, and by its loops, flung like a lariat across the white plain, he knew his direction. I did not die in Omaha, but stepped on the platform, where an audience was waiting indulgently, because they had heard of our adventure and of this flight through a snowstorm to reach them.

13

PEARL HARBOUR

I was in a train which had pulled out of Baltimore when stupendous news came to me.

The guard—an elderly man with a dry New-England-looking face under his peaked cap—came over to my seat and whispered to me.

"The Japs have attacked Pearl Harbour. . . . Uncle Sam is in the war."

I was, I am ashamed to say, not very clear as to the geographical position of Pearl Harbour. But my heart gave a lurch, and instantly there came into my mind the thought that now Britain would have the aid of American man-power in a war which had become a World War. It would mean the downfall of Germany. It would mean certain victory. I did not know then how much of tragedy there was for the Americans in this dastardly attack which took them unawares and destroyed a great part of their fleet. I knew it only when I reached Toronto that night, when I grabbed the nearest paper and read the astounding and earth-shaking news. That evening I listened to a quintet in Hart House, Toronto, sitting in the gallery of a beautiful hall and listening to the music of Mozart. Here was a little sanctuary of civilisation in a world of flame and fury. I sat next to the great-niece of Mendelssohn, whose work was barred in Nazi Germany. Afterwards there was a reception and all the professors of Toronto University had only one subject of conversation. Uncle Sam was in the war! Isolationists would die the death. The American people would throw everything in against those who were out for world domination.

When I left Canada and went back into the United States I found a changed people. They had changed overnight. No longer was there any reservation in their minds about 'Aid to Britain' and 'No Expeditionary Force'. We were all in together now. They were at war with Germany as well as with Japan. Together we should win, though the road ahead would be long and bloody.

I was deeply impressed by the way the American people took this blow, and this call to arms. At first they were stunned. Such a thing had never entered their imagination. But when they recovered from the first staggering sensation they were very quiet about it, and very grim. There was no boasting, no flag wagging, no hysteria. I talked to the ordinary folk at street corners and in drug stores and at the counters of coffee shops. They all took the same line.

"It'll mean hard work, lean times, and plenty of sacrifice. There's nothing we shall be called upon to do which we won't do. We've got to win this war, and knock hell out of those dictators, whatever the cost. I'm thinking of my boy. He'll be in it. Just old enough. It'll be hard on the boys."

So said one man I met, and so said many others. They were ready for self sacrifice. They asked for it. They knew the cost would be heavy. They would take it whatever came.

The worst came, or almost the worst, for them and for us, in the Far East. The Japanese won all the first victories, and with incredible speed seized Malaya, the Dutch East Indies, and a chain of islands which were the stepping stones to Australia. After heroic fighting General Mac-Arthur and his men had to abandon the Philippines. "I shall come back," said the General. Singapore fell—the greatest single tragedy which befell us in the war. The *Prince of Wales* and the *Repulse*, our very latest battleships, were sunk by Japanese dive-bombers.

The Pacific and the Indian Ocean lay wide open. Australia was in mortal peril. Over in Egypt we were holding on precariously when Australian troops left to defend their own soil. Supposing the Germans took possession of Persia? Supposing the Japanese linked up with them in the Persian Gulf? They were grim and terrible possibilities. The Germans were advancing towards the gates of Moscow. If Russia were knocked out the entire German Army would be flung westward at Britain. It needed supreme faith to see any gleam of light in all this darkness.

14

THE GREAT MAN

There was one man I met who had that faith. It was the President of the United States—Franklin D. Roosevelt. I went to see him in the White House and had a long talk alone with him, after attending his Press conference. He sat there at his desk, crippled from the waist down. But there was no sign of that, no reminder of it, as he talked and

R

laughed. He looked the picture of health, with a fine ruddy complexion under his white hair, and with very blue luminous eyes. He had been amusing, witty, gay, with the Pressmen, chaffing them all, enjoying himself, as afterwards he told me. He liked those Press conferences which he had held for nine years. In our private talk alone together he was calm, serene, and confident. He made light of the immediate disasters, and looked ahead to the turning of the tide. He had put out, some months before, a stupendous programme for production of ships, guns, tanks, and all weapons and munitions of war.

"People said my figures were impossible," he told me with a smile; "even my best friends thought them crazy."

He fingered some papers on his desk.

"We're doing better than schedule," he said; "my figures were all right."

He spoke with enthusiasm of a friend of his by name of Winston Churchill.

"We see eye to eye. We understand each other."

Only once did he tell me that something he said was "off the record". He talked with great candour, and sometimes dangerously, I thought, of personalities in his own country, trusting me not to let him down. Bad news, and I saw him on a day of bad news, did not cast a shadow over his mind. There was something almost supernatural, I thought, in this vision of future victory, this certainty. Some inner radiance seemed to come from him, and when I rose to leave him I felt uplifted with new hope.

"Come again!" he said cheerily, holding my hand for a moment.

By a section of American opinion he was the most hated man in the United States. I had sat at dinner tables when the most bitter and cruel things had been said against him. Some people could not bring themselves to speak his name. They called him "that man". One literary man I knew called him a "Swindling Messiah". On the very day when I write these lines there is a letter on my desk, just received, from an American woman who still denounces him with anger and contempt.

About his domestic policy there is great argument. He was a shrewd politician, with perhaps a touch of ruthlessness, vindictive against his enemies. But personally I remember—and many Americans remember —that it was his clear vibrant voice, his cheerful resolution, which lifted them up, as though by a call of the spirit, when they were sunk deep in despair, with their Banks shut, millions of workless men, stocks and shares almost worthless, at the time when he first became President.

From first to last in the World War he was our greatest friend. He strained the American Constitution when he sent us 200 destroyers to replace our losses from U-boat warfare. His Lend-Lease Act saved our economic life, and sent us supplies which enabled us to carry on the war. Step by step before Pearl Harbour he led his people forward to the conviction that if Great Britain went under, they would go under, and that civilisation itself was at stake. He "sold" this idea, as they say, to the Middle West, to Texas and Kentucky, where, as I have said, it needed a great intellectual effort to see the danger of isolationism. His leadership in the war was magnificent in its courage, decision and confidence. I am glad to think that one day I sat by his side, and talked with him, and felt the pressure of his hand.

15

HENRY WALLACE

I met another man in Washington who impressed me very deeply. It was Henry A. Wallace, the Vice President. He was very different from the President whose personality was everything. Henry A. Wallace had no appeal to the crowd. He was quiet, almost shy, and without Roosevelt's radiance. But I had read some of his articles on the kind of peace worth fighting for, and when I met him I drew him out on those lines. They were brave ideas, and noble, and demanded a generous vision from the American people to put them into action after the war. They would have to lower their tariffs. They would have to grant great loans to stricken nations to restore their purchasing power. They would have to tighten their belts to prevent widespread famine and disease. He told them that they were in no small measure guilty of the war which had happened by shutting their doors to world trade and so causing a repudiation of debts, vast unemployment, and economic misery. 'Starry-eyed Wallace' he was called by his critics, but here was idealism based on realism.

I told him how deeply I agreed with his point of view about liberating the world from its tariff barriers and trade restrictions.

Once he smiled and said quietly: "I don't get much support for these ideas from England. I don't hear any enthusiasm from the other side of the Atlantic."

I reported these words to friends of mine when I went home again, and the result was that the Liberal Party under Sir Archibald Sinclair asked me to form a committee to do something about it. The outcome of our work was a book called *Bridging the Atlantic*, of which I was editor, with seventeen contributors of great distinction. We faced all the difficulties of Anglo-American co-operation, frankly and squarely. There was no evasion or soft soap. The book still stands, I think, as a valuable contribution to a healthy understanding and friendship between the United States and ourselves.

16

THE OLD COTTAGE

I was an exile from my own house. Before going to the United States for nearly a year I had let it to Lord Esmé Gordon-Lennox and his pretty wife, and when I came back I could not regain possession from them. I found refuge in an old cottage round the corner in Sweetwater Lane, swarming with village children, and there I lived winter and summer with my nephew Barry Rowland, who was unfit for military service, and with Dorothy Webber who owned the cottage and acted as my secretary. It was not all honey for any of us. Small though it was, the cottage became a sanctuary for relatives and friends who wanted relief from bombing nights in London. A camp bed was put into the sitting room at night and removed by day. Washing up after each meal became the routine. Food was an obsession, but by some miracle there was always a meal on the table at appointed times and Lord Woolton kept us from starvation.

There were restless nights under the old beams. Bombs fell far or near, shaking the walls and the floor boards as though by a giant hand, and presently, as time went on, there was the roar of our own bombers over the chimney-pots, hour after hour, on their way to Berlin and other German cities. Their deep, heavy, throb pounded in one's ears, and the sky was crowded with their black wings, and one's heart followed them into the fiery furnace in which many of the boys up there would be burnt like moths.

Sometimes I would look through the iron gates of my own garden and think: "I used to live there once. Shall I ever get back?" There were many times when I thought I should never get back to that house which Agnes had made beautiful and where her spirit dwelt for me.

I was often ill and darkly depressed, and presently there crept upon me an affliction which might have got me down if I had not resisted the demon of despair.

But there were compensations. There was no lack of laughter. Barry Rowland is one of the world's laughers, with a great hearty laugh which greets any small comedy of life, and a friend of mine named Ulric Nisbet, devoted in friendship, came for six months to act as secretary, relieving Dorothy Webber for a time, and he was a laughter-raiser when not getting down to serious talk to which he warmed up at midnight, discussing the meaning of life and philosophy and religion, as interpreted for him by Rudolf Steiner and occult visionaries whom I could not follow into the deeper mysteries. My call for evidence was answered by him with a tolerant smile, and a fresh line of argument which I cut short by staggering to bed. Those old beams in Old Stonnard's Cottage must have strange vibrations, for great talkers came, and great arguments ensued, and my typewriter went tap-tap-tap when I was left alone.

One consolation I had in dark moods was the friendship of children. The children of Shamley Green 'adopted' me as their friend. They whispered to me their secrets. They came running from all parts of the Green whenever I appeared. In Sweetwater Lane they swarmed about me like frisky lambs, and the school children going to the little school at the end of my garden, shouted—"Mr. Philip!" and made a dash at me when I came passing by. Their names were like a nursery song—Christopher, and Jennifer, and Anthea (my very particular friends), another Christopher with Sally and Janie and Peter (very special friends also) who all sat on top of me in the green bus from Shamley Green; Susan and Sally and Gillian, Timothy and Patrick and two Johns, and Oliver and Julian, Gay and Elizabeth, Ozzie who is also a Jennifer, and Gordon and Shirley, and very many more. Before two seconds had passed in their company I had lost my hat and stick. There were chases across the Green and battles in Sweetwater Lane. Their mothers called me 'The Pied Piper' but were not afraid that I would lead these little ones astray. Each year I gave a Christmas party for them, limiting the number to twenty or at most thirty. But there were taps at the cottage door. "May I come to your party, Philip?" I heard the patter of feet after me. "May I come to your party, Philip?" There were ninety in the village hall when at last the party came with a Punch and Judy one year, and a conjuror the next. They sat at two long tables laden with cakes and jellies, in spite of war-time rations. It was a pretty picture and hilarious. Next year there were a hundred and twenty.

Timothy and others gave birthday parties of their own and I was invited. Timothy sat at the end of a long table in the centre of which was a cake with six candles.

"Tell me a funny story," said Timothy, like an eighteenth century gentleman presiding at his mahogany board.

"Well," said Henry Tottenham, in deep base voice, "the other day I swallowed some food and it came out at the end of my nose."

Great laughter went round the table at this Rabelaisian anecdote.

I took part in a children's play. My part was that of a poet and it ought to have been played by T. S. Eliot who lives on the hill above our village. But he was too busy at the time and a man of shy reserve. But he was interested. "How did you make up for the part of a poet?" he asked me. "How ought a poet to dress?"

I wore a pair of corduroy trousers, a blue shirt and a very floppy tie. The children recognised me instantly as a real poet, or as a real poet ought to look. The adorable Jane Casson, grand-daughter of Dame Sybil Thorndyke, made her début. Aged four, and as pretty as a rosebud, she was the Announcer and spoke her words in a stentorian voice. But there was a little trouble behind the scenes and Jane lay curled up in my arms, tearfully, because, as she confided to me, she hated the people clapping her, and the whole beastly business of acting. But she made her curtsey with Dame Sybil and I prophesy that one day great audiences will come to see her play.

17

DIM LIGHT

It was annoying, to say the least of it, that my eyesight failed. The creeping disease of cataract stole upon me and put a mist before my eyes. For nearly two years I could not read, and that was a severe deprivation. I could not recognise my friends at a yard's distance and cut them dead in the village street. I did ridiculous and humiliating things like a blind man in his first clumsiness and once, at Helen Blacker's tea table, swept off a sugar basin of priceless porcelain, smashing it to bits on the floor. I had to memorise the whereabouts of chairs and tables, and unexpected stairs and steps, but it was a long time before people realised how blind I was, because I still walked quickly across the Green or on swinging walks up country lanes. The children never guessed that they were fading away from me. I had perilous adventures in London, especially in tube stations, or crossing the streets. Sometimes I had to ask for help. Always it came with almost embarrassing kindness. People would lose their trains and go out of their way to give me a helping hand. Policemen would hold up the traffic and lead me across. Boredom was the deadly enemy. Not to be able to read, to sit around thinking, not to see people's faces and expressions, to miss so much of the colour and form of trees and flowers—all that was very trying and needed a constant fight of the mind to avoid dejection. But I would not let it get me down and I had one way of escape which was never failing. I could not read but I could go on writing. I could still pound a typewriter so that something like words would appear on the paper. What did appear was a jig-saw puzzle of letters which had to be interpreted and deciphered.

"What does '*D X* %—mean?"

"Why, that's easy! It means—'*the*'."

"What's this word—'*Eazaspwratnio*'?"

"Why, it's obvious!—'*Exasperation*'!"

In that kind of cryptogram I wrote three novels—*The Amazing Summer, The Long Alert,* and *The Interpreter,* and apart from a few errors, because I could not read the proofs, they read as well as their author could hope. But I owe a great debt to the patience of those who helped to decode and decipher them, and to Ethel McGuinness who typed them perfectly, and never let me hear her cries of anguish.

One has to be patient with cataract and get worse until one can get better by surgical operation. My time of waiting ended at last. My oculist was hopeful of success with my right eye—a fifty-fifty chance perhaps, and I could have the greatest confidence, he told me, in Colonel Bickerton who would do the trick.

So I walked one day into Fitzroy House nursing home in Fitzroy Square, where the matron received me brightly and introduced me to the nurse who would have me under her special care—Sister Frieda Smith.

"Is she a kind and human soul?" I asked in the presence of that young woman.

The matron laughed.

"Very kind and very human."

She was also beautiful and gay. The other nurses were equally kind and human, and night after night they made a rendezvous in my room which was filled with laughter and cigarette smoke. Now, strange as that may seem, it was due to Adolf Hitler or Hermann Goering. For my stay in the nursing home, the oldest in London, coincided with a February Blitz. Night after night the German bombers came over, and the neighbourhood of Fitzroy Square seemed to be their special target. Fires raged in the Tottenham Court Road and streets not far away. Our guns put up an infernal barrage, heavy crashes shook the old house in which I lay abed, or in which I paced up and down my room in a dressing gown with my right eye swathed in bandages after my operation which I was told had been very successful. It has been an almost painless operation with a local anæsthetic except for seven unpleasant moments, and Colonel Bickerton had given me full marks as a patient for remaining motionless.

"You never moved by a hair's breadth," he said. "That was very helpful to me. Some patients are very restless."

During the nightly bombardment the nurses never turned a hair. Discipline and tradition, and their own spirit came to their aid. As soon as the sirens sounded the matron, who had donned a steel hat because she was a fire watcher, visited each patient and said: "Would

you like to go downstairs?" Only one went below. It was a big burly
man whose nerves went to pieces so that he had to be taken away from
Fitzroy Square.

The night nurse carried in some tea to my room. I handed out
cigarettes. Nurses and patients drifted in and out. We had quite
cheerful little parties in spite of "noises off".

My particular night nurse was Irish, by name of Sister Mortell. She
had been a schoolmistress in Ireland and now was studying for a
medical degree.

"We must have a talk about Ireland", I said in an incautious moment.

"If once we start on that . . ." she laughed.

She came into my room about midnight. All her patients had settled
down.

"Did I hear you say you wanted to talk about Ireland?" she asked.

"Let's have some tea and talk", I suggested.

We drank tea and talked about Ireland for two hours. She was a
psychologist. She understood her people. She even made out a case for
understanding Mr. de Valera. But then Sister Mortell is a very clever
lady with a great sense of humour.

I had many visitors while I lay abed with that bandage round my
head, having my eye dressed three times a day by Sister Frieda Smith.

One of them was Frank Swinnerton who made me laugh so much that
he might have ruined the success of the operation by shaking me up too
much. He is a born mimic and would make a cat laugh by his im-
personations of famous people, and a most comical story teller who
enjoys his own gift. He told me stories of his own experiences in a
nursing home, and I laugh even now when I think of them.

I went home before my bandages were removed. I was blind in one
eye and couldn't see out of the other, as the old lady said. But I played
a game on a putting green with my nephew Barry and with my first
stroke at a long putt holed out in one. It was, of course, a miracle.

It was a long time, nearly three months, before I was given my new
glasses. I had been dejected. Oculist and surgeon had both declared
that the operation had been a success, but here I was blinder than when
I went in. Then one day Colonel Bickerton sat me down before the
usual letters which meant nothing to me. He put a frame on my nose
and a lens in the frame.

"Good God!" I cried.

I could see all but the smallest letters with clear and wonderful
definition.

I went out into the streets of London. The black-out had gone up. I
could see as never before for many years. I could see the numbers on
the busses, the advertisements on the walls, the names over the shops,

the expressions on people's faces. I could see with the eyes of youth, with the eye of an eagle. In my garden that day, and in the lanes round about, I walked with delight. I could see the colour of the flowers, intensely bright. I could see each little leaf and each petal, and the play of light and shade on the little low hills. I could see once again the enchantment and the beauty of the world about me. I could see the faces of my friends again.

18

THE MIRACLES

The war went on, but for us it was the turn of the tide.

It was as though a page had been turned over in the book of fate.

Before then the record had been black, with defeat and retreat on our side. Now by the Battle of El Alamein and the pursuit of Rommel by the Desert Army our enormous peril was relieved, and the next chapters of history were a story of increasing strength and a weakening enemy on all fronts.

Looking back on this war we have to acknowledge five major miracles which saved us:—

The evacuation of the B.E.F. from Dunkirk by the little ships.

The Battle of Britain and the victory of the R.A.F. against enormous odds.

Hitler's decision to attack Russia.

The Japanese attack on Pearl Harbour which brought American man-power to our aid against Germany.

The Russian victory at Stalingrad and the turn of the Russian tide which swept back with irresistible force.

Miracles, or events of amazing luck—call them what you will. If even one or, say, two of them had failed we should have lost this war and all that we have. Historians of the future may ask whether our statesmen had any right to count on five major miracles in reckoning the chances of war and flinging everything into the scales. A very pretty argument. Surely it was a risk never to be taken again by a great nation which began a war without the means to fight it. But that argument now is academic. If there is another world war there will be no more world for mankind.

In Berchtesgarten Adolf Hitler must have been sunk in gloom over his maps. In Russia, in North Africa, and then in Italy, his armies were in retreat. But he may still have had a gleam of hope and the fanatical light of faith. His scientists were having a race with time. They were devising merry things for the annihilation of their enemies. "This war will be won by technology", said Hitler, and it was no empty boast as now we know. Their V.1 and V.2 might have done the trick for them if they had had six months more for mass production. Up in Norway German scientists were experimenting with heavy water and certain metals. If they could split the atom they could blow the world to bits, or that part of the world inhabited by the Allied nations. They were very near to the heart of the mystery. Another six months! A little more of that precious thing called Time.

The V.1 arrived. I saw one of its first arrivals. Stepping out of a bus at Shamley Green I was startled by an apparition in the sky. It was lunch time and there was no one on the Green except myself. There overhead, travelling westwards, not towards London, was a thing which looked as though it had come out of a Christmas cracker.

It was rather a pretty toy with lights in front and a long red flame coming out of its tail. I thought it very odd indeed. I could hear the thump-thump of its engine as it travelled across. Presently the engine shut off and ten seconds later I heard the crash of an explosion. It was one of the first "doodle-bugs", as the American soldiers nicknamed them instantly.

19

THE "THINGS" ARRIVE

As it happened I was in London a good deal during that time of pilotless planes, having taken a flat which I shared with my son, in a big block of flats round the corner of Cadogan Gardens, not far from Sloane Square. Many times during those days, and many times during those nights, the flying bombs arrived, sometimes at the rate of one every few minutes. They were not amusing. They caused a very heavy toll of casualties, mostly from glass splinters which cut their victims about terribly. "It isn't surgery," I was told by a nurse in a hospital who was dealing with the wounded, "it's butchery."

Many people were more afraid of them than they had been of the old type of bombs. The taxi-cab drivers hated them, not being able to hear them coming. After the long strain of the great Blitz some people could stand no more and lost their nerve. So I was told. But my own experience was different. Personally I did not find them so abominable as the old bombs which smashed up London. It seemed to me that they gave one a slight chance. One could hear the thud-thud of their engines. One could tell, or one thought one could tell, how long and how far it would be before they dropped after the shutting off of the engine. "There it comes! . . . Over!" So I heard men and women in the streets shouting to each other when one of those things was overhead. And because of the inescapable power of self preservation people would laugh when the Thing had gone over. Somebody else would get it. We were all right.

I saw no sign of panic, and hardly a sign of fear, among the Londoners at this time. On the contrary, I was amazed again at the *sang-froid*, the courage, and the contempt of most of them, and especially of the young girls, who walked hatless into the parks or hurried from their offices in lunch hour.

"There's another of those beastly Things!" they would say as they strolled along the Serpentine, or sat on the grass while one of those Things cut through the blue sky and went, generally, in the direction of Kensington where they made a hideous mess in Exhibition Road and Church Street and other places.

I was in a little restaurant at the corner of Lowndes Square one day when three of them came over during lunch time. Through the windows we could see a few people running. We could hear the thump and thud of the familiar noise. But no one moved. A young girl, being entertained by a naval lieutenant, smiled at him and said: "Pass me a cigarette, darling." No one spilt the soup. These youngsters are wonderful, I thought.

"Do these Things worry you?" I asked the waitress in the restaurant of the service flats where I had a room.

"Worry me?" she answered. "Good heavens, No! I never bother about them."

She looked out of the window in a great block of flats, which were nearly all windows—the delight of the "doodle-bug", which killed most of its victims by cutting their throats or slashing them with flying glass like knives. Twice the thought of that flying glass made me sufficiently nervous to drag the mattress off my bed and carry it into the small bathroom which had no windows at all. My nephew Barry did the same in the passage-way. Now it happened that the manageress opened the door with her pass-key and saw this arrangement for the night. She saw it with contempt for the cowardice of men. Not a single pane was broken in that house of glass, though flying bombs seemed to make a particular target of this neighbourhood. There was a tragedy not far away when one of these pilotless planes fell on top of a block of flats in which 300 American soldiers were billeted at the end of Lower Sloane Street, killing sixty of them, and wounding many others at breakfast time one morning. I talked with the men who escaped and they were much shaken.

But one of the worst of these tragedies was on a Sunday morning when a pilotless plane was brought down above the Guards' Chapel. Hardly a soul escaped from that shambles which killed many officers and their wives and mothers. A nephew of mine in the Coldstream Guards should have been there but overslept himself, having been to a party the night before. Other friends of mine were going, but for some trivial reason were prevented at the last moment.

Those "doodle-bugs" did heavy damage to houses as well as to human life, though great numbers of those Things were brought down over the sea or the coast and their sources of supply and transport were heavily bombed by the R.A.F.

V.2 arrived—the rocket bomb—and there seemed to be no answer to that weapon except the destruction of its bases. Rising into the stratosphere it fell with incredible speed, and its victims were dead before they heard it. A triumph of science! A glorious success for the inventive genius of the scientists! Another little gift for human creatures to play with in their childish games! The Germans were filled with exultation at the results of these new forms of slaughter, just as some of our own newspapers, but not many decent people, exulted over the wiping out of Hiroshima and Nagasaki by the atomic bomb.

Dr. Goebbels and his menagerie went far in imaginative description and excited their readers by the stories of the roads out of London being black with panic-stricken crowds, when hatless girls were sunning themselves in Hyde Park, as I have said, and refusing to be frighened. But there was no exaggeration about the effects of the atomic bomb. It was "highly successful".

20

DELIVERANCES

D-day, the day for which we had all been waiting with hope and frightful apprehension, because of inevitable and perhaps ghastly losses, came at last. The armies which had been held and trained in England— British, Canadians, Americans—were landed on the coast of Brittany. The "Western Wall" had seemed to the Germans impregnable. Every ingenious and diabolical device for destroying landing craft and men had been prepared against us. Great prongs, tipped with high explosives, stuck out into the sea. The beaches were strewn with mines. Coastal batteries commanded the sea and the cliffs. The risk was appalling, but the invading troops—it was our turn for invasion— supported by our battleships silenced the enemy's batteries, cleared a way through the mine-fields, and scaled the heights, without enormous losses.

We were there, in France again, on the continent of Europe which was waiting for liberation.

There followed the break-through into Brittany, the advance into Normandy, the close, bitter, and bloody fighting by British troops at Caen and the Falaise pocket, the failure at Arnhem where our airborne troops were surrounded and checked. The Americans fought with magnificent dash and courage, like veteran soldiers, though to most of them it was their baptism of fire. But as usual the British took on the hardest job, and endured the worst ordeal, and cleared the way for the American drive through France to the gates of Germany.

I was envious of the war correspondents when they followed, and could hardly keep pace with the American and British spearheads. I was out of it this time. It was a glorious and thrilling adventure for them, more spectacular and exhilarating than anything that had happened in the last war, and they did supremely well, not sparing themselves, taking all risks with great dash and gallantry.

It was the beginning of the end. Our complete supremacy in the air was a formidable factor on the way to victory. It broke up the enemy's transport system, isolated his armies, annihilated them on the roads, smashed every attempt to bring up supplies and reserves, destroyed his railways and rail heads, pulverised his concentrations of tanks, guns, and ammunition, caught his troops on the march and flayed them. Never before in the history of the world had such a terror been let loose upon masses of men, nor over great cities where women and children were massacred in the ruins. It was a war without chivalry, without mercy, without morality.

That is to say, it was war, as we moderns now make it, and as Germany first made it.—Total War, and ruthless.

Germany was doomed. On the Eastern Front Russia was winning great victories. Hitler's frantic orders to his generals to hold on to their positions to the death were unavailing. German troops fought with desperate, and let us say, generously and truly, with heroic courage, killed in many places to the last man, in obedience to their Führer's orders, or retreating to die elsewhere. Zhukov and his fellow generals gave them no respite, but struck sledge-hammer blows on the right, left, and centre, with alternate strokes of irresistible might. The Russian Armies were reckless, ferocious and exultant. The German Armies were outgeneralled, outfought and overwhelmed. To Hitler there was nothing left but madness and death; and the end of those Nazi leaders, and that man whom they had set up as a tribal god, was as *macabre* as any vision of apocalyptic doom, or as the damned souls in Dante's

Inferno. They had declared war upon the Christian tradition and creed.
They had invoked all the devils of hell, and now they paid the price of
devil-worship.

They had derided pity, justice, and all the noble instincts of humanity.
They had practised brutality. They had revived torture and all forms of
cruelty. Hitler had deliberately sold his soul to Satan, tempted by
power over all the world. Now his Master claimed him.

May 7th and Victory Day. The United States, always quick—too
quick—to get ahead of the news, had gone wild before the final and
official announcement of the German surrender. In England the
B.B.C. gave it sombrely, and seemed to announce two days' public
holiday to celebrate the end of the war as though giving news of a state
funeral. The Announcer of these glad tidings had a stern hard voice,
and was very gloomy about it.

No gloom oppressed the spirit of the vast multitudes who surged up to
Buckingham Palace, cheering the King and Queen, and giving Winston
Churchill a great ovation—though afterwards they voted against him.
There was no disorder among those crowds, but only a sense of joy and
deliverance. God knows they deserved this holiday and this rejoicing.
It was their victory. They had endured much, toiled much, and looked
death in the face for six years. History will record all that, and will tell
the tale of an heroic England which rose to its greatest heights in those
darkest years.

In Shamley Green, as in ten thousand English villages, there were
bonfires on Victory night and the children watched effigies of Hitler
consumed by flames. I went out on to the Green to watch the fire and
hear the laughter of the children, kept late from their beds.

The end of another war—a war which ought never to have been
fought, and need never have been fought, if, after the last, there had
been a little more wisdom, a little more morality, a little more virtue in
us. Was it the end of war itself? If not, then the world is just a lunatic
asylum and we are all poor fools.

21

LABOUR WINS

Before the German surrender I was asked by Sir Percy Harris, leader
of the Liberal Party in the House of Commons, to sit on two committees appointed to consider and report on two important problems
from the Liberal point of view—the word 'Liberal' being interpreted as
'liberal-minded', rather than confined strictly to party men and women.

The first was on the subject of "What to do with Germany after the War". Our Chairman was Lord Perth whom I had met in the old days as Sir Eric Drummond, Secretary-General of the League of Nations—a man of experience, judgment and good nature. Among the members were Sir Andrew McFadyean, who had been my fellow passenger in the flight from Lisbon to the United States. No man knows more about the economic side of German life, and his knowledge and point of view were very valuable in drawing up the report. He combined severity with fair-mindedness and a broad vision of European conditions and necessities. Among other members was Dr. Gilbert Murray, whose mind is steeped in Greek philosophy and who can see further than most men in the realm of civilised ideals because of that learning which does not grow old. Our report still stands as a thoughtful, practical, just and liberal-minded plan for preventing any further German aggression, but for Europe's sake as well as Germany's, allowing those people a reasonable economic life, and a chance of moral and spiritual regeneration. Few people read it, perhaps, though it had a good Press. Now, nobody reads it. It is just waste paper, like so many other reports by men of knowledge and foresight, dropped with a heavy thud into many waste-paper baskets. The name of Lord Perth, alone, guaranteed that his plan for Germany would be just and wise and free from the spirit of black vengeance and blind hatred. That is to say he has a civilised mind as rare as Christian charity.

He was Chairman of the other committees on which I served to consider the recommendations of the San Francisco Conference.

Among its other members were Sir William Beveridge, a fellow member of mine at the Reform Club, Lady Violet Bonham-Carter, and Dr. Gilbert Murray again. I advanced upon that committee's room at Liberal Headquarters in Gayfere Street, Westminster, with a number of doubts, reservations, and points of criticism on the plan for the "United Nations". I thought I should have to summon up a considerable amount of moral courage to put these forward bluntly and squarely, but I found that all my fellow members had the same anxieties and doubts, caused by the outstanding fact that if one of the Big Three—say Russia —became disunited in these United Nations, the whole plan would fall to pieces. The elaborate foundation laid down as a blue print by the San Francisco Conference would be utterly undermined and upheaved. The powers over the Assembly seemed to us too great, and we were critical of a Big Power being able to veto any action which seemed contrary to its own interests. It seemed to me personally no advance towards international peace if nations contributed a quota towards an international police force to prevent aggression but remained fully and heavily armed in the background. Sir William Beveridge had strong views, which he afterwards expressed on public platforms, regarding the necessity of some surrender of sovereignty' in the dominion of international law, and Lady Violet Bonham-Carter, like others of us, was anxious about the rights and liberties of the smaller nations, already being violated. Lord Perth with his long experience of the League of Nations thought the San Francisco plan far from perfect but much better than nothing at all, and better in certain ways than the limited powers of the old League. Without some sort of international organisation of this kind, he thought, there could be no peace and no security. Finally we produced a report which pointed out the weaknesses and limitations of the San Francisco plan while welcoming it as a step towards perfection, and giving a clear analysis of each clause. Again, a good document, I think, and, as far as I was concerned, an interesting experience in the English spirit of finding a common ground of agreement in spite of intellectual differences and free expression of disagreement. Subsequent history is not reassuring. The expulsion of the Germans in East Prussia by the Poles, and of the Sudeten Germans by the Czechs, without mercy for their agony and loss is the violation of every principle of justice and every instinct of humanity.

As it happened I was a guest at a luncheon party given by Philip Inman, Chairman of Charing Cross Hospital, to the delegation appointed by the Labour Party to attend the final sessions of the San Francisco Conference in which would be decided the future structure of international co-operation for the establishment of international justice and economic security among nations, noble principles and glorious ideals which have already fallen to the ground in a quagmire of vengeance, cruelty, hunger, disease, chaos, and all forms of human misery which, as I write these words, combine to form the present picture of European civilisation.

It was the first time I had been in the company of the Labour leaders and I did not guess that the quiet little man who sat opposite would, before long, be Prime Minister in succession to Winston Churchill. Next to me sat a little lady, as bright as a new pin and as perky as a canary—Miss Ellen Wilkinson. We talked about the international situation but not very deeply. Mr. Herbert Morrison, a fair Saxon type with blue eyes behind his glasses, exchanged smiles with "Ellen" and once beckoned her to his side for a private joke. Down the table was a cheery fellow with a strong Yorkshire accent who in the course of a speech told some good Yorkshire stories. That was Mr. George Hall who was under the fire of his colleagues' chaff. They urged him to keep on talking honest Yorkshire in San Francisco, and thought it would make a good impression on the Americans who couldn't abide the Oxford accent.

They spoke about their coming visit to San Francisco, and Ellen Wilkinson seemed to express the general feeling of the Labour delegation when she said that she was going out with a mixture of cynicism and hopefulness. But all of them, including Mr. Attlee, emphasised the point, that if they did not succeed in reaching agreement with the Allies there would be no hope of future peace. "We *must* succeed!" said Mr. Attlee. . . . It was before the atomic bomb had fallen in Hiroshima, beginning—or ending—a new era in human destiny.

Some weeks later I found myself reluctantly involved in the General Election. My son Anthony had become Liberal candidate for East Harrow and sent me an S.O.S. to speak for him and take the chair at one of his meetings.

Liberal Headquarters had for some time prophesied a Liberal renaissance in England, and in the new constituency of East Harrow there was some evidence thereto. Canvassers reported that the women in small houses were going to vote Liberal, even though their husbands were voting Labour and had put Labour bills in the window. Certainly Tony had fine meetings, attended by intelligent people of the district, among whom were many women, obviously well educated and thoughtful because of the questions they asked after the speeches. They looked to me like the people who read books borrowed from the libraries, turned on the wireless to good music, never missed the Brains Trust. They had been the heroes and heroines of Civvy Street during the war, with night raids over their little houses, while they did fire-watching, huddled in Anderson shelters, and had suffered without a whine all the discomforts brought about by ration books, queues, crowded busses, and shortages of stockings, soap, coal, pots and pans, and almost everything. Now they were going to vote in a General Election and were, it seemed, a little undecided. The Conservatives were too far on the Right for them, Labour too far on the Left. Had not Lord Samuel made the best and most intelligent speech? They were sick and tired of the Tory Government. It was time to change that, anyhow, though Churchill was still their hero. He had been great—magnificent—as a war leader. They loved his personality. But would he be so good for the Peace? It was all very difficult, and they wanted to vote sensibly, without being carried away by sentiment or false loyalties. Something of that kind was working in their minds, I think, in East Harrow.

I listened for the first time to a speech by my son Anthony, and felt nervous, as one always does when a member of one's family appears in public. It was a good speech, well delivered in a voice astonishingly like my own.

He spoke with great sincerity and seemed to impress his audience.

S

When I took the chair for him one evening he had the support of a young man named Air Vice Marshal Bennett, famous as " Path Finder ". No one could doubt his courage. Had he not led the way, time after time, above Berlin, through storms of flak? But I thought he showed another proof of courage that night when he addressed this audience. He was still on active service. He was one of the heroes of the war, but he would not let these people get away with false ideas about the nature of war.

"Ladies and gentlemen," he said, "war is just plain murder."

I saw the whole audience sit back as though taken by surprise, and I turned in my chair to look at this young man who dared to tell the truth in such straight unflinching words. He was out to stop all future war. All other things—housing, demobilisation, financial problems—were insignificant compared with that one duty of the human race.

At another meeting I had to make a speech lasting three quarters of an hour in one hall while my son spoke in another. I did not indulge in abuse of Conservatives or Labour, and freely admitted that there were liberal-minded men of great sincerity in both those parties, but I tried to show that Liberalism represented more clearly than any other policy the mind and spirit of the English people, hostile to extremes, believing in the liberty of the individual, warm in its humanity, on the side of little people and little nations, the age-long champions of social reform and freedom from tyranny. That sounds boring but I tried to keep my argument light and lively, and anyhow I made one convert to this creed. A respectable-looking man rose in the hall and said: "Ladies and gentlemen, when I came here to-night I did not know which way to vote. I was all bewildered. But now I am going to vote for the Liberal candidate." I had rounded up one lost sheep astray in the wilderness of political controversy, but, poor lamb, he went to the slaughter-house with the rest.

It was a wholesale slaughter of the Liberals. But the overwhelming victory of the Labour Party surprised even its most optimistic prophets and was a staggering blow to their Conservative opponents.

I felt sorry for Winston Churchill. His election speeches had not done him any good. He had jumped too abruptly into the mud and dust of the party arena, and had been unfair to men who had been his faithful colleagues in the Coalition Government. For a man who had been an inspired leader during all the war it was a descent from the sublime to the ridiculous. He was betrayed by his schoolboy pugnacity and love of a scrimmage after school hours. It was, he thought, the merry game of catch-as-catch-can. But there is hardly a doubt that if he had spoken with wisdom and dignity above the arena, his Party would still have been defeated. Every grievance and grouse which had been stored up in

men's minds for six years, every petty injustice among the fighting
services, the long strain and weariness of the war, the discipline, the
restrictions, the ordering about by little Jacks-in-Office, made for a
change of Government. The Service votes weighed down the scales.
It was, as a friend of mine said, like 'cocking a snook' at the sergeant-
major when the fighting man registered his vote against the big lads who
had controlled his way of life for six years.

But Labour had its fervent disciples, its fanatics, and its idealists.

"The Bastille has fallen!" wrote one of my enthusiastic friends on the
Left when the election results were known.

He meant, no doubt, the Bastille of privilege, vested interests, and
other bogies. But there is another Bastille being built. The Bastille of
Bureaucracy with the *lettres de cachet* of little tyrants, directing labour,
and arranging a hive-like system of life for men and women who
formerly loved freedom and often died for it. That is, to my mind, a
great danger lurking ahead, though if it comes it will be stealthily and
for a time not very noticeably. Mr. Attlee, as Prime Minister, is leader
of a Girondin Government—a Government of moderates. But on the
back benches are the Jacobins, and one day we shall hear from them.
We have already heard from Mr. Laski, the little round-faced Robespierre, who sits behind the scenes.

22

What Hope?

Now I come to the end of these reminiscences.

What have I learnt really from all my contacts with my fellow men and
women? What philosophy have I gained during this pilgrimage, if any?
What is to be the outcome of this peace which coincides with the race to
split the atom, which we won by a short length? What can humanity
hope for next, if there is any hope?

Looking back on my experiences in many countries I still think, as
always I have thought, that the common man and woman, the ordinary
folk, the little people, are extraordinarily decent everywhere. Meeting
them as individuals over a café table or in a railway carriage, or in an
inn, or an American road-house, or a French *pension*, or a German beer
garden, or an Arab tent, one finds—I have found—pleasant, kindly,
intelligent people. They do not want to kill anybody, unless they are
first made mad by political passion or mob mania, excited by their
leaders. There must be a lot of bad people in the world to commit the

s*

atrocious cruelties which have been perpetrated in this war. "In your novels, Sir Philip," said a young friend of mine, "you always write about good people. Won't you write a book about evil people—the utterly depraved?" But they haven't come my way along the roads of life, and yet I have been in many strange spots and poked about the places where the bad men dwell. I think, perhaps, I have met only one bad man and had personal conversation with him. That was Himmler, who, when I met him, was unlike the portrait of a human fiend, though certainly he was one. I may have been lucky. I may have been deceived, but I do not think so. I believe that the people I have met about the world, decent and kindly, are the normal average people—not angels but not devils, with a fair standard of intelligence, with very reasonable ideas as to what life should be—the first item on their list of desires being peace and security. If that is true, how is it that they are utterly unable to control their own destiny, and that in time of national hysteria and passion the individual is lost in the mob? Why does the mob follow its leaders like sheep, when decency, intelligence, and kindliness, are overwhelmed by the forces of unreason? One has to dig very deeply into human psychology and history to answer those questions. The 'herd' instinct, the spirit of the tribe, jealous of its totems, hostile to other tribes, still lies in the subconscious minds of men, and surges up when war is threatened. It is sublimated into national or racial loyalties, and even by the noblest minds, into patriotism. *Dulce et decorum est* . . .

Poets and heroes glorify the virtue of patriotism, and it has great virtues and inspires them in brave and noble minds. The love of one's own country, readiness to die for it, cannot be ridiculed or condemned, and in this last war it produced marvellous deeds of heroism and endurance, and a common courage transcending the ordinary spirit of men and women. But even patriotism may have a quality of evil and ignorance in lower forms of character. "My country right or wrong," is not the highest form of morality. It is not morality. Totem worship lurks still in the civilised mind, and more strongly in the uncivilised. I remember at the end of the first World War meeting a Belgian lieutenant and a Guard of Honour carrying their national flag. "Salute the Flag!" he shouted at me with glaring eyes in which was a fanatical light. I had every intention of saluting the flag, but this young Belgian was in a state of patriotic hysteria quite divorced from reason, and ferocious in its expression. The Trooping of the Colour, very fine as a little pageant, is another form of totem worship which produces an almost religious fervour in the minds of the spectators. Because it is a symbol of our old history and tradition, steeped in the spirit of our strongest loyalties, it moves us deeply, but there is no reason why the sight of a flag should make us want to rush out and kill some neighbouring tribe which happens to have a different kind of flag.

Even patriotism has to be controlled by intelligence and morality. But it is not so controlled. Its symbols, its totems, are made use of by ambitious power-loving men to inflame national hatreds and to dupe their own peoples, as Hitler did, as Mussolini did, and many others.

"Patriotism is not enough," said Nurse Cavell before she faced the firing squad. Nationalism is not enough, especially after the advent of the atomic bomb. Unless we extend our sense of morality and our range of intelligence beyond our own frontiers, by an international control of war and the weapons of war, it will be the end of civilised man, quite certainly. We have that choice now.

We had that choice and missed it after the last war. But as far as this country is concerned, we as a people stood on the side of peace and international law. Were we foolish in supporting, as a people, the ideals of the League of Nations? Were Ramsay MacDonald and his fellow pacifists, or semi-pacifists, so wrong as their critics now assert? Was Neville Chamberlain wrong in making a last desperate effort by his policy of 'appeasement' which now, because it failed, is denounced as a moral iniquity?

Were all those people—millions—who signed the Peace Pledge, wrong in putting their faith in Collective Security? Was I, poor ant, wrong and foolish, and blind, and sentimental, in recording the abomination of war, and striving for peace by a better understanding of other peoples, and by a comradeship of men and women across the frontiers, in so many of my novels and my books? "You are one of the goody-goodies," said Winston Churchill, who, perhaps, had read some of these books. But I was a greater realist than he, foreseeing the destruction and ruin and agony that would happen if another war happened.

I do not think that those who strove for peace were wrong, even though they failed. The causes of that failure lie with the so-called realists and with those who criticised and ridiculed the so-called idealists. One has to go back farther than Hitler's advent. Would not a more generous spirit towards the German people after their defeat, and a more active policy towards international co-operation in a warm, human, spirit across the frontiers, have prevented the coming of Hitler? Who was it that held up general disarmament in Europe for seventeen years? The 'realists', who by so doing played into the hands of Hitler. Who refused to abolish bombing aeroplanes against the advocacy of the League Assembly? The 'realists' who proclaimed that bombing was an economical way of maintaining order on the N.W. frontier of India, and of punishing Arab tribesmen in Mesopotamia for refusing to pay their taxes.

The 'realists' who imposed astronomical and impossible reparations on Germany (Keynes pointed out the absurdity of all this in his *Economic Consequences of the Peace*) led the way to the inflation of the German mark which was completed by the 'realistic' occupation of the Ruhr, causing such misery and hopelessness that Hitler had a fertile field for his propaganda. The 'idealists' were the better 'realists', when they worked for a general reduction in arms, a better peace than that of vengeance, and a vision of international justice and fellowship.

All that is now in the past, and as I write all the peoples of the world know that these ideals, so much derided by the so-called realists, so much resisted, must be fulfilled lest all of us perish by the Frankenstein monster we ourselves have created. We have to pick up the broken threads of those very ideals which went down into the fiery furnace of war. We have to establish a new League of Nations. The San Francisco plan has been adopted with stronger powers. We shall have to yield some claims of sovereignty in respect of declaring war and maintaining separate armies which formerly enforced national decisions or defended national interests. All that must be controlled by international authority. Was that not advocated years ago by Lord Davies and his New Commonwealth, and by all the 'sentimentalists' of whom I was one?

The atomic bomb has forced this need of a super State, with supreme international authority and control of destructive weapons, upon all peoples, for they know that the alternative is death. I should perjure my soul if I defended the use of those two bombs against Japan. I am certain that the verdict of history will condemn it as a terrible crime against human life. The argument that it shortened the war and saved the lives of many thousands of American and British fighting men is not valid. In the first place the Japanese had asked the Russians to mediate on their behalf three weeks before the bombs were dropped. But the argument of shortening the war and saving the lives of our own men would cover every crime against humanity, including the use of poison gas, the dropping of disease germs, if that were possible, the machine-gunning of refugees on the roads—to impede military transport—any kind of ruthlessness, any kind of massacre of civilian populations. Having used that bomb to shorten war what will be our plea, what value our indignation, if some other nation decides to use it later to shorten their particular war and to save the lives of their own young men, and to wipe us off the face of the earth if we refuse to surrender?

"Why boggle at an atomic bomb?" say the defenders of its use at Hiroshima and Nagasaki," when Flying Fortresses and Lancasters were doing the same kind of job, less effectively but with highly successful destructive results?" There is something in that, but not much, because of the enormous quantitative difference. But in my belief, looking back on this atrocious and murderous war, the civilised mind betrayed its morality, and stepped down in the scale of humanity, when orders were given to switch over from the bombing of military targets to the wiping out of cities with their civilian populations, when women and children and all civilians were deliberately and intensively bombed with complete ruthlessness. Three million German refugees were gathered round the railway stations in Berlin during the last phase of our war with Germany. Would it not have been a chivalrous act to give them a few days respite and due warning with time to escape? Would it not have placed us rather higher in the verdict of history?

But no! Night after night we intensified our air-raids and dropped thousands of tons of bombs on the stricken city. The Germans have no right to complain, we say. They started all this. They did their best to destroy London, Coventry, Bath, Exeter, and many other cities. But our moral indignation at their machine-gunning of refugees and killing of civilians is weakened and falsified by a tenfold vengeance. In writing this I shall be accused of 'sentimentality', but many of our young pilots share this view and regarded their job as dirty work. One of them is Air Vice Marshal Bennett who was the Path Finder on these raids over Berlin and other cities. "War", he said, as I have already recorded, "is just plain murder. Do not let us pretend otherwise."

No further pretence is possible. The atomic bomb takes the 'glory' out of war, makes human heroism futile, annihilates fortifications and all means of defence. Battleships will be powerless against one bomb. An air armada will be burnt up like moths by one such explosion among them. War can no longer be waged by the former instruments of destruction which are now obsolete. We must get rid of war or it will get rid of us. Which way will men choose? There is no certainty that all nations will choose the way of life. There are minds so evil, so malignant, so possessed by wickedness that they may let loose this horror, caring nothing for the consequence and gloating over the end of civilised man and all his works. It seems fantastically incredible. It seems like a bogy invented as a scare to make our flesh creep and frighten us into being good. None of us can really believe it as an actual fact. We have—I have—a kind of mental resistance to such possibilities. They must be exaggerated. Imagination has run riot. The little devil 'Doubt' whispers to us: it's not really true. The scientists are pulling our legs. . . . It is true. Its proof lies in the ruins of Hiroshima, and in the wreckage of ships near Bikini atoll.

So far, as I write, there is not much excitement about it. An Atomic Commission has been appointed, but mankind is going on as though nothing had happened to alter the relative importance of things —nothing which demands a new morality among the world of men and women, a new conception of human life and law, a complete surrender of old nationalistic traditions and claims.

Bishops and clergy of the Anglican Church, who did not raise a protest during the war against the bombing of civilians, have—after the war—deplored the use of such a devilish weapon. But the ordinary folk go about their business or pleasure without even a meeting in a village hall to express their sense of apprehension or their demand for international action to save their children. The problem of housing, the difficulties of demobilisation, the clothing ration, the political plans of the Labour Party, seem to be of first importance in their minds. The cricket matches on Shamley Green, and all the greens of England, are played as usual, while scientists are searching for a cheaper and better way of splitting the atom and intensifying its explosive power.

An unjust peace is being arranged. The organisation of the United Nations, hardly differing from the old League, is designed to secure the rights of the smaller nations, to prevent aggression, to uphold justice and liberty. The rights of the smaller nations have already been violated in the case of Estonia, Latvia, Lithuania and Poland. There is no liberty in Russia, or in any country within the Russian zone of influence over which there is a black-out of censorship and silence. Russian statesmen, up to the time I am writing, have not made the slightest approach to friendly co-operation with Great Britain or the United States. The expulsion of millions of farmers and citizens from East Prussia and the Sudetenland make a mockery at the very outset of those ideals proclaimed as the high purposes of the United Nations. The German concentration camps with their horrors have been cleared away in cleansing fires, but in many countries there are new concentration camps crowded with political prisoners, and the *Ogpu* and other bodies of secret police in other countries have their tortures. Vengeance, vindictiveness, brutality, bloody mindedness, masquerades under the names of "Justice" and "Liberty" and "Democracy" in many countries of Europe, and in the minds of people who still call themselves Christian, though they betray every word of Christ. He preached pity, and forgiveness, and love, and peace. Christendom has answered with high explosives, Tommy-guns, concentration camps, rubber truncheons, and gas chambers.

I am writing these last lines in the summer of 1946. In many countries there are hunger, disease, and death.

Pestilence may sweep across the world and take a terrible toll of life especially among the children who were the hope of the world.

That is not a pretty picture with which to end my book. It is grim and

horrifying. It is the result of a war which need never have happened if
further back in history—not very far back—there had been leaders of
vision among those who pulled the wires of this puppet show, seeing
beyond their own frontiers and taking just one short step forward
towards human comradeship. It need not have happened if the peoples
themselves had cut the wires which made them puppets, and had
advanced across the frontiers, not with guns and tanks but with the
spirit of fraternisation which once took place on Christmas Day in No
Man's Land.

Now already there is talk of a third World War. In "The Children's
Hour" of the B.B.C. a distinguished speaker warned these little ones,
I am told (I did not hear him) that they must prepare their minds for
that next war. How damnable and how terrible that the young people
of the world should have their minds darkened by that fear in the
springtime of their life. If we go drifting on as now we are doing, if
Europe is to be divided into Western and Eastern *blocs*, as seems likely
at this time, and if Russian suspicion and hostility are not broken
down, or the iron curtain raised, the danger will be menacing. But a
third World War must not be allowed to happen. It must not be
accepted as a possibility. The minds of men and women everywhere
must refuse and reject that idea. There must be some leap forward
of consciousness and morality and spiritual power, getting across the
frontiers, reaching out to the common folk everywhere. There must
be a revolt of the peoples against the doom which may be imposed
upon them not by their own wills but by the power politics of evil
leaders. We must force the pace for general disarmament and some
form of international police to uphold international law and prevent
aggression. But that cannot be done unless there is some new spiritual
force, some tremendous awakening of human consciousness, some
tidal wave of mass emotion powerful enough to break through iron
curtains and to dispel the darkness which hangs heavily over the
human scene.

Every wireless in the world ought to be tuned into that wavelength.
Every voice of power ought to reach out to the common folk across
the frontiers in a spirit of comradeship and with a call to peace. We
need a new nobility of spiritual leadership to speak those words. We
should enlist all the fine and civilised minds in many countries to join
in a crusade for the rescue of civilisation itself and for the destruction
of the destroying things, which are the weapons of war and the atom
bomb and the evil spirit which would make use of them.

I have looked at life. I have seen and loved the beauty of the world.
Everywhere I have met pleasant, kindly, intelligent people, missing for

the most part the evil ones and the torturers. It is because of that that I still hope for the survival of civilisation.

If I have learned anything it is that pity is more intelligent than hatred, that mercy is better even than justice, that if one walks around the world with friendly eyes one makes good friends.